INDUSTRIAL PEACEMAKING

INDUSTRIAL PEACEMAKING

by ANN DOUGLAS

COLUMBIA UNIVERSITY PRESS

NEW YORK AND LONDON 1962

Copyright © 1962 Columbia University Press
Library of Congress Catalog Card Number: 62-14463
Manufactured in the United States of America

To

the memory of

ALBERT EINSTEIN

pioneer psychologist

ACKNOWLEDGMENTS

When a study has been in progress all of a decade, it cannot have failed to accumulate indebtedness. In the present instance, some of the debts which most deserve recognition have to be passed over because of the very nature of the undertaking. I refer to the parties and persons in the field cases which are the cornerstone of the work, who must remain anonymous in line with my original agreement to protect their identities in exchange for the opportunity of firsthand contact with their confidential proceedings and inner council. Although the major cases have, subsequent to that agreement, been released for use in the text upon condition of thorough masking, the decision to make them thus available, as the decision in the beginning to provide access to closed sessions, was not uniformly easy for parties to arrive at, and came about in some instances only after thoughtful weighing up of the balance between protecting important private interests as against denying students a look at the real world behind the conference room door. It is a special privilege to acknowledge here this high order of response in the non-scientific community which has attended the study throughout its long course.

Fortunately, certain contributions can be named outright, with expressions of particular gratitude to:

The Federal Mediation and Conciliation Service and the New York State Board of Mediation, for far-reaching cooperation during the field-work phase of the research;

The Office of Naval Research, for generous grants—under Contracts Nonr-401(04) and 1433(00)—underwriting in full the two years of field operations; the Committee on the Allocation of Research Funds, the University of Buffalo, for a small grant and loan toward transcribing of the case materials; the Quaker Program at the United Nations and the Ford Foundation, for grants enabling preparation of the book manuscript;

The School of Industrial and Labor Relations, Cornell University, and the Business Office of Northwestern University, for administration of funds from the above grants; and Deering Library of Northwestern University, for special library accommodations;

Arthur L. Adams, William H. Buch, Howard E. Durham, William J. Ehlers, William G. Hosie, Eleanor A. Jacobs, James L. Macpherson, Irving Paster, Rolf Valtin, and Martin A. Wersing, for their patient work in connection with the tedious sub-study on identifications;

Drs. John W. Cotton and Donald Paull, for advice on statistical procedures in the sub-study;

Herman Amster, for imaginative disguising of the engineering terminology in the Atlas transcript;

Mrs. Del Gerow and Mrs. Shirley Duane, for their combination of technical skill and matchless care in the reproduction of the recorded materials and the typing of the book manuscript;

Finally, six individuals—Arthur L. Adams, James W. Greenwood, Jr., Elmore Jackson, John R. Murray, Martin A. Wersing, and William Foote Whyte—who have left their mark indelibly on the better parts of this work through their common gift of uncommon support or loyalty when and where these counted most.

For permission to quote from other published materials, recognition and gratitude are equally owing to the following authors and publishers: Harper & Brothers, *Harvard Business Review,* Holt, Rinehart and Winston, Inc., Industrial Relations Research Association, *The Journal of Conflict Resolution,* George F. Kennan, The Library of Living Philosophers, Inc., and The Open Court Publishing Company on behalf of *Albert Einstein: Philosopher-Scientist, Life,* The Ministry of Education of the Government of India, *The New Yorker* and Bruce Bliven, Jr., Jordan M. Scher, *Scientific American,* Charles Scribner's Sons, *WFMT Perspective.*

ANN DOUGLAS

February, 1962

CONTENTS

BOOK ONE

THE COMPOSITION OF SETTLEMENT

CHAPTER I

Introduction

In any serious reckoning of inventions and discoveries which have issued from man's earnest to alter his own condition, negotiation in the conference manner deserves to rank with his finest achievements—with those successes which have habitually been attributed to rare and superior creativity. A thinking person who takes the trouble to explore this field will be bound to wonder how it could have escaped the human disciplines so long. It would be difficult to point to another thoroughly pragmatic development on the national scene making use of keener psychological insights.

I

Notwithstanding the commendable record of American labor, management, and government agencies in resolving industrial discord without interrupting production and employment to do so, illiteracy about their efforts preceding agreement runs high in the society. A poverty of even raw information must lie back of the language habits of a people who, from persons in high places to the daily press, confuse mediation with arbitration, and interchange the terms "negotiation" and "compromise."

There are several approaches to industrial peacemaking, in all of which outsiders (one or more) enter stalemated cases (either on their own initiative or by invitation of the principals) to assist in the settlement process. Among this family of peacemaking services, mediation and arbitration are probably best known, although in practice, when a choice is being made, their resemblances are less apt to be noted than a fundamental distinction between the two based on the degree of independence left to the disputants. Whereas in arbitration the parties call on an outsider for a judicial-like decision on the troublesome points, binding themselves in advance to accept and abide by the arbitrator's ruling, in mediation the "third person" remains attached to a case only on continued sufferance of the parties. Throughout their case it is understood they reserve judgment until a time of their own choosing on whether to heed or disregard the mediator's counsel. And though initially they may welcome his entrance into the case, if at any point in the proceedings they come to regard him as persona non grata, they are within their rights in dispensing with his person and his services.[1]

In a belief that wider recognition of the mediation approach to settlement waits on its delineation, the study reported in this volume was undertaken. It opened with a period of field work given over to observing and tape-recording the proceedings of live cases in which staff mediators from the appropriate Federal agency and one state agency were working with labor and management negotiators who had deadlocked, to bring about peaceful settlement in lieu of a strike. By the end of two years, four cases stood complete enough in recorded materials and in confidences provided by the parties to be drawn on as primary source materials. In the chapters which follow, the fictitious names assigned to these four cases are used as titles in referring to them.

The Marathon Case (extending over five months' time).

Observing and recording began while the parties were still making preparations for their forthcoming negotiations, lasted throughout the two-party negotiations until a deadlock was reached, and continued until final settlement some two weeks after a mediator had taken over direction of the case. Although the company was part of a diversified corporation, staff specialists in the main office in another state acted only in a consultative capacity to negotiators drawn from the local plant. The union, which had never affiliated beyond the local level, brought its attorney to the table to handle its presentations. Contract renewal was the target of negotiations.

The Crescent City Case (involving a total of five sessions with a mediator, and terminating in strike).

The union, recently certified by the National Labor Relations Board, was

---

[1] Industrial mediators in this country are generally the employees of Federal, state, and municipal mediation agencies, hence are financed by tax monies, but important exceptions exist. There are, for instance, some industries in which the parties to the contractual relationship in effect maintain for themselves a private mediation service through the office of a permanent "umpire" or "impartial chairman," who may mediate as well as arbitrate controversies between the parties. Within the decade just past there has been some encouragement for more extensive development of such privately-sponsored mediation.

attempting to negotiate its first contract with this new branch plant. The parent International already held a contract with the main plant of the company in another state. The management team was constituted from the local staff and headed by an attorney engaged from a near-by city. The union team was led by two representatives from the International staff augmented by a third at one session.

The Irving Mining Case (brought to settlement in two days of meetings by the same mediator who handled the Atlas case).

Spokesman for the union was a representative from the staff of the International. On the company side, the senior Industrial Relations man, who was also an officer of this local concern, led that party's group. Expiration of the contract accounted for the negotiations.

The Atlas Case (covering approximately four weeks' time).

The transcript of proceedings of all seven sessions with a mediator is reproduced in full in Book Two of this volume, accompanied by a roster of the participants. The background of the case is enlarged upon in the transcript.[2]

II

Away from the conference room, the question of the responsible agent in negotiations is largely disposed of before it arises. In the public eye, once labor and management engage each other at a table, their representatives cease to count as individuals as long as they remain at their posts. In cases which fail to settle, the negotiators will not be held personally accountable, nor will their superiors who relayed instructions from behind the scenes. Neither will any persons receive the public's plaudits for success, these being handed out in the names of the parties. It is not only that the public's absence from the table disqualifies it to say which particular persons are entitled to the credits. Under the sanctioning system of the society, negotiation is treated as an affair of two institutional bodies—and their private affair, at that. Unions and managements admit the necessity of taking note on occasion of dissident and otherwise specialized elements within their ranks, sometimes to the extent of buying extra benefits in their name. Even so, such pressures follow no

[2] In succeeding chapters many passages are quoted from the transcripts of the Marathon, the Crescent City, and the Irving Mining cases. With few exceptions, quotations from the Atlas case have been avoided, as this material can be consulted in context. Some preliminary familiarity with the Atlas transcript is assumed when reference is made in the text to that case. It will more than repay the reader to turn at the end of this chapter to Book Two for an inspection of that material before proceeding with Book One.

fixed pattern and can be kept subordinate to the larger aims of the organizations—of the union Local and International, of the corporation, of the trade association. The single-minded pursuit of institutional survival and prosperity, deeply entrenched in negotiations between labor and management for historical reasons, now extends beyond the principle of self-preservation. Clear-headed parties which no longer rely on instinct for strategy have refused more than once to allow their representatives at the table to push over a company tottering on the edge of bankruptcy or a union weakened internally by a militant political minority.

Inside the conference room, a different picture takes shape. To be sure, there are token groups here whose seating arrangement—union representatives on one side, management facing them from the opposite—bears out the party alignments; whose exchange of viewpoints on the issues carries the articulation of parties another step forward. But here, as elsewhere, each advocate is also a fragment of his own kind, like and unlike all other human beings. Almost from the beginning, one looking on from the sidelines is reasonably certain that individuals qua individuals will not become extinct in the final analysis of negotiation. Again and again in real cases it is borne in upon an observer how psychological resources work their way to the forefront of negotiating situations, as though by design. One walks out after firsthand experience in the conference room convinced that somehow it is within the jurisdiction of flesh-and-blood people, not legal entities, that agreement is reached, regardless of whether these persons have been commandeered to take stands which they repudiate on the side.

It is on the occasions when a third classification in the person of a mediator enters into calculations about negotiation that the student is in optimal position to reflect on the possibility of an analytic unit superior to either party or person.

With the current equivocation of American opinion regarding industrial mediation, any strong, steady identification for the mediator to match that of union and management negotiators is lacking. It follows that a mediator cannot, under ordinary circumstances, be as effective with parties as with persons. Sometimes that fact can be circumvented if government is believed to be lined up behind the mediator, as was demonstrated several years ago in a case involving the East Coast longshoremen. The White House had dispatched the director of the Federal Mediation and Conciliation Service to New York City to see if anything could be done to get a contract signed without further delay. The FMCS Director entered the conference room at 2:00 P.M., with an ultimatum to the parties to produce a settlement by 4:00 P.M. "or the Government will take action." By 4:00 P.M., though agreement was still not in sight, the parties had settled down to hard work and were begging for grace on the deadline; by 4:00 the next morning, agreement was a reality. With his assignment fulfilled, the FMCS Director returned to Washington, checking in at the White House to report his success. The President heard him out, then inquired: "You say you told them the Government would 'take action.' What would the Government have done?" The answer that came back was: "Damned if I know!"

A mediator entering a case with the presumption of well-placed government concern would naturally take on unusual stature and an aura of authority in the eyes of the parties; but an unreserved partnership between mediators and government coercion is lacking in the bulk of American industrial mediation, despite the fact that government agencies provide most of the mediators working in the field today. Some students of the field express belief that mediation services, as presently constituted in government agencies in this society, have limited effectiveness, for all their heavy caseloads. They point to the poor record of settlements in disputes of widespread public concern—the so-called "emergency" cases like steel, coal, transportation, foodstuffs, and communications—as evidence that the cases which really matter to the general public do not yield to normal mediation effort; that, in the past, powerful public pressures have had to be applied before the parties to such cases have budged. Nevertheless, as mediation is carried on in the field, government mediators do not present themselves to disputing parties as possessing any special authority by virtue of having government for their employer. Quite the contrary, the impression is gained that they avoid that spotlight as scrupulously as they do all others.

It would be something of a paradox that mediators who are ineffective with parties for lack of power can become effective with parties' *cases*, were it not for the assailability of the American conception of power. The provincial origins of the term have been retained in its industrial usage: in the public mind, the power of labor and management to negotiate their way out of an impasse is equated almost exclusively with their economic condition. Mediators who regularly shoulder responsibility for turning stalemates into settlements know full well that, whatever the balance of economic power with which parties come into the conference room, the exercise of negotiating skill at the table will in time bring forth its own brand of *table*-power. A pre-conference imbalance in the respective strengths of two parties can be partially recouped during negotiation if the party which is initially disadvantaged on economic grounds is fortunate enough in its representation; and when deficiencies in negotiating skills come to light early enough in a case, an able mediator can help a very great deal in repairing them.

With increased insight into the manifoldness of table-power, the narrow preference for mediation which dominated the early days of the industrial project gave way in time to an outlook on peacemaking which did not discriminate pointedly in favor of any of the nominal units in a case. Certainly it was indefensible to accord to the third-category mediator any privileged status or function which the two principals did not also possess, else how to explain those many cases where labor-management parties conclude agreement without calling for outside assistance? Some larger, more inclusive "nature" which could be ascribed to all peaceful settlements seemed to be called for—in analytic terms, a plane where the ostensible negotiating units, whether parties or persons, could be thought of as working in concert with the equivalent of a mediating unit, which might or might not be a physically present mediator.

III

As negotiators close the door of the conference room, they turn their backs on reality in any of the senses in which science and society use that term. Their attention shifts to finding keys which will unlock a potential whose existence is fixed, space-wise, only in the mind, time-wise, only in the future tense. With no perceptible instrument but the human voice, and without stirring from their seats at the table, they move and change position, to attain what they refer to as a meeting of minds. Whether two parties, two parties and a mediator, or two parties and a mediator and a research observer, they achieve the same result: a slow but steady approximation in the group of absolute equality of all parts— equal units, equal distances, equal intensities. Since "parties" and "persons" enter the room already prejudiced by their histories against anonymity, labor and management, and negotiators, mediators, and scientific investigators must undergo reconstruction into an anomaly more nearly resembling the geometer's classical point, capable of taking on this quality.

Upon development of equality of points at the table, not only has the conflict originally separating the disputants been neutralized as a secondary effect; the justification has vanished for continuing the separation of parts which have been demonstrated to be interchangeable.

A student who has not given thought beforehand to the possibility of an effect upon himself from occupying the observer's seat in such a setting may return from a period of field work deeply shaken by his experiences. Today's would-be observer of peacemakers and peacemaking, his training for research in all probability received in one of the formal sciences, carries no precedent from classroom, library, or laboratory to prepare him for what lies ahead for the parties, and for himself. Nor, as his problems become manifest to him, will he find solutions in conferring with his contemporaries in related fields; they ply an altogether different course from the peacemakers—like the psychiatrists and clinical psychologists, who press their indirect claim to be carrying the benefits of negotiation and mediation (though more often it is arbitration) to the civilian population. For a theory of human conflict ample enough to circumscribe skilled negotiation and mediation among industrial groups, it would be necessary to call on American psychiatrists to forsake favorite portions of their current raison d'être. In the clinical theory from which American psychiatry still takes its cues, anger goes unquestioned as a corollary of disagreement. Anger-letting is, therefore, standard practice among psychiatrists. If it is not spontaneously forthcoming in the psychiatric encounter, the clinical procedure is to work to elicit it; failing in this, to alter the diagnosis to impute a severer degree of pathology than was originally charged. Plain men watching for the door of a conference room to open again may reason, in the same way, from the quarrels that went in that explosions of hot words are following when, in truth, inside the conference room anger in any form is verboten.

The most knowledgeable of the sciences—the physical—have been spared the burden of the concept of pathology, due in large part to an acute consciousness of their dependence upon the concept of nature. This did not spring from an artificial choice between these rival but incompatible concepts. In the history of the physical sciences, the vaster the compass of knowledge attempted, always the more outspoken the approach to harmony. Not until the *life* sciences (together with their applied extensions, the service professions) did the concept of pathology invade theory construction on a scale to be reckoned with. Where the assumption of natural orderliness failed to catch hold at all, as in the behavioral sciences, human beings evolved into foils for Nature, and the concept of pathology was fashioned into a counter-foil for use of the theorist going in to do battle with the phenomena of inter-personal and inter-group relations, under the beguiling label of "social problems." As a result, some so-called social scientists have very nearly persuaded themselves and their colleagues that their loftiest aim is the differential diagnosis of disease in their own kind.

Not only is this a crude declaration of belief in the supremacy of one mentality compared with another; it infuses a certain presumptuousness into the search for knowledge. One is led to ask, as a result of experience in the industrial project, if the behavioral disciplines have changed course from pursuing knowledge to professionalizing the circumlocution of modern men who, in this way, are actually settling their affairs with each other. Among peacemaking practitioners, notably the mediators who are invariably sought out by sophisticated parties because of their known skill, there is no rush to be accredited as the experts they are. Within the conference room proper, to raise the question of skill would serve no purpose but an academic one. Today, the emphasis in professional education and practice is contrary to this. Where else in the society, one asks, is there another professional group which eschews the claim of superiority over other men's minds in the very respect in which it serves them? It should be noted that the equalization process in negotiation never works from the premise that a more skillful and powerful adversary must temper his resourcefulness to match a modestly endowed opponent. In a process which begins with the future tense and comes full circle in running its course, the seeming less advantaged is seen as capable of exercising the same skills as the already expert, if the way is cleared for him to do so.

The only person in the conference room who can provide such clearance for anyone is that one's "other." Initially, at least, this implies that the only person in the conference room who can afford to be aware of the skill element is an observer located outside the immediate action field. But even while proposing this exception, one is reminded that such observer status must also be illusory, for the grounds on which one argues that negotiators cannot attribute skill to themselves while in action— only someone not engaged with them can properly do that—are grounds compelling one to argue that an observer should not expect to see himself while in action as apart from the observed—only a non-observer could aspire to do that.

In fact, the conference room has pitted the student against a profound problem in modern-day science: what to do with the evidence that on the frontiers of knowledge the method of scientific observation, as it has been transmitted from generation to generation of students, is already obsolete? Psychologists should have been the first to recognize the inevitability of this event and to begin to prepare for it. It is, instead, the physicists who are performing that function in science by asking the discerning questions—in this instance, relating to the identification of potential and of motion, terms which have already appeared in the industrial study:

Thus we have followed the history of the laws of conservation of momentum and energy up to their amalgamation in the recent state of physics. Every thinking person cannot but be strongly impressed by the last consequence, which is extreme, but confirmed by experience, that at least for electrons the mass is nothing but a form of energy which can occasionally be changed into another form. Up to now our entire conception of the nature of matter depended on mass. Whatever has mass,—so we thought—, has individuality; hypothetically at least we can follow its fate throughout time. And this is certainly not true for electrons. Does it hold for other elementary particles, e.g., protons and neutrons? If not, what remains of the substantial nature of these elements of all atomic nuclei, i.e., of all matter? These are grave problems for the future of physics.

But there are more problems. Can the notions of momentum and energy be transferred into every physics of the future? The uncertainty-relation of W. Heisenberg according to which we cannot precisely determine location and momentum of a particle at the same time—a law of nature precludes this—, can, for every physicist who believes in the relation of cause and effect, only have the meaning that at least one of the two notions, location and momentum, is deficient for a description of the facts. Modern physics, however, does not yet know any substitute for them. Here we feel with particular intensity that physics is never completed, but that it approaches truth step by step, changing forever.[3]

[3] Max von Laue, "Inertia and Energy," Chapter 19 in Paul A. Schilpp, ed., *Albert Einstein: Philosopher-Scientist* (2d ed., New York, Tudor, 1951), p. 533. Einstein, commenting in the same volume on the various essays by distinguished scientists treating of his work, had this to say of von Laue's contribution: "An historical investigation of the development of the conservation postulates, which, in my opinion, is of lasting value. I think it would be worth while to make this essay easily accessible to students by way of independent publication" (p. 686).

Has the very ingenuity of science become its own undoing? The rigorous outlook and procedure of science as it is known today in the Western world will have to give way to some radical innovations, else certainly it is destined for eventual decline as a preferred means to knowledge. The West is as beholden to the traditional thought- and work-ways of science as to those of political democracy. Do the two exist in support of each other, revision or decline in the one a harbinger of the same in the other? Modern high-energy microphysics, where the revolutionary call has already been sounded, is reaching a stage where its province is no longer easily distinguishable from that of psychology. Is a new generation of psychologists to be born and reared in a different house of science? [4]

Problems of this nature, and more, have been in mind in the present study. It was not so at first, only gradually came to be. Perhaps in the chapters to follow there will show through something of what it meant to one student, searching for a mode of analysis big enough to comprehend the mind's demands, to have had the fortune to come upon the conference room and its negotiating table occupied with the problem called "peace."

[4] Einstein, in his "Reply to Criticisms" referred to above, concluded a discussion of considerations determinative of the future conceptual basis of physics with the words: "I close these expositions, which have grown rather lengthy, concerning the interpretation of quantum theory with the reproduction of a brief conversation which I had with an important theoretical physicist. He: 'I am inclined to believe in telepathy.' I: 'This has probably more to do with physics than with psychology.' He: 'Yes.'" Schilpp, ed., *Albert Einstein*, p. 683.

I. AT THE NEGOTIATING TABLE

CHAPTER 2

Phase 1: Establishing the Negotiating Range

In projecting the long-term trends in negotiation, it is useful to speak of a steady process build-up to settlement, but when the role of analyst is laid aside for that of observer, straight-line development is less discernible than a series of step-like movements combining to form a central tendency. Changes in overt behavior come as spurts, often rather abrupt ones, following periods of prolonged circular activity which appear to accomplish remarkably little in a forward direction. In the present study, the sporadic progress toward decision has been broken down into three distinct "phases." The goodly amount of time consumed in each of the phases, and most markedly in the first two, imparts an impression over the long haul that these are steps measured in clock hours, but this is illusory. As a matter of fact, it would be difficult on a temporal basis to locate cut-off points when one phase might be said to have been exhausted and another to have opened up. Only later when the raw data are treated by the analyst in terms of functions can the behavioral overlappages be drawn sufficiently apart to reveal the unbroken threads beneath.

The teamwork between a party and its representatives at the table creates the basis for such a step-like movement. The parties face a task which in itself emphasizes the need for an analytical breakdown of the negotiating sequence along functional rather than chronological lines. There is, first of all, the need for amassing a body of data bearing on the problem, where is the tolerable point at which the two sides can come together? Any data gathered by the parties with respect to that problem will be fragmentary and inconclusive until ordered into place with the aid of meaningful criteria. This ordering can be accomplished only by subjecting the data to psychological assessment, a feat dependent on capacities at the command of private individuals. Thus, of sheer inner necessity, the negotiating process must sooner or later fracture the institutional parties who are the nominal negotiators into more critical units of single persons, the representatives who face each other at the table. The notion, therefore, of "phases" in negotiation derives from the general deduction that the individuals at the conference table will receive increasing degrees of surcease from institutional control over their operations. As conditions existing outside the conference room decline in usefulness as terms of reference for the negotiators, while conditions at the table are taking on increased significance, the successive transformations of behavior which a negotiator adopts will express both the fact and the degree of compensating autonomy coming his way. The gamut of relationships between a negotiator and his organization can run all the way from a condition of committed delegate bound by rigid instructions to that of autonomous agent with wide powers of discretion. The fact that these negotiator-party relationships are not haphazard and unpredictable in their order of emergence in successful negotiating makes plausible the notion of a sequence of the phases—in other words, the notion of a negotiating *process*. Unlike a developmental sequence which culminates in a foregone conclusion (for example, locomotion in the human infant, in which intermediate steps like creeping and crawling may be by-passed without impairing the later walking performance), negotiation involves a process which cannot be telescoped without sacrificing harmony that is evident when the phases keep to their appointed times.

I

The first phase of the negotiating process often runs for a relatively long time, with all the outward appearance of deep and irreconcilable cleavage between the parties. The speeches of participants have the quality of public oratory; compared with the rest of the conference, they are exceptionally long. The number 1 negotiators carry the verbal load, seldom interrupted by each other and almost never interrupted by any others bidding for the floor. Speeches flow with unusual smoothness and rhythmic regularity, as though they had been prepared and rehearsed in advance. For local color there are forensic fireworks and dogmatic pronouncements. There is a great show of muscles—verbal, of course (with the promise of other kinds to come)—augmented by lengthy statements about firm positions which everyone knows will eventually give way, though the principals continue stoutly to deny this. There are vehement demands and counter-demands, arguments and counter-arguments. Each side shows prodigious zeal for exposing and discrediting its opposite, and sooner or later there almost invariably comes from each side a conscious, studied, hard-hitting critique of the other. These attacks are typically vigorous and spirited; not infrequently they are also derisive and venomous.

This is the phase which is the most universally standardized in its trappings. Seasoned negotiators understand perfectly well the strategy of the opponent, and they profess to relish the opportunity for parrying verbal thrusts. In private caucus immediately following a joint meeting in which a bitter attack has been delivered from the other side of the table, they have been heard in this research to speak with admiration of the skill and accuracy with which the adversary delivered his blows; in the case of a weak and ineffectual presentation, they have also been heard to pine for a stiffer challenge against which to pit their own prowess. The layman might assume that a really skilled negotiator would welcome the prospect of a weak and inept opponent, the better to enhance his own chances for success, but, with skill as with power, gross imbalances at the table prove a handicap for everyone. The spirit is much like that among contestants in a game, with the same competitive savor to which Riddle alluded in a study of poker players:

It turns out that the betters are not, in general, eager to win against those from whom they could most easily win; the weak player is not the one against whom the bluffs are directed. Quite contrary to the hedonistic interpretation, the goal here, even when measured in money terms, is very specific. It is not simply a desire to win money where it can be won most safely or in the largest amount, but rather, where an aggressive attitude and an exhibition of skill afford a direct challenge.[1]

Some of the most misleading interpretations of the behavior during this first stage have been contributed by psychologists. Having gone into this field with the idea that a negotiating conference is merely another example of the small, autonomous problem-solving group which has engaged so much social science attention in recent years, they have pointed to the donnybrook of outbursts and denunciations as evidence of anxiety, hostility, and aggression as clinicians are accustomed to deal with these.[2]

[1] Gardner Murphy, Lois B. Murphy, and Theodore M. Newcomb, *Experimental Social Psychology* (rev. ed., New York, Harper and Brothers, 1937), pp. 705–6.

[2] As an example, there is McMurry's proposal for diagnosing the industrial negotiating conference as a play of personalities at the table: "If possible, [the union

In their haste to extrapolate in a straight line from clinical observation of troubled persons to relationships between modern-day power aggregates, they have mistaken purposive social action for individual re-action. The running "work notes" kept by a clinical psychologist in the course of inspecting some of the Atlas transcript betray this typical bias: [3]

SESSION I

(Page 3)
I suppose this is being a clinician, but somehow I get the feeling Michelsen is basically insecure in his presentation. Cue: calls for support from others relative to points he makes; appeals to the "we" feeling of the total group; plugging for group solidarity on *his* terms of what the situation is; appeal to unite against competitors; appeal to pride in the company's product.

(Page 5)
Meaning of Gambon's being sorry? Does he wish he, too, had charts, rising to the challenge of the company presentation?

(Page 13)
Union representative is warming up to his rebuttal. Does he feel more secure now? [Near end of his speech] Did he check his impulse to aggress here?

(Page 14)
Union representative seems to be attacking the "elite" (executives not present) —a safer method of aggression than previously tried.

(Page 19)
Feeling of Michelsen's insecurity continues to suggest itself.

---

leaders'] personalities should be evaluated *clinically*. (This is not as difficult as it sounds; it is only necessary for a man with clinical training to observe them in action at the bargaining table for a few sessions to make a fairly accurate diagnosis.) The reason for making a diagnosis of this sort is that, as numerous case studies have revealed, the personalities of the negotiators are the controlling factor in many bargaining sessions. Hence, from the standpoint of strategy formulation, there must be an answer to the question: Are the persons with whom the company must deal normal, healthy, well-adjusted, and integrated individuals; are they paranoid and hypersuspicious, i.e., fanatics; are they attempting to compensate for underlying anxieties and insecurities by bluff and bravado; are they 'acting out' a neurosis or psychosis of some sort; or are they typical psychopathic (gangster) personalities, almost wholly without moral or ethical scruples? . . . All executives and supervisors [on the company side] who participate in bargaining sessions ought to be appraised in the same manner." Robert N. McMurry, "War and Peace in Labor Relations," *Harvard Business Review*, Vol. XXXIII, No. 6 (November–December, 1955), pp. 55–56.

[3] The sub-study in which these "work notes" figure was built around the Atlas transcript, and is described in full in Chapter 7.

(Page 6)

Michelsen again refers to outside data (newspapers) to substantiate his point. Somehow he needs such outside support. Is he self-conscious at this point or just insecure? He's hesitant without his figures.

(Page 7)

Michelsen acts insecure and apologetic again.

(Page 8)

Did Michelsen feel it necessary to continue? Was he unable to tolerate the "rather long pause" at the conclusion of his talk? A further cue to his basic insecurity? I'd love to have a Rorschach on this man.

(Page 9)

Michelsen gets hesitant as a defense against aggression? He *is* insecure in his relationship to Gambon.

(Page 14)

Gambon getting a little aggressive again at this point.

(Page 62)

Gambon getting openly aggressive again, huh? Michelsen also getting tough in return, but still not too secure in doing so.

This orthodoxy of the psychologists has overlooked the considerable evidence that there is a tenable distinction to be made between the inter-personal and the inter-party climates in negotiation. The importance, both theoretically and in practice, of making an early distinction between these two levels is simple and plausible in the case of Phase 1. The real actor units in this stage are the sides, or parties. The negotiators at the table are properly seen as representatives, not as contenders in their own right. As "committed" delegates of the parties, they operate at this stage with no prerogative of independence or free choice but under instructions, explicit or implicit, aimed at accomplishing the party's ends. This rather unequivocal identification of the negotiators with their respective parties probably does not approximate identification in the psychoanalytic sense, but comes closer to a sort of social adaptation or role-taking which can be observed and checked on by others, resulting in the standardized behaviors which are quickly spotted by anyone at all familiar with conventional negotiating procedure. Here, then, where the conflict of interests between the parties is forced into bold relief by the very design of the situation, inescapably it follows that the schism within the original conference body is enlarged and deepened for the time being, and the dominating spirit at the conference table is rendered highly competitive and "self-seeking." It not infrequently happens in Phase 1 that while the parties are busily engaged in depreciating each other, at the level of inter-personal relationships there flow warm currents of personal good-will and friendly respect between and among individual negotiators.

Previous to the opening of the Atlas case, both union and management spokesmen were interviewed at length about the coming negotiations. Two excerpts from the field notes on those interviews depict the good status of the relations of these two people who were to prove, once negotiations got under way, to be among the most redoubtable opponents in dealing publicly with each other to be encountered in the whole of the project.

After the investigator's interview with U 1: [4]
I distinctly felt that what he did (and did not) say about C 1 indicated wide respect for him. He referred at least twice to the reputation C 1 has established "in the community," even in so short a time; he applied the term "competent" to him. But as though to make sure I didn't get too favorable a picture of C 1, he added: "He doesn't have *wings,* you understand!"

After the investigator's interview with C 1:
His feeling about U 1 seemed, on the whole, to be respectful. I noticed that he made sure to say several times, "Of course, he has made mistakes"; but he acknowledged that U 1 has done a good job. In the time he has been associated with him, he said, no one has shown greater concern for the company than U 1.

[4] In excerpts from the field materials throughout the chapters of Book One, negotiators are generally designated by party and rank within the party, "C" referring to company and "U" to union negotiators. The key to these abbreviations is as follows:

C 1   spokesman for the company party
C 2   second-in-command for the company party
C 3, etc. company representatives below the C 1 and C 2 positions
U 1   spokesman for the union party
U 2   second-in-command for the union party
U 3, etc. union representatives below the U 1 and U 2 positions
M   mediator
AD   Ann Douglas

In a post-settlement interview with U 2 of the Marathon union committee, just after its long negotiation with a management against whom committee members expressed grievances to the very end, the investigator raised the question of residual acrimony at the inter-personal level. This is a condensation of the conclusion to that exchange:

AD: Do you feel any differently about C 1 than you did when I first came down here? You folks—you know, back in those sessions you used to have fellows made a lot of remarks about him. Do you still feel that way about him?

U 2: No, all those remarks you might have heard us make, we weren't really too serious, you know, because we've had fellows in here even worse than C 1. We know that regardless of who the men are, if it wasn't C 1 it would be somebody else, so what's the difference? Personally, I like C 1 as well as I do anybody so far. I don't know why, but I really do.

AD: You all talked about him as though he were a hatchet man or something, you know—some terrible character. And I wondered if you still felt that way about him.

U 2: No. No, we never really felt the way you think we do.

The Marathon management negotiators, too, were able on occasion to muster spontaneous displays of goodwill over and beyond their oft-expressed dissatisfaction with the union group. A pertinent example is lifted from a joint meeting on time study in which, preceding this exchange, the union group had voiced strong sympathy for workers in the shop who became nervous when a company engineer hovered over them with a stop watch:

U 1: And then—then see—what, did I break the mike? (Laughs)

C 1: Look, pay no attention to me. You're doing all right. I'm just having a little private conversation over here.

C 2: Well, you're makin' me nervous. (Several laugh quite heartily)

U 1: He can't—he can't perform on his rate now. (Laughing continues a little longer)

Perhaps it is not strange that persons unfamiliar with negotiating exchanges should find this stage of the proceedings almost incomprehensible. Negotiating, by definition, makes it mandatory that the positions taken up in the beginning must be modified in part or abandoned in whole by the time final agreement is reached, else negotiating "in good faith" cannot be said to have occurred. Yet the principals, in full knowledge of this, strive for a convincing demonstration that they are impossibly at loggerheads, taking up stolid, adamant postures in defense of which they marshal an elaborate factual exposé. Then, in the end, many of these points so painstakingly worked over in the early stage may suddenly drop out of sight, with no sign whatsoever that they have been satisfied, even in part. The great expenditure of time and effort which goes into the building of defensive bulwarks that are known to be slated for ultimate abandonment does not fit easily into conventional business notions about economy and efficiency of operation, and certainly not into the American sense of what is moral and ethical.

The vivid monologues of this stage do, however, have important over-all utility for the parties. That function may be referred to as the setting up of the negotiating "range"—that is, the stretch of territory within which the parties propose to move around while they reach for consensus on a single settlement point. Negotiators and mediators encountered in the field talked freely about the implicit design back of the redundant activity at this stage. One company negotiator applied some very apt similes in his discourses about Phase 1. "I try," he once stated in interview, "to develop first *the sphere* in which we are working, because it leads to quicker agreement and the quicker clearing of—of the issues." In another interview he made the observation that "This sort of thing, of the long, drawn-out negotiation sessions and the hammering—you *must* go through this. You must 'suffer' it, in order to get a contract." On still another occasion, when explaining to his union counterpart at the table that his demands were statements of company goals, not replies to union demands, he put it that "unless ya have two poles from which to start, you don't get anywheres, see. I mean, otherwise you develop into sort of a 'Yes, I did,' 'No, I didn't' argument." In referring in private to the set of original company demands with which he followed the union presentation of its demands, again and again he added the postscript, "It was pitched for bargaining!"

Much of the literature in this field has depicted the parties as searching from the very beginning for a central point at which they can divvy up the losses and gains between them. In the live setting, however, it turns out that the first transaction between the parties is given over to an exhaustive determination of the *outer limits* of the range within which they will have to do business with each other. This calls, in other words, for preliminary *emphasis* of the disagreement factors. The debt of the negotiating process to the conflict element which fuels it is easily overlooked. Indeed, unless an issue provides reasonable grounds for cleavage between parties, it is not suitable for negotiation. If the parties to a case cannot afford to concentrate at the outset on the divisive aspect of their case, the issues at stake may be better assigned to a problem-solving than to a negotiating set-up. In many modern contract arrangements, the date for formal overtures between management and labor rolls around so regularly that conflict sufficiently virile to sustain the negotiation— that is to say, *genuine* conflict—does not really exist until it is first worked for.

The positions propagandized by the opening salvos, far from representing bona fide expectations, serve the more immediate purpose of flashing to each party an impression of the degree of obduracy to be contended with in the other. To a not inconsiderable extent, what is settled for in the end will reflect the determinations about original positions which the principals have imparted and detected in this first stage. Strength and vigor in a party and a ring of conviction in its presentation can help to spell out an impression of intractability which becomes part of the accounting data of party A as it goes about determining how far and how long it dares continue to press party B for concessions, in lieu of modifying its own position. It should be apparent from this that the net effect of Phase 1 is not essentially negative but positive. That is, though seeming to dwell on the outer limits, or vastness of difference between the parties, Phase 1, by drawing the attention of each party to the fact that the opposite is equally prepared to resist attack, insures that the expectations and predictions on each side are significantly enlarged beyond anything with which either could possibly be equipped on first approaching the table. It cannot be emphasized too strongly how effective this contribution can be in softening up at the heart of the range a wider stretch of possible settlement points which, if they are not all equally desirable, still may emerge at the end as acceptable. Since the outlines of the negotiating range are compounded out of the activities on both sides of the table, this phase cannot be exploited fully unless both parties participate energetically and wholeheartedly in it.

II

The quick-freezing of positions to avoid weakening of the conflict element is a temporary precaution, and subject to definite ground rules. The hard core of resistance must be properly placed (it belongs in this stage of activity, not in later ones); it must be properly timed (it should be tractable when the requisite change agents have been introduced by the developing situation); it applies to the inter-*party* relationship (inter-personal relationships shall at all odds be protected from it).

Antagonism between the parties is the life blood of this stage; antagonism between persons would be highly detrimental as a precursor for the psychological activity which is to come to the forefront in the next phase. Negotiators vary with respect to the tone they claim to prefer in working with their opposite numbers, but among mediators there is wide consensus on the gravity of the contamination which comes with emotional stress. The late Arthur S. Meyer once commented that "the economic aspects of a dispute never account entirely for the asperities that accompany it. Rudeness, irritation, and the habit of not listening—these are as vexing as the untenable arguments that accompany them. Progress has been made through the mediator's presence, though that presence has brought nothing more than temperate speech." [5] In general, from the moment mediators enter a stalemated case, they work continually to insure that moderation shall prevail in all things inter-personal, no matter what dispositions of an inter-party nature may develop.

An excellent demonstration of the mediator's concern in these matters is to be found in a sequence from the Marathon case. The mediator had intended to begin with a joint meeting between union and management. However, upon his arrival at the company premises this plan was quickly revamped when he learned that relations among the participants were already so strained from previous meetings that another joint encounter could only widen the breach. His decision was reached in a preliminary caucus with management representatives.

M: Well, it almost appears as though what is needed from me is not a joint meeting with you gentlemen, but a private session with U 2. (C 1: I—) I might find out just where he expects to go in this and with what means and how we can get to work in a business-like fashion to get something resolved.

C 1: I felt that, in the light of the situation, you would—probably would wanta do that. As a matter of fact, I think I remarked to you about it, C 2, that I felt that probably—

C 2: Yes, we felt that. How—how shall we go about it?

M: Do you suppose that if we have a joint session that fireworks might emanate from it, or in it?

[5] Arthur S. Meyer, *Some Thoughts about Mediation* (Mimeographed, 1950), p. 6.

C 1: I think there's that possibility right now.

M: Is that good or bad, from your point of view? At this point, I mean?

C 1: Well, we've got 2 weeks. I'm wondering whether a meeting, M, is going to do anything but stir up tempers or recriminations at this time *unless* we have a grounds on which to meet, an area of discussion described for us.

M: Yeah! That's exactly what I'm thinking, and I—I had in mind merely sitting down and having each of you define just where *you* stood and then try to create some relationship between the 2 positions, but in view of what you've said so far it would appear that I better find out individually, first, where you stand before risking putting you together, if part of that risk is that there will be fireworks which I'm not so sure are going to do anything other than make the thing more difficult at this point. We can avoid—fireworks sometimes are (C 1: Good) good, *but* not necessarily on the first session that the mediator sits in.

C 2: That's right.

M: So I think I'd better at least talk with them first and see how it lines up.

In a management caucus with the mediator long after he had begun work in the case, it first became suspect that C 1 might have had more than a casual hand in sullying the inter-personal climate during the pre-mediation stages. A condensed excerpt from that caucus exchange discloses:

C 1: I don't know. I'm—I'm a little bit afraid that when you get us together again, I'm gonna jump him. I'm getting to the point where I've taken about *all* that I can take!

M: *You* haven't taken a thing for a week! (C 2 laughs riotously)

C 1: I have taken a cock-eyed (M: I've been protectin' you like a baby!)— that cock-eyed thinking of his! (C 2 continues laughing)

M: (Loudly) Oh! Oh! (C 1 says something) Here I am, cut and bruised, bleedin' all over, and *you're* complaining (laughing slightly)! You're hurt.

C 1: He—he's getting warped. (C 2 laughs again) If he stay with U 2 long enough, he'll be just like him. (Laughs heartily)

C 2: I think he's aimin' to get away from him. (Laughs. Pause) Leave us have coffee.

C 1: (Emphatically) Look, what you've got there is not gonna budge one Goddamn ounce until U 2 budges! And that means a strike!

M: Hurray! (Pause)

C 2: Nobody's gotta have 'em, M. You're gonna be worn out. We're gonna be worn out, and it—

M: Well, now, let's see. U 2 has budged on Point 4.

C 1: Huh? What Point 4?

M: U 2 has budged on Point 6. U 2 has budged on Point 8. U 2 has budged on Point 9. U 2 has budged on Point 11 (C 1: He hasn't budged on anything *important*), 12, 13, 14, 15.

C 1: The company has budged on Point 1 in *3* respects. (M: Uh-huh) The company has not budged on Point 2. The company has budged on Point 3. The company has budged on Point 4. The company has budged on Point 5. The company has budged on Point 6. The company has budged on Point 7. The com—company has budged on Point 8, on Point 9—no. It's not over our original proposal. We've budged on Point 10—

C 2: Yes, we have on 9.

M: Sure, you've budged on 9.

C 1: On 9 we did. Yeah. We've budged on 11 considerably. We budged on 12. We've budged on 13, on 14, on 15, on 16, on 17—no, did we?

M: I don't know. No. Union budged on that. Don't be takin' credit for their budges.

C 1: (Over M above) No. That's 2 we haven't. O.K. Take it back.

C 2: About 17, you mean this—

C 1: (Over C 2 above) 18, say "No." 19, say "No." O.K., add 'em up. Now let's see U 2 move! And our budges are *substantial* ones, in most instances —not this Goddam piddling business! I want action!

M: Want me to run down the hall?

C 1: (Laughing slightly) I don't give a damn what ya do! I want it! And I'm tellin' ya, I'm ripe to talk to U 2.

M: Well, I think I'll keep you away from him. I wouldn't care to have all my slow, careful building (C 1: I'm warnin' ya. You're runnin' the show but—) knocked over before the concrete gets dry.

C 1: You're runnin' the show, but I'm tellin' ya.

M: Naw (laughs slightly), I think you're enjoying yourself. I'm willing to—

C 1: No, I'm not!

M: Oh, all right. All right, let's get serious and—

In the course of several subsequent interviews between the investigator and the management spokesman in this case, all doubt was removed about C 1's calculated efforts to make a personal target of certain persons on the union committee. As he verbalized his conscious design in all this, if his blows failed to elicit personal annoyance, he interpreted this to say that the point was not significant to the opponent; on the other hand, when he "drew blood" with one of his attacks, he took it as a sign that he had hit sensitive ground, a fact which he noted mentally for future use in trading off negotiable points. When asked what cues he utilized to distinguish bona fide from synthetic emotional reaction on the union side, he replied: "I don't think it is anything that is said, but I notice flushing of the face, and mainly I watch the neck muscles in the other fellow." His recorded comments make clear that he knew what he was after:

C 1: The other—the other point that I thought we might talk about a little bit was the mediation session that you sat in, and as I indicated to you before we went in, I was going to get a little rough.

AD: How much feeling is there when you do that sort of thing, or is it actually because it amounts so much to a sort of strategy that, you know, it's like turning it on and off?

C 1: I turned it on just like I turned on a spigot last time. For a reason. I'm the whipping boy to a degree with this union, and *will* be for a while. Not that I like it, and I don't think that it's good, but we have other problems that I have to consider, and until we can get [these] at the proper level, I'm the whipping boy.

AD: Are you gonna be able to change roles from that, with this same group?

C 1: Well, I'll tell you what I've done—some of the things I c—yeah, I—I think so. It's not—it's not as bad as it appears. Now, don't forget that I was after some definite effect in that—in that mediation session, and I was the *so-and-so,* and I *was*. Now, I know that a lot of people wouldn't agree with that strategy. A lot of people will *dis*agree with me on that strategy, perhaps for a number of reasons, and I think some of 'em haven't got the courage to do it. You run a great risk of not being able to come up—off the whipping post, once you're on it. I'm not saying that it's not possible for me to have been wrong, either, in what I did. When ya first get into collective bargaining, the thing that amazes you is the reactions that you get when you say something, which are *not* what you expected because you expect—normally, from a pattern you expect a more—a certain normal reaction that you and I have when we're talking. But in collective bargaining the reaction is not that. The reaction is a very *definite purpose* behind it (AD: That's right) to undermine what the other guy said. (AD: It's a studied thing) It's a sadistic approach.

AD: Well, that's interesting. I never heard that term applied to it, but I don't see why not. That does describe it, doesn't it?

C 1: Yeah! And you have to have a rough, tough hide to stay in negotiations. This fellow Falkenthal that [preceded me] had been a—he—sh—sh—I don't know why he was that way. He had been a union organizer, so he said, or a steward or something. (AD: Uh-huh) And the union would bait him, and he'd blow up! And we sat in there and U 3 would say to me, "Yeah, just like Sid Falkenthal." And C 2 says, "And you sit there and let the damn thing roll off ya." He says, "You—you—you sit and grin at him and then—" I said, "Certainly, C 2. All I have to do is let U 3 know that when he says I'm like Falkenthal that it bothers me." (AD: Uh-huh) And I said, "Then I'm through being a bargainer."

AD: When you used to talk to me about the way you were going to m— manage this thing, once the bargaining got under way—and I assume that meant mediation, too—gonna be the whipping boy. You were gonna be the fellow who came in and pounded the table at certain times. You really haven't done much table-pounding since this—this whole last thing came along.

C 1: Well, I kept—I'm the one that kept the—the driving on the piston. I kept the push behind the thing, though. And (AD: Except you—) I was the one that was harsh with the union.

AD: Well, you know, I didn't feel it the way I thought you had meant to do it, that you were gonna be—

C 1: Oh, I wanted to a couple times, but M held me down. 'Course, I think U 2 needs some of that, myself. I mean, really nasty stuff, right across the board. I think he needs it. Because if I judge U 2 rightly, you can break him because he has a *tremendous* desire to be loved (AD: Yeah), to be a—a—well—well, to (AD: He thinks that he—)—to have approval, see. And I think a direct personal attack—a vicious personal attack on U 2 would break him. Just—he—he'd—he'd just break under the thing. (AD: Uh-huh) And I have had a feeling all along—C 2 held me back, the vice-president held me back, M held me back, so I dropped it finally. But I was *itching* to make a direct personal attack on U 2. I felt sure I could blow him higher'n a kite. Didn't dare do it in the last few days, but if I could have done it a week ago, or 2 weeks ago, before ready—U 2 was ready to take the strike, he would have had to gather himself together again and come back into the bargaining. And at that point U 2 would have been whipped psychologically and we could have gotten almost any kind of a contract we wanted. Now, that was my theory.

AD: You couldn't afford to do it, you mean, this late?

C 1: Not at the end, no, because then U 2 would say, "To hell with you. We'll strike." (AD: Uh-huh. Yeah, I see) And—I've used that before. You get certain situation and the union just gets stubborn, see, so you give 'em a good strong personal attack and they get so mad about the personal attack they forget what they were doing and start talkin' about something else, and after a while you're all back into bargaining again.

How the circumspection of the Marathon mediator paid off could hardly be summed up more simply than it was by the very U 2 whom C 1 had had in mind for his chief target. When queried in a post-settlement interview about his reaction to the use of mediation, he verbalized the point which is at the heart of the mediator's custodial role in these matters:

U 2: It was the way he conducted himself that was good. I really believe that if it wasn't for mediation we would have been on strike today. We were so far apart from the company I honestly don't believe, you know, that the agreement would have been signed at all. It was due to the fact the mediation, where they—I don't know what you'd call it—it has a third party there that automatically—somebody you're not mad at. See what I mean? You can talk to him and you can listen to him. However, if it were the company doing the talking you wouldn't trust him any more at that stage of the game. If someone from the company had come in there and said those same things the fellows would have gotten awfully mad, and once they got mad they would *never* give in then. You wouldn't get no-where. I really believe mediation stopped the strike.

The mixed auspices under which industrial negotiations take place make it reasonable to anticipate that the negotiating process would tax the individuals at the table to a not inconsiderable extent. Perhaps the wonder is not that negotiators produce no more settlements than they do but that they succeed in so many cases without having to call on outside assistance. After a long, hard look at Western ideologies and Western conditioning, one can ask what in a negotiator's personal experiences in this society has equipped him to take on the job of functionary for an institution like labor or management, moving in and out of the behavioral variations which are woven into progress toward settlement. It is tempting to posit the thesis that a "mature" or "adjusted" man as projected in the idealized Western image would be handicapped by his very personality in carrying the burdens of industrial negotiation. There are good reasons for querying how Western negotiators could avoid at the table a stimulation of unresolved personal problems, since neither Western experience during the formative years nor formal Western training professes to prepare individuals for responsible behavior from the standpoint of formally organized social structures like present-day industrial groups. It would be an instructive exercise to examine the most popular theories of personality development and of clinical rehabilitation among contemporary behavioral scientists, to see how many recognize that adjustment to modern Western society requires some working relationship with large-scale, impersonal groups. How, for example, experience in the communistic-like primary family, which clinical theories generally regard as the main influence upon the young child's forming personality (meting out gratifications according to need, rather than contribution), prepares him for responsible association with large groups (meting out rewards according to contribution, without regard to need) is not entirely clear. It seems a not incredible possibility that in Western society organizational assignments would be prized by poorly socialized individuals whose developmental deprivations and distortions keep them foraging constantly in the environment for just such toe-holds as the authoritarian structures of modern organizations provide. Needy personalities would be expected, in other words, to look for organizational niches where, under the protective guise of organizational prerogatives, they could act out their private problems. This is not a way of hypothesizing that the good negotiator is necessarily a specimen of skewed ontogeny, but of saying that an earnest adaptation to Western cultural demands may be an almost incongruous recommendation for one who is to attend seriously to the demands of the conference table.

Incentives of hostility and retaliation may be particularly intensified by group enterprises which seek to rectify the condition of members, as Jawaharlal Nehru has pointed out about Mahatma Gandhi's long and fervent crusade in India against British rule. Nehru's remarks were occasioned by a seminar of world leaders convened to examine the applicability of the "Gandhian outlook and techniques" in the treatment of contemporary world tensions. His analysis of political phenomena seems very pertinent to the industrial scene:

[Gandhiji] calls, as you perhaps know, his autobiography *Experiments with Truth*. There is that in them, that quality of inflexibility, that is, to say, not surrendering to what he considered basically evil, whatever the consequences; but having decided that, always to be friendly, always to be cooperative, always to stretch out your hand to your opponent and enemy, always to keep a door open for reconciliation.

These two things are very difficult to have at the same time—to be firm and inflexible and to fight evil with all your might and yet always to be prepared for reconciliation. The two do not normally go together. You work yourself up to a fury of hatred of your opponent as normally happens today with wars. . . . And yet Gandhiji could combine the two, and of the many miracles he wrought in this country this was one, that he made us in India . . . also somewhat receptive to that technique, to those ideas and even to that behaviour; so that, while we struggled, we did not have that much of bitterness and hatred in us which normally accompanies such struggles. . . .

Now that was good of course, but another virtue was also attached to that general approach, and that virtue was that when the time comes to end the struggle, it can be ended graciously, gracefully, and with a minimum of bitterness.

When the approach is according to what might be called the Gandhian technique, first of all you are not supposed to paint the other party as the devil. . . . You separate always the individual from the system. If I can give you an example, Gandhiji was always saying: "I am fighting British imperialism, I am not fighting the Britisher; I am not fighting the Englishman or anybody. They are my friends but I will fight British imperialism." . . . That itself of course rather toned down the opposition of the opponents. . . . So firstly there is the struggle and hitting out, in a non-violent way, but hitting out; . . . [yet] the door is open to reconciliation all the time, but not by any compromise on any basic question of what is considered wrong and evil.[6]

Certain conditions prescribed by the negotiating sequence so surely promise some deterioration of inter-personal relations that antidotes may need to be introduced consciously into the developing set-up. There is no small danger that the castigations which spark the institution-to-institution exchange in Phase 1 will be mistakenly absorbed into the inter-personal system in its embryonic state, before it is robust enough to operate outside the inter-party system. The assaultive blasts and propaganda pressures, applied to impress and to dislodge, may prove overwhelming as tension-generators and thereupon be interpreted as personal attacks to be reacted to in kind. When negotiators are new to conference work or to one another, these hazards are compounded. But sabotage of the negotiation from such inter-personal imbalances is not to be attributed solely to the novices. The mediator will sometimes run into experienced negotiators whose life conditioning has left them with such poor frustration tolerance for anxiety and uncertainty that they will easily turn, under stress from the invective fall out, to an emotional cathartic for relief. He is also likely to find some negotiators whose personal inclination is more toward scrapping than negotiating and who are simply spoiling for a good fight—a personality attribute which may erroneously be identified as ingenious strategy for flushing out cues about the opposite side.

The Marathon mediator had a story in a lighter mood with which he made the point in union caucus one day:

M: One of the nicest collective bargaining tricks I have bumped into is one that—well, it's not collective bargaining. It's a girl who is chief shop

[6] *Gandhian Outlook and Techniques* (New Delhi, Government of India Press, 1953), pp. 13–14, 16.

steward in a plant which is part of an amalgamated Local with a number of plants in the —. She does not get along with the business agent, and, oh, they've had a lotta trouble. And the workers support *her,* and they're always threatening strike. In fact, they've been out on strike, I guess, twice this past year. So, they come up to mediation to see if we can help them settle the thing, and she wears a hearing aid. So she will give off with a long, impassioned diatribe against him. Then when he starts to speak, she unhooks the hearing aid and lays it on the table. (All laugh heartily) Yeah, I thought it was kinda cute the first time she did it. (Laughs) But, oh, she drives him wild. (U 3 and M laugh slightly) He just can't talk to her; won't listen. (Laughs again)

Among the field cases there were several tailor-made opportunities for comparing interaction when an accustomed pair of negotiators representing the two sides was broken up and a third person took over from one of the original persons. In three such instances a strong impression was created that the quality of the inter-personal relationship was so radically transformed by the change as to have wide repercussions—sometimes favorable, sometimes not—on the over-all drive for agreement.

Atlas Case. The pairings in question here are U 1 with C 1, and U 1 with C 2.

C 1's departure from the concern for a new position catapulted C 2 into the position of chairman at the beginning of Session VI. The investigator seemed to sense an ameliorating blanket spread over the entire proceedings by this shift in personnel. It was not that there was any noticeable decline in firmness on either side; the mediator saw strictly to it that this did not happen. But the stepped-up frequency with which verbal gestures of goodwill were exchanged seemed to temper a certain bristliness which had existed in the conference room before.

It cannot be claimed that the final settlement was higher or lower than it would have been if C 1 had remained chairman throughout. At the same time, a few remarks dropped by the union committee in caucus with the mediator hinted that that group was dealing with C 1 not only on an institutional basis but on a personal one as well. Had he remained till the end, it seems likely that the union committee, which proved itself most resolute with C 2, would have challenged C 1 to as tough a bargain as it could exact.

Some of C 2's personal mannerisms seemed to induce a friendly response from the other person: for example, his tendency to personalize many of his comments by addressing them to a specific person whom he called by name; his earnest emphasis on the purity of his *intent* toward the opponent, however distasteful the deed, and his assumption of the same attitude in his opponent; the cushioning of his "No" answers with background explanation about the management position.

Crescent City Case. The first pairings in question are C 1 with U 1, and C 1 with U 2.

It is typical of this case that U 1 incessantly needled, and that C 1 salvaged the situation again and again by providing the comic relief or the needed topical exit. (Incidentally, it would make an interesting sub-study to examine this case from the standpoint of the reversal of roles between M and C 1, on the hunch that it was C 1 who more often made the saving conciliatory gesture.)

U 2 was far less active in these proceedings than U 1, often remaining silent for long periods, unless time-study problems were raised. In sharp contrast to U 1, however, his manner tended to reflect amiability even when firm. What is perhaps more important, he was also able to concede the possibility that the company negotiators were acting in good faith when opposing his side, a belief which U 1 seemed entirely unable to entertain. The field notes for the last day of negotiations, when U 2 was replaced by the spectacular U 1–A, say in part: "The mediator remarked to me on the side several times during the day that the bargaining today needed U 2. I think he felt he could have worked with him, but not U 1, and *never* U 1–A."

The other pairings of interest in the Crescent City case are C 1 (and M) with U 1, and C 1 (and M) with U 1–A.

It is hard to conjecture with confidence whether this case would have settled without strike if one or another condition had been different. On the surface, the rigidity of U 1 appears to have been highly obstructive in effect, though C 1 and the mediator were both able on occasion to rescue the proceedings from U 1's influence and to breathe fresh life into the weakening situation.

There are grounds for contending that a major crisis developed in Session V (on the last day of the proceedings), being centered in (1) the theatrical appearance for the first three-quarters of the day of U 1–A, a time-study specialist brought in by the union from its International headquarters, whose performance created an uproar; and (2) the abject failure of the mediator to capitalize on the extraordinary relief which seized the main participants upon the departure of U 1–A in the early afternoon.

U 1–A's capacity to arouse personal antagonism proved destructive in two directions. He first incited C 1, who had previously been so successful in moderating and controlling the inter-personal atmosphere; later, in union caucus, he succeeded in working the mediator in the same vein. To a certain extent both of these people succumbed to U 1–A's ill-tempered cavils, some of which were literally shouted across the table.[7]

The strong negative reactions stirred up by U 1–A were so abruptly reversed upon his sudden departure that the investigator, watching from the sidelines, predicted that some definite agreements would be consummated before the day ended. The field notes on that session record the disappointing aftermath: "At 2:55 P.M. the joint meeting resumed downstairs, this time without U 1–A. I want to observe right at this point, since the mediator had speculated with the company in caucus upstairs immediately before this meeting that the atmosphere without U 1–A might noticeably improve, that I was on the lookout for this. I *clearly* had the feeling that until somewhere near the end the whole tone was so decidedly different and more conciliatory that the mediator might have gotten the union committee to agree to recommend the company's offer. When the mediator and I talked about this afterward, he too said he felt the atmosphere had improved. My lament is that the meeting *degenerated,* I felt, after it got off to this renewed and healthier state."[8]

[7] This portion of the Crescent City transcript can be consulted in Chapter 3, pp. 52–54.

[8] Two excerpts from the field notes bear on this point. One quotes the Atlas mediator during the Irving Mining case: "The mediator characterized as important the slight agreement reached before lunch—(it was *so* slight I can't even recall at this writing what it was)—because the atmosphere thereby generated augured well for starting up again in the afternoon. In other words, an atmosphere of agreement had been generated. The mediator asked if I had noticed how U 1 had written it down, apparently indicating that this informed him of the importance the union attached to the matter. He said this was something the company was going to have to give anyway, in the end, hence *in agreeing* they had not given up something unduly, but rather *in the act of* agreeing they had made a contribution." The second note is a reference to the second joint meeting in the final thirty-six-hour session of the Marathon case: "I have a feeling that the atmosphere is conducive this morning to settlement. Once the point has been reached where agreements are being made and commitments decided on, it *seems* a great deal easier to get further agreements on other points."

CHAPTER 3

Phase 2: Reconnoitering the Range

I

Phase 1 audits the range in terms of the areas of *dis*agreement; Phase 2 seeks out the areas that hold some promise of agreement. If the former is often long, the second is apt to be much more so, length resulting here not from extended speechmaking but from intensification of inter-person interactions. The outside observer is treated to a splendid exhibition of tactical maneuvers, both offensive and defensive, as the parties "jockey for position"—that is, spar for the choicest location, as each party sees it, on the negotiating range. When dexterously managed, the headwork and footwork of this phase form some of the most brilliant display in the negotiating repertoire.

So far as formal exchange at the table is concerned, there is often not much visible or audible to distinguish Phase 2 from Phase 1. The parties continue the same outer appearance of firmness as before, still insisting noisily that they will not recant their positions. If before they were given to philippics, these, too, will likely continue, even if the acrimony is now somewhat watered down. They press the opposite side to confess its basic weakness and capitulate; they themselves yield ground only after many protestations of reluctance or else self-proclaimed magnanimity. This familiar breast-beating carried over from Phase 1 preserves the atmosphere of the public forum, insuring a continuity of role for the organizational bodies. But the acute observer who is on the lookout for something new can detect soft spots already showing through the brave public fronts as the negotiating opens a second front backstage amid a new set of props and the institutional actors undergo recasting for another set of roles. Excellent examples can be found in the Atlas case to illustrate how negotiators begin to search earnestly in the background for signs of tacit agreement long before in their public exchange they can afford to profess anything but continuing disagreement, because of the loss of sparring advantage which would result from such a show of "weakness."

If it is handy to think of the first phase as a period for the parties to get on the record a turgid edition of what they wish to say about themselves and their positions, it could be said that the second phase is brought on by the fact that inevitably each side has to pull back from this public show of strength in order (1) to form some estimate of the *real* strength of the other—how far *can* the opponent be safely pushed for concessions before it will turn from negotiating to force a showdown?—and (2) to decide how long and how far to continue pressing its own claims—when would it become institutional suicide to get caught in a showdown with the opponent? In other words, it eventually becomes incumbent on each party to begin moving, or to assume a posture conducive to moving, toward a modified position which bears some relation to the position assumed by the other side. The shift in emphasis which this entails was once put very pungently by a mediator in the field, who counseled a party in caucus to "Stop talking about your own position, and start talking about the other party's." Serious negotiating does not, cannot begin until the parties have recognized that such a shift has become imperative.

The necessity to begin preparations for movement holds serious implications for the real decision-making centers of each party. If the terms of settlement have been immutably laid down before Phase 2 begins, the basis for attempting a *negotiated* settlement no longer exists. The prospects for mutual agreement grow in direct relation to the willingness of party advisers to let their best-laid plans face the hard test of surviving this phase. In the negotiating model the indeterminacy factor is provided for by the introduction of a distinction between negotiable and seriously intended positions. Time-wise, the major portion of the negotiation is taken up with a measured retreat from the former in search of the latter, which cannot be ascertained until demands are pursued at the table, then rebuffed or conceded. Even in those instances—and they are not unusual —when special circumstances force a party to decide its limits on an issue before negotiation gets under way, the party can put forward its minimum with enough padding attached so that later shrinkage will assist the parties in coming to terms. To one party which labeled every demand it discussed in caucus as "minimal," a mediator commented: "Well, minimums, when they're put on paper, become maximums."

Hard tactics and stances devised outside the conference room, so useful in season for holding firm inside that room, may become a liability to negotiators if insisted upon past their natural time. Once the charge is leveled in earnest at the table that a party's position ignores the existence of the other, that party's advisers are in effect being challenged to pay closer attention to the reports reaching them about what the opponent is doing and saying at the table. To serve his superiors well in this connection, a negotiator's reports must be more than simultaneous translations of the copious raw data reaching him in his capacity of observer. From the standpoint of the party, the premium is on the negotiator's distillation of his experiences with the data. Hence, by Phase 2 the negotiator who is proceeding on schedule will, in addition to maintaining his share of the organizational fanfare, be engaged in highly sensitive mental operations. The splintering of the negotiator's assignment in this phase between institutional and individual functions implies that he has been relieved in fact as well as in theory of a large measure of direction from outside and invested with considerable autonomy to act and react on his own. In the field one often hears plaintive comments by practitioners that too few of the top echelon in organizations are aware of the impotence which overtakes a conference when negotiators are deprived of the freedom they require if they are to carry out the psychological functions which are integral to Phase 2.

The specialized know-how for engaging the opposition in this phase is at wide variance with some of the standard practices for striking a deal in American commerce. In particular, the linear concepts employed to evaluate business gains in this economy—rewards for parsimony, logic, efficiency; penalties for circuity—prove harshly antagonistic to the production of negotiated gain. It is non-linear behaviors such as delays, retrogressions, resistances, and crises that bring the experiences of a psychological order which negotiators draw on in their final accounting. For the traditional business leader, Western style, this fact may be extremely difficult to reconcile with the exacting demand in Western circles for conscious speed toward the goal. Some of the saddest stories one hears recounted in the field concern high-level business executives who, on their first visit to the negotiating table, think to clinch a settlement with the same aplomb and the same techniques with which they close business deals over the luncheon table. It is not surprising that at the negotiating table they are often ruinous in their effect and that a whole new class of industrial relations specialists has inevitably developed in the society to look after this conference function. By virtue of this arrangement, the institutional groups are saved an immense amount of possible embarrassment and entrapment. Until the threshold of Phase 3 is reached, negotiators can, on their own initiative, make innumerable pilot runs on the data, trying on modified positions for fit without involving their respective bodies in a single firm commitment. It can scarcely fail to stand out how intolerable such marauding behavior becomes under circumstances of real combat, whereas under the auspices of the conference table the opportunity for negotiators to behave in this way can be of great assistance to all parties.

To the lay mind, some of the disconcerting aspects of this period are the nonchalance with which negotiators make assertions of fact, then subsequently deny them; with which they make critical issues out of special demands, then barter them away *in toto*—the famous *quid pro quo* —for something entirely different; with which they enter into agreements on specific items while reserving the right to abrogate the agreements later on; with which they examine numerous minor points exhaustively, then cavalierly dismiss them with an announcement that their fate hinges on a still undefined "package deal" to be worked out later. Confronted outright in Phase 2 with the stark competitiveness of their aims, the parties come face to face with a strategy problem which did not beset them in Phase 1. Any public show of change from one position to another will be a source of cues to the opposing party about what it can rightly expect and hopefully push for. If, accordingly, a management team has solid outer limits beyond which it cannot (or fervently hopes not to have to) go, it must stay *at some distance* from these to convey to the other side a sense of the real point. To state forthwith exactly what its limits are would be to state instead, in language of negotiation, "We offer this now, and you may legitimately figure that there is more to be had where this came from." An uninitiated observer of these delicate side-steps may disagree with negotiators that this is not wasted but constructive use of their time together. Indeed, without extensive exposure to the conference table, one is almost bound to be inadequately prepared to deal with the content of negotiation proceedings. Unlike the models of communication which rate clarity and precision as top values, at the table indirection is willfully incorporated into the verbal system. That this prolongs uncertainties and delays development of conclusions which must come before decisive action can be taken is not regarded in negotiating circles as a cost of doing business. The communicant at the conference table knows better than to scorn non sequiturs—gaps can be made more telling than words—or to grow impatient with long-winded sentences—some messages cannot cross the airways unless shielded between spoken lines. An extract from an interview with the Crescent City mediator subsequent to Session I of that case articulates the kind of open-ended evaluation to which the table conferees, including the mediator, must continually subject the talk from the other side of the table:

M: Toward the end of the day, after final caucuses with each of the parties, I determined that I should like to have both parties come together again, put their last positions on the table, and then get each of them to comment on their own last position as well as to refute the comments made by the other side. At this point I delivered a short talk on the—what seemed to me to be the unnecessary position that both parties were taking in that they wanted to resolve a question only by the show of economic strength. At this point the union restated its position as to why it would not give up all of the so-called economic issues in return for what they called the "privilege" of discussing the economic issues which could conceivably end up by being nothing, anyway, and if they had given up their non-economic issues in return for "your discussion" of economic issues, they would be left completely without bargaining position. The company then began to reply to the union's statements, and also restate its position. At this point I had the very peculiar feeling that the attorney for the company was taking too many *words* to *say No*. Our meeting had been very clear in such things before this in saying *No* just because he said No. Here, however, I thought that the speech that he delivered was much longer than was necessary if he wanted to maintain the same position, and that—I had the impression that maybe he wanted me to come up with some other solution, or at *least* was finding some way to have another meeting at which these problems could be discussed.

The popular difficulty in grasping this feature of negotiating was forcefully demonstrated in a Congressional hearing in which a mediator from the Federal Mediation and Conciliation Service (referred to in that Service as a "Commissioner") was quizzed on his activities in a certain case which was under Congressional investigation.

The occasion was a joint hearing before special subcommittees of the House Committees on Education and Labor and on Government Operations, held at St. Joseph, Michigan, June 9–10, 1953. In addition to Representative Clare E. Hoffman of Michigan, who was presiding officer, participants included Commissioner Chester E. Ralston of the Federal Mediation and Conciliation Service and William F. McKenna, general counsel for the Committee on Government Operations.

The investigation centered on labor difficulties in the Benton Harbor Malleable Industries of Benton Harbor, Michigan. According to testimony, labor-management relations in this concern had been in a state of strife for several years, involving slowdowns and work stoppages. Eventually a contract had been signed between the parties for a period of three years, prohibiting strikes or slowdowns and providing for a reopener at the end of one year for the specific purpose of discussing a pension plan. A three-day strike which occurred during the life of the contract prompted the company to institute a suit against the Local and International for $1,000,000 "for damages and breach of contract." Upon the occasion of the reopener, after several meetings between the parties one of them requested the presence of Commissioner Ralston, who then convened several sessions with the parties.

Testimony brought out the fact that the union had expressed itself to the mediator in private as being less interested in negotiating on the pension question than in persuading the company to drop the lawsuit and to remove the arbitration clause then in the contract.

It will be seen in the following condensed excerpt how Commissioner Ralston's subsequent testimony brought impatient rebuke from one of the investigators, who was hard put to fathom how the mediator thought to help the disputing parties as long as he maintained an uncommitted stand on issues.

Mr. McKenna: Did you report to the management of the conference group what the conditions of settlement would be or what the matter of dispute was?

Mr. Ralston: We first held a joint conference. Following that the parties separated, and I did report back to the company my evaluation of what the issues were, which included arbitration, pensions, and the lawsuit. We did discuss their relationship in the dispute at that time.

Mr. McKenna: What is the nearest you can give us to a direct quote of what you told the management conference group?

Mr. Ralston: I advised them that I was of the opinion that possibly the union knew that the company, being in the position they were financially, could not possibly pay for a pension, but in the background of this situation was the union's request that a suit be dropped.

Mr. McKenna: Did you not understand that under the contract only pensions could be raised?

Mr. Ralston: Yes, sir.

Mr. McKenna: What did you do after you talked with the labor group?

Mr. Ralston: I transferred to—I submitted to the company the union's position, and as to the question of what was open in the contract or could be opened in the contract—I do not think it is an abnormal procedure that other issues might arise during an opening that it is necessary to settle before a dispute can be completed.

Mr. Hoffman: Did you at that meeting in substance say to Mr. Bell that the union was not interested in pensions, but in the dismissal of the suit? That in substance?

Mr. Ralston: I possibly indicated in my discussion that a major point that seemed to be between the parties was the suit.

Mr. Hoffman: Dismissal of the lawsuit?

Mr. Ralston: That is right, but the pension was still an issue. It was never taken out of not being an issue between the parties.

Mr. Hoffman: Did you not say in substance at that meeting, directing your remarks to Mr. Bell, and in the presence of several, perhaps 10, of the company employees, that the union was not interested in the pension?

Mr. Ralston: I may have indicated that possibly the pension issue could have been dropped at that time; that is right.

Mr. Hoffman: That is right. You did tell them that the pension issue was out, that in substance, I mean?

Mr. Ralston: Well, I probably—

Mr. Hoffman: I do not intend to give you the word.

Mr. Ralston: I probably indicated it could have been dropped if the suit could be eliminated and something done about arbitration.

Mr. Hoffman: But you did give the company employees, and it was your intention to give the company employees, to understand that if the lawsuit was dropped, if that issue was out—

Mr. Ralston: There was a possibility of pensions not being pushed any further.

Mr. Hoffman: Did you not tell them flatly in substance that if the company dropped the lawsuit, the pension issue would be dropped, and had you not been so instructed by the union representatives? There are two questions there in one if you want to separate them.

Mr. Ralston: I think at all times one was contingent upon the other to the extent that I do not think the union at any time said that the pension was out of the way, but if something could be done about the lawsuit, there was a possibility of it being taken out of the picture.

Mr. Hoffman: You keep saying "possibility."

Mr. Ralston: That is right.

Mr. Hoffman: Did you not give the company employees to understand that if the lawsuit was dropped, that the pension issue would be dropped?

Mr. Ralston: There was a possibility it could be eliminated.

Mr. Hoffman: No, do not go back to "possibility." Did you not go farther than a possibility and tell them it was your understanding—I will put it this way: Did you not believe at that time that if the lawsuit was dropped, the pension issue would be dropped?

Mr. Ralston: I did believe that, that is right.

Mr. Hoffman: You did believe that honestly and sincerely, did you not?

Mr. Ralston: That is right.

Mr. Hoffman: You were trying to settle the labor dispute?

Mr. Ralston: That is right.

Mr. Hoffman: Then did you not tell them so?

Mr. Ralston: I possibly indicated to them in a way that that could be done, yes.

Mr. Hoffman: Did you not understand from your conversation with the union's bargaining agency that it was their position that if the lawsuit was dropped, the pension issue would be dropped?

Mr. Ralston: That was their indication.

Mr. Hoffman: That is what you understood, was it not?

Mr. Ralston: That was their indication to me.

Mr. Hoffman: You believed it, did you not?

Mr. Ralston: Yes, sir.

Mr. Hoffman: You were there trying to settle the labor dispute, were you not?

Mr. Ralston: Yes, sir.

Mr. Hoffman: Did you not then give the company's representatives to understand that if they dropped the lawsuit, the pension would be dropped? Did you not so state if flatly in substance?

Mr. Ralston: I stated that if they would move off the suit, there was a possibility that the union would drop the pension.

Mr. Hoffman: Every time you bring back "possibility." I do not want to quibble about this thing. Here you are, trying to settle a labor dispute. The issues in that labor dispute as you got them from the union bargaining representatives were two, a pension that they wanted, and a lawsuit that they did not want.

Mr. Ralston: There was another one. There is arbitration there.

Mr. Hoffman: Arbitration—but that got out of the picture pretty early, did it not?

Mr. Ralston: No, I think it is still there.

Mr. Hoffman: Just for the moment forget it. There were those two issues, were there not?

Mr. Ralston: Those 2 were involved, yes, and 1 other.

Mr. Hoffman: You have already testified that you gathered from what the union bargaining representative said that, if the lawsuit was dropped, the pension would be dropped, have you not? You have already so testified, have you not? You have already so testified?

Mr. Ralston: They indicated that that was the possibility, yes.

Mr. Hoffman: Why do you always stick in a "possibility"?

Mr. Ralston: I think that it is a matter of the way we operated as a service of trying to work between the parties and still hold the confidence of the parties.

Mr. Hoffman: What is the use of going to the company representatives with a possibility? You go to the company representatives as a mediator with some proposition, do you not?

Mr. Ralston: No; not necessarily.

Mr. Hoffman: Do you not carry the word back and forth between the two?

Mr. Ralston: Not necessarily, no. We—

Mr. Hoffman: How in the world can you ever adjust anything unless you tell each side what the other one—

Mr. Ralston: We make an effort to move into a position that we ourselves know that certain things can be done, and when we find that those things can be done, we can generally find some basis of a settlement.

Mr. Hoffman: What did you find from the union representatives before you went to the company representatives in your opinion that could be done to settle that?

Mr. Ralston: I knew in the background that they would, in my opinion, and in their opinion, possibly drop. But I did not say to the company that they would drop. I said there is a possibility of the union dropping the question of pensions.

Mr. Hoffman: Do you think you and I would ever get together on the price I should pay for something you had to sell if I said that perhaps I might give you so much and you said that perhaps you might accept it if I would name it?

Mr. Ralston: I think there is a possibility, yes.

Mr. Hoffman: Wouldn't you want a firm offer if you were going to buy or sell something?

Mr. Ralston: Of course I—

Mr. Hoffman: If a fellow had a crate of strawberries and the farmer comes in and says to the buyer, "Possibly if you offer $10 I might take it," and the fellow says, "Possibly if you agree to take $10, I will offer it."

So where would they get?

Mr. Ralston: Mr. Congressman, I had no offer to give. I had something to carry back to the company that was an idea that could be worked out as a settlement.[1]

II

With the parties working simultaneously in two directions, both to give and to obtain cues, concessions ahead of schedule benefit no one, not even the receiving party. Not only does a party tantalize and mislead the opponent if it relaxes its firmness too quickly, but the parties also need the opportunity to experience exhaustion of their demands before they can be satisfied that they have drained what was there to be had. Premature movement robs them of this experience. Though each party can be reasonably confident that positions taken in this stage will not be maintained intact to the very end, when and how much movement will ultimately be made away from these starting points—how firm *is* firm?—is not yet known; and when a negotiator is at last convinced that "This is all" means just that, it will not be because the opponent has told him so but because he has personally experienced the futility of seeking more. The outsider looking in on the conference room for the first time may recoil from this as a filibuster of sorts, interpreting it as evidence of reluctance on the part of the negotiators to get down to agreement. To the contrary, the exhausting of topics offers one of the most useful criteria for measuring the timeliness of movement.

A young mediator-intern who sat in as an observer on the Crescent City case began reacting from the opening session to the mediator's management of the talking-out requirement, a theme which he returned to in trying to evaluate his own capabilities:

M: Look, I want to establish one thing before we get a—too far away from Crescent City. Harry was very persistent in continually discussing, rediscussing, 'n going over ground that was—had been gone over again and again and again. As I said before, knowing full well that these people had established, that they were testing each other's strength, and had evaluated each other's strength, and were aware of stre—strengths and weaknesses, correctly or incorrectly, but—their analysis, that is, but they—they—they were aware—they had determined this—he continually—it was notable, I think —that it was notable on both parties that they *never evidenced* any annoyance

[1] *Joint Hearings before Special Subcommittees of the Committees on Education and Labor and Government Operations, House of Representatives, Eighty-third Congress, First Session,* Hearings held at St. Joseph, Mich., June 9 and 10, 1953 (Washington, D.C., U.S. Government Printing Office, 1954), pp. 24, 34–38.

at this harping—and it did amount to harping. Harry has an ability to say in 20 words what can be said in 2 or 3, which helps. It—it kills time. Now, do I—do I—am I too curt and therefore not allowing myself time?

Then Harry—Harry made notes of each of these issues in dispute, and when they were finished with their comments—their ad lib comments, shall we say—then Harry pres—went over the list and asked leading questions about each item, and it appeared to me that he didn't need the answers, but he wanted to get them talking—even if it was repetitious, he wanted to keep them talking to each other, or in the presence of each other. And there were 5 or 6 items there. He asked them for the reasons behind it and induced the statement on the part of another party on some angles or aspects about it, and kept a conversation going fairly x^2—normally. The reason I emphasize that, you see, is that it struck me, and again I—I think of myself as a trainee, as a learner here—if I were on this alone, would I ask as many questions? I knew that as a matter of technique I would have asked some questions, but I want to know would I, of myself; and I couldn't answer the question. In fact, the answer I gave myself was one that, no, I don't think I would have, and that would have been bad, you see. Then I thought also that I would like to have more of this kind of experience with Harry and other mediators just to—to find out how much of this sort of questioning, this sort of asking obvious questions and the leading questions is useful and necessary.

On the opening day of the Atlas case that mediator was probed on the same subject. The field notes from that conversation say, in part:

At lunch I asked the mediator a number of questions about the morning session. (Why did he break the session up just at the time he did?) His first answer— "Because I felt hungry right then"—ended in a laugh. Actually, they were running out of things to say and beginning to repeat themselves. They were also beginning to put on a show for him, and that he does not like! (How did he know this was intended for him and not as a display for their own people or the other side?) There are ways of telling the difference: (a) He watched the union committee; they would frown when the company made a good point and smile when U 1 scored a point against the company; (b) U 1, at one point, had said about a point that it was "for the mediator's information." (What will he do if, during the afternoon, they get into this same kind of an act and he has no lunch recess to resort to?) He will call a recess and keep them apart for a while. (Why is he bringing them *together*

---

^{2} x indicates a word which was not audible in the transcription. The number of words lost is signified by the number of x's, up to a total of five; any greater loss (such as an entire sentence) is denoted by the maximum of xxxxx.

again after lunch, if they are already beginning to repeat themselves?) These parties have only had one bargaining session before today; they have a lot to talk about yet. A lot of mediators made the mistake of rushing in and starting to mediate too fast. The parties have to talk a certain amount before they are ready for mediating effort. He is giving them a chance here.

Through its record of stability (or instability), every negotiated settlement measures at some future date the degree of the parties' success in ruling out at the time of negotiation the feasibility of any other agreement. If the time differential needed to acquire this knowledge could somehow be narrowed, perhaps the opportunity to pre-test settlements before their formal conclusion would prove as economical of time in other negotiations as it did in the Marathon case. Because the parties in that instance worked so close to the strike deadline before reaching a settlement, the understandings on most of the items were left in oral form, with a post-settlement meeting set up for one week later for the purpose of putting the agreement into written form. C 1, U 1, and the mediator attended this latter session. To everyone's surprise, six issues came out at that time as still actively in dispute or misunderstood, and had to be re-mediated by the mediator. The mediator was asked in private later for his interpretation of this unexpected turn of events. The field notes record his answer as follows:

The 6 points which U 1 contested and brought up for adjustment, the mediator said, indicated that there had *not* been a full meeting of minds in the negotiations. He expressed it with a customary phrase of his: "Not all the i's were dotted nor the t's crossed." With reference to his own role in the matter, he made 2 points. Some of the misunderstandings he "subconsciously let get by." Others he recognized at the time; but saying to himself that "The parties are adults, so why should I take them by the hand and point everything out to them?" he *deliberately* let these slip through.

In the Marathon case, it was the investigator's private conclusion that a deficiency which had developed in Phase 1, long before the mediator had appeared on the scene, had not been adequately repaired and had bred a problem situation between the parties which came forth in the post-settlement difficulty. This was the fact that the union had not been allowed or encouraged to talk itself out on its original set of forty-three demands. All through the later sessions with the mediator there were outcroppings of union complaints and criticisms on this score, and again and again both mediator and company team had to contend with efforts of the union group to reintroduce one or another of their original demands which had since been washed out.

C 1 recognized the problem at the very time it was created in Phase 1. Excerpts from a private interview with him after the second meeting between the two parties reveal that he was already weighing the consequences in strategy terms.

C 1: I was a little disappointed in the meeting.

AD: Why?

C 1: Well, in the first place, we sat in the caucus and discussed the matter of drawing the union (AD: Uh-huh) out on these things for all of this meeting, and I had hoped all day. (AD: Uh-huh) In the beginning, the meeting was cut off at noon, and it necessary in al—all this meeting and the next meeting and if necessary, a *third* meeting, because I wanted to get impressed *thoroughly* on the union's mind the ridiculousness of their demands, that they came in and made demands without reason (AD: Uh-huh), to eliminate some of the tension or to try to eliminate the deadlock later on so that they don't get—the company doesn't sit down and say, "Well, these are your demands," and so on, and then they become set in those demands, because they're not thoroughly discussed, and later on when you get into a crisis *it's too late!* (AD: Uh-huh) And be—try to—to wear them down, and—and I tried to give C 2 that tip-off several times: "Hit 'em. Hit 'em." At this time we can afford to get the union mad; they won't strike at this point. This is a time to rile them up, if we *have* to. I don't say that we should. But we don't—we don't run any risk in riling 'em up at this time. (AD: Uh-huh) So that this is a time we should ridicule. (Slight pause) Because if we don't, we're not going to get the improvement in our contract. We—we're aiming at 2 things, now: one is to negotiate these demands with the union's, the other is to get an improved contract, from *our* standpoint. (AD: Uh-huh) And I feel that in order to do that we have got to—to do a pretty thorough job on going over these fellows. Now, we're either—we're gonna have to do one of 2 things. We're either gonna have to go back in the next meeting and start this over again, which I think now is a very difficult thing to do, or change our strategy slightly to accomplish that end by different means. The other thing I was disappointed in was the fact that even though we had discussed it before, C 2 said that we would present the union with our demands. Well, as a matter of fact, I have no intention of doing that unless I have to. So that just now I—I was in C 2's office. I said to him, "What's the matter? Did you run out of words?" (AD: Yeah. Uh-huh) And that was a tip-off to him that I *wasn't* quite satisfied. Now, I was just in here talking to him *now,* and I brought up the point *again.*

I said to him then, I didn't understand why he cut it off. (AD: Uh-huh)
He feels that there'll be a lot more discussion on this, but—there will be,
but I think there's a lot of difference in just having discussion on it and
having a discussion at the right time, that is, a time that is timed for us
(AD: Uh-huh), to our benefit. (AD: Uh-huh. Uh-huh) I don't think any
particular damage has been done, but it *is* one of those situations which I
indicated to you that I was gonna have to deal with. And—(pause).[3]

Somewhat later, after outside assistance had been called into the case,
he restated the problem in the first management caucus with the newly
arrived mediator.

C 1: I think the break came too fast, M. Let me tell you a little bit about the
meeting between us to this—this is Tuesday a week ago. We had been
going over—in essence going over these company proposals, article by article, and section by section, because, you know, one of the things that we
wanted was to straighten out this contract. And we had been getting some
agreement, and some disagreement. We were defining, in other words, our
areas of disagreement, and—it took a sudden turn. I—I—I felt something
there but kept moving along in the normal pace, so as not to upset anything,
and we were reviewing a rewritten proposal of the company on the grievance procedure, and we got to a certain section and U 1 says, "Well, we
don't want that. We have to tell you that that won't go." He said, "We
have to take that out"—something to that effect. I looked at him and I
said, "Well, that's what you asked to have put in there last time." U 1 said
something or other, and ended up by saying, "Well, I'm just walking on
water. I don't know where I'm going." He said, "We're going through this
whole contract," he said, "and we're going over a lot of stuff we already
have," and so on. And I said to him, "Well, ya wanta sign last year's contract and forget it?" "Well," he said, "would you sign last year's contract
and talk about wages?" (M: Uh-huh) And I said, "You make a proposal."
So he kept after me to talk about wages. I said, "No, you make a proposal.
If you have a proposal to make, you make it. I suggest you caucus." And,
so they did caucus, and they came back with these 9 points (M: Yeah)—the
contract had 9 points. And that was about midnight. So we recessed at that
point. Then we came into this meeting this week on Tuesday and gave them
the company's counter-proposal, because—I thought—it looked as though

[3] In the field notes C 1 is recorded as putting the same thoughts in this way:
"He thinks things are going all right, if he can keep C 2 from going too fast. C 2
gets impatient, and C 1 has to hold him down. C 2 will say something isn't important, for example, and he'll be inclined to let it slide out from under them.
C 1's reaction is that it isn't whether it's important as an *issue*, but *extremely* so
whether it's strategy."

we were hitting into the package deal, counter-proposal for counter-proposal, to work out. And, immediately U 2 began to draw out 4 or 5 more points —you know the technique that he uses. (M: Uh-huh) We listened patiently to those, and I didn't think that any of them were really major points. I mean, they were just certain things that apparently are to U 2. And U 1 kept trying to calm him down and explain it away, and particularly on one item U 1 was with us, right down the line, obviously, and—Ann has remarked before, or asked me before, why it is that U 1 advises the union in front of us, and it dawned on me at that time that the only reason that I could see was that he was trying to indicate to the company that he could make an agreement with us but he was blocked by U 2, see. He was just trying to get U 2 to forget this and get back (M: Uh-huh)—but she went dead. They asked for caucus and they were out about—oh, 15 or 20 minutes, C 2?

C 2: At the most.

C 1: —and said they were all finished, and I said to C 2, "Well, it doesn't look good, because they certainly haven't considered the company's proposals and what's in them in a matter of 15 or 20 minutes." And when we got back, in essence what they said was, "We don't want any of it. Let's go back to our 43 demands." So at that time *we* asked for a caucus, and we felt that this bargaining area had been narrowed down. Now, if it slipped away from this point at this *time* of the negotiation, it would spell trouble. And, on the face of this block—I hesitate to call it a refusal to bargain, but i—it's not—i—in essence it was a refusal to discuss the situation (M: Uh-huh), and I seriously—we felt that in the light of that, it was time we had your assistance. So we went back in and proposed to the union that, in view of the situation that as it developed in this meeting, that the assistance of mediator would be called for and we felt that it would be helpful. Would they like to make it a joint request or should we call him (laughs slightly)? And U 1 *immediately* said, "I think it's a good idea and I think we should do it and I would like to have it a joint request." U 2 didn't say a word. He just got blank in the face and stuffed his papers in the bag. Now, that's the way we saw it u—I's just covering the last couple meetings, C 2, with M, and he's got a file here—all the submissions and proposals and the agreement we made on x.

M: What—what I don't—I—I don't look forward to this possibility that, now that I'm in we may have to start all over again, that there may be a— a xxx—

C 1: (Over M above) I'm gonna throw—I'm gonna throw the block right at 'em, because my demands are on the table—my proposals are on the table, and if they go back, I wanta go back to all of ours, too. (M: Uh-huh)

And we're gonna—we're just gonna start all over again and I'm gonna keep right on plugging—

M: (Over C 1 above) Well, that's just exactly what I mean (laughing)!

C 1: Because I can't afford to advise my company to move any differently. Now, at one point U 1 did say something about using some of these things that we've initialed. Generally speaking, as a counter to that, I would say, "O.K., let's use *all* of the ones that we initialed," because we have an agreement there that if either party withdraws anything that's initialed the other party has the right to withdraw *all* of the i—initialed agreements. (M: Uh-huh) And I told him that the company—

M: (Over C 1 above) And that's part of your pre-bargaining x—

C 1: (Over M above) There're some things in that initialed section—those initialed sections that I want very dearly. And—we were willing to throw *those* over to go with 'em. We have tried to keep pace with 'em, M, but when you open the door and a guy won't walk in, I don't know what to do.

M: Well, I can well imagine the confusion, because I—

C 1: (Over M above) Now, here's this—here—

M: (Over C 1 above)—I've become the third of this triumvirate—

C 1: Apparently it's fear on their part—

M: (Over C 1 above)—each part of which confesses don't know what to do with a circumstance such as this, and one of the things I didn't hope to have to do was to begin with the first item in the contract and start to bargain with each side (C 1: Well—) all the way down through it.

C 1: I don't know what stops them, M, but we set it up for a deal, see (M: Yeah), and then we hit it. We—we just go *boom*. And that's what threw U 1 off, because he didn't come back on the bargaining principle of trade, see. (M: Uh-huh) There was no trade set-up so that management when necessary could give gracefully (M: Uh-huh), see. I mean, you—you lost that little technique of face-saving through the thing, and the union was moving in *jumps* rather than in *steps,* and they jumped right out in—into the—from the fire into the frying pan. Well, in order to save it we decided we'd jump along with 'em (M: Uh-huh), and when we jumped with 'em, apparently it boiled down to such a small package that when they boiled down the package we thought, well, they're interested, see. (M: Uh-huh) We're—we're in a trading area; we're in a—a movement area. But as soon as we came back because we didn't accept this proposal of theirs carte blanche and we came back with one they didn't even wanta talk about ours. (*Long* pause) I think we're in a realm of agreement. We've got the basis of agreement. We've got 2 things. We got timing for 2 weeks, and to work out a little bargaining—a little horse-trading.

M: Uh-huh. (Pause) Assuming, of course, that there is a possibility of this proceeding on the basis of some give and take. If, however, the thing is going to start going backwards rapidly, it looks like the situation is gonna take *quite a while* to get straightened away before it starts goin' ahead again.

In a post-mortem interview C 1, reflecting upon the usefulness of turning to mediation in this case, once again returned to the theme that the union had caused trouble all the way through because it had not used its *positions* to establish a coherence about its *movements*.

C 1: The—the problem with it, ya see, was not (slight pause)—I don't think you could have really done it under s—I don't know. Maybe you could have, but, see, here's U 2—look at U 2 and w—his reaction when he gets something written from the company, see. Look at the way he shifted his positions all the time, and look at the way we'd go in there. And one time we'd be talking about one thing and another we never—so many things that, instead of going through and cleaning that one up and setting it aside, and then the next one and set it aside, and taking it by slices, we were jumping all over the lot! (AD: Uh-huh) Well, you can't write on that basis (AD: Uh-huh) because you don't know where it's fitting in. (AD: No) And that's another reason for that start-off that I had of the whole agreement, see? With any union that has had any experience in negotiations, they *want* to do it that way for the simple reason they always know what their position is and so does the management. And it makes collective bargaining easy because you keep—as I said before, you define the area of difference. (AD: Uh-huh) And then you sit down across the table and you look at the other fellow and he looks at you and you *know exactly* what your differences are. And then you begin to whittle them away (AD: Uh-huh) till it finally gets down to this package, and close it. And at all times both parties know what their—they are and what their bargaining position is. (AD: Uh-huh) And if U 2 had done it, I don't think I'd a-gotten away with the money.
AD: Well, would that have helped him to realize better what was happening?
C 1: Sure!
AD: But, as it is, he doesn't have any *framework*.

With an occasional practitioner, the usefulness of the hard rounds of talk in exhausting topics is mistaken to be one of exhausting negotiators. If a party requires this kind of annihilation of its opposite, it is not prepared to participate in legitimate negotiations. The concept of victory or conquest by one over the other is complete anathema in negotiation, even in Phase 1 when the conflict-waging is at a peak. To say that a negotiation in industry has "terminated in" strike, or that a strike has been "ended by" negotiation, reflects a conceptual contradiction. A strike and a negotiation are power contests of unlike order; they are neither comparable nor complementary.

The really pressing problems related to over-talk do not in general originate with the few persons bent on wearing out the opposition; instead, they derive from the process in which practitioners must engage. From its very inception, negotiation is fraught with the danger that rigor mortis may set in during one or another period of repetitive activity. The attractiveness of stiffened positions can be rendered well-nigh hypnotic by an interval of hard-hitting Phase 1 exposition, with its remarkably singular purpose. The Crescent City case, which passed through a strike before a contract was signed, gave evidence of suffering from this defection on one side of the table. The union's position on the wage issue, usually denominated in the joint exchange as getting "within shouting distance of the Chicago rates" (that is, the rates paid at the parent plant in Chicago), remained essentially unchanged and unspecific from beginning to end of the negotiation. Unlike the Marathon union, which seemed not to alight long enough on any point to turn it into a position, the union in the Crescent City case continued to send arguments and counter-arguments of the Phase 1 type flying across the table even in final Session V—only now delivered through a megaphone: namely, U 1-A, a representative of the International staff paying his first visit to this conference table. The following is only a sample of the exchange that took place.

C 1: That's right. That's the proposal.

U 1: Well, that certainly makes (laughing slightly) it the—the more ridiculous. Retroactive date only if the contract is settled this week—well, I certainly would like to settle it this week, too, but I don't see how we possibly can agree to it on the basis of what you offer. And no improvement factors —no improvement factor at all. If—if anybody is entitled to an improvement factor, these people are, based on the production that you're getting here. And then the offer that you make here—I don't see how we possibly can get together on 5¢ and 2¢. It'll just—well, I mean, I—I thought that you'd come up with something better than that. Believe me, I—I can't see the way clear at all to even go to these people and recommend it. If something w—some half—half-decent here—it was a fair offer, I might see my way clear to go to this membership and recommend acceptance. But I just can't see it on—on the basis of what you came back here with. I think it's— I'm just wondering if you—you actually give it any real thought at all.

I—I wonder if you're—if you're actually joking in the—in some of the proposals that you have made here. Come back here and say that you're willing to give us an over-all increase of 5¢ and 2¢, why, I think it's ridiculous.

C 1: Well, what d'ya mean, / ridiculous? [4]

U 1: (Over C 1 above) Well—well, I think it is. It—'course, you're—you're gonna give us the old area song and dance and—well, I just can't see it at all. You gave no consideration at all on what you're—the requirements that you're asking here and what is bein' done elsewhere in the corporation. Why, I don't see how you expect these people to s—to accept this kind of a package at all. I certainly can't go there and—and recommend it. I (C 1: Well, I—) just can't.

C 1: Well, I'm sorry about that, Curt, but (U 1: Well, I am, too!) I like to an—I'd like to answer first that we've giving—given it *very* serious thought. Secondly, I wanta repeat that our desire in this plant is—I've stated many times that the take-home pay of the people that work in Crescent City is comparable, if not better than, what is generally taken home in the area. I think we've *maintained* that, the people *know* we've maintained that, and we will *continue* to do that. Now, you don't like to hear "What's the area earning?" argument. I understand that. Y—you don't like to hear it because you *know* that the employees' earnings compare *quite* favorably with the area. Ya know that the benefits they have / compare.

U 1: (Over C 1 above) It's not a fair picture. It's not a fair picture at all. It isn't.

C 1: Well, only because you're looking at a different p—differen (U 1: Well—)—looking through a different / set of binocular.

U 1: (Over C 1 above) As I told ya last week, you certainly wanta compare these people with some sausage factory over in Richfield (C 1: But, of course—), why, we don't wanta be compared that way at all (C 1: Well, Curt, if you would show me—), and you know it. You're—you're in a— you're in a wealthy industry. You're part of the television industry, and you can pay. And I don't wanta be compared with some shirt factory down the street that is makin' a couple nickels an hour. You're—you're —you have the ability to pay. You're a wealthy organization, and you're part of a wealthy industry, and you can—and you can do it. You can pay much more than you're offering here.

C 1: Well, you're entitled to that opinion.

U 1: I think that the—I think that the—the Textile Workers did a—did a fair—a—a fairly good job in their industry, but *you're not* in the textile

[4] / indicates the point at which the speaker who has the floor is interrupted by another who continues after him.

industry, or (C 1: I'm not—) you're not in the meat industry (C 1: I'm not com—I'm not com—), or somethin' like that. But that's what you wanta compare with, though!

C 1: No! No! Not at all. (U 1: Well!) Not at all.

U 1: Let's compare a little bit with what your—what your people are earning in C—Chicago, in Milwaukee, and the requirements that are being asked there in—in those plants.

C 1: Well, I—I—I can't—I can't foreclose you from making any comparison you wish, any more than you can foreclose me. It's another thing, however, for you to *persuade* me. And you haven't, and you won't, if you use that argument. You can *use* it; I can't stop you.

U 1-A: I don't think he will if you live by a double standard. You see, if you live by a double standard economic philosophy, which the television industry has tended to live by for many, many years and which we have broken down, we are *never* gonna convince you. The only way we're gonna convince you is to try to convince you that you can't apply a double standard. You can't apply one economic philosophy to the product you sell and another economic philosophy to the workers whose wages you pay. You (C 1: Well—) see, you don't charge different rates for receiving tubes anywhere all United States. There's a standard rate that you charge for receiving tubes. It's the same argument with a television set. The Consolidated Industries Corporation makes sets in Decatur and they sell 'em for the same price in Dallas, Texas, as they do in Decatur. (C 1: I'm very aware of that) And so we say that if Consolidated Industries opened up a plant in Dallas, Texas, they gotta pay the same rates they pay in Decatur.

C 1: That's what *you* say.

U 1-A: We say that because we think that's—it's *only fair play*. It's only fair play to apply an economic philosophy to your workers as you do to your product.

C 1: That's all right. That's what you say.

U 1-A: I w—no, it's not—not only what I say, but it is fair play! It (C 1: Well—) is *admittedly* fair play. (C 1: Well, xx—) The Consolidated Industries Corporation goes along with this philosophy. (C 1: Well—) The Acme Electric Company goes along with this philosophy, the Monarch Corporation (C 1: H'm) goes along with this philosophy. (C 1: Then there are a lot of companies that won't) The New Economy go—well, you name 'em. (C 1: Pardon?) (Speaking loudly) You *name* 'em!

C 1: Oh, well, I—I know lots of corporations (U 1-A: Name 'em!) in—in the television—

U 1-A: Don't tell me there are lots. Name 'em!

C 1: Oh, well, there are lot of companies that (U 1-A: [Shrilly] Name 'em!) have mills in the South / or in the West.

U 1-A: (Over C 1 above, loudly) Who? Who? Who? Name 'em!

C 1: Well, I didn't come prepared to name them.

U 1-A: Well, ya see, that's the point! Every time the question is asked, "We're unprepared to name them."

C 1: Well, you know the reason I won't—*no!* I—I'm—I can name *some*. (U 1-A: Well, I wanta hear. I'm willing. I'm willing to hear) There's a reason—there's a reason why I won't. There's a reason why I won't. Because if I do, then that word is immediately flashed to the Textile Workers, or the Steelworkers, or to somebody else. I know lots of companies that have differentials in different plants.

U 1-A: I'm talking about television / companies.

C 1: (Over U 1-A above) Oh, I'm not! I'm not. (U 1-A: Well, I am) I don't know any—I don't know anything about the television / industry.

U 1-A: (Over C 1 above) I am. I'm—I'm—well, I do! I / do.

C 1: (Over U 1-A above) Well, I'm not interested in your point of view (U 1: Well!) so far as the television industry—

U 1: Well, I (U 1-A: I do!) think you—well, you should become / interested.

U 1-A: (Over U 1 above) I *am* interested (C 1: I'm not!), because these people work in the television (C 1: That's right. That's right. But—) industry, and we're not gonna permit *any* company to apply a double standard— a double / standard—

C 1: (Over U 1-A above) Who are you? The— / who are you, now?

U 1-A: (Over C 1 above) The *union* (C 1: Oh, well, I'm not interested in what you're gonna permit and what you're not gonna permit!) is not going to permit *any* company to p—apply a double standard to its product and its workers.

C 1: Well, I don't—am not interested in what (strongly) the Electrical Workers Union's gonna permit, if you please! (U 1-A: Well, I tell you what we're gonna—) (Loudly) Because an employer is gonna pay only what he's willing to pay, I mea—and not what Electrical Workers Union says he's gonna pay. / I don't give a damn about your double or single standard!

U 1-A: (Over C 1 above) Well, I didn't say anything about what C 2 is going to pay, or Crescent City (C 1: And I don't care what your International president says) Manufacturing is gonna pay. (U 1 laughs shortly) I don't—I didn't say anything about / that.

C 1: (Over U 1-A above, loudly) We're gonna pay the wages we're *agreeable* to pay (U 1-A: All right. Now, I'm telling you—), not what you say, or what your philosophy is.

U 1-A: I'm telling you again one of the things which makes for unfair treatment, for lack of fair play, for lack of genuine bargaining on your part is your inability, or your refusal, to apply the same standard to the human beings whose wages you pay and to the p—than to the products you produce.

C 1: Who are you to come here today and tell me what my genuine bargaining is?

U 1–A: Well, I am / a representative—

C 1: (Over U 1–A above) You just met me today.

U 1–A: I'm a rep—I've / *heard*—

C 1: (Over U 1–A above) You've never bargained with me before.

U 1–A: I've heard *considerable* here.

C 1: Oh, well, I'm glad you can judge after 5 minutes.

U 1–A: Oh, I've been in this business a *long, long* time.

C 1: So have I! But I (U 1–A: Yeah) don't like to be told by any union what *they're goin' to permit,* because that's im—the worker only gets work because the employer supplies it, and he only gets paid because the employer *pays* him! You don't supply a *day's work* to *any* employee, or *a day's wages,* except the people that work on the Electrical Workers Union payroll! So who are you to permit industry to do thus and so?

U 1–A: Well, I tell you very frankly / and very honestly—

C 1: (Over U 1–A above) Socialistic philosophy is what it is, emanating (U 1: Uh-h-h!) right from your International headquarters.

U 1–A: I tell you very honestly and very frankly that the union (emphatically) will not permit any employer in the television industry to apply the ph— the economic philosophy of the double standard.

C 1: Well, then, let's get up and leave (U 1–A: Naw), because we're (loudly) not goin' to pay the Chicago rates here, if you call that a double standard.

U 1: Well, I told you before that you're not acquainted with your facts, and you certainly haven't *got* yourself acquainted with the (C 1: Well, I'm very close. I'm—I am—) facts. The jobs are not—the jobs are not the same! (C 1: Well) There's a different wage payment plan and everything else.

C 1: Well, I'm—I'm—I'm not—

U 1: (Loudly) And I said there and I say to you again the same thing here, we expect to get within *shouting* distance of these rates that are being played in Chicago. (C 1: Well, we'll all—) And we said the same thing in Midwest Electric. And somewhere down the road we're going to get the *same* amount of money, and we're going to pro—produce the same amount of pieces. I said that we don't expect to 'complish in—in a first agreement, but, by God, if you come here and say that you're going to give us 5¢ and 3 cent or 2¢ and that's within shouting distance, believe me, it—it's not anywhere *near* what *I'm* thinking about.

C 1: Well, we've got in shouting distance to a lotta things this / morning and—

U 1: (Over C 1 above) Well, you're the one (C 2 laughs) that's been shouting. Believe me, you have.

C 1: Well, I assume you'll submit this to the membership.

U 1: Are—are you—are you telling me now that this is your final—final offer on these / things?

C 1: (Over U 1 above) Well, I've made you a package proposal. You've—(rather long pause).

III

In this industrial system, there is a general feeling that calling for outside assistance is legitimate only after the parties have bankrupted their own private resources. Actually, the effectiveness of a mediator in liquidating a dispute case hinges to a not inconsiderable extent on the status of the situation when he inherits the case. This is an important dictum about mediation which deserves wider circulation and respect in industrial circles than it now enjoys. Mediators in the field often lament that they are too seldom called into cases early enough, before all the elasticity has been stretched out of the disputed items. The point is akin to Leiserson's contention that to talk about mediating a strike is a confusion, if not also a perversion, of the mediation function. C 1 of the Atlas management team is recorded in the field notes as making the same point in an interview just prior to the opening of that case: "He quoted the mediator as having warned them in advance, 'Don't bring a dead cat down here.' He indicated that he knew he had to give the mediator something to work with. He would not, he said, consent to mediation if he had already offered the union all he had to give."

From the standpoint of giving the mediator "something to work with," the Marathon case was essentially poverty-stricken on the union side when he entered the situation.[5] The union's original forty-three demands had been replaced in a single sweep by a new set of nine demands that were now being termed "minimal." On the side, the mediator quoted himself as having taken U 1 severely to task for this wholesale move:

[5] The advantage of expertness weighed heavily on the side of management in this case, largely because their C 1 was so alert to matters of strategy at the table. This comment appears in the field notes at the end of an interview with C 1 very early in the two-party negotiations: "His way of reacting to this morning's meeting was rather typical of him. He gives the impression of a person who has been sitting through the whole performance with his eyes narrowed to a slit, aimed on targets ahead, so that the by-plays that inevitably develop in the course of the session distract him very little. At the end he is prepared to report at once his reactions in terms of the rather clear-cut goals he has had before him." After a number of fruitless sessions between the two parties, C 1 contrived to get the consent of all concerned to call for a mediator.

M: Well, when you knock out 43 demands—and I quizzed him on this, "How come you throw them out?" I said, "You know, you've always had the notion that perhaps mediation was going to come in. Why throw things away, if you're pretty certain it's going to come in? Why not wait till it comes in, so that you can give them to *him* to throw away, in exchange, perhaps, for something?"

The notion of a transition from the unilateral "demands" of Phase 1 to elasticized "proposals" in Phase 2 was particularly difficult for the union to comprehend. For anyone concerned with the special attitudes and table strategies called for in this connection, the following sequence from the Marathon transcript (condensed at many points) will be highly instructive, particularly in those stretches where the mediator turns union caucuses into classes on the internal design of Phase 2.

From the mediator's second caucus with the union:

M: Well, look, fellows, to get this started, I don't know how much I rea— how much time I really need with you. I had a pretty good idea last time of just what you wanted, what were the basic demands, and, more prob'ly, I have more work to do with the company at this point than with you. However, I do want to do one thing tonight. I wanta go over with you what the company has responded with respect to each of the 9 basic demands you substituted, *plus* get your thinking on each of the company's counter-proposals. Now, before we get into that, I want to spend a minute or 2 with something else. I wanta remind you of something I used as a compari-son in one of the early classes we had. You recall at that time I said that, in a sense, we *all* do bargaining in one form or another on many occasions, and I used the example of any one of you who might have an automobile that ya wanted to sell. What ya did was dress the thing up, make it look as attractive as possible, and put the highest price you felt you could rea-sonably ask on it. When a prospective purchaser came around, you gave him the best sales talk you could give, *but* ordinarily you did not expect he was going to say "Yes." Ya expected he was going to haggle a little bit, and when he did, ya tried to think up some arguments to counter those that he advanced. Ya try to indicate to him that the lower price he was offering was not a proper price. Maybe you would even go back in the garage and dig up another spare tire or something else to make the car a little bit more attractive, and you would keep on haggling with him over price. And eventually he would offer something that was worth while to you, for which you would make the swap. Now, in that sort of thing, you didn't get overly mad. Ya took it as part of the game you were playing.

I'm not saying that in collective bargaining, where you're dealing with—with much more serious things, and things which are not quite within your control as is the sale of an automobile. You can either sell it or not sell it; you don't have to. With a contract, though, ya do have to conclude it, and ya have some compulsion here which was not present in any individual bargaining you might do over a personal effect. *But* there are a lot of elements of sameness; and just as you would do in a private transaction, so, in part, you must do here. When you make a proposal, until ya come right down to the end of the wire, where ya have most everything settled and it's a matter of saying "Yes" or "No" to a couple of final propositions, ya got to expect that what you're going to get is a tentative "Maybe," usually a—to which is usually added a couple of other propositions, and it becomes a switch back and forth, a jockeying to try and get the most of what you want, knowing that the company is going to do the same thing. Now, I mention these things *because* I want to remind you that last time I said that *I* did not think the company counter-demands, which you felt pretty strongly about, were things to get too seriously concerned with, for, as far as I knew at that point—they may be, but as far as I know, they do not represent a final company position. If they did, then I think that you would be logically entitled to say—and holler every sort of implication you could think of. But I don't think that that's what they represent. I think what is called for after this is some further thinking, some further proposals on your part. What I want to do is to find out, how *much* that the company offered in connection with the counter-proposals they made to your 9 proposals is acceptable to you, either as they have stated it *or* in some modified form. I want to find out, secondly, what there is in the company's additional 9 proposals you think have any merit or that you're willing to go along with, either as they stated or in some modified form. This is for my information. Tomorrow I have to do the same thing with management. *How much* of what the union—of what they said in their counter-proposals did they say for bargaining purposes, how much closer to what they know the union wants are they willing to go?—that, again, is confidential with me. When I have those 2 things, then I can see how *really* far apart you are, and becomes a problem, then, of trying to get you to go a little bit this way on that business, gettin' the company to go a little bit your way on some other matter, until we reach the point where it looks like we have something that is an agreeable thing with you, something that's agreeable with them. And the only way we can do that is through this point-by-point discussion. I want to repeat that what you have to say concerning it is between you and I. Concessions that you tell me you are prepared to make are not told to the company. Concessions the company tell me *they* are prepared to make are not told to you at this point. For what you will be willing to do, what they will be willing to do will be to perhaps make concessions on one item, providing they get a counter-, or you get a counter-, concession on another item. So until the whole thing is squared up, I have to be the repository of your confidence and of theirs. So, to get to this, then (pause), let's start with their response in connection with No. 1, 2-year contract. And this is what I want to know. If you gave them a 2-year contract, what would you want in return? Of what advantage is it to you to say, "We'll give you a 2-year contract"? What can you get out of them in return?

. . .

M: Well, d'you still feel that way? Now, remember this is merely on this point. Actually this has nothing to do at—this right now with (U 2: Holi—holiday, vacation pay) this. If you didn't get other things, it might not make any difference to this, and it might. You'd have to see what the whole of it looks like. That's why this is between you and I. I can't go to the company and say you'll give 'em a 2-year contract if they will give the full General Motors' formula, *period;* because the period isn't there. There's a semi-colon, and then all the other things before you will sign *any* sort of a contract, whether or not it's 2 years or one year. But if, assuming that everything else were satisfactory (pause) (U 1: Well, i—)—is satisfactorily adjusted, would a 2-year contract be O.K. with you if the company gave the full General Motors' formula, which is a penny-an-hour wage increase for each increase of 1.14 in the index, plus a 4-cent-an-hour annual productivity bonus, or what General Motors calls "improvement factor"?

. . .

M: Well, now, wait a minute. That—that, however, is a completely separate matter from the length of the contract, and—

. . .

M: Well, now, look. Look. If—if a 2-year period is completely out, that's the answer, *but* when you—(pause).

. . .

M: Well, I'll put it down, but that is all this and heaven, too. Ya understand that? Not even General Motors—not even the strength of the United Automobile Workers could get *that.*

. . .

M: No, I'm not saying that you should do one thing or the other. *I* wanta find out exactly what you *will* do *if* this becomes a point where (U 1: The company—)—where you want to seriously consider a 2-year contract. Now (U 1: I think we do), I—I want to remind ya, too, that you're not considering this all by itself. This is not the only point. (U 1: Yeah) This is merely one of them. And when you have said, "These are the things. This is what we will do to give in to the company"—the company proposed 2—2 years. There's some bargaining advantage to say, "O.K., we will *accept* your proposal, *if*," rather than say "No." You put the other guy in the position of being forced to accept the fact that his proposal is *partially* acceptable. (Pause)

. . .

M: Well, I—I don't think I get my point across a-tall. (U 1: I—I think we understand your point) When a offer is made to you, there's a psychological advantage in taking a good, healthy look at it; and if ya can say, "Yes, *if*" (U 1: Uh—), you always stand to gain just a little bit if you can give in to the other guy and then add a "but" (U 1: Well—), and by so giving in, get more of what you want than you're giving away (U 1: Uh—) by agreeing. (U 1: Now, look at our—) That was the only thing I wanted to get at.

From the mediator's third caucus with the union:

U 1: What's their attitudes on—their position as to our minimum demand? Are they altering those?

M: Well, you have their counter-proposal which is very definitely not acceding to your minimum demand. See, I—I don't understand minimum demand (U 1: Well, you gotta remember that—)—what you mean by minimum demands. If you have to have everything such as this, then there's no room for bargaining.

U 1: No. But we'd like to know if their counter-proposal to ours is *their* final position.

M: Well, I just explained it. I've just told you the answer to that.

U 2: Which?

M: That I've found that there is things in their position (U 2: That's what—) that are bargainable (U 2: Well—), which merely means that they are not saying *to* you, or they're not saying to me that "What we have answered the union is as far as we will go."

U 2: See what's happened, U 1? We—when we went through—pract'ly went through all of these here and gave 'em our minimum demands, now what they're doin' is just knockin' *them* down to where—

U 1: Yeah!

U 2: The way it is now, we want all of ours.

U 3: That's where the stalemate is.

M: No! The stalemate is that after you gave the company this offer, the company made a counter-offer and then you quit bargaining.

U 1: We didn't quit bargaining. *They* did.

U 3: They did.

M: All right. There was no cause for further reaction on your part directly to what they had said and that's what I am trying to get. Ordinarily in these things, it's a series. You demand, they reply; you demand, they reply; you demand, they reply; you demand, they reply. Somewhere in there—and this is exactly the way it looks—you start here with your demand. They reply. Then on down, each counter-demand is met with a counter-reply until you reduce the difference (U 2: Well, the—) the point where you reach an agreement. Now—

U 4: Fact, all the time we're in there, M, we're t—all the time we were talking about *their* proposals. We hardly, if ever, mentioned our own proposals, because we figured when they got through we'd have our chance, and we never even got our chance to talk xx.

U 5: (Over U 4 above) U 4, as far as language is—is concerned, the whole thing is in a package and what—C 1 is sittin' back, like a—oh, one of these here chess players with the idea he just—he can take and move us fellows like we's just pawns or somethin' there. He just tryin' to xx.

U 4: We never ran into that before. I mean—

M: (Over U 4 above) Well, look. How—how would you propose that you go about—about reaching an agreement? What's your idea of how you do these things?

U 1: They never once discussed any of our demands, never (M: Well—), and that's what we were asking for. (M: And—) Uh—

M: If they didn't discuss them, it was because you didn't insist on it, because you certainly have a right to discuss your own demands. (U 1: We insisted on those) If you start, then they got to respond. You'll haggle back and forth until you get what is reasonably satisfactory. Now, when you tell me that you'll take 4¢ plus—4-cent improvement factor each year plus the cost-of-living adjustment, I am not going to tell them that. If anything, I might tell 'em, well, you'll take 10¢ plus their—no, I won't tell them you'll take. I'll ask them, "Well, what do you say—give 'em 10¢ plus the cost-of-living, huh?"—to give *me* some room to move around. I gotta bargain with you and I gotta bargain with them, so I can't—I'm not gonna give them minimums. (Laughs) I'll stretch the minimum so I can come back a little bit.

From the mediator's fifth caucus with the union:

M: Well, now, from your own review of it, U 1, you show me what is world-shaking about anything the company demanded x—

· · ·

M: All right. What's (U 1: In fact—) world-shaking about that, providing you have what (U 1: All right) you want in a 2-year contract?

· · ·

M: W—w—w—here. That's what I wanta know. What is world-shaking? What looks as though they're tryin' to destroy the union and destroy the contract with the proposals, which are bargaining proposals? They're not saying, and they have not said, "You either will accept these things or we'll do nothing."

. . .

M: I—s'pose they did say that. D'you believe 'em?

. . .

M: Here's the—here's the point. See, if I believed that (U 1: D'you believe our—) your minimum demands are completely unsusceptible of any change whatsoever, that you either get them exactly as you wrote them or strike, then there'd be no point in my wasting any time here or wasting yours! We might just as well wait until the 28th and let you go on strike. (Slight pause) Obviously, that isn't so because we've gone over them and you've indicated, in various directions, where you would compromise. Now, that's the only way you can ever work out a settlement. And you're either going to work it out that way now or you're gonna work it out later. You're gonna settle it, one day, whether it be before the 28th or after. (U 4: H'm. I tell you what—) Important thing is to settle it now, if it can be settled. And the only way it can be settled is to have some give-and-take, because if you don't have an attitude of give-and-take on it now, you're gonna have to develop it later.

. . .

M: *Well*, I don't blame you! If you're gonna—you're gonna (U 3: Let me—) agree on 2 years, you want something in return for it. That's how you bargain! When the company says, "We want a 2-year contract," you reply, "Sure. We'll give you a contract for 2 years, *if*."

From the mediator's seventh caucus with the union:
U 1: Now, we've got something in here that we'd like just talk to you about—the unused sick-leave situation.
M: Oh, now (U 1: Well, I just mention it to you!), look! This is rough now (U 1: All right) as it is, and when ya add and add (U 1: That's right), you can't do anything (U 1: All right) with it. (U 1: Yes, I'm just sayin' that these are the ones that come up—) I'll—I'll agree that they're good, sure! (Laughs) I can't argue with whether they're good or not. (Laughs)
U 1: These are the ones that you left out, see.
M: But that would never—that has *never* been brought up. (U 1: H'm) It has never (U 1: We'd like a clarification on this, see) appeared in anything since I entered the picture. It doesn't appear in anything that (U 1 laughs slightly)

you put on the table up till now, and we've got enough (U 1: All right) trouble (U 1: O.K.) with what you got on the table. (Laughs)

U 1: All right. Don't—don't (laughs)—don't throw a fit.

M: It's something brand new. The sick-leave. (U 1: All right. Sick-leave— that—) But I (U 1: That doesn't amount to very much)—as soon as I (U 1: This doesn't amount to much) bring something like that up (U 1: It—), the company says, "All right, if they want to discuss that, why, we'll throw one in the hopper then." (U 1: Well, these 2 aren't so important) We won't—won't get anywhere if we keep (U 1: 100% of unused sick-leave) puttin' wood on the fire. We gotta get a match under it and get some of this burnt up.

In Phase 2 the hypotheses which each party develops about the other will be of limited value unless they are validated. This calls for a series of experimental runs to determine what is in store if a party attempts conclusive action based on one or another of its tentative deductions. The most serious hazard which besets all such verbal reconnaissance in this phase is the possibility that an intransigent or a dull party may try to pin on the other as a firm commitment what was ventured purely as exploration. C 1 of the Crescent City case was reminded several times of this problem during the exchange over the issue of retroactivity.

From Session III (condensed):

U 1: Look-it, on the—on the progress or the procedure of the thing, we're willing to sign an agreement on things that we have negotiated if they're written up the way we'll—after subject to check by us, the understanding that we will continue on in negotiations on the over-all wage picture—includes everything—and the understanding that after a reasonable length of time and there's no agreement arrived at, the union has a right to strike, also with the understanding that we have an agreement on a retroactive date on whatever we arrive at. We're willing enter into an agreement on that basis.

C 1: Well, I won't agree to any retroactive date, Curt, but I'd be inclined to go along on the other basis. I think it's—I think it's giving—giving you a distinct advantage.

U 1: Why?

C 1: Well, because you—there—there are many things in this agreement which you can hold us to if we sign it—the thing that I have submitted—and yet, at the same time, we're constantly threatened with a possibility of a stoppage because we're still negotiating other items. I think you have an advantage, now—just 'cause the retroactivity factor is still a factor. It's a negotiable factor. As I say, I'm not foreclosing any—any retroactivity date; I'm not saying we will agree to one. But I'm not gonna commit the company to one. It'll just be a—it'll be a part of our discussion.

U 1: And you will agree to negotiate on the retroactive / date?

C 1: (Over U 1 above) Oh, yeah! Yeah! Sure!

After lunch:

U 1: Well (C 1 starts to speak), you get a chance to discuss our proposition on—(voice dies out)?

C 1: Are you—are you in a position to indicate any favorable inclination toward a fixed period during which the no-strike clause would be applicable?

U 1: I would go on record as saying a 30-day period. Get down to serious business, and in 30 days.

C 1: Well, let me—let me—let me ask further question. Let's assume—let's assume that we agree—and these are all ideas I'm—s'pose we agreed that on the day this is signed that becomes the effective date of anything we should agree to in the future.

U 1: Oh. I—*I* don't think ya could say that. I failed to say at my last stating of the proposition that the question of the effective date would be subject, too, and I think that prior to going to lunch that you said that you would—

C 1: Oh, well, I understand be subject to negotiation.

U 1: Yeah.

C 1: Oh, no. I wou—I wouldn't, of course—I wouldn't expect you to give that up. No. I'm throwing something further out. I'm just exploring. Suppose—suppose we would sign this—you and the union and the company would agree to be bound by this, and we would agree that the effective date of any adjustment we might agree upon later, either on incentives or on time x, could be effective as of the date we signed that—let's assume that (pause)—provided that we had a specified period of time, from the date of signing to the date you could strike—have the *right* to strike—during which both sides would sit down and in good faith try to find out if there's an area of an agreement on incentives and on that—this Blue Cross point and on the day rate / that you—

U 1: (Over C 1 above) Oh, I don't think that your—your date is fair— / a fair one.

C 1: (Over U 1 above) I didn't say—I didn't say date that last—in that last statement.

U 1: Date of the signing (laughing slightly) of the—(slight pause).

C 1: Oh, you mean the effective / date?

U 1: (Over C 1 above) Yeah.

C 1: Oh, well. (Pause) Uh—we don't propose—

U 1: We asked for a—in our demands to you—

C 1: Well, I know you did.

U 1: —a much better date than that.

C 1: I know you did.

U 1: I don't think that it comes anywhere near what we asked for. However, we're willing to consider some fair one, but I don't think that's / a fair date.

C 1: (Over U 1 above) Well, let me—let me s—say i—say it this way. If we can agree on—if we can agree on the effective date of any adjustment (long pause), is the union willing to go along on a 6-month period for negotiating? In other words, you're not *hurt* by it. Uh—

U 1: It's too long, though; too long.

C 1: Well, if you're willing to g—30 days obviously is—is ridiculous, Curt, / because—

U 1: (Over C 1 above) I don't think / it is.

C 1: (Over U 1 above) Oh, sure it is! Just the—sure, it is.

U 1: Aw, it'd be different if we had the whole contract to go through, but we only have 2 issues here, and that's the wage issue and the small issue on dependent coverage.

C 1: What do you consider a reasonable time to discuss this incentive problem, if we can agree on a retroactive date?

U 1: Well, I su—I suggested to you 30 days. You—you made the remark that that was ridiculous. Now, I don't think that it's ridiculous at all. I (C 1: Well, I do) think that, considering the 2-week period now that there'll be no negotiations and from then on that we'll get into this thing and spend some time with it, I think a whole lot can be accomplished, and your suggestion of 30 days—I don't think that it at all is a bit ridiculous, and—

C 1: (In a low voice) Well!

(At this point C 1 takes C 2 out of room for private consultation, returning in about 5 minutes)

Why, Curt, I'm—I'm not prepared to—to bind with finality the company to this proposal which I am going to—not proposal, but this (pause) proposition, the final answer to which I wanta give you—or you—or the committee to you, later. These are the points:

(C 1 outlines 6 points)

Now, as I say, I'm—I'm filling this out w—with the understanding that I'm not in a position to bind the company with finality any more than you're able to sign this today with finality. But on—I'm—I'll expect an answer from you at—on this proposal—signing this, and I'll be—be able to tell you the first of the week through the president if that is a fixed proposal. S—so you don't have to commit yourself on that now.

U 1: Oh, well, we can—I can give you a commitment on a rather strong basis, and I (C 1: On this?) am quite convinced (C 1: On this?) that we can—we can get that approved.

C 1: This approved.

U 1: Yes.

C 1: Uh-huh.

U 1: However—

C 1: And I'm—I'm—I'm—I am reasonably certain that I can persuade my principals that they should go along on this thing which I have—I have evolved.

U 1: Well, there's only one thing—there's only one thing here in your proposal. You—the effective date of the adjustment—you're proposing Monday, May the 11th.

C 1: I—I—I—I know I have no authority to go back. That's why I'm making—

U 1: Well (pause), I think that there would be a lotta merit to your suggestion and would open the—could see our way clear to go along with the proposal if we could get some kind of a better date here.

C 1: Well, Curt, I'll take that suggestion (U 1: Well—)—in other words, what you're saying to me is you feel—you feel certain that there can be no question about going along if we had a better—you get a better retroactive date. Is that what you're saying?

U 1: Yeah! And th—also this, too, that you—you—you were making a point all during negotiations that (pause) we have it right here in our hands to make the decisions.

C 1: What?

U 1: I say you were makin' the point during negotiations that you have it in your hands to make the / decisions.

C 1: (Over U 1 above, in mumbling voice) Uh-h-hun. I don't know / about that.

U 1: (Over C 1 above) Well, so—so far as we're negotiating here in Crescent City.

C 1: Oh, / yeah!

U 1: (Over C 1 above) Well, can a d—can a decision be made on—on that point here?

(Reel changed on recording machine) [6]

C 1: Oh, Curt, don't let me m—mislead you. That's what I'm saying. That's why I said—I said that I would give you a statement—I would give you a final answer. That is, I would give you through him, the president, or

[6] *Observer's Note:* Between reels, U 1 pushed the point that he had thought they were working through an attorney who was a spokesman for the company; was he or wasn't he?

directly to you a statement as to whether or not you can take this as a fixed firm proposal to be accepted or rejected by you. I cannot do that now! I can do it—I can do it Monday, or Tuesday. (Slight pause)

U 1: Well, I don't know. It's—you're here as a spokesman of the company, and the—the company is here and the officials of the company are here. I—I—usually these things are resolved in a little adjournment and recess and come back here and—and (C 1: Says he, with a twinkle in his eye) tell us about it. (M and C 1 laugh) So (C 1 laughs heartily again), I think it could be handled very easily that way.

C 1: Well, if it could, why, I'd be delighted to do it, Curt.

U 1: And I might suggest, too, that if (pause) needs any approval from somebody else, perhaps we could shoot through a telegram or telephone call to somebody that's helpin' to make the decision and arrive at it this afternoon.

C 1: I don't know that you got to have that decision this afternoon.

U 1: Well, the thing is that the—the date that your suggestion is so far from what we proposed in our original draft that—

C 1: You mean the retroactive date?

U 1: That's right. It's going to make—make it mighty difficult for us to—even though your other—your other suggestions have merit (C 1: Uh-huh), might—

C 1: Well, I see what your problem is. It's / on a—it's—well, I have—I just can't—

U 1: (Over C 1 above) It's—we've been negotiating here for quite a while, and certainly the retroactive date isn't just gonna be washed out by saying that next Monday—from next Monday on. Pretty hard for us to make a decision on that basis. You got something better to offer than the—Monday, why, we might see my way clear to accept the thing.

C 1: Well, I—I—I can—heck, I can say—I can say 1950, for that matter. This is only (laughing) my idea. As I said, I can't make—

U 1: Well, then—then the whole—this whole thing is subject to—

C 1: Oh, yes! Golly. I made that clear, I thought (laughing slightly)! This whole thing is my idea. I have no authorization / whatso—

U 1: (Over C 1 above) Well, maybe—maybe we could ask C 2 if he any— has any ideas on the thing—if get any x on—

C 1: Well, Curt, there's no use of being *cute* about it, now. Let's—after all, the—C 2 doesn't own Crescent City Manufacturing Company. You know who owns it. So why—there's (laughing slightly) no use being—kidding (U 1: Well [laughing slightly], I'm—I'm not—I'm [laughing slightly again] not—say I'm not being cute—) about it or shadow-boxing about it. Now, I—th—this is a very—this is a (speaking emphatically) *very fundamental problem*. It's a question of now or later. Now, I'm perfectly willing to recommend to my principal, rather than to have a showdown now on something that needs exploring, to try to work out a formula whereby it can be explored amicably, peaceably, without any problems, and—and I think there's a solution there in 60 days from 2—from the—2 weeks from Monday. I think there's a solution. I think that if reasonable people confine themselves to these narrow issues and that's all that's in the picture, that you'll—that they'll reach a solution.

U 1: Well, w—we—we have the right to discuss—or we can discuss the thing on the basis of *you* making a better suggestion (C 1: Sure!) than May the 11th, and that's what—that's what I'm tryin' to put across to you. I think that we're entitled to a—a better date than that. I think that you—you can —you can see your ver—your way clearly, very clearly, to make a—a suggestion on the basis of—of 90 days retroactive from—from this date. And you can make the suggestion, and I'm *sure* your suggestion is going to carry some weight with the powers that be. And you can do that! (Slight pause)

C 1: I (U 1: So—) tell you what I'll do. I'll put in here as my suggestion, as a proposition to my principals, April 1st. Our first meeting was March 27th, 1953. I—I don't know what day of the week that was. Well, make it March 30th, beginning of the work week (slight pause), which is the— for—beginning the first work week following our first negotiation meeting, which was March 27th. (Pause)

U 1: And you say that you'll be able to give us an answer on Monday (C 1: Yep) with a—

C 1: We'll get the word to you (gesturing toward U 3), and you get in touch with them?

U 1: —company will go along with your / suggestion.

C 1: (Over U 1 above) That—that—that is a firm proposal. Yeah. For you to accept, if you wish. (Long pause)

From Session IV (condensed):

C 1: All right. (Long pause) Now, let me—do I understand that—that the union is opposed to a contract longer than a year? (Pause)

U 1: That's right. (Rather long pause)

C 1: Well, then, are y—are we prepared to—to execute this agreement for this —for June—effective—let's say make it effective June the 1st? (Pause)

U 1: Well—

C 1: (At same time as U 1 above) This—this much of the agreement. You said you wanted to put it into effect. We're willing to put it into effect.

U 1: Well, w—we are, too. However, there's a little matter here of the agreement that we—or at least a—it was a suggestion on *your* part when we left here at the last meeting. However, when we got your proposal, why, it certainly is far from what we thought you suggested. Apparently you weren't able to put it across.

C 1: Obviously.

U 1: Well, that's (laughing slightly)—we're not prepared to sign on that basis. We feel it falls far short of what we did. However, I felt sure with what we at least—well, as a suggestion on your part we could go to the membership and recommend the acceptance of it. However, when we received it, it was far from wh—the understanding on these—these issues. However, we did take it to the membership, regardless.

C 1: This.

U 1: This (C 1: Uh-huh)—this document here that you've given us. And the membership turned it down. However, they did make this reservation in it. If the company is willing to institute the question of retroactivity here and nail it down as of March the 30th, and (pause) give us the Blue Cross and Blue Shield coverage for the individual, husband, and wife, and family, a one-year agreement, why (pause), we'll go along on the basis of signing it.

C 1: Well, it doesn't make any difference to us whether ya sign it or not (U 1: Well—), actually. I mean, it doesn't make a bit of difference! It's to your advantage to get this thing signed, not ours!

U 1: Well (laughing slightly), th—that's true! However, y—*you—you* made the suggestion (C 1: Yeah) on the question of retroactivity, and we accepted it in all good faith! And we thought that we'd have that nailed down. Now the thing is wide open! Unless I'm not hearing right this morning, I—that's the—that's the (laughing slightly) way it stands.

C 1: That's right.

U 1: Now—

C 1: It's an open issue.

U 1: Well, it wasn't an open issue when we left / here. At least we—

C 1: (Over U 1 above) Oh—oh, it—oh, it was! I made it very clear that m— what I s—what I threw out on the table was my own thinking.

U 1: Well, that's true, you did. But, nevertheless, we know that you're the— the spokesman for the company and we're—we're dealing with responsible representative of the management, and we thought that there'd be no question about this thing. However, there—*now* the thing is (laughing slightly) wide open.

C 1: (In *very* low voice) That's right.

U 1: Well, we just can't go along on that basis of s—

C 1: Well, I—I—I—I'm not saying you need to go along / on that basis.

U 1: (Over C 1 above) Well, all right. But if—but if that's the position that we're—we have to take from—if that's the understanding we have to get from you people every time we—we tentatively agree to something, why, then we're gonna have some mighty difficult negotiations.

C 1: Well, we didn't tentatively agree to anything. I couldn't have made it any clearer than I—

U 2: One thing that puzzles me, Norm, is the fact that all through the negotiations you took a pretty positive position that the working agreement be worked out first (C 1: [In low voice] Yeah), and you wouldn't discuss any economic issues until that was done.

C 1: And we've done it! There it is!

U 2: But then when we get to the point of completing that and we had a tentative agreement, you kinda switch horses on us in the middle of the stream.

C 1: But, Al, I sw—no. I didn't switch anything! I—I said last time—I said this is my idea and mine *only*. / I made it *very* clear.

U 1: (Over C 1 above) That's right. There's no question. But we also know, Norm, that you're—you're the spokesman of the company and we're—we're s'posed to be dealing with responsible people of management, so you don't make those statements! You don't make those statements and—and then come back here with something like / this, I—

C 1: (Over U 1 above) Well, Al, on the contrary—or, Curt, on the contrary, I—when I made that statement, I had no authorization from my superior to agree to any retroactive date! I had none—no authority at all! So when I made my statement it was my idea *only*. And I was reversed!

U 1: Are we to take from that, then, that anything that you say that we—we don't know whether it's nailed down / until the following meeting is held?

C 1: (Over U 1 above) Oh, I—I know what my authority is.

U 1: Well, then, / xxxx.

C 1: (Over U 1 above) Only last—only the—only last time was the only time I conditioned anything I said. Whenever I agree to anything before that, it was agreed.

U 1: Aw! Even though ya did condition it, after all, we're no children in this game. We know that you're the spokesman for the company and that—and that when you make those statements you have some freedom in making 'em or you wouldn't make them, and you feel sure. And—and I—I *emphasized* my remarks that you go back and sell this to the people and—and come up with a thing on Tuesday—and y—and—or Wednesday, there'd be no doubt—there's—be no question about me going to the membership and putting this across. And I didn't hear any response to that from the management, which indicated to me—well, I certainly believed the—you people were gonna live up to your statements, even though it *was* a suggestion on your part. (Pause)

C 1: Well, I'm sorry, Curt (U 1: Well—), if I—I—if I m—mis—misled you in any way. I didn't think that I misled you.

U 1: Well, if that's the position of the company, all I can say is, then, that we better get into negotiating the—or—or tryin' to reach a settlement on the rest of the agreement very quickly, because patience of our people are just about exhausted on this thing.

C 1: Well, I—I can't—I'm sorry to hear that, but let me—let me explore this thing a little bit more. There are 4—4 items, the hourly rates, the incentive, retroactivity, and this dependency coverage. Are you prepared to—let's assume that we—that we could nail down some retroactive date, are you prepared on *that* basis to go ahead with this contract and then discuss the other 3 items? (Slight pause)

U 1: You mean the question of retroactivity?

C 1: No. No. / If—

U 1: (Over C 1 above) What are the other—what are the other / 3 items?

C 1: (Over U 1 above) Dependency coverage, incentive, and hourly rate—those—those 3 economic items. In other words, let's assume—let's assume that we agree that X date was the retroactive date. Are you prepared on that basis to sign the agreement, put it into effect, and discuss those 3 ec—economic issues during this no-strike period of 60 days, or whatever the total was? I'm—our—I just—there was some hope that we were gonna meet today and get these issues op—that're open resolved and sign it today. I guess that's the only reason for picking the date, and today is May 25th, so if we—if we—if we initialed this today, making it effective June 1st, let's say—and I think we oughta do that, because it—it would give the company a week to wind this thing up and get the contract into effect. Then it would be 60 days from June 1st. (Pause) Be 60 days from next Monday. Monday would be the 1st, effective date of the agreement. (Pause) Well, y—you think we could work that sort of thing out if we could pin down the retroactive date?

U 1: I think so.

(C 1 and C 2 retire to confer in small room adjoining conference room. Finally C 1 reappears to say, "Why, we'll have to ask for a—about, maybe, 15-minute recess." He asks C 3 to leave with them. They return in a short while)

C 1: Why, I am sorry but I cannot agree, so we'll just have to go ahead and—(pause).

U 1: The only thing I'd like to see us go away here with these issues narrowed down a little bit / xx—

C 1: (Over U 1 above) I can't narrow them any more / now.

U 1: (Over C 1 above) Oh, I think that you can, Norm. I—

C 1: Well, I know what I can do, Curt.

U 1: Aw, you've got some of these things here ya (U 3: If you tried)—matter of 5, 10 minutes' caucus, you could agree to these things here.

C 1: Well, let me decide that, Curt. (U 1: Well, let you decide—sure, you can—) I—I think I—I think I, as management's spokesman, know what I can do and what I can't do, what I'm prepared to do and what I'm not prepared to do. Why should I tell you otherwise—like to do con—otherwise? I mean, why—what would I gain by it? If I were able to say—I—I said to you, you're—you're pressing me for a final answer, I'd say *No!* I don't wa— that may not be my final answer.

U 1: You can say No. Sure (laughing slightly), you can say No.

C 1: But I can't say Yes!

U 1: Why can't you?

C 1: I'm tellin' you I can't! I know my authority. (Slight pause) I know what power I possess, Curt! My gosh!

U 1: These things could be very easily narrowed down to about 5 issues here.

C 1: I—I—I—I went out on the limb on this one business, on retroactivity, and you keep he—throwing it back at me, in spite of the fact that I made it perfectly *plain* what my th—authority was. Then you say, well, you left here with the understanding that you were gonna be—March 30th was firm date. Well, hell, it wasn't! (U 1: *Aw!*) I—and so w—w—and I was re—I was reversed in su—if you wanta put it that way. Least my—my idea was not a—was not approved.

U 1: I don't think you were reversed.

C 1: (In fairly low voice) Well (C-2 laughs heartily), too bad. I wasn't. I'll tell ya someday. (Pause) I'll tell ya someday. Remind me. And I—I—when this becomes history. (Pause)

CHAPTER 4

Phase 3: Precipitating the Decision-reaching Crisis

I

This is the period during which the sides, or parties, again take the center of the stage, bringing the interaction to an end with announcement of their formal agreement, or else going on record as having reached an impasse. The union will likely follow up the latter by publicizing the failure of the negotiation and its intention to move on to strike action.

The lines of communication between the conference room and those to whom negotiators answer on the outside begin to hum for the first time in Phase 3. As their representatives at the table explain, it is the outsiders who have the final word on the key issues, and the most serious of these—involving money and strike—are, by the very nature of negotiation, reserved for the end.

From the field notes on an interview with C 1 in the Crescent City case:
I raised the question about his relationship to the management of the parent company—about how much of his limits he has known about, or did he have to keep determining these as he went along? He said he has known everything with which he had to work, except money. He still doesn't know that and believes that his principals don't even know themselves yet what they will give. He mentioned at one point that they have to depend a lot on him and C 2 to get the tolerance of the situation for them as a guide. Between now and the next session he will go over with his principals the union demands that are now before them. He will get from his principals their position. When he goes into that session, therefore, he *will* know what his principals will do on money. He says he already has a figure of his own in mind and thinks he can "buy the situation for that."

From the field notes on an interview with C 1 in the Atlas case:
I asked him, is the management negotiator prepared with his *last* position

when he goes in, or do his superiors hold back from him? He claims that in his own case he knows what he has to work with. However, he added that during negotiation there may come to light (a) facts which were not previously known, or (b) a new turn of events. At such a time he might see that a cent would make a difference. Without refusing to negotiate any more, he would call for time out so that he could go back to the company and talk it over. As he put it, "They run the company; I just have a job to do." He himself might recommend to the company that they hold firm at 5¢, because it is a time when they ought to hold firm at 5¢ to show the union that they mean a thing when they say it. The company, however, might answer him with, "No, C 1, we would rather settle for 6¢ and give the extra cent, rather than go through such-and-such."

From several interviews with C 1 in the Marathon case:

C 1: See, things begin to crystallize after the union has placed its demands and we have discussed it. (AD: Yeah. Yeah) It's difficult to get management to crystallize its thinking on anything except perhaps technique and policy, even on getting a commitment as to how much money is going to go—someday I'm going to have a—go into a negotiations with the management—the management will say to me, "C 1, there's just so much money and that's all," so that we can pitch the negotiations from the outset to end up at that point.

AD: Well, when they don't tell you that in the beginning, is it an indication that they have a flexible amount on hand?

C 1: No, it's usually an attitude of "How much can we get away with?" An awful lot of it depends on whether the manage—the management is convinced prior to negotiations that they can afford a strike, because when they say—see, what they're saying—management is saying to the negotiating committee, "You have"—let's say—"all told"—make it ridiculous—"all told, you've got 35¢." They're in essence saying to the negotiating committee, "We'll take strike for anything more than that."

AD: Do they actually know before negotiations what—to—know at what limit they would take a strike, or do you think that that tends to be formulated later on under certain pressures?

C 1: It usually is formulated later on, and I've heard many managements say that, "Well, by golly, we're not going to give any more than this much money, and if they want more than that they can strike," and when it comes down to the point where the union says, "Either this or we hit the bricks," the management will say, "Well, maybe we better give 'em another nickel." (AD: Yeah) So that in the negotiations your committee is usually standing on sand, not rock. That's why I said to you that the pre—the meetings prior to the negotiations are—the fact that you might not get in on a management meeting if they call it suddenly—are not too important, because the real decisions will be developed during the negotiations. We all know ahead of time what we want (AD: Uh-huh), and during the negotiations we find out how much we really want them.

Following one of the early sessions after exchange got under way at the table, the investigator inquired of C 1 why he and C 2 had consulted with their superior so early in the negotiations; were not top-echelon people reserved for major points only, and then near the end?

C 1: Personally, I approve of the practice thoroughly. I think that the executive of the company should be completely informed and should be interested enough to know *every detail* that occurs in negotiations. You see, if we suddenly find that we have $20,000 too much inventory in some item out here, that somebody's made a mistake, the skies fall down. But with a stroke of a pen we can say, "We give 'em 2 more holidays; there's $20,000." Then all of a sudden, at the end of a year, they suddenly wake up to the fact that their labor costs are too high. We should work in such a way that [the top management] realizes [its] responsibility in this. It's not unusual. Now, ya see—as a matter of fact, at—before I came here, they—all of the officers were much closer to the negotiations than they are here. And with every negotiating session, *immediately* when it was over, within 5 minutes, we were in the president's office with the executive vice-president, and we reviewed the entire negotiations of that day—what occurred that day—in detail and made our recommendations. Well, then, very often we came back for another meeting and—to make our recommendations of what should occur in the next meeting, which they approved or disapproved. You see, you're aiming toward one of 2 things in negotiations, either complete agreement or a strike. And it's only the brass that can decide whether or not they want a strike. When a personnel man decides that the company's gonna have a strike, he can go look for another job.

Some time later, only fourteen days before the contract expiration date, C 1 was still discoursing on the same topic.

C 1: You can't know this early what the union really wants. It won't come out until the day before or the very last day. *Then* you can go to top management and tell them what it will cost them to prevent a strike.

C 1 maintained his point to the last, as he reflected over the several weeks of negotiation which had preceded the agreement reached the night before at 8:50 P.M.

C 1: Should teach [U 1] never to come in and boast to a company man about what they're going to do, or a company man to the union about what they're gonna do, because, by golly, Ann, you don't *know* what you're gonna do. And we didn't know until 25 minutes of 9:00 *last night* what we were gonna do!

AD: Well, that was the thing—

C 1: —when M said to the union, "Is this acceptable?" and U 2 said, "Yes."

Parties will not infrequently round off Phase 2 with some difference between them which has not been erased by any of the reductive operations performed on it. If the difference is small enough, they may weigh it as not worth the expense of a further struggle on the strike front and so be willing to chip away at it from their separate positions until it is entirely eliminated. Forfeitures of this sort are not losses in any momentous sense. Evaluated against results from the whole of the negotiating enterprise, these can, to all intents and purposes, be written off as a part of the normal expense of negotiating. By the same token, there are no real gains here such as have accrued through the sparring and jockeying operations in Phase 2. Much conjecturing about the role of compromise in negotiation has confused these minor concessions which are natural to Phase 3 with the complicated modifications of position in Phase 2 which are essentially forward-bent movements—movements which are not, in well-managed negotiation, really "compromises" at all.

The real work of Phase 3 is concerned less with reducing any areas of difference carried over from Phase 2 than with another type of determination which has not hitherto been so prominent. In this last phase the parties finally come up against a dead end in their negotiating procedure, for somewhere and somehow there must be answered the question toward which all the explorations of Phase 2 were directed: how firmly will each side hold out against the other? At this late stage it takes not relaxed but greatly sharpened perceptivity to sort out the irreducible last offer which is not just another negotiating ruse, both sides having on so many earlier occasions used "This is our best one" as an open invitation for still another counter-proposal. This is an important fact to be kept in mind about negotiation, because it points out the vigilance which attends good negotiating to the very end, in contrast to the popular conception that agreement "grows" by steadily increasing degrees of confidence.

The strategy of one side becomes increasingly instrumental to the other in connection with the narrowing-down which engages the parties in

Phase 3. The field materials turned up three different forms of such strategy, each estimable for some singular effect.

1. *The categorical "Yes" or "No"*

At an earlier stage of negotiation than the final one, the Atlas mediator was particularly fastidious about sealing off all possibilities for the parties to answer each other as definitively as this.

From the field notes:

The mediator had said to the company that they should put their counter-proposal on the table before adjourning for dinner; then, without allowing any time for discussion and possible No's, the meeting would adjourn, which would give the union a chance to go over the proposals at dinner and come back in an amenable frame of mind.

After C 1 had read off to the mediator the company's proposed counter-proposals, the mediator advised him, in his presentation to the union, not to present any of them simply as "No change." His suggestion was that a refusal should always be couched in an explanation of *why* no concession, so as to take the bluntness out of that fact. He dramatized this to C 1 by pointing out one stretch of successive "No change's" that could be softened with something like, "We don't feel we can do anything different on the —— one because ——."

From a union caucus with the mediator:

M: This thing is beginnin' to roll a little, and after they submit their counter-proposal I think we oughta take around 45 minutes, go out and get somepin' to eat, come back for no more than 2 hours. It'll give you fellows a chance to look over what they're gonna present to you and I think, in all fairness to them, instead of rejecting anything when they submit it, you should say, "Well"—in fact, I'm going to introduce these remarks that I'm —I'm suggesting that you, immediately after the company presents 'em, that we retire for 45 minutes or an hour or so, get something to eat, come back and—with the understanding that we'll just work 2 hours. In—and it will give the union a—an opportunity to study the un—the *company's* proposals. See, I wouldn't want you to comment at this time—say, "We don't like this" or "We don't like that." See, I've got them moving on the whole thing, which wasn't too easy because there was differences of opinion on that, and we had to reconcile those differences on their committee. Now, we got 'em moving in that direction, and I wanta *keep* 'em there, see. And then, too, you will owe it to these negotiations also to spend a little time with *your* committee and give your reply *formally* across the table tonight.

In marked contrast to the foregoing is the presentation by C1 in the Crescent City case of the last offer of the company, an offer which was ultimately followed by strike. The wisdom of C1's insistence on getting a "Yes" or "No" answer is not the concern of the analysis at this point as much as the effect upon the union position of C1's pressure for an *immediate* reply. The following excerpt is a condensation from the last part of the last session in that case:

C1: Well (rather long pause), I did indicate to the mediator (rather long pause) my thinking on the over-all picture, and after further discussion of the problem with him I told him that (pause)—that it was my conclusion that I was gonna come down here (pause) and I was goin' to state what management's position is—its final position (pause)—and I wi—I'm gonna do just that. But before I do, I want to make a few observations. First off, I—I want you to realize—you, the committee, to realize—I know Curt does, but I wanta say it publicly, that (pause) any—any apparent anger or bitterness is really just here. I mean, we forget about those things when we go out. And I don't—I'm not critical of your—of your desire to shoot for what you call the Chicago rates. I understand that argument, just as you sh—must understand ours, that we don't here want to get outside of the area. I sincerely hope that we *can* work this out and we can have good relations over the next year, and then if we have problems then, we can work them out in the next contract. But, in any event (pause), I wanta make this further statement, that I'm gonna submit to you what is our final position so that these negotiations will not be further prolonged. When I say final, I mean final. And I mean that they'll either—they're either goin' to be accepted by the membership and we have a contract, or they're—the membership is gonna have to decide to take other action. Now, it's gonna be up to them. I'm saying to you—I—I'm saying this to you because I don't want you to come back or ask for a meeting—to come back and tell us you have strike authority or something of that sort and you're asking for more, because— well, I'm telling you that this is our final offer. I'm not—it's no—I'm not joshing or kidding or joking about it, and I hope that you will see fit to recommend it. (Pause)

(C1 then enumerates the several points of the offer)

U1: Well, I don't know. I—I don't know whether we're going to be able to sell this at all, I'll tell ya the truth.

C1: Well, are you gonna recommend it, is what I wanta know.

U1: Well, I—I don't think that I can. No.

C1: Well, I don't question whether you *think* you can. I wanta know officially from this committee whether they're gonna recommend our—

U 1: Well, we'll have to determine that ourselves, and you'll have to find that out later on. But as it stands now I don't think that we can.

C 1: Well, it isn't a question of finding out! I'll—let me ask you specifically.

U 1: Well, at the moment say No.

C 1: May I ask you specifically?

U 1: *Ask* me.

C 1: May I ask you a / specific question?

U 1: (Over C 1 above) Yeah. Go ahead.

C 1: Question Number 1. (Pause) Will you—will you—will the committee— and I assume the committee has *something* to say, Curt (U 1: I guess they do), un—unless you can speak for them without even talking to them. Maybe you can do that. But I'm asking you this question. Will you tell this company whether or not you're gonna recommend the—our final offer to the membership?

U 1: Well, we will have to—we will have to recess on that question. (C 1: Well, that's—a—a—) Frankly, I—personally, I don't think that I can. I don't think that *I* can recommend it. (Pause) What's your n—did you have another question?

C 1: Well, yes! If you say that you will tell us whether or not you will recommend it, then I'll—my next question is, will you recommend it? (U 1: [In low voice] Uh! Well—well [laughs shortly]—) Like the—the answer to each of those 2 questions. If you say, "x we will not tell you—company whether or not we will recommend it," then tha—I don't need an an— there's no answer to the second question. If you say you will *tell* us whether you will recommend or not recommend, I'll ask you what—what—what is your position goin' to be before the membership?

U 1: Well (laughing slightly), I'm sure if we tell you that we're gonna recommend it we'd do that same thing before the mem—the membership.

C 1: Oh, I—I ag— / I agree, Curt! Sure. I understand that.

U 1: (Over C 1 above) Well, there's no—no need to ask us that.

C 1: (In fairly low voice) I mean, how! Well, I'm—I am—did I—didn't make it clear (laughing) wh—what my question / was?

U 1: (Over C 1 above) I—I don't think that the—we'll recess on it, but certainly the offer that you've made isn't—isn't enough. Believe me, it isn't. / That's all.

C 1: (Over U 1 above) Can't help what you think about it.[1] That's what it is, and I—I—I just want to again emphasize to you that that's *it!* Now, that's—that's our *position.* And if—I—I—when I started out this statement, I made this offer. I told you, and I made it clear to the mediator, that I was coming down here and I was gonna state to you our position. You could

[1] *Observer's Note:* C 1 put all of his papers away. U 1 sat looking at the paper in front of him.

take it to the membership. We would like ya to recommend it; we hope you will. We'd like to know whether you will or you won't—you're going to or you're not going to. But I want you t—want *again* emphasize that this (tapping table) is our *final* offer! Now, / I'm just makin' it very clear.

U 1: (Over C 1 above) Well, O.K., then. The only thing is I'm tryin' to work out some—tryin' to get some of the rough spots out. There's a lot of rough spots in your offer! Tryin' to work those out! (C 1: Well, they're not—) But if you don't wanta even *talk* about 'em and—and try to discuss 'em and work 'em out, that's it. / I'm not xx—

C 1: (Over U 1 above) Well, they're not a question of rough spots, Curt. I know— / I was—I was aware of what I said. I—when I—

U 1: (Over C 1 above) And—and—and as far as giving you a commitment now, we won't give you no commitment now. We'll discuss it amongst ourselves and we'll make our recommendations to the membership. (C 1: Well [laughing], we—) And you can wait—you can wait until we met— hear it a—after the meeting or at the meeting.

C 1: Oh, well, then you've of—then you've answered my first (U 1: Aw, that's—) question.

U 1: But—well, in view of the—your offer, we'll want to—this is it, so as soon as—I think, mediator, that it's not gonna be satisfactory. Only attempting to discuss or—reason I discuss it further is to try to work out some of the —because we do have—well, we do have a problem. Even if your money— even if your money *is* accepted, we do have a problem on these things— how we're going to resolve 'em in the event of a dispute. Because (pause) of the—the offer that you've made, well, we *have* to take that into considera- tion. If you were making an offer here that you could buy and we could close our eyes to these things for the year, O.K., then I could go along with ya saying that all the present time studies are accepted and there'll be no question about—we—well, we could question 'em, but that's all, with the grievance procedure. I can't leave that w—that thing wide open.

C 1: We have no—we—we certainly aren't closing—we haven't closed the door to intelligent discussion in the grievance procedure of whether the time studies are erroneous or should be adjusted (U 1: Well, then you shouldn't—), but we are not—what we are not willing to do is to submit the—the—these rates which we have lived under and worked under these years, to arbitration. That's all.

U 1: Well, why not?

C 1: Pardon?

U 1: Why not? If you say—if you say that they're all that they're s'posed to be, then there's nothing to our case. You can shoot our case full of holes and the arbitrator will uphold you. The only thing I'm saying to you that in view of your offer, present studies—the union has a right—and we will present it on the basis that the arbitrator should rule and rule alone whether the study is right or wrong. If it's wrong, then we have a right to sit down and work out the answer; and if we can't work out the answer, the union has a right / to strike.

C 1: (Over U 1 above) No! Well, of course, that won't do. (Pause) I said—I said 9 meetings ago that I would never agree to a right of a union to strike during a one-year agreement. Never!

U 1: Well, this—that's—that—*you* said that.

C 1: Damn right I said it, because (U 1: However—) I—I said and I'll repeat, the union and the emp—the union gives *nothing* (pause) in the—in collective bargaining. *Nothing!*

U 1: Well, that's true! (C 1: Right) We're the ones that asking. We're asking. / That's x—

C 1: (Over U 1 above) Right. And, therefore, when management agrees to limit *its* rights (U 1: Well, you're—) and—and agrees to spend more money, it's not goin' to—it's not goin' to have that p—the production which it hopes to get for one year, at least, interrupted by a strike because *you* don't like the fact that the company doesn't agree / on some of xx.

U 1: (Over C 1 above) We're not asking—only on one (C 1: Right! A—any one! Any item! xx) problem. xx. The rest of the grievances are all subject to the / regular procedure.

C 1: (Over U 1 above) Anything at all that's—makes (U 1: Oh, no)—gives you the right to strike is o—any management that agrees to that I think is foolish. (Rather long pause) God knows management gets very little / from the union.

U 1: (Over C 1 above) Youse are the givers! There's (C 1: That's right. That's right! That's right!) no question about it. We're the ones that are asking (C 1: That's right) for this thing. (C 1: So—sure!) The whole—the make-up of this collective bargaining is—is in that scope. The (C 1: That's right) —we—*we're* (laughing slightly) not giving anything! (C 1: That's right) We're the ones (C 1: God knows you're not. That [laughing]—that's— that's quite obvious. And nothing that you—) that're doing the asking there. We have nothing to give. You're the ones that *have* it to give.

C 1: That's right. You have nothing to give. (Rather long pause) The only people that have to give are the employees and the employer, not the union. Gives nothing.

M: All right? (Pause) When is your meeting scheduled for?

U 1: Well, we're contemplating one for Saturday.

M: Uh-huh.

C 1: Now, may I—may I just repeat once again—I'd like to ask the question once again before I leave. Will you or will you not recommend the offer? (Pause) Guess I should say recommend the *final* offer.

U 1: Personally, I won't. But we'll discuss it / and—

C 1: (Over U 1 above) Would you tell us before we leave today, if / you caucus with the committee?

U 1: (Over C 1 above) Well, I won't—be impossible to tell ya today. I don't think we can.

C 2: Well, we'll—

U 1: It'll take quite a bit of thought on the part of the committee, and I don't think they can do it in—in an hour or a day or 2 days. I think they'll have to give it quite a bit of thought. I have to say t—again to you that the only way that you'll be able to find out is to—

C 1: Wait until the meeting.

U 1: That's right.

C 1: O.K. Just want to know what your position was.

2. The "forced choice" between alternatives

The Atlas case can be consulted for one illustration, in the surprise introduction late in Session VI of an alternative proposal by the union spokesman which worked to the decided advantage of the union party in the final settlement. The staging of the proposal, kept private even from the mediator, was handled with considerable finesse.

An even more clear-cut specimen occurred in the Marathon case in connection with the company's efforts to finalize the contract on a two- rather than one-year basis. A skeleton from the transcript covers the history of the issue of the two-year contract as C 1 steered it through the final hours of the case.

This item had been introduced by the management committee some- time earlier in the case, but it did not become a major issue until the final day of negotiation. Up to this point the union committee had been resistant to all suggestions that they be bound by anything beyond a one-year arrangement, and among the other things on which they were very demanding was a special three-week vacation plan for workers with fifteen or more years of service. The following excerpt comes at a point in the negotiation when the parties had been meeting with the mediator in continuous session since 9:00 A.M. of the previous day. Shortly after lunch the management committee, in caucus with the mediator, first indicated to him that the company had put them in position to offer the union an additional holiday in return for a two-year contract.[2]

[2] The field notes record the following exchange just prior to the mediator's ap- pearance for this caucus: "When I returned sometime after 1:00 P.M., I found C 1 and C 2 already there. C 1 said they were waiting for the mediator. I felt that there

C1: What do we have to pay for a 2-year contract?

M: I don't think ya've got the price!

C1: What d'ya think is the price?

M: A couple of times I thought I had the price of it. The last time, I discovered they didn't want a 2-year contract, so what w—had been given the—in a previous session as an alternative proved to be no alternative.

C2: We are being pushed [by our top management] for a 2-year contract.

C1: (Over C2 above) Now, let me tell you what we've got, but we're not—this is only in the realm of bargaining for a 2-year contract.

C1 stated the concessions, which now included, for the first time, the offer of one additional holiday.

C1: Now, we cannot get hung up on this unless there's the 2-year contract in it. Those are our orders.

M: You mean it's a 2-year contract or no contract.

C1: No, no.

C1 explained the difference between concessions on one-year and two-year deals.

C1: This is what I'm wondering. What would happen, without revealing our hand at all, say, if you went back to the union and indicated that the company was stuck on a 2-year contract? Ya get—the 3-week thing is out, so ya have that. That's out under any circumstances, no matter which way it goes. What would happen if you went in there and indicated to them that our big hurdle in acceptance of this thing is the term of the contract? And then they say, "Well, we can't do it." And this way, "Well, have you considered making a counter-proposal on it?" Then if we don't—or can't meet the counter-proposal, we drop back to the one-year contract and settle on the basis of what's on the board.

Immediately after receiving this new information from management, the mediator went into separate caucus with the union, presenting the management proposal to them as follows:

M: No, they won't be up for a while yet, and, if ya like this, why, this won't take too long. You gathered, from the pressing I did over these several days, that the company wanted a 2-year contract. That want still exists, and the

---

was something on C1's mind but that he wasn't going to give with it until the proper time. He finally told me that when the mediator came he thought I would be interested in recording the conversation, since I was to see a sample of 'bargaining in reverse.' "

proposition advanced exactly as it was advanced this morning cannot be sold. However, a 2-year contract can, with considerable benefit to you, benefits which, I think, will be the sort of things that stand out and make it something your membership can go for. Just as the Steelworkers were able to make some capital out of a 3-week vacation x, so, too, if you will accept a 2-year contract you can make some capital out of a point that up until this morning the company was *not* prepared to even consider. Now, let me indicate to you just what it 'tis. Everything this morning, as was tentatively accepted, except the 3-week period and the one-year contract. In return for a 2-year contract, you can have a wage reopener at the end of one year; you can have one extra holiday, making a total of 7, which will cost the company about 3 times as much money as that vacation thing would do, but, nevertheless, that is the way they want it; and they will give you a 60-day retroactive feature in connection with the job evaluation.

The union's announced reaction, largely under the persuasion of U 2, was to reject the company proposal unless it was augmented to include the three-week vacation item. When the mediator reported this to the management group in caucus, he was rigorously quizzed by C 1 as to how the holiday item got onto the table with the union. It seemed to the investigator, in observing this latter caucus exchange from the sidelines, that C 1 was visibly shaken over the mediator's handling of the affair.

C 1, in private interview the day after settlement, verbalized his reactions to what had transpired with reference to the holiday item.

C 1: Now, I made one big tactical mistake, in my mind, during the whole negotiation. It was one things I was mad about. I was mad at M. I could have killed 'im.

AD: Why?

C 1: Because, when I told him about the holiday in the 2-year contract, I *explicitly* said to him, "Don't put it on the board until you find out what they will *take* for a holiday."

AD: I knew you were mad because you asked him point-blank yesterday afternoon, "How was it presented?"

C 1: Yeah.

AD: Right?

C 1: "How did it get on the board?" I wanted to know *how our offer* got on the board.

AD: (Over C 1 above) Yeah. Yeah. I knew you were, C 1.

C 1: I had no right to be mad at M. I'm old enough and experienced enough to know that that kind of a tactic I should never have trusted to anybody else. So then, the problem was how to recuperate from that. And the way we recuperated was to play the vacation *for* the holiday. And it worked in this case because of U 2's mind, but any mature union would have hooked me for both. And that's what I was concerned about. And so I was *raving* mad when that was done!

AD: How could—how could they have hooked you for both?

C 1: Why, a—a—an—another union would have just held right out to the bitter end for *both*, but—

AD: Instead of taking your alternative.

C 1: (Over AD above) And we had both to give!

AD: Yeah. (Pause) Uh-huh.

C 1: But M is not used to me and I'm not entirely used to M. M is a very slow and deliberate person, which was the best thing we could have had in this negotiations. And I—I realize that at that end of the negotiations he was tired and he just didn't get the pitch of what I was driving at. And I was tired. You don't get enough explanation of the thing. But the whole trick at that time that I was building for was to make U 2 feel that he got the last ounce of blood out of us. That he got a good contract. Well, we did it. We did want a 2-year contract, so I used it as an excuse to keep goin'. And at that point the situation was such that I felt that at the point, if I wanted more, oughta give more. What I should have done, instead of putting it in M's hands, was say to M, "I want to talk to the union." And go back to the union and say, across the board myself, "We'll take the union proposal except for this and this and a 2-year contract." Then let M—M call the caucus and come back and tell me what the union would take for the 2-year contract. Then he would have been mediatin', but I did the unfortunate thing of making M a negotiator at that point.

AD: Uh-huh.

C 1: I got him out of his own role. He was tired; I was tired. If he'd a-been sharp, he wouldn't have taken it. He would have told me to do it. And if I had been sharp, I wouldn't have asked him. So to me, that was the only slip of any major importance that we made in the negotiations, and it certainly wasn't a major slip because we crawled right out of it (AD: Uh-huh) by forcing the union to make a choice of either-or. And what did they take? They took the package that I sent M up there with to put on the table!

AD: But you feel it was because you put it in different wrapping (C 1: Yeah!) x by making alternatives.

C 1: Well, making U 2 make a choice! (AD: This—) That's all!

AD: Yeah.

C 1: And I knew that U 2 was dead tired at that time and it was the last second. He was ready to go to the meeting and everything else, and I figured, "Now's the time. If I put something on the board, U 2's going to say 'No' or he's gonna say 'Yes.' But if I put something on the board where he has to make a *choice,* he'll forget about saying 'No' or 'Yes' and make a choice." And he did.

AD: Uh-huh. Uh-huh.

C 1: Because M said right up to the last minute U 2 was ou—up there arguing with them about what else he could get out of the company. And when I gave him the choice to make, it washed it out (AD: Uh-huh), because psychologically U 2 felt that he had *both* of them (AD: Uh-huh), and he was satisfied. (AD: Uh-huh) All he had to do was make a choice.

AD: You—I know that you were sort of vexed at—at the way M handled that—that business of the 2-year proposition yesterday, and I sensed that yesterday when you asked him that question, I'm *sure* that's the reason you were asking it.

C 1: (Over AD above) Oh, I was boiling mad.

AD: Well, I—I felt you were asking it because you were—you were su— suspect.

C 1: Oh, when M walked out of the door, I said to C 2, *"Je-sus Christ,* what happened?"

3. *The "official" / "unofficial" context*

Adroitly engineered and supervised by the Atlas mediator, this distinction was ushered in to create a two-level graduation in the seriousness of negotiators' verbal commitments. As such, it proved a splendid auxiliary for the exploratory work of Phase 2, but the peak of its usefulness was not realized until Phase 3.

The "official" level. In the main, "official" transactions were reserved for joint meetings. These gatherings were organized around the parties' reports to each other about the status of their respective positions, along with renewed efforts to dislodge and move each other. In the vernacular of negotiators, these were the transactions which were "on the record." Since changes of position would be announced here, it was in these meetings that the crises and breaks, or transitions, showed up boldly. The Atlas mediator spent considerable time with each party ahead of these meetings, preparing them for what might be expected from the other and rehearsing them in the proper response. He was most emphatic that a party should never *reach* a decision in one of these meetings, only *announce* a decision arrived at earlier in "unofficial" context. It was thus incumbent on negotiators to maintain the greatest discretion in what they said and did in the "official" contacts. Not only were they looked on by the opposite as their parties' mouthpieces in these meetings, hence pronouncing firm commitments for their parties, but the mediator encouraged everyone in the belief that sundry speculations which had stretched out interminably over the caucuses, when thrown out on the table in "official" exchange could safely be read as, if not firm offers, certainly ones to be worked with with some degree of confidence. In line with this belief, the Atlas mediator made very certain that "official" encounters were ringed about with prohibitions which would stifle indiscretions before they had a chance to occur. The more advanced the negotiating sequence, the sharper the strictures he levied and the more stringent his supervision over the digressions in which negotiators might indulge.

The "unofficial" level. As a rule, "unofficial" business transpired in the private party caucuses or in "side bar" conferences between mediator and single negotiators. The distinction, however, was not as rigid as joint vs. caucus meetings. In a joint meeting it would be possible for parties, if they chose, to go "off the record" for brief periods. The critical condition was the understood level of operation. "Unofficial" gatherings were given over to strictly exploratory work: to hypothesizing about possible lines of action and the probable consequences, to weighing expected advantages and disadvantages, to clarifying uncertainties. Indulgence in spontaneous and speculative talk was confined to these contacts—but here it was the typical approach, and entirely permissible. Indeed, the high point of these meetings was the freedom they provided for talk about points without the implication of any commitment whatsoever. It seems clear that the "unofficial" meetings were always reaching for outlines and boundaries within which agreement could later be nailed down at the "official" level; hence the first understandings to be arrived at—the tentative agreements, that is, on general principles and broad terms of reference—were sought here far ahead of outright commitment in the "official" meetings, where binding concrete details necessarily would have to be hammered out on a vis-à-vis basis.

The fact that advance understandings could be kept intact through the "unofficial" mechanism was particularly serviceable to the mediator in shuttling between caucuses when the parties were separated. Far from holding in secrecy what he had learned from a caucus, he was more likely to put into the hands of the opposite his knowledge and interpretation of what the other had given him. As is made clear at innumerable points in the Atlas case, the mediator was working with those parties on a presumption that the negotiators involved could utilize in a responsible fashion the confidences thus relayed to them. He put this rather succinctly in one caucus when, after reporting on something gathered from caucus with the other party, he added: "So, *unofficially* you have it. You can't use it, because they didn't give it to you, see." In other words, it might be used in planning action and in building expectations about the other which would be in readiness once real deeds came through at the table, but in joint meetings no transactions utilizing these data could be initiated until such time as the originator party chose to make the data explicit. The Atlas mediator's practice with respect to the caucuses was not peculiar to him; other mediators have been heard in the field to follow the same procedure, sometimes adding the warning, "If you ever say that I told you this, I shall publicly deny it." In a Western society there is apt to be apprehension about the moral and ethical implications of such a practice, and a deduction that intrigue and machination are at work. By standards of personal conduct in this society, this could be condemned as bald dishonesty; by standards of power politics, within the framework of which negotiations are undertaken and should be evaluated, it may be opportunistic but is not necessarily misleading.

II

A vigorous conference group begins to quicken its pace, once termination is in sight. Inevitably, then, any announcement that an offer is accepted will fall on the ear with the sound of brusqueness, far more than will rejection. The effect is not confined to the outsider scanning a negotiation scene in its final hours; up to the taking of the last official position, a degree of haunting uncertainty besets everyone in the conference room, particularly noticeable by hindsight in those cases in which settlement is reached.

One recalls the Atlas mediator's numerous reminders that settlement would come on the heels of a crisis. This strained finale—what C 1 of the Atlas case referred to as a "photo finish"—may well be labeled "crisis" as a way of describing appearances, but the build-up to it, often long and sometimes labored, is reacted to in the conference room as almost pleasurable. The Atlas mediator not only implied that it is useless to think of eliminating a fateful juncture, but that the sequel of crisis-into-settlement fulfills a natural, if obscure, requirement of the negotiating process. Early to late in the Marathon case C 1's readings of the tension level were similarly put, as confirmations of progress.

From the field notes before the case had gone into mediation:
He was pleased at the morning's negotiating session. (What did he particularly like about it?) It was a "quiet" session where "We just sit back when they make a point and let them talk." (I could not help reflecting at this point that this was precisely what I had heard U 2 tell the union committee, before the session started, *their* side should do!) C 1 hopes the next several joint sessions will continue along this same quiet vein. From a strategy standpoint, he sees in this the advantage of working the union side up to a state of anxiety in which they get the impression they aren't going to get anything, so that they become willing to give a little in order to get. By sticking with *non*-money items the union's anxiety about the money ones will be greatly increased, C 1 contends.

From the field notes two days later:
He was greatly pleased at the day's proceedings. He said they didn't make a single change that mattered. He doesn't *like* all of the new arrangements, but they are still all right because the original *intent* was preserved. They are working in layers, and the layers are coming along on schedule. If they started off with the tough questions and deadlocked, "They have you over a barrel. Management can't afford to prolong a strike over small issues, so they begin to give away things in order to settle; and when it comes to the *big* issues later on, they're really caught." The idea, he said, is to build tension in the union group. Get them so anxious about whether or not they're going to get anything, and what, that finally they say: "Oh, we'll give you this if you'll give us that."

He says the incentive issue will remain the very last one to be disposed of. It will keep appearing, as it did today, then be dropped, then reappear, and so on. At this point in the negotiating continuum, minor issues are the appropriate agenda items. Why? They can be discussed, left dangling in uncertainty while other considerations are attended to, and later returned to for *clinching*. But this won't work on major issues; on those only a final Yes or No can suffice.

From an interview after settlement of the case by mediation:
(The investigator had asked C 1 for examples of items on which the manifest content which appears in the transcript is misleading so far as the company's real intent was concerned)

C 1: Take a maximum rate range for the tool-maker. (AD: Yeah) How would you know from anything in negotiations that we had 2.30 as a— in mind for the top?

AD: You wouldn't. As a matter of fact, do you think M sensed it? You revealed something when you told him that this morning, didn't you?

C 1: Yeah.

AD: That has been one of the things that has terrifically impressed me, how M was trying to estimate. Even though you told him—

C 1: (Over AD above) What *each* side would do. And the caginess of both sides. See, and—and the—the slow washout. Now, you see, if either side— if you jump, you lose your bargaining position. (AD: Yeah) So the mediator's trick is to keep that level going this way, very slowly up, to the c— crescendo, to the crisis.

AD: Yeah. Yeah. And he does have to make guesses about these things.

C 1: (Over AD above) All the time. Just as we're tryin' to guess him and the union. (AD: Yeah. Yeah) You notice how I always try to drag out of him what happened when he talked to the union? [3]

The mediator comes under the same spell of crisis and uncertainty as the parties, regardless of how well he has performed or how close to inner confidences it appears he has been permitted to work.[4] If the heavy rounds of interaction in the two earlier phases have misled one into thinking of the mediator as a flexible figure aligning himself closely with first one, then the other party, it may come as a surprise to discover in Phase 3 the common denominator of *distance* which he shares with the two contenders; moreover, to discover that the parties have never intended that it be any other way. As a matter of fact, fairly early in the field observations suspicion was aroused that negotiators behave differently in the presence of a mediator than they do without him. Attention began

[3] Cf. a field note from the Atlas case: "It is part of this mediator's strategy not to inquire directly for all the information he needs to appraise a situation. Today, for example, he pointed out to me that I could notice he is leaving the company free to choose, *without a definite recommendation from him,* their next steps; he is only helping them estimate the situation. When I summarized his meaning as, 'By leaving them free to make their own judgment at this point, you get a better picture yourself of their *real* position,' he came back with a hefty *'Right!'*"

[4] The investigator recalls waiting with the Atlas mediator in an outer office while the two parties caucused separately during the evening of the last day in that case. After nearly a month of joint meetings alternating with caucuses, it came as a surprise to hear the mediator declare on this occasion: "This is it! When we go back in now, we get either a settlement or a strike." When asked which he expected, he replied, "I *think* it will be a settlement, but I cannot be sure."

to center on this possibility in the Marathon case, the first case to be followed to completion and one, fortunately, in which observation of the parties began with their two-party negotiations before stalemate brought the mediator onto the scene. A sequence from various parts of the transcript and the field materials picks out some of the threads in the arm's-length relationship between mediator and negotiators in that case.

From the field notes on the first contact between management and mediator:
There was an interesting change in C 1 today. I would not call it dramatic, but for a person who had watched him in operation at the negotiating table, there was some changing of roles with him that was clearly discernible, I thought. I suspect I would have been able to report a parallel change in the union, particularly U 1, if the union's previous negotiating behavior had been better organized, but it was in C 1 more, I think, that I sensed the shift. Whereas before he was at least "reaching out across the table," so to speak, to find some point for establishing contact with the union, today he was taking a strong stance *only in behalf of his own side.* In other words, he was busy girding himself for the struggle ahead, making as good a case for his side with the mediator as possible, strengthening and reinforcing his position. The conciliator role (i.e., taking into account the other side as well as his own) had now slipped off onto the mediator's shoulders, and C 1 could concentrate on only the company's angle. I certainly sensed the difference in him, although it is not so easily conveyed in words.[5]

From the field notes on the second contact between union and mediator:
I had a thought during the union caucus this evening which the recording points up. It seems to me that I detect 2 voices for almost every one of the people involved in this case, and they use these according to the occasion before them: (a) back and forth *informal* conversation gets one kind of modulation—a low one, not beamed to carry broadly, while (b) *formal* addressing of something to the other side gets a strident, deeper voice. The reason the typists and I have had so much difficulty with the transcription of this case is partially that much of the conversation on the union side has been of the first type, aimed for circulation just among themselves. This is important, I think, not only with respect to mechanical problems in recording and tran-

[5] In a field note set down much later than the one above, C 1's own words verified the investigator's surmise: "He added that he always tried to remember, in discussing anything in private with the mediator, that he was in essence discussing it indirectly with the union, hence it should be presented to the mediator as though it were being presented to the union directly."

scribing, but as an indication of the lack of cohesion among mediator and principals when they come together. U 1's voice shifts when addressing the mediator, as compared with his comments to his fellow union negotiators, first suggested it to me tonight, and I began to realize it applies widely throughout the union committee.

From the second management caucus with the mediator:

M: Well, what I'd like to do today is go over the company's counter-proposals to the union's proposals and see how much it means, actually, how much room there is to move around in connection with the various points you have made, and I want this for my own information. I've already discussed a good bit of this with the union, so I have some notions on what they will and will not do. I wanta get similar notions from you and see whether or not actually you're really closer together than you appear on the surface. I'll say this pretty frankly, that quite probably there's goin' ta have ta be a lot of shaking down before you get to an agreement. The union is undoubtedly holding out for more now than you're prepared to give and they're going to have to come down (C 2: Uh-huh) in a number of respects.

C 2: Any particular areas?

M: Ul—(slight pause) I won't say now. Just (C 2: Uh-huh) as a general proposition, they would appear to be holding to *some* things which are unlikely to come their way. I mention this because I think in *part* they're holding to them out of a belief that you, in *your* counter-proposals, have advanced some rather unreasonable notion.

C 1: You mean unreasonable to them.

M: Oh, of course (laughing). Not to *me,* never! (C 1, C 2, and M all laugh) Not for recording on tape.

C 1: Well, M, you don't expect us to give away our whole bargaining position, do you, now?

M: No, but I expect to get at least part of it today.

C 1: What you're tryin' to do is find out where the soft spots are.

M: Yeah, and without presenting as notions the union might have to you, I shall discuss these things from the point of view of softening your position. Again I say that this is between us and for my information to see where I can then approach the union to get them to do likewise, and if we can get enough of that done, why, the thing may not look quite as black as it appears to the union to be.

Considerably later, in the same caucus exchange with the mediator:

M: On a 2-years' contract they would have to wait 2 years.

C 1: *All right!* What's unusual about that? General Motors is waitin' 5 years.

Two-year contracts are predominate right now because of the trend of the Labor Board. That's not unusual. They lived under this agreement for 2 years!

M: They claim to be very unhappy about it, too.

C 1: Well, that's tough. So are we. We wanted to negotiate a whole contract. There it is.

C 2: Oh, I think they have to get off the idea that it's just a one-way street, M. They would like to write a contract and bring it in and just have it signed.

C 1: But we don't wanta negotiate every—every month or every other month. We want a contract for 2 years, and if they've got any sense, so do they. And if they've got a reopener on that strike clause at any time they want, they're—they're just *ripe picking* for an organization drive. (M: Uh-huh) *Very* ripe. Some guy gets in here who's a good organizer for the C.I.O. and he gets the guys on the street, unbeknownst to this union, and no contract for protection and we're in the soup. We're the guys that lose the money.

M: (Over C 1 above) Well, it's an interesting question, and, frankly, I'm concerned with it. If we should *not* get something worked out, what happens if they do get on the street? A one-day strike is a simple matter; a 2-, 3-day strike is likewise a simple matter; but let it stretch for a week. Well, I take it that, as exactly written here, you are not insistent—

C 1: It's a proposal on it!

M: —that you're amenable to changes here and there, providing that the substance remain—

Some time later, still in the same caucus:

C 1: No. 3, open door for a little dickering. Open door that they can't see. (Slight pause) If we get, we give. (Rather long pause) That's all I'm gonna tell you about that now.

M: (Over C 1 above) Subject to bargaining.

C 1: (Laughing slightly) Tell me what ya can get for it and I'll tell you what I can give ya. (Laughs heartily, joined by M)

M: Oh, I'll commit ya to something really handsome and come back and say, "Look, for this you *can* get—" (C 1 laughs again)

C 1: Don't be surprised if I caucus and come back again. (Laughs slightly)

M: Uh-huh. (Pause) So that's the area for bargaining?

C 1: What is?

M: That 5 hours.

C 1: You're wringin' my arm, my friend. No comment.

M: Enough said. 'Nuf said. O.K.

From two management caucuses without the mediator, near the end:
C 1: And don't forget that Mr. M is puttin' the heat on us, too.

C 2: Yeah, I s'pose.

C 1: In his own little subtle way.

C 2: Yeah. Let's find out what he means.

C 1: I'd just say "No" to that.

C 2: I'd be willing to modify it.

C 1: Let *him* (laughing slightly) find that out, then. Goddamn it. He's gonna get tough with us; let's get tough with him. Lis—don't forget this isn't the union; this is the mediator.

C 2: Yeah. (In low tone) O.K.

C 1: 'Cause after we answer *this,* he's gonna wring our arm some more.

From an interview during the negotiation:

AD: I wanted to ask you if you behave any differently when you have a mediator in, and I think you're saying now that gave you a chance.

C 1: Normally I don't, but that time I did. Yes, I—I'll take that back. I think —I think we do. I think we put on a little bit of an act in front of a mediator. You see, you've got an outside person coming in that has a *very* short time to absorb your entire problem, and one of the ways that you can get your problem across to that person is the use of dramatics. So I—I would say, yes, there is a certain amount of—of dramatics put on in those hearings that would not normally be put on if the mediator weren't there.

AD: Uh-huh. So really you're playing to the mediator as well as to the other party. Right?

C 1: We're both there for the same thing, to convince the mediator that we're right. Now, you can do that by a number of techniques. One is to simply put the facts out on the board as you see them. One is to ridicule the other party in one manner or another, disparage them. And a third is to dramatize your case. I tried to use all 3.

A good mediator is not only altogether cooperative but complementary to parties in instigating relationships in the conference room which will make the most of the tension-drawn lines and angles. On first thought, it might seem natural to expect a mediator, once entered upon a case, to attempt to spearhead and then stabilize within himself the central assault upon the sticky items, but the experienced Atlas mediator emphatically abrogated any such role for himself. An excerpt from the field notes shows how resolutely he tried to enforce with the parties this qualified status for himself: "I made a remark to the mediator during the day that I notice that when he recesses a conference, he gets out of the room awfully fast. He admitted this. Says he does it to prevent anyone from coming up to him and adding something else." It is not until the proceedings move into high gear in Phase 3 that the mediator's intent on this score comes into clearest focus. Then it becomes an instructive exercise to follow him in the transcript, weaving the parties back and forth between increasingly longer, ponderous caucus meetings and increasingly shorter, succinct joint meetings. (In an outer office of his agency, several staff people who were gathered at the water fountain one day broke out in laughter when, after watching the mediator pass with the Atlas management team on the way to a joint meeting with the union, they saw him less than three minutes later rush by again as he swept the management group back into their own caucus room before they could become entangled with any too penetrating questions from the union spokesman.) These crisp joint meetings come more and more, as the case unfolds, to take on the aspect of trial balloons in which the mediator takes a quick reading on the state of the developing tensions, then hurries the parties off again to their private sanctums to build more "head," until at last he is satisfied that the equation is sufficiently balanced to provoke decisive action when the principals come together for the last time.

In helping the parties stake out these "tension distances" in the conference room, the Atlas mediator took full advantage of the fact that he alone of all the conference group had the depth of perspective that came from *continual movement* between the sides. The horizon of parties is naturally enlarged when they acquire a second source of information, such as a mediator's reports of his contacts with the opponent. In the Atlas case, however, it could not be claimed that the mediator provided verbatim or literal accounts in his reports. His transmittal was of a highly selective sort, coming after he himself reacted to what was put out in caucus; then, concentrating on those aspects which he wished to emphasize, he relayed *an analysis* which presented the caucus data clothed in the special meaning which he assigned to it. A perceptualizer of each to the other, he might appropriately be called; and in the course of fashioning ready-made perceptions about each for the other, he appended his own embellishments in such manner as, not to deceive, but to highlight, intensify, or otherwise single out certain elements for special attention. The sense of adamancy and pressure which he stepped up in his reports of one to the other; his screening of the data reaching the parties; the inaccessibility to countering data which his separation of the parties imposed—such tactics would unquestionably influence a party's estimate of the status of the conflict. This function the Crescent City mediator once condensed into the witticism that "Mediators are the exclamation point." The outsider's difficulty in reconciling this behavior with standards he has acquired through his own inter-personal relations came out in the reactions of a lay person to portions of the Atlas transcript. In reference to the mediator's conversation in caucus with the management group:

When he repeats to the company what he said to the union the content of the statements is couched in stronger terminology. I wonder why? He doesn't sound quite this tough when he actually talks to the union people. Somehow, and I really don't know why, but I'm beginning to *dislike* the mediator. He's either *very* clever, or else he doesn't seem to be playing fair. I get the impression that he is on the company side, or tries to give the company that impression. It's like "talking behind the union's back," trying to humor the company into a mood of "These union boys *are* calling the shots. Let's find out their strategy and then I can help you." He (the mediator) sounds more like a "cloak-and-dagger private eye" than a mediator. Maybe I'm underestimating him at this point.

Then immediately following the above, in reference to the mediator's conversation in caucus with the union:

I guess I have underestimated this mediator. He uses the same tactics with the union. If this is on purpose, I wonder if eventually the two sides have to unite together against the mediator, [and] in doing so, they get together. It is a clever method, but somehow I can't agree with it on ethical grounds.

The Atlas mediator was customarily active only in the caucuses, but he was responsible for one tactic in the joint meetings which, when carried over to Phase 3, charged anew the already tense atmosphere. It has been brought out how rigorously this mediator followed the practice of pre-viewing and rehearsing each principal in private on the agenda of "official" meetings before he permitted the parties to come together. A surprising twist, then, was his penchant for opening these joint meetings with a dignified speech of his own delivered, sometimes at length, before the conference was allowed to get on with the agenda. Since the parties had already been well briefed about these matters, what of pertinence the mediator could add now is in some question. One can fantasy the entire conference group rather sitting with tongue in cheek as he droned out a recapitulation of his earlier speeches to them in private—or did he? Inspection of the transcript indicates that he went well beyond the private rehearsal. What one seems to witness in these last-minute addresses to

the parties is his attempt at *equal* indictment of *both* for the still unresolved state of affairs between them. This stands in gross contrast to his
previous operations in the private caucuses. There his pressure tactics had
been sweetened over and over again by aspersions on the activities of the
other, with remonstrances that he considered himself a collaborator with
each in pursuit of its special goals. But here, in the joint meeting, the
heavy judgmental hand reaches out indiscriminately, dealing with the
two contenders as one, chiding them both. Watching the Atlas mediator
publicly reverse his former private position in relation to the parties, one
picks up a strong impression that the mediator is urging the parties to
catch up with him in calculating their latest positions. For if, to ascertain
their respective locations, both parties now sight in the direction of the
mediator for their fixed point, then compare findings, they cannot fail
to discover that at last they are in step with each other.

No practitioner in the field verbalized this effect in this way. The
Marathon mediator came nearest to doing so at a time when he had under
advisement the idea of moving the mediation sessions from company
property to a downtown hotel. The recording of that interview includes:

M: Well, since we already have a meeting scheduled tomorrow in which I
am going to be more the interested observer rather than the active participant in, there's no reason why it shouldn't be in company premises. When
I start taking over the joint meeting I want them to be under *my* auspices.
I want them to be—to feel—that they're no longer on their own ground,
that each is on a par, and the only way you can establish that is to take
them into neutral territory.

III

If all goes well, Phase 3 ends in happy accord for all at the conference
table. For the observer on the sidelines, however, it closes on the dissonant
note of an unsolved paradox.

An observer can easily fall into the habit of practitioners, in calling on
the term "tension" to venture a guess about the inner experience of negotiators during the outer "crisis" between their parties in this final phase.
Yet experience leads one to conclude that the reactions stirred up in
negotiators by their joint exchange have such poor stamina that they are
not likely to survive and to grow into decisive action unless they are
strongly reinforced, sometimes over a very long time span.

The usefulness of taking account of this fact was first brought home to the investigator while negotiating with a group of university students over a working relationship with them as their instructor. The negotiation was being observed and wire-recorded by a graduate student who was interested in the verbal exchange for research purposes. At the end of each thirty minutes the exhausted spool of wire had to be rewound before it could be removed from the recorder. In order to lose none of the exchange, the graduate student had obtained everyone's promise to suspend all remarks, upon signal, for this five-minute rewind. The procedure worked fairly well until the negotiation reached the item of grading, an issue which, it turned out, aroused sensitivities all the way around the table. On a day when this topic was under discussion, a faculty colleague collaborating with the investigator in the negotiation—normally an unusually placid and well-controlled individual—was caught by one of the rewind intermissions in the heat of something he was presenting. Turning to the investigator, he blurted out with considerable spirit, "I'll be damned if I'll stop talking now!" Nonetheless, he managed to lapse into cooperative silence. At the end of the five-minute recess, the reduced intensity with which he again picked up his arguments proved almost startling.

When practitioners in the field have been asked about this apparent diminution of tension following forced breaks, not one has failed to recognize what was being referred to, and not one but has agreed that it coincides with his own experiences. One mediator put it this way, in explaining why he called lunch recesses when he did: "If they go to lunch now they cool off, and when we reconvene afterwards, they start in again on a different keel."

This awareness that high pitches of intensity burn out rapidly in negotiation unless reinstated bears scrutiny in relation to another observation in the conference room. There is general consensus that the final positions adopted at the table must be sanctioned by top management and the union constituency, with whom negotiators step up their consultative contacts in Phase 3. And yet in no case did negotiators leave the table to put through a telephone call just before giving out a party's final reaction to the last-minute maneuvers of the other. The witness on the sidelines was entirely confident that, whatever advice and direction negotiators submitted to from outside the conference room, a party's decision *was not solidified until the closing hours of the case—and then solely by the negotiators at the table.* Moreover, the observer became convinced that although the outer "crisis" was somehow essential to the parties in achieving settlement, they did not necessarily reach *the point* of settlement at the same time. The Marathon case provides a particularly useful illustration here. C 1 of that case has already been cited as believing he prompted the union decision by his use of a "forced choice" between alternatives, but the transcript, synchronized with the observer's notations of clock times for the various events, reveals that the union committee had already taken a decision before C 1 arrived to announce his alternatives.

From the last union caucus:

At 7:30 P.M. the union was meeting without the mediator. The observer had just entered the room. The committee was in process of writing out what they were going to say at the membership meeting at 9:00 when they presented the contract terms. U 1 was dictating; U 2 was writing the various points down.

U 1: Don't you squeal on us. We're not gonna strike tonight, per—maybe.
AD: You're not gonna strike?
U 1: Well, maybe.
AD: Oh, I was looking forward to the strike. (U 1 laughs slightly)
   (Two or three talk at once with AD)
U 2: (Over others above) It's not final—it's not final yet.
U 1: No, it isn't, but assumin' that things go along as they are.

At 7:50 P.M. the mediator and the observer joined the management group in their caucus room, where C 1 and C 2 were working with C 1's secretary on a new statement of their "final offer." Meanwhile, in the union caucus room upstairs, the recording machine was taping this exchange:

U 1: This is a fantastic x—
U 2: (Over U 1 above) Isn't it, though? It—I mean, gee, do you think the Wage Board will approve that? (Laughs) What else? Does that cover everything?
   (Low conversation follows among U 2, U 1, and one or two others. U 2 remarks, "That's a good contract.")
U 2: Gee, that'll stop all the talkin' on the first ones, when they get—because it builds up better and better and better as it goes along.
   (Several talk at once)
U 3: (Over others above) Jesus, as I listened it sounded amazing.
U 5: Well, why don't you get it and read it back, U 2? Go on. Stand up and read it.
U 4: (Over U 5 above) It does after you listen (U 2: What?) to it, don't it?
U 5: (Over U 4 above) Come on. Read the whole thing off. It's serious.

U 1: Now read it slow.

U 2: (Over U 1 above) O.K. If we have a mistake, we'll correct it now. Right?

U 5: Yeah, read it back. xxx—

U 1: (Over U 5 above) Well, read it slowly, too, U 2, as if you're explainin' it—

U 2: (Over U 1 above) Well, I will. Now (U 5: All right), I'll (U 1: Just—) kinda—

U 1: Just look at that as a note, U 2. D'ya understand?

U 4: I'll bring ya a glass of water and set it on table.

U 2: (Speaking impressively) "We've decided on a 2-year contract, with a wage reopening clause, April 28th, 1953, for these reasons: to be protected from government interference"—

U 6: There he is.

The mediator entered the caucus room.

U 2: (In lower tone)—"to keep the best for ourselves, xxx"—it's good. I've put it down just the way we—

M: They'll be up in a couple of minutes.

U 1: Do they wanta further discuss this?

M: Uh—

U 1: They do?

M: I've asked them to put their best foot forward in form that it's all in front of you so that in case there's any report you have to make to the union you have it all in typed-up form, so—

From the field notes:

At 8:20 P.M. C 1, C 2, the mediator, and I joined the union group in their room for the final joint session, with C 1 leading off with a presentation of the company's "final position." It occurred to me later, in matching up these events, that the timing of the union's decision not to strike was very interesting, since it preceded the entrance of the management group with its "final offer." If the management group downstairs had only known at 7:30 P.M. what was going on in the union room upstairs!

The timing of union and management events showed enough disparity to encourage an observer to conclude that decision to settle "existed" before it took hold at the table, and that wiping out the time lag between the two phenomena was somehow the main business of the conference in the final joint meeting. If decisions to settle are made before they are reached, an investigator working only from behavior observed in the conference room will most certainly be handicapped in trying to explain the negotiatory process.

II. BEYOND THE CONFERENCE ROOM

CHAPTER 5

The Lore about Negotiations

Apart from case studies of negotiated agreements, a rich source of data about this field lies in the things practitioners have to say about themselves and their work. In the present research it has been impossible to overlook certain discrepancies between observation of mediators in action and the accounts of their work which mediators offer for public consumption. In general terms, in their rank-ordering of the factors which determine the outcome of any case, these professional peacemakers deny that the process in which they participate with negotiators at the table is a major variable.

I

When mediator groups get into discussion among themselves about their objectives in working with dispute cases, something like a normal distribution curve of attitudes emerges.

At the one extreme are a few mediators who seem to have achieved a rather complete psychological insulation from the troublesome question of committing themselves to any specific goal. By maintaining that the contending parties are wholly responsible for the decisions taken in the end, these mediators can accept in consciousness *any* outcome—a strike just as well as settlement—without incurring guilt feelings from within or risking condemnation from without. These are the mediators who decline to evaluate a settlement as long as the parties are willing to sign it, even if the terms do not augur well for an amicable day-to-day relationship between the parties.

One probationary mediator encountered in the field would be slotted on this end of the curve. For his first casework on his own, his agency had docketed him for one case each of mediation and arbitration.[1] He con-

[1] Not all mediation agencies handle arbitration cases, as does this one. Mediators

fided to the investigator that the mediation would not bother him, since the parties in dispute would have to come up with their own solution. The arbitration, however, worried him, for he would be required to render a decision and he had not yet made up his mind what position he would take "on the two approaches to arbitrating": should he base his decision solely on the evidence which the parties elected to present, or regard the issue as a symptom that the over-all relationship between the parties was awry? The second position would doubtless oblige him to probe for information not volunteered by the parties in their formal presentation.

At the opposite extreme is an equally small but insistent group of mediators who declare outright that they seize the initiative and then exert pressure, if need be, to steer the negotiating toward an end they deem advisable. Among these mediators, some will express greater concern over the future day-to-day relationships in the shop than over the fate of the issues being negotiated; hence these mediators will be able to condone an occasional punishing strike as the outcome of negotiations if it promises to clear the atmosphere between the parties on a long-term basis. The balance of this group will just as earnestly maintain that if the mediator succeeds in circumventing a strike deadline with a signed agreement, even a not so good one, he is sufficiently rewarded for his efforts. "Labor disputes," charged Meyer, "are exhausting processes and the mediator, like the participants, will think of nothing so much as of a settlement, any settlement, for according to the conventions of the game, each settlement is a victory and there is little to choose between one and another. Catalysis is the guiding principle and peace the constant objective." [2]

The great bulk of the mediator population is distributed between these two extremes of the curve, forming the familiar middle "hump." The peak which rises out of this central tendency suggests that the majority may actually be caught between a pull to play the responsible peacemaker and an equally strong pull to keep out of the spotlight. This analysis was repeatedly confirmed by observation of mediators who strove verbally for immunity from personal liability for success or failure in the cases in which they participated, in the face of evidence that these same mediators applied themselves energetically to disputes in the hope of bringing about some sort of peaceful conclusion.

---

who are called on to function as arbitrators of course don a different cap at such times.

[2] Arthur S. Meyer, *Some Thoughts about Mediation* (Mimeographed, 1950), p. 15.

It was the continual preoccupation of mediators with mechanical matters which first raised the prospect in this research that those in the mid-group might be perpetrating an ambiguous status for themselves as peacemakers. The seeming readiness of mediators to dispense with frank discussion—the medium of their successes with disputing parties—when their own procedures come under inspection is illustrated by one group observed in the field. Ease of agreement in this instance was more apparent than real, for these were specialists who knew better than most the bearing of experience on knowledge, now setting aside their own differences of experience as though these did not count.

A committee of staff mediators had been assigned responsibility by its agency for compiling a "Grab Bag" of techniques. The name "Grab Bag" was a clue to the function intended for it as a collection of techniques to which staff personnel could turn with confidence. An agency official who explained this objective to the investigator particularly emphasized its usefulness for the inexperienced mediator who, when he felt the need for something with which to rescue a collapsing case, could reach down mentally into the "Grab Bag"—here the official dropped his hand to the side of his chair and gestured dramatically—to come up with a new saving grace.

The committee's procedure for assembling the "Grab Bag" was to invite various staff mediators to appear before it as expert witnesses, to testify about their experiences with various techniques. The appearance of each new witness brought steady growth of the list. It had reached several score techniques when suddenly an alert member of the committee pointed out that for every technique being added it seemed someone had already supplied an anecdote to illustrate success with precisely the opposite. One mediator had reported that he found story-telling an effective device for dispelling tensions at the beginning of a session; another mediator had been just as firm in claiming success with a serious, straight-to-the-point approach. This discovery was welcomed with open pleasure by the committee, though no committee member inquired how unlike techniques could lead to like ends or what conditions should be kept in mind when choosing between the opposites of a pair of techniques.

Considerable deliberation developed over whether or not the list should be classified as top secret within the agency and its circulation controlled, to prevent leakage to mediators in other agencies. A few members took the position that techniques are to a mediator as a kit of tools to a plumber:

without a requisite skill in using them, they are of no value whatsoever as mere statements of things to be done. But the committee decided against this point of view. When the completed list was finally reported out to the total personnel of the agency, the copies were numbered before they were distributed, and at the end of the meeting members were not permitted to leave the room until they had returned their copies to a member of the committee stationed at the door. It seemed clear that here were mediators who looked on their applied procedures as a sort of stock-in-trade having competitive value in the professional market place, hence jealously to be guarded.

The outsider following a mediator discussion of techniques will wonder why the prolonged attention given to these matters does not arouse discussion of the related matter of ends. Sometimes the observer can discern the possibility of extrapolating to very dissimilar results from a single technique being recommended. Mediators themselves may not be entirely unaware of this possibility; a consensus matching their unity on operational details is conspicuously absent when goals are under discussion. Whereas the lay person may assume that the very creation and maintenance of mediation agencies commit their personnel to work wholeheartedly for peaceful settlements, a lively controversy will almost invariably be provoked when a mediator is asked in the presence of his colleagues what he is trying to accomplish in his work.

A condensed sequence from the stenographic transcript of a staff conference in one of the government agencies brings out the lack of unity among mediators on this subject. The first excerpt is taken from a panel discussion on "Responsibility of Mediator for Results of Settlement: Should He Have Any Goal Other Than Agreement?"

Mediator A: Talking about "goals" opens up a large field. The panel members have discussed several of these points among themselves and there is no unanimity of opinion as to any of the particular points that will come under discussion. When we speak of what goals a mediator should have other than an immediate settlement, it opens many avenues of discussion and many differences of opinion.

Mediator B: We have to consider the extent to which a mediator should go in attempting to arrive at an immediate settlement, and whether an immediate settlement might be a primary objective. We have to look beyond the settlement even though we must get it. [The mediator] should look to the fact that he must meet with these parties at some other time. If he is aware of the fact that one of the parties is attempting to use him, he may effect a settlement, but he must not make himself expendable where the confidence of either party in another case will make him less effective. He may be aware that the settlement will have a bad effect upon one of the parties, and he must retain the confidence of the parties for future relations.

Mediator C: Define what you mean by "being used by the parties."

Mediator B: There is a difference in parties "using" the Service and making use of it. Being used is when one party insists that the mediator use his good offices to advance their ideas with the other party and put the other party in a position where they will accept them. The mediator may be able to obtain an immediate settlement, but he wouldn't be in a good position with that party who had to take what they didn't want to take because of the mediator.

Mediator F: If a mediator is called into a case by the union which has set up a deadline, and the union hasn't called him in to conciliate but just to get management to say yes or they will put up the picket lines, is it the job of the mediator to get management to capitulate completely to the union's demands if he is interested in averting a strike? Does the mediator have an obligation to go in and bludgeon one side to avert a strike? In an actual case, management was determined if the strike had to go on, they were willing to sacrifice $25,000,000 to fight the union on the union shop proposition. The mediators had the job of going to management and selling them on union shop or getting out entirely. They worked on the management representative and pressured him for hours on union shop. He was able to fight them off and not give in to their demands that he go along with the union and accept its proposals. I wonder whether those mediators didn't overstep their ethical bounds as mediators in attempting to effect a settlement that way.

Mediator C: I think when a mediator is faced with that type of situation he has one obligation and that is to see that both parties attempt to effect a compromise. Even if the issue is union shop, I think he must attempt to impress the parties that they must accept a compromise.

Mediator K: Our function is to aid the parties themselves, to be impartial. It seems to me an attempt to "bludgeon" comes close to forsaking the role of conciliator and becoming a union spokesman. Our jobs have elements of right and wrong. I would rather not see an agreement at all than one which I felt was brought about through any unfair means. To what extent is our job amoral? I feel that we can pay too high a price for something. You can't lay down categorical rules that are going to cover each situation.

Mediator E: Human beings being what they are, we have to work on the level of the calibre of the people we are working with. Perhaps we sometimes have to blend the high goal with a little expediency.

Mediator L: Who is to pass judgment as to what is right or wrong in an agreement?

Mediator K: There are many different opinions as to what is right and wrong.

Mediator G: What do we do in a situation where we have the so-called "sleeper clauses" in a contract? The consensus of opinion has been to leave them alone.

Mediator J: The meeting of minds is something we can't say is good or not, but we have an obligation to get it. If the mediator knows the parties are in disagreement about the way a clause is written, but they are willing to sign it anyway, I think he has an obligation to point it out and maybe even avoid a settlement.

Mediator L: Do you think if they go ahead and sign it anyway, that the mediator's obligation is ended?

Mediator J: Yes.

Mediator L: I agree with you there.

Mediator H: If you find sleeper clauses which had not been issues, what would you do?

Mediator J: I wouldn't touch them with a ten-foot pole.

Mediator M: I had a case which was all settled except the contract duration. Under the wage reopening, the union thought it had a right to strike, but I saw it didn't. Should I have pointed it out to the union?

Mediator G: Not if they didn't ask you.

Mediator M: They didn't ask me, but I pointed it out and it was changed.[3]

When a second panel discussion reached the question of the strike, the division of opinion on the mediator's goals came out even more sharply.

Mediator M: It is commonly understood and believed that the main job of a mediator is to resolve the conflict between labor and management over the proper distribution of the economic benefits that our economic system provides.

We all know that no two people can agree on any exact measurement or formula of what this proper distribution is or should be. . . . Very few settlements are reached based only upon agreements reached which are predicated on straight economic arguments advanced by the parties in negotiations.

It is at this point that we find that possibly the most basic factor influencing the reaching of an agreement is the fear of open conflict, or a strike, in our field of endeavor. One of the most potent weapons of a skillful mediator can be an intensification of these fears by opening up the books on the costs of a strike. He can build up these fears by pointing out to the

[3] Mimeographed minutes of meeting.

company the cost of strikes or to the union the difference in the pay checks if they win or lose. With the union it can be the approach of a detailed breakdown of the exact cost differences that the strike might gain or might lose. With the company he can emphasize the loss of employee goodwill, of customer dollars and orders; he can emphasize the fact that under the present tax laws the government would assume more than one-third of any wage increase. He can also emphasize what seems to be our experience that in probably 19 out of 20 strikes, settlements are reached by management making concessions that if made prior to the strike would have resulted in agreement without a strike.

If only one party in a dispute fears a strike, it can make the mediator's job very difficult due to the absence of an equal pressure to force the will to compromise on both sides. Should not the mediator attempt to install this fear in the other side? In cases where no strike has been mentioned, but nothing is being accomplished in negotiations, and the mediator wishes something would happen, should he suggest putting economic pressure on the company, or is such a move too dangerous in all cases?

Conversely, in situations where the union has the company "on the run," and the company is prepared to give the union more than it expects, should the mediator act as a "buffer" and release some of this pressure on management and prevent something that might be detrimental to labor relations in the future, or should he sit by and let management be forced to make a settlement that could later rebound to the detriment of future sound labor relations?

It has been my belief that the soundest, most workable contracts and relationships are generally found where bargaining powers are relatively equal. If this be the case, cannot the mediator contribute to such a sound relationship by attempting to balance off unequal powers if found at the bargaining table? If pressure gets too great and a rupture at the bargaining table threatens, the mediator can refuse to transmit a position that he knows would blow everything apart.

A significant part of the good mediator's duties can be to graphically paint "the one-or-two-month-after strike picture" in the minds of the parties in the week before the strike starts. If we can do this job effectively, we meet our primary obligation which, as I see it, is to prevent strikes, not to settle them.

I pose again two fundamental questions: (1) Should the mediator use the many resources at his command to play upon the fears of strike? (2) Should the mediator play the dangerous game of motivating pressures which lurk in the vicinity of every dispute?

Mediator J: Persuasion must be keyed to the specific desires of the parties, whether they are reasonable or unreasonable. Regarding bargaining strength, which one do we push? Regarding counseling a strike, I agree with the position that a strike is better than prolonged negotiations with nothing accomplished.

Mediator A: Regarding the financial standing of companies or unions, outside of being a guide to him on judgment as to the ability to strike, I think a mediator is clear out of his field if he attempts to get such information. I think it is none of our business what the financial standing of a company or union is, except for our own judgment.

Mediator C: There might be one exception: if you have a union that is "hell bent" on a strike and hasn't much money.

Mediator L: Are you really telling them anything if you tell them they haven't any money? Sometimes some poor unions have had strikes by tightening their belts.

Mediator C: I believe a mediator should warn the union of the pitfalls.

Mediator J: Where there is a lag between the union leadership and the members, shouldn't the mediator advise the members even though it is against the interests of the leadership? [4]

The debate over objectives is discreetly waged and, by and large, is kept a private controversy within the profession. For the public ear, mediators manage a near-united front, declaring that the only admissible position for one of their number is a "neutral" one. The intense insistence on this score prompts one to guess that defenses may be at work in the background, for the assumption that a mediator can be both effective and neutral in the same situation embodies a contradiction. If one argues, as some practitioners do, that neutrality is meant to reflect only the mediator's conduct of a case, not his secret judgments, there remains the question of why it is necessary for mediators to call attention to the standards of their profession.

Other self-images circulated in the professional propaganda of mediators can be read, like that of neutrality, as attempts to discourage curiosity which might lead to examination of the mediator's part in the settlement process. In one of these images, well put by Meyer, the mediator corresponds to a chemical agent which can be reclaimed virtually intact after its work of excitation is accomplished.

Pure catalysis at times is sufficient. I recall that on one occasion, after a disagreeable strike had begun, I brought together the presidents of the union and the employer corporation. I came with a complement of facts and a theory of

[4] Mimeographed minutes of meeting.

settlement. But I waited to see what would happen. The presidents started to talk. By the end of a quarter of an hour it was clear that progress had been made. By the end of the first hour the rough outlines of a compromise had been blocked out. By the end of the second hour the details had been filled in and the job was done. I had contributed nothing but my presence.[5]

Another well-worn image singles out the uniqueness present in every case, and depicts the mediator as acutely responsive to this demand. To indicate how such "artistry" precludes any general formulation about the mediator's line of action one can hardly do better than to quote Meyer again:

You will not, I trust, gather from what I have said that the task of a labor mediator is an easy one. The sea that he sails is only roughly charted and its changing contours are not clearly discernible. Worse still, he has no science of navigation, no fund inherited from the experience of others. He is a solitary artist recognizing, at most, a few guiding stars and depending mainly on his personal power of divination.

The only mediation that a mediator really understands is his own. In the early days of the State Mediation Board we attempted mediation by committees and, in one instance, mediation by the entire Board. The plan was found to work badly. Speaking for myself, I soon discovered that other mediators would speak at the very moment I would have remained silent, pursue a line of inquiry that I would have dropped, frown when I would have laughed, and keep the parties together when I would have separated them. Of course, I do not mean that I was right and the others wrong. I only mean that we were different and that in the practice of a subtle art, where timing and inspiration are everything, you can no more collaborate with others than you can improvise music together. . . .

The final demand is still for patience and endurance. Be patient, be patient, and evermore be patient. Be not too patient! Never tire, but watch for the gathering signs of fatigue in others. Then push over the pins that are already trembling. How? I cannot tell you. A sudden change in attitude, a deepening of the voice, a strident, unexpected urgency . . . But no two cases are alike and, even if they were, no two mediators would attack them on parallel lines.[6]

"Timing is everything," Meyer opines above—the magic slogan advanced uniformly in the field in behalf of the mediator's plea for the same freedom granted the artist. More often than not, however, the diagnostic guidelines for analyzing situations on a time basis and for matching up remedial actions with their situational counterparts are curiously missing.

[5] Meyer, *Some Thoughts about Mediation*, p. 6.   [6] *Ibid.*, pp. 5–6, 13–14.

"Each mediation problem is unique because the parties and particular issues are always different," wrote Cyrus Ching to the Congress in one of his annual reports as director of the Federal service, and mediators themselves seem to agree that they want this view of their work to stand. If the artistry concept were to be taken literally, it would be an acknowledgment that the mediator improvises continually, on an *ad hoc* basis, a redefinition of his function and role—a most convenient public image for a mediator who finds himself in need, for whatever reason, of avoiding too firm a commitment about what he does in dispute cases to bring about a settlement.

For all this sensitivity about appearing to be anything more than cooperative with the parties, there are grounds for believing that many mediators, surreptitiously or otherwise, may in practice be much more directive in handling their cases than they care to publicize in statements for the record. Indeed, some mediators readily admit to pressing influence on the developing situation if they can transfer the credit for their acts to the parties. In such vein, one mediator speaks of a "hope that the parties will take up the alternative solution as their own. It must not be attributed to the mediator if it is going to do its job." Another mediator advises his colleagues in staff conference that "Unless the mediator gets the parties to believe he is impartial, he is not able to get the full effect and the full weight of success out of [his persuasive ability]. If we can leave the parties thinking they have done it, they will have a deep respect for the Service and for the mediator." Meyer, somewhat less subtly than either of these, proposes that the mediator

can manufacture a desire for some objective which he believes is reasonable and obtainable. . . .

It may happen that you wish, on a certain point, to favor one side and yet are aware that you will meet with strong, if misguided, opposition from the other. Sometimes the result can be achieved by uniting your decision with a reprimand of the favored party. The criticism will act as so agreeable a stimulus that the adversaries in their pleasurable excitement will not realize what has occurred.[7]

II

As an alternative to implicating themselves or anyone else in explaining how peace is brought about, mediators have adopted a brand of determin-

[7] *Ibid.*, p. 11.

ism which links the terms of settlement to popular sources of authority outside the conference room. Negotiators (and one presumes mediators to be included, too) are said to be flanked at the table by a trio of stage directors who see to it that no one departs too radically from the traditional script for ending disputes: "The Strike" takes over as the disciplinarian; "The Compromise" is the guarantor of justice; "The Economy" holds the purse strings. This writing-off of the conference group as relatively impotent is accompanied by a spate of fictions which have all the character of a kind of symptomatology, particularly in light of the evidence from actual cases that a different point of view might bring more profit to all parties concerned.

FICTIONS ABOUT THE STRIKE

The dogma which attaches to the strike in this society is very great indeed. For many, perhaps most, persons who claim some sophistication about the workings of industrial negotiation, at the center of attention throughout a case is the prospect of interrupted production lines and pay envelopes—the hard taskmaster by which all settlements are at last wrung out of contenders.

The strike thesis holds that when negotiation ends in agreement, it is less because of the intrinsic merits of the terms agreed to than because agreement is forced on the disputants as they weigh the gains to be bought with peaceful methods against those that open combat would likely produce. The difference between the two estimates may simply not seem to warrant the risks and added expenditures involved in an all-out fight. By and large, mediators in the field insist that negotiated settlements would probably not be made at all if the strike did not loom on the horizon. To reason in this way is to argue that the purgative and punitive effects of a strike are just what is needed to bring recalcitrant parties into line— if not before, at least after the event. For peacemakers, as Leiserson pointed out, this is fallacious logic.

A strike or a lockout is a method by which the parties themselves try to settle their disputes, but once production is stopped or services are discontinued it is plain that the method of peaceful adjustment has either not been attempted or has failed to settle a dispute. Nevertheless, mediation agencies as often intervene after work stoppages have begun as they do when peaceable adjustment is still possible. And whether they settle strikes or settle disputes before they break out in strikes, both are called mediation, as if a strike were the same thing as a dispute. True the duration of work stoppages may be shortened by settling strikes, but such settlements do not substitute peaceful adjustment for a test of strength, nor do they help to reduce the frequency of strikes or the numbers of workers who are involved in them. Mediation can hardly have much effect in preventing work stoppages if its purpose is as much to settle strikes as to adjust disputes before they break out in strikes. And the available strike figures seem to show that it hasn't had much effect in reducing the national trend of strikes.[8]

It is frequently contended that recourse to strike must be factored into industrial agreement-reaching to protect union memberships against infringement of their "right" to control their own destinies. But anyone who has watched the procedures by which memberships are made ready for the taking of votes of "instruction" to their negotiating committees will be somewhat skeptical about the amount of *de facto* guidance which experienced negotiators look to the membership to supply. Notwithstanding the strongest urge to believe that the machinery of negotiations continues the historical promise of turning out democratic products, union memberships are actually without access to the data they must have if they are to participate intelligently in the negotiating process. This research has indicated that *any* parts of the industrial human structure which are not present in person at the table—union memberships and company officials alike—acquire an incapacity from that very fact. The evidence suggests that for skilled negotiators at the table, union membership becomes just another unit in the system of signals by which the opposing sides communicate with each other: the union team, to reinforce the points at which it eventually decides to take up its most assertive stand; the management team, to gauge the strength or weakness in back of the union committee when it directs pressure tactics against the company—as witness an excerpt from an interview with the Crescent City mediator after Session I of that case:

M: I tried to discuss at great length with the company why it was that they wouldn't pay for third-step grievance, in view of the fact that they had agreed to pay for first- and second-step. I wanted to know why they wouldn't grant a greater union security than maintenance-of-membership, in view of the fact it had become pretty much accepted practice. The company's posi-

[8] William M. Leiserson, "The Function of Mediation in Labor Relations," *Proceedings of the Fourth Annual Meeting,* Industrial Relations Research Association, 1952, Publ. No. 8, pp. 4–5.

tion was very flatly that third-step grievance procedure payment opened up the door to unle—limited grievance time, and they did not propose, at least in a first contract, to grant the union payment for third-step grievance or to give them more security than they were able to muster in a union election. The company was very frank to admit that had the election results been 240 for the union and 10 against the union, their strategy might have been completely different, and that they might have conceivably taken a different position on these 2 very important issues. But, the situation being what it was, they felt that they were in a position to dictate to the union certain terms, because the union wasn't strong enough to go to its membership and say that "We want you to vote for a strike on the basis that you—you are not going to be paid"—or, that is, "your committee is not going to be paid for third-step grievance," which amounted to roughly 10 hours a week. They were sure that the union could not muster sufficient strength in the rank-and-file of the membership to support a strike on the question of union security.

It might be supposed that the strike threat could not possibly carry weight at the table unless backed up with serious expectations of the real thing, but in a true negotiation expectation of failure, if held at all (and this is highly doubtful), would be held provisionally. Comments of "strike" may crop up throughout very nearly all of the proceedings of a case, and an undiscriminating observer may deduce from this that it is the shadow of the strike, kept dangling like Damocles' sword, which takes over the situation, after all. But this does not seem to be knowledgeable observing. Somewhere in the course of negotiations the possibility of strike will have to be assigned a weight in the calculations taking shape around the question: what price agreement? In this form, it can take its place alongside all the other verbal pressures which the parties exert at one time or another, presenting no more frightening prospects than any other given. Once it has been disposed of in this way, as is true for all the pressures flying about in the conference atmosphere, the real substance of negotiations can follow. Negotiators who are genuinely bent on peaceful solutions are not apt to possess a mentality which holds on to the strike theme indefinitely. Their reputation for competence is a contra-indication, as one negotiator admitted in a post-settlement interview:

AD: Well, where—from just your point of view, not your superiors, now, or
   C 2, even—where would you have refused to budge any more?
C 1: Well, I don't think the company would have taken a strike for a 2-year
   contract. I don't think they would have taken a strike for the description

of a grievance. I think they would have taken a strike for the no-strike clause.

AD: Uh-huh.

C 1: I was in a position of getting something into the bargaining unit with a very doubtful situation whether the company'd take a strike on anything they wanted. Yet they all agreed it was very important to the contract, very important to our labor relations. But that's what your negotiator is paid for. That is the—the skill of negotiations that you get paid for. That's your job.

In appraising the role of the strike in conflict-handling, it makes some difference whether it is regarded as demonstrating the failure of peaceful methods to do the job or as demonstrating the superiority of open warfare. If the efficacy of the conference method must be operationally pre-tested each time against another which is considered to be basically more powerful—will the conference method, or will it not, get agreement before a strike breaks?—then work at a conference table is obviously not being conceptualized as a first-class method for dealing with dispute cases. Negotiators with a deference for the strike can be expected to operate at the table to implement it, so that the strike can acquire a higher rating because the conference method has not been given an equal try. But if the picket line is given priority over the conference table, its endorsers must be prepared to accept its weaknesses along with its anticipated strength. Aside from its obvious costs of destruction, the strike approach is inherently inefficient on one score in which the negotiatory excels in particular—that is, in the explorations which consume such a large portion of the total time spent at the table. When negotiating, for whatever reasons, has deteriorated sufficiently that strike follows, it is fairly safe to conclude that this normal exploratory work has been prematurely terminated. Theoretically, at least, if the explorations in the conference room had been carried to completion, what could be learned from engaging in a strike would already be known and would have been taken into account. Being able to test little besides economic solvency and endurance, the strike has nowhere near the elasticity of the conference instrument, and hence is apt to add little worth-while knowledge that could not be gained by less expensive methods. The fact that strikes seem inevitably to end and the parties thereafter to return to the conference room in no way minimizes this deficiency of the exploratory capability, for no parties ever return after strike to their status of pre-strike days. Once a strike baseline has been established between labor and management, it is wishful thinking to believe that the conclusion which is agreed on will not bear the strike stamp. What takes place upon return to the table at that point is not negotiating, but the sealing and delivering of the victor's conquest.

The clamor to preserve the indispensability of the strike has become increasingly suspect in the course of this research. If the indications have been correctly interpreted, the strike is fated to become passé with something of the same speed at which the potential of negotiation picks up conceptual vigor and boldness. One may well inquire, then, why the strike is promoted (as it still is) as the grand solvent for all manner of labor-management problems, and why its defense as such calls forth so much heat.

FICTIONS ABOUT COMPROMISE

For all the reassurances that benevolence is embedded deep in the concept of compromise, whenever that concept turns up in negotiating practice an equally strong element of gloom seems to accompany it. An informal incident which occurred during the field work illustrates the effect of this attitude upon negotiators at the table.

At the end of a day's session in one of the cases, the company spokesman invited the investigator, together with an electronics salesman who had been testing some special recording equipment during the session, to join his party for a steak dinner in town. The steaks arrived at the table just as the salesman was inquiring of the group how the mediator (who had been relatively inactive during that day's proceedings) fitted into the case. Immediately the company spokesman seized the salt shaker and, giving a vigorous dash over the salesman's steak and another over the investigator's, dourly remarked: "There you have it! The mediator takes whatever there is to be had and divides it up between the union and the company. You get part, she gets part."

Two aspects of this compromise formula have a special bearing on settlement work insofar as they shape the expectations of negotiators about what will happen at the table—an impact reaching further back into the whole negotiating process than is at once apparent. In emphasizing that what can be had will always prove to be less than either party sought, the formula plainly instructs the parties to accept the inevitability of loss as a result of their work: "The demands of the parties may be represented by two large circles that barely touch, but the important fact is that they do usually intersect and that it is this common segment that represents the not impossible area of agreement. . . . It is the willingness to step away from the rest of the two circles and approach the common segment which [has been] called 'a willingness to lose.'"[9] Since the best of negotiating work would presumably not eliminate this built-in negativity, the compromise formula comes to center on the hope of softening the impact, accomplished by pooling the losses and then distributing them equally between the disputants. Ask a lay person what compromise means, and the first thought to come to mind will likely be this familiar operation of halving the over-all difference, with a share going to each. A group of Federal mediators, enucleating in staff conference the purpose of their agency, made it clear that this standard approach permeates thinking even in professional mediation: "For what it is worth with regard to our objective, a simple analysis of our name [Federal Mediation and Conciliation Service] is as follows: (1) conciliation, coming from Latin *conciliare*, 'to draw together'; and (2) mediation, from Latin *mediatus*, p.p. of *medio*, 'divide in the middle.'"

As a way of depicting either the course or the aim of negotiating, the compromise formula is considerably at variance with the perspective which has emerged in this research. Take, by way of example, the matter of positions and the forced retreats which are assumed to be incumbent in compromise. As the field cases well document, parties almost certainly will have some objectively determined restrictions which prohibit them from conceding where otherwise they might. When these limitations are fed into the main stream of negotiating action through the formal structure of the negotiating "range," a bonus of resiliency is added to them. Use of the "range" for this purpose, however, accomplishes more than the concealment of minimal positions on a temporary basis. In the early stages when the parties are broadcasting their maximal demands, they are filling in a period when they can in fact have no accurate vision of final outcomes. They *may* claim otherwise, yes, and their very doing so may force closure at just such points. Yet opening demands which harbor anything more than a modicum of fixedness are antithetical to a bona fide negotiating approach. In other words, by the very nature of negotiations, the really possible outcomes can at best be only roughly sketched in at this stage, and if expectations are curtailed, then losses at the end will

[9] Meyer, *Some Thoughts about Mediation*, pp. 3–4.

also be curtailed. Mediators, perhaps more than any other group, can appreciate the insurance this provides against the hazard familiar to them on entering stalemated cases, where energetic negotiators have sometimes so shored up their public stance around a party's minimal demands as literally to have impaled the party on its own position.

None of this is meant to suggest that the practitioners observed in this research made no use of compromise, but only that its function was limited. There was not, as a matter of fact, a single case followed to completion where compromise was not resorted to before the proceedings were closed. Appended as a sort of mopping-up operation after the main negotiating is transacted, it fits admirably into a scheme of peaceful settlement. The distinction came out with great clarity in a caucus exchange between mediator and management spokesman in the Marathon case:

M: See, I don't want you to misunderstand me. I do not think that it's going to be possible for me, through my back-and-forth efforts, to completely resolve all this stuff other than time study. (C 1: Oh, no! We wouldn't expect that, M) I do think, however, we can bring it to a point where it will (C 1: That's right) become a good idea to put you across the table and let you try and folish—polish off—well, as I described it to the union, if I can get you down to that little bit of difference, then you should be able to close the gap yourself. Right now you got that much of a difference, and—

C 1: If you get to that much of a difference—

M: One side or the other will give enough to—

C 1: Well, both sides'd have to go a little and clean it up, and then everything would be—

Negotiable points are thus separated from *compromisable* ones, and come as the first order of business. The prospect for gain or loss is considered to lie with the negotiable issues; hence the parties are not expected to begin splitting differences until they have reached agreement on these crucial matters. They are ready for compromise when the differences remaining between them are so diminished that, as the Atlas mediator was wont to put it, "They wouldn't strike for that." In that case, no one seemed to anticipate that the eventual compromise adjustments would take the form of really regrettable cuts. This representation of the compromise act as a modest part-function in the total negotiating sequence is a considerably reduced version of the picture portrayed in much of the literature, where the parties are seen at the end as facing a choice between halving their demands in an atmosphere of acknowledged loss, or else striking in bitterness and disappointment to maintain a last show of dignity and "self"-respect.

Why, amid evidence that it would be better abandoned, is the compromise theme still a favorite one with some practitioners? Mediators in the field have offered one explanation: that all positions advanced at the table must be accepted as possessing intrinsic merit which entitles them to representation in the final settlement. To a Western society professing to cherish democratic tenets, this has an appealing ring and comes as welcome confirmation that its ideals are being translated into practice. Judging from some of the literature in the negotiating field, the concept of compromise, as rationalized at the negotiating table, represents a direct translation of a more general inclination to assume equalities in human relationships. Whatever the reasons which explain why industrial negotiating persists at the conscious level in clinging to a social mode which is manifestly archaic for its purposes and out of keeping with its structure, it seems reasonable at this point to suspect it of playing carrier for some ideological remnants-with-a-history in the society at large.

FICTIONS ABOUT THE ECONOMY

Students who talk and write about industrial negotiation insist that positions invoked at the table will be vulnerable if they are not in line with current trends in that section of the economy into which the industry fits. This is in part what is meant when a party is said to negotiate "from a position of strength"—that is, to claim at the table the right to make demands or refuse concessions on the basis of inclusion in an economic system where such things are happening in negotiations elsewhere. In the industrial idiom, this article of faith in economic determinism passes under various labels—"the market," "the economics of the industry," "area patterns," "competition," "what the traffic will bear." Any aspirations at the local level to jostle the giant are ruled out on a priori grounds:

Before we left for the day the mediator and I exchanged a few words about the day's events. We discussed the question of how "right" it is for him to take a hand in stimulating the union here to quicker action. He said he does not know whether he has any "right"; that he is not really taking such initiative. One reason why it doesn't matter if he does something to hasten the coming together is that, whatever the extremes of position at which they now stand, the small area of coming together is rather inevitable and he serves them by helping them get there sooner than otherwise. I asked how absolute and fixed that is. Within a cent, he replied; i.e., his, the union's, or the company's calculations of "what the traffic will bear." He admitted that a cent miscalculated in all the annual bargainings of the country could add up to a good many dollars; but he pointed to some Bureau of Labor Statistics booklets on his desk and said, "Those books on the industry tell pretty close where U 1 *has* to settle finally."

This impersonal approach to negotiation denies that the work around the conference table can affect the outlines of settlement in any substantial way. The presumption of predetermined strengths leads to a conceptualization of the power to settle as a property bestowed or withheld by centers of control with which negotiators have no reciprocal relationship. The location of this centralized power is definitely outside the conference room though, beyond that, vague. Its existence has been established statistically, in keeping with the proposition that individual acts and preferences which are indeterminate in the singular acquire the status, when combined in sufficient number, of compelling "forces." These hypothetical centers of determination are taken to function as sources of stimulus control which play upon and through negotiators to bring about a settlement which was already pretty much "in the cards" when the negotiators came together. The function of the negotiating conference is then envisaged as giving expression to these impersonal environmental factors, underlining them, and, if need be, becoming insistent about their weight; and the table process becomes, as some accounts have attempted to depict it, a rather perfunctory ritual or ceremony, in the sense of playing out the hands which have already been dealt from a stacked deck.

Yet, in the field, rather than a conclusion of inexorable outcomes, one develops the impression that no skilled negotiator or mediator operates at the table as though conceiving the substance of final agreement to be so fixed that he is bereft of all chance to influence it. Questions having to do with the concrete terms of agreement often persist quite late in the sequence to take second place to matters of strategy, not, it turns out, because negotiators and mediators believe themselves bound to submit to some predetermined score but because successful outcomes are expected to follow only if certain conditions have been prepared in advance. The long-continuing preoccupation with strategy matters, often with decided indifference to what the strategy will net, can be a deceptive oversimplification of what amounts to real astuteness in the struggle to win bigger and better concessions. A newcomer to negotiations may be surprised at the small concern shown by the mediator for the actual amounts which will change hands as a result of the negotiating transaction—the verbal fuming and noise-making at the table concentrate on these, so how can he risk a show of indifference to them? But quotations from the field materials will point out not only his *apparent* lack of concern with these but also his genuine preference for steering clear of too early confidences which the parties might like to divulge on the subject. The field notes on informal conversations with the Atlas mediator reveal clearly that this was his point of view on the subject.

After Session I:
The mediator made one last remark, that I will notice in his cases that he never asks specifically about money. He cited the Irving Mining case [which I sat in on] as an example, saying he didn't ask the union if 20¢ [which it settled for] would do, nor did he ask the company to give 20¢.[10] He estimates it this way. He can find out just as well without asking.

After Session II:
Between these caucuses with the company and union the mediator took me aside to point out that he does *not* want a money commitment yet. If he got it at this point it would "dig the parties in" and make them less flexible for further moves. As a matter of fact, he himself, if given a "realistic" money figure at this time, would tend to drive toward that and hence become less flexible himself. What he is doing at this time is working on both to loosen them up. He remarked that U 1 doesn't want to move, so he has to work on that angle. He said that in reporting back to the company caucus about his efforts in the union caucus to get the union to move, he would be giving the company a hint to do the same thing themselves.

[10] In the Irving Mining case, in caucus with the union late in the day on which settlement was reached, the mediator is recorded as saying: "Now, here's exactly where ya stand. We're in complete agreement on everything, since Blue Cross is a wage question. (Pause) He still hasn't committed himself on money, but I'm saying to you here and now that we've got 20¢. We've got it, although he hasn't yet said so. When he speaks about it, he refers to the subject as 'wages.' And I don't—I haven't pressed it. I mean I haven't once suggested, 'cause I'm following the theory that you take it for granted you know what it is, I know what it is." Again in conference with the union somewhat later, the mediator added: "So I'll go in now. For the first time I'll talk money but, of course, I'm willing to wager. (Pause) Strange thing, we've been workin' all through this thing without mentionin' money and yet we each knew what the figure was—all 3 of us! I mean, more or less, and we've never mentioned it."

After Session VI:
Tonight while we were waiting to be called into the management caucus, the mediator pointed out again that I should notice he never asks them what they have to give, nor does he recommend.

It can be argued, of course, that the mediator knows from past experience that figures given out early in a case are bound to fluctuate widely, sometimes wildly, in the course of the negotiation, hence do not deserve to be taken seriously. This is true. But the mediator's willful avoidance of money discussions turns out to be confined only to his dealings with the parties. In the field, mediators were heard habitually exchanging guesses on the side about the final settlements that could be expected in cases they had under way. A résumé of the frequently revised predictions in a single case, illustrated here from the field notes on informal conversations with the Atlas mediator outside the conference room, will point out how remarkably little stability these guesses may possess. In light of the drastic changes which the negotiating situation underwent in that case, some of the guesses appear in retrospect to have been exceedingly rough.

Session I:
At coffee before the day's session began, I asked the mediator what settlement he sees at this time. 2–3¢, he replied. (What has the company given him to work with?) 1¢—but the union doesn't know this. (Why does he give this 2–3¢ estimate?) "The economics of the situation." He says there ought to be *at least 2¢.*

Back in the office at the end of this day's meetings, the mediator was in perfect fettle for information-giving about the case. He is ready to "up the ante" on his estimate now. (What is his new calculation?) *More* than 3½¢. (How does he arrive at this?) The company knows it got by easy on the last reopener when they gave only 2½–3¢; the economic picture presented puts the company in the position of being able to pay; because of the decentralization move, the union is going to force the company to compensate them well. He showed me some figures he had jotted down in his notebook while the parties were talking, indicating what had been gained elsewhere—3.42¢, e.g., at one place.

Session II:
As regards what he meant by a "realistic" offer, I tested the mediator on 10¢.

This was not realistic, he said. Then I tried 4½¢. He said this was "right on the nose."

Session III:
During coffee break the mediator made several observations about the case. 5¢ *at the outside* will be the settlement. (How did he arrive at this?) He knows what is being given in the industry.

Session VI:
In the hallway I asked the mediator if C 2 meant 4¢ as absolutely final or did he have more. The mediator said he could go more; his superior would give him more. The 5¢ he (the mediator) mentioned to them last week was a seed planted; their 4¢ today is in answer. He asked me again what his original estimate had been; wasn't it 3½ to 4?

Session VII:
At coffee before beginning the day's session, the mediator predicted that the company will try to get the one-year deal. They may offer 8¢ and give 10. Yesterday, I recall, he had predicted the company would buy the one-year for 10¢—5 and 5.

After his side-bar with U 1, the mediator informed me that the union, in figuring the over-all cost of what they wanted, had come up with about 9-plus cents. The mediator declared to me he would "eat his shirt" if he couldn't sell that 9¢ deal. I thought he seemed very confident of himself.

The mediator was obviously pleased with the movement in the union caucus just finished. He predicted that U 1 will finally settle for 8¢.

In the hallway sometime after 8:30, the mediator told me that C 2 would give a package of 7-8¢ and that there were several possible ways of dividing out the amount. Sometime later in the hallway he said he felt the company would get short-changed on a 6 months' deal and that they would be wise to buy a year for 8¢. The union, he said, would also be doing all right on the same basis.

If the guesses are destined to range over a wide territory and to be toppled one after another almost to the very end, how is any useful purpose served by such liberal speculation? The answer was summed up in rather straightforward fashion by a young probationary mediator in the field:

You—you run into—you make a rough estimate, and something happens which requires you to change your estimate. It's a lot like some mechanical operations, let's say trimming metal to a certain tolerance. You make rough cuts, and then you make finer and finer cuts. Now, if you set your machine a little bit faulty at the rough stage, it—it's not too much of a problem, you see. It means e—either if it's short you—th—then you've got to—th—yo—you don't make as much of a fine—your fine cutting doesn't take as much, and if it's long, then you have to do a little more fine cutting, you see.

I think the mediator demonstrates his confidence or his control of the situation to the parties by his conduct. Now, by his conduct people judge him, and that is the basis of confidence. It's the confidence that you would have in a plumber, rather than in a confessor, as I see it now. I think the interpretation that most people put upon confidence in this Service when they talk about confidence, they talk about the confidence the parties have in you, they're thinking in terms of the confessor: are they willing to tell you their secrets? —that is, how much they're willing to settle for, how much they're willing to go to, or something like that. To my way of thinking and on the cases I've handled, I've found that once I get into it I'm really not too *interested* in that point. I know this might be wrong. I mean, I might be way off the beam on it. But I'm not too interested in a specific figure. What I'm interested in is a direction of movement. I can guess very well without them telling me, I think, ab—about what—what the area of settlement is going to be, or what their range of settlement is going to be. So that I don't have ta bother them to s—tell me something that they don't wanta tell me or would feel that my knowing it would interfere with their operation. *But* what I do want them to feel is that when I am pursuing a certain strategy, it is because I think, and I'm qualified to think so, that it is a good way of accomplishing the settlement, or of achieving a settlement. Now, that's—I—I'd rather have the confidence of a plumber than the confidence of a confessor.

The concept of remote power concentrations emitting radiation-like "forces" appears of limited value in understanding the derivation of settlement terms. In this study the data lend themselves readily to interpretation of the parties' activities as negotiating *to bring about* positions of strength, and the same data have repeatedly demonstrated that pre-conference power imbalances can be rectified by the table-power to which negotiating expertise gives rise. The present analysis has been founded on a presumption that negotiating effort is taken up with the actual mobilization and organization of the energies to be put to work in the interest of bringing settlement about. By assuming widely dispersed sources of energy whose effects are insignificant except in large-scale combination, the "forces" concept avoids scrutiny of some matters which this study considers relevant to the power problem.

The disclaiming of concrete, localizable human responsibility for the outcome of negotiating is in itself an arresting social phenomenon. To be sure, the issue of power has long been surrounded with ponderous and troubled reactions in American society generally,[11] a fact which may help to account for the vigor with which it has so far been shunned as a legitimate issue for inquiry in this field. If the society is uneasy about admitting that negotiators constitute a new and independent power resource, there must be something in the over-all process of negotiation, or else in the society itself, which make it inadvisable to see negotiators and mediators as free architects of settlements.

[11] Cf. George F. Kennan on the point: "We Americans have a strange—and to me disturbing—attitude toward the subject of power. We don't like the word. We don't like the concept. We are suspicious of people who talk about it. We like to feel that the adjustment of conflicting interests is something that can be taken care of by juridical norms and institutional devices, voluntarily accepted and not involving violence to the feelings or interests of anyone. . . . We like to feel that if this principle were to be understood and observed by others as it is by us, it would put an end to many of the misunderstandings and conflicts that have marked our time." George F. Kennan, "Training for Statesmanship," *Atlantic Monthly*, Vol. CXCI, No. 5 (May, 1953), p. 41.

CHAPTER 6

Negotiation and Democracy

One cannot go far in search of the prevailing attitudes in the economy without uncovering a tendency to applaud any labor-management relation with a record of staying clear of government aid in its contract negotiations. This outlook is phrased in the affirmative as the national policy of encouraging "free collective bargaining." Two-party negotiation is thus depicted as the modus operandi of American "industrial self-government," to borrow the words of one of its best-known proponents.[1]

Enthusiasm for self-rule among industrial principals has so thoroughly permeated thinking in the American economy that it is a major factor to be reckoned with in evaluating the scope of dispute settlement in this society. Such a point of view expresses confidence that the contenders will more often choose to act wisely than foolishly, for in espousing independence of interaction for disputants it pushes out of range of public scrutiny the background events leading up to a settlement or a strike. On the American scene this takes the form of a painstaking effort in the society to absolve anyone in particular, including the parties at the table, of the weight of responsibility if negotiations wind up in failure. Certainly the society does not speak out in any formidable way to hold the parties to account for their conduct in the course of negotiation, or, at the end, to pass judgment on the merits of whatever agreement is arrived at. Public reluctance to apply external standards to negotiated agreements—reluctance to demonstrate interest in ascertaining if the parties negotiated resolutely and *well*—has been a token of the over-all American attitude toward labor-management negotiations, and has without doubt been taken over as a guideline by the principals themselves.

[1] George W. Taylor, *Government Regulation of Industrial Relations* (New York, Prentice-Hall, 1948).

Government, which normally contributes form and instrumentation to many of the society's attitudes, has not yet been assigned a function in the negotiatory scheme of things. The assumption has been widely held that the only alternative to an independent two-party system is a tri-party set-up which embraces government as an added power contender. Although no one any longer expects government to retreat from its numerous invasions of the traditional prerogatives granted "free enterprise," in the public eye government participation in dispute matters continues to be branded as government interference. Since this is held to constitute abdication of the spirit and letter of the cherished belief in "free" negotiations, the current temper clings tenaciously to the position that there is no really desirable role for government in this field.

The personnel of government-provided mediation services have been among the staunchest verbal advocates of this position. Presumably it was public concern over labor-management behavior which prompted legislative bodies in the first place to create such agencies. But staff representatives of these agencies have been heard again and again in the field to contend that "good" mediation implies a mediator who is working himself out of a job in the sense that he aims constantly to get the parties back to a state in which they can get along without him—a criterion which one mediator in staff conference pithily summed up with the pronouncement that "We have to believe fundamentally that we are the guardians of [two-party] collective bargaining." In his annual reports to the Congress during his years as director of the Federal Mediation and Conciliation Service, Cyrus S. Ching repeatedly enunciated the policy of that Service to side with the competitive tradition of the economy in the contest with government:

The courses of action that might follow upon reaching a deadlock vary. One course is a work stoppage. The deadlock and the resulting work stoppage continues until the economic power of one of the parties defeats the other or the cathartic effect of the stoppage produces a settlement. As a Nation we have decided that the value of such a free system far outweighs the cost in occasional lost production. . . .

In the vast majority of cases it would appear to be wise to restrict Government participation and intervention in such disputes to the usual and normal processes of mediation. If these disputes cannot be resolved through collective bargaining and mediation the parties may decide to resort to economic force. In terms of the public interest this means loss of production and services, loss of pay rolls and purchasing power, and loss of taxes. Frequently the cost to the public of permitting the parties to indulge in economic conflict is high, but I feel certain that the American people are prepared to pay that cost as the price of retaining the freedoms which they enjoy.[2]

Ching remarked on another occasion that the Service's "conception of the role of government in labor relations is that the less government you have in labor relationships, the better the labor relationships will be." [3]

Much lip service to the contrary, there is considerable indication that in those segments of the society in position to influence industrial disputants, the propriety of government entrance into the labor-management relationship through its mediation services is viewed as an uncertain good and the industrial mediator as a controversial change-agent figure. In this research the task of finding a meaning to fit the observation of mediators peddling rationalizations about their work to the outside world first raised the suspicion that the very society to which they were accounting might, in its continual noise-making about democracy in industry as elsewhere, have laid the groundwork for a pernicious attitude toward peacemaking work.

I

A critical examination of certain aspects of the democratic scheme of social organization, about which American introspections undertaken in public are so boastful, is overdue. Students of American history find it easy to explain how a strain like this took hold among the founding groups who, pondering their experiences in other contexts, had determined to reap a different harvest in the new setting. Less easy to understand is the fact that among those who have singled out the democratic motive as a fundamental key to the American national character are late generations who have not undergone the provocative experiences of the founding fathers in deprived environments.

Or have they? It could be maintained that the democratic prescription, projected as a series of recommendations on group life, is intended not so much as an accurate description of the outer condition of the American

[2] Federal Mediation and Conciliation Service, *Fifth Annual Report, Fiscal Year 1952* (Washington, U.S. Government Printing Office, 1952), p. 1. *Second Annual Report, Fiscal Year 1949* (1950), p. 6.

[3] Cyrus S. Ching, "Government's Role in Labor Disputes," *Commercial & Financial Chronicle,* Vol. CLXX, Pt. 2, No. 4862 (December 8, 1949), p. 2295.

people as an account of their recurring inner experience, generation after generation, that it would be humanly good, were it so. For this seems to be the sense, and the only one, in which one can come to terms with the doctrine of equality of persons. Democratic theory utilizes the leveling factor of equality to assure all of the "rights" entailed in membership in the human group. Objectively speaking, a condition of absolute equality would imply indifference among parts; and among parts respected to the degree that human personalities are said to be in this society, such a condition could reign with no more stability than that of an oil-and-water blend. For an individual participant in such a system, as seen through the eyes of an observer located outside the system, abstractions like "human rights" and "equality" would be negatively derived as a matter of course —that is, acquire significance precisely because the system defaulted in providing for experiences of such nature. This is equivalent to saying that democratic concepts appear to arise more in response to *the objective observation* of someone else's, or one's own, experience than to the direct experience of social participation taken alone (which is to add that such concepts must include a hidden time element that would have to be factored out before the essential nature of the concept would be disclosed).

With democratic concepts thus delineated on the basis of external and internal implications, depending upon whether the contemplator places himself in or out of the system while reviewing it—e.g., is "equality" to be regarded as generated between man and man, or between a man and himself?—democratic thought comes close, but apparently not close enough, to making a decisive and long-needed distinction. In their summing-up of experience, democratic concepts are coterminous with the life span of single persons, hence cannot be held in trust for the unborn— harking back to John Dewey's reminder that democracy has to be re-achieved in every generation. Historically, democratic theory has countered this negation of its generality by positing hidden potential of unknown amounts and kinds at the disposal of all individuals who enjoy reasonable longevity. By proposing to make the most of such inherent tendencies in the face of time limits, democratic philosophy presses its claim to represent the perennial hope of man that his kind will sometime be set free by one of its own social inventions to fulfill its implied greatness. To make good on this claim, democratic thought would have to advocate a conception of time coordinated with disappearing (i.e., *equal*) parts. The trend of official democratic declarations has been otherwise, taking the shape of pronouncements about environmental aids to private persons striving to retain their identities.

As democratic philosophy moves over into the area of social organization, it retains this individual focus, its portrayal becoming that of the single person related through the medium of action and reaction to the whole community of his fellows, who, for the benefit of the one, are now made the ideal environmental backdrop which this philosophy sets such store by. Even when the individual turns up in situations involving him in *inter*-action with his fellow men, democratic ideology is prone to strike a defensive posture in his behalf, as though to say that in its constant attention to single-person "rights" in such situations it asserts at the same time an assumption that the individual is in need of protective custody when set down in the midst of other individuals. This conservative feature of democratic ideology, whether from the standpoint of outer behavior or of inner experience, means that it has actually not ventured to any appreciable extent beyond a single level of conceptualization. Thus it follows that the model will inevitably be cast in terms of units the size of individual organisms; that probably it will not be prepared to identify problems of social rights and social welfare as something distinct from personal rights and individual welfare; that it will not concede to social relations any uniqueness which it has not already taken cognizance of with single persons.

It has become a thesis of the analysis here that the long-standing implicit indifference of democratic philosophy and democratic institutions to *inter*-personal and *inter*-group relations has placed the democratic approach so out of line with the contemporary world that it fails to accommodate modern social reality. This is not to say that the democratic model is archaic; at the level on which it concentrates, perhaps it is as fresh and pertinent in present-day America as in an earlier day. But the modern world is populated not only by single-person units which lack noticeable influence in the horizontal dimension; there are other, more recent structures of people whose interrelatedness in the vertical direction endows them with strong and commanding capacity as actor units. The negotiatory approach, modeled to fit such formal *organizations* of people, calls attention to how highly selective and limited are the principles and methods provided by the so-called democratic approach when integers like modern business firms and labor unions and nation-states become involved in transactions with each other. When a society which is riddled with such large organizations continues in public to espouse democratic principles as its source of inspiration in executing its regulative responsibilities, it is almost certain to be doing so only because the model it operates with has a hidden face which takes care of the discrepancy. In the area of social relations, traditional democracy has so far not only failed to show any remarkable luster or brilliance, but in malpractice of some of the very doctrines it so stoutly adheres to with the tongue, it seems literally to reverse itself. The observation to be made on empirical grounds is that social action, with or without explicit guidelines from democratic theory, does in fact attempt to cope with group-generated phenomena, but must do so strictly by indirection. Its preference for camouflage in dealing with social conflict, one of the patent problems in the society today, has become particularly conspicuous in this research, where the more straightforward position characteristically taken by negotiating experts now stands out in vivid contrast.

The tightness of unilateral, or authoritarian, organization is ruled out by definition in the democratic model, leaving the horizontal plane as the only direction in which bona fide interrelationships can develop. This arrangement has the effect of catapulting into the foreground in a truly democratic society a continuous stream of internal differences as the many individual units, encouraged by the democratic message to do so, ventilate their respective self-interests. This competition is not looked on askance, but rather is taken as a mark of the healthy operation of the system: to wit, the American extolling of such variations on the democratic theme as the so-called "free enterprise" system. In the light of the history of democratic thought and value, this is understandable, for political democracy originated and flourished in social orders which had above all else developed keen regard for the distinctiveness of the human personality and which were disposed to take an unusually permissive attitude where the private autonomy of the person was concerned. Thus the democratic credo came naturally to underwrite as fundamental the doctrine of self-interests, and it has been at pains throughout its history to attempt to arrange conditions which would guarantee freedom of expression for just such vested interests.

This partnership between the democratic ideal and the clash of differing interests is easily overlooked, but it is important to recognize that consistent translation into action of a theoretical position like this, no matter the level, is bound sooner or later to court larger and larger conflicts. If the negative atmosphere which is so often discernible to Americans in their social relations could be traced simply to the failure of democratic theory to provide them with guidelines for interaction as persons and groups, this finding, however illuminating, would almost certainly create unease among thoughtful persons. But the matter shapes up as even more sobering, for what at the point of take-off in the democratic approach has the ring of a promise to do something about human emancipation turns out in raw empiricism to resemble a case of Democracy vs. The People. Social conflict, when it occurs in disruptive proportions, has to be checked even if a cure is not to be tried, and the democratic system is found, on examination, to nibble away at this problem from a sheltered position, in typically roundabout fashion.

Outwardly, the model proves fairly sophisticated in dealing with the problem, essentially by denying a priori the hypothesis that human disagreements can lead to disastrous results. The exercise of inimical self-interests is not ordinarily advanced as a critical issue for democratic orders. With equality imputed to all the member units, none taken singly is presumed capable of giving rise to any really overweening effects. The possibility, therefore, of a really devastating aftermath to real conflict is theoretically canceled out by assigning an indeterminate and insignificant status to the crucial units. In what may well be its singular gesture of profound self-consciousness, democratic ideology gave away to The People the very possibilities for a power build-up which attract such healthy respect wherever vigorous pursuit of settlement goes on at a negotiating table. With this radical dissolution of central power and authority, democratic action has had to face the imperative demand for some form of control which would abate and depress the massive power threat which is unleashed in democratic theory, without at the same time distorting the delicate balance already achieved in favor of individual freedom and self-expression. The feat has been accomplished in part by a theoretical addendum in which the status of power has been changed from that of a product of local centers of human activity to an impersonal "social force," attributable to masses of units whose only significant relationship accrues from the brotherhood of a statistical accumulation. In democratic thought the problem is thus dispensed with simply by denaturing it.

Power is known in real life to originate in the opportune application of resources; therefore, to randomize its source of origin in theory is to deprive select people of the right to lay claim to it—in other words, to dissociate it from expertness and the exercise of skill. In theory, the meta-morphosis appears to work well enough: power is visualized with a po-tency beyond anything which flesh-and-blood men are said to be capable of taming; but since it is allowed existence solely in abstract form, power is not considered to be a property of real people who can be singled out of the mass and held to account for wielding it. Democratic training, in con-formance with the ideal, leads to muted sensibilities and an accent on refinement and diminution of responsiveness, particularly with respect to displays of power potential. The true democrat is not only offended at Nature's natural exhibitionism because of the rawness of her resources; paradoxically, this product of what is probably the biggest noise-maker and propagandist among political systems has already had trained out of him the kind of curiosity which is required for exploration of natural potential of the human variety. What this can mean when applied to at least one area of human interaction must already be apparent from the discussion in earlier chapters, for if expertness and skill of exploration were to be omitted from the life story of negotiations, there would be no real story left.

Democratization seems perennially to follow a sequence similar to the treatment of the power factor: an original set of ideals born out of deep personal experience is projected into the outlying environment outside any particular persons. Here, in time, the ideals become encapsulated in man-made institutions endowed with human characteristics. Successive generations then become the captive market for these ideals, as the institu-tions become sources of standards and purposes which individuals take over as their own and interiorize into personal value systems. Whether as moral and ethical or legal, religious or scientific standards, the annexation to the democratic armament of social sanctions which are readily adaptable to the single-person level works directly to fill in the authority vacuum created by the theoretical dispersion of power over a massed population. Indeed, in order at all to maintain an effective level of operations, demo-cratic systems must rely upon their mildly phrased external standards to grow in strength and compellingness as they are converted into intra-personal value systems.[4]

[4] The present-day condition of science (in the sense of a popular method of investigation) and of the sciences (in the sense of various organized areas of knowledge) stands in intimate relationship to the whole matter under inspection in this chapter, particularly to that of control systems induced within as a result of the establishment of outside institutions. There is need for examination of the

For all the public protestations to the contrary, first hand experience with modern society teaches even democrats that there are actor units which are undoubtedly powerful enough to victimize segments of the society that are not even involved with them in their conflict engagements. Democratic adherents, in search of mutations of the democratic theme which would permit them the outer appearance of faithfulness while strengthening their hands to deal with these hard social realities, have arrived at a form of indirect authority for situations which hold the prospects of spontaneous and unregulated social interaction. By stifling social conflict before it has a chance to come forth into the open, they have developed an amazingly potent brand of control—what has very appropriately been referred to as the seduction practiced by this society. Under the guise of majority rule and consensus, powerful pressures are brought to bear within groups to induce agreement via outer conformity, whether or not inner conviction accompanies it. And, as if for further protection against the bare chance that a desire not to conform will take over in the individual, his consent to lose some of what he wants is added as an integral requirement of participation in the group.

Small wonder, perhaps, that the so-called political democracies are easily made uncomfortable by the suggestion that subversive tactics may be used to infiltrate them from without, for this is their own preferred method of working among their member units and they are scarcely prepared to contest it. Perhaps this helps to explain, too, why social scientists have persistently come up with "cohesion," "harmony," "cooperation" —sometimes referred to as "round-tableness"—in studying problem-solving groups, while to date they have so assiduously avoided the study of negotiating groups working from opposite sides of the table. They have turned much of their work into a treadmill, for having set out to demonstrate the efficacy of the democratic procedure in the group setting, they have persuaded themselves in advance to see group members as moving away from their differences toward a state of unity. This kind of discomfiture in the presence of open and vigorous disagreement stands in striking contrast to the confrontation and harnessing of the conflict elements— indeed, even their exploitation—as it was witnessed among skilled labor-management negotiators during this research.

---

possibility that the institution of science has been fashioned by the Western world into such an authority system, functioning with almost mesmerizing effect to meet certain concealed demands of the democratic approach.

A society which is not prepared to recognize and to grapple openly with conflict is not apt, either, to have developed a forthright position on the issues of peace and peacemaking as separable from the absence of conflict, or conflict held in check. Democracy in this society, taken either as practiced or as promulgated, has never been notable for a strong, decisive advocacy of peaceful human relations. The uneasy status of peacemaking in the industrial system borrows from a broader societal reservation about the proper limits for tolerating unregulated conflict, for it is not clearly unequivocal that peaceful means to terminate disputes are strongly preferred in contemporary American society over combative measures.[5] The fact that a non-destructive state in group interrelationships is not incorporated as an overriding, even a substantial, value in any of the control systems which have broad influence in this society is a fact of the very greatest importance in appraising the society's management of its large-scale disputes. But even if this were brought forward as a respected and desirable goal and came to be recognized as such in the society, any active pursuit of it would have to contend with certain conservative conceptual trends which, in the form of mechanistic operations, are invoked again and again in this society to reinstate outer control over the range of choices to which the individual is allowed access.

Indeed, one handy short cut to comprehending the difficulties experienced by peacemakers in American society is to realize that they have not yet been provided by the society with concepts capable of encompassing the magnitude and unique character of the special human relations which they are called on to deal with. In democratic thought, time and space and change, concepts which are indispensable in the analysis of peacemaking, yield to the system's demands. Movement is desirable only if it is forward, which means that, once started, it is expected to continue in the same direction in a straight-line sequence—for which it is rewarded with the label of "progress." Change is allowable only if it is predictable, which means that it is expected to be cumulative, irreversible, and permanent—for which it is rewarded with the label of "growth." Human outcomes are prescribed in advance of human effort, which means that supreme ex-

---

[5] In the Great Seal of the United States, the eagle which forms the central figure holds in the right talon an olive branch, to symbolize the quest for peace; in the left talon, a sheaf of thirteen arrows as token of the determined reluctance, after all, to forfeit preparedness to fight. Apparently the ambivalence in this regard has not changed greatly since July 4, 1776, when the Seal was authorized by the Continental Congress of the thirteen founding states.

cellence is reserved for the achievement of equilibrium between inner and outer worlds—a rejection of unfettered exploration and discovery by the simple expedient of starting off with some measure of the outer world as pattern and cutting the inner one to fit it, then rewarding the ensuing silence with the well-known labels of "maturity" and "adjustment." [6]

After the discussion in earlier chapters, it is hardly necessary to point out that such an approach is at odds with the negotiatory one, where indefiniteness is welcomed as adding elasticity to movement and the *ad hoc* situation is deliberately dedicated to the derivation over time of the principles which will govern the relationship at stake. In this latter type of set-up, standards of judgment and of control have to be suspended for the period in which the derivative process is going on. In the world outside the conference room, condemnation is probably intended if "circular" and "regressive" are used in reference to observed behavior; yet both of these are descriptive of appearances in negotiation when, it turns out later, progress is most imminent. The distaste of democratic action for amorality of this sort is well known; the hidden expectation seems rather to be that, from the very beginning, interaction of persons will reflect some rules of government which will make it possible to drop the prefix "inter" and get down quickly to pure action.

II

How, then, is public reluctance to become involved in real-life peace-making activities to be reconciled with a rising public consciousness of possible interrelatedness between the industrial situation and the general welfare? The concern is unmistakably focused on the effects of the uncontrolled exercise of powerful self-interests, but this time, as William O. Douglas points out, it is "not Marx's struggle between management and labor. The foremost problem—the one most pregnant with conflict—is the relation of that industrial power to the whole economy. It is between that industrial plant and society that there is the greatest potential conflict." [7] The Committee for Economic Development once based a plea for a re-

[6] One familiar with modern-day psychiatric literature and practice will recognize these terms as standard currency in the professions which dispense psychological-type services. The question is warranted whether the therapeutic professions may not, like scientific scholarship, have unwittingly come under the influence of the thought system which is presently dominant in this and other Western societies.

[7] William O. Douglas, *Democracy and Communism* (University of Chicago Round Table, No. 807, September 27, 1953), p. 14.

furbishing of industrial negotiating on the same grounds: "that the general public has a vested interest in industrial peace, that labor disputes are no longer the sole concern of management and labor, that in consequence the general public through government has an obvious right to impose rules upon both management and labor which will promote peaceful bargaining." [8]

Persons close to the work of the field who have otherwise expressed confidence in the two-party system have from time to time come forward to caution the principals against ignoring the public stake in what goes on behind closed doors at the negotiating table. "The mediator's principal tool in breaking down the refusal to compromise is the public interest," wrote Warren and Bernstein, who continued with the warning that "The disputants cannot ignore this pressure of public interest: it is the yardstick against which their attitudes are measured; . . . and it clothes the mediator with moral authority." [9] Likewise, Meyer, in concluding an account of the struggle of the New York State Board of Mediation to dissuade the Ives Committee from recommending subpoena powers for the Board, cautiously added the postscript: "Here was a joint legislative committee asking an administrative board to accept more power, . . . and here was the board answering: '. . . If [management and labor] are swayed by any consideration save their own interest, let them continue to be swayed, as they have been in the past, by public opinion and a growing sense of the importance of public relations.' " [10] Of the advocates of "free" negotiations, Taylor has perhaps gone further than most others in placing squarely on the two principals the onus of patrolling the peace:

It has become apparent that the theory of free collective bargaining stops short of explaining how the use of strikes and lockouts can be reconciled with the over-riding right of the community to carry on its life and work. . . .

It is high time to realize . . . that conscious and purposeful efforts have yet to be made by organized labor and by management to develop fully the agreement-making potentialities of collective bargaining. . . .

Whether or not industrial self-government will suffice is still the challenge.[11]

[8] Committee for Economic Development, Research and Policy Committee, *Collective-Bargaining: How to Make It More Effective* (New York, 1947), p. 8.

[9] Edgar L. Warren and Irving Bernstein, "The Mediation Process," *Southern Economic Journal*, Vol. XV, No. 4 (April, 1949), pp. 443–44.

[10] Arthur S. Meyer, "Function of the Mediator in Collective Bargaining" (1951, unpublished), p. 4.

[11] Taylor, *Government Regulation of Industrial Relations*, pp. 31, 32.

The defense, on the one hand, of a "free" and private negotiating situation for industrial disputants and, on the other, of protection of the public interest when it rests in the hands of powerful disputants like organized labor and management betrays unresolved questions within the society about the importance to be accorded certain values—values having to do with freedom of interplay among competitive self-interests as contrasted with decentralized responsibility; with constructive as contrasted with destructive effort; with single units as contrasted with the body politic. Twentieth-century American society, caught in uncertainty between uniting for common action and abstaining from action, is floundering, too, in formulating a definition of the mediation function and a clarion charge to its mediators.

Mediation agencies, in going about their work, reflect this dichotomous strain in the public attitude toward them. This was put cogently and tersely by Leiserson in his 1951 presidential address before the Industrial Relations Research Association, as he pointed to

a vagueness on the part of Congress as to the functions of mediation in promoting peaceful adjustments that is common also among mediation agencies and the public generally. We speak of the agencies intervening in industrial disputes, at the same time we expect the parties to take the initiative in invoking their services and making full use of their facilities. . . .

The uncertainty as to the time when mediation begins is matched by the vagueness of the procedures after it has begun. . . . The process seems to be "to bring the parties together again," after they reach a deadlock or break off negotiations. But what the mediators do to bring them to agreement on the issues in dispute and how the mediation procedures differ from the collective bargaining procedures, is generally a matter of doubt.

If you inquire of the mediation agencies, you will usually be told that the proceedings must be informal, that different mediators get equally good results by pursuing different methods, that there cannot be any set rules. As an officer of one of the oldest State Mediation Boards has recently written: "In spite of its venerable age, the agency has developed no formal rules or regulations, no elaborate forms, no 'red tape.'" But what the process of mediation consists of is not explained.

Informality is indeed desirable in mediating labor disputes, as it is in arbitrating them, or trying to settle them by the fact-finding process, or in the original collective bargaining negotiations. But these have some procedures, some commonly understood customs or rules governing the manner in which they adjust disputes, while nobody seems to know the normal requirements for orderly and effective mediation. This lack of definiteness as to procedures reflects, I think, the general absence of common understanding of how the process of mediation works to bring about peaceful adjustment of labor disputes, how it functions to achieve the results it seeks. Adding to the confusion is the fact that strikes are mediated as often as they are prevented by peaceable adjustments.[12]

One effect of seeing the field in this particular way is to reappraise it in terms of the quality of mediation which can flow in the economy while these circumstances persist. The absence of a cultural endorsement for the peacemaker's work penetrates to all the participants at the table, manifesting itself in the expectations of disputants about the use they can make of a mediator, as well as in the amount of initiative which a mediator envisages as his prerogative. The still uncrystallized American attitude with respect to the value of mediation thus casts a shadow of uncertainty over every occasion when a mediator is called on to retrieve a case in which parties have deadlocked. It is, in other words, a thesis of the analysis here that the mediator who attempts to operate on the American scene does so without benefit of a clear-cut delineation of his social status as public servant or of his role responsibilities to the disputants. This does not say that mediators are necessarily aware of their professional problems on a conscious level; probably few of them are. But it does imply that in the daily pressure to get cases taken care of and off an agency's docket, mediators on the American scene can scarcely fail to sense at some level of understanding that the society to which they ultimately account provides no directives for choosing the steps to be pursued, and may even indict any assumption of authority which they decide on their own to hazard. In some direct proportion as they feel themselves subject to this popular ambivalence toward them, mediators will feel endangered and hence immobilized against assuming any conspicuous role.

With specific reference to the process which takes place around the table itself, it has been pointed out earlier that in the lengthy intermediate portion of negotiations, where the situation is acquiring shape and where practitioners—mediators and negotiators alike—proceed largely on the basis of touch and an ear kept close to the ground, considerable strain from uncertainty will almost certainly develop. For persons confident of their own ability to "read" the environment accurately and to force the inconclusiveness toward greater and greater finality, this period may pre-

[12] William M. Leiserson, "The Function of Mediation in Labor Relations," *Proceedings of the Fourth Annual Meeting,* Industrial Relations Research Association, 1952, Publ. No. 8, pp. 3–4.

sent few untoward difficulties. But if the natural uncertainties of the table process are to be supplemented by artificially compounded uncertainties from outside the conference room, the already uneasy position of the mediator will be made further unsure. For the mediator, then, it becomes of immediate practical concern to work out procedures which can stave off undue pressure from the society while he is proceeding to execute his own privately defined objectives. Among mediators who deliberately choose to pursue the peace, one would look in particular for means to have developed which would filter out the societal quandary as to whether peace is to be sought with such determination.

Just such a solution is suggested by the phenomenon of a central tendency in the mediator population to avoid public commitment to the goal of peaceful settlements. The clichés and idioms which confuse the discussions of the professionals in this field are not to be taken literally but are rather to be traced backward as purposeful inventions—the "fictions" referred to in the previous chapter—which have been introduced to free great numbers of industrial mediators to work for settlements while doing obeisance to the public demand that they shall be factored out as decisive elements in fashioning such outcomes. It should not, however, be concluded that the lore which purports to purge mediators from liability in their work is their profession's unique creature instituted solely for protection of its particular membership. On the contrary, in the broader context of the total society there is evidence of a counterpart tendency to displace responsibility for social decisions away from live people to abstract environmental centers of determinacy. The fictions which mediators have adopted have thus come to them ready-made and possessed of full-blown respectability. Not only does the societal reinforcement contribute powerfully to their usefulness for the single mediator, by alleviating his anxieties lest he be censured for seeming to take undue liberties at the table; with the mediator cloaked in a sort of pathology already existent in the society, it seems almost certain that the impulse toward imaginative experimentation with the peacemaking process will not only be curbed but will likely atrophy among mediators. Surface appearances to the contrary, in a society as unsure as this one about its attitudes toward peace-seeking, the latter effect can prove a not inconsiderable safety measure. Experience in the field tends to confirm this expectation, as one notes in the prolific "shop talk" among mediators about cases long past how often what was done turns up as what should have been done. In their nostalgic analyses-by-hindsight, mediators repeatedly seem to say that they choose to validate the negotiating process ex post facto rather than to reason forward from a set of hypotheses which would have to undergo testing in future cases.

The microcosm of mediators in the mid-group thus takes on unexpected capacity to instruct the observer-analyst about the larger social macrocosm. The dilemma of the American mediator in the mid-group is but a small-sized version of the society's ambiguity about the whole matter of a proper disposition of its internal disputes. The conclusion presented here—that democratic ideology and democratic institutions inhibit development of a forthright American interest in peacemaking which can be publicly acclaimed—raises two questions of considerable import. In a society which makes political capital out of "informed public opinion," how are negotiating parties, in the midst of their delicate and tenuous unofficial, off-the-record explorations, to be protected from outside pressures to hold frequent open-house so that the public can inspect their work with that yardstick of "progress" so beloved by it? (The public, long under the impression that a democratically managed event is a publicly accountable one, often entertains exceedingly unrealistic notions about what it can rightfully demand that the parties reveal of their encounter at the table. Insistence that the public be informed of these proceedings through running reports in a "free" press and radio and telecast will often run afoul of the interests of the parties in maintaining a strategically flexible and uncommitted situation up to the very point of settlement.) Why is negotiating expertise still so conservatively valued in the society, even by the scholarly elite? (Those in the best position in the society to provide the conceptual tools needed for an all-out development of negotiation have not informed themselves of the intuitive wisdom long-standing in the negotiating field. The coming-of-age of a body of knowledge presupposes some degree of formal mastery of the respective functions of time, space, and motion—those three—in mental life. Although the tendency to mental triangulation is a universally recurrent human phenomenon, heedless of all proof that it misrepresents physical reality, none of the life disciplines seems to have penetrated its mysteries as sensitively as have the skilled in negotiation.)

These questions, in particular the last one, pose the task of the concluding section: to attempt to bring together some findings from the present study in the interest of uniting men at the negotiating table with man at large.

III. THE INQUIRER TAKES OVER

CHAPTER 7

The Identifiability of Negotiators

At the time of the field work, the spoken exchange at the table was valued most highly among the several forms of data being collected. This emphasis on verbal products seems in retrospect to have followed an assumption similar to that of Hilgard and Lerner, that "verbal behavior is a form of human behavior, that the communication process is an aspect of the historical process, that the flow of symbols is a variable in the flow of events. What is *said* in any situation, therefore, is an index and agent of what is *done.*"[1] One effect of this concern over verbal matters was to catapult into great prominence the mechanical task of converting the tape recordings of case proceedings into faithful transcripts. After experience had indicated some of the problems, a set of comprehensive instructions was worked out to guide the transcribers; for further precaution, the investigator painstakingly proofread all of the transcripts, word for word, against the original tapes. It was agreed with the transcribers that the investigator would fill in on the transcript the names of negotiators speaking as their voices were recognized on the tape. All in all, many hundreds of hours of labor went into the recording feature of this research.

In the course of the proofreading, a mechanical slip opened the way to a new type of thinking about events in the conference room. The investigator, struggling with a particularly difficult stretch of exchange one day, happened to back-space too far on the tape and was forced to wait for the tape to catch up again. The time was put in by glancing ahead on the typist's copy and guessing which negotiators had delivered the speeches

[1] Ernest R. Hilgard and Daniel Lerner, "The Person: Subject and Object of Science and Policy," Chapter 2 in Daniel Lerner and Harold D. Lasswell, eds., *The Policy Sciences: Recent Developments in Scope and Method* (Stanford University Press, 1951), p. 24.

about to come up. When the tape finally caught up with the copy and moved on, to the very great surprise of the investigator it turned out that gross errors had been made in some of the guesses—errors such as crediting speeches of union representatives to company representatives, and the reverse. Consternation followed, for the uncovering of this kind of inaccuracy was not easily acquiesced in. The investigator had sat in on all the live sessions as they were being recorded; had, in the course of every case, been associated for long periods of time under a variety of circumstances with every negotiator who was appearing on the tapes. By the end of a case there had always developed—indeed, there continues to persist —an impression of intimate familiarity with special verbal manners which tagged the different negotiators, so that an assumption had quite naturally arisen that these negotiators could be differentiated from each other on the basis of their speech. The notion that individuals are denoted by their unique "styles" of speech is not original in this research; by some persons who deal with conference work it is said to be a variable which is regularly isolable from the institutional factors. Nevertheless, a preliminary follow-up of this accidental experience in the present study reinforced a growing suspicion that any expectation of internal consistency in the verbal behavior of negotiators was perhaps mistaken, at least to this extent: whereas in the early sessions of a case it seemed easy enough to assign speeches without quibbling, as the case wore on such assurance faded.

Immediately the matter is recognized in this form—a second experience with data from the conference room which contradicted earlier experience —it will be evident why in this study it became necessary to side-track onto a sub-study of the question, can negotiators be identified "blindly" by referring to their verbal productions only? The transcripts provided the means for putting this to test much in the way it had been stumbled onto in the course of the proofreading.

I

From the seven sessions of the Atlas case, a sample was selected composed of Sessions I and II and the first and third thirds of each of the two lengthy sessions which brought this case to a close (hereafter referred to as VI-a and VI-c, VII-a and VII-c). This was not an arbitrary choice of transcript parts: Sessions I and II were taken to constitute a block most representative of the early stage of the negotiation; Sessions VI and VII appeared to set forth the heightened activity which surrounded the closing out. Because of their unusual length in comparison with the other sessions, Sessions VI and VII lent themselves to subdivision into beginning and end stages within single sessions.

The original transcript had already been edited for clues that might lead to identification of the parties and persons in these proceedings, and had been retyped with fictitious substitutions for proper names, dates, and process terminology. On the copies which were to be used in the sub-study, the fictitious names assigned to negotiators were now deleted, along with the labels attached to meetings (i.e., Management Caucus, Union Caucus, or Joint Meeting). When the fourth and final edition of the transcript was ready, it was pockmarked with cut-out spaces replacing names of speakers and meetings. Copies of this last edition of the transcript were distributed to a group of judges across the country—one, a clinical psychologist; the others, mediators and union/company negotiators—who were asked to determine, on the basis of the verbal exchange, to what participant each verbal contribution was attributable. Judges were asked to make their identifications in terms of party affiliation (this refers to company, union, or mediator) and function within a party (this refers to rank-in-importance of a negotiator within his party group).[2]

Once the identifications were in from the nine judges who completed the assignment, and the raw tabulations and scores were taken care of, analyses of variance were undertaken to establish the presence or absence of significant differences in accuracy of judgment within the total range

---

[2] If one looks in this sub-study for a meticulously constructed piece of laboratory procedure, there can only be disappointment. Nothing of the sort was intended, nor would it have been justified. This does not mean that less care was exercised than would be true in any kind of inquiry, but the objective and the circumstances for carrying it out had something to say about the kind of sub-study this should be.

No more was expected than some refinement of what, originating as surprise, turned into wonder and then suspicion. From even this modest beginning the sub-study was forced along the way to countenance further restrictions, so that it ended as a far less ambitious affair than had been hoped for. For example, it seemed eminently desirable to get identifications on both the Atlas and the Crescent City cases, as this would have made comparisons possible between a case that was settled without strike and one which was not settled. It was hoped that the entire Atlas case, rather than segments, could be used, and if this had proved feasible, the character of the changes at the conference table would have had an incomparably stronger demonstration. As it turned out, the task of making identifications on the six selections from the Atlas case was so time-consuming that of the more than twenty who began as judges, only nine saw it through to completion.

of sessions (and within single sessions, in the instances of Session VI and of Session VII). Seventeen such analyses were run.[3] Since all seventeen indicated substantial significant differences at the one percent level of confidence, it was necessary to determine where within each of the seventeen categories—between which whole sessions or parts of sessions—the differences in the accuracy of the judges' identifications were significant and where not. For this purpose each category was analyzed internally by means of the Duncan Multiple Range Test.[4] This treatment of the judges' identifications culminated in the representations in Figures 1–6.

How to Read Figures 1–6

Key: Upper bars $=$ 1% level of confidence
Lower bars $=$ 5% level of confidence

Beginning on the left, sessions appear in rank order, from least to most accurately identified. Any two sessions spanned by the same horizontal bar do *not* differ significantly from each other; any two sessions not spanned by the same bar *are* significantly different from each other. (According to Figure 1, at both 1% and 5% levels of confidence, Session VII-a differs significantly from all other sessions or parts of sessions, in the direction of greater accuracy. In the Over-all category, Session I differs significantly from VII-c at the 5% level of confidence, but not at the 1% level. Although the 1% bar is broken in this instance, its segments overlap, with the result that it must be read: "At the 1% level, Session I is not significantly different from II or VI-a. Neither VII-c nor VI-c is significantly different from II or VI-a; therefore, neither VII-c nor VI-c is significantly different from I.")

Figures 1, 2, and 3 involve two scores for each identification: accuracy in terms of party, and accuracy in terms of rank-within-party. Figures 4, 5, and 6 are concerned with accuracy of party only. (Thus, if a judge identified U 1 in the transcript as U 2, he was right on party but wrong on rank-within-party. In Figures 1–3, this identification would be treated as inaccurate; in Figures 4–6, as acceptable.)

[3] Figures 1–6 give the appearance of a total of twenty categories (i.e., Company, Union, Mediator, and the three taken as an aggregate). Actually, the three titled "Mediator" in Figures 1–3 are the same three titled "Mediator" in Figures 4–6, as this category carries no rank-within-party.

[4] D. B. Duncan, *Multiple Range and Multiple F Tests* (Blacksburg, Va.: Virginia Agricultural Experiment Station, Virginia Polytechnic Institute, Technical Report No. 9).

IDENTIFICATION OF PARTICIPANTS IN JOINT MEETINGS
IN TERMS OF PARTY AND RANK-WITHIN-PARTY

Over-all

Session VII-c	Session VI-c	Session II	Session VI-a	Session I	Session VII-a

Company Negotiators

Session VI-a	Session VI-c	Session VII-c	Session II	Session I	Session VII-a

Union Negotiators

Session II	Session VII-c	Session VI-c	Session I	Session VI-a	Session VII-a

Mediator

Session VII-c	Session VI-c	Session I	Session VI-a	Session II	Session VII-a

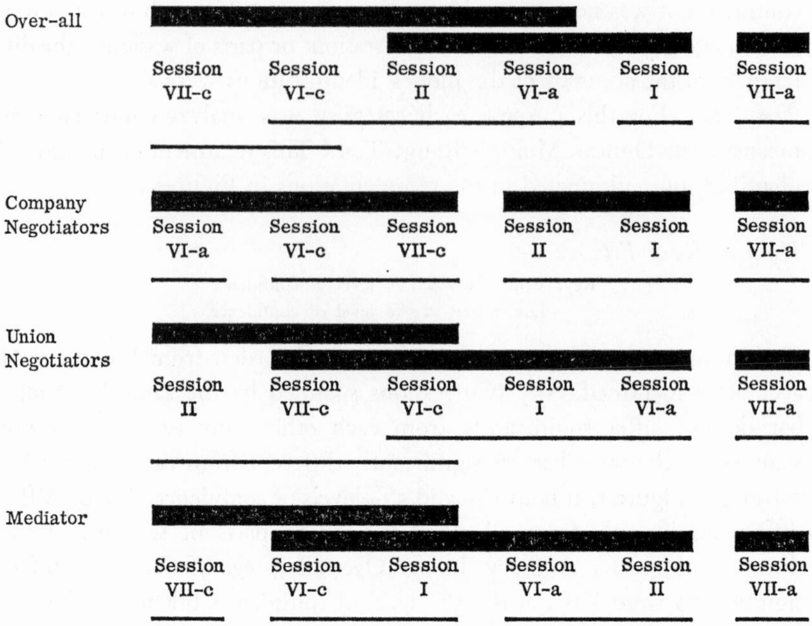

Figure 2

IDENTIFICATION OF PARTICIPANTS IN COMPANY CAUCUSES
IN TERMS OF PARTY AND RANK-WITHIN-PARTY

Over-all

Session VII-c	Session VI-c	Session II	Session VII-a	Session VI-a	Session I

Company Negotiators

Session VI-c	Session VII-a	Session VII-c	Session VI-a	Session II	Session I

Mediator

Session VII-c	Session II	Session VI-c	Session VI-a	Session VII-a	Session I

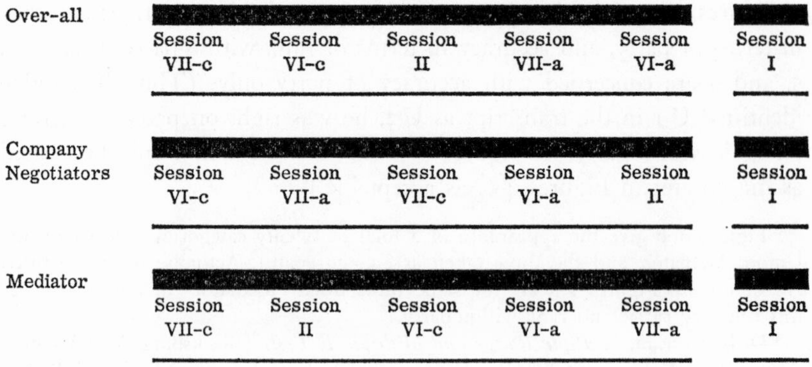

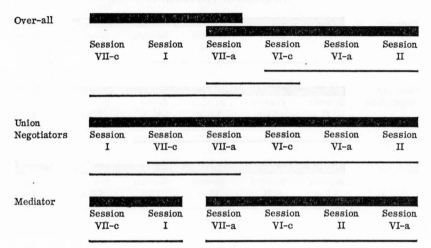

Figure 3

IDENTIFICATION OF PARTICIPANTS IN UNION CAUCUSES
IN TERMS OF PARTY AND RANK-WITHIN-PARTY

Over-all

Session	Session	Session	Session	Session	Session
VII-c	I	VII-a	VI-c	VI-a	II

Union
Negotiators

Session	Session	Session	Session	Session	Session
I	VII-c	VII-a	VI-c	VI-a	II

Mediator

Session	Session	Session	Session	Session	Session
VII-c	I	VII-a	VI-c	II	VI-a

Figure 4

IDENTIFICATION OF PARTICIPANTS IN JOINT MEETINGS
IN TERMS OF PARTY ONLY

Over-all

Session	Session	Session	Session	Session	Session
VII-c	VI-c	II	VI-a	I	VII-a

Company
Negotiators

Session	Session	Session	Session	Session	Session
VI-c	VII-c	II	VI-a	I	VII-a

Union
Negotiators

Session	Session	Session	Session	Session	Session
VII-c	VI-c	VI-a	II	VII-a	I

Mediator

Session	Session	Session	Session	Session	Session
VII-c	VI-c	I	VI-a	II	VII-a

Figure 5

IDENTIFICATION OF PARTICIPANTS IN COMPANY CAUCUSES
IN TERMS OF PARTY ONLY

Over-all						
	Session II	Session VII-c	Session VI-c	Session VI-a	Session VII-a	Session I

Company Negotiators						
	Session II	Session VI-c	Session VII-c	Session VI-a	Session VII-a	Session I

Mediator						
	Session VII-c	Session II	Session VI-c	Session VI-a	Session VII-a	Session I

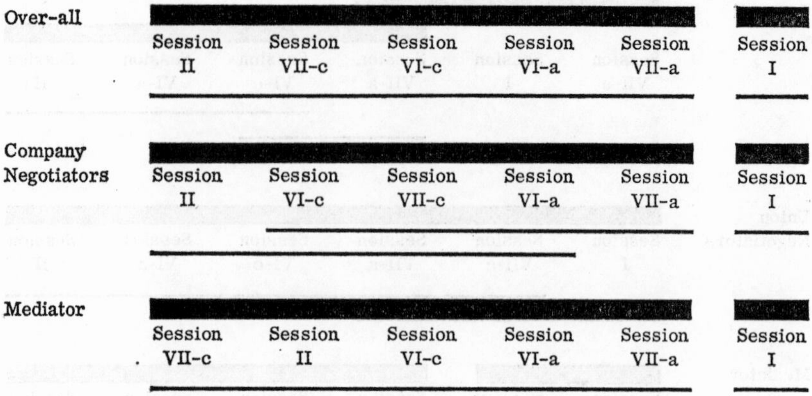

Figure 6

IDENTIFICATION OF PARTICIPANTS IN UNION CAUCUSES
IN TERMS OF PARTY ONLY

Over-all						
	Session VII-c	Session I	Session VII-a	Session VI-c	Session VI-a	Session II

Union Negotiators						
	Session I	Session VII-a	Session VII-c	Session VI-a	Session VI-c	Session II

Mediator						
	Session VII-c	Session I	Session VII-a	Session VI-c	Session II	Session VI-a

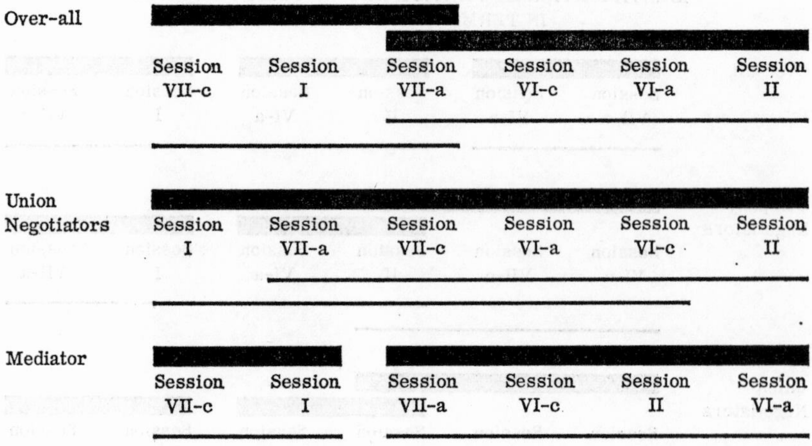

II

Statistical dissecting of the Atlas case was intended to improve the vision in searching for changes in behavior which coincide with progress to settlement. Inspection of Figures 1 and 4, representing the full negotiating body at work, reveals a distinct decline in accuracy of identification in the direction of settlement, hence the sub-study might conceivably be a welcome demonstration of the transitions intrinsic to an analysis of negotiation by "phases."

Curiously enough, however, the immediate findings of the sub-study on this score led not to enlightenment but to an analytical impasse. The analysis in Part I had relied heavily on the proposition that negotiators play both ends of a functional continuum from institution to individual. This was tantamount to declaring that the investigator had accepted parties and persons as the primary units of negotiating analysis. With the sub-study now providing a different location from which to make observations of negotiators at work, the new body of data could be employed with almost equal success either to support or to refute the person/party dichotomy.

The very fact of declining identifiability vetoes the suggestion, raised in advance of the sub-study, that personalities distinguishable along "style" lines can wield an overriding influence at the table. If psychological specialists are correct in insisting that human organisms exhibit sufficiently reliable response tendencies, each in terms of his own history, to warrant title to a basic personality structure or "integration," it is reasonable to assume that such a private condition will prevail in the conference room with a degree of constancy which can be detected and tracked. At least, this seems to be the sense in which the concept of a static "personality" is usable, if at all, within the negotiating context. The unmistakable evidence of judge variability seems without question to rule out that possibility.

In the Atlas case, this was put to concrete test through the happenstance of C_1's departure from the company after Session V and his replacement thereafter by former C_2. The judges had received advance warning of the replacement, because it was discussed at length in the transcript materials with which they were working. However, to make doubly sure about the matter, if it seemed remotely possible that a judge had overlooked this fact, that judge was interrogated, on turning in his work, to see whether or not he had been aware of the personnel situation. Every judge so questioned admitted to having recognized that a switch of company spokesmen had taken place.

In view of their standard knowledge about the change, a question arises as to why only three of the nine judges caught the fact that the new spokesman was former C_2. The remaining six took the new leader to be an import from outside or some team member other than former C2. To quote from their comments on the matter:

The spokesman for the company in Sessions I and II is different from the spokesman in the following sessions. I did not identify the latter spokesman as being present in Sessions I and II, and I presume that he did not enter into negotiations until later. The person who becomes the new management spokesman from VI on is not someone who had a number in the first sessions; he is a brand new person and consequently he is not the same C2 as originally labeled.

My recollection is that the C3 man who took over from C1 in the later sessions was the same C3 referred to in the earlier sessions. He did not appear to be an entirely new man on the scene and became C3 only because he was the third man on the management team in Session I who spoke—or so it seemed to me. I didn't think a new man was brought in. It seemed to me that C3 developed quite a bit of skill through the series.

My impression was that the chairman of the company team had been changed and that "a brand new person" had appeared on the scene, entering for the first time.

When I say "new C1" [from Session VI-a on] I mean no more than that a different person has become the company's chief spokesman. I figured you would want 1 appended not so much to a particular individual as to have "1" designate "chief spokesman." I do not know, couldn't guess, and felt it was irrelevant for your purposes whether the new "C1" was previously a member of the company's negotiating team and got elevated to the status of chief spokesman, or whether he was brought into the negotiations when the original "C1" left. I think this much could be discerned: the new "C1," whether or not previously on the negotiating committee, had been with the company (Treasurer?) for some time and was not a newly hired Industrial Relations Director.

It now seems certain, upon second thought, that as primary units of analysis, individuals were doomed from the beginning to fail the test of the sub-study. This was not for lack of a discernible structure per se; but no structure, personality or otherwise, would be consonant with the task facing a negotiator if it did not lend itself as a base from which to unravel a history of change. An unwinding structure is hardly consonant with the task facing the judges—a conclusion echoed by several in remarking at the end on the lack of confidence they had felt in making this type of identification:

I have done my best to identify company and union people but find it very difficult to get beyond the point of merely identifying which side of the table is talking. Images of people per se were difficult. There was not too much difficulty in identifying the utterers of the longer speeches, but the short interjections which were not trimmed with any characteristics left me totally without clues. In this final session it was difficult to pick out separately any of the subordinate negotiators. One had a feeling that the committee was somewhat larger than it had been in the early sessions, but during the caucuses when figures were discussed everyone cackled so that identification was almost impossible. Even C 3 became lost in the general mumbling. The same situation seemed to prevail in the union caucuses, but not to such a great extent. The union committee seemed fairly large. Some were not very clearly identifiable, except as off-stage noises.

My only real difficulty was the determination of who on the union committee was talking when in caucus and who on the management committee was talking when that group caucused.

Conceding that suppleness could be identified only where its opposite had once flourished, it would be predicted that decline in identifiability would be associated exclusively with the joint meetings, which are known to have been constituted in the Atlas case as the official forum of the institutional contenders. According to the data of the sub-study, this is precisely where the judges fluctuated in performance in significant degrees. No comparable trends for the private caucuses show up in their work.

Perhaps the claim of "parties" to primacy—their loss of identity with progress toward settlement qualifying well enough as historical trend—would have survived at the hands of the judges, had it not been for one wholly unexpected development, disclosed by the sub-study, which is too striking to be written off as random deviation. In the early portion of the final session of the Atlas case (i.e., Session VII-a), in which agreement was reached after a month of negotiations had taken place, a most remarkable return to accuracy occurs among the judges. This session ranks alongside Session I for accuracy in terms of party; when rank-within-party is added to party affiliation, it outranks all other sessions in accuracy, including Session I. Even the mediator, whose functioning was most clearly discernible in the intermediate stages, comes forth in a fresh burst of clarity in VII-a: in this, his last major appearance with the parties in joint context, he reaches the highest point of his clarity anywhere in the sub-study.

The joint meetings of Session VII-a were not the most productive ones, measured in number of participations; but, taken as a percentage of the productivity of VII-a over-all, they were almost identical with the joint meetings of Session VI-a taken as a percentage of VI-a over-all. Notwithstanding this similarity, the judges distinguished significantly between VII-a and VI-a—*markedly* so with company negotiators, boosting the accuracy level in VII-a appreciably for seven of the nine judges.

In the advance formulation of what would be likely to appear in the sub-study, there had certainly been no expectation that accuracy which could rival the beginning phase of the case would turn up so near the end. As a matter of fact, the expectation was nearer the opposite: that by this point accuracy would have deteriorated beyond repair. The discovery of this last-minute break in an otherwise straight-line tendency in the changes taking place, particularly when the break seems to bespeak a regressive return to the earliest form of identities, has all the appearance of a "collapse" into settlement only after a restitution of the original condition of intense conflict. On the basis of the external signs, one may ask in practical terms whether a crisis dramatizing the prospect of non-settlement is indicated as a forerunner of the decision to do the opposite; [5] but in theoretical terms it must be asked how one is to reconcile the disparate findings that come out of the sub-study packaged together—resurgent conflict interrupting accumulated readiness to agree.

There is one figure in the sub-study materials—the mediator—who was surely called on, in the line of duty, to take a practical stand on this whole theoretical question of the dichotomous classification into parties and persons. It was declared in Chapter 1 that in his own and negotiators' eyes the American mediator has no party affiliation to substantiate his actions, making him less useful to negotiators who are agents of parties than to negotiators operating as autonomous individuals. For this reason alone, his distinctiveness as a mediator would be expected to vary over the whole of a case, moving in early and late joint meetings into a kind of background obscurity in deference to the all-out party activities at these times.

[5] The practical question is rather easily answered at the level of analysis maintained throughout Part I. The demands of Phase 3, as these were seen through the eyes of a witness in the conference room, make a return of conflict like this seem entirely reasonable and acceptable, perhaps even imperative. When in need of exceptional proof of firmness, as is the negotiator in making his last-time "final offer," there may well be no more resplendent symbol of the power to sanction and/or punish than a reply rendered in the name of the institutional parties, whose outlines the judges so accurately picked out.

From the Atlas mediator's comments recorded in the field materials, it is already known that this mediator claimed to make his choice of behavior on other grounds. The orderliness of the variability with which judges distinguished him in participation with the parties supports his claim that he deliberately manipulated their opportunities for relating to him. There is no conspicuous difference between the mediator's clarity for judges in the joint meetings of Session VI-c and VII-c, although in VI-c he was more active, in terms of gross participations, than in VII-c. The poor visibility which he has acquired to such a marked degree by Session VII-c has apparently already set in by Session VI-c. With respect to Session VII-c, the decline in his clarity is achieved without sacrificing his rate of activity, for his gross productivity here was about equal to that of Session II, where his functioning as mediator is so significantly more certain to the judges than in VII-c. His "obscurity," in other words, must be related to a condition more widespread throughout the conference room than mere personal withdrawal into passivity or blacking-out in the shadows cast by the more gigantic party figures.

One way to break this analytical impasse created by the sub-study is to call in question the working ideas of the sub-study itself. "Identity" proved applicable as long as it could be paired with parties; this, in turn, proved to equate it with a state of conflict. "Identity" and "conflict," in other words, turn out to be analytically useful where, but only where, the adjunct of space makes possible a conception of withdrawal of object from object, point from point. Time being the psychological, or experiential, counterpart of space, it might be surmised offhand that the sub-study was fortuitously supplied with the very mathematical properties required for on-going identity, since any assumption of "progress" toward settlement, as here, embodies the additional assumption of a time sequence. But it is now quite clear from the sub-study that a time dimension equated with the space dimension but independent of it does not provide a profitable line of analysis for negotiation. For the materials of the sub-study yielded not a progressive trend, but retrogression and reversal of direction; and yet neither of these can logically be labeled "deterioration" when agreement is the aftermath.

III

Each transcript sent to a judge was accompanied by a set of instructions including, among other points, the following:

Start identifying as soon as you start reading. In other words, don't read in advance with the idea of building up any mental picture of the negotiations or negotiators and then going back to mark identifications down. Thus, your Union 1 will be the first representative of the union side you encounter in the transcript, Union 2 the second one, etc.

Under no circumstances are you to go back and change, on the basis of hindsight, an identification you have made earlier. Let all identifications stand, once made.

After you have completed all the transcripts, I would like a sort of thumb-nail "personality" sketch of each of the negotiators you have identified with numbers, so that I can see which person represents for you the chief spokes-man on each side, which the second-ranking one, etc. In this sketch I would like particularly to get indications of the *cues* you utilized throughout to help you in making the various identifications.

One may ask how a conscientious judge would set about deciding on an identity that he was not allowed to test before having to vouch for it. It had been presumed by the investigator that, because of their occupational pursuits, these judges were virtual counterparts of the subjects they would be judging and would accordingly prove an apt lot for purposes of the sub-study. Judges such as these, all but one of them with extensive ne-gotiating experience, had well-stocked memories of other negotiations to draw from in embarking on their assignment. Until criteria could shape up out of the transcript itself, these advance expectations could serve judges judging negotiators in exactly the same way they serve ne-gotiators judging other negotiators on first contact at a conference table. Use of a clinical psychologist was thought to be especially high in promise; do clinicians not profess to be dealing daily in conflict resolution and in promoting one kind of peace—adaptations of men with their fellow men? And, to the extent that the verbal exchange can be assumed to be the vehicle of events at the conference table, the judges, in their exposure to the transcript, were presumably operating with opportunities for experi-ence similar enough to those of the negotiators. The fact that the accuracy scores held up so well in the early stages compared with the mounting in-accuracies in later ones prompts one to conclude that the negotiators at the Atlas table may indeed have started off in conformance with the images the judges had in mind. Yet the unmistakable evidence that judges tended to grow less accurate with progress toward settlement suggests that, in some way or ways which need to be ferreted out, the universes of negotiators at the table and of judges poring over transcripts, after taking off from a common matrix, parted company in ever expanding degree until at the end they shared little if any ground between them. Since this is just the opposite of what took place between the contending sides, it is meet to ask what happened in the course of the Atlas case to draw negotiators together in the conference room which eluded judges in working with the historical record.

The question is easier to work with if it is turned around and asked in reverse. When one searches in the work of *the judges* for the needed clues, one suspects quite early that in summoning up stereotypes out of bygone experiences to get a yardstick for measuring the stature of speakers, the judges may have reached deep into self for the traces of an outline to be applied. In three sets of thumbnail sketches submitted by as many judges, it will be seen that only one stuck closely to the objective verbal behavior as an index of functions performed for the parties. The other two judges went considerably beyond this, seizing upon non-verbal grounds for passing judgment on matters of personal and social attraction and repellence, and of efficiencies and inefficiencies—these all, presumably, measured against the standard that "if *this* judge had been in place of the speaker, the transcript record would have read differently."

From Judge A:

C 1: In the initial sessions this individual was chief spokesman in his capacity as Industrial Relations Director. Clues used were his predisposition for engaging in long monologues concerning industry economics, well illustrated with graphic material.

C 2: Management spokesman after C 1 left the company for other employment. He is the Treasurer of the firm. Identification of this person became easier after he took over as chief spokesman. C 2 is a good role player.

C 3: Appeared to be the Sales Manager of the firm. I must confess that I endeavored to identify him mainly by his references to industry problems or comments in the nature of "fillers."

C 4: Was, in initial sessions, the Assistant Industrial Relations Director, and after the resignation of his superior moved to the top post. *However,* he did not take over as chief management spokesman. C 4 was largely identified by his "advisory" comments, made generally in the separate caucus. He appeared also to have been responsible for grievance handling, and comments relating to same were accorded to him.

U 1: The chief spokesman for the union committee. He is an International representative. My impression of U 1 leads me to believe that he is a very capable negotiator and strategist, extremely articulate, and possessed of a good sense of humor. Clues used in identifying him include his use of the first person when referring to the union, his well-developed sentence structure and tightly reasoned arguments.

U 2: This person is, in my estimation, an official (perhaps Secretary) of the Local union. His main role in the negotiations is to supply supporting, corroborating, or explanatory statements. I have used speeches which support positions taken by U 1 as the main clues in identifying U 2. U 2 is apparently trying to follow U 1's lead into the International union.

U 3: This is the rank-and-file negotiating committee member whose chief role concerns asking the embarrassing question and/or making the wry comment. In short, the baiter. The clues resorted to in identification of U 3 include tartness of subject matter and informality of sentence structure.

U 4: Appeared to me to be a resource person who had a good knowledge of shop practices and conditions in the subject plant. Identification in this instance was based upon statements which reflected a familiarity with plant operations.

M: I feel confident that greater accuracy has been exercised in identification of the mediator than any other negotiating personality. The major clues included his repetitious style of speech and his neutral attitude. The mediator appeared to be a well-experienced, even-tempered individual.

From Judge B:

U 1: Here is the International representative, the skilled and experienced negotiator, well-poised, articulate, sure of his skill and his leadership. U 1 is probably the strongest man in the situation: stronger than anyone [else] on the union side of the table, stronger than the mediator, and stronger even than the characters on the management side.

U 2: This one I see as the strong member of the Local committee, probably the Chairman, not too bright or experienced in negotiation but not as stupid, really, as he appears in his earlier speeches. He is completely overshadowed and dominated, however, by U 1.

(The union committee seemed fairly large, and there seemed to be several women on it. Some of the union committee below U 2, such as U 3 and U 4, were not very clearly identifiable except as offstage noises.)

C 1: Another windy character whom I have met many times, probably the Personnel Manager of the company who, by his charts and graphs and figures and volubility, has convinced himself and management of the soundness of his position and the "logic" of his reasoning.

C 2: An individual who plays a very minor role in labor relations of the company but who seems to keep a wary eye on the dollar. Quite possibly he is Treasurer or Comptroller of the company. His presence during the negotiations seems to be for the chief purpose of giving support in depth to the management spokesman.

C 3: He appeared on the scene in Session VI-a. He appeared to be a man without too much experience in negotiation who was forced reluctantly into the role of negotiator by the departure from the company of C 1. I thought he was a notch higher on the management organizational chart than his predecessor but not high enough to operate without limitation. His uncertainty in the beginning was the chief clue to his identity. He developed as the sessions proceeded, and he became more sure of himself.

(I couldn't find clues to any other management people at the table.)

M: A wordy, windy, apparently indecisive character, who rarely finishes a sentence or a thought but who, by these very characteristics, manages to move the principals out of the dreamy area in which each, during the earlier negotiations and the early mediation sessions, has managed to entrench himself behind a bunker of rationalization and self-justification. During the early sessions I was afraid he was going to be completely ineffective because of his lack of aggressiveness—but it is possible that this approach was just what the parties to the dispute needed. Occasionally I have the feeling that his peregrinations in discussion with management approach the boundaries of ethics. There seems to be in his mind a sort of haze surrounding the status of confidences he obtained from the union representatives.

From Judge C:

U 1: Represents to me an International union representative because of his skill in tactics. He is a clever bargainer and uses many of the standard approaches to shifts in position. In other words, when he had the company coming to a point he would suddenly shift his proposal without even telling the mediator and thus draw the company out even further.

U 2: Seems to me to be the usual would-be tough guy from the shop who stirs up enough activity to get himself elected President of the Local.

(Obviously there was a woman on the union committee, but I could not identify either her or the several other members of the committee.)

C 1: Represents the original spokesman for the company, who, from what little we had, appeared to be a tough bargainer. I would like to have seen him in the clutch. However, I think he made a bad blunder in the beginning of the negotiations by revealing his charts and data *before* the union had been fully drawn out. This data could have been used to better advantage later in the negotiations and perhaps in not so formal a manner. It would have then been more effective in answering points raised by the union. There was no attempt to make the union justify its own position, so these points could have been used to knock down union arguments and put them on the defensive.

C 2: Could have been C 1's assistant, but he certainly was not a strong man. He was too uncertain and placed himself in the hands of the mediator, which is a fatal mistake! I like to bargain with the mediator, which makes him tougher with the union.

C 3: Did not appear too definite, but I get a feeling that he was the strongest of the management committee. At least he was the solid thinker.

(There seemed to be two other members of this committee, but I cannot identify them.)

M: The mediator had a pipe dream with this one! Apparently he is very capable, but he only had the union side of the table to worry about! And I suspect—just suspect, mind you—that he knew long before the end what would settle the deal. Not sure if he gathered this from a side-bar with International rep of the union or because he was forced to put himself in management's position and shot for definite goal in his own mind. Certainly, management did not seem to have a pre-negotiation goal to drive for.

(My conclusion is, if you are interested, the company paid more than it had to!)

An inspection of the errors made in identifying conferees suggests a second trend among the judges: to seek a *consistent* and *unitary* way of beholding the transcript speakers. To manage the contradictory strains of behavior which originated within a single negotiator, some judges openly resorted to the ingenious technique of transplanting each strain to a synthetically created "mythical" person endowed with a static but *perceptible* structure. Once a single real negotiator was thus reconstituted into more than one person, the judge could proceed to distribute between the hypothetical figures the total crop of verbal statements which had issued at the table out of the same mouth.[6] An excellent illustration is afforded by the clinical psychologist serving as a judge, who offered thumbnail sketches of two new creatures substituted for the *real* company spokesman:

C 1 created by judge:

A "we" man. Identified by his pauses, speech interruptions, apologies, half-treading argumentation, compulsive details of his charts, hesitancy. He is gen-

[6] This way of proceeding was made quite explicit in the case of two of the judges; for a third, it was certainly indicated. It seems not at all unlikely that it may have been the basis for inaccuracies among the other six judges and was simply better masked.

tle, insecure, systematic, compulsive. Is good as long as he can hold onto things cited above. Shows courage, then retracts. Operates on a minute detailed level.

C 2 created by judge:
Much more like U 2 than C 1. Little more aggressive; takes firmer stand; doesn't retract. Secure. Supports other statements with "Uh-huh." Gives a "I'm with you, Joe" feeling. Will turn out to be top company representative. Flow is smoother. Operates on principle level.

For the single *real* union spokesman, this judge likewise created two "mythical" persons:

U 1 created by judge:
More like C 1. Easy-going. Means business, but willing to move halfway. Optimistic soul. More willing to work with people. Subtle guy. Not open about it, even if is dangerous. Will be chief union spokesman in end. Will be more respected than U 2.

U 2 created by judge:
Is a "me" man. Has trouble in getting attention. Others laugh at him. Has to make strong statements, flippant remarks to company. Demands so much. Tries to check himself but can't. Others fear him but don't give respect to. *Aggressive.* First subtly, then more and more openly so. Won't budge. Could be openly aggressive, but holding self in check and using humor as a cover-up. Could make it acceptable. First differentiation between U 1 and U 2 was a difference in "flavor": i.e., their difference in gentleness and aggressiveness.

Theoretical considerations about the settlement process argue for just the opposite of the judges' tendency to *require* negotiators to be seen as consistent in action at the table. Hence, the spectacle of judges bifurcating live negotiators to derive segments sufficiently solid-like to support a perception as units is highly provocative. The necessity to recognize and to theorize about the possibly natural occurrence and functioning of some such "splits" in human materials is decidedly not the fashion in contemporary Western psychology, absorbed as it is with its norms of personality "integration" and "social adjustment," its distaste for behavioral withdrawal and inner isolation. Such a necessity was forecast in this study as far back as Chapter 1, though to postulate it, as was done there, along lines of "parties" versus "persons" now appears, in the light of experience with the work of the judges, insufficient for analytical purposes. The indications that have emerged as a result of the sub-study point rather to single per-

sons who, in the course of a successful case, are somehow to be understood as fracturing from their original status as parties into persons and
then into still more significant units than either of these—but units whose
outline and make-up have most emphatically not been captured in "personalities" psychosomatically wedded to physiological "bodies," or "individuals" reciprocally defined by and defining "families" and "secondary
groups," small-to-large "societies," and "institutions" and "cultures." From
the point of view necessitated by the sub-study, therefore, the notion of a
level of activity in negotiation which is represented in scale units of interactions or trans-actions (whether personal or party), while a decidedly
convenient one up to a point, eventually has to be abandoned because,
under the weight of inquiry, it simply is not durable. It was the ostensible
search of the judges for just such a level on which to commute between
themselves and the speakers in the transcript which threw the first shaft
of light on what was amiss here. At least in part, the judges had said
through their work that until the people of the transcript were brought
to life as real people like themselves they could not deal with them.[7]

IV

Out of such reflections, at length a thesis began to take hold that somehow a fundamental distinction obtained between being in, as opposed to
not being in, the conference room. At first it was thought likely that the
emphasis belonged to *in* vs. *out* in a geographical sense, a distinction based
on a physical perspective which has to some extent survived all of the
analytic metamorphoses. But further reflection tended to minimize this
degree of emphasis and to shift it instead to *being* vs. *not being*. That is
to say, to define who or what was in the conference room was a more
devious thought development than was required, and amounted to a lure
away from the theoretical main stream. The fact that "is" could be said at
all about the conference room seemed in itself sufficient, perhaps even
momentous. It could almost be said for the time being that this rather
primitive way of reducing the entire organization of the conference room
to the fact of "life" there had about it the first look of genuine reality to
come about in the research. It did, as a matter of fact, prove to be a land-

[7] Practitioners who have worked with the transcripts have repeatedly remarked
on the deadliness of the verbal exchange in its typed form. All of the parties who
were recorded were supplied with transcripts of their proceedings, and more than
one negotiator has complained that the transcripts have an irreality which is hard
to reconcile with his memories of the live proceedings.

mark in thinking about the whole matter of peacemaking, and it made possible for the first time a grasp of a certain type of observation about negotiation which before had not seemed comprehensible.

All of the fragments of observation of this type were concerned in one way or another with a wholesale transformation which various negotiators had been reported to undergo, once seriously engaged in the work at the table. The investigator could recall having remarked to the Atlas mediator on one occasion, "The minute you walk into the conference room you become a different person." That fact seemed certain enough to the investigator; it was the Atlas mediator's response that carried the surprise element: "And did you realize that you do, too?"

A related report can be cited from a very different source—an account which appeared after the death of John Foster Dulles regarding his last appearance at the international negotiating table at a time when he was already acutely stricken with cancer:

There was seldom a moment on this trip [to Europe] when he was without pain. He was unable to keep down a single meal.

I asked him how he was able to carry on.

He answered, "I told my associates that they were to watch me carefully and that they were to inform me immediately whenever it appeared that my physical condition in any way impaired my ability to carry on the negotiations in which we were participating." But he was never better at the negotiating table than at this most difficult period of his life.

He afterward told me, "I never felt any pain while the negotiating was taking place. Then at the end of the day it would come down on me like a crushing weight." [8]

In none of the reports about the display of unusual response tendencies is there any suggestion of bizarreness or abnormality. On the contrary, it seems to be implied that the transformations are accompanied by the acquisition of extraordinary and highly useful strength and command capacity, so that the conferee possessed of these new-found qualities now more nearly resembles his opposite in the conference room than himself outside the conference room. Though it is individual negotiators who bear testimony in their persons to such a phenomenon, the transformation is represented in the evidence as a trend throughout the conference room rather than a localized or personalized event. An all-inclusive tidal effect

[8] Richard M. Nixon, "Vice President Nixon Writes about Dulles," *Life,* Vol. XLVI, No. 23 (June 8, 1959), p. 36.

is inferred to spread out over the group, sweeping into its compass things which ordinarily do not combine in any such indiscriminate manner. This could hardly mean other than one thing: interchangeability is a more accurate description of the conference units, at least at this level of development, than is identifiability.[9] If parties and persons are to be retained as useful units of analysis, it will be necessary to make room for a third category, the units of which are characterized by bona fide *equality*—that is, equality to the point of indistinguishability.

It was beginning to seem by now that it would have been impossible for the judges to fulfill the mission on which they had set out—on the basis of spoken words to identify units that may not be dependent on speech at all, to attempt to identify when it is not certain that identifiability is even an attribute of the units. The only possible way of managing some of the foregoing revelations from the sub-study is to posit that negotiators bring with them to the table not only perceptible bodies and cognizable personalities in the idiom of the clinician, but freely moving, unbounded, infinite potentialities for interchange of energies which are not contained, much less molded, by any conceptions which start with conventional "space" and "time" as features of the universe of thought to be employed. This not only lays the groundwork for some new and untoward propositions specific to peacemaking matters; eventually it necessitates the raising of questions about the investigation of such matters. In the internal schematization of Western science, scientists and their objects of study fall into rigidly separated groupings. Can it be foretold now that the tradition of an impeccably sterile operating theater will someday wane in favor in science? If this particular study has shaken the grounds for maintaining that negotiators can successfully remain distinct from each other, or judges from negotiators, it also has shaken the grounds for isolating the investigator as a special person. At least, to one investigator it seems

[9] One case in this research which was dropped before completion involved a union whose spokesman was an International representative brought in from headquarters in another state. In talking informally with him after one of the early sessions, the investigator dropped the remark that he must have come to his present position the hard way, up through the ranks, because he spoke so persuasively in joint meeting about the problems of the men in the shop. "Not at all!" he replied. "I am an engineer by training and have just finished twelve years with management. When I decided I wanted a change of employer I began looking around, and ran across this opening with the union. It makes no difference on which side of the table I sit; I can do equally well on either."

dogmatic to claim that anything more than transitory comfort can be derived any longer from the classical dichotomies of inside:outside, of environment:person, of observer:observed, of macrocosm:microcosm, of objective:subjective.

CHAPTER 8

Movement and Change in Negotiation

In one of its feature "Profiles" *The New Yorker* honored the head tone regulator for Steinway concert grand pianos, William Hupfer. The tone regulator's job is the testing of hammer felts for variations of tonal quality, in distinction to that of the piano tuner, who concentrates on pitch. Hardness in felts is corrected by jabbing them with needles; tired felts are rejuvenated by filing off worn grooves. Hupfer is quoted in this bit of musing about his unusual occupation:

Now, I will admit that the effect of the felts on tone is a small thing compared to all the other influences. Most of your tone, of course, is built right into the instrument. It's not just the sounding board but the entire piano, down to the smallest screw, that vibrates, and that's what sets up the sound waves. Even the stage of the concert hall vibrates with the piano, so you have to count that in, too. Well, the felts *are* just one part of the whole thing, but you can't do anything about all the rest of it unless you want to go out and start from the beginning and build yourself a completely new piano. The felts are the one part you can change. When you look at it that way, they are very important.[1]

By parrying his final estimate of the respective contributions to the complex of tone until he has assayed the speed with which tonal changes can be effected, Hupfer manages to demonstrate that the time factor is on the side of the tone regulator's job. This touch of the philosopher's genius on Hupfer's part must bear some relationship to his capabilities as a self-regulator, for his reckoning, arrived at sheerly on the strength of foresight to "look at it that way," savors of exemplary command over mental resources. It is remarkable enough that he should have decided to rest his case for the tone regulator upon an amalgam of change with time.

[1] Bruce Bliven, Jr., "Piano Man," *The New Yorker,* Vol. XXIX, No. 12 (May 9, 1953), pp. 54–55.

More than this, however, it is a piece of first-rate shrewdness that in an empirical setting he should have come so close to embracing the uncommon idea of the tractability of Time.

To acquit oneself with the evidence from peacemaking as creditably as the piano man with his, radical change in thinking is sooner or later made incumbent upon an investigator, much as it is taken to be incumbent upon negotiators in the conference room. The piano man's story anticipates developments in this respect which were forced upon the present study. Here, for example, in attempting to decipher the inner reality of outer or apparent change in settlement work, it proved necessary to give independent thought to the tenuousness of Space in the hands of skilled negotiators, and, as a consequence, to be prepared to question the fate which would befall Time at the hands of the same negotiators. Once the general issue of change had acquired this two-pronged form, a re-examination of the field experiences turned up cogent substantiation for the thesis that at an advanced stage of negotiation there is a mutation of Time from its ordinarily ponderable state to one which is new and imponderable. This thesis, ramified in various ways, has come to play an indispensable part in opening up improved ways of thinking about the stated objective of getting parties in disagreement "to move" at the conference table.

I

If the symptomatology presented in the preceding chapter is accepted as significant—whether negotiators and mediator, or judges and investigator, once inside the conference room these people all appear to become more like each other than like themselves on the outside—it would be in keeping with conventional analytical approaches to attribute to *the conference room* some special status as an environmental center of influence. But special status of this sort is spatial status, and wherever in this study an attempt has been made to fix a theoretical position on any such basis, sooner or later the ground beneath has turned out to have shifted. It is not only that the investigator in this study has gradually become wary of a thoughtway linked too firmly to an objective Space which is playing host to its contents; the implication looms large that negotiators manage to divest themselves of some of their spatial dependencies in the course of their work at the table.

The ontogenetic acquisition of a spatial axis in the course of coming to terms with reality is thought to be one of the best-kept phylogenetic promises among the human species. The adaptations of the sensorily handicapped in catching up again with their fellows in this regard become a source of pride in Nature, as expressed by non-handicapped members. From one point of view this natural phenomenon provides a most durable, probably the most authentic, base from which to look forward to a brotherhood of men, for it is said to be in conjunction with their spatial perceptions that men learn to distinguish each other and eventually to recognize the imperativeness to make room for others alongside self. Democratic societies in particular, in the name of the common welfare, hail a distribution of space-perceptual habits as uniform as possible. Under such circumstances, to denounce one's natural developmental history as a perceiver of the external world is to court the charge of deliberate flouting of the social surrounds, especially so if the universal and time-honored perceptions are to be put in doubt on the basis of abstract conceptions about the structure of the world which average sensory experience, culled over a lifetime, would confirm very meagerly if even that much. It should surprise no one to find that the freedom to topple absolute Space is actively curtailed in these societies, vigilance over the individual stopping just short of the point where not to stop would put the society in jeopardy of losing certain highly prized creations which only free individuals seem able to produce. In this society that concession is made almost exclusively to the labors of physicists, of philosophers, of artists; the same phenomenon in a person who is not an accredited member of these protected deviations is apt to be diagnosed as pathology, and to be subjected to pressure (informally referred to as "help," professionally, as "treatment") in the interest of restoring a greater semblance of typicality (frequent terms here being "normality" and "contact with reality"). It is entirely conceivable that the lore which practitioners invoke relates in part to a well-founded apprehension that, should "the public" become apprised in full of what goes on at the negotiating table, its myopia regarding such matters would lead it to brand negotiators as aberrant and to strait-jacket their activity.

What, then, is the student of peacemaking to make of an implication that the adult model of reality which seems unfailingly to earn the blessing of both Nature and society is forsaken under the impact of work at the table? One is straightway thrown back upon the very concepts of space and time which the question is supposed to query, in the sense that since the possibility of spatial dislocation in negotiators is referred strictly to their presence in the conference room it is made a phenomenon of temporary duration. There is no suggestion whatsoever that negotiators walk out after a negotiating session into a physical and social world which they deem to be greatly different from the world they left behind when they entered the conference room. Yet, in reflecting upon the matter, one comes to ask whether it could in fact be so, that negotiators doff and don their perceptual habits at will; indeed, if so, how so? The question serves to point out that although the concept of a spatial orientation *en* process appears eminently serviceable in the analysis of negotiation, it is still crudely and vaguely defined when it turns up in this field, and one cannot be comfortably sure yet just what is entailed in borrowing from the physicist's idiom for use in a non-physical sense. One can only be certain that the problem is not envisaged, much less taken on, by diagnostic tests which purport to evaluate the efficiency of the sensory modalities and of the central nervous system. With little more to start with than an intuition of correspondence between the physicist's and the negotiator's world-views, this line of thought nonetheless has the ring of soundness and must be pursued.

II

No comments are forthcoming from practitioners to indicate that they are cognizant of coming to terms with something called spatiality. This must be deduced by the outsider on the basis of his own experiences with the evidence. With regard to time, however, heightened sensitivities are the rule rather than the exception. Contact with mediators in particular creates an impression that the temporal commands a degree of respect which normally is accorded only to causative agents.

There are numerous occasions when the subject is freely and frankly brandished between the parties. Announcement of a strike ultimatum invariably precipitates such an exchange. Even without status as an agenda item, the subject of time is certain in due course to arouse active consideration, if only because parties which trace their origins to a mutually binding productive obligation outside the conference room cannot allow divisiveness inside that room to flout their raison d'être interminably. There are on record some notable exceptions to the generalization that labor and management parties behave as though their negotiations are no more than seasonal variations in an otherwise harmonious alignment;

but, by and large, negotiators for American industry have of their own accord perpetuated a tradition imputing to both parties a responsibility with regard to the time factor.

These are gestures, almost perfunctory, to a brand of "time" brought pre-packaged into the conference room. To temporize in this mode in negotiation, as elsewhere, synchronization with standardized clocks and calendars on the outside is absolutely essential, since it is by means of such hardware that the senses are able to take note of efforts to simulate in "reality" the presentment in experience of smooth, unbroken continuity. For the present, it does not particularly matter whose effort or whose experience is referred to, inasmuch as the analyst's assumption of a universal attitude gives him leeway to deal with one as equivalent to all, therefore to deem each negotiator a co-author of the public "time" which clocks and calendars purport to measure.

Yet from the very outset it must be clear that there could be no reasonable basis to hope for a perceptible facsimile in the world of the senses of a concept like continuity. A breach, described in spatial terms, is necessarily constituted between the source of inspiration for the time idea and its ultimate execution in an authorized agency like worldly time. The human organism must feel sorely pressed to keep up in daily life these round-trip vaults between concept and percept, for in order that the student, bent on analysis, may establish the plausibility of theoretical linkage here, several layers of abstraction must first be worked over. Time in the objective mode settles, as the language puts it, for "a sense of" movement, since the sensory equipment is prepared to deal with physical change of position as such only on an alternating or episodic basis. So that movement is already a new version of a state which is not accessible empirically, but rather must be derived by extension of the judgment that *change* has taken place when comparison of perceptions reveals some discrepancy. Movement thus becomes reality upon extrapolation of continuity from its opposite, change. Continuity, in short, is 100% idea; it cannot be experienced as physical. In normal everyday life, the question left open in theory whether time is to be treated as precept or percept—as an active regulator or a passive register of events—is continually being arbitrated out of existence by a recording system so thoroughly automated that it has, in taking over large areas of the human task with regard to time, pre-empted even the perceptualizing aspect. Time ordained under these circumstances could be nothing other than Euclidean space in disguise, and its espousal in the conference room should signal any keen student that negotiators so oriented are probably space-bound.

The reader will recall from the Atlas transcript the early concern of the mediator on this very score. If the vigor and seriousness with which he pursued the problem are not still sharply etched in memory, the reader would do well to review the first half of the transcript before going any further. Lacking confirmation, particularly from the union, about its intentions with regard to a date for terminating the negotiations, the mediator put all other business aside to concentrate on this one question —not, as he tried to make clear, with the aim of taking over from the union its planning prerogatives, but rather to ascertain *what work pace* was being proposed by the controlling party.[2] The point of his concern, reiterated in numerous union and company caucuses throughout the early sessions of the case, is summarized in one passage worth repeating here:

M: The one thing that bothers me a little bit with these negotiations is the (pause) *lethargy* of the—on the—the union just doesn't—isn't hot. They're in no hurry. And whenever a union is—or a company—isn't in a—in a hurry to settle, it—well, you gener'ly have to do one of 2 things. Yo—ya have to either ride it out, sometimes called baby-sitting, or step up the tempo. I could see from last week that these people weren't in very—now, it may change, but I'll ha—I haven't had the pulse beat this morning, but I think we'll get that this morning. Then we'll be able to ascertain whether we can—we should come back at 3:00 o'clock—whether there's any worth in it. 'Cause if they're still dragging their feet, then instead of wasting time on the conference room, we'll—we'll have to de—devote more time to stepping up the tempo.[3]

In both cases in which this mediator was observed and recorded, he chose the alternative of driving for an increase in tempo. In the two-day Irving Mining case, which preceded the Atlas case (and which he cited

[2] In the pre-negotiation days of the Marathon case, while preparations were being made for the forthcoming exchanges, C 1 summed up in an interview the responsibilities which lay ahead for him as the most experienced negotiator on the management team: "It'll be my job to try to judge the pace and the timing and the tactics."

[3] Atlas II, Management Caucus A. It is recorded in the field notes, in reference to an interview with C 1 of this case on the day before Session I: "He spoke briefly about his reactions to mediation. He feels he hasn't had much experience with mediation, but what he has had was good. He hastened to add that he was re-ferring to [the Atlas mediator]; he would not say this about all mediators. [The Atlas mediator] is so effective, he says, because (a) he has an unusually fine sense of timing, and (b) he is fair. He spoke almost with awe about the former."

for illustrative purposes to both Atlas parties), his tactic was to urge on the company giant-sized rather than baby-sized steps in getting on the table its contemplated wage offer to the union.[4] The following condensed sequence from the transcript and the field notes of that case is reminiscent of corresponding moves made by the same mediator in the Atlas case.

From the field notes:
I knew that the mediator had had a private talk with U 1 Friday, and with C 1 on Saturday, before the negotiation opened on Monday, but I hadn't been very successful in finding out what they discussed except rather generally that it pertained to the coming negotiations. However, on Monday evening after the first session, in my presence the mediator remarked to a colleague that "pre-mediation has certainly been effective in this case." I quizzed him then about what he had done in the encounter with C 1, and his explanation was that he coached C 1 on how to present his stuff when the parties came together in joint mediation. He made a remark to the effect that he had observed in other cases how much damage could be done by faulty presentation of otherwise good stuff. With C 1 in this case, it specifically related to the wage offer. He encouraged C 1 to make a *substantial* offer early—at least 75% of the company's final figure—contrary to their former practice of dragging it out so long by offering pennies-at-a-time.

From a union caucus on the first day:
M: In discussing these issues in caucus with the company (pause) and at the same time keeping my eye on the clock, I noticed that from the way we—the company was talking about these issues they were time-consuming—the way they were talking about them with me in there. So, to make a long story short, I have convinced the company that they have got to come out and make a counter-proposal to the union. They've got to—they can do it by coming in and taking these points and discussing them one by one and wasting a lot of time. Shouldn't say wasting but—well, maybe I should. Yes. Now, I pointed out to them that we've got to move faster. We've had a good long day at getting the background of these various issues, and the time comes where we should move, and I did it in a manner of taking it for granted that, (1), that a counter-proposal was coming. I mean, I did no selling or convincing or pushing because I treated it in a manner that there's more there. There is! I—no question about it; it's just a question of how much. The sooner we find out, why, the sooner we're g—going to know where we're going. So, getting the vehicle for doing it was the next step.

[4] Atlas II, Union Caucus D and Management Caucus F.

I haven't asked 'em for anything other than a counter-proposal, but I wanta get it on the table.

From the field notes:

The mediator had been called by the company into the management caucus to hear the package they were going to propose and to comment on it. I cannot remember at just what point, but somewhere about this time he informed C 1 that an offer of 7.5% was not enough, since it would only bring the wage offer from 11¢ to 13¢. Tonight, he said, it was "psychologically important" that the union feel it had *gained* some. Otherwise, as he put it to C 1, "Tomorrow they may just drag their feet." I remember his adding, "I've seen this happen!"

At dinner tonight the mediator remarked that the day's progress has been so great that the mediation is running "2 days ahead of schedule." Incidentally, the mediator confided to me later that in an aside during the evening U 1 had thanked him for getting such a good offer out of the company. He said it had "softened the committee considerably."

From a union caucus on the second day:

M: Going back to last night, the only mention—the only move we made in the direction of wages was when I learned that when they were going to make an offer it was to be a-cent-and-a-half. And in our caucus last night we convinced the company that that was the wrong thing to do. We didn't tell 'em how much that they should give you as a first offer in our negotiations, but we told 'em that a-cent-and-a-half—that we knew well settlement was going to be more than that and that a-cent-and-a-half would aggravate the situation and do more harm than good because it would prolong the negotiations. "The union has a pretty good idea of where they're going on the wage question, and we think you do, too"—meaning the company—and that to put a-cent-and-a-quarter or a-cent-and-a-half out would put this union committee "in the frame of mind that—that maybe some of the things that were said about the company before they came down here are right. Maybe the people that said them are—are right. And you're gonna—you're gonna throw these negotiations out of a conciliatory atmosphere and into a non-conciliatory one. So, we would say that if you're going to make an offer tonight it oughta be a substantial one," avoiding the—we didn't tell 'em what to put—what to do—how much. When they called us back in there and told us what they were offering, we were satisfied.[5] We thought that

[5] Apropos of this first offer to the union, on the second day C 1 reported to the mediator in caucus: "The Executive Committee [at the plant] nearly fell off their chairs when I told them our wage offer of 17¢."

was a good step forward, because it certainly showed—should show the union committee that they were acting in good faith, and we think, too, that it did just that. We think that you fellows reacted accordingly. We think that your counter-proposal [to deduct from your demand for 23¢ in wage increase one cent for each cent added by the company to its offer of 17¢] was a good one—reasonable. (Rather long pause) So—so that's as far as last night.

The Atlas mediator's preoccupation with the rate of change of the parties' manifest positions can be deceptive if it is relegated to the category of substance brought up for discussion, to be followed by disposition. Offhand, it does seem that he contrived in both cases to get it entered in first place on the conference agenda, but it proves to have none of the history of a topic that has been negotiated to settlement. Was his call for acceleration, then, a token of sensitivity to deadlines brought in by the parties? He himself disclaimed that interpretation in his rejoinder to the Irving Mining union committee when they pressed him to hurry things up so that they could be on their way to a membership meeting; "I never try to beat a clock" was his phrasing. Something more subtle seems to have been posed, in effect a challenge of the profligate rate at which the parties were spending their resources at the table—profligate because the negotiators had not yet disengaged themselves as parts of the system they were purporting to evaluate. Negotiators could make no incorruptible assessments of their situation if they did not make them from the observing side of a mental one-way screen. So far these negotiators had remained cloistered on the reflecting side only. The mediator was not there to describe the image that would emerge when a negotiator exchanged his former viewing post for one behind such a screen, but he could predict with remarkable accuracy the main phenomena augured in re-positioning the observer outside the immediate sensory system ("to close that gap into the area where *both* sides will know whether that *is* their position or not"; "They should be satisfied, you should be satisfied, and I should be satisfied that everything was done to get into that area of *at least finding out*"; "Now, that doesn't mean that you could even reach an agreement. But the answer that you're seeking is, *can* an agreement be reached"; "I don't know *myself* whether this thing could be resolved"; "You're going to get this thing down to the crisis point. Then you're going to know whether it *can* be settled or it *can't* be settled"). Until this indispensable condition became accepted among the negotiators, no mediator would render them much assistance ("I would be very, very wary of applying mediation technique or action at the wrong time"; "We can be here for [a] long, long time if we play. The sooner we get down to the realistic zone, the sooner we start to move because I—I can't really be effective until we get down to that area. I'm not talking money with you, I'm not talking money with them until I know that we're down to where I want you").

In retrospect, it can be speculated that the hallmark of the Atlas mediator's excellence as a mediator may have been his ingenuity in hitting on the creation of a "generation" of time in the conference room as his test of whether the cycle of re-positioning from sensory to non-sensory had been fulfilled. The materials of this study offer grounds for asserting that when, in the course of negotiation, sensory documentation ceases to be a sufficient or trustworthy guide to reality, able negotiators will respond by restoring temporal functions which must have been indigenous to the organism before the physical orientation of everyday life became fixed as the modus operandi with the animate and inanimate alike. This rolling-back therefore revives a semblance of junction between the perceptual and non-perceptual, and reinstates the experience of existence as integral to reality. The willingness of the Atlas parties (given the capacity) to cooperate with the mediator as he presided over this aspect of their work together may have given some prognosis of their chances to profit from a mediator's presence.

Practitioners put none of it this way.[6] Nevertheless, one indication of the soundness of thinking along these lines is the fact that connections to a main stream can be established for certain trends among the data in this study which had formerly been resistant to interpretation. Incidentally, these trends all involve data which came as unexpected bonuses from working with the transcripts. If this heralds a clue of some significance, it must lie in the fact that when, as here, multiple presentations of data occur within the same observational system, the observer's experiences in seriatim bring him into possession of a most sensitive instrument for detecting variations. It can hardly be a matter of surprise that under such circumstances an idea magnifying serial order, as does the concept of time, should have come forward to be tried on for fit and adjustment.

---

[6] Perhaps the closest was a quip by C 1 during a management caucus in Atlas III. The group was discussing the possible significance of a union meeting scheduled for the following week. Still holding firm at his 4/10-of-a-cent offer, C 1 countered lightly: "Long time to go a short distance." Connoisseurs of Bach's music may detect in C 1's statement something familiar to them.

Now for examples of the experiences put to use in this way.

The investigator had decided to designate in the transcript as a "session" any continuous clock-sequence between an official coming-together of the parties and their official adjournment. In this way sessions could be numbered in serial order. During a single session the parties might not sit together continually within the same physical space, but they were presumed to be more occupied with the negotiation than with other matters and to be available on short notice for vis-à-vis contact. Presumably, too, negotiators were released upon adjournment from these conditions, even though informal contacts which were not rated as sessions might continue. (In one recorded case these involved the mediator and individuals of both parties, sometimes with the investigator present.)

It occurred to the investigator one day to wonder what it meant to have arrived at a mechanical means for designating something now to be known as a session. Does a "session" embody an idea, or is it merely an operation?

Some sessions broke up after only a few hours; some followed rather routinely the workday of the business enterprise; some extended into the night; in the Marathon case the final session ran from 9:00 A.M. one day to 8:50 P.M. the following day. During that lengthy session both management and union groups left the hotel where the session was going on, to attend to other matters (including a meeting of the union committee with the union membership). But there was no doubt on anyone's part that the thirty-six hours held together as a unit. The recording caught U 1's good-natured resignation to that fact on glancing up at a window in the late afternoon of the second day: "It's gettin' dark again, huh?"

In the final Marathon session most of the recesses which were taken simultaneously by all were spent in pursuit of food. Not a single meal was missed by anyone. No suggestion that it should be was tendered even in jest, although nutritionists would probably agree that well-fed persons like these could sustain life without further nourishment for a period far in excess of thirty-six hours.[7] There was even a trend toward supplemental

---

[7] Coffee consumption reached a very high level, but this went on in conjunction with the session, demanding no special time allowances. The field notes contain this memorandum from the second day of this session: "At 9:45 A.M. C 1 sent me down with a $5.00 bill for coffee for the crowd from the Coffee Shop. This may be as good a place as any to comment on the gallons of coffee consumed during the meetings of the last few days. It usually fell my lot to do waitress duty on

feedings between regular meals. During the night which followed the first day of this session most of the union committee used a recess beginning at 2:40 A.M. to go scouting for a diner open at that hour. (They succeeded in finding one, for the field notes record that "when the fellows returned, they had 2 plates of hot cakes with syrup and sausages, one each for U 1 and me, and lots of hot coffee for everyone.") This recess was followed by the first joint meeting of the session, which convened at 4:25 A.M. It proved a most productive get-together, and afterward C 1 and C 2, in high spirits, were predicting that the close would come within a few hours. A notation in the field notes reports about that meeting: "About 6:15 A.M. a good deal of restlessness seemed to develop in the group. I made a note at the time that it was an 'awfully droopy bunch.' Several of the group began walking around the room (I remember C 1, for instance, at this), even though the meeting was still going on and they were talking as part of it. U 4, I recall, had great difficulty keeping his eyes open, as did the Observer!" The antidote came about 7:00, when the calls for food began again. The following condensation from the transcript gives the mood of the group at that time:

U 1: We wanta reserve strike in cases where the company would readily give us good cause to strike, anyway.

C 1: M, I don't know. We're in a funny position here. We got it here—

U 1: (Over C 1 above) I—I'm tanglin' him up, M, in a lot of different ideas, and I've got myself a little lost, too.

C 1: Well—

M: Well, I—I would suggest this. I believe that (C 1: I believe we oughta eat breakfast) No. 3, No. 9, . . .

(Discussion of various issues continues for 12 pages of transcript)

C 1: Well, I'm—I'm not too clear on this whole (U 1: All right) thing, and— U 1's expressed a number of ideas and it sounded to me like a—a package.

U 1: That's what it is. (Pause)

M: (C 2 talks at same time) Well, let me sum it—

C 1: (Over C 2 and M above) I would like to have somebody develop that package clearly for us. (U 1: Let M do it) We're—we're—we're all a little groggy, and we don't wanta make any mistake.

---

this score. C 1 and I took turns financing these, and once each, I recall, C 2 and the union crew did so. The union fellows occasionally ordered beer, also, for their private meetings. When I handed C 1 his cup this morning, he gave with a loud stage whisper: 'Ann, I've got coffee running out from under my fingernails!' "

U 1: How come you look so (U 2: What we need is a good breakfast) fresh, now, in the early morning, M?

(Brief joking follows)

M: Sit down and get your pencil!

(Several pages of serious work follow)

C 1: (Yawning) Ho-ho-ho. Company would like a caucus. You wanta get breakfast and then come back?

U 1: It's early, isn't it, for breakfast? Oh, it's 7:00 o'clock.

C 2: It's 7:00 o'clock.

M: We'll be awful hungry by breakfast time.

C 1: Well, we can eat *another* one then. (Laughs)

M: Now, how about that? Do you wanta caucus—wanta grab some breakfast (?: Change shirt), company caucus, and return?

C 1: Uh-huh.

M: No. If anybody goes home for a clean shirt, we're gonna lose about half-a ya. So better not go home for a clean shirt.

(Several talk at once)

C 1: (Over others above) The guy that goes home for a clean shirt pays for all the breakfasts.

U 2: All right. Who needs another shirt here—white, blue?

M: I think U 5 liked that idea. He's not gonna home for a clean shirt, I see. (Laughs)

(Considerable discussion follows re police tickets for parking overnight. M suggests parties will have to go up 10¢ on the wage figure "to pay all these parking fees," and U 1 jokes about making "Company has to pay parking" demand No. 21 by union. Discussion ensues about places open at this hour for breakfast. M compliments someone because his hair isn't mussed, but accuses him of not having worked. As the recording ends, someone remarks that it's getting daylight.)

The matter of clean shirts had come up before. During the previous night, while a poker game was going on in the union group and the management group was caucusing with the mediator, the investigator left a recording machine running in each room and went to her own room in the hotel. Upon reappearing in a fresh blouse, she was chided by U 1 with: "That's not fair! Anybody puts on a clean shirt can't come back in these meetings!" In the same vein, when the union president addressed the membership body at 9:00 P.M. on the second day, he prefaced his report of the settlement with "We don't want—we hope none of youse'll laugh at us. We've got the same suit on for the last three, four days."

Those last thirty-six hours in the Marathon case constituted the longest session in the present study, but by no means did they set a record for negotiations.[8] Several days of round-the-clock negotiations preceded settlement of the 1953 New York City milk strike, prompting a veteran labor reporter for one of the metropolitan newspapers to complain: "After a week without sleep, the industry and union conferees were so groggy that minor differences became the basis for violent recriminations, and the ability to compromise flew out the window. The peace talks had more ups and downs than a roller-coaster, and the supposed peacemakers were repeatedly on the verge of blows."[9] Representatives of the press and of seven mediation services were standing by outside the conference room during the final long session of that case. One of these reported later that as the conference room door opened one evening he succeeded in getting a glimpse into the inner sanctum. What he saw was a large table set banquet-style, indicating that the parties were preparing for a hearty meal. The public representatives had been cooling their heels on the outside under the illusion that the weary negotiators inside were deliberating about milk for the city rather than food for themselves.

During the last third of the thirty-six-hour Marathon session there were numerous comments on the loss of sleep: union members checked on one another (always in light spirit) to see if they were awake; the parties commiserated with each other because everyone was said to be "tired." But just as frequently evidences were offered of revival and new bounce; and U2 went so far as to declare after the case was finished: "I still didn't recover. I kind of liked it, though, after the first night. I got to the point where I wasn't sleepy or anything any more. I kind of liked it; I knew what was going on." His remarks are reminiscent of something said by the Atlas mediator during the Irving Mining case, when he was musing with the union group about so-called "marathon sessions" in labor-management negotiations: "Sometimes it's—this is strange business. Some-

[8] An unofficial report circulates at United Nations headquarters to the effect that during the Suez Crisis of 1956 the late Secretary-General Hammarskjold had no sleep for five continuous nights except for a half-hour respite each night while sitting at his desk. When the President of the United States was queried in press conference afterward about the Suez affair, one of his first reactions was to marvel at the Secretary-General's physical feat.

[9] A. H. Raskin, "Milk Parleys Point Up Folly of Continuous Negotiations," New York *Times,* November 2, 1953, p. 16.

times you get s—latched into one of these things and lose all time—concept of time and you figure, 'Well, just about another hour,' see. And it's another one, another one, and—"

After pondering these irregular practices of negotiators in meeting the needs of the human body during a negotiation, the investigator came to the conclusion that the only discernible criterion of a "session" is the willingness of negotiators, as if at some behest, to exchange sleep for food. This conclusion was at first taken half humorously, but there now appears to be more than wit here. Human inability to continue indefinitely without sleep readily enjoins confidence in a mechanistic interpretation of Nature's prescience. The body, somehow set to anticipate the limits of tolerance for environmental stimulation, intercedes in time to head off any irreparable damage. In this sense, to forfeit sleep during negotiation could be taken as flying in the face of commonplace experience, especially if acuity to deal one with the other were impaired. But negotiators take a position more like that of Dostoevsky's character in *Crime and Punishment* who challenged the doctrine that man is paced by Nature, as though to disavow any authority couched in terms of absolute limits: " 'Oh well, brother, but we have to correct and direct nature. . . . But for that there would never have been a great man.' " The tempo of a negotiation attuned to the daily sleep cycle will be relatively fixed, tied as is the sleep habit to the rhythm of light alternating with dark in the physical world. That relationship can be broken, however, if the system of reference for denoting tempo reverts from the planetary one to another more immediate to the conference room. As a case draws to a close, the unusual vigilance of negotiators in holding themselves available for perceptual activity underscores a strong possibility that sensory operations are slated to undergo drastic curtailment. From the evidence in this study, Voltaire must have been alluding to the system which subsequently takes over when he wrote in one of his letters that "Thought depends absolutely on the stomach." [10]

A second cluster of experiences to suggest that time enters negotiations through a special door grew out of the investigator's objective of making the transcript as representative of the live sessions as possible. From the beginning of the study it had seemed to be inevitable that by the time expertise with the materials of any case could be assured, they would

[10] The sentence following the above in the original puts one on guard not to oversimplify Voltaire's intent: "In spite of this, those who have the biggest stomachs are not the best thinkers."

already be one sieving operation removed from original tapes to transcripts. So far as the verbal exchange was concerned, this made it obligatory that the greatest possible care be exercised to preserve along with the palpable contents the structural character of the verbal situation. In actuality, to keep to this goal with the exchange in these lively labor-management cases turned out to be a really formidable undertaking on two scores.

For one thing, a babel of overlappages and interruptions among speakers assailed the transcriber from the earphones more often than an orderly and well-mannered sequence of voices. Someone would break in over another who was still talking. The person interrupted perhaps came to a gradual stop; in rare instances he might rebuke the offender and demand that the floor be returned. Not infrequently an interrupter would break in to have his say, then lapse again into silence with the gratified air of one returned from a mission accomplished, while the first speaker continued on, paying no noticeable heed to the intrusion. When, as occasionally happened, several began to talk at once, the last vestiges of order collapsed completely in the melee that resulted. No one addressed anyone in particular, but merely added to the sum of noise and confusion that came through the earphones. The worst of these conglomerate sections of tape became the transcribers' nightmare, necessitating frequent intermissions away from the machines for relief from the nerve-racking effect.[11] The expediency followed in both transcribing and proofreading was to try to attend to a single voice at a time, rewinding the tape as often as required to sort out the complete speech of each voice. This amounted to giving each speaker a turn at playing the leading voice.[12] In the final

[11] Before the present study the investigator had worked briefly with mediation transcripts produced by a court stenographer, who had recorded in shorthand the proceedings of two live cases. Those cases turned up in typed form as neat, orderly dialogues unlike any of the transcripts assembled in the present study. Not until the investigator had had the experience of sitting in on cases in the conference room and then of hearing the tapes of the same cases played back over the earphones did it become apparent how the court stenographer's notes had produced such pretty copy. In the conference room one unwittingly cuts through the plague of overlappages, selecting the parts of the jumble to attend to; if the massing is so bad that the voices are not easily disentangled, one turns a deaf ear to the whole. It took a mechanical observer like the recording machine to bring back into the record those parts which the human observer had already eliminated before taking even a first step with the exchange.

[12] This procedure involved so much back-spacing that the rewind mechanisms on the machines were literally worn out again and again. In the second year of the field work the replacement of all equipment with binaural machinery greatly

copy all speeches were to appear in serial order. The criterion was to subdivide the scrambled content into respective speakers *on a time basis* —i.e., the first to start speaking came first, and the speech of any interrupter was joined to the first speech at the point of the interception. The result in the final transcript was an exchange spread out like a solid piece of fabric reinforced with bulky seams wherever a contest had been fought out between speakers.

Speakers not only interfered with each other but also got in their own way. Much of the articulation, whether of words or of thoughts, was halting and strewn with self-corrections. In this instance, all the disturbances took place within the individual person, who interrupted himself, who uttered pronunciations foreign to the language, whose own ideas abruptly seized the floor from others of his ideas. A reader who strives to cooperate with the original speaker in one of these stumbling, bungling passages is very apt to discover at the end of the speech that he has no idea whatsoever about the content he has just covered. Two devices were employed in the transcribing to reproduce these effects of raggedness and incompleteness of expression: dashes (—) to indicate breaks in syntax or the evolution of an idea, or to announce the introduction of entirely new thought material; "uh" when its use was equivalent to a pause. ("Uh" is not uncommon in everyday speech, but the rule here was to include it only when the speaker clearly seemed to be trying in this way to retain the floor for himself until he could come up with something further to say. The "uh's" are therefore the spoken counterparts of the silences which were labeled "pauses" in the transcripts.)

In the course of proofreading the transcripts against the original tape recordings, the investigator fell to devising rules of thumb which would equate the technical difficulties in transcribing with specific states of progress toward settlement. For example, the studied presentations— those speeches which appear in the first stages of a case, of a session, of discussion of a particular topic—are seldom broken by others bidding for the floor. These speeches, customarily delivered by U 1 and C 1 during periods of partisan exposition, have the aloofness and the closure of soliloquy. Whether or not it can rightly be said that their speakers are trying in advance to fend off any analysis or rebuttal by others, at least

---

facilitated the unscrambling problem and to some extent also reduced the back-spacing, since it then became mechanically possible to subdue the input of the left-hand microphone when concentrating on the right-hand one, and vice versa.

the opposition cooperates by refraining from attempting it. By the time an observer recognizes intuitively that movement has set in, in all likelihood none of the foregoing trends is any longer empirically manifest. Gone is the confident delivery of prepared thoughts, and in its place is heard the staccato of the unrehearsed speech; immediate and succinct reactions replace circuitous explanations; meaning ceases to be obliquely or opaquely put; voices are intensified enough to require a downward adjustment of the volume control on the recording machine; the distribution of individuals getting something on the record covers most of the conference group. In fact, the investigator debated for a while whether a scheme for plotting the movement of a case could be developed around these physical indices of change—the contraction of speeches, the focusing of content, and the like. What confounded the schematizing was the fact that among the indices of progress would have to be included the multitude of overlappages. From the standpoint of the listener at the earphones, this meant that progress was being equated with increase in confusion and disorder, a point of view which did not seem to make sense at all.[13]

Now, the investigator was struck by the fact that the judges, working with these same transcripts in the sub-study, intermittently rejected the unit of analysis selected by the investigator—i.e., judging on the basis of a single speech at a time—in favor of a *block* of consecutive speeches. At times when they were hesitant about attempting to identify, they applied this reaction to every contribution in a block, with the result that some individual speeches which seemed to the investigator to be quite revealing, simply by virtue of well-rounded content, were labeled with a string of question marks. At the other extreme, when judges were willing to commit themselves, single words like "No" or "Uh-huh" were assigned to specific negotiators even though, from an objective point of view, content like this seemed void of any clues to its source. But at least if one wanted to catch the mood of the judges in working with the transcripts, their practice hinted that there must have been a metronome of sorts in the background. Furthermore, suspicion was aroused that

[13] Cf., for example, a note set down by the investigator, while proofreading transcript, on page 153 of a recording which totaled 154 pages: "Whereas the early part of this session's recording was singularly orderly (in the conventional sense), these last 10 or so pages have been most *dis*organized and muddied by overlappages and interruptions, and increased short participations competing for the floor. Particularly noticeable in listening to the tape."

back of the metered timing lurked some measure of an optimal length of speech, for when speeches extended onto a second page the judges occasionally, on turning the page, credited the continuing portion to a different speaker, though the previous page had ended in mid-sentence. Put facetiously, the judge seemed to be saying as he turned the page, "Now it's someone else's turn." The predilection of the judges to mark off these neat cadences, in combination with their earnest efforts, noted in the previous chapter, to establish the behavioral consistency of chief negotiators, could mean but one thing: structural outlines had assumed a greater importance for them than content fillers, and words were proving their adaptability to the architectural task.

If one inquired more specifically about the blocked units, it began to appear that the judges had proceeded as if to assemble a representation of stacking which they found necessary for their task.[14] A careful look at the transcripts could leave no doubt that this meant reinstating a physical structure like that of the overlappages which the investigator had been at such pains to break down in the processing from tapes to

[14] One of the judges was given the preliminary task of identifying the speeches from Atlas I when cut apart and presented as an assortment of single speeches out of context. The judge kept the following running notes on the experience of trying to identify speakers under these circumstances:

"1. Began by making one slip for mediator, four for company, four for union.

"2. Tried to begin by separating within each of [the] three categories. Doesn't really work. So decide to use three large qualifications only, at first.

"3. After four slips placed in mediator, realized there should be a three-fold breakdown here, too. Made one: mediator with both groups, mediator with union, mediator with management. Doesn't really work at this point, either. Go back to straight large sub-division. Separate within subdivision later, I guess.

"4. I need a '?' category. Wonder whether it's the small length of statement? Can't get enough cues.

"5. Use of language cues giving me trouble at this point. 'Ya' in a formerly-sorted one [I categorized] as union. Not appearing in what I believe to be company statement.

"6. At this point I don't believe the '?' category is based on short length; just placed three very short ones in other categories without trouble. I wonder why these appear so clear?

"7. Realize now [there] should be another breakdown of union members talking in meeting with mediator vs. in joint meetings. Probably same for all three groups. Even with [that] realization, don't feel free to make such separations at this point.

"8. I get the vague impression some of the smaller statements are identical or similar to segments of larger ones. Can't fit them when out of context.

"9. Is there more than one mediator, I wonder?"

transcripts. In the investigator's format, speeches were expected to proceed down the typed page one after another in single file. To carry the format out in an overlappage, if the interrupter continued past the first speaker, his speech was set down as the successor of the first one; otherwise, it was necessary to embed it in parentheses within the first speech to indicate that it had not survived the competition. In some sections of the proceedings this transcribing rule resulted in very high mortality among speakers merely because of the absence of any response to their words. Accordingly, the unheeded interruptions did not turn up in the final transcripts as influential parts of the exchange, and judges were not expected to bother to identify them. In brief, it would have to be said that in the transcripts the various speeches in an overlapping mixture were granted separate and equal status entirely on the basis of success of an interrupting speaker in outlasting in time the one he had interrupted. This was serial ordering of the severest sort, built as it was on the premise that action took place in one plane and one direction only—the straight-line sequence of verb tenses, running from the past through the present to the future. But, in addition, it was ordering made to conform to a democratic ethos, and what stood out about that ethos in the picture brought forth here was the expectation that persons would derive their social identity from putting to rest their opponents. To all intents and purposes, persons who could not meet that test were non-existent when credits were handed out to those who had impressed their images on the historical record.

In the case of the solitary speaker, whatever his motley of thoughts pressing simultaneously for release, with only one voice at his command he was compelled to deliver his pronouncements arranged in consecutive order. As a result, single speeches reached the transcriber's ear already formed into simple successions producing no outward quarrel with the investigator's format. But now that the work of the judges pointed to the possibility that a significance other than competitive attaches to the multidimensionality inherent in overlappages, one would need to take a fresh look at the plight of the lone speaker who did not have the assistance of interruptions. From the numerous word and thought fragments left dangling in the single speeches without provocation by outside interrupters, is one to conclude that even the individual negotiator inclines toward some experiential equivalent of the outwardly perceptible overlappages? If he does, he must stand in very special need of his fellows, especially his opposite, at the table.[15]

These various considerations aroused doubts that the standard communicative function assigned to speech can be absorbed into the scheme of analysis for the negotiated settlement without some overhauling, at least to the extent of dealing separately with the form and content of speech. The simple unit of the two-way interaction, as it was strained out by the judges in working with the transcripts and reconstituted into equal intervals appearing in rhythmic succession, echoed a sound heard over the earphones each time the words parading across the tapes broke rank (a regular occurrence for the listener) and swarmed the pathway of movement, as though to block the course of action and thereby deflect it at an angle. From the evidence, the conclusion has seemed inescapable that the movement at the table inscribes a curved course, prognosticating the eventual demolishment not only of the points which define the separation of the disputants but also of any abstract relationship by which they may be construed to be held together. If the reaching of settlement coincides with this process, is agreement correctly represented by zero-point, or by unity? The one has overtones of the absence of disagreement, the other gives agreement the undertones of an entirely new and different state.

A third group of research experiences to crystallize on the basis of

[15] If this point is to be consistent with the over-all analysis in the study, it is necessary to conceive of a natural provision whereby an individual (negotiator or not) can come to his own assistance if his fellows are not forthcoming on this score. Such an inference about schizophrenic behavior, for example, can be backed up with descriptive detail which comes close to recapitulating the negotiating scene: "Experience with the schizophrenic, particularly intimate and protracted as in the course of therapy, leads one to the conclusion that the patient is often acutely aware of behaving and communicating in a manner which is related to, but not immediately representative of, his ongoing process of thought. . . . Thus in the examples given earlier [if he cocks his head to the corner of the room he is said to be hearing voices; if he waves his hand, to be warding off a face; if he removes his shoe and swats the floor with it, to be killing an imaginary demon] the observer almost gets the message though *not quite;* an educated guess, however, may often be made. In each of these examples it is as though the individual has acted not in terms of a dyadic, but a *triadic,* or *three person system.* It is not surprising that in such instances we should assume the literal existence of the third person, on the part of the patient, and behave toward him as though to him this was a reality, since he does nothing to dispel our judgment and may even confirm it on being asked. His conversation or behaviour may quite persistently infer the presence of the third party." J. M. Scher, "Indirection: a Communicative Basis for a Theory of Schizophrenia," *Congress Report of the IInd International Congress for Psychiatry,* Zurich (Switzerland), September, 1957, Vol. III, p. 71.

the time factor can be traced to the fact that case proceedings were registered in permanent form, making it possible for the verbal content to be reviewed at a later date. In going into the field to gather data from live cases, the investigator insisted on taking recording equipment into the conference room and on being allowed to sit in in person. This procedure brought on dire warnings from many on the outside that data gathered under such auspices were bound to be superficial and unnatural. It was argued that no group which was really serious about its negotiations would permit confidential proceedings like caucuses to be recorded and the tapes carried away by a stranger. Against these forebodings the investigator pitted her own firm belief that in due time the sight of her and her equipment would become so familiar in the conference room that so far as the conferees were concerned it would be nondescript. In the early days of the field work, when someone in the conference room turned to address a comment to the investigator sitting on the sidelines, the investigator's reactions were mixed with discomfort and a fervent hope that the negotiators would soon settle down and get on again with their business. No doubt everyone in these cases who might have been quizzed on the point at the beginning of a case would have agreed that anonymity was the only proper role for investigator or machinery—a sentiment echoed by the Atlas mediator in opening the Irving Mining case, his first venture with the research project:

M: The (pause)—(addressing Observer) oh, yo—you—you—you mentioned you wanted their names (slight pause) in this thing?
AD: Could we?
M: Just so she can decipher who says who later in the conversations, would you just announce your names and who you—
(All do so)
Thank you. (Pause) Now we can forget all about her and just go on like she wasn't there.

The request to have the recording equipment and the investigator admitted to the conference room set up an insurmountable hurdle for many parties and mediators. Again and again the investigator was turned down, and sometimes many months were spent before a case could be located in which everyone involved would agree to cooperate with the study. Even after the investigator was admitted, apprehensions still lurking in the background sometimes asserted themselves. In view of this generally unfavorable beginning, the fate of the observer and recording machine took a surprising turn. In the four cases which were recorded, recording machine and observer figured in every transcript. Numerous references sprinkled throughout the Atlas case demonstrate that that mediator sought to use the observer as his "rememberer" (to use his own term) when he reported to one party caucus about events from the other party's caucus; and he once informed the observer outside the conference room that if she had not been able to supply the wanted information, he would have asked that the tape be played back to refresh his memory. In a very similar way C 1 of the Marathon case pressed the observer into service at the first management caucus with the mediator, when he attempted a résumé of the two-party negotiations that had stalemated: "And, Ann, check me on this, will ya? I mean, whether I've got the right highlight, because sometimes when you're sitting back you can interject a little bit here." Far from achieving anonymity as the cases progressed, the research instruments acquired increasing status as participants and, judging from comments within the groups, the further distinction of being annexed as an asset when a party or a person needed supplementation. The permanent tape recording, particularly, came to be honored as an ally of the parties.

From the Crescent City case (following a bitter joint exchange on the topic of union security):
C 1: You know, it's a good thing, U 2, that this doesn't record what you're —you're (laughs heartily)—how you're lookin'!

From the Marathon case (excerpts from union and management caucuses during the final thirty-six-hour session):
M: Well, we'll prove it when it's all over by having the record played back (U 1: Here's what they told you. Here's what they told you) (laughing) if Ann can find it in all those records.

. . .

U 3: There is also on that recording my voice stating, quote (U 1: We'll check on it), that if the grievance is . . .

. . .

M: See, on some of this it's difficult for me to do much, because you get a *completely* conflicting story. See, you can't get a meeting of the facts a-tall on which to really make an argument. (C 2: Yeah) And, in a case like that the only thing to do, I—what I told 'em—I says, "All right. We'll get the company in here and we'll discuss that. Prob'ly a few other things will have to be cleared up. You talk to them as volubly as you have to me and as freely and with as many illustrations and with as much philosophizing as you've done—good! I think ya can get it worked out." I did that for 2 purposes—3 purposes, really. I thought of Ann while I was saying it. It would be interesting for her to take that section of their tape and compare it with the section of tape that will record their conversation with you on this. Because they do *not* talk as freely in front of you. Now, whether it is because they can say things to me which I can only argue it not only in the abstract *but* from the point of view of what is history, not what is fancy. And, secondly, I wanted to put them on notice that if they're so damn right, O.K. They shouldn't have any trouble convincing. (Laughs) Well, we'll see what happens with it.

From the Marathon case (excerpts from a post-settlement joint session for writing down the agreement):

C 1: I can't help but take a strong position in the fact that we should not even change anything that was agreed to in the negotiations, and I think that this is one—is one point where we are definitely changing wording which—which changes the intent as far as the company goes on its proposal.

U 1: I think if you'll open up the record—open up that tape recorder, you're gonna find that that was our squawk all along.

. . .

U 1: You probably never h—gave it the attention that—it's one of the minor points definitely, I think, in the whole negotiations. I really do. Uh (pause) —how many miles of "uh" have I got on the recorder? Must have about 2 miles of "uh." (Long pause) That last deal, there. . . .

. . .

C 1: U 1, could I talk to M a little bit alone?

U 1: Oh, sure. I'll—I'll listen to it on the recorder afterward (laughing heartily)!

. . .

U 1: How many miles of tape does that (laughing heartily) cover?

AD: I'm x shivering already over it.

U 1: We oughta—

M: (At same time as U 1 above) Human relations is expensive!

U 1: We oughta call in that friend of yours from the newspaper and give a little plug for Miss Douglas. (Pause, then laughs heartily)

C 1: Yeah (laughing heartily alongside U 1), I mean that's a good idea! (Laughs again) Get *her* in hot water, too.

U 1: (Still laughing) Yeah. "They used up 3 miles of tape recorder." (C 1, M, and U 1 all laugh slightly. Pause)

From the Irving Mining case (excerpt from the field notes):

On his own, the mediator had obtained advance clearance for recording the joint conferences. C 1, however, adamantly refused to allow me to record management caucuses. So the mediator and I decided that I would simply follow him into these, without paper or pencil, at least to hear what transpired. At the first such company caucus, the mediator took pains to explain that he had "frisked" me before I came in. No one but C 1 responded, who remarked, "But I think she has a good memory."

After the case was finished, the mediator told me that C 1 asked him about the research I was doing, and had added that it "wasn't so bad, after all" to negotiate in front of microphones. In the final management caucus on the last day of the case, when the management group was considering the advisability of drawing up the written form that night, C 1 suggested that they could turn to the mediator if disputes arose in writing it up later on. He put it to the mediator this way: "You've sat through all of it, and we have the tapes, too." With the greatest of inner glee I heard this respectful reference to the tape, and I had to suppress an urge to remind C 1 that, had he cooperated more generously in the beginning, we *could* have had more tapes!

At noon of the first day, after the morning's experience with the first session, the mediator volunteered to me that the microphones weren't bad at all. He didn't elaborate, but it was my impression he was saying it for himself, not from observing the parties. This was my first clue that he might have had any prior personal qualms about being recorded.

In retrospect, it is clear that it was useless to hope for physical imperceptibility, at any rate. Microphones were planted between the parties on the table in full view of everyone; yards of cord were strung across the room from microphones to the recorder, actually obstructing traffic to some extent. With the change to a binaural recorder in the second year, poundage and size of the physical equipment grew appreciably, and now the investigator, top-heavy from wearing leather-thonged earphones, sat monitoring the input like a broadcast engineer. Nevertheless, certain incidents involving the physical equipment could hardly have taken place if it had not to some extent been incorporated by negotiators. The investigator recalls distinctly such an incident in the Atlas case during a long management caucus between dinner and midnight. A peculiar

noise coming through the earphones prompted a look toward the microphones, revealing a weary negotiator lounging on top of the conference
table, apparently quite unaware that he was vigorously rubbing his
stomach with one of the microphones.[16]

The investigator's intentness about getting accurate and complete recordings communicated itself in time to the negotiators. This might have
become grounds for resentment and resistance; but, actually, the parties
themselves came to express in sundry ways an interest in insuring a good
record. U 1 of the Marathon case caught the sentiment, even if he put
it facetiously to his fellows: "Don't say it so loud. It's bein' recorded for
posterity." One mediator volunteered that if the investigator would signal
when the reel of tape had to be changed he would gladly halt the proceedings if nothing crucial were under way; the same mediator stopped
himself in a meeting one day when he saw the investigator about to
turn a reel, and asked if he should wait. When C 2 in one case suggested
adjourning a management caucus to another office which would be nearer
loud shop noises, C 1 replied, "Ann Douglas is gonna scream." Union
and management negotiators commented of their own accord on new
microphone equipment on the tables one morning. In one case, one
of the key management negotiators had been very uneasy in the beginning about allowing recorder and observer in on the negotiation; yet
in the last session of this case, after a siege in which condensers in the
recorders unexpectedly began blowing out, this same negotiator took the
trouble to call an electrician from the plant to come to the building where
the meetings were in session and check the investigator's equipment and
the outlets. The investigator had queried U 2 in the closing hours of the
final long session of the Marathon case about the possibility of recording
the union membership meeting at which the terms of settlement were
to be voted on. U 2's response was: "Down there? Why, sure. I think it'd be
better off to record it"; and as he faced the membership that night, about
to begin his report, he admonished the group, "During this talk, we'd
like to have you be quiet as possible due to the microphones that are
up here."

---

[16] One reaction to the recording equipment was repeated a number of times by
the Atlas mediator. After addressing a question to the observer, he would occasionally add, as though in an aside to himself, "Oh, I forgot. She can't hear." (This
was a reference to the earphones, which looked like thick ear muffs.) In reality, of
course, the earphones increased the observer's sensitivity to sounds in the conference
room, including the mediator's comment.

In each of the four cases completed in this study the research was singled out for favorable comments from within the conference group before the case was over. Letters written to the investigator after the close of cases leave no doubt that the research "presence" was considered not to have hampered the parties in their work. In one case U 2 thanked the investigator several times for bringing them "good luck." How was that? "We *never* got so much before in any contract." In another case the investigator was thanked by two of the management group for joining in the proceedings. Why? U 1 and U 2 had been more temperate in manner and speech than in previous negotiations, and the observer was credited as the braking influence. In both of these instances the party expressing gratitude had been outdone in some term agreed to at the table, hence the investigator was at first inclined to suspect the parties of having poor insight into their real situation. On later thought, however, this began to seem less likely. Even if it might not be immediately clear how the presence of the recorder and observer could benefit the work going on at the conference table, the idea could not be wholly dismissed that it might, after all, have done just that. Indeed, reflection upon the course of this research indicated that when the grafting of Recorder and Observer onto a negotiation successfully "takes," reception of the foreign material will open the gateway to unexpected phenomena in the host territory, so much so, in fact, that one now wonders if here is revealed with special illumination some of the possible effect of a mediator's intercession.

More than eight years after it had been set down in the field, the following forgotten note was discovered among some materials of the Marathon case which had been brought out of storage for review:

After the recording machine was cut off today following the interview with C 1, I asked him if he would like to hear his voice played back. His secretary stopped at this point to listen, too, as I played back a final portion of the recording. C 1 listened extremely solemnly. No smile crossed his face —and he smiles very easily. I had the impression he was listening intently to himself, and I also got the impression of some sort of studied reaction on his part.

As I was leaving, I expressed, as usual, my gratitude for the interview, whereupon C 1 replied that these interviews we are having are proving very helpful to him. He said that as he discusses negotiation with me it becomes necessary for him to think more carefully about these things than he would be apt to do if the interview situation didn't face him. One way he put it was, "Unless I were doing it this way, I would be much more apt to react without thinking through the situation; therefore, I would act on the basis of my past behavior and past experiences, and tend to develop a pattern for handling these things."

I have been tempted several times in the last week or 2 to enter into the record the fact that I think we are going to have to remember in the end that the recording is an aspect of the study. I felt this particularly with the —— union group, and am coming to see it now with the Marathon union group. Always when I play back a recording to a person or to a group, there seems to be some kind of detached examination on their part of what they have just done that has been recorded. The first experience of this was with the recording of Jim Slocum, which had run 2½ hours. I had secured his consent to record the interview partially by promising that he could hear himself back after he had recorded. (Incidentally, I have found that this eases the tension for people being recorded for the first time, the fact being, I guess, that they themselves will be able to pass judgment on what they said.) Jim sat for 2 hours more after the 2½ hours of recording, listening to his record played back. I think it is fair to say he was literally fascinated with it, and after that I heard him refer a number of times in union committee meetings to his experience in dictating. I think his fascination was not solely that of listening to his own voice; that would have been satisfied in less than 2 hours. But I think he was also reviewing, in hearing it repeated back, what he had reported onto the tape, and this gave him a new angle for looking at the data.

When I have recorded a union committee meeting and then played it back, in every instance the crowd has been intrigued with listening to itself. Some of the interest, I know, pertained to recognizing voices, and they'd get a big bang out of laughing at some of the remarks which they hadn't particularly laughed at at the time they were made in the meeting. Always they are impressed with the overlay of talking, that is, the fact that many people in a group are apt to talk at one time. When the machine plays it back it has the effect of drowning out all distinctiveness, leaving the impression of just one mass yelling. As one of the Marathon union fellows describes it, "It's just like hearing the animals being fed at the zoo." I've noticed that once one of the union groups gets used to having a meeting played back after adjournment, they expect this to happen each time and they'll stay quite some time—until I turn the machine off, in fact—listening and commenting and laughing. The fact that the recording is going on I definitely feel does not inhibit the material I am getting from these committee meetings. Various of the fellows will from time to time call down a member who is yelling above somebody else or not speaking loudly enough, by making the point that it's going "to ruin her recording," as they put it. They'll adjust the microphones on the table and monkey around in other ways enough to indicate to me that they're cognizant of the presence of the recorder and feel it is a part of the situation. Last night, at the end of their committee meeting, we all went downstairs to the bar for drinks. One of the questions which the fellows asked me then was, "You're going to take the machine in when we have our bargaining, aren't you?" The question was clearly put in the sense of "We hope you will." I think they want to hear *that* played back.

It proved a fruitful experience to stumble onto these various evidences that those involved in negotiation came to welcome the tape recording as a means of functioning simultaneously as negotiator and observer-of-oneself-as-negotiator. It was particularly important to be reminded of this fact about C 1 of the Marathon case. Since he had been desirous from the very start to cooperate with the research, he had given many hours of his time to recount his personal experiences at the table and to discuss the rationale and tactics of negotiating. Being astute at observing and analyzing himself, as well as adroit in the actual give-and-take with others, he became one of the most valuable resources to which the research gained access. Just as soon, however, as the case involving his company got into full swing, he did a complete about-face, resolutely resisting all of the investigator's efforts to tempt him into continuing these post-mortems in the abstract. In an interview recorded after the case was settled, he set forth his reasoning (somewhat condensed here in being lifted from the transcript).

C 1: I've been very much interested in the [research] thing all along because it's given me a chance to talk out a lot of things that are in my mind and it clears thinking. And it—as a matter of fact, I think that being able to talk about it has helped me with the situation.

AD: Well, that's interesting. That's really interesting. If we'd been able to get these recordings through, especially after bargaining started—

C 1: No, I wouldn't have listened to them.

AD: You wouldn't have even gone back and looked at them then?

C 1: Not at that point, no. I'll do it now it's over. Because, Ann, if at any time—particularly in the last few weeks, I *did not dare* have *any* doubt, in any way, that I was going to get a contract and not a strike.

AD: Oh, this is interesting, because you're saying that that was no time to be analytical.

C 1: Right. Of myself!

AD: Yes, what you were doing. Or—or even the situation.

C 1: I had to be absolutely objective. I had to analyze the situation at every step *as we went* and what it was then, not what it was yesterday!

AD: I see. Each time it was a different situation.

C I: Yeah.

AD: Yeah. Uh-huh. It's very interesting.

C I: Every time you sat down across the table from the union, it was a brand-new situation. You didn't know what the atmosphere was going (AD: No) to be.

AD: That's very interesting you're able to verbalize that. That's—yeah, that's very interesting.

C I: Now's the time to analyze what happened.

AD: In the over-all.

C I: Yeah. Well, you—I guess you recognize by now that when you get into these n—negotiations, you get on a certain key which is not your normal key.

AD: I guess you have to, don't you?

C I: You just close out almost everything.

C I's testimony about his change of approach, once engaged at the table, coincides with testimony from an entirely different quarter of the research. The transcriber whose unscrambling of the tape recordings had proved most reliable had been asked to set down any notes that might prove helpful in future work of this sort. Her summary reports discoveries of great value in the present discussion.

In attempting to analyze the techniques which I used to get the most material from the recordings in the quickest way, during the actual transcribing process I think it helped to listen ahead for perhaps a paragraph or two (in the more difficult parts) before putting it down on paper, and in that way pick up key words and phrases and the general thought of the section, so that sounds would automatically develop into words of meaning.

In particularly difficult spots where this method failed, repetition was my final step. The machine was so constructed that when using the handle designed for the purpose of back-spacing, usually a whole line, or two, were back-spaced with one turn of the handle. It seemed to me that this was too long a span to remember and allowed too much time between repetitions, so I began retracing the difficult spots by turning the reel manually, and developed a technique of *very fast,* short repetitions (from 3 or 4 to 6 or 8 words, depending upon continuity), with up to a dozen or so repetitions in succession. The repeated sounds in many cases seemed to develop automatically into words. While using this method I tried to close my mind to active thoughts, did not attempt to figure out the meaning, but rather let it become an automatic process of striking a familiar chord simply by hearing the same sound over and over. If transcribing equipment could be regulated to back-space in this way, it would be most helpful. Of course, this method was not successful with all material, but worked in many cases where ordinary "listening" failed.

As far as separating several voices speaking at once, I think that also becomes an automatic process, with a little practice, of listening for and "hearing" just one voice at a time.

The recording machine was the only participant in the conference room which approached ideal input and output neutrality. It altered or forgot nothing once noted; it encompassed in entirety the most congested overlappage. That participants were not averse to having in their midst such a detached and efficient observer hints strongly that it performed a service recognized as taking place in conference rooms with or without machinery designed specifically for such purpose. It can even be ventured that to negotiators the recording feature of the research was equivalent to a flashback of their own condition which, because it was abstracted out and away from the unit designated "a person," dramatized a breach with which they were already familiar.

C 1 had insisted that in the decisive period of his company's case he had stood still in the ever-present awaiting the oncoming always-new (from the standpoint of language alone, a tax on one's credulity). Although he had declared verbally that his confidence had been stout and unflagging throughout this period, he had testified earlier in the same interview that such confidence in a negotiator is foolhardy, otherwise negotiators will undertake no critical judgments of their parties' situations.[17] The transcriber had spoken of recognition upon "striking a familiar chord." Did C 1, too, have means in readiness to keep track of the effects produced by his actions during the interregnum of decision-reaching? If so, there is a vital part missing from what he says here.

One accustomed to look to stimuli followed by responses as the way to knowledge may dismiss C 1's assurance as a kind of whistling in the dark. But if C 1 had abandoned the sensory system as necessary, even desirable, in the acquisition of knowledge, then his words can be read quite literally to say that he (along with all other thinking persons in the conference room) *could in truth know ahead of settlement* that settlement would come to pass. It must be noted, however, that C 1 would know this, *could* know this, first of all only from himself, not from the environment.

A mechanism for knowing in C 1's fashion is conceivable if it can be

[17] Cf. Chapter 4, p. 75.

established that there is a possibility of mental transmission at such fantastic speeds that the ingredients of speed, time and space, are self-obliterated. When space and time are united, physically or conceptually (or, conceivably, psychophysically), the result must be the same: that is, there is movement, expressed in units of speed. The rate of motion will be determined by the inner relationship of the space-time unity. If that relationship can be slanted in the direction of either factor sufficiently (without severing the union), the other factor should be rendered negligible. Presumably, too, if the factors can be sufficiently equated, they will both be rendered negligible. Under such circumstances, "When . . . ?" and "Where . . . ?" would no longer be applicable; only "Is . . . ?" would remain. C 1 and the transcriber were obviously engaged with the latter question.[18]

[18] An innovation belonging to this century is the appearance on the international scene of a potential full-time caretaker for the time element in international controversies. Formal and public aspects of the work of the United Nations in particular bear on this point. Certain trends in the General Assembly can be taken as evidence that the world organization has been driven to the production of time for its own consumption, with an effect not unlike (albeit more sophisticated than) that brought to attention by the recording machine and the general research framework in the present study. The reluctance of various organs of the UN to recognize failures with issues is a trend in point, resulting in what the late Secretary-General Hammarskjold referred to as the "hardy perennials" like disarmament, apartheid, etc., reappearing on the Assembly's agenda season after season—and often resulting, too, in verbal difficulties at some of the Secretary-General's press conferences when reporters tried to extract from Mr. Hammarskjold tangible justification for the never-failing "hopefulness" and "optimism" they detected in his outlook, which so puzzled them.

CHAPTER 9

The Moving Observer

The far-flung enterprise of nature is conceded, by definition, to hold the record for peaceable adjustment internally (provided socio-politico-economic man is not counted among her constituent parts). For purposes of the present analysis, it would be preferable if the *fait accompli* could be exchanged for a close-up of Nature in the act of reconciling some of her semi-autonomous divisions. What the student specifically has in mind is that a properly directed search of the natural world should turn up the archetype of the successful intercessor.

I

In the one autobiography which Albert Einstein was persuaded to write, some psychological sidelight is again and again put forward as utterly integral to his reading of the physical universe. Such a passage occurs in his review of the mental events which culminated in the first paper on relativity theory:

Reflections of this type made it clear to me as long ago as shortly after 1900, i.e., shortly after Planck's trailblazing work [on heat radiation], that neither mechanics nor thermodynamics could (except in limiting cases) claim exact validity. By and by I despaired of the possibility of discovering the true laws by means of constructive efforts based on known facts. The longer and the more despairingly I tried, the more I came to the conviction that only the discovery of a universal formal principle could lead us to assured results. The example I saw before me was thermodynamics. The general principle was there given in the theorem: the laws of nature are such that it is impossible to construct a *perpetuum mobile* (of the first and second kind). How, then, could such a universal principle be found? After ten years of reflection such a principle resulted from a paradox upon which I had already hit at the age of sixteen: If I pursue a beam of light with the velocity c (velocity of light in a vacuum), I should observe such a beam of light as a spatially oscillatory electromagnetic field at rest. However, there seems to be no such thing, whether on the basis of experience or according to Maxwell's [electromagnetic field] equations. From the very beginning it appeared to me intuitively clear that, judged from the standpoint of such an observer, everything would have to happen according to the same laws as for an observer who, relative to the earth, was at rest. For how, otherwise, should the first observer know, i.e., be able to determine, that he is in a state of fast uniform motion?

One sees that in this paradox the germ of the special relativity theory is already contained. Today everyone knows, of course, that all attempts to clarify this paradox satisfactorily were condemned to failure as long as the axiom of the absolute character of time, viz., of simultaneity, unrecognizedly was anchored in the unconscious. Clearly to recognize this axiom and its arbitrary character really implies already the solution of the problem.[1]

Einstein's original paper on relativity theory (since designated special relativity, distinguishing it from general relativity, which came some years later) appeared in 1905 with the title "On the Electrodynamics of Moving Bodies." His drastic revision in that paper of certain ingrained notions about the universe occasioned a now famous lecture on "Space and Time" by Herman Minkowski, professor of mathematics at Göttingen. Of that lecture in 1908, as well as Minkowski's over-all part in disseminating Einstein's thoughtways, Infeld has written:

The first words of Minkowski's lecture were a prophetic statement of the profound influence which Einstein's ideas would exert on modern thought:

"Gentlemen! The views of time and space that I wish to develop before you grew on the soil of physical experiments. There lies their strength. Their

---

[1] Paul A. Schilpp, ed., *Albert Einstein: Philosopher-Scientist* (2d ed., New York, Tudor, 1951), pp. 51, 53. Like others of Einstein's oversimplified, idealized experiments, the pursuit of a light beam, though impossible to execute physically, is highly susceptible to imagery. The few ingredients a reader will need to realize the light-beam experiment for himself are presented in order in Leopold Infeld's small volume on Einstein, under the heading "A Paradox? A Paradox! A Most Ingenious Paradox!": "From the time Einstein was fifteen or sixteen years old (so he has often told me) he puzzled over the question: what will happen if a man tries to catch a light ray? For years he thought about this very problem. . . . Indeed, in the case of a man who catches and runs with a light ray we see the great puzzle that led to relativity theory. For such a man, because he moves uniformly, all phenomena should be the same as for the man who stands still; but, on the other hand, he always remains in front of the light wave, and for him light stands still." *Albert Einstein: His Work and Its Influence on Our World* (rev. ed., New York, Charles Scribner's Sons, 1950), p. 41.

tendency is radical. From now on, space in itself and time in itself should descend into a shadow and only a union of both should retain its independence."

Minkowski's mathematical genius put Einstein's ideas into a new geometrical form that fully revealed their beauty and simplicity. Sometimes we hear that "time is a fourth dimension in relativity theory," and we are impressed by the mystical sound of these words. But there is nothing mystical about them. Events in the world must be described by four numbers, three of them referring to positions and one to time. Minkowski showed that it is much more convenient not to treat space alone as the background of our events, but spacetime. The splitting of such a space-time background into space and time depends on the *system* of observation.[2]

Since 1905 confirmation has piled up that the unification of space-time makes for a superior scientific assault on the problems of the physical universe; still, there has been no evident conversion of non-scientific minds from the familiar dichotomy into space *and* time. The introduction of an observer (recorder) function into the light-beam experiment indicates that Einstein was essentially working with a three-cornered schema. The question ripe for inquiry is one for psychology rather than physics: is the bringing together of space and time in man a work of recurring settlement in nature?

II

The conception per se of a space traveler enjoying a free ride at the front end of a light beam does not seem to *require* that the traveler should "know, i.e., be able to determine, that he is in a state of fast uniform motion." That necessity was foreseen exclusively by Einstein. The subtlety with which he introduced the subject of the space traveler's mind and its prerogatives belies the potential significance of the responsibility he assigned to "the observer." Henceforth no major calculation of physical motion can be entirely credible unless it takes into account the possibility raised by Einstein's experiment that motion originates in conjunction with mentality.

Earthbound observers, being lifelong space travelers, have no choice but to make their observations, of whatsoever sort, while in a state corresponding to the light-beam traveler's.[3] The experience of uniform physi-

[2] Infeld, *Albert Einstein*, p. 45.

[3] Cf. Buckminster Fuller on this point: "Students often say to me: I wonder what it would be like to be in a space ship? What would it feel like to be flying through

cal motion—the registration of continuity in the unconscious—is thus involuntarily fed into every attempt at impersonal, objective cognition of "reality." Einstein remanded this experience to further elaboration in the mental realm. Was it only an exceptional mind, one the caliber of his, which could afford to propose such a step? According to the evidence, no; for Piaget, stimulated by Einstein's express interest in the matter, devised a simple means of ascertaining that the very young, when presented with a situation modeled on lines of the light-beam experiment, will resemble Einstein in their reactions:

Does a child's first conception of velocity include comprehension of it as a function of distance and time, or is his notion more primitive and intuitive? Albert Einstein himself posed this question to me in 1928 when I was demonstrating some experiments on causality to him one day. I have since performed a very simple experiment which shows that a child does not think of velocity in terms of the distance-time relation. We place before the child two tunnels, one of which is obviously much longer than the other, and then we push a doll through each tunnel with a metal rod in such a way that the dolls arrive at the other end of both tunnels simultaneously. We ask the child:

"Is one tunnel longer than the other?"

"Yes, that one."

"Did both dolls go through the tunnels at the same speed, or did one go faster than the other?"

"The same speed."

"Why?"

"Because they arrived at the same time."

Now we take the tunnels away and push the dolls along the floor in full sight, over the respectively different distances, both arriving at their destinations simultaneously as before. This time the child recognizes that one doll traveled faster than the other.

"Why?"

"Because this doll passed the other." [4]

All reference to motion imputes the contradictory events of continuity and change as occurring simultaneously in the same locus—in short, as

---

space? And the answer is: What does it feel like? That is all you have ever been doing! You have to remember that Earth is a very small space ship. I've learned to feel the Earth as a space ship; it is really a very small little ball." Studs Terkel and John Walley, "An Interview with Buckminster Fuller, Part II of III," *WFMT Perspective* (Chicago), Vol. X, No. 11 (November, 1961), p. 24.

[4] Jean Piaget, "The Child and Modern Physics," *Scientific American,* Vol. CXCVI, No. 3 (March, 1957), p. 51.

equivalent to each other. In the realm of mentality, when identical or interchangeable factors appear, regardless of their genus, they are known to tend toward reconstitution, consequently to be short-lived in their presenting form. Continuity (uniformity) is unknowable either sensorily (as physical stimulus apart from an observer) or immediately (in the absence of time). But, rotated on its mental axis a simple ninety-degree turn, it automatically converts from on-goingness into out-thereness—the best-known attribute of the space world over which prepositions preside. Converted and consolidated into enduring form suitable for further use, the constant production of continuity can be brought within the scope of reality, there to serve the organism as an ever replenished stock of building material.

In commenting on the child's reappraisal of the physical facts in the second half of his demonstration, Piaget points out that "passing" simply reflects a change of order between the dolls. In the case of two bodies in motion in the same direction, the change of order involved in overtaking would reach an Einsteinian observer as motion in reverse. Obviously, it cannot be claimed that the physical path of either doll has altered direction. A more reasonable conclusion is that motion emanating from the observer in the first place eventually returns to him over a second route, providing a basis whereby he can estimate positions, including his own. Who wields the power to originate motion must control the main accesses to time; for the concept of motion *requires* the Siamese-twinning of space-time.

Can a rule of reversibility be demonstrated to hold in negotiations? To meet this test, it will be necessary to produce evidence that negotiators calibrate their progress in such fashion that they can be informed by the senses when the time for decision has been reached. A most striking and convincing piece of evidence comes from the sub-study, in that completely unexpected revelation that immediately preceding settlement the judges interrupted their trend of increasing inaccuracies in making identifications, now reaching a new peak of accuracy. If to a non-participant this looks like a return to the conference table of the intense conflict of the early days of the case, the reflective observer will see beyond to the bending of the time dimension, a psychological event of the very first magnitude.[5] Time experienced in backward flow, as here, becomes a yard-

[5] Two splendid lines suffice for Robert Frost to state the psychological case for reversibility in "A Masque of Reason": "When time was found to be a space di-

stick in the hands of the experiencing organism, assuring the measurer that he has at last escaped the attraction of a system upon which he proposes to report. In his experience of refracted Time he has been simultaneously informed of the separate existences of himself and of a system apart from himself, the only condition under which it is possible to say that even limited objectivity has been achieved.

One can now make a prediction about the content of final settlement which was not possible before—namely, that the final settlement figure (or arrangement) will fail to incorporate everything that is literally obtainable. In other words, there will be something left over after settlement from the total resources which the parties bring to the table prepared to spend if necessary. It should be feasible to test this prediction in concrete cases. What the present study has to offer is a finding which at first seemed incredible: that in the Marathon, the Irving Mining, and the Crescent City cases (the reader will be left free to make his own judgment about the Atlas case) there was one party in each instance which did not have to yield to the ultimate limits for which it was in readiness at some point. In these cases it can be declared with the greatest confidence that a party's failure to tap with its minimal demands the maximum available to it from the other did not prohibit it from accepting the settlement with satisfaction.

---

mension/ That could, like any space, be turned around in." *Complete Poems of Robert Frost* (New York, copyright 1945 by Holt, Rinehart and Winston), p. 594.

BOOK TWO

A CASE OF INDUSTRIAL MEDIATION

THE ATLAS CASE

Mediation Proceedings [1] between The Atlas Recording Machine Company and Local 89, OPQ International Union
March 21–April 18, 1953

ROSTER OF PARTICIPANTS

For the Union
(U 1) John Gambon, full-time Business Agent, OPQ International Union
(U 2) Bernice Meyer, full-time Secretary-Treasurer, Local 89
 Tom Saunders, President, the Local
 Katie Moran, Vice-President, the Local
 Walt Denk, Vice-President, the Local
 Peg Healy, Recording Secretary, the Local
 Shirley Comeau, Trustee, the Local
 Les Baker, Chairman of Skilled Trades Committee, the Local
 Stan Wollman, representative of night shift, the Local

For the Company
(C 1) Bill Michelsen, Industrial Relations Manager
(C 2) Len Loring, Vice-President and Treasurer
 Erwin Espig, Assistant Industrial Relations Manager
 Bob Pranis, Works Manager

Mediator
 George Thomson

Research Investigator
 Observer

---

[1] The transcribed proceedings preserve the verbal content as it was originally tape-recorded except for alteration of clues which might lead to identification of the field source. If any names, places, processes, or dates appearing in the transcript suggest a resemblance to known persons, parties, or cases, this is contrary to intention and is to be attributed to coincidence in the masking.

TRANSCRIBING SYMBOLS

/   Indicates the point at which the speaker who has the floor is interrupted by another who continues after him.

x   Indicates a word which was not audible in transcription. The number of words lost is signified by the number of x's, up to a total of five; any greater loss (such as an entire sentence) is denoted by the maximum of xxxxx.

...   Indicates loss of material while the recorder was inactive for one or another reason (tape being changed, machine warming up after being turned on, someone talking again after recorder turned off, etc.).

Joint Meeting - A (10:35 A.M.)

Mediator: Well, I understand that your negotiations have opened, and you
held a meeting, and this is on a reopener. Is that correct?

Gambon: That's correct.

Mediator: Yeah. / And what is the —

Gambon: (Over Mediator above) April 1st, 1953, is the reopening date.
(Rather long pause) Copy of the letter, George, that was sent to the
company (pause) — notice of our intention to bargain during the reopening period. (Long pause) A copy of the union's demands presented to the company, at Bill Michelsen's request. (Long pause)
Think maybe you should have a carbon copy of the actual letter,
George, rather than that, if you prefer.

[A quite long interval follows, during which the two parties sign on
separate sheets passed out by the Mediator.]

Mediator: Well, in opening the conference I would suggest, if you will,
w — that both sides give us a little résumé, a brief history of your
positions — your negotiations and positions, and then we'll pick it
up from there. So, if the union will, suppose you kick off first.

Gambon: Well, I think our position is pretty well outlined in the — our
letter of March 6th, 1953, to Bill Michelsen, stating the union's bargaining position at that time, and as of this time, also. It was presented to the company previous to the first negotiation meeting in
order to give them some time to look ours program over and to possibly give us some answer as to what they could do in regard to that
particular program. Company and the union had met on one occasion,
March 12th, on the company's premises, which time the company made
one offer after a discussion of their position — financial position and
so forth, an offer which was entirely unacceptable as far as the union
goes. That's just about where we are at this moment. It appeared to
me and the rest of the union's committee that there didn't seem to be
much hope of sitting across the bargaining table with the company and
trying to talk about the meeting, in a much more substantial way, the
request of the union. Result is we're now back down here, hoping that
the company's position will get to be more realistic than it has up to
this point. (Pause) I think that would conclude any statement that I
wanta make at this time, George.

[Pause. Mediator looks toward Michelsen and nods.]

Michelsen: Well, George, essentially what John has said is true. We've
had one meeting. Company stated its position. It — it supplied some
information in support of that position. I intend this morning to submit
some additional information, because I'm quite interested that everybody here have complete understanding to the degree that it's possible
for me to submit information, so that there's a complete understanding
of why the company's position is the position that it is. At our last —

I'm gonna ask you to bear with me so that I can do that. I'm not gonna
be long. I'll promise I'll be as brief as it's possible for me / to be.

Mediator: (Over Michelsen above) Take as much time as you want.

Michelsen: I'm not known for my brevity, sometimes. However, at our
last meeting we reviewed essentially about 4 things that you could boil
our story down to, and that was that the year of 1952, our sales had
gone down 9%, our costs of operations had gone up — material costs
and costs of employing people had gone up, and many other costs. Our
selling costs, the costs which we have to pay in order to sell recorders
to people who are goin' to buy them, have gone up. Along with those
rising costs, we had profits which dropped considerably and — quite a
drop. Before our taxes were deducted those falling profits were something in the neighborhood of 42%, I believe; we have the exact figures
here. Along with this drop in sales and rise in cost and falling profits,
we are in a much more difficult competitive position than we've been
in the past, for several reasons. Number 1, we've got more competitors than we used to have. A lot of people have gotten into the recorder
business, into the products in which a small company can get organized and equipped easily. The larger companies who formerly gave
us a good run for our money are now larger, they're multi-product
companies like ours, they're in a position to do what we for awhile,
along with a few other people, were the only ones able to do, and that
was to handle large requirements from our big customers. We now
have several competitors who can do that, and who do it as well, in
some cases a little better than we do. So we have that kind of a background. One of the charts which I wanta show now — I'm gonna have
to use some of my people here as easels.

[Period of light remarks follows. Michelsen laughs heartily in announcing, "I — I hope you'll forgive the — the background in some of these
easel charts." Joking follows over whether Michelsen said "easels"
or "weasels."]

Michelsen: (Over Espig from above) Here's the one which — which we
showed — it — it showed what happened for 3 years in terms of profits.
The blue figure is profit after taxes; the black figure is sales; the red
profit is profit after taxes; and the green figure is our tax bill. I
showed you this chart before. I just wanta emphasize and to bring out
this point, that here in 1952 you see a 9% fall-off in sales accompanied
by a 42% fall-off in profits before taxes, which is a measure of the
company's operating efficiency. After the tax bill had been paid, the
profits after taxes declined 23% in '52 over what they had been in '51.
Now, you get some greater concept, or a sharper contrast, of what's
happened when ya look at the relationship between '52 and '50. Not
that the numbers on the years mean anything, but the sales are relatively the same. In 1952 our sales were about 7% higher than they
were in 1950; and yet with this increased sales of 7%, our profits for
this year, even with those increased sales, were less — 56% less
than they were in 1950 before taxes. This year, after taxes — comparison of one tax bill against another — they're 55% less. And this
relationship of taxes — the point that I was tryin' to make here, that
we have these lower profits in 1957 as compared with — or, '52 as
compared with '51 — 23% less after taxes, even though our accrual
for taxes in '52 is about half — 663,000.00, as compared with what

we had to pay in 1951. Now, that to me was a — a dramatic presentation, in a sense, of what actually happened in our operations last year: falling sales — slight fall-off in sales, 9%; rapid fall-off in profits — 42% before taxes, 23% after taxes. And here on a comparable year in terms of sales volume you have, even though sales in '52 are 7% greater than '50, profits 56% less this year than they were in this year. As far as I'm concerned that's — that's not a good picture. Now, the only thing that — that I can — can't stress too much in this meeting is this business of competition. Atlas generally, except for our leader model, is just about undersold on nearly every recorder it manufactures in one area or another. We showed you this chart. I'm not gonna labor this point any more. This shows you just roughly the percentages by which these prices of the products of ours are overpriced in terms of the market. This black column is the definite overpricing. For instance, in this recorder here, our deluxe custom unit with amplifier and so on, we are anywhere from 20, or 15, to about 35% over the market. And in this product particularly and some others of this kind, we're getting the kind of — of competition — these are the areas in which small companies are coming into being, getting equipped and under way quickly. The — not as much capital equipment required to get into the production of amplifiers, for example, as there is in a — a tape recorder. They're getting in, they're giving us a good run for our money, which you people well know. But the point is that c — c — competition generally is getting tougher. We're having a hell of a time with — with — competition. In the instances where we manufacture our brand for the big national chain outlets they are really making us get competitive, and as you of course realize, we need their volume badly. They're doing everything they can to bring the price of this particular type of item down. The same thing applies to the component manufacturers. But they're in the same squeeze. They have 2 — 2 commodities that go into their product. They are the labor which puts it together and the raw material which they have to buy from somebody else. But that's getting tougher. Some of you may have seen evidences of it in the paper recently when Chrysler reduced prices on automobiles, and it's quite possible that you're going to see some price reduction moving in that field now in order to get the automobiles moving. And the same thing is gonna be true in any group of appliances or — we certainly feel that there's gonna be real price competition in the whole field of home recording devices, and that moves back very quickly to the people who make the units. We don't sell our products — and you know this — we don't sell our products to the ignorant consuming public — and I use that term not to depreciate any of us, but most of us don't know whether we buy a good refrigerator or a good television set. We — we listen to the advertising. If we like Bing Crosby's voice and he's selling something, our daughter likes that, we go buy it, or we buy something else based on advertising. But we are not, most of us, competent engineers to be able to determine whether or not the product which we bought, which we think is the best, is the best. But we don't sell products to that kind of a consuming public; we sell 'em to people who have an understanding of fidelity, of tonal quality, and, what's more, who are often recording their children's first words and things of that sort for posterity, so to speak.

These people are real critics and don't buy a unit because they like
the cabinet style. And what's more, they look around and compare.
They know what they're buying, and they know what they want in a
product, and they either get it or they buy it somewhere else. Now,
I told you last week and have confirmed this, that we see no possibility of any rise in our prices, and (slight pause) — so that we're going
to be facing this competitive situation with a price structure that's
relatively stable but with costs that have risen, and it gonna be a
tough situation to keep our competitive head above water. Now, in
this chart here where you see this fall-off in profit, this means here,
where you've got a profit of $577,877.00, that we've got less money
left over at the end of the year to do things with. It means that we
curtail our research and development programs, the things that 4,
5, 6 years from now make us more competitive than we are at this
moment, or make us even — put us in a better competitive position
than we may be at this moment. Our dividends have been cut back;
and I mentioned that last time, that in the last 2 quarters of '52 we
reduced dividend payments to stockholders by 50%. They were cut
from 10¢ to 5¢ a share. Now, those dividend payments in 1952 totaled $395,949.00. That — they were dividend payments which were
made to 4,488 stockholders. Now, actually, if you want a comparison
— these dividends to stockholders — to the 4,488 stockholders, about
twice as many — a little more than twice as many stockholders as
there are employees — of $3,995.00 — was just about the money that
we spent on vacations and holidays last year. Our bill for vacations
and holidays to our employees in 1952 was just a little less, by 15,
20 thousand dollars, than this dividend payment to our more than
4,000 stockholders of $395,949.00. Now, that's, as far as I can see,
studying other reports, not a very large profit, and — Len, can you
hold that one? I — I don't wanta lose sight of that chart. (Someone
laughs) I'm just (Gambon laughs) — but I want you to look at another
one which I think is quite interesting. In your union's SPOTLIGHT
this week, 3/11/53, Al Hughes was making a statement about Lashley
Equipment's profits, and of course that's one of his favorite subjects,
Lashley Equipment Company; and he said that here were their profits
— and I'm gonna read from the SPOTLIGHT which I've had reproduced so you can see it. "Profits based on reports for the first 3/4ths
of 1952 will average $2,039.00 per employee, compared to a $1600.00
profit per employee in other companies in the electrical machine industry. Thus Lashley makes $430.00 more per employee than its
competitors." Then it says, "Though these are before-tax figures,
the / after-tax" —

Gambon: (Over Michelsen above) Well, why don't you read the rest of
that, "a figure (Michelsen: Uh?) equal to 21¢ an / hour per employee"? That's —

Michelsen: (Over Gambon above) — "a figure equal to 21¢ an hour per
employee. Although these are before-tax figures, the after-tax profits show the same high ratio. Af — after taxes, Lashley profits per
employee will be more than $800.00 per year, as compared with the
approximately $540.00 for the rest of the electrical machine indus-
try. This extra profit, $260.00 per year after taxes, is equal to more
than 13¢ an hour per employee." Well, that's an interesting r — ratio.

I don't necessarily subscribe to that, but we took Atlas's profit and divided by our employees, and we have, in comparison with the $2,039.00 per employee before taxes — we have a profit of $645.00 per employee, which is the division of our number of employees into our before-tax gross. Then if you compare that with this $800.00 figure, which is what he says is the profit Lashley will be making per employee after taxes, our profit after taxes per employee comes out to $300.00. So that if this is a comparison, you can see that our profits per employee or per anything are quite low in comparison to at least one company. And I made this comparison simply to show you that — that while this is a substantial figure, according to Al Hughes, this is a very unsubstantial figure here, and it — it's — it represents the fact that last year we didn't make very much profit. Now, the other thing that I tried to show you last week was what happened to the Atlas employee during this period when sales were dropping and profits were dropping and costs were going up. Well, the Atlas employee, as you know, got increases which, in terms of the cost of the package, came to about 18¢ an hour: a 15-cent increase which came out of this room in April, and another 3-cent which came out in October of 1952. And, of course, that is one of the things and a big factor in giving us our rise in costs during 1952 — the increased cost which we had to bear. And I showed you last time, although it has gotten to be a — not fashionable any longer to discuss consumer prices — to show you what happened, this line which is plotted here is the Consumer's Price Index based on — it was at about 100 in 1941; it's now up around 195. I don't know what the latest index is, and I doubt whether anybody does at the moment, but it's up around 195. In other words, it's gained 90% over its 1941 level. Well, then I plotted along here the average hourly base rate — this is the guaranteed base rate, not take-out — guaranteed base rate, and plotted it from its level of 47¢, which was its average in 1941, up to its present level. And that, put on the index, takes it up to about 310%, so that there's been a rise in that since 1941 of 210%, as compared with a 90% change which has taken place in the cost-of-living. So that I don't think there's any question about it but that our rates of pay have more than kept pace, to the tune of about almost twice as much, with the rise in the Consumer's Price Index, which has been accepted by a great many people to at least reflect the changes in what's called the average consumer's market basket. So that we had that kind of a change. And certainly that rise and that widening of the gap between the — the line which shows here what it costs a family to live based on certain commodities which are regularly priced and what the people have been taking out — this difference has more than absorbed the rise in the cost-of-living in terms of — of what has happened in terms of our wage rates. Now, that, of course — and I have to show you another chart here, is the — the increase in the payroll dollar. This chart, which for 3 years since we've been keeping it this way, shows the divisions of the sales income to the company. In other words, this represents every dollar coming into the company, and this represents how it goes out: employees, materials, supplies and services, depreciation on our plant equipment, taxes, and profits. And you can see here this — this payment to employee, which is all employees,

from the janitor right up to the president of the company. In 1950 it
was 48.6%; it's now 57.7%. That's about a 20% increase in this percentage ratio from 48.6 to 57.7. In other words, our cost to employees, or our payments to employees, have risen over this 3-year period about 20%. Our profits over the 3-year period — and I'll just
use the extreme ends of the chart at this point — have dropped from
9.4¢ out of each dollar, or 9.4%, to this year 4.8%, and that's roughly
a little — a little less than 50%. So that there you see a confirmation
of what I said earlier, increasing costs, falling profits. We don't show
the relationship of sales here. But to — and I wanta — well, some of
the information which you haven't seen which I wanta show you is
gonna relate to that later on. Now, there, again, you can see, since
we have these increased sales in '52 but with lower profits at this
blue point here (pause), as compared with what we have here, w — what
we have here — these are profits before we pay our taxes. In other
words, this is what we had left over before we pay everybody but the
government. It's what we have left over aft — before we declare any
dividends or anything else. In other words, just pay your bills for
producing recorders. You pay for your materials and for the people
who make 'em. You had this left over in '50; you had that left over in
'51; you had this left — only this left over in '52. Which means that
this rising here — these materials rising are eating away at what
should have been coming out at that — at that point. Now (pause), this
(pause) — just wanta show you one other chart right now. (Pause) I
wanta go back to what happened to the employee during this period and
again show you some — some figures which will be helpful, I think.
Here's another quote from the SPOTLIGHT which I thought and hope
will be significant. This is from the National Association of Electrical Manufacturers' statement of — report of a meeting in which they
say: "The electronic industry in the last 3 years, in spite of its tremendous growth and prosperity, has not made any progress in reducing the differential between it and other industries. While all manufacturing wages gained 28. — 26.8¢ since January of 1950, durable
goods gained 30, electrical machinery gained 27, home entertain-
ment devices such as radio, TV, and sound recorders" — which is our
industry — "gained only 24¢. Thus they slid further behind by 2 to 6¢
an hour. On a percentage basis, they also did worse than these other
industries." And, also, over here, while I didn't intend to show that,
i — is a comment on the fact that Hercules had a honey of a year this
year. Their net profit was 6% over their 1951. And I just don't want
you to forget that our net profit was 23% less than our 1951. Well,
what I wanta show is where Atlas stacks up against this sort of thing,
so I went to the source of this information, which is the Bureau of
Labor Statistics, compared it with what happened to us in Atlas. Erv,
you havin' trouble with this? (Laughs)
Espig: No, I'm all right (Michelsen: D'you wanta hold this one?), i — if
it's all right with you.
Michelsen: Well, here's some — here — here are our figures, and here
are the Bureau of Labor Statistics figures which were used in this
article here. Hold that over, so we can check these. (Pranis laughs)
Here's the industry classifications. These are taken right from the
Bureau of Labor Statistics, and I have the basic documents right here
so that we can check 'em. All manufacturing, as the article says,

went up 26.8¢; durable goods, 30; electrical machinery, 27; radio, TV,
and home recorders, 24. Well, it just so happens that since January,
1950, to November, 1952, the gain in our average hourly earnings has
been 35¢. In other words, 8.2¢ better than all manufacturing, according to the Bureau of Labor Statistics average; 5¢ better than durable
goods; 8¢ better than electrical machinery; and 11¢ better than what
has happened to other — to the average in the commercial electronic
industry. So that in this case where it says that — that the industry
gained only 24¢ and slid further behind 2 to 6¢ an hour, we slid further ahead by 11¢ an hour, which is a considerable slide, believe me,
to go that far ahead of your industry, and that's in this period of time,
just from 1950 to November of 1952. Now, these are figures right
from the — the B. L. S.; and since they were used here to stress a
point, I just wanta further emphasize it that while these are facts,
what happened in Atlas is not comparable to what happened in the average in the electronic industry, which increased 24¢ since January
of 1950. We have increased, in terms of average hourly take-out,
35¢. And I wanta just go a little bit further into some of that, so —
got some more of these (slight pause) figures here, if I can — (pause).
Here are the — the figures from the — Len, can you (laughing) hold
that? (Someone laughs) Let's put these down here. (Slight pause)
Here are the figures from the Bureau of Labor Statistics as they're
published in the earnings i — s — analysis in the MONTHLY LABOR
REVIEW. Here's the review from nineteen f — Ja — June of 1950. I
picked that because it had the January average. Some of these averages which come out very close to the month after publication are —
are temporary estimates and are not — not — are later adjusted, if
they need to be, so that taking the month of June, this January of 1953
was the final figure. And there it showed that average earnings in the
electronic industry were $53.05 based on a 41-hour week, and that
their average hourly earnings, $1.294. Then, the same point taken
later on, the average for 1951 — and I'm — I picked these out because
I'm gonna show you Atlas figures which correspond with these — the
average for 1951 was a take-out of 58.40, or $58.40, based on a work
week which averaged $40\frac{1}{2}$ hours and an average hourly earnings of
$1.442. Today, which is November of 1952, the last figure which has
been published by the B. L. S., but it's reasonably — it's — it's not
only their latest figure but we haven't had much fluctuation in our
wage rates because our last increase went into effect in October, so
that the only changes we have is fluctuation from jobs moving up or
down, or mixes of — of people starting f — more at the low than at the
high rates — those sort of things, which do give you a fluctuating average from week to week but shouldn't distort it too much. But in
November of 1952, which was the last published figure, the weekly
take-out was $63.35, based on a 41-hour week, or an average hourly
earning per hour of 1.54\frac{1}{2}$. Now, what does Atlas's picture look
like — and let's see if I can find it. (Pause) Well, here's — here's
the story, looking at it from one angle. In January of 1950, the industry average — and these figures can be checked back on these charts
that we have here; I can assure you they're correct — in — industry
average for electronic industry — the average hourly earnings at that
point were $1.29. At that time ours were $1.36 per hour; or, we were
7¢ an hour, or 5.4%, ahead of this figure, difference between 36 and

29 being about 5.4%. Now, we pick off our next figure, which is November of 1952, which brings us up to the present date as far as the record is concerned. We find the industry has come along to $1.54; Atlas's average hourly earnings at this point are $1.71. Now, that's important, but it's not as significant to me as this last figure, and that is that instead of being 7¢ ahead of the industry average, we're now 17¢ ahead of it; instead of being f — a difference between the industry and Atlas as existed back in 1950, a difference of 5.4%, there's now a differential of 11% between the average hourly earnings for Atlas employees and the average hourly earnings for those people working in the electronic industry. Now, let's look — forget what happened to A —
[Tape changed]
... 25.7%. Now, that's what I'd like you to look at. The industry changed from January of '50 to '52 by 19.4%, or 25¢ an hour; Atlas changed during that period by 35¢, or 25.7¢ an hour. You hold this, x? I've got just one more and we'll be finished. Here I've taken some of the week's earnings which are shown in this column and some of the work weeks to just carry out that comparison completely. Here you see the January, 1950, figures, and the industry averages are what you would see on this chart here for January, 1950. The industry was taking out $53.05 for a 41-hour week, $1.29 was the average hourly earning; Atlas was taking out $53.46, only 41 cent — only 41¢ an hour more, but they were taking it out based on a work week which was 39 hours instead of 41. Average earnings were $1.36, a differential of 7¢ Now, here I've done something which is pure arithmetic, doesn't reflect anything real. I've adjusted our work week so that it can be compared on the same basis as the industry, so that I've added 2 more hours at this rate, I've put in no overtime premium. So if these people who are working 39 hours and taking out 53.46 at this average earning of $1.36 were given 2 more hours of work at straight time, they would be taking out 56.18, so that on a comparable basis, both working 41 hours, difference in take-out is 53.05 compared to 56.18. Now, I've done the same thing for the other 3 periods of time which I wanted to just check on. The average of 1951 showed that the industry took out 58.40 on a 40.5 work week, $1.44 average; Atlas, 59.43 per week on a work week which averaged 38.8, average hourly earnings, $1.53. I adjusted the work week show that it showed a 40.5, no overtime, and it came to a take-out of $62.03 which would have been taken out by our people at a minimum — it wouldn't have actually been taken out, 'cause they'd been getting overtime, but a minimum, just for comparisons, based on the same work week, of $62.03. Now, we go up to November, 1952, which is our last point of comparison. We see that the industry is working 41 hours a week again, what they were doing back in '50. The average earnings — weekly take-out was 63.35 — based on that work week, $1.54; Atlas is taking out $67.00, difference of $3.65, on a 39.1-hour work week, a difference in work week of 1.9 hours, and the average hourly take-out is $1.71. So here, again, I adjusted the work week of 39.1 up to a 41-hour work week. We see that our take-out would be, compared with 63.35, $70.25, average hourly earning of $1.71. Now, the only other chart which I have was the one we showed you, and we did it to make a little more legible (laughing

slightly) this time, was what's happened in our industry and what happened in our area. And here are these figures to the best of our ability to procure them. They show that Atlas — and we've put down here just wage increases, none of the costs for the — any of the fringes which we've given, which were originally included in these packages of 15-point-something cents in April and in the 3¢ which we gave last week — last October. They're not in here; these are just wages. It shows that this is 20 — about 20 — almost 21¢ — 20-3/4¢ which we have given. These other companies — Viking has given 15½; Hercules, 19.2; Lashley, 25 — more than we have; Standard Products, 17 — they're now negotiating, I know that; Dayco, 20 — they're now negotiating, I believe; Aristocrat's gonna be negotiating, given 18; Timmons, a parts industry, 11¢; Tri-State Wire Products, a parts industry, 16¢; Fletcher-Knowles, parts industry — they compete with us — 16¢; Mentor Associates, a parts industry very definitely, given 8¢; Old Reliable, parts industry, 17¢; Eureka, good competitor of ours in our leader model, along with Old Reliable, 12¢; Master Craft, good competitor of ours, 17¢; Solar Sound, 19¢. Now, the only thing I can say in conclusion — and, believe me, this — I'm gonna stop now; this is (Someone laughs slightly) the conclusion — if you were faced with this situation, what would you do? And I think you'd do just what we've done. We've said that we're gonna bear an extra cost of the group insurance, we don't wanta take away the benefits, but that's all we're gonna do. And that's the end of my little speech. (Rather long pause)

Gambon: Well, I might comment that your presentation was excellent.
Michelsen: Thank you, John. I tried to make it that way.
Gambon: Your presentation.
Michelsen: Well, I — I say, I thank you for that.
Gambon: I hope I'll be able to do as well in commenting on your presentation. (Someone laughs)
One of boys: The only thing was lackin' was a stands for the music.
Gambon: I don't want any charts to hold up; I just wanta fire some things (Michelsen laughs) back to you on the basis of comments (Michelsen: O.K. Well, I —) that Mr. Michelsen had to make. (Slight pause) Well, to begin with, statements made in the very beginning by you about the competitive situation are (slight pause) just about exactly the same kind of statements that we listened to in April of 1952 and again in that October of 1952. (Michelsen: No question about that) Despite the fact that com — competition existed, at that time, at — on those dates and even prior to that, the company has made some tremendous strides in the last 3 years. You comment on the fact, in using one of your charts, that sales fell off in 1952 by 9%. (Michelsen: Yeah) I wanta quote for you from your own financial report (pause), and I'm quoting (rather long pause) — I wanta quote Clarence M— Haas. No, this isn't Clarence Haas, I'm sorry. But the — in your financial report under the heading of the year's business you very definitely point out that during the latter half of 1952 your sales were 14% higher than those for the same period of 1951. I think it's very significant (Michelsen: Uh-huh), and I think that's much more significant than your pointing out to us that sales dropped off 9% for 1952. (Pause) '51, you talk about the sales being 7% higher than in 1950, and again I come back

to the 14% in the latter half of '52, and on the basis of information which you gave us concerning the first period, it seems that that trend which developed in the last half of '52 is now extending into the — at least the first period of 1953 at the same rate.

Michelsen: Yep, that's true.

Gambon: Now, you mention the overpricing and amplifier units on your chart there, and you also showed deluxe custom units with amplifier, among others; and the comment that I make here is that these are items — Number 1, most of the manufacturing facilities for the production of amplifier units, test equipment, and so on which the company has already moved out of the metropolitan aree — area to Aiken, South Carolina, and that the winding and potting of power transformers, along with a couple of other items not mentioned by you, are due to be moved out in the very near future. All of these were listed by the company, in information which I requested, as being responsible for losses during the year of 1952. In the case of transformers which we produce here — that's all types — out of a total loss during 1952 of $776,994.00, power transformer — transformers alone accounted for $583,828.00. I make a very pointed remark at this point that that loss should no longer exist since the company has moved it from the metropolitan area to an area where the rates of pay being paid by the company are _much_, _much_ less than the rates of pay given to employees in the metropolitan area here at this plant. Now, you talk about this business of having less money to do things with. We can only assume ya mean less money to continue a very broad decentralization program; and, of course, if that's what you're talkin' about, I know you don't expect to get too much sympathy from the union in — on that particular kind of thing. You talk about dividends and the dividends going to 4,488 stockholders. It's interesting to note something that you haven't said here, that the company issued some $250,000.00 worth of — or, 250,000 shares, rather, during 1952, and that the (slight pause) shares, therefore, increased — outstanding shares increased — uh (rather long pause) — well, they increased (pause) — my count was 258,000 shares was the increase, rather than the 250 that you had mentioned in your book, probably as a general figure. But the earnings on the original shares that existed before that new issue, according to your statement, ran around 71¢, and in '52 you say it was only 42 — or, 44¢. (Slight pause) I'm sorry I don't have my information lined up, but I didn't have as much time to do it as you did (slight pause), in view of the fact that a good bit of the information ya gave us here is entirely new. To make that straight, 71¢ for each of the 1,067,163 shares of stock ac — outstanding on December 31st, '51, and 44¢ for each of the 1,325,163 shares outstanding on December 1st — 31st, 1952. So that while the 44¢ certainly is lower than the 71¢ per share, it must be remembered that ya paid it on 258,000 more shares of stock. (Pause) Now, you mention the fact here that the amount of dividends that ya paid out was _matched_ by the total cost of the company for vacations and holiday pay, and I wanta point out to you, too, that the _largest_ — the _very largest_ stockholders (slight pause) in — of this organization happen to also be (pause) officers of the company paid salaries, and they, too, receive vacations and holiday pay (Michelsen: Sure) that is deducted from the company's profits, if

you wanta take it that way. (Pause) You talk about not being a large
profit. Now (slight pause), I might comment and say that according
to the information I received from you, Bill, you point out that had you
not had these several lost items which totaled the 776,994, that you
would have had approximately $160,000.00 more profit. That's inter-
esting to note, particularly when all those items are being rapidly
moved out of the plant. (Pause) You made some comparisons there
about Lashley and Atlas on the basis of breaking (Michelsen: Uh) it
down to what it meant by employee, but you very (laughing slightly)
(pause) — maybe you done it unconsciously, but you forgot to make
the comparisons between sales of Atlas and Lashley and all the other
related subjects, to make that have any real worth to us. (Michelsen:
Well, the sales, John — we're talking percentages) You talk in terms
of 12 — or 11, 12 million dollars here when — in sales in Atlas, and
then you forget to mention the fact that the sales in Lashley run into
millions of dollars, if not billions.

Michelsen: Yeah, but the product which I used, which was the profit per
employee, is — is the <u>product</u> of / dividing into — into the number of
employees.

Gambon: (Over Michelsen above) By your own statements, year after
year, we have been told that there shouldn't be any comparisons made
between Atlas and a place like Lashley because they don't manufacture the same kind of an item. We manufacture an item that sells in
terms of hundreds of dollars, if not dollars in some instances; whereas
the type of product sold by Lashley are term — are sold in terms of
<u>thousands</u> of dollars.

Michelsen: That's true! I / was thinking you were referring to this
SPOTLIGHT x.

Gambon: (Over Michelsen above) Now, you talk a — about this business of
— of wages. You showed us a chart where we've advanced from 47¢
an hour all the way up to — I forget the figure you quoted, at the moment — as of 1952. I wanta point out to you that until about 1945 or
1946 the wages in Atlas were abnormal, to say the least, not only in
our industry but in the area — very abnormal, and in (Michelsen
starts to speak) 19 — 1945 or '46 was when you began to meet the
kind of pattern that was generally being set, not only in the industry
but nation-wise, beginning particularly in 1946 with the steel increase. (Pause) Now, your pro — your payroll dollar, particularly
that part of it showing the increased labor costs, again, as I've mentioned to you before, we pointed out to you that you have included in
that labor cross — cost all increased costs by virtue of what the company has given to non-union people, which includes, among other
things, the profit-sharing plan for your executives and (pause) manufacturing (Michelsen: Uh-huh) supervisory group, which began in
1950 and went through '51 and again in '52, for very appreciable
amounts, amounts which, if they were put into terms of cents per
hour to employees, would have accounted for appreciable wage increases over and above what we have already received.

Michelsen: It's also true, John, that if we took — took the wages of the
employees, or some of them, and gave them to the executives, the
profit-sharing plan would be higher, too, / wouldn't it?

Gambon: (Over Michelsen above) It's i — it's interesting to note that despite the fact that you're talking to us in terms of — of 4/10ths-of-a-cents-per-hour business as an added cost, which, of course, you limit to one particular item, that you have already paid out for the first period of 1953 some profit-sharing to your non-union employees which includes, again I say, the executives of the company, which, though I don't have the figure here for the profit-sharin' for the first q — first period of '53, I would be quite willing to bet and give you odds (Michelsen: xx) will show a lar — much larger cost / than 4/10ths of a cent.

Michelsen: (Over Gambon above) I gave it to you. Payments for the first period to this group were / twelve thousand xxx.

Gambon: (Over Michelsen above) I said in profit-sharing. Where — did you put that in my letter?

Michelsen: Yeah.

Gambon: I'm sorry, you do have it here. 12,472 cents — or, 72 dollars. Well, that's much more than 4/10ths of an hour, even if you prorate it for all the employees in the shop. (Pause) Now, y — you talk about this comparisons for the last 3 years, '50, '51, and '52, and show that Atlas gave out 35¢ compared to industry — our own industry — radio, television, and home recording industry — of 24¢ (pause); and then you gave us some hourly wage increases and hourly earnings — average hourly earnings, and things of that kind. But you very carefully restrict yourself to 2-year period, 1951 and 1952. I've done a little checking on the situation generally in our industry compared with some of the same companies you showed us on your chart. (Michelsen: Uh-huh) And you say Atlas got 20¢ and so-and-so got 17, and things of that kind in a 2-year period. And I'd like to read some of those to you. (Pause) I go back to 194-s-6, which I think is the proper thing to do here, and I find that without (pause) probably any argument from you — you can argue with me if you want, but I don't think you gonna be in a position to — that we have, for instance, in 1946 Standard Products receiving, in wages alone — now, this is just wages — $23\frac{1}{2}$¢; Lashley, $18\frac{1}{2}$; Hercules, $18\frac{1}{2}$; big steel, $18\frac{1}{2}$; Precision-Made, $18\frac{1}{2}$; Dayco, 18; Atlas, 15. In '47 —

Mediator: Fro — excuse me, from what dates? From what year are you —

Gambon: This — that was 1946 that I quoted. Uh — 1947, Standard Products, $6\frac{1}{2}$¢; Lashley, $11\frac{1}{2}$¢; Hercules, $11\frac{1}{2}$; big steel, 20.18¢; Monco System, 11¢; Precision-Made, 15¢; Dayco, 11¢; Atlas, $13\frac{1}{2}$¢. At this point I'd like to comment that, while the union was able to negotiate in 1946 the $18\frac{1}{2}$-cent package set by steel, the final $3\frac{1}{2}$¢ of the total of $18\frac{1}{2}$¢ was not paid until, I believe it was, February of 1947 (Michelsen: Yeah), so that the increased cost is properly reflected in the year 1947. In 1948 Standard Products received 12¢; Lashley, 12; Hercules, 12; big steel, 13; Monco System, 15 in 3 separate increases; Precision-Made, 8¢; and Dayco, 10.48. At the same — during the same year, Atlas received 9¢. In 1949 most of all the unions in the area, including our own industry, were engaged in fringe negotiations, and I think the kind of fringes negotiated were pretty general in the form of pensions and health insurance plans. In 1950 Standard Products had 10¢; Lashley, 10; Hercules, 10; big steel, 16; Precision-Made, $10\frac{1}{2}$; Dayco, in 2 increases, 11.27. Now, Monco System, during 1950, first received a 3-cent increase and then a 7% increase which was approximately total around 12¢, giving them approximately 15¢. In 1951 / Standard Products —

Meyer: (Over Gambon above) xx Atlas in / 1950.

Gambon: (Over Meyer above) Did I — oh, I definitely wanta (Meyer
  laughs) make that statement. In (Meyer continues laughing) — in
  comparison with those increases, Atlas received 5¢. In 1951 Standard Products received 9¢; Lashley, 15.3; Hercules, 15.1; Precision-
  Made, 12½; Dayco, 9 and, oh, .18, I guess you would call that; and
  Monco System in 1951 — they received a 3% increase, which was approximately another 5¢. In '51 in comparison to those increases,
  Atlas again received 5¢ an hour. In 1952 Standard Products, in 3 different — on 3 different dates, received a total of 13¢ an hour; Lashley,
  10¢; Hercules, 10¢; big steel, 16; Monco System received a percentage increase of about 3/4 of 1%, which resulted in about 2¢, and then
  later a 10½-cent wage increase, giving them approximately 12½¢;
  Precision-Made, 13.66¢ per hour; Dayco, 8.4¢ per hour; during which
  time Atlas received in wage increases 14½¢ an hour, possibly slightly
  above that because of the 5¢ additional to day workers and skilled
  trades. Taking those things into a total situation, you find Standard
  Products over those years receiving a total of 74¢ an hour; Lashley,
  77.3; Hercules, 77.1; big steel, 83.6; Monco System, 68¢; Precision-
  Made, 78.1; Dayco, 71.3; and Atlas with 62¢. Now, I think that sets up
  a much fairer comparison, because I want to make note here that during 1950 when we got a 5-cent increase in the face of a pretty general
  10¢-an-hour increase, and during 1951 when we got the 5% increase in
  the face of anywhere from 9 to 15-cent increases, that those were the
  years when the company's profit-sharing plans for executives and
  their supervisory officials first began to be reflected in their costs.
  (Pause) I'd like to comment at this time to this extent that as far as
  I know right now, Lashley and, of course, our union is in n — are in
  negotiations. The request, as you have correctly stated it, is 21¢ an
  hour from Lashley. Standard Products is right now in negotiations
  with a request for 16¢ an hour plus some fringes. There are many
  others. I know, as you state, that Aristocrat and many more of these
  plants that you have given us (pause) are just about ready to go into
  negotiations. Now, I will later on — I didn't — didn't purposely stay
  away from Aristocrat, but I had requested this type of information
  from them and had not received 'em prior to this meeting. I am
  quite sure that the total figure in wage increases paid out in Aristocrat from 1946 through '52 will exceed the total of 62¢ which we received over those years.

Michelsen: You're right. It is.

Gambon: Well, I just wanted to make certain that you understood I wasn't
  by-passing it because I thought it might be low. Now, almost all of
  these particular companies that I name have been named by you, and
  while you confine yourself to a 2-year period, I think it's only fair to
  go back and follow what you started to do in 1946. At least some attempt was made by Atlas to keep pace with the 3 wage patterns which
  were set pretty much by steel — big steel — during '46, '47, and '48.
  In '50 we lost track of that situation entirely and, of course, we got
  into quite a bit of — uh — difficulties, I should say, in trying to find
  out whether we had any tandems that we could latch onto during the
  last negotiations for the new contract back in the early part of this
  year, and because the company had not followed big steel, at least we

couldn't establish any tandem, even though we were successful in getting things proven. (Rather long pause) Well, I s'pose I get down at this point to this particular kind of a situation. Keeping in mind everything you have to say, I ask a direct question and that is, what has all of this got to do with the company's ability to pay? There is no doubt in my mind that the company <u>does</u> have the ability to pay and to absorb additional costs which are <u>much</u> greater than anything like 4/10ths of a cent an hour. The union's bargaining position remains the same! We see no reason to begin making overtures to the company in an effort to have you get away from a very unrealistic position of a 4/10ths-of-an-hour — 4/10ths-of-a-cents-per-hour wage offer, which in reality is not a wage offer but a continuation of a cost which the company says it will now continue after it has absorbed that cost from October, 1952, to date, without any complaint to the union or without any request to the union that the benefits be cut back because the contract itself only provides for premiums of $6.00 per member, whereas your actual cost, according to your figures, is $6.60. (Michelsen: H'm) (Pause) We find, again I say, that particular position of the company very (pause) unrealistic, to say the least. (Michelsen: Well, John, just —) I would like to wind up at this point, for the time being, at least, with the (pause) comment, Bill, that your financial position is much, much better than it used to be back in these days of '46, '47, '48, and so forth, when you were giving out large increases, and I think you ought to note that your comment that the last wage increase back in April was the very largest that Atlas had ever given out doesn't hold too much water, because we have received, in terms of cents per hour, larger wage increases at a given time other than in the early — April 1st of 1952. You've given a great deal of publicity to that in your publications and your letters to employees and everything else, and I wanta comment here that the record doesn't show that to be true. The (pause) — there are some interesting (pause) items (pause) in your financial report, particularly in your statements. (Rather long pause) There is a particular sentence here under your heading of earnings: "Current sales volume and industry forecast for 1953, together with strong emphasis on cost reduction, point towards increased profits for 1953." (Michelsen: Amen) I'd like to point out that we have always bargained with you not solely on the basis of what you have done in the year just ended or the period just ended, but also based on the company's outlook for the subsequent period we're coming up to. The company itself introduced that kind of bargaining procedures long time back, and I find it difficult to agree with the company's approach to these problems these days in that one time you negotiate with us you don't wanta talk about what the rest of the industry does; the next time we find you making comparisons with the industry. One time you don't want to talk to us about what you did the last year, you wanta talk to us what the outlook is for the coming periods ahead; the next time we bargain you don't wanta talk about the coming periods ahead, you wanta talk about what you did before. I think you're fairly well convinced that the union doesn't p — isn't particularly happy about the fact that Atlas has planned such an extensive decentralization proposition here, and I think it should be understood that the union has no intention of <u>refraining</u> from <u>requesting very</u>

strongly that the company take on increased costs (pause), because we have no intention of paying for your decentralization program, which will in effect reduce the number of jobs in the metropolitan area. (Pause) We think that we are entitled, as the company has always said, to a fair share of what the company is doing. In the face of your own statements about the coming year of 1953 and its pro — its prospects, for which there is good evidence that if the continued rate of business shown for the first period of '53 continues, that Atlas is going to have the best year that it's ever had in its history, because if that period means anything and if we use that as a — an average for what can happen, your sales will probably wind up somewhere between 14 and 15 million dollars, if not higher. And that certainly bears out to me the reason comments are made that there certainly will be increased —

[Tape changed]

Michelsen: I have a couple of comments, George. (Pause) Number 1 — and Len can check me if I'm mistaken — made several references to cost of decentralization. Cost of decentralization is not being borne out of our operation — operating statements. That's being privately financed from, you might say, outside funds. The money that's being earned by Atlas as an operating entity up at 1122 is not financing the decentralization but private loans and — paid privately. The mention was made that stockholders, in addition to receiving dividends, also receive vacations if they happen to — those stockholders happen to be employees of the company, and it's quite true that the officers of our company are large stockholders in the company. And it's an advantage in many respects for everybody that the directors of the company and the principal stockholders are employees of the company, because I think you can be assured that they're quite interested in the progress and development of the company. And they did receive vacation pay, and they did receive dividends. They received / vacation —

Gambon: (Over Michelsen above) The major portion of the dividends went to a small group of stockholders (Michelsen: Yeah) who are also employees of the company. Isn't that true?

Michelsen: That — I think that's so. I don't have the / tabulation. The figures —

Gambon: (Over Michelsen above) Out of 4,488 stockholders you have — well, I don't — I can give you the exact number; you know 'em as well as I do, but they're only a small group of people. (Michelsen: Yeah) And I would say that they probably take almost 70 to 80% of the total amount of the dividends paid out because of the large shareholdings they have.

Loring: That's not right, / John.

Michelsen: (Over Loring above) That's not true, John. No.

Gambon: How much is it, Len?

Loring: It's in the neighborhood of 30% — 30 / to 35.

Gambon: (Over Loring above) 30% of the total?

Loring: 30 to (Michelsen: Yeah) 35% / total x.

Gambon: (Over Loring above) Well, that's one way of findin' out how much it was in total / xxx.

Michelsen: (Over Gambon above) Well, another way is to just ask.

Loring: (At same time as Michelsen above) Well, and that — that was — and that's everybody, John. That's the — that's the entire group.

Meyer: Well, don't this — this same stockholders — that small group — this 30% are also included in that sales dollar and the amount of wages?

Michelsen: Oh, definitely. (Gambon: Oh, yeah) They're a part of that. (Gambon: We —) The thing that I might — I wanted / to point out —

Gambon: (Over Michelsen above) We wanted to make that clear for George's benefit in his efforts to try to have us get together for an agreement. I mean, I didn't want the matter to stand as the s — these labor cost increases were supposedly all for union labor.

Michelsen: Oh, no.

Gambon: A very <u>appreciable</u> amount of it includes the non-union benefits.

Michelsen: Yeah, that — that's — that (pause) — let me just show you a few charts, to go back to that point. You're saying that — that this figure here, as it does, contains payments to all employees, that it contains payments to the president, the vice-presidents, and other people. It includes — contains bonus payments to those people, too. (Gambon: Uh-huh) And you'll notice that this chunk here has been getting larger. Now, there's no question about it, we have increased the benefits to our salaried employee. The one thing which is quite interesting and which I'd like you people to understand is that while this has been getting larger, the profit-sharing plan — while this rose in '52, profit-sharing plan to our executives — last year we paid to 114 people who participated in that plan $174,000.00; the year before we paid to 97 of them $223,000.00. In other words, we had a greater cost in — in the bonus plan in '51, we had a <u>lesser</u> cost in '52, but yet our sales dollar — the portion going to employees rose. Now, it didn't rise because we paid less bonus to these people. If anything, it should've come down if that had a great effect. But the important thing was that — that this — this portion of the sales dollar went up, because we are paying employees generally — and if you were to take out of that that chunk here — if you were to take out of this what we pay to our salary people and leave only the payments to hourly people, you'd see them rising! You have to see them rise when you see this (Gambon: Well, look —), because back in '50 we were paying $1.36 an hour average take-out; we're now paying $1.71. Well, you don't rise from $1.36 to $1.71 without having this rise. So that, while it's quite true, and I'm not saying that — that in this figure — this is total payments to all employees — there has been a rise. This is a trend which is reflected <u>definitely</u> in payments to hourly employees. / xx —

Gambon: (Over Michelsen above) Well, I'd like to comment on the figures you give out for your bonus earnings — for executive bonus earnings as they're listed here for 1950, '51, and '52. (Michelsen: Yeah) You paid out to 66 participants the total of $204,913.00. (Michelsen: Right) That averages out, on a yearly basis, at $1.55 per hour increase for each employee. (Michelsen: xx) That in itself — that total amount you paid out, measured in terms of increases for 1400 union employees, is 7¢ an hour. (Michelsen: Uh-huh) In 1951 ya paid out a total of $223,177.00 to 97 participants, which is an average of $2300.79 for each employee, into 97, or $1.15 per hour increase. As against that, that would be approximately an 8-cent-an-hour increase for the 1400 employees. In 1952 you paid out $174,882.00 to 114 participants, or an average of $1534.00 for each one, an increase of 76.7¢ per hour for them, which would average out to 6.2¢- per — cents-per-hour increase for 1400 employees. In 1953 for the first period, for 114 employees, I assume, you paid out $12,472.00, which averages out $109.40 each, or 54.7-cent-per-hour wage increase for the first period, which is equivalent to a $4\frac{1}{2}$-cent-an-hour increase for 1400 employees, and you've already given out that $109.40, or the 54.7-cent increase, and then come along and tell us that the best you can do for us is 4/10ths of a cent! (Michelsen: Yeah. Well — uh — John —) I suggest that you do a little more thinking about what the employees' fair share of this situation is.

Michelsen: Well, we've done plenty of thinking about that. You — you're discussing these payments to these people in the bonus plan. I can (slight pause) pull off the records — and I certainly couldn't do it here — what our payments have been to people who work on our incentive system. / They — they're —

Gambon: (Over Michelsen above) That's fine, but for the incentive system — the money you pay out in the incentive system is reflected in reduced costs (Michelsen: We think it —), and that's (Meyer: Does he consi —) production (Michelsen: Yeah) up, up, up. (Michelsen: Right. Well, one of the reasons —) And there is definitely 62¢ an hour that you get production on for which you pay no incentives whatsoever! Let's remember that, too.

Michelsen: John — and it's qui — also quite true that the reason that we have this executive bonus plan is that we feel that it's an incentive which adds to the company's profitability and its operation, and that's why we have that. We don't have a plan for these executives simply to distribute the company's profits because we don't know what to do with 'em; we have it because we feel that it's just as much an incentive for them to be working under this as it is for people in the plant. And, believe me, the take on the incentive system out in the plant is far in excess of anything that's been paid to these people. And I'm not questioning / its — its — it — the rightness or wrongness of it.

Gambon: (Over Michelsen above) Well, you — your (laughing slightly) people — your people may be doing a good job for the company. In fact, they are doin' a good job as evidenced by the way the policies are developing and what's happening in Atlas. But let's remember, I mean, that the people out in the plant are the people who, with their own sweat, are producing these profits, to a much greater extent, I think, than a small group of people who are receiving money and benefits from the total business of the company every year far in excess of (Michelsen: Well —) what each individual out in the plant is getting! The union employee, I'm talkin' about, and that's the only one I'm really concerned with here. (Michelsen: Well, there's no question about it —) Will you — will you show me a percentage — or an average of 54.7¢ an hour over and above a man's salary which you've given to 114 employees already (Michelsen: All right), and then you turn around to me and say, "I am willing to give you 4/10ths-of-a-cent-per-hour increased cost in the form of continuing the increased insurance cost" (Michelsen: Uh-huh), I can't see in any way, shape, or form where you're takin' a fair approach to what the employees'

fair share of the company's business for '52 is, or a fair share of
what we should expect to get during '53 in the face of a <u>very good</u>
<u>year</u> in <u>prospect</u>, by your own statements — responsible officials of
the company — the Board — chairman of the Board <u>and</u> the president
— the new president of (Michelsen: Uh-huh) Atlas (Michelsen:
They're statements you —) — their <u>public</u> statements. (Michelsen:
Sure! And we certainly hope that they're going to come true) And
then we sit here at the negotiating table with you and we listen to
your comments, your statements of factual information that you present here, which in themselves may be factual but they don't go far
enough to show the true picture of what's goin' on in Atlas.
(Michelsen: Well, th —) They don't reflect — and, anyway, to me
your charts be damned (Michelsen: Well —), that we are getting
our fair share of the over-all benefits that should come out of Atlas.

Michelsen: Well, John, the eternal question in the field of industrial relations is always going to be, I'm afraid — in fact, I hope it will always be, what is the fair share? When we get to the point where
somebody determines for us by legislation what the fair share is, I
— / I doubt xx that.

Gambon: (Over Michelsen above) Bill, I don't think you want, and I certainly know I'm not interested in havin' anybody legislate for me
what a fair share of the profits of this company or any other company is. I think that we have provisions now by law, for that matter,
if we can sit down across the bargaining table and negotiate these
matters out between the parties concerned. I'm willing to continue
on that basis.

Michelsen: All right. Well, then, what you're saying is that (Gambon:
I'm not xxx) your concept of a fair share and my concept are always
gonna / be different.

Gambon: (Over Michelsen above) Now, if you're talking about, perhaps,
the government passing a law where every company in the country
must guarantee an annual wage, maybe I'll buy it.

Michelsen: Yeah. Well, you've been reading the newspaper. So (Meyer
laughs) have I. Uh — the one point that / you made —

Gambon: (Over Michelsen above) I've been reading the newspapers
(Michelsen: Yeah), but I might comment at this time I remember
the now new president of Atlas Recording Machine Company quite a
number of years back telling me he was definitely in favor of an an —
an annual guaranteed wage. I am waiting for a proposal from Mr.
Harold Fuller showing me in a very concrete form his favorable approach to an an — annual guaranteed wage, and we'll begin to bargain
with you on that and remove the present demands.

Michelsen: Uh-huh. All right. Well, I'll so inform him. (Several smile
broadly and laugh quietly) This thing that you mention (pause) in
your statement here about this being a — a — perhaps not improper
but (Meyer: Subnormal) abnormal comparison to show this trend from
1941, let's assume that's a fact, because, while it's not — it's not
abnormal, there'll — there — this was — this was a low rate, and you
say that from '45 on is a better comparison. So let's strike out the
chart from here on back to '45, and you'll notice that in '45 our rates
jumped up and went up. But the point I'm tryin' to make is that here
where you have the — the Consumer Price Index line, you get a

terrific jump-up here, and it — even striking out those 3 or 4 years
which preceded it, you get a terrific — in fact, it's at this point that
the gap widens back here — / that the wage rates were so little.

Gambon: (Over Michelsen above) Yeah, but, Bill (Meyer: That's precisely —), on — on the basis of this sheet / that I read to you showin'
comparisons, didn't everybody do it?

Meyer: (Over Gambon above) Yeah, but you don't have it balanced beginning, Bill. You would have (Michelsen: Yeah) to pull that red
line down (Michelsen: Sure, yo —) about 16 squares, and (Gambon:
Uh —) it would still be a (Michelsen: That's —) — a little above the
cost- / of-livin' xxx.

Michelsen: (Over Meyer above) You — you would pull it down here, but
you would find here, Bernice, that it would / widen out. It would go
up quite a bit.

Meyer: (Over Michelsen above) It would still be a — it would still be
(pause) higher, I grant you it will, but (Michelsen: Sure) it won't be
high to the extent that ya / have it there.

Michelsen: (Over Meyer above) Well, John, the other things which I —
I just wanta reply to a couple more of these — these statements here
that — that you've gone back and you've made these comparisons back
to 1945 in wage rates, and I'm not questioning your figures at all.
They're / undoubtedly right. Uh — I don't want —

Gambon: (Over Michelsen above) They're authentic. I can guarantee
that because good many of 'em came from the files that I don't think
anybody can question.

Michelsen: I — I'm not questioning 'em. I'm saying that that comparison
back to 1945 can show those things. I can do the same thing and I can
show you that over that period of time a lot of the people who make
our business profitable or unprofitable — and I'm talking about our
competitors. I'm not — again I have to emphasize that, and that's why
I said, when I showed this profit figure for Lashley Equipment, I don't
necessarily submit this as a comparison. It was just interesting to see
the — your union people using it as a — as a — as a source of — of
information to convince the people who read their paper / that — uh —

Gambon: (Over Michelsen above) Well, keep that straight, that Hughes
was pointing up the position that our union has taken with the Lashley
Equipment Company (Michelsen: Yeah), and he is pointing up the
comparisons between industry generally and what he thinks that
Lashley should do to be even on a comparative basis with industry
generally. (Michelsen: Well —) Now, let's say this, that the comments that he was making were directed solely to Lashley. They
were not — those figures were not set up to develop a comparison
such as you were tryin' to make here.

Michelsen: Well, he used them that / way, though. He — he used those
to compare against the average.

Gambon: (Over Michelsen above) He used them because of the fact that
our union is definitely (Michelsen: Yeah) in negotiations with Lashley (Michelsen: But the point is he —), who have, by the way, offered
a 2% increase.

Michelsen: Yeah. I — I know about (Gambon: H'm) that. He used them
— not — not only the Lashley figure was used here, if you remember,
but he compared it with the electrical industry (Gambon: Uh-huh),

and the figure there is just about twice what ours was. The point I'm
making, in addition to the statement that you made that we have to understand that Lashley sales are much greater than ours, the ratio i —
may not be any greater. We're — we don't happen to have 250,000 employees, which is something in the order of what Lashley Equipment
Company have, so you divide that 250,000 into their sales and you keep
pretty much the same ratio, although the dollar billing for a great
many of their items, I have to certainly agree with you, is far greater
per unit than ours. But the — the other thing which — which I want to
make mention of is that I could go back to 1945 and I can show you
what Eureka has given over that period of time, what Mentor Associates has given, and I can in many cases show you totals which don't
come up to what we've given. / That's why I have —

Gambon: (Over Michelsen above) You can show us Old Reliable, ya can
   show (Michelsen: Yes) us Master Craft, / too, if — (voice dies out).
Michelsen: (Over Gambon above) Right! Sure! I can show them. But,
   for that reason, I have attempted here to get away from that and show
   you just what the industry is — average is (Gambon: Well, let me —
   let me —), and it's $1.54 now as compared with our $1.71, or a 35-
   cent change / over that period of time.
Gambon: (Over Michelsen above) But just one — just one comment. You
   mentioned many, many times Solar Sound as a (Michelsen: Yes) terrific competitor, and on your own chart, taking a limited 2-year period,
   you show that Atlas got 20¢ (Michelsen: Sure) and Solar Sound got 19!
Michelsen: And there was — very definitely (Gambon: All right. Well,
   some ti —) you told 'em you were gonna help 'em catch up.
Gambon: Huh? (Laughs slightly) Well, / there be — there's some evidence there, isn't there? Huh?
Michelsen: (Over Gambon above) From a very low point they — that 19¢
   (Gambon: Yeah) was put on top of a base rate of (Gambon: x) something like 7 — 75¢ / an hour.
Gambon: (Over Michelsen above) There's some evidence that our union
   is trying to do something about those competitive situations.
Michelsen: Well, John, that's (Gambon: Uh-huh) — that's your mission
   in life. I don't (Gambon: Uh-huh) wanta urge you to do it. / Uh —
Meyer: (Over Michelsen above) Yes, but, Bill, ya must remember that
   these wage increases that went to a lot of these places, they have a
   non-incentive system. Their production has remained the same for
   that increased — used the figure of 20¢, I think you had in there —
   where in our 20-cent increase, that went into the payroll add, and you
   have gotten increased production over and above that that you saved
   that 20¢ on. Those other people don't do that.
Michelsen: Bernice, that's an observation on your part. I — I'm not
   questioning what you said. I visited the Solar Sound plant — not recently. No one'll ever convince me that those people were producing
   any less than the people were producing in our plant. And when I observed 'em when they were in Canfield they were being very closely
   supervised, and they were workin' like hell, frankly. The same is
   true in a great many of these other plants. True, Solar Sound's
   (Gambon: Well —) does not have an incentive system / xxxxx.
Meyer: (Over Michelsen above) Neither does Master Craft; neither
   does x.

Gambon: (At same time as Meyer above) You don't mind if I disagree with you. I've been (Michelsen: Sure) all through the Solar Sound (Michelsen: I haven't been there recently) plant. I never see anybody breakin' their back in that plant. (Michelsen: Well, I don't see any —) And I wouldn't agree with (Michelsen: I didn't see anyone breaking their back) you if you're tryin' to imply that they're workin' at a faster pace than we do at Atlas.

Michelsen: I would also disagree with you — and this — we're getting a little bit into a fuzzy area (Gambon: Uh-huh) — that our profits are being provided by the sweat of our employees. That's a — that's a descriptive term, but highly inaccurate (Meyer: Not with Ted Shrout in there x) in terms of our operations at the present time. Well, the other thing that I wanted to — to make point of in terms of these trends, Atlas — and I — this is not intended as a trite statement — Atlas isn't in business to follow any wage patterns. Our business is to produce recorders. We're in business to produce a useful product at a price that people will buy it and at a quality at which they'll accept it. And we're in business to get as many customers as we can. (Gambon: Without considering what's your employees' fair share?) Now, along with that we're tryin' to do — we are trying to do as good a job for our employees as we feel that we can do, and we think there is plenty of evidence to support that, and we intend that we will continue to do that. / If you feel —

Gambon: (Over Michelsen above) Does the new president of the company still continue under the policy that Atlas will stay with the leaders in the industry and if necessary even go ahead of them?

Michelsen: I don't know the answer to that, / John. I haven't asked him that question.

Gambon: (Over Michelsen above) Well, I mean, it's interesting to find out whether or not policy in that particular point has changed the way everything else has been changing.

Michelsen: Now, you say this — one other thing you say / here —

Gambon: (Over Michelsen above) We have yet to wait — or we have yet to find ourselves in the very desirable position of having the company come to the union when it was doin' good, which it has been for several years past now, and say, "We're not waiting for you to do anything about demanding wage increases. Here's something that we think you should have." And that was said directly to the union's committee some few years back when the company was in a bad position, "You won't have to wait. When we're doin' good, we'll come to you!"

Michelsen: Well, John, suppose / somebody came to you and said that, would you take it?

Gambon: (Over Michelsen above) I ha — I hate to keep bringin' that up all the time, but I'm an optimistic soul and I hope some day that Hal will do exactly that. And I think now is a very appropriate time for him to do something like that, particularly in view of the fact that ya've had a good year in '52 / and excellent prospects for 1953.

Michelsen: (Over Gambon above) Well, he's — can't do it now. You've already asked for somethin', so he couldn't take the initiative. (Meyer laughs)

Mediator: Let me — let me at this time suggest that we recess for lunch, and we'll resume in joint negotiations about 1:30. (Slight pause)

Michelsen: O.K.
[The meeting recesses at 12:05 P.M.

After lunch the management group returns to its caucus room, and
Mediator spends a few minutes with them there before leading them back
at 1:50 P.M. to rejoin the union group. As the joint meeting gets under
way once again, there is a considerable period of light informal talking.
Several, particularly Meyer, joke about Michelsen's charts, voicing
doubts about the statistician who helped prepare them. Michelsen participates in this, remarking at one point, "These aren't statistics; these
are facts." Gambon starts to tell a story and then suddenly reneges,
amid much laughter, upon remembering the recorder. Observer offers
to turn the machine off. As it goes back on, there is much laughing and
talking, Gambon closing the incident with "I was gonna say 'bull,' ya
know." Michelsen again makes reference to the charts, including, "Well,
that's why I brought along all the collaborating data."]

Mediator: Before lunch, before we recessed (pause), I think you had just
    concluded a point, or you — both of you were still speaking on the po-
    sitions of the industry — the comparable positions, so, if you wish, you
    can take — pick it up at that point.
Gambon: Well, I — I think Bill has concluded his further statements that
    he made after I commented on his presentation. Uh (Michelsen: Well,
    the only thing that I was gonna do was to xxx —) — I have a couple
    more comments to make that I — that I wanted to make on the come-
    up — company's financial position (rather long pause) — point up,
    'course, that the company's working capital has increased by almost
    a million dollars over '51. (Pause)
? : Yes.
Gambon: And I'd also like to —
Michelsen: Primarily by the issuance of stock.
Gambon: I'm talking about — not the issuance of stock. That's reflected
    later on in your report, to show the increase investment for the stock-
    holders to about a million and 300 thousand-odd dollars. I'm talking
    (Michelsen: Uh-huh) about the figures that show a million dollars'
    increase in working capital in your net current assets without that /
    sale of stock.
Loring: (Over Gambon above) Well, that resulted from the sale of stock,
    John. We sold 250 shares of stock at $5.00 a share. That cash came
    in. (Michelsen: The net was about a million, wasn't it?) It — it —
    it increased the working capital.
Gambon: Well, it doesn't show it th — here (Michelsen: No), Len. It
    shows it in the net worth of the company. Now, if you wanta talk about
    (Loring: Well, I mean, i — it's in both places, John, see) — well, if you
    wanta talk about that, Len, then you have to go back to December 31st,
    1951, to look at $1,549,000.00 as your net current assets (Loring:
    Uh-huh) and then go down and look at your total working capital and
    assets, including the share of stocks, which goes to 4,644,000.00,
    which is more than a million dollars, too.
Loring: John, when your working capital increased like that, that is also
    reflected in your net worth — your — your capital outstanding. Other
    words, it's a balancing proposition there.
Gambon: Uh — the point that I wanted to make this morning — I mean,
    based on the first period of 1953, would reflect, if that continues, very

close to 15 million dollars in sales and almost $2\frac{1}{2}$ million dollars in profit before taxes. (Pause) Now, based on your — your report here and the comments from both the new president of Atlas and the chairman of Board of Directors, think everybody has every reason to believe that that's going to pretty much come true. (Slight pause)

Loring: Hope so. (Laughs)

Gambon: Uh — so do we, Len, and we (Loring laughs again) — again I make the statement that I usually make, we're extremely confident that the company will make it come true because of the way they're operating these days (pause), with the emphasis placed on reduced cost and things of that kind — decentralization, and so forth, getting away from lost items and that kind of business. Uh — the interesting thing to note is that your last 3 periods of 1952, the 8th, 9th, and 10th (pause), was pretty close to about 40%, p — plus or minus either way, I suppose, of your total sales for '52.

Michelsen: And if they hadn't been, we'd been in a hell of a sit — fix.

Gambon: Well, that's despite the fa (laughing) — despite the fact that you might have been, you didn't get into a fix, Bill. And, frankly, if I recall correctly, you were looking forward to that kind of a 2d half of 1952. And now we're looking forward, again, to (Michelsen: We're always looking forward to better [pause] year, John) a good year in '53. I mean, it's not just the company predicting a good year. The whole industry — the industry reports — N. E. M. A. reports indicate a very good year for the whole industry because of many things which you point out — some of which you point out, as the general increase in activity in the home recording field and so forth, which would create a higher market — not a market, but aroused activity means the sale of more recorders, which we expect to continue to produce. What is it? — 60% (pause) of the industry's demands?

Michelsen: 40.

Gambon: 40%.

Michelsen: We — we would love to be able to do that much.

Gambon: Uh-huh. What, 60?

Michelsen: 40.

Gambon: You would love to be able to do 40? Well, don't you do that much now?

Michelsen: I don't know the latest figures. I think that the business in the recorders with amplifier units — and Bob may — / well, he may know better. We're about xxx.

Loring: (Over Michelsen above) We're in the — in the low 30's on that. We made some very special studies last year, and we find that it's around 32, 33%, as best we figure, which, of course, is a pretty difficult thing to do.

Michelsen: Business in that particular product, as I gather, is pretty well split between Old Reliable and Eureka and ourselves, with some other companies doing the smaller — very small percentage of it, but most of it between those 3 companies.

Gambon: Well, the (pause) important thing to note is that you had that 14% increase in sales in the 2d half of '52, and accordin' to some news re — paper reports that I read back in February you — first report for '53 showed about a 20% increase in sales over the same period for '52. So the trend is definitely on the upward move. (Michelsen: Yes. That does not necessarily —) Which gets us back to the proposition that we

wanta discuss and carry on negotiations the same as we always have
on the company's ability to pay. And, in answer to your present offer,
we — it does not reflect your ability to pay, by / any means.

Michelsen: (Over Gambon above) Well, I — John, let me just make a
point here in reply to what you were saying there. (Pause) Let me
just use this as an example. In the chart which very definitely indicates that increased sales do not <u>necessarily</u> provide increased profits — we certainly <u>hope</u> that increased sales <u>do</u> provide increased
profit — that your cost increase as your sales increase — the net effect is that you're handling more units and you're handling more paper
work in terms of handling customers' orders, but you're not necessarily making any more money. Now, as evidence of that, look at 1952
as compared with 1950. '52 we did 7% more sales than we did in 1950.
Here we did only 11,085,000, where here we did 11,986,000. And yet,
with this 7% increase in sales — fine, it's a better sales picture than
'52, yet our profits before taxes are 56% less! Now, how you figure it
out? The only way you figure it out is that the cost to produce that
much goods in '52 is greater, and the reasons it's greater, we're paying more to our people who are producing these things, we're paying
more for materials, we're paying more for services. In other words,
we've got a fixed price structure as far as our customers are concerned, but we've got a rising cost picture as far as what we buy!
And we buy human energy, we buy wire, we buy ceramic products, we
buy advertising time, we buy sales. Those things are rising, so that
here you see your — your picture. So let's assume sales go up. Fine.
We hope they're gonna go up and profits are gonna go up with 'em, but
it's (Gambon starts to speak) not necessarily a fact. And this is
stark evidence of the fact (Meyer: Yes, but —) (Gambon: But speaking
—) (Meyer: Wait a minute) that rising sales here does not produce
rising profits.

Meyer: No, wait a minute. In there — in 1950 you have that 2 million
dollar profit. (Michelsen: Yeah) In 1952 you have 1 million dollar
profit. Also in the year 1952 you had expenses that you did not have
in 1950 that were not all labor cost. (Gambon: H'm) (Michelsen: Oh,
I — I x I said that, Bernice) You have increased the assets of the
company by other things that the total worth of the company is much
higher than that profit figure leads ya to believe, because you have the
land in Aiken, you've got / the plant in Aiken.

Michelsen: (Over Meyer above) I'm talking just — I'm talking just about
/ the relationship of sales to profit.

Meyer: (Over Michelsen above) Yes, but, Bill — yeah, but, Bill, I could
do the same thing. I could make (Gambon: H'm) $5000 in 1952 and
say at the end of 1952 I only had $50 in the bank, but I bought a house
for $4500 that I can live in the rest of my life. / So, I mean, that —
those figures — those figures don't show <u>anything</u>.

Michelsen: (Over Meyer above) Right. That's true. You're s — you're
making some capital expenditure. But you'll y — yeah. But the point
is this, and I think the records will show it, that in 1951 and in 1952
— or, in '51 and '50, our appropriations for capital goods were greater
than they were in 1952. Now, I'm not sure of that. I <u>am</u> sure of / 1950.

Loring: (Over Michelsen above) Well, actually, the — the point is, anything you spend for capital — plant, or like that — doesn't affect the

figures that we show here, Bernice. I mean (Meyer: What d'ya
mean? The —), that's capital. It's — it's a ch — change of —
[Tape changed]
Gambon: ... $8,344.00, a couple of hundred dollars less in sales, but you
    show profit before taxes of $240,975.00 before taxes. Now, that is
    about — well, roughly almost $25,000.00 increased profit on practically
    the same amount of business that you did in — in '48. So (Michelsen:
    That's right) comparisons can be made on your chart, and I can take
    your own figures and make comparisons, too. (Michelsen: Yeah, ex-
    cept that you —) It depends on whether I wanta point up a nice bright
    picture, or you wanta point up a very dull one.
Michelsen: Well, the point is that you may there have an expense not oc-
    curring in that period which may / be picked up in the next.
Gambon: (Over Michelsen above) Well, isn't that true of your figures
    there?
Michelsen: Yeah, but your — your — your annual — your statements of
    operation are based on one year's operations. Now, there are fluctu-
    ations within that year. Everything that we use in the 10th period isn't
    billed to us by our suppliers in that period. You may get it in the fol-
    lowing period when sales may be down. And you get that kind of a
    fluctuation. But usually those kinds of fluctuations are not carried
    from one year to another. They're — you make interim adjustments
    of that kind from year to year (pause) — from month to month, I
    mean.
Meyer: Well, if you increased your labor costs, wouldn't that cut down
    on your excess profit tax, though?
Michelsen: Probably.
Gambon: I'd like to ask you a question here that's not clear to me in this
    report. You mentioned among your other assets an investment in a
    wholly-owned British subsidiary.
Michelsen: Yeah.
Gambon: Is that wholly owned by Atlas?
Loring: Atlas, John.
Gambon: Now, as an asset you list there $8,348.00. Yet over under one
    of your notes you stated the net worth of that company is 44,791.00.
Loring: We do that because that is in blocked currency, John. We
    couldn't take that out of England if we wanted to. There's no free
    exchange / with —
Gambon: (Over Loring above) Yet it's wholly owned by the company.
Loring: Right.
Meyer: Well, you'd have to (Gambon: H'm) go to England to live up the
    money, is that the idea, / if you liquidate it?
Loring: (Over Meyer above) Well, that's (Several, including Meyer,
    laugh) — right now I guess you'd have to, Bernice. We hope some
    day you can get it back, but —
Gambon: Well, you got $22,119.00 out of it (Loring: That's right. Uh-
    huh) in dividends last year, anyway, didn't ya? / xxxxx.
Michelsen: (Over Gambon above) That's a wholly-owned subsidiary, and
    it has been for some years, / John.
Gambon: (Over Michelsen above) I understand that. But I was just point-
    ing up the fact that the company is worth s — some 44,791.00, yet you
    only list an asset of 8,300.00 (Michelsen: Yeah), and — although you

do reflect that you got 22,119.00 in dividends from that company, which has been continuing for some years (Michelsen: Uh-huh), variations in the number and amount of dividends you get.

Loring: Well, John, that's the first dividend we've got in over 10 years. We couldn't take it out before, but this year they let us take that much (Gambon: Uh-huh) out.

Gambon: Well, that's continuing, / will it not?

Loring: (Over Gambon above) Our employees — no, no. (Meyer: Just —) No, that was just the / one —

Gambon: (Over Loring above) Just this year?

Loring: Just that — just (Gambon: Won't get it in '53?) last year. It ex — it expired at — the permit ex — expired December 31.

Gambon: Well, I mean, you — you will not get it in '53, / or is it continuing?

Loring: (Over Gambon above) I doubt it. That we don't know. Something / x might come up.

Gambon: (Over Loring above) Well, it's a doubtful amount of income, is that right?

Loring: The reason we only show the 8 thousand is that is what it cost us originally in U. S. funds. We can't even get that out in U. S. funds now. It's blocked. It's — it's — it's in / xxx.

Gambon: (Over Loring above) I'll give 10 thousand for 22 thousand back any day. (Rather long pause) Well, George, I don't know where we are in your opinion at this moment, but seems to me we have reached the point where the union can reasonably request the company to do a little recessing and to begin approaching this table with an idea of tryin' to reach a reasonable settlement with the union, considering the fact that we don't think they have any realistic position at this time and considering the fact that we don't expect that they're gonna come back and hand us the full scope of the union's demands. I think that ra — the only reason we've been commenting on this financial statement a'tall is to — to bring out the fact that we're (laughing slightly) not unaware of certain things, despite charts and everything else, some of those things bein' that the increased worth of the company continually is on the way upward and has been for several years; that the company's position financially is much more sound than — than it has been a long while; their outlook for '53 is brighter than it has been for a long, long time; and we have every right to believe that the company can and should make a substantial wage increase — a local substantial wage increase at this particular time.

Mediator: I understa — go ahead.

Michelsen: Well, John, the fact that the company's net worth increases does not necessarily mean that it's in a better position financially, and by that I mean that the company's net worth increases darn near every time that we add people to the company in jobs, because we have to provide them with equipment on which they work and usually that's capital equipment and it gets to be a part of our net / worth. So as the company —

Gambon: (Over Michelsen above) More equipment, more production (Michelsen: So as the —), more profits, more dividends (pause), / more wages.

Michelsen: (Over Gambon above) But as the company gets larger — all

right. As the company gets larger, necessarily it — it — it has more
equipment, its capitalization gets up because you purchase more equipment. Now, I tried to — to make a point — and I'm not gonna show the
chart again — that it is possible (pause) to have higher sales, as we
showed between '51 and '5 — or, between '50 and '52, where our sales
were up about 7%, and yet we have profits down, only because in '52
with those higher sales we had much higher cost of operation. Now,
the other thing I wanted to mention was that to say that — that — that
the employees have not gotten a fair — a fair shake — a fair return
on their efforts is — is making a statement in the face of these facts
/ here. In terms of the industry —

Gambon: (Over Michelsen above) Now, just a moment. I mean, don't
put words in my mouth. I didn't say they hadn't gotten a fair shake!
I said that we expect a fair share of what's being done in Atlas. And
we're talking in terms of what's been done in '52 and the outlook for
'53, which is no more of a different approach than we've ever used
(Michelsen: Uh —) in all — all our bargaining with you. (Michelsen:
All right. Now —) You're tryin' to confine the discussions here to
comparisons that you come up with on charts, which doesn't reflect
the true situation in Atlas as far as this union is concerned. (Michelsen: Well, it reflects —) We've always said to you we're not interested in what Standard Products does or Viking does if they do less
than we do, but certainly we expect ya to keep up with what's going on
in the area as well as the industry. I've given you some area comparisons, the same companies that you used on me here — or, on the
committee here — for 2 years. I've gone back to 1946 in order to get
a much clearer picture of this situation.

Michelsen: Yeah. Well, John, you could back into those — back into '45
and '46 and you can make comparisons. I wouldn't question the fact
that it might be possible for me, or for you, to go back to the time the
company started and to show comparisons which were favorable or
unfavorable to either party. I think that — I think that's possible.
The important thing, as I see it, is here you can see what the — has
happened to the industry, based on this fact: they have moved up since
(pause) 1950 an increase of 25¢; Atlas's gone up 35¢, or 25.7 in advance of the industry! Now, to me that — that's significant, the fact
that — that we're just not keeping up with the parade; we're 25.7%
ahead of it and have gone a — ahead of it in — that much in that period
of time (Meyer: Our productivity has increased) — or we've gone
the difference (Gambon: Uh —) between 19.4 and 25.7, / or 6%.

Meyer: (Over Michelsen above) Bill, our productivity has increased to
reflect that. Because you have a lower number of people working
here right / now than you did in 19 —

Michelsen: (Over Meyer above) Yeah, but you can't say that it hasn't
increased in these other companies, Bernice.

Meyer: No, because of — we're more — we're more incentive than they
are, and you know it, and rated / within the industry.

Michelsen: (Over Meyer above) Some com — I know some companies
that don't have an incentive system where the rate of productivity is
higher, and I — if — if I could take you, I'd take you to Monarch Engineering in — in Trenton — M. P. S. — / and see people producing on
base rates.

Meyer: (Over Michelsen above) Yeah, but Monarch — yeah, but Monarch
Engineering's — Monarch Engineering's rates will be pretty darn
close to ours.

Michelsen: That's right. But their take-out (Meyer: Uh-huh) won't be.

Meyer: No, / but —

Michelsen: (Over Meyer above) But the — the / imp — the thing I'm tryin'—

Meyer: (Over Michelsen above) Maybe not, but for every — every hour
of take-out, don't forget you're — you don't have the overhead or anything else. And I bet that their production doesn't / equal ours.

Michelsen: (Over Meyer above) You don't have the overhead, period. /
That's the only thing that you gain.

Meyer: (Over Michelsen above) And you don't have the 62¢, either. You
don't pay it.

Michelsen: But here — here you have this comparison of — of us going
ahead of the industry by about 11%. Now, to me that — that is (pause)
/ — seems to point out that we've done very well.

Gambon: (Over Michelsen above) I — look — Bill, I wouldn't particularly
care right now whether we were 50¢ ahead of the industry. (Michelsen:
Oh, well, I do, even — even with those people) I'm still saying to you
that on the basis of what kind of business you're doing in the year and
the outlook for the coming year we shall continue to expect you to negotiate with us on the basis of your ability to pay. (Michelsen: Well,
we're not negotiating on the ability to pay, John) And you have not
said all during this discussion, or during the first meeting, that you
do not have the ability to pay. Your cry, as I interpret it here, is that
you don't wanta pay out any increased (Michelsen: Uh) benefits to the
workers in the plant. You wanta retain as much as ya can in order to
develop this program that ya have, which includes, among other things,
decentralization. (Michelsen: Uh) Now, we're not gonna buy that kind
of a package, my friend. We expect to share in the increased benefits
that are going to be coming up durin' the year. We don't intend to sit
by, for instance, and take 4¢ of a — 4/10ths of a cent as your offer to
us and see, on the other hand, that you've already paid out an average
to us of 4½¢ an hour to a small group of people (pause) (Michelsen:
Well, we've —) — 54.7¢ an hour to 114 people, and (Michelsen: John
—) you have the gall to offer us 4/10ths of a cent increased cost!
[The recorder is temporarily turned off for mechanical reasons.
Exchange in the intervening period is confined to Michelsen and
Gambon.]
... that you can prove to me satisfactorily that every one of the people
that share in your profit-sharing plan is efficient.

Michelsen: Well, I'm not sure that I would care to, or want to, at this
point. The other thing is this, that in terms of — of the (pause) — I'm
not arguing this thing on a technical point of our / ability or inability
to pay.

Gambon: (Over Michelsen above) Neither am I. I mean, there's nothin'
technical about the company's ability to pay.

Michelsen: I'm saying that in the face of what I have presented here, in
the face of the way the company views the — the operations of the company at this point, in the face of what we have done for the employees,
we do not feel that we should add any additional costs.

Gambon: Why? (Michelsen: Well, how come you —) Why?

Michelsen: Because we feel that our — our costs for — we've done enough
for the employees at this point and that we need to make a little more
profit so that it can be diverted into areas that are gonna do the company some good in terms of research, development, better capital position that's goin' to attract (Gambon: And more profits) more capital
investment into the / company.

Gambon: (Over Michelsen above) More profits, as you said to us in your
letter to all the employees regarding decentralization. More profits.
Now, if you continue to make more and more profits, do you expect to
do anything more? Yo — you're telling us now, "We've done enough for
you." (Michelsen: That's a problem —) You're — keep — keep in
mind, my friend, that you sat down here in this very room and worked
out an agreement with us in March — the deadline around March 31st
of 1952, and in that agreement you agreed, in addition to what the settlement was at that time, to wage reopeners. (Michelsen: Yeah) Your
position ever since that time has been that you don't wanta do anything
under these wage reopeners, and your attitude to me expresses a desire on the part of the company to forget that there is any such thing
(Michelsen: Oh, no. No) as a wage reopener, despite your ability to
pay, and to forget about anything more in form of benefits to the employees until the expiration of the contract. In the meantime, you will
expand your facilities, you'll buy new equipment, you'll buy other
plants, you'll decentralize on us and everything else, and we're supposed to sit here and watch you do it. Now (Michelsen: Uh —), go
ahead and expand, Bill — fine. And we'll go along, and we hope ya
prosper. But we wanta go along, too. We're not gonna sit (Michelsen:
Uh) back and let ya use money that could be beneficial to us to expand
and, in fact, in lots of cases reduce the number of jobs that are gonna
be available in this area.

Michelsen: Well, I've tried to show you, John, how you've been going
along in terms of your — the / increases —

Gambon: (Over Michelsen above) Well, don't ask us to put the brakes on
now.

Michelsen: — in terms of the statement which was in the SPOTLIGHT,
which was — said that the 24¢ which the electronic industry has
gained since 1950, / which included —

Gambon: (Over Michelsen above) Are you bargainin' with Al Hughes or
with John Gambon? (Meyer laughs)

Michelsen: No, I'm using (Gambon: But I —) a fact. Uh —

Gambon: Well, I'm — I'm talkin' about facts. (Michelsen starts to say
something) You bargaining with Al Hughes or John Gambon?

Michelsen: I'm bargaining with Local 89.

Gambon: I don't care whether Al Hughes goes to Lashley and accepts 2%
wage increase. If that's acceptable to Al Hughes, that's fine.

Michelsen: I'm not — I'm not discussing Lashley Equipment Company.
I'm saying that Hughes's statement in which he said — and he was
quite right, because he was quoting these facts from the Bureau of
Labor Statistics — / that the electronic —

Gambon: (Over Michelsen above) Well, let me ask ya a question at this
point. If we were to pull the brakes on, will you guarantee that the
average of $1.71 that ya quoted around here will continue?

Michelsen: I won't guarantee any average, / John.

Gambon: (Over Michelsen above) Well, then, why x the — the air about a thing like that? We get $1.71; will you guarantee it?

Michelsen: No, I won't guarantee it! I won't guarantee that that / average of $1.54 will stay.

Gambon: (Over Michelsen above) Well, you're tellin' us how much you've done. Well, look. You've told us how much you've done for us up to this point. "You're now getting $1.71 against the industry's figure of" — what? (Michelsen: O. K.) — "$1.54½."

Michelsen: All right.

Meyer: 1952 that was then.

Gambon: Was that — in 1952, and you're sayin', "Well, we think you guys oughta stop right here because you're ahead of the industry, and you oughta (Michelsen: Uh) stop right here and let us go ahead and do what we wanta do with this pro— this increased (Michelsen: No, I didn't say that you should stop you —) profits and all we'll make." But will ya guarantee the $1.71?

Michelsen: All right, I'll answer both of those questions. I didn't say that — that — that we had gone ahead of the industry in that way. We were <u>ahead</u> of the industry back in 1950.

Gambon: Well, I thought, according to your remarks, that you had showed that it had increased from '50 to '51 and from '51 to (Michelsen: All right) '52 (Michelsen: Uh —), from 7 to 9 to 17, didn't ya?

Michelsen: That's right. I (Gambon: All right, then) showed that — that — I showed that back at that time we were 5.4% ahead of the industry. (Gambon: Uh-huh) We have not only maintained that differential, but the gap has widened to the point now where we're 11 / %.

Gambon: (Over Michelsen above) All right. If this is gonna mean anything to us, will you guarantee the $1.71? (Michelsen: No, I won't guarantee $1.71) You were asking (Meyer: Why?) us to s — look, you were saying —

Meyer: Why, Bi — Bill?

Michelsen: The $1.71 is based on the rates of pay and the effort which is performed by the employee working, because this includes incentive earnings.

Meyer: Go a little bit further, Bill; tell the truth. (Gambon laughs quietly) Why don't you (slight pause) guarantee the $1.71?

Michelsen: I don't think we can ever afford to guarantee (Saunders: Not payin' it!) anything for the future, Bernice.

Meyer: (Laughs) Why? Because it / xxxxx?

Saunders: (Over Meyer above) You're not payin' it! Not to the Local, you're not payin' $1.71. You <u>know</u> it!

Meyer: And you won't pay it in 1953, / either.

Michelsen: (Over Meyer above) In — in take-out, that's what it is.

Saunders: Not (Meyer: You do not) in Local 89!

Meyer: No, you won't.

Michelsen: (At same time as Meyer above) Well, the only thing I can do is show you the rates / xx.

Gambon: (Over Michelsen above) Well, I suppose one of the reasons that Bill would find it difficult to guarantee $1.71 is because a great number of the jobs that were in the higher wage base have already disappeared (Meyer: And —) and <u>will</u> disappear (Meyer: They will disappear at the end of the year) when the — the (Michelsen: Did

they?) profit's up. (Michelsen: Did they?) So that eventually, if the
program continues, we'll have some difficulty in (Michelsen says something) finding ourselves with any jobs above Grade A. So your $1.71
means nothing to us.

Michelsen: Well, John, what happens to the fluctuation of the rate depends
on a lot of things. The only thing that — that we can guarantee is that
we're gonna s — try to stay in business and try and satisfy our customers. / They're the people who, in effect, guarantee our rates of pay.

Gambon: (Over Michelsen above) Fine. But don't just satisfy your customers and don't just satisfy your stockholders at our expense, see.
(? : I think you —) Because your position has generally been, throughout the years, that, "We'll always do something for our employees
when we have good years, and we've"— even went to the extent, as I
mentioned this morning, of saying, "One of these days, when we have
a good year, you won't have to come to us; we'll come to you." We're
still waiting for that happy day. But you — we know you've had a good
year in '52, and we know you've got even a better year coming up in
'53. We have every right to expect that because you're looking forward to it, you're planning on it. (Michelsen: Right. Well —) You're
selling stock on that basis.

Meyer: And your over-all labor cost will go down, Bill. You've taken
al — everything above B out of the plant so far.

Gambon: You've taken an average earning figure of — what is it? —
$1.60-some-cents, plus or minus, down in power transformers that
we had, and ya take it down to Aiken, South Carolina, and you pay a
dollar? (Slight pause) Oo! (Pause) Don't — so don't tell us how
bad off ya are, Bill, because the same thing will happen in regard to
choke coils, which you've told us no matter what we say or do or suggest it won't have any bearing on the fact that the company definitely
is gonna move those products.

Michelsen: Uh-huh. (Meyer: And they're all skilled labor) That's right.
But they're not moved yet.

Gambon: Huh?

Michelsen: They're not moved yet.

Gambon: They're not moved yet, but what does Mr. Chatham say?

Michelsen: He says it's planned to move — there are plans to move.

Gambon: Definitely. Well (Michelsen: Yeah), what did you tell us?
And what did (Michelsen: Same thing) your attorney tell us? "No
matter what ya say or do or suggest, definitely it's gonna move. The
(Michelsen: Right) union can't do anything about it."

Meyer: And your D labor grade, and multiple-machine winders will be
another one. Your trap coils — well, they're (Michelsen: Uh-huh)
not too good; I wouldn't even mention them in — / (laughs). They're
(laughing) xxxxx. (One or 2 others laugh)

Gambon: (Over Meyer above) Incidentally, ya must have been a little
bit worried about the union's unfair labor charge. (Meyer: Even outside you couldn't pay any lower than that) (Pause) Pointed up in your
financial report for the benefit of the stockholders that we had withdrawn it.

Michelsen: It's not a question of our being worried about it; it's a
question of our giving them a factual statement of / what happened.

Gambon: (Over Michelsen above) Well, you should've told 'em, if you

wanta be factual, that the union (laughing slightly) reserves the right
to file another one soon as we get enough on it to do it.

Michelsen: The law guarantees you that (Gambon laughs) right, John.
We (Gambon: I know that) don't quote the law in these reports, but
we do try to keep our stockholders advised. (Pause) Well, George,
that's all I have at the moment.

Mediator: Somewhere along the line I heard it mentioned that — in your
early statement, that the uni — the company had made an offer to you.
You said it was a small offer, but I heard nothing about it. I did not
hear it described.

Gambon: Well, as I understand it, George, the company said to us on
March 12th in the first meeting (pause), "Since October of 1952 we
have been paying a insurance premium of $6.60 per employee per
month to cover your insurance and health benefits for the employees
and their dependents, and the contract calls for only the expenditure
of $6.00 on the part of the company. It — we estimate that cost to be
4/10ths ¢ per hour to the company."

Mediator: The difference of a 50¢.

Gambon: It's 60¢.

Mediator: 6 — or, 70¢.

Michelsen: (In fairly low voice) Figures / close to 60¢ x.

Gambon: (Over Michelsen above) Uh — "We will continue to pay — we
will continue to absorb that additional cost." In answer to my question
as to whether s — Bill was offering us 4/10ths-of-a-cent-per-hour
wage increase if we didn't elect to take the increased benefits which
might be reflected by the additional 60¢, he said definitely no; it was
only in one form. They would continue to pay the $6.60, despite the
fact that the contract only provides for a $6.00 expenditure. Now,
that's the extent of the offer as I understand it. It's limited to the
in — increased premium on insurance.

Michelsen: (In low tone) That's right.

Denk: Well, what was that based on? How many m — how much people
was that based on, Bill?

Meyer: (Says something but cannot be understood)

Michelsen: (Over Meyer above) Based on our experience of the last
year, which is the way our premiums are determined.

Denk: Well, I mean, since that time there are — amount of people has
dropped, though, hasn't it?

Michelsen: The unit cost has not dropped. That has no effect on — the
premium under the group insurance plan is based on your experience
under each one of the coverages, and each year the insurance companies figure your — your — your experience against each one of
those, your life insurance, your hospitalization, your sickness and
accident, your surgical, and they adjust your premium based on your
experience. Our experience has been bad. The cost per person is
adjusted so that now, paying for each one of those coverages and adding them up, it comes to about 6 dollars and 60-some ¢ per person.
(Gambon: Well, what does —) Has nothing to do with the total cost to
the company in terms of how many thousands of dollars it costs. Certainly it's gonna cost us less in terms of the total mondey — money
expended if we have 500 people where last year we had 1,000 people.
But the unit cost has no relation at all to the total cost. The unit cost
has gone up, because we've had bad experience.

Gambon: Do you take into consideration in fixing that $6.60 cost the fact that you have dividends?

Michelsen: We had no dividends.

Gambon: You didn't have any?

Michelsen: No.

Gambon: Uh-huh. (Slight pause) Well, it's strange to me that in October during the negotiations under the October 1st — the '52 negotiation you made no mention of the decentralization plan until after the negotiations were out of the way. At that time you talked about your bad first half of '52 and you admitted that you expected to have a better 2d half. But you had the union in a position where we were tryin' to give fair consideration to your financial picture, and we wound up with a sum of money which I assure you, and I think you know, would not have been the settlement had we known your decentralization plans at that time. Now you come along at this point and you start tellin' us about an increased cost of insurance which must have been getting into the picture at the time we were negotiating then. You made no mention of it, and you haven't objected to that increased cost all these months. You wait until the period — now, actually, the 4/10ths of a cent, as far as I'm concerned, is not gonna interfere one way or the other with the settlement that I think should be reached here that should be a reasonable settlement, reflecting a substantial wage increase. So that I — I don't consider it, George, a legitimate offer, really, because of the circumstances involved in this whole situation. They've been paying this since October of '52, accordin' to their own statements, without one word of complaint or without once saying to us, "We're paying more than your contract provides."

Mediator: I have another question. The union's proposals amount to 7 points. Correct?

Gambon: Uh-huh.

Mediator: I haven't heard the company mention this, and I haven't heard the un — union mention it. Have you broke — broken down the cost of your proposals as they stand now? Is / there a figure on that?

Gambon: (Over Mediator above) No, we haven't, George, and I — it would be hard for the union to estimate some of these items as far as cost goes. I don't know whether the company has come up with any breakdown on cost of these items. (Pause) Some of them can be readily figured out, such as the 2d item / xxxxx.

Mediator: (Over Gambon above) Well, before you start — before we start, let's find out whether (Gambon: Uh-huh) they do have them. Do you have them? (Rather long pause) All right. Now, you — take 'em as you were doing it there. (Gambon: Uh-huh) First one ya have is the 35-hour week.

Gambon: Yeah. (Pause) Which I might say is the (pause) point of most interest to us. (Rather long pause) You — do you want me to try to give you estimated costs here, George?

Mediator: If it's possible. It — with the understanding, of course, it would be approximate. You wouldn't be held to it.

Gambon: Well, I'm not sure that I can do that without possibly putting the union's position in a — perhaps in a bad light — I mean, to — to making it a impossible situation. (Mediator: Well, all right. Let's —) Let me say this much, George. The information here was given to Michelsen at his request (pause) rather quickly without any opportunity to estimate costs. I think Bill was more or less in — interested in the shape that our demands were taking at this time, which I point out at this time as what we — date of March the 6th the position we were taking. (Pause)

Michelsen: Well (Gambon: Uh —), I was interested in this, George. John sent me a letter, which he's given you a copy, saying that the union intended to meet with us and present the demands. I was interested in the (Gambon: Uh-huh) business of saving time, not particularly in having them go to work and develop demands. I thought if they're gonna give us demands we could save time, rather than have a meeting at which he handed me somethin' and I said, "Well, that's fine. We'll read it and meet ya next week." If he gave it to us in advance we wouldn't have to have that unnecessary meeting.

Gambon: Well, you've had this thing since March the 6th, 1953. We met on March 12th, 1953, for the first time, and it is now March the 21st, 1953. And in my letter containing the union's demands I asked that you place this before responsible people who could make decisions that would reflect increased benefits to the company. If you have no cost figures a'tall, it appears to me that not an awful lotta consideration — not much consideration, I should say — was given to these demands, whether totally or individually. (Michelsen: Well, I don't think that that's necessarily true, John) I mean, it seems to me that the company's position seemed to have been that, well, they looked at this, didn't bother to make any estimates, or they (Michelsen: We have no exact estimates, if that's what you mean) took a position that said that, "You're" — or telling us, which we interpret to mean, "Well, this time we've made up our mind we're not gonna do anything for 'em," and if I recall correctly, you've made pretty much of a flat statement along those lines at one point here this afternoon — "That's all we're gonna do," or s — words to that effect.

Michelsen: Yeah, that's true. (Gambon: Now, that remains [laughing slightly] to be seen) But — but that doesn't mean that we had not considered these demands. Some of them were relatively easy to calculate; others it's easy to determine that they're reasonably large sums of money. And (pause) we made no exact computations of their cost, that's true.

Mediator: Ya have a copy of the reopening clause (pause) (Gambon: I —) handy? (Rather long pause) I should know it. (Several laugh)
[Several begin reminiscing about the earlier negotiations implied in Mediator's statement, sometimes talking and laughing at once. Mediator remarks, "I think we were here till about 4:00 o'clock in the morning that morning that was written, wasn't it?" There are several contributions, then, regarding the time, including: Michelsen, "Oh, it was reasonably late"; Gambon, "No, it wasn't that late"; Meyer, "Well, it was only a quarter of 3:00." Saunders has produced a copy of the contract from his coat pocket. There is much talking and joking over whether Michelsen has a contract.]

Mediator: Why d'you make that contract so big, so you don't lose it?

Gambon: Well, I — we don't make it big, George. I think the company writes 'em out so long and lengthy so they'll have room to make interpretations (Meyer laughs), see. (Several laugh heartily) We've had so many interpretations of this contract since it's been written

it's not even funny. Incidentally, for the first time in the history of
the labor relations between the company and the union, we're getting
to arbitration on some of these interpretations, now.

Mediator: Reason I asked if — in the hotel (Michelsen: Is that good or
bad?) generally every —

Gambon: I don't think it reflects a good labor relations policy. I mean,
it's very interesting to note that the kind of policy we've introduced
in Atlas run along the lines of things that happen in Precision-Made,
and I don't consider that to be good labor relations up there. Oh, it's
curious! I mean, I don't know whether you guys get your heads together — I mean, you personnel managers — but letters to the employees, reports of negotiation meetings to employees before the
union itself reports to 'em — they do the same thing up there. You
guys must have a union of your own. The reopening provisions,
George, provide: "The determination of changes in rates of pay or
fringe issues of a monetary na — nature may be brought up for consideration on October 1, 1952, and April 1, 1953, and October 1, 1953,
by either party giving at least 30 days' written notice to the other of
the intention to propose changes." You'll note that our notification is
dated January the 23d, I believe.

Mediator: O.K., that's what I wanted. (Rather long pause) At this time
I want to separate the 2 committees. I'm goin' to talk to management,
and then I wanta talk to the union committee. So, if the company will
retire into the other room, I'll join you there and then later join you
here. Think you'll find a deck of cards there.

[As Mediator prepares to leave, Gambon calls out to him to determine if they are to play cards or to do something else. Mediator lingers briefly with the union group.

The management group remains alone for some time in their caucus room. When Mediator enters he almost immediately excuses
himself "for about 15 minutes."]

Management Caucus[1] - A (3:25 P. M.)

Mediator: Uh (rather long pause) — all we did was (pause) go over
some points that you people have gone over before and are most familiar with (Michelsen: Uh-huh), and (pause) — uh — seems to me
that the one thing that throughout all of their discussion — the one
thing they touch on and evidently are — all their negotiating is — develops from this — let me put it this way. One thing that appeared to
be most in their mind was the fact that this decentralization — that
they are paying for this — or contributing to the (pause) decentralization program, and I guess you've noticed that in their arguments
that they were very (Michelsen: Yeah) strong on that and the

_____

[1]All caucuses in this transcript include the mediator as a participant.
With the Atlas case it was not attempted to record, as had been done earlier in the field with the Marathon case, those caucuses of each party from
which the mediator was intentionally excluded.

inference being that they're in a tougher spot with their membership
this time because of that. Their people will say, "Well, we have to pay
for them to move their plant out and eventually knock ourse — selves
out of a job." Uh — however, that's s — s — a theme (Michelsen: Yeah.
Except it's not a fact), and (pause) I let them talk about it. Now, as
far as today is concerned (rather long pause), there's not a lot can
be done today. I mean, we've — we've had them state their case and
you've had your presentation, and we're not going to attempt to do
anything today (Michelsen: Uh-huh), because it just would be the
wrong time. (Michelsen: Yeah) There wouldn't be any point in it.
Uh — now, the thing that I wanta talk about now before we talk about
anything else is time — dates. Their contract expires on Saturday,
or Su — Sunday.

Espig: 1st.

Michelsen: (Laughs slightly) Yeah, if it can be accepted as an expiration. I don't know that it necessarily means that in the agreement.
We've never had to test its meaning.

Mediator: Did they take a strike vote?

Michelsen: No. Not that I know of. Certainly haven't heard of any, and
I'm sure I would have. The only report that I've heard of a meeting
was that the report to the membership at the meeting, which was a
very small meeting — a very short meeting — was that there has been
no prōgress — progress yet, there haven't been enough discussions
for them to even record anything, and that they would advise 'em of
this at the next meeting, which is the one thing I don't like to hear,
'cause at the next meeting they may mean that they're gonna drag this
thing on by saying, "Well, we'll leave this as an open-end reopening.
We'll come back in the next period and see what's happened." But
that, of course, is a very — could be a very inaccurate report. But
impression I got was that they told the membership that, "N — there's
not enough taken place yet to even report, and we'll keep you advised
at the next meeting." Now, whether they meant special meetings
they would call for it, or at the next meeting which is the 2d Friday
in April, I don't know. The agreement — the agreement — I mean, I
have the date here for the — (voice dies, while looking something up).
That'd be the eleven — 12th. The agreement says that either party
may bring up these things for reopening on this date. Doesn't say that
anything expires on that time. There's nothing in the language in the
reopening which says that. (Mediator: No) It does not prevent them,
in my opinion, from making that kind of an interpretation and saying,
"If there is no meeting of the minds on this point, we're going to exercise our economic strength" — for instance, a strike. I would say
it would be possible to say that they had a right to do that. (Mediator:
Uh-huh) Uh (pause) — I don't know. Of course, as you've seen today, there's been very little heat in this whole thing up to this point.

Mediator: This — this — this case is cold. It's (Michelsen: Yeah) in
the cold stage now. (Michelsen: Yeah) It's — I — I would even guess
that you did more talking today than you did at your last meeting.

Michelsen: We did. The last meeting they had just 4 people. As I told
you, they brought in enough people to — to — to be able to say they
showed up for the meeting. Well, I don't make much progress tryin'
to convince the professionals in that group. I'm working on the

commission, so today I pulled out a few more stops. (Mediator: Uh-huh) But (pause) I don't exactly agree with their conclusion, or their feeling, as you've given it to me — not that — that — that you're not giving it to me properly — that — that they can't go back to their membership with this —

Mediator: It's an argument they'll use.

Michelsen: — argument, yeah. I don't give it any weight at all. I don't think the membership is, at this point (pause) — feel as though they're — they're — they're gonna get <u>tough</u> with us because of decentralization. I f — think the feeling is that, "Let's hold on to as many jobs as we can and that we're reasonably well paid now and company's doing a good job for us. Let's not be pushed." Now, I'm quite sure that that sort of a feeling has been transferred to the mem — to the leadership of the union. I know that after the decentralization there was a reaction which was <u>entirely wrong</u>, and it was (laughs slightly) — I can imagine how the union leadership felt — was that, "You people who have pushed the company too far are responsible for this thing, and we've been tellin' you that all along. Your policies have been too aggressive." Well, that was wrong because that wasn't the thing that prompted the decentralization. But I know they felt that. And I think that feeling's a hell of a lot stronger on the part of the rank and file who are working there and earning their incomes than the vindictive feeling that, "Now we're gonna give it to 'em, because we're not gonna pay for decentralization." The other fact is that they're not paying for decentralization. Decentralization is being financed privately, not out of the company's operating revenues but out of loans from lending institutions which were secured for that specific purpose. It's not coming out of our income, and we've said that. I've tried to make that point a couple times here today. Now, it's also true, by the same token, that those loans are gonna have to be paid. They're gonna have to be repaid eventually out of what we hope will be revenues from those decentralized operations. So that they will, in effect, totally stand on their own feet, both as to the capital which financed 'em, and also the income which comes back from 'em will help to reduce those loans. So that there <u>is</u> no great burden of replacing those people here to pay for that. As a matter of fact, those profitable operations are gonna make this operation here in the metropolitan area more profitable. But I have tried this morning, without (pause) distorting any facts, to show them where we stand financially, and that this company, in terms of its position in the industry as far as its employee —

[The balance of the caucus covers only 2 topics: (1) a rather long discourse by Mediator about the Hercules discharge grievance he settled a week earlier; and (2) discussion of the date of the next meeting. On this latter, Michelsen first agrees to Tuesday, the 26th, since Mediator says he is not free for the 25th. Later Michelsen returns to the 25th, asking Mediator about the possibility of his making that date, after all. Mediator is generally hazy on this point, saying he has a meeting tentatively scheduled but there might be a chance of having it changed.]

Union Caucus - A (4:07 P.M.)

[Mediator refers to the day's session as "a very healthy exchange, and I'm very satisfied with the way it went on both sides of the table." He lauds the committee, on behalf of both himself and Observer, on their good negotiating work. He describes the case as still in a cold stage, adding, "And there's no point in pushing this thing any further today. Yo — we've got the thing on the table where we want it, and the — the next point to take up is the next meeting." Gambon quickly asks that it not be before next Friday, the 29th. Meyer questions meeting on Good Friday, in case the Mediation Service —]

Meyer: ...offices are closed for (Mediator: No, we're open) legal holidays, or anything like that?

Mediator: Good (Meyer: I'm not x —) Friday, / Christmas, New Year's —

Gambon: (Over Mediator above) Well, I — I'm not gonna la — raise any objections on that score, unless the committee does, or —

Meyer: No, I (One of girls: No. No) — I wasn't raisin' objection. (Gambon: All right) I just wanted to point it out.

Mediator: Now —

Gambon: If there's anybody wants a recess for a period of time on Good Friday, we could do that, I think, and we m — might (Mediator: That can be arranged) go — go for a / longer —

Mediator: (Over Gambon above) You'll see conferences in every room here (Gambon: Uh-huh), all over the place, on Good / Friday.

Gambon: (Over Mediator above) Well, I would — I would prefer that, George. (Pause) Actually, we have a little organizational work to engage in next week, Tom and I, and —

Mediator: Have to beat the drums.

Gambon: Huh?

Mediator: You have to beat the drums.

Gambon: Well, I mean, it's very directly connected with (laughing) Atlas. (Laughs heartily) (One of boys: One of those charts. [Laughs] xx) Aiken (laughing), South Carolina, to be exact (laughing).

Mediator: They're set up there? / They operating?

Gambon: (Over Mediator above) Oh, they're operating, yeah. Yeah. We — we have to pay 'em a little visit, begin to let them know we're around. So that's one of the reasons for saying Friday. I don't expect to be back here much before Thursday / x.

Mediator: (Over Gambon above) Well, that will suit me fine (Gambon: Uh-huh), and (pause) I'm going — I'll go in there and talk to them about it, and then I wanta bring 'em in for joint adjournment.

Gambon: Uh-huh. Well, there's one thing that I want to say here that I think y — you can check, if you want to, but it's come to my attention in a pretty direct way, and I have no reason to doubt it. Now, you may or may not be familiar with a chap by name of Ray E — Horton, who is a vice-president of Atlas in ch — in charge of sales. He has commented to Herb Jenkins a week or so ago in discussion there that — something about the offer the company made, but he thought there would be some settlement reached. So I know from that — in fact, I knew before we come in here that that 4/10ths of a cent is not a real position. My own thinking (Mediator: It's entirely — it's entirely

too —) xxx — they wanta get away as cheap as possible, George, to
push this expansion program. That's what it amounts to. (Mediator:
Uh-huh) And we (laughing slightly) have no intentions of lettin' 'em
get by with it, because I pointed out that had we known in October
last year that during September that they were planning this particular move, after all the years that they were telling us "big family
business" and all that, you know — "Stay with us" — and as Wollman
pointed out, they cried all over our shoulder, got — to go along with
'em so they wouldn't be forced out of business when they owed us all
that money. (Pause) They d — they done it in a very nasty way. They
didn't tell us a thing about it until after the plant was under construction and everything else, and then they suddenly — in fact, they ignored the union as an organization. They sent out letters to all the
employees and then came — the — the day they were ready to send
'em out, noon of that day Michelsen drops into my office and he says,
"Here's what I'm sendin' out this afternoon at 4:00 o'clock." That's
the kind of notice we got from 'em. (Mediator: Uh-huh) Spelled out
the complete decentralization plans of the company. We've held
meetings with 'em — 3 or 4 meetings, now — on this problem of decentralization, trying to get some transfer rights for full seniority
and pension severance benefits rights and all the other kind of things,
for people that wanted to go down there. / No soap.
Mediator: (Over Gambon above) Are there any unions down there?
Gambon: Uh — / there's some textile —
Mediator: (Over Gambon above) Well, Aiken is a — Aiken is a winter
    resort, isn't it?
Gambon: No, it's a year-round (Mediator: A year-round resort) resort.
    Yeah. It's right in the sandhills — a beautiful country down in there.
    There's (Saunders: You can't eat the scenery, George) not a great deal
    of organization, but there are some textile mills around in there, and —
Mediator: Are they organized?
Gambon: Yeah. Yeah. CIO, Textile. And we've — well, we just won an
    election in Durland-Dolley down in Hendersonville, and couple of
    other spots in around North and South Carolina there have some or-
    ganizational work goin' on, so the name of our union is not entirely
    unknown in that area. And we intend to see that it's not unknown in
    Aiken, South Carolina, either.
Mediator: I know you had one down in Kingsport. (Gambon: Yeah) No.
    (Gambon: Tennessee, that was) No, no — Bristol.
Gambon: Well, that was a Hercules (Mediator: Yeah) job. That — they
    folded that plant up.
Mediator: Yeah, they took it out.
Gambon: Yeah.
Mediator: It was formerly a Lashley lamp plant.
Gambon: Well, we have a very tough problem here, George. We have
    not yet been able, after 3 meetings with the company on this problem
    of decentralization, to get them to commit themselves to what's — as
    to just exactly what's gonna remain in the metropolitan area. The
    only thing we can go on is the fact that they had a lease that runs un-
    til 1962 on that building at 1122 West Oak Street, and in that lease
    there's an opportunity for them to get out of it in April of 1956. So
    that we feel fairly safe in saying that, well, at (laughing slightly)

least we'll have something here until April of '56. But beyond that
point we know nothing. They have this plant up in Rome, New York,
that's all set to operate under a Navy contract to run electronic recording units, breathing down our neck. We haven't yet got an answer
as to whether there's d — section in that contract with the Navy which
would permit the company to buy up the equipment and the plant and
put it into operation for their own use. So that it's a pretty <u>dark</u> picture from where we're sitting. And if anything does remain here —
one of the reasons I kept battin' at him about guaranteein' that $1.71,
all the high-grade jobs are goin' out of that plant in these products
that they're moving. We'll finally have practically 80 or 85% of all
the jobs that will eventually remain here after they make these <u>2</u>
moves will be all in the very lowest labor grade and the 2d lowest labor grade. (Mediator: Uh-huh) Beyond — beyond that, you'll prob'ly
have some of your skilled trades in one or 2 spot sections of x, but
— but that — that's male work. But the average wage of that plant by
the end of this year'll go down terrifically, because the next move is
planned for November of '53. (Pause)

Mediator: Uh-huh.

Gambon: So we don't — we don't intend to have them do what they've done
now completely behind our backs. I mean, after all these years of
this "partnership" business — see, that's what's got us corked off
but good. We were (laughing slightly) always partners until it come
(Meyer laughs) time now that things are gettin' good, they don't like
(Meyer laughs again) us for partners any more. I mean, to give you
an indication, George, of what they're doin' down in (slight pause)
Aiken, the average rate of pay on power transformers in the metropolitan area here was running anywhere, I would say, from a do — about
$1.55 to $1.65 an hour, and they're gonna s — make the same thing down
there for $1.00. They're gonna pay $1.00. That's gonna be a high
rate for that area, incidentally, because it runs somewhere between
75 and 80¢. But they're takin' all their incentive standards that we
had up here, and they're not gonna put an incentive system <u>in</u> the
plant, but you can bet your bottom dollar that those people in that
plant are gonna be producing probably at a level, for a buck, that we
produced at $1.65 for. That's what's gonna happen in Aiken. (Media-
tor: Uh-huh) And that's what'll happen with these other products.
And what they wanta do is to let — leave off here. They don't want us
to bother 'em. They've done this twice, now — 3 times (pause) —
twice, I should say, since we signed that contract in this room. They
gave us the same business last time in here — in this same room,
cried the blues all over the place. But after th — after they got the settlement, which was a very skimpy affair — I mean, I didn't wanta push
'em too far. I thought we'd done right well in '52 there in the first
contract there, and I figured, all right, we'll give 'em a breather, see
how they do. So we settled for a cost-of-living increase of $2\frac{1}{2}$¢, as
you know, and an extra holiday. And immediately after the reopening
negotiations were over, decentralization announcement is made in
November. (Pause) So they're — they're in no position to give us that,
"We're playin' nice and fair and square with you boys and girls."
It's gonna be a tough proposition this time, and they'd better understand that. We're not gonna pay to have them expand and hire more

time-study men. We have jobs in that — places that have increased just since October — 40% increase in production. Guy still gets the same amount of money. They don't take those — they didn't talk about those kind of things when they say, "Well, you've got a take-out on that job of $1.96 an hour." In October the guy got $1.96 and he produced X number of pieces; today he still gets $1.96 and he's producin' 40% more. They take the money they don't wanta give us and hire time-study men to find new ways of increasin' production to get more and give us the same dough. That stuff is — they've been doin' that now for several years. We have lots of departments where the increase in production are <u>well</u> over 100% in about — since '41 and on. They've done a very methodical job and a very / <u>good</u> job.

Mediator: (Over Gambon above) New changes?

Gambon: Lookin' all over the place. They hunt all over that place for — tryin' to find changes in jobs, and if they can't find changes, they'll pull out an entire element out of a job and they'll say, "That's a 100% change." And under the contract they're — they have a right to change your rate.

Mediator: They putting in new machineries?

Gambon: In (One of boys: Certain, like —) — in here? Some (One of boys: Some, but not too much) — some new machines in — such as a KM — what we call a KMT machine. That's a machine that —

Saunders: Automatically assembles / the wire-wound unit.

Gambon: (Over Saunders above) — automatically assemblies a wire-wound unit on cord and cuts it off to a proper length and so forth — puts wires on it, and all that sort of — (slight pause). They're goin' — they have come a long way from a hand or manual proposition to automatic machinery over s — past several years.

Denk: Well, they still been pickin' up the methods of the people themselves and usin' / our —

Gambon: (Over Denk above) Yeah, that's — they (One of boys: That's right) do all that kind of business, but they're (Wollman: They don't want —) — they do anything they can get away with under the contract. And as I say — I mean, we — we — right now we have 4 cases going to arbitration on this new contract — on the contract interpretation, tryin' to cut corners to cut cost. And they say right in here, "Cost reduction program." (In low voice) Huh? Oh, I'll have to try to get you a co — this is the fir — I got a-hold of this just accidently. We didn't get any of these booklets from the company. (Mediator: At least they mail —) But the statements they make in here!

Mediator: Didn't they mail 'em to you the last time we / were in here?

Gambon: (Over Mediator above) Well, I have mimeographed / copies such as I gave you, see.

Mediator: (Over Gambon above) I think one of you was — was a stockholder, weren't you?

Gambon: Huh?

Mediator: Weren't — was this the case where one of you was a stockholder?

One of girls: No.

2d girl: No.

Gambon: No, no. (2d girl laughs) No.

2d girl: No (laughing). (One or 2 others laugh)

Gambon: (Over laughter above) We — way back when they had that (Mediator: I had one case here where —) problem they wanted us to buy stock, see.

Saunders: It was —

Mediator: One of the union committee had $5.00 worth of stock, and they used to mail him the (pause) (Gambon: Yeah) — these / statements.

Gambon: (Over Mediator above) Well, our union does that in some places. I mean, for instance, / we hold — the union — we got Lashley stock. Yeah (laughing), that — that's in —

Mediator: (Over Gambon above) Well, Hughes — oh, Hughes is a — Hughes's a m — holds stock in Lashley (Gambon: That's right) (One of girls: Yeah) and Hercules. I think he has about / $10.00 worth. (One of boys laughs)

Gambon: (Over Mediator above) That's nuisance xx. (Laughs slightly) / Annoys the —

Mediator: (Over Gambon above) Every now and then he'll say to Klinger, "I'm a stockholder (Gambon and Saunders laugh), and I wanta go to your stockholders' meetings."

Gambon: Yeah, but remind (Mediator: They'd gladly give him his $10.00 back) Michelsen he's not — tell Michelsen I'm not Al Hughes. (Several laugh) I'm not — I'm not sayin' in — that to a — a derogatory way to myself, but, I mean, he — he's talkin' to me in Local 89, not Hughes in Lashley. I hope Al gets a million bucks, as far as I'm concerned, but (pause) — but I'll settle for less, provided it's enough.

Mediator: Well, with that outfit, every time you get a half a cent it's a million (laughing slightly) bucks.

Gambon: Well, that's true. (Mediator: So getting a million would be easy) And they — they have a 2% wage offer on the table now. (Pause)

Mediator: All right. I — I'll go in there and s — have a few minutes with them. (Meyer: [In low voice] Tell him not to say anything about Aiken) Then I'll bring 'em in here and / see if we can't set it up for Friday.

Gambon: (Over Mediator above) Yeah. George, I'd appreciate it if you don't mention the fact in there that we're goin' down to Aiken. I mean, I don't wanta be (Someone laughs) (Mediator: O.K.) met by a welcoming committee. (Saunders laughs)

Mediator: No.

Management Caucus - B (4:25 P.M.)

[This caucus lasts less than 3 minutes. Mediator reports that his meeting with the union group went better than he expected; they had agreed to meet again on Friday, the 29th. Two or more of the management group comment that the 29th is Good Friday. Mediator states that the union group had also raised this point and had asked if government employees worked then. He had assured them, he says, that the rooms will be full of meetings that day. Michelsen inquires why the union wants the next meeting delayed so long. Mediator answers that they want "to look into some of these figures you presented," that it is "going to be a job," that they could not be ready before Friday. He ends with, "So, it won't be a sneak preview.

That I'm sure of. So it's O.K. with me." Then he suggests that they reassemble jointly, officially set the date for the next meeting, and adjourn.]

Joint Meeting - B (4:28 P.M.)

Gambon: You gonna drag that chart out again? (Michelsen laughs heartily) Not this time of afternoon! (Michelsen continues laughing as does someone else) You know the one chart I miss, though? The one about the pie. You know (Michelsen: Uh-huh) — remember the one you had the pie and everybody (Meyer laughs heartily) had a slice?

Meyer: That pie. (Laughs again)

Michelsen: I'll bring / that the next time.

Mediator: (Over Michelsen above) Let's get some pie on this (One of boys laughs) table the next meeting, huh?

Michelsen: Mince pie the next (Gambon: Yeah) meeting. O.K.

Meyer: (At same time as Michelsen above) Maybe the executives ate it. Don — don't you think so, John?

Gambon: I don't know. But if they hogged all of that / pie, I — I hope it was green apples.

One of girls: (Over Gambon above) They had their finger (laughing slightly) in it, anyway.

Michelsen: (Laughs slightly) O.K., I made a note of that. I'll bring that one.

Mediator: I've asked the both committees in to joint meeting here for the purpose of recessing the conference. First, I wanta say, in summing up, that we think both committees have submitted — or, rather, have been in what we call good, healthy ne — negotiations. Both committees certainly were prepared with their facts and their figures, and there's certainly material here — plenty of material for both committees to consider. It's not a situation where we have an empty sack. So (pause) — by that I mean, not a situation where the parties come in and state their positions and let it go at that — nothing else to work on. So, from where we stand, we're quite satisfied with the — with the — the day. Although you — your — both positions are the same, nevertheless we feel it has been a productive day in that we had to get over these particular preliminary presentations. And now, on the question of getting together again, I first talked with the union, later talked with the company, and Friday, Good Friday, is agreeable to both committees and is agreeable to us. So we'll set Good Friday, 10:30, as the day and the date — uh — time.

Gambon: May I ask if we could set an earlier starting time, George, considering the fact that we may wanta recess / for —

Mediator: (Over Gambon above) Yes. That would be in order. It's all right with me. How is the (Michelsen: Yeah) company — (pause)?

Michelsen: Any time.

Mediator: Now (pause), what time do — what time do ya have in mind?

Gambon: Well, I think 9:30 instead of 10:30, if that's agreeable.

Mediator: 9:30 it is. All right with the company?

Michelsen: Sure. (Slight pause)

Mediator: All right. Fine. We'll consider the conference recessed until Good Friday, 9:30 A. M.

[As the group disperses, conversation goes on about Good Friday. Michelsen says, "Don't forget it's a holy day." Gambon follows this with, "It's a paid holiday some places, too," to which Michelsen replies, "<u>Some</u> places it is paid." Mediator withdraws immediately; the time is 4:30 P.M.]

SESSION II (March 29)

[At 9:30 A.M. Mediator checks in with the management group in their caucus room, inquiring if they would like some time together. Michelsen replies that they "might have a short review of the situation," whereupon Mediator withdraws to await their call. He stops by the union caucus room to inform that group about the management caucus, and then departs.]

Management Caucus - A (9:45 A.M.)

Michelsen: Is this session supposed to end at 12:00 o'clock for Good Friday / observance?

Mediator: (Over Michelsen above) I have a feeling that it will. I — I imagine that (slight pause) — what are the hours — 12:00 to 3:00, isn't (Michelsen: Yeah) it? — where they observe?

?: Yeah.

Michelsen: My associates tell me these people are all dressed up ready, look like they're going to church, or something.

Mediator: Yeah. So I — I feel it prob'ly end about 12:00 and —

Espig: They aren't gonna give, Bill.

Loring: Can we arrange a break around noon, anyway — I mean, if — if it's gonna go on — for lunch?

Mediator: Uh — yeah. Well, here's — here's — here — here's what we'll have to determine. We'll have to determine whether or not, (1), there'll be any point in coming back. (Michelsen: Yeah) If there is, then we can recess at 12:00 (Michelsen: Uh-huh), come back. The one thing that bothers me a little bit with these negotiations is the (pause) <u>lethargy</u> of the — on the — the union just doesn't — isn't hot. You can see it (Michelsen: Uh-huh) in the bargaining room. They're in no hurry. And whenever a union is — or a company — isn't in a — in a hurry to settle, it — well, you gener'ly have to do one of 2 things. Yo — ya have to either ride it out, sometimes called baby-sitting, or step up the tempo. I could see from last week that these people weren't in very — now, it may change, but I'll ha — I haven't had the pulse beat this morning, but I think we'll get that this morning. Then we'll be able to (Michelsen: Yeah) ascertain whether we can — we should come back at 3:00 o'clock — whether there's any worth in it. 'Cause if they're still dragging their feet, then instead of wasting time on the conference room, we'll — we'll have to de — devote more time to stepping up the tempo.

Michelsen: George, one of the th — thoughts I had since — since last week was that — as for this lethargy, was that they were waiting for Standard Products, who are negotiating a contract, and I have talked to those people and they're s — 3 or 4 weeks away, from what I can gather, from any conclusion on this thing. They're just getting into (Mediator: Yeah) discussions. And it's a contract negotiation, not a wage

249

reopening, so there are reason to believe they could last some time, even for Standard Products. (Mediator: H'm) So that they may be waiting for that to pop. Now, I think Dayco is also in the process — is that true? (Espig: Yeah) — of discussion. So they may be just holding off to see what's gonna happen, which —

Mediator: Well, then, again, question comes up on retroactivity. (Michelsen: Yeah) If they — I don't know what their thinking is, whether they believe that anything that they negotiate here will be retroactive or whether it has to be negotiated. (Michelsen: H'm) Some unions are — well, they're concerned about that because it can mean losing money, and it (Michelsen: H'm) can — but of course, if they have a retroactive feature, the — uh — retroactive agreement, they don't lose it and they'd take their time.

Michelsen: Yeah. Well, we don't have such an agreement in our contract, and of course the discussion between the parties up to this / point —

Mediator: (Over Michelsen above) I may (Michelsen: Yeah) raise that question (Michelsen: Yeah) today in the joint s —

Michelsen: But we haven't offered anything that retroactivity would — would mean anything to 'em.

Mediator: Uh-huh. (Pause)

Michelsen: Uh-huh.

Mediator: I think toward the close of the meeting I may raise that question, / say —

Michelsen: (Over Mediator above) I can't agree to carry these insurance costs retroactively because we have been carrying 'em. We're agreeing to continue them. This is a question of being a date on which we terminate these benefits and reduce them, which is for me not a very serious threat and I think they recognize that, that (rather long pause) — well, we haven't gotten to that point. (Mediator: Uh-huh) We're not gonna consider any retroactivity. We're not even going to — I mean, as — as I've told you and I repeat, we're not considering wages at this point. (Slight pause)

Mediator: There (slight pause) — there's just no life there on that side of the table. Now, the last time that I had this case — or the last time you were in it was an entirely (Michelsen: Yeah) different.

Michelsen: Well, I'd certainly be interested in advancing the resurrection day if we can do it. (Laughs)

Mediator: Uh — we'll know. Now, what I'm going to do is get together now and just try to flush out a few questions and get you started on (Michelsen: Uh) joint discussions. I don't intend to hold you there very long (Michelsen: Oh); prob'ly 10, 20 minutes, then break into caucuses, then start to move. See if we can't find out what's behind their timetable or what it — what the timetable is. (Michelsen: Uh-huh) So I — I'll prob'ly call on the union or the company for the (rather long pause) statement on their position as it is now. That's a good place to kick off, because I think anything that the company says will — I think I'll call on the company first, see. (Michelsen: Uh-huh) And anything that you say I'm sure is going to (slight pause) ha — Gambon will (slight pause) be in a better position to — he'll add more to the joint conference by following you than he will by leading. (Slight pause) So, if you're ready — or if you want a few minutes —

Michelsen: Well, I just wanta make a chart. (Laughs)

Mediator: Go ahead.

Michelsen: I have here a recent communique from Mr. Durkin, and he points out that wages since February of 1952 as compared with February of this year gone up 10¢, or 6%. That's his statement on — for the average, and — factory production workers, and ours have just gone up 19¢, or 12½%, in that period of time which I — I'd just like to keep 'em abreast of what the Labor Department is issuing. (Mediator: Uh-huh) (Slowly, while writing) 1.52, 1.71. (Rather long pause, pencil work continuing) Won't be able to have this printed very attractively, but they get the point, I hope. (Long pause. Pencil work continues) O.K!

Joint Meeting - A (10:00 A.M.)

Michelsen: Well, Brother Gambon, how are you-all this morning?

Gambon: I'm fine. How are you-all?

Michelsen: Good. (Mediator laughs slightly) (Rather long pause)

Gambon: Gonna sign the contract now? (Michelsen laughs heartily) Gonna wait a little while? (Michelsen continues laughing)

Michelsen: (In low tone) I'm gon — gonna wait.

Gambon: Huh?

Michelsen: I think there should be a considerable time of waiting, John.

Gambon: Why considerable? (Pause) Huh? (Long pause)

Michelsen: (In low tone) Well —

Gambon: Save wear and tear on my constitution runnin' back and forth between the metropolitan area and Aiken, South Carolina.

Michelsen: It's nice time of the year to be there.

Gambon: Nice country. (Pause)

Michelsen: Take me down the next time you go down.

Gambon: Huh?

Michelsen: Take me down the next time / you go.

Gambon: (Over Michelsen above) O.K. We might even be shorthanded givin' out leaflets. We can always use you. (Several laugh)

Michelsen: Well, I'm capable of giving out leaflets, / I xx. (Several laugh)

Meyer: (Over Michelsen above, laughing heartily) That's true. (Several laugh heartily, including Gambon and Michelsen)

Michelsen: No one ever questioned my ability (Several continue to laugh) to hand out paper.

Meyer: Postin' notices on bulletin boards.

Michelsen: (In low tone) Yeah.

Gambon: Did ya get one? (Pause)

Michelsen: Did I get one?

Gambon: Yeah. Didn't x mail ya? We gave him enough. (Several laugh, including Michelsen) / xxxxx.

Michelsen: (Over Gambon above) Oh, I've seen them. (Laughter continues) I've seen 'em. Very nice letter. Very nice.

Mediator: Ladies and gentlemen, at our last conference you — both sides presented their positions, and most of the day was spent in hearing the positions of both parties. And we've called this conference to resume, or pick up at the point where we left off, and a good point in starting

might be to call on the parties for a statement of their present position. So, without further ado I'll call on management, and then following that, call upon the union. So, Bill, you take it — (pause).

Michelsen: Well, George, I'm — I'm <u>really</u> gonna be brief. (Pause) I
tried to make these points at last meeting — I'm gonna repeat them
without my visual aids this morning — and they were that our past
performance in '52 was characterized by 4 significant movements,
and they were lowered sales to the extent of 9% over '51; profits which
went lower still, percentage-wise — before taxes, 42% fall, which is a
pretty long fall, and 23% after taxes. Along with those downward
movements on the escalator there were some movements in the opposite direction, and they were that costs were up — cost of everything
which we buy, pretty much. That's speaking in terms of the categories. There are prob'ly some materials that didn't go up, but generally our materials and services costs rose. Our labor cost certainly went up. And along with that we had a — a more vigorous competition. You might say our competition is going up. We have more
of it, it's getting more vigorous, not alone because of our competitors
because they're trying to be nasty to us, but because our customers
are very much interested now that competition is — is getting keener
and that they're having more difficulty in — in — in selling. The market is — well, not saturated — getting to the point where supply and
demand are pretty much in balance. It's at that time that the — the
customer gets in the driver's seat and makes his choice. In the field
of electronic equipment, particularly in consumer goods, that kind of
competition gets to be pretty keen. And you see all around you in the
newspapers and great displays that are being made in an effort to sell
television sets and refrigerators and other consumer goods of that
kind in which there is a reasonably large financial investment on the
part of the consumer. The same thing's true in auto fields where you
now see the prices on — on the way down in some companies and in
most of their models. Another — there are evidences that — that what
I'm saying is — is going to be more and more the situation in the year
to come. They were the 4 movements which concerned us greatly,
the — the fact that it's tougher to — with the competitive situation, the
fact that our profits and sales have been down and that our costs have
risen. That produced — aside from the l— lack of profit, it produced a
profit which we feel is insufficient to meet our needs for research and
development. It — the reduction of our dividends to our stockholders
is a bad record. We think, in a sense, that it's not the sort of thing
that attract investors to the company, and our business is the kind of
a business — it's a — in the electronics industry, and particularly in
our end of that industry, we're in the kind of business which is — it's
very dynamic. We've gotta be in a position to move to meet our customers' demands. And our customers' demands are — are not static.
We — I mean, we've got to be in a position to — to give him the kind
of recorder, in terms of quality performance, and in terms of modi-
fication, in terms of variations in the product, that will satisfy his
needs, and if he doesn't get them from us, he'll get them from somebody else. And one of the very significant things is that Atlas and the
recorder industry today is a great deal different than Atlas and the
recorder industry of 10 and 15 years ago when we were <u>predominantly</u>,

by far and away, the — the — the only producer of — of wire recorders
that made a complete line. And while that's still true, we now have
competitors — smaller competitors in many cases, but in some others,
larger companies than Atlas at the moment — in the recorder industry
who — who can handle the requirements of a great many of our large
customers, as well as the general consumer for direct sales, both in
terms of the quantities which they demand, in terms of the prices
which they more than demand, in terms of the kind of delivery which
they require. So that's the — the situation. The only other thing I can
mention, and I mention it simply because it's a problem which concerns us, there has been no question in our mind that 1953 is gonna be
a good year. We certainly hope that it will be. We certainly need it.
One thing which frightens us, and — and I mention it only to — to bring
you up to date, is — is this problem of binaural sound, which in the
long run is — is one of the best things that will ever hit us, because it's
gonna mean increases in the appeal of home recordings in terms of the
quality of the results possible, it's prob'ly gonna mean additional recorders. But the thing that bothers us is gonna be the development of home
recordings using conventional type records. If the record changer industry comes out with some type of cutting device to produce home
recordings of good quality, and can utilize existing reproduction equipment, we are in for some very severe competition. It is quite possible
that that Viking electronic system could be used. Viking engineers
have indicated that it can be. And you've been reading this in the
paper — and that's all I've been doing. You may feel that they do.
Duo-Sound at the last (pause) I.R.E. meeting — its 2 recording engineers said that such a development was a couple of years away; Viking
claims that it's around the corner. Neither company is in a perdit —
position to mass produce it, and it's quite a — a fact, I believe, that it
would be some months before such equipment could come off the assembly line. That's the big problem. Knowing that home recording
equipment using conventional records was feasible and being cognizant of the distribution agencies that could be utilized, and just reading what accurate or inaccurate statements happened to appear in the
paper, you can imagine what the person who's contemplating buying a
tape recorder is going to do. He's gonna do nothing. He's not gonna
buy a tape recorder, and he's not gonna buy it until the — he's assured
that he can get one. And in addition, he's certainly not gonna buy a
conventional recorder if he knows that — or thinks that what's coming
off the line in the near future is gonna be something different — binaural sound, to be exact — although I don't know what — what is gonna
be coming off the line, whether it's just gonna be an adapter that can
be used on the regular set, or not. I don't know that detail, and I'm
not trying to speak authoritatively. I'm just saying that this great to-
do about this thing — it's — it's gonna bear some of the similarity
which developed, you remember, when we got into the record changer
problem where, with all kinds of speeds being developed and if you
wanted to play all 3 kinds of records, originally ya had to buy 3 different kinds of — of players. But the point is that a great deal of
buyer res — consumption may temporarily be halted until this great
controversy, which is now unfortunately getting played up in the paper
— the fact that binaural sound may soon be within reach of the general

public, it may soon get to be a reality. Great many people who — on whom the industry's surveys were based as being potential consumers may not be consumers next month or the month after. So that while there's nothing in — that's — that's tangible to substantiate what I've said, and I'm not saying it as a substantial prediction, I'm saying it's something that has concerned our industry, and the parts industry, very much, because our customers are certainly not going to buy any more than they can need for their inventories. They don't stock great inventories of recorders and won't want them. And they certainly are gonna be concerned with this thing, as I know they are, with the premature release of — of this whole process until the mass production techniques can be set to produce it to satisfy customer demands so that there won't be this great drop-off in demand. The other thing which — which just recently came to my attention — and (pause) I submit it just for what it's worth, which is an index — the United States Department of Labor just recently, in one of their latest releases, sent out this release for earnings in February in which Martin Durkin says, "The hourly earnings this February were 10¢, or 6%, higher than a year earlier. This gain reflected cost-of-living and other wage rate adjustments, increased overtime work, and a larger proportion of workers in the higher paid durable goods industry." So that this over-all average of — from February of '52 up until February of '53 was 10¢, or 6%. I pulled off the — the figures for Atlas for those 2 months in these 2 years of '52 and '53, and we find that our average earnings in February, '52, as compared with February of — of '53, have gone up 19¢, or about $12\frac{1}{2}$%, as compared with this 10¢ and 6%. It's just another (pause) look at this thing from another 2 — 2 other dates which are reasonably recent, that certainly what has been happening to the Atlas employee has been far and above what has been happening to the average in industry. And I submit these, knowing that averages are composed of high and lows and that there are some high people in here and there are some low ones, but it's — it's — it's one of the reliable indexes which are used, and I submit it for that reason. That's pretty much, George, our case. We feel that — that based on our past performance in terms of the last 2 — the contract negotiation in April and the reopening which we had — seems like just yesterday — in which we've — we've made — given appreciable improvements to our employees, that that's all the company should do at this time. We have another reopener in October, which will be here tomorrow, practically, and we feel that this thing should be passed up with the exception of this small improvement or maintenance of the — the group insurance benefits which I've offered. And that's (slight pause) my quick recap.

Mediator: Uh-huh. (Rather long pause)

Michelsen: I might also just add one thing since, Tom, you mentioned this at the last meeting. You felt that — that our earnings were gonna drop off after the transformer moved out. I checked those. I'll just give 'em to you; these come from our payroll register. The week ended — these are week-ending dates — week ending March 1st, the hourly rate — and these things fluctuate from week to week couple of cents, but — but I's — that's why I've given you averages over a long period of time, but these are the weekly averages. Depends on the mix of people who happen to be working that week and who are not in the plant, absenteeism, and things of that sort which changes your proportions, but they vary a couple of cents. Week ending 3/1/53 — these are all prior to the termination of the Power Transformer Department — was $1.71; 3/8/53 was $1.72½; 3/15/53, 1.74 — that was the last week in which Department 9 was operating; then week ending 3/22, which was the week in which the Power Transformer Department was not in the metropolitan area plant, $1.72. So that there has been no change. You've — we observe this sort of fluctuation every week. / So that —

Meyer: (Over Michelsen above) Simply because ya had a lot of M-G and because you had that overtime with the maintenance work. Right?

Michelsen: Could be, Bernice. It also could (Meyer: Uh-huh) be down because there were a lot of people had been moved to new jobs that they hadn't worked on before and (Meyer: Uh-huh) their incentive earnings might not be as high as they would when they got to be experienced on the job. There're all sorts of things. The — the variations are — that I'm tryin' to point out are very slight. (Rather long pause) The — the reason — I might add that — that we see no reason for the average dropping; that with moving out the transformer jobs you're moving out a large number of comparatively low-paid jobs, and that your skilled trades jobs and molding jobs and that sort of thing are virtually unchanged so that their effect on the average is actually heavier than it was before.

Meyer: Except for that group of people who are on D and E jobs, / and C jobs no longer x —

Michelsen: (Over Meyer above) Yeah. Well, they're — but they're still — they are still lower paid than the — the — the skilled trades people, so that you have now the skilled trades group which hasn't —
[Tape changed]

Meyer: ... future cuts in Tr — Transformer Potting and M — Multiple Machine Winding Department will take practically all of the D jobs out of the plant, and you take Transformer Potting'll only be left with spot checkers and handwinding machine operators. And when you take multiple machine winding out, you'll do away with all those C jobs in the (Michelsen: xx) power transformer production that you could n — not possibly absorb in the plant / xxx.

Michelsen: (Over Meyer above) That's — that's certainly possible, Bernice, / and may not change the average.

Meyer: (Over Michelsen above) And the B jobs mostly — the B jobs mostly were transformer mounting machines and — and allied machines, and in Department 4 your welders and your riveters, too. So that by November of next year you will have predominately A grade, you'll have your Plating Room, you'll have very little of your Press Shop, and you'll have your skilled trades. So while the number of people will be cut ya can still come up with this $1.71 or $1.72, but, over-all, the people who are left, the people with seniority who'll remain working, will actually take a pay cut, because I think ya can check anyone that left Department 9. / There's very few of them have made up anything.

Michelsen: (Over Meyer above) Well, that — that — you'll — you'll find that there'll — that some of those jobs will be removed but they haven't been removed yet, and, / in fact, I had —

Meyer: (Over Michelsen above) Well, they have. They've started, Bill,
in Department 9. / They have started. Yeah.

Michelsen: (Over Meyer above) In Department 9, yes. But I mean they
hadn't been (Meyer: Uh-huh) removed any place else.

Meyer: So that (Michelsen: Yeah) it's an inflated picture one way or the
other. / It's according to what you wanta use the figure for.

Michelsen: (Over Meyer above) And there's no — there's no definite —
there's no definite (Meyer: Uh-huh) date d — determined as to when
they'll be removed, at this point.

Meyer: Well, so far as I'm concerned, I thought it was November. I
thought that was / verified.

Michelsen: (Over Meyer above) My — my statement before was that that
plan had not been changed. (Meyer: Uh-huh) I said that there was no
reason why it shouldn't or couldn't be. I mean, the — the date of November — we saw no reason to extend beyond that (Meyer: Uh-huh)
date, but that doesn't mean that we'll be ready to move in November.

Gambon: Doesn't mean you won't, either. (Laughs slightly)

Michelsen: That's true! And it also — but it also means that November
is 5, 6, 7 months away. This is the end of March.

Meyer: Yeah. And so what does it equal, then?

Gambon: (At same time as Meyer above) That's true, so that the figures
you're giving here, I mean, of $1.71, 72$\frac{1}{2}$, $1.74, and then again $1.72
after the transformer move, in my opinion it's a little premature to
try to maintain that you're holding that average and it won't go below
that. It's a matter of opinion. You say you think it will, as a matter
of opinion. We say we don't agree with you. We don't think that average is gonna hold up after you make these other moves, particularly
after you make these other moves.

Michelsen: John, what the conditions in — in November or October will
be is a subject we can discuss in the (Gambon: H'm) October reopening.

Gambon: Well, we prefer to discuss the question of (slight pause) wage
increases under this reopener, and that's what we're here for.
(Michelsen: Right! And I'm tryin' to give you the facts which xxx)
When the company signed a contract with us, you signed it and agreed
to reopeners on (slight pause) April 1st, 1953, October 1st, 1953, and
then an expiration of the contract (Michelsen: Uh-huh) in April of
1954, plus the reopeners that have since passed from the signing of
the contract. Now, last reopener you came here with the same kind of
a proposition: you didn't think we should be asking for any increases.
We have no doubt that it comes October you'll be takin' the same kind
of a position. (Michelsen: Well, let's say I'm more convinced of it
now, though, I mean) The company has expressed, and you're continuing to express for the company, its very great interest in its ability to
continue this what you call improvement program. Well, it's not an
improvement as far as our position goes. It's lesser jobs, lesser paying jobs, and many other problems connected with that kind of thing.
(Michelsen: Well, there are — there are no — there are no —) I don't
think the company has any right to agree to reopeners and then complain about the fact that the reopeners are so close together.

Michelsen: John, up to this point you haven't noticed any fewer jobs in
the plant. We're still / employin' the same people.

Meyer: (Over Michelsen above) And 160 / people xx?

Gambon: (Over Meyer above) Look! We have a hundred (Michelsen: Huh?) and (Meyer: One hundred —) — it's 160 people / already laid off?

Michelsen: (Over Gambon above) Well, as I remember reading your letter to the Aiken people, you said that none of your people were laid off. / I remember that.

Meyer: (Over Michelsen above) We did not. We said they were placed in other jobs.

Gambon: (At same time as Meyer above) I didn't say they were placed in other jobs. / Let me read it to you.

Michelsen: (Over Gambon above) Well, I — I've forgotten the text (Gambon: Oh! Well, don't forget it), but it was / a very nice statement, and —

Meyer: (Over Michelsen above) Uh-huh. Placed in other jobs. It didn't say they were laid off.

Michelsen: Yeah.

Gambon: Here's what we (Meyer: They're not laid off, rather) said. "There is no need for any of you to feel even the slightest twinge of sympathy for Atlas employees in the metropolitan area who were displaced when transformer production was moved to Aiken, S.C. (Michelsen: Yeah) We are happy to report that every one of the employees affected by th — the move has been placed in another job." (Michelsen starts to speak) I didn't say in Atlas.

Michelsen: Oh, would be placed in other / jobs.

Meyer: (Over Michelsen above) That's right.

Michelsen: I see (Gambon: H'm), now. You sure of that?

Gambon: Yep! I said "in other jobs." (Michelsen: Well —) We're taking care of our people.

Michelsen: Well! I think you're gonna find — and — and — that — that (pause) — that people who were displaced by this transformer thing — most of 'em will be back at work.

Meyer: They're not / working right now in Atlas.

Gambon: (Over Meyer above) Well, they're not working at the moment. The people who are working (Michelsen: It's quite clear they are) have been placed in other jobs through the efforts of the union (Meyer: Uh-huh) and in cooperation with other Locals of our union in the area here, and we're gonna continue to do that. We had no — no way of assuring those people they're gonna come back to Atlas just / because you tell us that.

Michelsen: (Over Gambon above) No, that's right. You had no way of assuring it.

Meyer: In fact, you're laying off today again; you laid off last Friday. These layoffs started on the (Michelsen: Uh-huh) 8th of March and they haven't stopped yet.

Michelsen: But that's not due to any decentralization; that's due to a lack of business.

Wollman: Just had some laid off last night.

Meyer: Uh-huh.

Michelsen: Yeah.

Gambon: Well, let's (slight pause) say that as far as the union position goes, George, we're pretty much in the same position. I don't wanta

be repetitious, but I have to take issue, of course, with this point of
9% lower sales in 1951 because Bill is not reporting what the company itself has already made public, that during the latter half of 1952
our sales were 14% higher than those for the same period of 1951.
Now, I — I'm quoting from the company's financial report — the year's
business under heading of sales. That's what they say. (Michelsen:
That's quite true, John) They go down to earnings — under their statements about earnings — and they say, "The current sales volume and
industry forecast for 1953, together with strong emphasis on cost reduction, point towards increased profits for 1953." (Michelsen: I — I
think you'll find xx) Then we go over under dividends and they explain
that they had reduced the earnings for the first half of 1950 — or r —
rather, "reduced earnings for the first half of 1952 and a necessity to
coserve — conserve resources for desirable expansions, the directors
reduced the last 2 quarterly dividends from 10¢ each to 5¢ each. This
action did not establish a new annual dividend rate, and it is anticipated that the quarterly dividends will be increased when it appears
financially — financially sound to do so." We have no doubt that they're
gonna increase it back to the 10¢ that they gave for each quarter and
possibly even increase it above the 10-cent figure. (Pause)

Michelsen: Well (Gambon: Uh —), I don't know whether you should have
any doubt about it, John. (Gambon: Let me finish my comments, will
you, Bill?) I would say that the company — company wants to do that.
/ Sure. I'm sorry.

Gambon: (Over Michelsen above) The president of the company now, Mr.
Fuller, states in his note here, in TRENDS, that "the advent of binaural
sound, which will provide new markets for tape recorders, the rapid advancement in electronic developments, and continued high level of defense expenditures all indicate increased demands for our products in
1953. With our emphasis on lower operating costs, new products, research and development, and market distribution, we face the coming
year with confidence that your company will improve its position of
leadership in the industry." It's hard to know what to believe when you
read these kind of things in a statement — a financial statement of a
company which is public property, goes to all the stockholders, and then
try to match it up with the statements being made by Bill here. Electronics production, for instance. Reading the — the very latest N.E.
M.A. report — industry report, which is dated March 22, '53, in one
part of it here they point out that the radio, television, and recorder
production for January and February of 1953 (slight pause) is — is
far ahead of the same production th — that they had in January or February of 1952 — well above the level of that month. In fact, they claim
that in February of this year that they established a new record for the
month of February in any year. So that the trend is definitely upward
as far as television, radio, and recorder production goes at this moment, according to — to their own industry reports. Now, we get back
again to this question of comparisons in wage increases, and I must
remind you again that as against the 62¢ that Atlas has given in wage
increases since '46 through '52, we have the same kind of wage benefits given to Standard Products employees, which total 74¢ for the
same period; for Lashley, 77.3; for Hercules, 77.1; big steel, 83.6
plus; Monco System, for instance, 68¢; Precision-Made, 78¢; Dayco,

$71\frac{1}{2}$. Now, many of these companies have been used by the Atlas to make comparisons in the past. In fact, some of these places were used in building our case for the W.S.B. to show that Atlas's rates of pay were lower than those companies in order to get approval back in — for the wage increases of 12¢ for people generally and 17¢ for skilled trade. That's when we signed that present contract. So that there's no reason why we shouldn't look at this particular picture, not just go back to 1950 and say, "Here's what we done in '50, '51, and '52." Go back to '46 where everybody was s — starting off on the same foot and bring it forward, and you — you get the kind of picture I just quoted for you. And we're not — we're not going to take a look at this kind of a situation on comparisons of wage increases granted, particularly in the area and in our own industry, and then (pause) look at the company's financial report and know that the company can well afford to do something substantial right now. 4/10ths of a cent, I mean, on the face of your financial report here is actually sort of insulting in — inte — the intelligence of this committee, Bill. You must think we can't read. I mean, I don't know — (pause). (Michelsen starts to speak) Well, I — that's — our position has not changed, George. The 4/10ths-of-a-cent-cost-to-the-company business, which is supposedly an offer here, is entirely out of the question in the face of all the information we have here, information, incidentally, issued by the company itself. (Pause)

Mediator: I think at this time I'm going to talk to both groups before resuming joint negotiations. So I would like to meet with management (Michelsen: H'm), and following that I want to meet with the union committee.

Management Caucus - B (10:47 A.M.)

[Mediator had broken up the joint meeting at 10:30 A.M., but he does not rejoin the management group in their caucus room until sometime later. He explains that he has been talking with another mediator in an outer office.]

Mediator: Uh (rather long pause) — I really didn't want to come — talk to you. I have nothin' to talk to you about at this time. I do have something to talk about with the union. (Michelsen: Uh-huh) And the things I wanta talk about with the union are those things we talked about this morning. I wanta (Michelsen: Uh-huh) find out — a — a — and now is the time to find out about them. I also wanta find out about this afternoon. But I felt it best to s (Michelsen: Uh-huh) — say I's comin' in here to have a talk. So the time I spent talking to my colleague — I can (Michelsen laughs shortly) use that (Michelsen: Uh-huh) here. So I'm going back with them. And I don't see any need at this time, or purpose, in discussing any of the issues till I find out those other things. (Michelsen: Uh) (1), I got — I have to establish the tempo of this thing. Wanta find out (Michelsen: Yeah) what the timetable is, if there is a timetable. (2) (pause), once — once that's established, then I can talk about the issues and their bargaining — the way they're bargaining and what they're thinking about, and so on. (Michelsen: Uh-huh) So! I've got to find that out first (Michelsen: Yeah) before we can talk about anything, even the — even talking — I gotta find that out before I can even talk about an adjournment. (Michelsen: Uh-huh) (Laughs slightly) (Pause) So (pause), enjoy yourselves, if that's possible. (Michelsen laughs shortly)

Michelsen: Well, we get along / xx —

Mediator: (Over Michelsen above) Why don't ya leave that on, Observer, let them do a little crooning (Michelsen and someone else laugh heartily) and play it back? (Laughter continues)

Union Caucus - A (10:55 A.M.)

Mediator: The — the one thing that I've b — observed here in these negotiations and the thing that I'm a little more concerned about than I am with the issues, and I wanta talk to you and your committee about it now. If you can shed some light on it, then I think the negotiations will start to move. I've observed that there's a deep entrenchment on the part of the company. I have not tried to move them, or I haven't even discussed issues with 'em yet. It's not the right time. I know that until other things are cleared up the negotiations won't move, and these negotiations are no different than any of the others. In all negotiations we have to first remove or find out about certain things. Now, the one thing that I'm interested in is your termination date. Your termination date is April 1st, and I didn't hear this discussed and I haven't discussed it with the company / yet. I will —

Gambon: (Over Mediator above) You mean contract termination date?

Mediator: No, your reopener.

Gambon: Reopener date, huh?

Mediator: Your reoperal — the re — your reopener is April 1st. I haven't heard discussed and I was glad it wasn't discussed until I had an opportunity to talk to you, when you go over your reopener date (Gambon: Uh-huh), what understanding do you have, if any?

Gambon: As to an effective date?

Mediator: No. Let us say you don't reach an agreement for a month. (Gambon: Yeah) Now, do you get retroactivity?

Gambon: We have always — in the last few reopeners it's been the reopening date. Now, for instance, we went past, if I remember correctly — a short while past October 1st. (Meyer: We went into November) Began negotiating in September, and we went into / November, didn't we? Yeah.

Meyer: (Over Gambon above) November. Remember, we had one — yeah, we had our meeting on the 1st of November.

Gambon: And the retroactive (Meyer says something) date was back to the date of the reopener, October / 1st, '52.

Mediator: (Over Gambon above) Well, how was that done? That's the point I wanta get. Was it —

Gambon: By agreement.

Mediator: By agreement.

Gambon: Yeah. / We agreed.

Mediator: (Over Gambon above) You negotiated it.

Gambon: We had said in here, if I'm not mistaken. (Rather long pause)

Meyer: Yeah, your original one, I think, John. Look at your original / x.

Gambon: (Over Meyer above) Oh, that. Prob'ly the original letter, if
it's in here. (Pause) I had intended in stating our position, George,
to make specific note of that, and then I thought afterwards, well, I'm
not too concerned with it. They know that our position is always that
the bargaining (pause) — or the reopener date as the effective date
for any kind of increases that they put into effect.
[Long pause follows, during which Gambon is searching through his
papers. Several, including Mediator, make remarks pertaining to the
search.]

Mediator: January the 23d?

Gambon: Yeah.

Meyer: (At same time as Gambon above) That's the one.

Mediator: "Article 5, reopening provisions, provide for the opportunity,
Local 89 to propose changes in rates of pay or any fringe issues of a
monetary nature under the regular reopener April 1, '53. In compli-
ance with Article 5 provisions" — and so on — "herewith giving the
company the required written notice of the union's intention to change
rates of pay, fringe issues of a monetary nature. As usual, it is suggested that the negotiations begin several weeks in advance of April 1,
1953, date, in order to allow ample time for satisfactory settlement
of the union's proposals. Will you please advise me as to the earliest
date convenient for the company to begin negotiations of our proposals?
Very truly yours."

Gambon: That part about ample time to get a settlement before April 1st
is clearly understood by them. We always — because they usually
bellyache to us about retroactivity we always tell 'em, "Well, let's
get started ahead of time so that you don't have to be concerned with
retroactivity." Now, while it isn't specifically put into it for the record that we said "effective April 1st, these are the wage demands,"
I have no doubt that Michelsen understands our / position.

Mediator: (Over Gambon above) Well, he probably does, and (Gambon:
And —) we haven't discussed it. (Gambon: Uh-huh. Well —) I mean,
the reason for me mentioning it now (Gambon: H'm) and — to —

Gambon: D'you wanta know whether it's a bargainable / proposition with
us?

Mediator: (Over Gambon above) No. No, that wasn't my concern as
much — I was trying to put my (Gambon: H'm) hand on the pulse
beat of the tempo of these negotiations. (Gambon: Uh-huh) Now,
sometimes both sides, either the union or the company, have a timetable (Gambon: H'm), and naturally it stands that first thing we try
to do is find out what the tempo of these negotiations or any other negotiations are and acquaint ourself with the timetable if there is one.
And you can understand why, because we — we, as mediators, won't
put our best foot forward until it's the right time (Gambon: Uh-huh),
and we don't — we wouldn't buck a timetable. Now, I don't see any
timetable in these negotiations. / I really don't.

Gambon: (Over Mediator above) Uh — if you're talking about deadlines or
anything of that kind, let me say at this moment we have not set any
deadline and tell them, "Unless you do certain things by this date
we'll take certain actions." Generally, I'd say, George, we're gonna
press for a (slight pause) wage proposition here — increased benefits, whether they be straight salary increases or fringes or both

(pause), one that we can take back to our membership on the 2d Friday of April (Meyer says something), which is a me — membership meeting. I would say that if there is any timetable on the union's part, that'll be our position if they're gonna continue to bargain with us on this basis.

Mediator: The reason — what motivated my discussing the — the (pause) — the retroactive date was that in their discussions I picked up 2 points. They didn't bring them out here. They were talking among themselves, and I'm not violating a confidence in mentioning this, because it was general discussion, and that was the Standard Products negotiations and the Dayco negotiations. (Gambon: H'm) Reading between the lines of their conversation, I figured that what they're saying is that probably this union is waiting to see what happens in Standard Products or what happens in Dayco. And what I'm — why I'm discussing it with you is that if that is the case (Gambon: Uh-huh), then, of course, I will know how to gauge the tempo of these negotiations.

Gambon: Well, I'll be frank with you and say this, that I'm certainly interested in what Standard Products's going to do. I'm definitely in contact with those fellows in there and (Mediator: Sure, you have to be) as they come out of a meeting — now, they — they're right, at this moment — they're in — well, not at this moment. I don't know whether they're in there today. They — they began negotiations, I think, a day or so after we started, and we are in close touch with 'em. I'm interested in what Standard Products does; I'm interested in the Lashley situation; I'm certainly interested in Dayco situation, I mean, because they're all right here in the area. (Mediator: Sure) Now, one of the things the company will probably do is that, if anything, I think they'll try to lie, because there was one time not too long ago, before we signed this present contract, that Atlas went out ahead of the industry on the matter of pens — not pensions, but on insurance and a few other fringes. We got about a $7\frac{1}{2}$-cent package at the time that Standard Products only came across with 1¢; and, as we understood, according to their own statements, Standard Products Corporation raised hell with Atlas for — for goin' as far as they did with their employees, because soon as that happened, of course, the union in Standard Products started breathin' down their neck.

Mediator: So they may be a little wary of Standard Products now.

Gambon: Right. And I think they've also been pressured from time to time by Viking. That is, we completed our contract here, this one which you were in on, before the negotiations were finished in Viking. It was interesting to note that on a couple of fringes which were sort of unusual in this area, at least, say, this paid time-off for death in the family (Mediator: Yeah. I remember that), Viking, bein' in close contact with us, got the identical provision in their contract, along with a / pretty substantial —

Mediator: (Over Gambon above) A number of unions picked it up, too, outside (Gambon: Uh-huh) of your industry. We had 'em in here later with those demands (Gambon: Uh-huh) in there. But yours was the first.

Gambon: Yeah. Well, it's the point that they make, I mean, of — of — without anything egotistical in the picture a'tall, I mean, we — our contract is, as such — particularly on fringes has been pretty much of a model in the area here. I mean, we (Mediator: That's right) were the first ones in the area that had 3 weeks for 10 years. We were first ones to get jury make-up pay. Workmen's compensation make-up — that's entirely new. And they take a position they wanta wait for competitors and all like that. That isn't necessary in Atlas's case. They keep groaning here about their profits goin' down and then they make statements (laughing slightly) here they got a million dollars and somethin' before taxes. (Pause)

Mediator: Well, all this — all this discussion and argument of position (pause), while it has its importance, of course, in any negotiations (pause) and I did pay strict attention to it, nevertheless, far more important than the positions of both the parties in <u>these</u> negotiations is the other thing that I'm talking about. Now, the company's saying now (pause) t — what they're saying is they feel you should forego your wage reopener at ti — at this time. (Gambon: He said the same thing in October) Now, I — I would have to be very naive to believe that they're gonna <u>hang</u> on that position as a last point. It's a bargaining position, I feel sure. But more — but far more important than that is removing the road-blocks. Now, the road-blocks could be this — and I don't know; I'm speculating. The road-blocks could be that if they didn't want to make a move, would they make it — would they — and I've gotta find this out — would they make it in the light of these pending negotiations in these other places which they mention? (Gambon: H'm) If they won't, and we can establish that, well, we'll all know how to gauge these negotiations without everybody getting into a wrong position. We can get into a wrong position when it's a wrong time. On the other hand, if these negotiations can be resolved before those negotiations and they can be convinced that this can be done, of course that will be our objective. May sound a little different to you, me discussing strategy and matters like that, but we'd be wasting time if I / didn't.

Gambon: (Over Mediator above) H'm. Well, we're certainly interested in Standard Products, as evidenced by the comparisons that I've made, '46 on — right now, in terms of wage increases, they at 74 against our 62, a 12¢ an hour there, plus the fact that Standard Products right now, as far as my information goes — they're pressing for a 6-c — 16-cent general increase and another additional nickel to take care of inequities, which includes their skilled trades. 'Course, that's a part of our program, too, this problem of (slight pause) knocking out this differential business that exists between skilled trades and production workers — incentive workers — and has been for quite some time, now. Company gives — gave some recognition to that particular problem back in January when we signed the contract, as you know, and, well, we feel that they should continue to give that in order to keep knocking down that differential. Of course, we say that the best way of doing it is by putting into effect Point 2 of our proposal to them, which includes that point of the x fixed bonus proposition. It was only — I would s — say, making a guess here, that I don't think there's more than — very many more than 100 people involved in skilled trades and other people who are on day work, out of around 1400.

Mediator: How many people?

Gambon: About 1400. 'S only about 100 of those people left. (Pause) They're losin' their skilled trades. I don't know — x, look, I'll be — this is off the record, I mean as (Mediator: Yeah) far as they're concerned. But we know definitely that they're inclined to do something for their skilled trades. They're — they can't compete with the price that's being paid in the market now. (Mediator: Uh-huh) They've lost about 4 or 5 men. (Mediator starts to speak) Les Baker here is the chairman of our Skilled Trades Committee in the shop, and he told me that he knows that some of these bosses down the line that are directly bosses over these thing are all in favor of a wage increase to the skilled trades.

Mediator: To hold their men.

Gambon: Yeah, certainly. Gonna have to do it, George! They're advertising in the papers now for two-and-a-half. Well, Dayco, let's say, is $2.36½ for tool and die makers; we got 2.27. And that — there're fellows up there are grumblin' and grumblin' all over the place because they want higher rates, so that Atlas can't maintain their position. It's — x much longer. Gonna have to do somepin' about it. They keep losin' men, and they're not bein' able to replace 'em at the rate of pay we got in the shop. (Pause) Th — they — we know that they're planning to do something. I mean, Ray Horton, for instance, the vice-president in charge of sales at Atlas, is a member of A.D.A. Herb Jenkins runs into him over at an A.D.A. meeting, so — Horton likes to talk. He — Jenkins asked him how things were going — how negotiations were goin'. He says, "Well, I think everything'll be settled." He said, "There'll be somepin' settled." Now, there's no indication to us (slight pause) that they wanta make any settlements at this point. I p — firmly believe that they're gonna get away from that position, 'cause this is not much different than October. They come out and they said, "We" — first Michelsen says, "We don't wanta do anything." The next meeting — well, they — "We don't think we ought to do anything." And finally he takes the position before we come down here, "Well, we — we won't do anything." Then when we get down here they come away from a zero position to position which we went along with because we — we recognize the fact that we took a good bite out of 'em in (pause) the early part of the year, so we settled with 'em on that — for what amounted to maybe 'bout 3-cent package, which was one holiday extra — election day — and a 2½-cent general wage increase, which was equivalent to the cost-of-living increase at that time. We were willin' to go along on that basis, but that was before we found out about this complete decentralization program. (Mediator: Yeah) Now, what they wanta do, see, they don't wanta pay out any more cost to labor, as far as they're concerned, if they can get by with it, and I think that that's not only true of this re-opener. That's until the expiration of this contract that they're gonna pull that stuff. (Rather long pause) Yeah, I — I firmly believe they'd like us to say to them, "Well, we won't bother you until the contract expires." It'd make 'em very happy to go out and take all the dough they've got and put it into this e — decentralization proposition.

Mediator: Is your position going to be better after the Standard Products negotiations?

Gambon: I don't know! I don't know whether it would have — put me in a better position or (Mediator: xx) — or not. But I — let me say this to you, see. At one time they would bargain with us and use Standard Products as a comparison, when they thought they were better off than

Standar — we were better off than Standard Products employees.
Today they don't wanta talk about Standard Products because of the
picture is right here — 74¢ against 62. They get back now to th — their
competitive situation. Now, we recognize that there is a competitive
situation. In fact, they're doin' it themselves! You get plants payin'
$1.00 an hour or $1.10 an hour out in these wide open spaces. I'm
concerned with one plant very much — I mean, this competitive shop.
We have it in one of our rival unions. It's up in Mooresville, Mass-
achusetts. We've gotten 19¢ in wage increases there and pulled them
up. Their o — rates now are only about $1.10 to $1.20 against the rates
of pay that we have. So it's — we know there's competition there, but
still they keep advancing. I mean, the competition that they have now
they've had for years, because this particular industry that we're in,
this recorder business, is — has always been a cutthroat industry, I
mean, as — from a competitive standpoint. Everybody's tryin' to put
everybody else out of business. And it's important to note that Atlas
went through that competition all these years with pretty much of a —
a manual job performance on the part of people. They're c — they're
coming every day — every year they're becoming more highly mech-
anized — automatic machinery all in there. They're reducing their
labor costs at a terrific pace. There's no question about that.
Mediator: In your opinion, how do you feel about this? Is the company in
 a better position to wait or is the company in a better position to settle before these other settlements?
Gambon: I don't know. I — I think that their — their opinions probably
 would be governed a great deal just how far the union's gonna go in
 insisting its demands and having its demands met with. (Pause) I'm
 not goin' to take any position at this moment as to what we're gonna
 do. About all I'll say to you generally is if they're gonna come around
 here with these kind of things that they're callin' an offer here, I know
 damn / well what I'm gonna do.
Mediator: (Over Gambon above) Oh, that — that — that that they've offered, I'd — I'd (Gambon: No) pay no attention to that. I'm not — I'm
 not a bit concerned about that, because, like I said, when — when the
 right time comes I'll be very, very surprised if they ever held to that,
 because (Gambon: Yeah), if the right time comes, they're going to
 make a move. The big question is, how much? But bigger than even
 that question is the timing on the thing. What I want to develop is the
 right time. I've talked no money, I've talked no issues to either you
 or the company (Gambon: Uh-huh), because, first of all, I wanta establish the right move now —
Gambon: But as far as I'm concerned, unless we have the kind of a wage
 offer from the company —
 [Tape changed]
Mediator: ... today, tomorrow, the next day. Would you still have to
 wait until April the 2d / — 12th for ratification?
Gambon: (Over Mediator above) No. Not — no, when we're in negotiations we can call / a special meeting —
Mediator: (Over Gambon above) You mean that April 12th just happens
 to be a regular (Gambon: That's right) business / meeting?
Meyer: (Over Mediator above) Uh-huh. That's right.
Gambon: Well, in other words, I'm not trying to set up a deadline and

squeeze 'em down to a position of sayin', "Now, you get a couple a days to make up your mind, or else." We've left the thing open. Understand, George, we only had one meeting with them. (Mediator: Yeah) When they took this position I knew there wasn't any use of — of foolin' around with 'em. I either had to take a position of saying, "Look, do somethin' or else we'll call a special meeting and take a strike vote," or I had to try to bargain with them, and the only place I could get them to do <u>any</u> kind of bargaining would be down here. 'Cause I — I asked Michelsen — I said, "Do you want me to take that offer to my membership?" (Pause) "Well," he s — "I guess you'll have to." I said, "Well, if that's the way you want it, boy, I'll do it." "Well, we'll go to mediation." I says, "Well, suppose we don't wanta go there?" I — I raised the question. I said, "Well, suppose I didn't wanta go there? Suppose I prefer to take your offer and tell the membership this is what you're offering," see. Yeah. He didn't insist the (pause) — from saying, "Well, we'll go to mediation," although at first he was giving the impression that he didn't care whether we took it to the membership / or not.

Mediator: (Over Gambon above) Has he raised the cost-of-living between — in the last 6 months?

Gambon: No, no direct comparisons. He's talked about the cost- / of-living —

Mediator: (Over Gambon above) He mentioned Lashley, but I didn't — I didn't hear him mention cost-of-living / in x.

Gambon: (Over Mediator above) Well, he had one of those charts there (Meyer: Only that chart about the —) where he was using the cost-of-living and how much better off above the cost-of-living we are and / so —

Mediator: (Over Gambon above) But he didn't come down to any percentage?

Meyer: Huh-un. / No, he didn't.

Gambon: (Over Meyer above) Not the — not the periods, you mean (Mediator: Yes. This one here) business, such as we had in October? No. In fact, I don't think there has been any, has there?

Mediator: Well, what was Klinger's offer based on? 1 — 1.4?

Gambon: I'm not sure. As I understand it, they offered a 2% wage increase.

Mediator: Is it 2?

Gambon: Uh-huh.

Mediator: 2% of the average?

Gambon: 2% probably of the existing hourly —

Mediator: Of the basic rates. Oh, yeah, existing, that would be. (Pause) I thought it was 1.4. xxxx. Uh — all right. (Pause) Now, about today. (Pause) I'm — I'm going to — I think I'd like to take a whirl at this today, take a trial (Gambon: Uh) run on it and put out a few trial balloons on this — on these 2 positions. Now, this afternoon you have the — your Good Friday. Now, you can suit youf — selves about this; I'll give you a blank check on it. You can — we can recess at 12:00 — the observance begins at 12:00, doesn't it (Gambon: Yeah) ? — 12:00 to 3:00? And if you want to, we can resume at — at 3:00, or you can recess at 12:00 without trying this. We'll try it at another time — another date. But either way is all right with me. And may — it may be worth it to get a look at this thing and s — see — put a trial run out and see how it goes.

Gambon: Well, I would say this, George. I think that I'll throw it out this way; I don't know whether the committee'll agree or not. I think our approach probably would be that since our people up in the plant have to work, we shouldn't object to goin' through it anyhow. I mean, it's not a question so much of anybody being so religious that we gonna stop there (pause), as much (Mediator: The union come back, then, at 2:00, or —) as it is that we feel that if people are — who are (Meyer: Yeah) workin' right on through there — they have no (Mediator: Well, it's all right with me) opportunity — we should work right on through / ourselves.

Meyer: (Over Gambon above) Yeah. Yeah, because there's one thing I would like to — it has no bearing on this, but to bring John up to date. There was a petition taken up in the plant la — about Tuesday of this week, the people who wanted to go out at 12:00 o'clock. I wasn't aware of it, but Bill Michelsen called about 10 minutes after 9:00 and said he had heard about this and the company's position is this, that nobody can go home at 12:00 o'clock today. It's an 8-hour day (Mediator: Oh! Well, that takes care of that) in the plant, and a notice is put — notice is put on the bulletin board that the company offered Good Friday for a paid holiday (Gambon: H'm), the union membership chose Easter Monday, so therefore production will go — continue all day long. So I don't even think it's good from our point of view (Gambon: Uh. Well, no) for us (Mediator: No) to take a recess.

Mediator: No, I think — I think / we can forget about —

Gambon: (Over Mediator above) Under those circumstances / I —

Meyer: (Over Gambon above) See, John, this came in this morning. I hadn't had a chance / to tell you that.

Mediator: (Over Meyer above) We will proceed on the regular schedule, then.

Meyer: Uh-huh.

Mediator: N — now, that takes care of that. I — I probably, even if we did take the 3 hours — I should go to church, but I prob'ly wouldn't. (Gambon: H'm. That's prob'ly what we'd do, too — some of us) And — so — 'course, I could drag in tonight (pause), but (Several girls laugh) (rather long pause) we'll do that. Well, I wanta — I wanta talk some more with them and then I'll be back here. So I think we'll give this a whirl in the afternoon session and start getting into the issues.

Gambon: Well, on that effective date business, just so they —

Mediator: Well, they didn't mention that, / see. That was my —

Gambon: (Over Mediator above) Well, I mean if they do bring it up and wanta know what our position is, it's April 1st, 1953, which is the re-opener date, and (Mediator: Well, what I couldn't understand was —) we assumed that they knew that because we had taken that position consistently.

Mediator: What I — what I couldn't understand was this. I felt that — well, the negotiations where they are now (Gambon: Yeah), see, they're — b — big gap. You're — you're far away from a settlement date right at this point. That being the case, and since you're almost over your April 1, I — I began to wonder, "Probably the union is" —

when — when they mentioned Dayco and Standard Products, I thought, "I wonder. Maybe the union's dragging their feet wanting to see what's comi — going to come out of these negotiations." And then I speculated, "Well, then why is the company draggin' <u>their</u> feet? (Gambon: H'm) Then <u>they</u> must have a reason, and what is <u>their</u> reason?" And talking to them I — I couldn't esfin — I couldn't establish one as clear as — for instance, in figuring yours out, I had Standard Products and I had Dayco, but talking to them I had nothing. Then I thought, "Well, I wonder if it's generally accepted that the thing is retroactive? If it is, this thing could go on and on and on and on, and if it does, I wanta know whether it's going to be real concrete negotiations or whether it's going to be a baby-sitting (Gambon: H'm) contest." (Gambon: No, it won't be on my part, I —) And when I established that, then I'd know how to proceed. But I've — you cleared up — you cleared up some of those points. Now, I've got to find out some of the same things from management. Then we'll plan on this afternoon.

Gambon: We're certainly interested in what's done in Standard Products and Dayco / xxxxx.

Mediator: (Over Gambon above) But it will not stand in the way of / a settlement.

Gambon: (Over Mediator above) It won't stand in the way, George. We're — we're — our particular emphasis is — is mostly this ab — ability to pay. And they — they said to us they're not takin' a position that they don't have the ability to make a better offer than what they have offered. (Pause) We're — we're bargaining with them the same as we always bargain. Either ya have it xxxx say you got it, see.

Mediator: O.K. Then April 12th is not a deadline. That's a business meeting.

Gambon: That's a business meeting, but it <u>can</u> be a deadline (Mediator: It could be), depending on the way these — what progress is / made.

Mediator: (Over Gambon above) Well, so could April the 5th.

Meyer: Yeah. So could today.

Gambon: (At same time as Meyer above) Yep, that's right! So (laughing) could today be. (Laughs, as do one or 2 others)

<u>Management Caucus - C</u> (11:25 A. M.)

Mediator: Uh (pause) — I put it to the union this way. (Pause) I said their — "Both the union and the company have stated their positions and stated their positions well, and I wanta talk to you about something outside of the subject of positions, or issues." Uh (slight pause) — I said, "I — there's a termination — or, rather, a — a mentioned date of April 1st in your reopening clause, and we've almost reached that date. The company hasn't mentioned anything about it, and the union hasn't mentioned anything about it, but I'm curious. And I'm curious for these reasons: (1), I want to know whether both parties are in agreement in this respect, that everything will be retroactive; (2), whether it's a question both of you don't discuss until the final settlement of the contract, and then you negotiate that question; or, (3), whether both of you have completely forgotten about

it. But most important of — of — of all is Number 4, and that is, what
effect is this goi — is — does that date have on the progress of these
negotiations? And to make myself clear I mean this, uh (pause) —
uh — the — is it going to slow down these negotiations, or does it control them? In view of the fact that you'll soon be past April the 1st
and you <u>believe</u> you're going to get retroactivity, in all probability
you could be dragging your feet. Now, is there any reason — because
there doesn't seem to be too much hurry in these negotiations. Now,"
I said, "I was getting a — a little suspicious, and I feel that it's important that I know — get the tempo of this thing, because I don't want
a baby-sitting contest. (Michelsen laughs shortly) I want to partake
in genuine negotiations." I said, "Now, one — another deduction or
a speculation that I've made is that in this area there are other
unions which your union has a contract and they're lar — with large
companies — there are other companies, I meant to say, such as
Standard Products and Dayco and some of these others. And I would
also like to know whether the union is waiting for these unions t —
companies to reach an agreement with the u — Local unions, and are
we just going through motions here? Do we have to wait for a settlement in those companies before either you or the company can have a
criteria to work on? If so, why, we'll all coast together." And I
said, "It would be very foolish to a — attempt to assist 2 people who
didn't want, at <u>this</u> time, to reach an agreement." (Slight pause)
Well, John said (slight pause) — on the first question, retroactivity,
he said, "We have never had any trouble with the company on that.
It was always generally accepted that when we reached an agreement
it would be retroactive to the effective date." (2), on the question of
the other companies reachin' a — reaching an agreement, "Sure,
we're interested in what they get." And he said, "We have a meeting scheduled for April the 12th with our union, and on that date we're
going to submit a report of these negotiations, if an agreement hasn't
been reached before that. But" — and the "but" is the big thing — he
said, "But Dayco or Standard Products or April the 12th has nothing
to do — doesn't mean that we can't reach an agreement without waiting for your April 12th or Standard Products or Dayco." I said, "Well,
I'm glad to hear that," I said, "because it has a lot to do with the
tempo of these negotiations and," I said, "we're all intelligent enough
to want to know these things, stop, so that we don't knock our heads
against the wall wasting time." I said, "I have not talked to either of
you about your respective positions, where you are at the bargaining
table, because I felt there was no point in it until I could establish a
clear road for these negotiations." He said, "If we can reach an
agreement, we can settle tomorrow." I said, "Well, then, do you
have to wait for April the 12th to get this ratified if you did reach an
agreement?" He said, "No." He said, "We would have a special
meeting and ratify." He said April the 12th is just a scheduled business
meeting. He said, "Now, we're n — we didn't set that up as a deadline."
He said, "I — that's not intended for — mentioning that doesn't mean
that that's our deadline and that we have that much time and that that's
to give them a warning that if they don't have it up within a few days
before that there will be a strike." He said, "That's not the purpose at
all." He says, "That is a scheduled business meeting." He said, "We

can have a strike tomorrow, or the next day." He said, "We're almost
over April the 1st." He says, "So April the 12th is not a deadline date."
He said, "It's merely a business meeting." I said, "All right. Fine."
I said, "That clears up a lot for me." And I said, "Now, the 3rd — the
next point is this. When we set this conference, we talked about it being
Good Friday," and I said, "The observance — the religious observances
take place between 12:00 and 3:00. Now, we can do one of 2 things. We
can recess at 12:00 o'clock and set another conference for some day
next week, or we can resume at 3:00 after the observances." And Bernice Meyer spoke up and said, "Well, as far as we're concerned on that
question, in our plant it is not a holida — it is not a time off and it might
be a little embarrassing if we took time off and plant had to work."
She would rather that — they would rather that negotiations be con —
continued in their regular schedules that we have, rather than any special consideration that the plant workers are not getting. (Michelsen:
Uh-huh) Well, I could understand that. Either that, or set another
meeting; see, one or the other. I said, "Well, that — that being the
case, I'm — I'll check that with the company and see how they feel
about it. I feel that they'll go along on — on that. There's no question 'bout that in my mind, but I'll take it up with 'em and I'll settle
it by saying we'll proceed along regular schedules," which means we
would meet in the afternoon session (Espig: Uh-huh) at the regular
time, 2:00 o'clock. So that was settled. Now, that's where we are.
(1) — (1), they contend that (slight pause) they're not waiting for anybody else to settle; that, (2), April the 12th is not a deadline date,
merely a scheduled meeting; and, (3), they're willing to continue negotiations today without any special considerations for observance
periods. So (slight pause), any questions there?
Loring: Well, we will readjourn a — we will return at 2:00, George?
Mediator: I would say that we ought to recess here about 12:00 (Loring:
H'm) and come back about 2:00. (Loring: Uh-huh) And (slight pause)
then we can really pick it up. There's no use of us starting any discussions on their positions or your positions at this time and having
to break it off at 12:00 (Loring: Yeah) o'clock. But I — I do feel,
based on the questions that I asked them, that they're not — I don't
think there's a plan on their committee — a — a pre-plan to hold these
negotiations off (Michelsen: Uh-huh) until somebody else settles. I
don't think that's — I don't think that's a — a plan with them. I do
think — I do think that if they didn't get a satisfactory settlement,
they might — they might take this position — and, again, they gave me
nothing to believe that they would do this; this is purely my own thinking — they might decide that, "Well, we're not satisfied with the company's offer so let's wait until the others settle and then we won't look
too badly. Or we can use it to point to the company, even though —
and say, 'Look what they gave, even though their contract expired.'"
That could be their thinking. I doubt very much that it is. (Michelsen:
Uh-huh) Because it could work the other way. Uh — it could work the
other way. It could work where — they're in a reopener now, and
they would be in a better position to settle before these other figures
come out, because these other figures will probably be higher, since
they're contract negotiations, than the figure that the Atlas people
would get. And, of course, the Atlas union could say, "Yes, but we

— we — we're only workin'on a reopener." But, psychologically, that — that would be a little difficult to overcome with the other unions and as far as Gambon's political position is concerned with other unions. So, that <u>could</u> work that way. But I'm convinced — I — I'm pretty sure that they're here to try to — I — I don't think that the other situations at this time have an effect (Michelsen: Uh-huh) that are — are a detriment, or a road-block, or are deliberately holding these things up. Unless you people have some information that I don't have. (Slight pause)

Michelsen: No. I — I don't (slight pause) — I'm not impressed with that — that delaying tactic. I — I just thought of it (Mediator: Well, I was very interested in it, more so than you) xxxxx. I know they're interested in what Standard Products will do. (Slight pause)

Mediator: But Standard Products is still a contract termination, isn't it?

Michelsen: Right.

Mediator: And I can't see them using crit — that criteria; I really (Michelsen: H'm) can't. Because if they were in — if — if your contract was terminating, I could see they (Michelsen: Oh, sure. I could, too) would be interested — very much so, and I doubt that you'd get a settlement (Michelsen: We're gonna be back here in October, again) before. And I think, too, that (slight pause) they're interested, but not to the point where they could use it in these negotiations. I think their 2 pos — the positions of the 2 people, Standard Products and Atlas, are in entirely different categories because of one being a termination of contract and the other bein' a reopener. So I think we're on pretty good ground that way. So, we'll recess at 12:00 and then pick it up at 2:00.

Michelsen: Uh-huh.

Mediator: I didn't talk any issues with 'em. I didn't touch the thing, 'cause I wanted to find out the — the other (Michelsen: Yeah) first. (Pause) And I also told 'em that company's — I said, "I haven't discussed issues with the company. The company's position is the same." And I said, "They're deeply entrenched in their position. They feel as though you should forego your wage reopener." Then, of course, Gambon followed up with all the reasons why, and you've heard all those. And — but I wanted to make it clear to them that it (Michelsen: Uh-huh) — we have not been discussing issues and that <u>I</u> have been steering these negotiations along the lines that I have been to establish first (slight pause) the <u>course</u> that we're to go on. And I made it very clear to them that if <u>I</u> thought for a minute that we were working on a timetable I would assure them — I assured them that I would <u>treat</u> that — the negotiations the way they oughta be treated under timetable conditions, which would be a lick and a promise to do more the next time and then stall it for another week and play around with it. (Michelsen: Uh-huh) "But if you're <u>genuinely</u> interested in tryin' to work out this thing, well, let's — let's <u>know</u> that." And the answer satisfied me. Now, that doesn't mean — and <u>they</u> know that that doesn't mean that — or isn't an indication, or a signal, that the company's position is going to be any different than what it is. The important thing was to find that out.

Michelsen: Uh-huh.

Loring: Do you think that there's a possibility of today of getting really into the thing, George?

Mediator: I think there's a good chance of — uh — I'm — I'm gonna — I plan on making a trial run this afternoon on those — on the positions. Now, here's what I intend to do. This can be established. (Pause) I can say, and will say, to the union, "This is the first time that I'm taking up your respective positions in 2 meetings. Your position — the union's position — these 7 issues — are not realis — a real — is not a realistic position. (Pause) I understand why you're asking for these issues, and I know how many of them are sticky issues and which ones aren't. (Slight pause) And you know."

[As tape is changed, Mediator explains what he will tell the union to get it to make a first move on its position, as a first trial balloon in the afternoon. If they reduce position by only small amounts, he says, he will know they are waiting for April 12.]

... or I know they're waiting for Standard Products. (Michelsen: Yeah) Everything'll be an — you'll get the answer there, 'll take 'em out. (Pause)

Michelsen: I'll be home dyein' Easter eggs if you come back with (Mediator laughs) that story xx. (Laughs) (Rather long pause)

[Some 5 minutes of conversation ensue on the union's distribution of material at the Aiken plant and the general problem of union organization in the South.]

Mediator: Uh — shall we make it 1:30 insteada 2:00?

Michelsen: Any time is all right with me, / George. I don't care.

Mediator: (Over Michelsen above) Is an hour and a half enough?

Loring: Whatever you say.

Michelsen: (At same time as Loring above) It's up to you. Yeah. If they wanta go to church for a portion of that time, which is (Mediator: Well —) certainly — I don't care. Any time.

Mediator: All right. (Michelsen: And —) I think — well, let's make it 1:30, then.

Michelsen: Sure.

Mediator: I think we can call it quits now and —

Michelsen: Do you see any possibility of this thing going over the Easter week-end?

Mediator: It'll depend on this afternoon.

Michelsen: I hate to think of / spending my Easter Sunday.

Mediator: (Over Michelsen above) I — oh, you mean hold conferences?

Michelsen: Yeah.

Mediator: (At same time as Michelsen above) Oh, no. / No.

Michelsen: (Over Mediator above) Well, all right.

Mediator: Oh, no!

Michelsen: No.

Mediator: Not on a reopener.

Michelsen: No. I don't (Mediator: No) — I don't think it's that critical. If (Mediator: No) it is, I want to adjust my plans. (Mediator: No —) Also, one other thing. You know Monday is a holiday in our plant.

Mediator: Is it?

Michelsen: Uh-huh. / So —

Mediator: (Over Michelsen above) Well, we've got — we've got that kinda time. We — I (Michelsen: I'm willin' to work then) — but a lot will — lot would depend on what kind of a move they make today. (Michelsen: Yeah) And even if they do it, if they make a good move, why, looks like there is common ground and could be settled, lot would de — that would — you'd have to answer that. Uh — that would determine our schedule. And even — even if the moves were good there isn't any reason why Easter should be disrupted.

Michelsen: No. I — I'm willing to spend all the time we need on this thing, but if they feel that it is necessary to spend a week travelin' around the country, even if it's far deep South, why, I'm not gonna be here Easter Sunday.

Mediator: I think you've got a lot of support on that. (Several, including Espig and Michelsen, laugh)

Michelsen: Good. Well, we've reached that agreement.

Mediator: Yep. That's one thing settled that wasn't on the — in — in the demands, huh? (Laughs slightly)

Michelsen: (In low tone) Yeah.

Mediator: All right. We'll see ya about 1:30.

Union Caucus - B (11:50 A.M.)

Mediator: I went over the same questions (pause) — well, not the same questions, but questions similar to those that I had asked the union committee, for the purpose of finding out the same thing with the company that I wanted to find out from the union, and I'm satisfied that the company has no particular reasons to drag their feet. And while I didn't talk issues with them, I did talk more about their desire to get this thing settled and if there was any reasons why they felt that it couldn't be settled at this time I would want to know about them and I would wanta talk about them, and if they were logical and reasonable, well, maybe we could all agree on them. But there weren't any. And so I'm pretty well convinced that we have a clear negotiating road. Whether we can use it and to work out the final settlement depends upon how all 3 of us operate from here on in. But that road-block has been removed and — well, I wo — I won't say removed. It evidently wasn't there to start with but — so, on the question of recessing, as far as the company's concerned, they're not holding to any 3-hour observance and they'll meet just on the regular hours, whatever r — shots we call. So suppose we recess for lunch now and come back at 1:30. That'll give us an hour and a half, unless any members of the committee feel they have to have more time to go to church or (pause) such. An hour and a half's enough for the company. It's enough for me.

Gambon: Well, let me put it this way. We'll be back at 1:30, and as far as I'm concerned, any member of the committee who wants to go to church, all right. It's — I'll excuse 'em for the time that they wanta go to church. W — we can continue here. (Pause) So we'll be back here — the union will be represented at 1:30 (laughing).

Mediator: 1:30.

Denk: Well, they're aware of that April 1st, now, aren — did you mention that to 'em, / George?

Mediator: (Over Denk above) Yes, I do. Yeah. I said, "I raised that point with the union and I wanta raise it with you, because nobody seems to be mentioning it and I was beginning to get a little worried about it, wonderin' what was the gimmick behind it." So I pointed

out that the union's reply was that they didn't raise it because, historically, it has never been questioned and the company always paid it. They didn't say they wouldn't pay it. They just listened.
[Mediator dismisses the group for lunch at 12:00 M.]

Union Caucus - C (2:15 P.M.)

Mediator: Uh — like I said earlier, I think the road is clear to start movin' this thing. (1), coming right to the point, it's my opinion that the position of the company — that the company's in right now is an unrealistic position. By the same token, the position that the union's in is not the position that they hope to settle this thing for. So we've gotta start moving. While I'm working with the company — I have some other things to talk about — I would like your committee to (pause) take a look at your position (Gambon: H'm) and s — getting it in ready for a — to get it in — getting it into condition for your — your first move. At the same time I'm going to talk to the company. Now, the gap between you is 4/10ths of a cent, and I haven't totaled yours, but I know it's a (Gambon: H'm) hell of a distance apart. The sooner we get down to that realistic area of bargaining the sooner we're going to settle. By the same time, I know the union has to protect its bargaining position, the company likewise is going to be very jealous of theirs. The time involved depends upon the steps that each side wants to take. Now — and that'll also determine the tempo of these negotiations. We haven't gone into costs of packages. We haven't gone into the ridiculousness of the company's 4/10ths-of-a-cent position, because I'm co — I'm convinced that both committees really want to find out where that area of realistic bargaining is. So while I'm with them I would like your committee to review your demands and see if you can't get them moving into the realistic area and we get the company to do likewise. / As soon —
Gambon: (Over Mediator above) Well, George, Number 1, we attempted to get the company to take a realistic approach to these negotiations in the first place. At their request I submitted the kind of things that we wanted. They supposedly wanted that so that they could consider the union's position and tell us what they would do. Now, since they saw fit to come out of the consideration chamber — I use that word very purposely — with the kind of an offer that they did, I'm not going to move from the position I'm in now until they make some approach to a sensible kind of an offer. I mean, I don't expect 'em to go all out, but I think they should make some kind of an offer that it at least indicates that they're tryin' to bargain here. I'll — I'm prepared to move away from my position here, but I want them to move away first. They're not makin' any kind of an offer that is any way reasonable a'tall (Mediator: Well —), or, as you say, very definitely un — unrealistic.
Mediator: It's unrealistic, and so is your position. Your position is unrealistic in this respect. (1) — not that I don't — wouldn't like to see you get every one of your demands; it would be a good thing if you could. But that would be wishful thinking in the light of the standard economics of the industry and area and so forth, things that I don't

have to tell you. I don't know how much yours cost. I believe the company said a rough guess, if they gave you what you wanted, would be 65¢ an hour. (Gambon: I realize that, George) So when I say it's unrealistic, I mean they're ahead (Gambon: Uh-huh) of you. When you're up at 65 and they're at 4/10ths of a cent, that's one wide (laughing slightly) gap to — to close.

Gambon: I suggested to them before they asked for this list of things — demands that we have here that we approach these negotiations on the basis that, "Look, you're gonna do something. Now, tell us what you can do. What do you say you can afford to do, and we'll start from that point and bargain the thing?" Now, that's when I get the request for a list. I told 'em — I said, "We gave you a long list once before. So we sit down and we haggle back and forth. Now, if you wanta clean it up quick, let's go at it without a lot of rigamarole." Now, they wanted this, and as I say, supposedly to consider before they made any kind of a — an offer or tell us where their position was. I will say to you at this point, not to be at this time communicated to them, that there are 2 particular points in this entire program that take first place. Number 1 is the 35-hour-week proposition and the other is the fixed bonus for skilled trades and day workers. They may or may not be our final position. It won't be the first move that I'm willing to make, but I'm — I'm telling that to you to let you know the 2 things that we're most interested — interested in. And I think you can understand our reasoning there because of the jobs that are being lost — already have been lost and those that were planned to go out of the picture by the end of this year — and the fact that we do have this problem of some inequities existing between the take-out pay of skilled trades and other day-work people as against the take-out of incentive workers in the plant. I — I wanted you to know that. At least it might help your thinking in the discussions with them, although I don't wanta make that as a formal, official proposition to them at this point. But it's still a bargainable proposition as far as I'm concerned. I mean, I'm not willing — I'm not unwilling to deviate somewhat from the list of demands in here.

Mediator: Yeah. W — w — well, here's the way — here's the way this committee — here — here's the position I believe this committee's in, as all other committees are in. This committee is standing pat. They have said, "We w — we want you to forego your wage reopener" (Gambon: Uh-huh), and this committee, like most all other bargaining committees, has to go back — and have to go back and report to their - report back to their superiors. It is my curbstone analysis that (pause) some members of this committee, on this side of the table, take their position seriously — some, not (Gambon: Uh-huh) all. I really believe that some of 'em would like to deliver that to their superiors (Gambon: H'm), that they got the union to forego their reopening clause. I think there are others on this committee who know that that's ridiculous. But, nevertheless, that kind of thinking is there and that kind of thinking is still going to be there as long as your position is where it is, because when they go back and report to their people and they say, "They're at 60¢" or "They're at 50¢" or "They're at 30¢" or wherever you are, well, their kind of thinking is goin' to be supported, because the company isn't going to make a

move, this company or any other company, until they get down near
that area where it's the 1-yard line. And I think both of you are miles
apart and both of you have a lot of latitude (Gambon: H'm), and just
now a question of who's gonna kick the ball off. I think that you've got
a lot of kicking material. Now — / but, by the same token —

Gambon: (Over Mediator above) I don't wanta be in the position where I
set the area of bargaining.

Mediator: What was that?

Gambon: I don't wanta be in a position where I set the area of bargaining
(laughing slightly). I'd rather they'd do it.

Mediator: Well, what I (Gambon: I mean, xx sayin' that) said to them —
what I said — yeah. What I said to them was this. I put it to them this
way. I told them pretty near the same thing as I have just said here.
(Gambon: Uh-huh) I have told them that I believe their position is not
a realistic position. (Gambon: Uh-huh) Now, there are some members on that committee didn't like to hear that because they — I think
there is at least one that believes in what he's been told (Gambon: Uh-
huh), that he's to get a settlement without paying anything. / Uh —

Gambon: (Over Mediator above) Well, I think there's some — some
soundness and reasoning — in fact, I'm quite sure that Bill Michelsen,
as the chairman of this committee, is very anxious to deliver on that
basis, because this is the 2d time that he has been in charge of negotiations and in both instances he's made the same approach. Now,
Bill has a big stake in this thing. He's getting himself quite a reputation in the industry and out of the industry. There's been some rum-
blings about the possibility of the guy going elsewhere. Certainly he'd
like to have it under his belt; I mean, that'd be a nice feather in his
cap, particularly with this union. This is a progressive organization
and a very militant outfit and has produced a damn fine contract over
the years.

Mediator: So you have a pretty good idea of the kind of work that's cut
out for me before these negotiations (Gambon: Certainly. Uh-huh)
are over. And I don't — I — I — what I — what I want to do — I don't
want the thing to be held up (pause) without good purpose, and I
think you have here enough material to start shaping (Gambon: H'm),
a — and I don't think you're going to lose any face or any bargaining
position in coming out with a — with a first offer upon / our request.

Gambon: (Over Mediator above) Le — let's you and I understand one
thing, and I think we know each other pretty good after a couple of
times we've been together, now. I'm not gonna bargain with anybody on
a personal basis. I'm interested in getting a fair settlement. However,
it makes it difficult for me to move away from a position when I know
that they're not taking a position solely because of the company's ability to do certain things. There are some personal approaches being
made from that side of the table, which you more or less indicate yourself, and I know that to be a fact. I've seen Michelsen operate before he
was the head man on these committees and I've s — I'm seeing him operate now, not only in these kind of negotiations but in grievance matters and things of that. As I pointed out to you, we're going into arbitration now, something we never done in all the years we've had contracts with 'em. So I don't blame the guy for trying to map his
strategy and keep it directed to getting away with nothing, if he can do

it, or with as little as possible, because I'm tryin' to get as much as possible. But i — it makes it a little bit tougher if I thought that he was makin' a — an approach — and I've said this to him on many occasions, "Look, lay your cards on the table and I'll do the same thing." I have no (laughing slightly) confidence if he throws somepin' down that that's his cards. I mean, he's s — still got a few up his sleeves. So I have to bargain the same way with him. I'll move away from that position. I'm quite sure the committee / will go along with my moving away.

Mediator: (Over Gambon above) Here's the — here — h — here's the way I think — here's the way I think you — here's the best position I — I believe you can get in — in these negotiations. When you make a move — Michelsen knows, when you make a move, whether you're sincere and you know whether he's sincere. For instance, let's say he came in here with a counter-proposal. (Gambon: H'm) He's offered you 4/10ths of a cent. Let's say he adds /4 —

Gambon: (Over Mediator above) 6/10ths. (Laughs)

Mediator: — or 6/10ths (Gambon laughs slightly again, followed by Meyer) more to it. You would know right then and there that this is the tempo that these negotiations (Gambon: Yeah) are goin' to follow. The man is insincere, or he wouldn't put that out. Now, while Bill no doubt is taking a adamant position in these negotiations, it's pretty hard for me to believe that Bill could even sell himself the idea that he could settle for 4/10ths of a cent in a situation and in an area like (Gambon: H'm) this, see. Now, however (pause), he's g — he's got — he has to be dislodged. He can't be dislodged if you come back — let's say your total package is 60's, or whatever he said it was — 60 or 65¢ — and you reduced it to 63. That would be just as ridiculous as him mak — mov — moving it up to 60¢. That gap has to be closed. The faster it's closed — you know the realistic area. (Gambon: Uh-huh) The closer you get to it, the tougher the position you can take. The sooner we get down to that point, the sooner we're going to move. Now, I'm not telling you what (Gambon: H'm) area that is. Yo — you're the judge of that. You know your own area. And I'm not telling ya what price or what figure you're to settle for; I'm not telling the company that. But I do know this, that I've gotta get the both of you down into that area (Gambon: Uh-huh), and you can get there fast or you can get there slow. It's up to both / of you.

Gambon: (Over Mediator above) Well, having been good bit of experience with his approaches to these kind of situations, I know it's not goin' to do me any good to make an appreciable cut in the union's position, because I would expect that his strategy then would be to do something like 6/10ths-of-a-cent proposition (Mediator: Well, if he does —) in hope that I would then make another big cut and come back with another cent or somepin' like that, / see.

Mediator: (Over Gambon above) No. Th — that will work this way. Let us say you made an appreciable cut and you get down to the realistic area and he came back with a — with a ridiculous (Gambon: Uh-huh) counter-proposal. You wouldn't have lost a thing, because when he does that, then I have the material I need to work on him.

Gambon: Well, let — let me say this to you, then. Suppose I do make a — a — an appreciable cut, recommend it to my committee and we go along and we say to you, "Now, look, George. Here we're gonna cut

down to this, and this is where we're gonna stand until this guy starts
gettin' into a — a position of coming somewhere <u>near</u> this kind of
thing." D'you want it that way?

Mediator: I think this, see. / If you make it to me —

Gambon: (Over Mediator above) If I make an appreciable cut, I'm gonna
xxx or I'm not gonna move.

Mediator: If you make an appreciable cut — there are all kinds of cuts.
There are (Gambon: Uh-huh) the appreciable — appreciable could
mean also miles away from a realistic area (Gambon: Uh-huh), and
then again it could be close. Now, I've seen one union come in here
and they said — they were up ar — their total package was around 50¢,
and they said, "Look, George, we wanta get this thing moving. We're
gonna get down to a certain position, and when we get down there you
will know where we are, that we're in that fighting area. (Gambon:
Uh-huh) Now," he said, "in the e — in the interest of getting these negotiations speeded up, we're going do that. If they come back with an
unrealistic figure, we're going to know where we stand. Now, we can
tell you that we're going to stand pat." Now — I'll tell you the name
of the company. It was the Irving Mining Company and their union. I
don't know whether you know him or not, Herman Schiff.

Gambon: (In low voice) No, I don't.

Mediator: Herman come in and he said, "We're up — we're up at the sky.
But," he said, "we're goin' to come back with a counter-proposal
that's goin' to put us right into that zone of no man's land (Gambon:
H'm) — a fighting zone," he said, "and from there on it's your baby."
Now, he did that and he lopped off (pause) a figure that was — put him
right in that zone. Company hasn't offered one penny one. Now, when
he did that — when he made that move it gave me what I wanted. I
went back to the company — Major Auerbach was the vice-president
for the company — and I said — and historically this company had
dealt in pennies — one move now, $1\frac{1}{2}$¢ (Gambon: H'm) now, $\frac{1}{2}$¢. Now,
this union had not had an increase in 2 years, so the settlement figure
was high, but ya have to remember (Gambon: Uh-huh) they didn't
have any for 2 years. They had a 2-year contract with no wage reopener. So the company — I said to the company, "Now, look. That
union has got right into the realistic area. If you come up with a cent
or 2¢ you are going to damage these negotiations beyond repair. Now,
you know you have to settle this and you know that you have a — a
limit. The question is — I know what you're tryin' to do. You're tryin'
to get to that limit without jeopardizing your bargaining position, and
I'm here to help you do that, but don't make it harder on me. The union
has made such a <u>substantial</u> move, and now you <u>know</u> they're in the
realistic area. If you come out with a penny you're gonna insult them.
You're go — you're goin' to make them feel that you're not bargaining
in good faith. If I were you I would throw out at least <u>80%</u> of what
you're going to give them" — and I didn't know what you were — what
the company was going to give them. So they held a caucus, and I was
more surprised than even the union. They threw a 13-cent offer out
which — soon as the union got it they went right into a <u>real</u> huddle
(Gambon: Uh-huh), because they knew here was a genuine step forward — the first step forward. I think within an hour and a half later
we had the whole thing wrapped up. It was a 20-cent settlement, but,

as I said, it was a 2- (Gambon: Yeah) year deal. But the point I'm
making is that moving — i — it can be done i — if they do it that way,
but if — if you make a substantial move and they come back with an
unsubstantial one, they have indicated that, (1), they're not bargaining
in good faith, (2), they've also indicated how they intend to move in
these negotiations, which assists both the union and the mediator, and,
thirdly, it puts me in a position where I can do a little stronger talking when I see the daylight. So it's for that reason that I mention these
things. We can be here for long, long time if we play. The sooner we
get down to the realistic zone, the sooner we start to move (Gambon
says something), because I — I can't really be effective until we
(Gambon: H'm) get down to that area. I'm not talking money with
you, I'm not talking money with them until I know that we're down to
where I want you.

Management Caucus - D (2:45 P.M.)

Mediator: Well — uh (slight pause) — here's a — here's a thumbnail
sketch or preview of (laughs slightly) (slight pause) my approach in
there at this time. Went something like this. (Slight pause) I told
John — I said, "John, I haven't computed the cost of your package and
the company didn't either, but in roughly figuring it I think it came out
to somewheres near 60¢, if granted the way it stands. Now," I said
(pause), "I've got to say — I've got to remind you of that, because I
believe that if this issue — if these issues, or this reopener, can't be
settled, you and the company will at least want to know how close ya
got to a settlement, or how much stood between the both of you. Now,"
I said, "we're never even going to get to that place if we don't move,
and the moving is the thing I wanta talk about. Now," I said, "you
want to know whether the company is bargaining in good faith; the company, no doubt, wants to know whether you're bargaining in good faith.
Your position is what you said it was; the company has said they feel
you should forego the wage reopener at this time. Positions bein'
what they are, you're in a ridiculous one, because it's unrealistic; it's
not a bargainable position; ya couldn't pull a strike on it, or with it;
you couldn't convince me or anyone else. So, cutting all the corners
and getting right down to cases, the sooner y — we — we get this thing
down to a realistic area, the sooner we're going to know whether
you're — you have a strike or whether you have an agreement. So you
are going to have to show me exactly what you are asking this company for before I can even write it down as the issue or the problem."
I said, "I couldn't write down that package that you have, because it's
unrealistic." He agreed (slight pause) that that was so. (?: Uh-huh)
So I said, "If these negotiations are going to mean anything, the union
is going to have to reconsider this and submit a proposal to me and to
the company that will indicate where you really are going, because the
company doesn't know where you're going and I don't know where
you're going at — where you're standing" (slight pause), which he
also agreed was so. (Michelsen: Uh-huh) So I said, "I want your
committee to take this package, review it, and reduce it. Now," I
said, "there are — there is all kind of reductions. You can review it

and ya can knock off a nickel, you can knock off a dime. The amount that you cut off is going to indicate just how soon you want a settlement, or how anxious you are, or how desirous you are of cleaning up these negotiations." I said, "You can — if you get your position down to the r — to a realistic figure that will indicate that your union wants to resolve these differences. Now, everything depends on what you do with it. Then there is the other way. You can s — you can start dealing in pennies, and you'd be here for a month of Sundays. I don't think ya want that. Well, if you don't want it, take a good look at your package and come out with a <u>sound</u> approach to where you wanta get to, because nobody can consider or take you seriously w — from where you stand. And you're just going through a lotta motion," which he again agreed was so. So, that being clearly understood, I left the committee. They are now revising their position. When revised, will call me and I'll take a look at it. Then we will then bring the company in, where they will formally present. Now, when they formally present it, I — I would suggest that — that the company make no commitments — uh — comments. (Michelsen: Uh-huh) I would like you to say (pause), "All right. We'll (slight pause) — we've received them. We'll (Michelsen: Uh-huh) have to think — we'll — we'll have a caucus and" (Michelsen: H'm) — or I might suggest it, right from the start, that when they come in, without any comment come back here and (Michelsen: Uh-huh) then take it from there. (Pause) (In low tone) So that's where we are.

Michelsen: (In low tone) O.K.
Mediator: So now, at ease, men.
Michelsen: Now? Starting (laughing slightly) right now?
Mediator: At ease. (Michelsen laughs)
Michelsen: I'd hate to define what we've been before. I had my feet up on the table then.
[Almost 10 minutes of varied conversation, some of it light, follow. Michelsen remarks at one point, "All this needs is a little Gilbert and Sullivan music to be a real comic opera," at which Mediator laughs.]
Mediator: What you said reminded me of — during the — right after the war, there was a manufacturer here in the metropolitan area who was ex — he — he — he was in negotiations with this union. And he knew that — he felt certain the union would accept 10¢, and I did, too, but under certain conditions and at — <u>at</u> a certain time. So — he was a — a very excitable man. He was very — he — he had high blood pressure. And these kind of meetings just aggravated heck out of him and he couldn't control himself. So he came in and he said — he said to me in caucus — he said, "I know what will settle it: 10¢. Now, let's stop all the bickering. Let's get 'em in here and give 'em a dime." I said, "Mr. Neifach, you may do that, but if you do, don't say I haven't told you." He said, "Do you mean to tell me they'd reject a dime? I <u>know</u> they want" — he said, "I know they — know they want 8¢." I said, "You put a dime on the table now and you can kiss it goodbye. They'll take it, but they — they ain't gonna stop there. Th — they've got another week." (Laughs slightly) "Well," he said, "they won't get anything." I said, "Then you'll — then you'll push them into a position where they'll strike." "I don't believe it."

Well, so (Michelsen: xxx 20¢?) he said, "Let's go." So we went in,
and he told them that he was a very busy man and (Michelsen laughs)
that he (laughs) (Michelsen continues to laugh very heartily) — that
was — he got — that — that was the start (Michelsen: [Laughs very
heartily] He read Dale Carnegie x) — and that he — that more important than labor was the sales and he had to — he was being taken
away from that end of the bus — and he had about 180 people in his plant
and (Espig laughs shortly) he was being taken away from that end of
the business, and the longer he was away for — from that, the more
they were going to suffer. "Now! I know there's going to be a lotta
haggling and I have a good idea where it's gonna end up, and I have an
offer to make. And here it is. I wanta end this thing up. I'm gonna
get — wrap it up and get out of here tonight. 10¢ an hour." And it
was 2¢ above what the union, you see. Union sat there; it was one of
the electrical unions. They sat there and not a word. And you could
see the look of disappointment on his face. He expected at least somebody'd say "Thank you," or — or (Espig laughs heartily) at least
coughed. So — Art Smith was the negotiator. He said, "Mr. Neifach,
we'd like a caucus to consider your offer." He says, "Consider!"
And he — his blood pressure went up. As I said, he was a very excitable man. I thought he was gonna jump out that window. And he
started. Oh, he just — he said, "There'll be no considering. You'll
take it or else!" And (laughing) he walked out. (Someone else, along
with Mediator, laughs) Boy (still laughing), if he didn't leave those
negotiations in a mess. Art came out to me and so he said, "What
the — what did ya ever let him get in that position for?" I said, "He
wanted to get in it." He said, "How am I gon — what am I gonna do
with it now?" He said, "And then him saying what he said." I said,
"Best thing we can do is forget this for about 3 days." So we did.
We got 'em back in the negotiations again, but he wouldn't come; he
sent his lawyer. That (laughing slightly) made it worse. Don't you
know he had a strike?
Michelsen: What settled it?
Mediator: 2¢ above what they gon — were gonna get. Because it was
   thrown out on the table at the wrong time. If he had waited and let the
   negotiations go their usual course, his timing had been right, 'twould've
   settled for 8¢. The union would've been happy and he would've been
   happy. (Michelsen: Uh-huh) So when you said Gilbert and Sullivan
   (Michelsen laughs slightly), that's what reminded me of Mr. Neifach
   (laughing). (Espig laughs heartily)
Michelsen: Yeah. (Pause) Yeah, some of these boys — they wanta —
Mediator: Huh?
Michelsen: (Raising voice) Some of these boys wanta apply pure logic to
   these things and (Mediator: Yeah) — well, did — didn't you tell me
   one time about — who was it? — one of the supermarket chains or
   somebody else ya had a situation like that with? (Mediator: Oh,
   brother! That one) The president wanted to get on the horse and take
   a quick ride.
Mediator: Well, what he did — see, he put the union in a box. He put the
   union in a bad box. The union was demanding union shop. But they
   were gonna back off of — of it for the r — if they could get I think it was
   10¢. If they could get 10¢ they were gonna back off it. (Michelsen:

Yeah) (Slight pause) But they figured getting the 10¢ as the — at — at the — at the last meeting. (Michelsen: Uh-huh) So all the executives of the company are in here and we're developing the thing up slowly, up to that point. And his negotiators are keen; they're — they're very good. They — they know the score. They knew which way it was going, and so did the union. And by the clock it looked like a midnight settlement. So for the first time comes into the negotiations the president. (Michelsen laughs softly) And he came in here, walkin' in here like the President of the United States (Espig laughs slightly), and — oh, he had about 9 on his team, and they were all top executives, too. (Michelsen: Uh-huh) Well, I could see soon as he came in the room, well, he really got attention. He was the head man; there was no question about it. They did everything but dust the chair off for him to sit on. So he sat listening, didn't say anything, and I was dealing with his labor rela — his industrial relations man, who knows the score from (Michelsen: Uh-huh) frontwards and backwards. So the union — we — we went into a joint meeting. He followed. Well, when he come in, the union figured, "Oh-oh." (Slight pause) No, this fellow had never been in any of them before. "What — well, this is a settlement. Why would he be here?" So, 'course you know what the union did. They just turned on a little steam and got a little tougher. So as negotiations were developing (slight pause) he says, "Mr. Mediator, I'd like to say a word. Could I?" I says, "Go ahead." (Slight pause) He says, "Gentlemen, we want good labor relations." He said, "I have" — and this is somethin' the union didn't know — he said, "I have" — I think he said — "$1,500,000.00 worth of produce perishable. If we don't have a settlement here by midnight," he says, "that stuff's going to waste!" (Michelsen laughs shortly, Espig utters an exclamation, then couple laugh) That was Number 1. His industrial relations director — I saw him sag. He just (laughing) — he — he went limp. So he said, "So, I can't afford that — perm — permit that to happen. Now," he said (pause), "there are 2 things I know yo — 2 important things here, the union shop and money." (Pause)
[Tape changed]
... I said, "Are we gonna have the president in the next negotiations?" He said, "Like hell we are!" He (laughing) (Michelsen laughs) said, "He's not gonna get within (still laughing) 10 feet of these — those negotiations." (Rather long pause)
Michelsen: Yeah. (Rather long pause)
Mediator: I had a — I had a — president of Precision-Made — he got in touch with me durin' — durin' these negotiations. (Michelsen: Uh-huh) He said, "George, what do you think about my coming into the (laughing slightly) negotiations?" (Pause) xx / xx.
Michelsen: (Over Mediator above) When is this? Recently? Or when (Mediator: Uh-huh. A couple of years ago) the other guy was in?
Mediator: Oh, it was Griffin. (Michelsen: Uh-huh) Jim Griffin.
Michelsen: No, but I mean your — the former president was — of the union was still in power.
Mediator: Yeah. It was Carl Kennedy.
Michelsen: Yeah. (Slight pause)
Mediator: And he said it — Jim said it like (slight pause), well, he was doin' us a big favor. And I think he really believed (Michelsen: Uh-huh)

it. I said, "Jim," I said, "if you come into these negotiations, you're gonna be — you're gonna set them back (slight pause) probably 2 months." He said, "Why?" "Well," I said, "they'll claw you so badly that you won't have a shirt when you get out of that room." I said, "You — the re — yo — you — you walking into that room," I said, "you're gonna do more harm to your bargaining team than you can imagine. You won't be — you won't see it tonight; y — you'll see it next year." I said, "You've given this bargaining team the authority to bargain. Back up that authority by staying out of negotiations." I said, "If you come in, next year they'll just use the bargaining team up to a certain step. Then they're gonna demand you. And if you set the precedent now, you better be prepared to come into every one of these negotiations. And the day ya <u>don't</u> come into 'em, you got a strike. Secondly, you're not a trained negotiator. You may be a good business man, but this is a specialized field. If you come into bargaining, those union negotiators are <u>sharp</u>, and if you start fencing with 'em, they'll box you into the corner and before you know it you've agreed to something that, well, it won't seem like the s — like you agreed to it the next morning. It'll be one of <u>those</u> things." I convinced him he oughta stay out. He did. For which Claude was very grateful (Michelsen: H'm), because if Jim had come in, they'da — they would have assassinated him. (Rather long pause) (Addressing Observer) Hey, am I on record here?

Observer: Naturally! (Someone laughs softly)

Mediator: I gotta watch what I say here. (Someone laughs slightly)

Michelsen: She's gonna collaborate with you, George, and publish a book, "The Memoirs of (pause) George Thomson." (Slight pause)

Mediator: H'm! (Rather long pause) I laughed at John Gambon when he was gonna tell a (laughing) joke and he'd look at that microphone (Michelsen laughs) and stall and (laughing) just change it. (Long pause)

[About 2 minutes of conversation follow among Mediator, Michelsen, and Pranis, centering about Gambon's use of a toy pistol on Michelsen at negotiations a year ago. Mediator relates his experience in another case where an attorney pulled a real gun on an opposing negotiator. Mediator is now called back by the union group, and he leaves.]

Union Caucus - D (3:15 P.M.)

Gambon: Boys makin' any progress in there? When I say / progress I mean —

Mediator: (Over Gambon above) Well, we're laying a lot of groundwork.

Gambon: Uh-huh. Well, we've (pause) come up with this kind of a position. (Pause) You have a — your copy there, or you want one of these?

Mediator: Yeah, I have one. (Pause)

Gambon: We are changing our position (pause) to —

Mediator: Is that this one?

One of girls: No.

Another girl: No.

Gambon: No.

Mediator: (At same time as Gambon above) No, I don't have it (Gambon: Here it is), then.

One of girls: It's a financial report.

Gambon: Here's that one.

Mediator: Thought I had a blue one in — yes, I do. Here it is. I'll use this. (Rather long pause)

Gambon: We're retaining Number 1 (pause), 2, 3, and 6. We've taken Items 4, 5, and 7 —

Mediator: Wait a minute. Retaining 1, 2, 3, and 6 (Gambon: Uh-huh), and what?

Gambon: Removing this 4, 5, and 7.

Mediator: You're deleting them?

Gambon: Yeah.

Mediator: 4 —

Gambon: 5, 7.

Mediator: — 5 (pause) and 7. 7 is increasing (voice drops to mumble as reads rapidly to self). (Very long pause) Uh-huh. All right. I tell ya what I would like to do with this. I'd like to bring them in here. I want you to make that proposal formally, and after that I wanta get them out of here and back into (Gambon: Uh-huh) their conference room.

Gambon: All right.

Mediator: Don't wanta give 'em a chance to say No to anything. Wanta get 'em right out and back (Gambon: Uh-huh) into that caucus room.

Joint Meeting - B (3:18 P.M.)

Gambon: We (pause) had some discussion with George about the x these negotiations going and held a meeting of our own committee here. We'd like to propose the following as the union's position at this time. (Long pause)

Michelsen: Wait a minute. (Gambon: Uh?) Are you gonna read from your —

One of girls: He's lookin' for his copy.

Gambon: Well, I'll — I'll give you the numbers — the items that will follow the wage proposals. D'you have a copy of it? / I'll give you an extra copy.

Michelsen: (Over Gambon above) Yeah, I did, John. Yeah, here they are. (Long pause) Yeah.

Gambon: We will delete Item 4, Item 5, Item 7, retaining Items 1, 2, 3, and 6. (Rather long pause)

Michelsen: Uh-huh. (Pause) 4, 5, 7. That it?

Gambon: Uh-huh. (Pause)

Mediator: If there are — if you have any questions, why, feel free to raise them. If you (Michelsen: Yeah) don't, I would suggest a caucus. (Pause)

Michelsen: O.K., George. I don't have any questions (pause), I don't think.

Management Caucus - E (3:21 P.M.)

Mediator: Oh, I'm — I'm for joint discussions, but not — not after a
counter-proposal is made. (Michelsen and Mediator laugh heartily)
Michelsen: Oh, my.
?: Well — (pause).
Michelsen: Didn't say much about that one. (Pause)
Mediator: Well, at least it's a start. (Pause) 2 holidays, extend vacation
allowances, increase nightshift differentials. (Michelsen says some-
thing at same time) They kept the 35-hour week, 20% fixed bonus,
elimination of payroll adds —
[Mediator, talking to himself, continues from above. Others converse
among themselves at the same time. There is some matching among
Michelsen, Espig, and Pranis of items and numbers. Loring, in low
tones, is calculating in the background.]
Michelsen: I would estimate that they'd knocked about (slight pause)
maximum of (slight pause) $3\frac{1}{2}$¢.
Mediator: Is that all?
Michelsen: Yeah.
Loring: Still adds up to about 53¢ xxx. (Someone laughs)
Mediator: It does?
Loring: (Laughing) Yeah.
?: Uh-huh.
Mediator: O-o-oh! Well, now we get (pause) — now I know where —
how they're bargaining. There's the tempo.
Loring: H'm. (Rather long pause)
Michelsen: Well, they wanta go home for Easter. (Slight pause)
Mediator: Yeah, I'm afraid so. (Slight pause) That's not a big enough
bite. (Pause)
Michelsen: Well — (pause). George, it's too early, I guess, to really
from — from this to get serious about this thing. I mean, I'm hoping
that — that — that my st — my strategy'll be st — at this point — and I
assume I'm speaking for my group at this moment. Even though we're
very democratic, they may change my mind. My strategy is to aban-
don every one of these demands and to have these people realize that
if they're gonna get something, it's gonna be little, 'cause I'm gonna
try and put it in something that it can sound like a lot. I mean, I want
them to talk — be able to go back to their membership and talk up
cents — or, pension improvements, group insurance improvements
which have a lotta words attached to the explanation but damn little
money. Now (slight pause), my sense of (slight pause) appraisal
and timing may be completely off. I mean, at this moment I don't see
them seriously concerned with — with any of these demands, at least
hoping to get them. Now, I may be completely off. This moment my
recommendation to the company would be that they not meet any of
these things. That's my recommendation at this point, that — I sincerely believe what I told th — those folks in that meeting and what
these charts show, that we've done a hell of a lot, regardless of what's
happened to Atlas in terms of other companies from 1945 to this point,
and from 194-X to this point. Our past performance last year doesn't
warrant our increasing our costs. They've got a reopening here. O.K.
I'm willin' to give 'em somepin' to take back, and somepin' they can

really talk about and explain and do all that they want with it. I mean,
they can mold it any way they wanta mold it, but it's not gonna mean
much dough.

Mediator: Well, I'm inclined to agree with you that this indicates their
seriousness, and they're not very serious, because I gave them a — an
illustration of how we moved on the Irving Mining Case. Uh — in that
instance I said to the company, who historically had negotiated in pennies and worked their way up to the top. However, in this Irving case,
there hadn't been an increase for 2 years, not even a reopener, and I
knew that the company was going to give X amount. (Michelsen: Uh-
huh) That I knew; I knew their limit. But the very important thing
would be how much they would put forth on their first offer, pretty
much as the union here (Michelsen: Uh-huh) is in the position of
makin' a first offer. And I said the same thing to the company (Michelsen: Uh-huh), Irving Mining, as I just said to the union. I said,
"You're going to be judged — your seriousness is going to be judged
by your willingness to get down into the realistic area. It is n — you will
not lose any bargaining position or face, or whatever you wanta call
it." I said, "It'll work the opposite. You come out with a — at least
75% of what you will give on the first offer in these particular negotiations, and," I said, "I'm willing to wager that the union, seeing that,
you will bowl them over (Michelsen: Uh-huh), and they will immediately go into a caucus, and the — you will get more from them by doin'
it this way than you would negotiating your old way." I said, "Take
my word for it. There are some things that I know about these negotiations that you're not in a position to know, and I know that this union
wants to settle. (?: Uh) But I know they wanta fight, too. And don't
give 'em anything to fight with." (?: Uh-huh) So Major Auerbach —
he talked it over with his committee — he's the vice-president — and
he decided to go along with that, so they came out with a — I think it
was a 14-cent — 13- or 14-cent first offer. In their case, as I said,
it was 2 years (Michelsen: H'm) back, and they did owe them
(Michelsen: Uh-huh) quite a bit. (Slight pause) Uh (?: Did —) —
geez, it worked just as we had said. The union went into a huddle,
came back, and, geez, they knocked out every — ev — nearly everything
that the company was worried about. (Michelsen: Uh-huh) (Slight
pause) One fell swoop! They said, "You moved; we're movin'."
And there was just a — an area of about that wide between us, and we
finally wound it up. We wound it up for 20¢; but while that sounds like
a tall figure (slight pause), it was 5¢ less than what they figured they
might have to pay. (Michelsen: Uh-huh) And the — they were quite
happy about it, and the union was happy about it. Now, I used that illustration, pointed it out to John. I said, "While their figures and the
arithmetic is not the same, the other holds, and if you're sincere and
you really wanta move it, find out whether the company is (slight
pause) not fluid, stuck right in where they are, the only way you can
find out is you move from your position. But when you move, take a
big bite." / And when he comes out with this —

Loring: (Over Mediator above) Way it works out here, George, it looks
as though they — they dropped about 3¢ and it still stands at about 57¢.

Mediator: Well, then, that shows that they are not doing — not approaching this thing the way we wanted to. Now, they evidently have more

time than we can put our finger on. Why, I don't know. I haven't been able to ascertain that. Uh —

Pranis: I have a question, George. Do they — do you think they understand the worth of those items ?

[Several talk briefly at once.]

Mediator: (Over others above) Uh — I — they're going to be told, / see.

Pranis: (Over Mediator above) Well, that — that was my next question. (Mediator: Oh, yeah) Shouldn't they know (Mediator: Oh, definitely) in a general way what — what each item's worth, / so that they —

Mediator: (Over Pranis above) You see, I would follow that up. I will follow that up, because, see, I'm the one that said to them, "Take a big (Pranis: Uh-huh) move, a big step." And I said, "If you're gonna haggle over — with pennies, you'll be here for a month of Sundays. If you're sincere you'll — you'll — you'll show it, partic'arly in that first move." And I'm going to say that I asked the company how much of a move that was and the co — company estimates about 3 or 4¢. (Slight pause)

Loring: Well, I have one other question, Bill. Is Item 1 a proper item to bring up at this negotiation, anyway? This is not really a wage or fringe issue; it's — it's something that's specifically defined in the contract, what the work week is — 40 hours.

Michelsen: Well (Loring: I think that —), I don't see any point in — in arguing its — at this point. Maybe — well (lowering voice), I agree / with you it's a technicality.

Mediator: (Over Michelsen above) Well, I think it's co — no, it's money.

Espig: Money — sure, it's money.

Mediator: It's a b — it's a big money issue.

Loring: It's the biggest one, yeah. But it — it also is the work week, which is defined specifically in the contract.

Mediator: Yeah.

Michelsen: Yeah, but you can — there are things in the contract which are defined right now. (Loring: H'm) Night shift bonus is defined, but it costs us money when we change it. (Loring: Uh-huh) Fact / of the matter, xx.

Mediator: (Over Michelsen above) And if you did win your technicality (Loring: Yeah. Yeah), they wouldn't move away from the (Loring: Oh) figure that they're — whatever they —

Loring: But, I mean, it's out of the question, anyway.

Michelsen: Yeah. Well, that's the important thing at the moment. It's out of the question.

?: Yeah.

Loring: But I was wonderin' if it might be an easy to get it out of the picture.

Michelsen: Well —

Mediator: I — I — I'm afraid that it might do this. If you started to talk about it, it might enlarge it — its importance, or — or they may — (slight pause).

Michelsen: Well (Espig: Confirms it the next time, too), the thing that bothers me somewhat, George — and that's the reason I mentioned this sort of — made this reference to the comic opera — these people are down here with — with — with, in my opinion, not only unprepared, but they had a meeting of their membership in which the only reference to this was, "Well, there's — nothing's happened so far. We'll report to you at the next meeting." They have no strike authorization. They can't back up any tough talk — to me they can't. I mean, they can talk it, but it doesn't mean anything to me. Uh — plus the fact that I'm — at this moment would — based on the past history of the — what's — we've done in the last year or so, and — not only in terms of benefits; in terms of moving 150 jobs out of that plant I don't think they're gonna get anybody enthusiastic about gettin' tough. Now, I don't know their — what they hope to accomplish, but — but we're — we're not gonna give any consideration to that.

Mediator: Well, I — I — I'm — I feel that (pause) this thing has to be heated. (Slight pause) (Michelsen: Yeah) Too cold. (Slight pause)/ Uh —

Michelsen: (Over Mediator above) Well, I — I question whether or not they wanta apply any heat to it (laughs) at this point. Now, maybe they / do.

Mediator: (Over Michelsen above) We have to find that (Michelsen: Yeah) out. And the one way to find that out will be this. Think, (1), I should go back there and I should talk about these issues and I should quote the cost of these issues, which then puts me in a good position with them because — not — I don't mean with them — I mean it puts them on the defense. They nodded in assent when — to the proposal — or to the principle of getting into the realistic area of bargaining. And then they come out and offer me 3¢ — cut 3¢ off a 60-cent package on a reopener. So, that puts them in a position where they've got to do s — some explaining relative to their sincerity. Following that (slight pause), we can get together jointly and you can give your reply to this counter-proposal without going into the merits of it. You can take a flat and a strong position that (Michelsen: Uh-huh) your position is (Michelsen: Boy, can I!) unchanged, you don't consider (slight pause) that you can make any other move, or whatever you want to say, in a manner, or in a way, that will build a little fire here. (Michelsen: Uh-huh) And then we can recess until a proper time. Uh — we better leave the recess subject to my call, without confirming a date, or setting a date. (Michelsen: Uh-huh) We can talk about the date later. (Michelsen: Yeah) But that doesn't look (pause) like a healthy move, and we've got to (slight pause) build more fire here. I was hoping they'd take a large step. Now, if they did, then I'd know that they wanted to settle. But they are playing cozy at this late stage of March 28. (Pause) So, I think we will do it this way. I'm gonna spend some time with them, talking about how they let me down (pause) — 3¢, or 4. (Pause) Following that, you be prepared to come in and give your reply to that counter-proposal. Following (Michelsen: Uh-huh) that, I will probably recess (Michelsen: Uh-huh), subject to call. (Rather long pause) 'Cause it just isn't there. (Pause) It isn't there. And if you spent another extra hour today, you'd be spending too much time. (Michelsen: Uh-huh) (Slight pause) I've (Michelsen: Yeah, I —) seen too many situations when it wasn't there. I've seen it happen too many times where both the union and the company and — or the mediator (Michelsen: Uh-huh) did everything to hatch the settlement, but they were working with a glass egg.

Michelsen: Well, the big problem, I think, right now is that — that — that they're more concerned with the Easter eggs than they are with this, frankly. I don't — I don't think they want to do this before the holidays. It's a very, I think, / big consideration.

Mediator: (Over Michelsen above) I buy that. This convinces me. So, that's the way we'll work it. I'll go in with them. I'll be back (Michelsen: H'm) with you later; and when I come back for you, it will be to call ya in the joint session, and (Michelsen starts to say something) you'll make your historical (slight pause) reply to the counter-proposal and then I will follow up.

Michelsen: Yes, sir. I will make it.

Union Caucus - E (3:37 P.M.)

Mediator: They'll be in — n shortly for joint session. They're in caucus now but takin' this time to discuss your proposal before they come in. They put it this way to me in — in there, that the 3 proposals that you withdrew amount to approximately 3¢.

Gambon: I would question that, George, because I think xx 4 alone is worth 2¢ — / paid holidays.

Mediator: (Over Gambon above) And they said that leaves you in a position of remain — the rem — the rest of the package cost 57.

Gambon: Well, let's look at their claim. Item 5 would provide for the 12-year service people, or rather the people who have now 10 years. They would get 10 additional hours' pay. Th — the next group would be getting 25 hours' additional pay; the next group, 40 hours' additional pay above the top of 120 hours which we now have. Now, th — that in itself, I think, would probably run better than a cent, without knowing exactly how many people we have in each one of those groups. I know we have an - quite a number of people over 10-year service in there. Wouldn't be too many with 15, although there should be, oh, at least — what, 20?

Meyer: About that. At the most.

Gambon: I think their estimate of 3¢ for the total of those 3 things — I mean, take the n — item Number 7. The wage differential now is 10¢ when the 2 shifts are operating. This 10% of gross pay would be much greater than 10¢ an hour, and if you used his — if you used his average figure of, say, $1.71.

Mediator: Loring did the figuring (Gambon: Uh-huh) — the treasurer.

Gambon: Len Loring?

One of girls: Len Loring.

Gambon: Well, I don't know how he can come up with a figure like that without knowing exactly how many people were in there unless he prepared it ahead of time.

Mediator: No, he didn't prepare it. Couldn't. How he'd know — he wouldn't have known — he wouldn't know — oh, I see what you mean. Broke 'em down (Gambon: Yeah) — uh — yeah.

Gambon: Well, you've got — how many people are on that night shift right now, Stan? Coupla hundred?

Wollman: Roughly about 275.

Gambon: 275. And if you use his average of $1.71 and take 10% of that, that's 17¢. (Pause)

Meyer: But they're only gettin' / a dime, not 7¢.

Gambon: (Over Meyer above) Yeah. And they're only getting a dime now. That's a 7-cent increase on that item right there, for 275 people. (Pause) I think he's quite a way off when he talks about the —

Mediator: How much did you figure the 3 up?

Gambon: I didn't, George. I — I couldn't come up with a — an estimate,
so I let it alone. The only ones that — that I've put an actual estimate
on was Item 5, and that's based on their own claims of cost. They
claim that a — a — a paid holiday cost 'em about (Meyer: 5 and 4) a
cent an hour.
Meyer: 5 and 4, John.
Gambon: What did I say?
Meyer: 5 and 5.
Gambon: Oh. I mean Item 4, the 2 paid holidays. (Pause)
Mediator: Well (rather long pause), like I said earlier, if — if — if it
is that figure, it's not a big step. (Gambon: No, if it were 3¢. But
I'm — I'm disputing the cost figure) There's 57¢. The only thing it
does, it indicates — it indicates the tempo in which the negotiations
are moving and will move, and that's a slow tempo. 'Course, if it's
to be slow, we'll have to go along with it as slow. Then we'll set our
sights on that — in — on that kind of a tempo. / Uh —
Gambon: (Over Mediator above) George, I — I can't help moving this
way, because I'm not convinced at this point that they're gonna do anything different than this. I don't wanta set what might be a fast pace
and have 'em come back here with their old snail's pace proposition.
When I'm convinced that they're ready to move, I'll move xx.
Mediator: Well, let me put it this way. They (rather long pause) —
they're — they have the money bags (Gambon: H'm); you're tryin' to
get a fair share of their profits. (Gambon: Uh-huh) They're on the
defense, and you're on the of — the offensive. You're — you're moving
to get it. (Pause) They have taken a position that, owing to all the
circumstances that they have related to you before you came here and
after you were here, they can't afford any more than 4/10ths of a cent.
Now, when they move, if they move, it won't be this — I'm sure you understand it won't be the same steps — or the size steps that you'd take.
You're at 57. If you moved 10¢ toward them they'd have to move 10¢
up toward you (Gambon: Uh-huh), and so on and so on, which would
break it down a half of 60, which'd be 30-cent deal. So that you can't
expect. (Pause) It's a good thing if they would, but hardly possible
you'd get that much without a strike. So, they, I think, were — was —
were watching very closely to see what your counter-proposal is going
to be, to see whether they had a hopeless situation or it — or one that
could be resolved. I was hoping you'd take a big bite, get this thing
down to a realistic area. Now, you may have reasons for not wanting
to do that, reason — reasons that will strengthen your position that I'm
— m — not familiar with, and I'm not going to argue with you about
that because you're entitled to do that. This may not be the right time
for you — things like that that I don't know about. But first reaction
is that the negotiations at this pace would go slow, and they, on the
other hand, would hardly make a c — counter-proposal when you move
at 3¢, or even 4 or 5 — whatever it is. / So —
Gambon: (Over Mediator above) Well, look, George. As far as I'm concerned right now, I — it's my humble opinion they have not made any
proposals yet. I mean, they're talkin' about continuing something that
they've done since last October without any question, and they had a
perfect right to raise that question at any time. Immediately that they
were faced with that they coulda called us on it right off the bat, because the contract is very specific. It says $6.00.

Mediator: Now, I don't know and you don't know what they are going to do. (Gambon: Uh-huh) So far they're goin' to do nothing, 's as it stands right now. (Pause) I'll be very, very surprised, and it'll be the first time I've been wrong in a long, long time, if that position holds in the final stages of these negotiations. The only thing is, I don't know how much. (Pause) I would be willing to bet a month's pay that this company is not going to terminate these negotiations at 4/10ths of a cent (Gambon: I would give a lot to —), especially in the light of that report that you read, where they were expecting good business in 1953, or the market was there, or whatever words they used. (Gambon: Uh-huh) The question is, how much? And we're — we won't know that until we get rid of the steps that are now in front of us that we have to take eventually. We're gonna take 'em later if we don't take 'em now. It's just a question of when. Now, I'm not hurrying the thing; I'm perfectly willing to go along with you. (Gambon: H'm) I've got lots of time x, and so have you, if you have. But if you want it to move fast, that's all I'm tryin' to find out. If you want it to move slow, I'll go along with it. So, it looks to me that the pace is going to be slow, so I think the company w — takes it that way, too, although they haven't said anything. I (Gambon: Uh-huh) think one glance at your counter-proposal indicate —

Gambon: Well, let me tell you what happened the last time, when we were in here last October — last September and October. We had to make several proposals downward each time before they even got off their cans and moved. Now, that's why I say I — I'm not convinced that if they say that "We wanta move fast," that doesn't mean anything to me because of the past experiences with / xxx.

Mediator: (Over Gambon above) But they're not sayin' it! / No, they haven't said —

Gambon: (Over Mediator above) I know that, but I mean I don't — I'm not inclined to think that you can sell these guys that idea, George. They'll say, "Oh, yeah, I'm interested." For instance, Michelsen says, "I — I'm interested in gettin' these things cleaned up right away. Give me your proposals so we can consider 'em." I hand 'em to him, and what position did he make? They start — that's even — to me it's worse than starting with a zero position, I mean, because of the type of offer they're making here, and why they're goin' on since last October without questioning the thing (pause) and then they bring it in here. No, I'd like to see just exactly what they're gonna do when they come in here.

Mediator: All right. Suppose we — we hear them out when they come in, and then we'll pick it up from there and decide where we're going on it. (Long pause) We don't wanta work Easter anyway, do we?

Gambon: Easter? (Pause) No — o. Don't wanta work Easter Monday, either. It's a holiday.

Mediator: If I had to work Easter you'd have a picket line around you by the Thomson family.

Gambon: H'm! (One of girls and someone else laugh heartily)

Management Caucus - F (3:50 P.M.)

Mediator: ... I told 'em that (pause) you were still in caucus and you said you would be coming in momentarily to give th — your answer to their counter-proposal. And I said, "Before they come in I want to talk about your counter-proposal myself." I said, "The company figures that your counter-proposal costs approximately 3¢." Before I had a chance to say any more, Gambon said, "Oh, I — I think it cost more than that." But when he started to look at it — he never did get to what he thought it costs — he got a cent for one of them and he (Michelsen: 2 holiday) didn't get any further. I said, "That leaves a balance, John, of 57. Now," I said, "I said to you earlier that one way of determining the speed of these negotiations and the sincerity of the bargainers would be to watch the outcome of your counter-proposal." I said, "Your move's — s a very small step and indicates that the union is not ready to bargain, or is not ready to settle this thing — first indication." I said, "That's — that's a bellwether." (Pause) And I said, "You may have reasons for wanting to go slow. If they — whatever they are, I'm un — I'm unfamiliar with 'em. And (pause) if that's going to be your strategy (pause), well, it's all right. We don't want to upset it, as long as there's going to be no strike in production. But (slight pause) you're not going to get it settled moving this way." Well, then he (slight pause) very weakly tried to defend his position, which he knew was just like (slight pause) — well, built on paper cards (Michelsen: Uh-huh) — fell apart. And (slight pause) I told 'em that (pause) he would have to make his mind up today whether he wanted to get into that realistic area or whether he didn't. He said, "Well," he said, "the last time we met," he said, "we hadda make 2 or 3 moves before the company even indicated what they'd do, and I don't wanta be caught in that position." I said, "But, John, you've got somethin' to move with." (Michelsen laughs slightly) I said, "The company hasn't got that. Now," I said, "you don't" — I said, "let's say you'd lopped off 10¢. D'you think the company oughta come up 10, and then you lop off 10 more, and they'd go up 10 more?" I said, "You'd have about 30¢," and I said, "30¢ on a reopener these days would make history, and I don't think the company's gonna let you make any history. So we're kidding ourselves, John. I've been in this thing a long time and am able to put my finger on these things. Putting my finger on this one indicates that we're not ready." I said, "If you wanta move fast, I wanta know it. I'll move fast with you. But this is — this indicates you wanta move slowly." So that's where the conversation died (Michelsen: Uh-huh), right there! So my conclusion is they're not ready. They are not ready, and the next step is for you to come in and give your counter-proposal, take any position you want. (Michelsen: Uh-huh) Following that, after — there'll be a discussion, and then I'll recess, subject to call. I (pause) — I've got to do a little more probing into their position. (Michelsen: Uh-huh) I've gotta have a talk with John after — after they leave here, prob'ly tomorrow or Monday. I've gotta find out what's behind this (Michelsen: Yeah), so we'll know.

Michelsen: Well, now, let's assume we do that and — are you gonna be available to talk to us afterwards (Mediator: Yes), or are you gonna wanta talk with them?

Mediator: No. And after we recess, you can come right back in here.

Michelsen: Uh-huh. O.K. 'Cause I'll wanta talk with you about what we should do next. I don't know whether to — why, my feeling is, in order to expedite this thing, that I'm — well — uh — somepin's gotta happen.

Mediator: They — they're (pause) — they're not shooting square when, on one hand, they say, "No, we're not waiting for the Standard Products or the (Michelsen: Yeah) — or the Dayco. We can settle, and April the 12th has no s — significance whatever, other than it's an annual meeting — regular meeting"; and, on the other hand, th — they chop 3¢ off a 60-cent package at this late date of a 2d meeting and almost past April the 1st. So —

[Espig engages Michelsen in a period of discussion about the union's state convention coming up the following week. Occasionally Pranis joins the exchange. The speculations are all bound up with the possible significance to the union of the April 12th date.]

Mediator: We'll talk about (Michelsen: Uh) the next step after we recess, and (Michelsen: O.K.) you can come back in here and we'll discuss it. Uh — but now, suppose we go in and you be prepared to reply to their counter-proposal —

Michelsen: Well, I'm gonna tell them simply that we've (slight pause) considered (slight pause) what they've asked us to meet, and our answer is still the same!

Mediator: Stronger, the better.

Michelsen: Yeah. (Pause)

Joint Meeting - C (4:00 P.M.)

Mediator: Go ahead, Bill.

Michelsen: John, we've gone over these demands that you've asked us to meet, and the only thing I can tell you, and briefly, is that our position's the same. (Pause) I went to great lengths try and have you understand why the company's position was why it — what it is, and that's what it is. We're goin' to continue our offer. (Pause) The reasons for it, as far as I'm concerned, are quite impressive. But these demands we just can't meet at all.

Gambon: Well, how do I interpret your position, then? That we're wasting our time bargaining?

Michelsen: Uh — I don't think you're wasting your time bargaining. (Gambon: H'm) I think in asking us to make these ki — consider these kinds of things (pause), we just are not going to consider at this time. I've tried to give you the reasons why I feel very strongly that the union oughta pass up this reopener.

Gambon: And we feel just as strongly that you shouldn't in — under any kind of consideration ask us to do that. You went into this contract with your eyes wide open, and that contract contains definite wage reopeners which you know the union would take advantage of. (Michelsen: John —) And I must re — refresh your memories th — that — that the settlement of that contract was on a — at a figure lower than what the union asked for, and it was only because of the wage reopeners in that contract that we accepted your final offer that day.

Michelsen: That may be so. The / fact that —

Gambon: (Over Michelsen above) That is so, but I mean (Michelsen: Yeah) don't — don't agree to wage reopeners and then complain about them. (Michelsen: Well —) And don't do it in the face of a financial report such as you've issued. And don't do it in the face of telling us you're gonna decentralize. And don't ask us to refrain from wage reopener requests so that you can continue to expend that money to move out of town! / You must think we're nuts!

Michelsen: (Over Gambon above) John, I'm not asking you to do — I'm not asking you to refrain from negotiating a contract with a wage reopener. I'm not asking you to refrain from coming in and exercising your option under those wage reopener. But don't get the impression that we agree to wage reopeners with the understanding that we're always gonna give something, / 'cause we don't.

Gambon: (Over Michelsen above) Any company that agrees to put a wage reopener in a contract and then does not expect to have the union request additional benefits is a little bit out of this world, and I don't think Atlas has any impression or any ideas that any wage reopener will be by-passed by this union.

Michelsen: I don't think that we consider it in terms of what is goin' to happen to 3 potential dates in which you're goin' to have an opportunity to come in and ask (Gambon: Uh-huh) for something. Nobody can specifically predict what's going to happen. / One —

Gambon: (Over Michelsen above) You might have some reason to think (Michelsen: Each one is settled —) that the union might by-pass a wage reopener if the kind of financial report ya put out would warrant the union considering that kind of a position. But you don't have that kind of a situation here. (Michelsen: John —) You keep emphasizing that the company wants to continue to expand and that / kind of business.

Michelsen: (Over Gambon above) To grow and to live.

Gambon: Expansion, to live — you're doin' good job of living. And you're doin' a good job of living, as far as we're concerned. (Michelsen: Well —) And you expect to continue to live and to grow and to expand. But don't ask us to have that done at our expense. We want our fair shake of what's being done by the people in that plant, making possible the kind of financial reports you can put out.

Michelsen: Well, John, I can go back into our chamber there and bring (laughing slightly) my charts in again and show you that it's not being done at your expense. It's being done with you people getting a very good share of — of / every improvement that's being —

Gambon: (Over Michelsen above) That's right. You put — you put up and show us the total cost for labor, but you don't come out and say, without being egged into it by the union, that that cost figure includes the benefits that were given to non-union people, to executives, and everything else. I mean, don't make it look like we took that whole thing there, that all the labor costs were — are responsible for benefits you gave to just the union people.

Michelsen: John, in terms of the one chart which showed the proportion of our income going to payroll, there was no attempt to show you that that percentage on over-all was applied only to hourly / costs. However —

Gambon: (Over Michelsen above) What you don't say — what you don't say either is the fact that pr — productivity in that plant has gone up along with your cost — labor cost increase.

Michelsen: I don't say that because I don't know that it's so (Gambon: Well, I know that it's so), but I know that to some degree it / certainly has gone up.

Gambon: (Over Michelsen above) I know that your Time Study Depart-

ment has certainly (slight pause) — legally, understand, under the
contract — changed rates and (Michelsen: Well —) that they're always on the move lookin' for that 25%.

Michelsen: All right. And that the — when — when they've changed
rates, John, they've changed (Gambon: They've gone up!) the rates,
not because the individual's effort has / been increased. We have no
right to increase the rate for that reason.

Gambon: (Over Michelsen above) Oh, look! You get — you're getting
— even if they get — even if they get the same money that they got
before, the result is that you're getting more production for the same
money. (Michelsen: For which we pay!) We've got some good examples of that right — it happened since the last reopener in the Mold
Room. (Slight pause)

Michelsen: O.K.

Meyer: You don't pay any more —

Gambon: (At same time as Meyer above) How many more molds is
that you —

Meyer: You don't pay any more (Gambon: My goodness!), Bill. You pay
/ the same, but you get more.

Michelsen: (Over Meyer above) We were paying in a sense that we buy
equipment which provides that technological improvement. There's
an expenditure of a c — of the stockholders' money which goes into /
that.

Meyer: (Over Michelsen above) Yeah, I know (Gambon: Well, let's —
let's take this example of it), and there's depreciation, too, that could
comes off so you can buy more.

Gambon: This is since the wage reopener in October — since the settlement. (Michelsen: Yeah) Ya had a TD-6 job (Michelsen: Uh-huh)
in the Department 7. The old (Michelsen: Yeah) rate was 29
(Michelsen: Yeah. Yeah) molds per hour. (Michelsen: Yeah) The
base rate's 96¢. (Michelsen: Yeah) The base rate is still 96¢. Now
it's 38 molds an hour (Michelsen: Yeah), see. Or it used to be out
of that (Michelsen: Why did they change the rate?) old — old rate
we got 13,680 units a day (Michelsen: Yeah), and for the same money
you're now gettin' 19,080, approximately a 46% increase of production.
There's no change in the wage rate there, not a cent (Michelsen:
Sure), as far as take-out goes.

Michelsen: That's quite true! But that's done because of the improvement in the molding / x.

Gambon: (Over Michelsen above) Look. I'm — I'm saying you — you're
talkin' and bellyachin' to me about labor costs, and I'm saying that
while that labor cost naturally is going up and you agree to benefits —
increased benefits to the union, you're not also coming around and
admitting that the productivity has continually gone up.

Michelsen: John, it has to go up. It has to go up. There's no way in the
world that this economy can afford to keep increasing its cost without
getting something from it. (Gambon says something) There's no way
in the world that we could afford to, Number 1, sell automobiles for
the price we're selling today and paying the rates of pay we're paying
for 'em if we couldn't do it with some of the technological improvement that we have, so that, therefore, you can't increase wages without
getting more pieces per hour. (Gambon: Look) But the — the — the

thing that's providing (Gambon: You — you realize that —) the more pieces per hour is not the blood, sweat, and tears of Local 89 members; it's the easier jobs that they have as a result of some of the technological improvement. / Go back to my example of — which I used xx.

Gambon: (Over Michelsen above) Well, I don't quite agree, I mean, it's always the easier jobs, because I've seen Time Study Department just take out an entire element that, as far as work load goes, don't mean much and as far as the effort that the operator's expending. But simply because they removed an element and that, in effect, is a 100% change, bing, they say, "We have a right to do it under the contract." (Michelsen: Sure. And then it — xxxx —) So don't try to tell me that it's not sweat — blood and sweat and tears business. (Michelsen: But the con —) In some cases it damn well is!

Michelsen: John, but the contract also says that the other elements in that rate are not restudied, / that if you take something out that the person had to do, xx paying for it.

Gambon: (Over Michelsen above) Look, regardless of whether it is or not, what is the usual result? An increase in productivity for the company without any increase in pay to the individual. In fact, / we have a —

Michelsen: (Over Gambon above) But without any increase in pay?

Gambon: Certainly! / Ya got an ins — you've got more —

Michelsen: (Over Gambon above) Don't you remember those charts when I showed ya how the rates of pay had gone / up?

Gambon: (Over Michelsen above) I'm talking about th — when the job changes the rate changes and you get more pieces per hour, you don't propose to pass that saving on immediately to that operator. (Michelsen: Well, we can't pass it along to that operator) What you say is — ya say, "Well, you sit down at a table and bargain with us, and as a result of this increased productivity and those things we give you wage increases and fringe benefits, / and everybody benefits." O.K!

Michelsen: (Over Gambon above) And we have given them to you, I mean, to a considerable degree.

Gambon: All right! But not to a considerable degree that's out of this world compared with what's being done around here. (Michelsen: Depends on what value ya — you put on the xx, John) I've given you wage comparisons. You have no right to go around beatin' yourselves on the chest in the face of some of the things that been goin' on in this town since 1946.

Michelsen: John, my — the facts that I presented to you w — were not presented in an effort to beat myself on the chest. They were in an effort to try and (Gambon: Justify your position) show you why we were not going to do anything at this point.

Gambon: Now, wait a minute. That's a very specific statement ya made, that you're not gonna do anything. (Michelsen: All right) And that's why I asked you, are we wasting our time here? Because if you want me to, I'll take your 4/10ths of a cent to the membership, and I won't wait for the 2d Friday in April! (Pause)

Michelsen: Well, that's — that's your decision, John.

Gambon: It's — it's — look, I'll have to make a decision if you're gonna lay it on the line that way, and I'll make it quick!

Michelsen: Well, I don't know how else I can say No, except to say that our position is still 4/10ths of a cent. (Pause)

Gambon: Well, I'm goin' to suggest, George, at this point (pause) that we break off here, and I'd like you to urge the company to go (laughing slightly) get a little bit realistic about this whole situation. And since I was under the impression that perhaps we were approaching the time when we could begin to do some bargaining here, and for that reason we made the 2d proposal, I'm gonna withdraw that proposal at this point and go back to our first position, since the company has taken the position they have at this point (pause), set up another meeting and see whether a few days thinking it over'll do any good.

Michelsen: John, I'm certainly hopeful that it will.

Mediator: I — can I say this? I feel that as far as today is concerned, we may as well re — recess. The holidays are upon you, and we can leave this meeting adjourned, subject to our calling you the early part of the week. Now, the reason for that is, I have a few tentative meetings that I have to rearrange and I won't be able to know until about Monday what dates I can set. But for — as far as today is concerned, I think that both of you have worked enough and it might be well to recess and I will get in touch with both of you and set the date for the next conference. / Uh —

Gambon: (Over Mediator above) W — we — we have a holiday on Easter Monday, so —

Mediator: It is a holiday?

Gambon: (In low voice) Yeah.

Mediator: Oh. I'll / remember that.

Michelsen: (Over Mediator above) It's one of our 8 holidays.

Mediator: So, if neither side has any further statements or comments to make at this time, we'll recess the conference and I'll be in touch with both groups.

Gambon: All right.

Michelsen: O.K.

[As Mediator is leaving the room with the management group, he asks Gambon to wait 5 minutes.]

Management Caucus - G (4:12 P.M.)

Michelsen: No, I just — I was just telling these fellows, now they know why industrial relations directors have a distorted sense of everything (Mediator: Yeah) — a distorted sense of humor, of logic, and everything else. (Someone laughs slightly) (Pause) I wish I could've egged 'em on to presenting it to the membership, but —

Mediator: Well, I think you — I think you (slight pause; someone laughs slightly) made it very clear. (Laughs) Uh (slight pause) — that — a lot of that is needed. A lot of that is needed. They're draggin' their feet. They're draggin' —

Michelsen: They sure are. They're draggin' mine, too. (One or 2 laugh, including Mediator)

Mediator: Uh (rather long pause) — now, you wanted to talk about the next steps.

[Tape changed]

Mediator: ... that it was crystal clear (?: Yeah) that they were not bargaining in good faith. Coming from me to the committee, John has got to come back and change his demands. Uh — when the next meeting takes place and John chops off 3 more cents, that's the time / to x.

Michelsen: (Over Mediator above) That's when I'm gonna walk out. (Someone laughs)

Mediator: Well, / we'll just xxx —

Michelsen: (Over Mediator above) I mean that! I'm gonna say, "This is not bargaining in good faith. Good-bye."

Mediator: Well, be careful. That (Michelsen laughs heartily) — but that's very dangerous. Uh — but after that meeting, there would be the real time to give it to 'em. But if I don't miss my guess, John is going to have a change of heart unless they are operating on that time-table. (Michelsen: Yeah) And what pur — for what purpose, see, I don't know. I don't know that they are, but it — it seems something's wrong that there's not a — a stronger desire to work this thing out quickly. April the 1st is almost gone! The — the time for the reopener — it (Michelsen: It has no significance, I think) — here they are. Dr — huh?

Michelsen: I don't think it has any significance for them.

Mediator: It might be just (slight pause) — might be just that they don't tach — attach as a much as important — uh — as much importance to that date as I do. Maybe I'm putting more on it than they do. But what-ever it is, I think that you should hold the other until the next meeting. Now, the other is effective, and it's been used in many situations. (Michelsen: Uh-huh) In fact, it has settled many cases. There's a calculated risk that ya take with it, but i — in some instances, that's worth it. I would — I would say to — I would like my remarks to be given a (Michelsen: Sure) chance, and a — and John is — will be faced with it (pause) — I told his full committee — I gave 'em the Irving illustration and showed 'em of the progress that those people made when they eliminated tomfoolery and got down — right down to the realistic area, in one big jump. He didn't do it. I gave him the illustration and he didn't follow it. Instead, he came out with a pit-tance. Now, that pittance — he knows how I feel about that, because I told him. I said, "It shows me that you're not ready to do busi-ness." Now he's in the position where, when he goes back to his shop, or his union, the thinking of that committee is going to be, "Well, look, John. Company is standing there. Even the mediator has made it crystal clear that he don't think we're bargaining. I think we'd better st — pull up the anchor and start moving." Or they're goin' to say something else. But I really believe that that committee is going to say to John, "Look. It's — the middle man here is — is beginning to see through your position, and it's not good. Maybe we'd better move." And I think he just needs a few days for that to sink in. I don't think he wants to be in a position where we can say, "You are not bargaining." I've already said that his — the — his position was almost fantastic. "And it's all right to kid — try to kid the company, try to kid somebody else, but I take it seriously when ya try to kid me. (Michelsen: Uh-huh) And I would think you were tryin' to kid me if you stuck on that position. And if you did, I'd say, well, you would have to get yourself another mediator, and probably another company committee, because" —

Michelsen: Another company. Another company.

Mediator: Or (laughing) another company. (Several laugh heartily)

Michelsen: (Laughing) You're not gonna deal / with anybody else in that company I know about.

Mediator: (Over Michelsen above) But John is a — now, I think John — I think John — comes the next meeting, there'll be a change. Yeah, if I miss my guess, then we have the other. But let's save that (Michelsen: All right. All right) other for one meeting. (Raising voice slightly) Not that I'm squeamish about (slight pause) putting a little (Michelsen: No. I buy —) heat. I — I've used stronger / mea —

Michelsen: (Over Mediator above) This is your party, pal. When we come down here, we'll let you drive the boat.

Mediator: I — I've used stronger t — methods than that sometime to blast open a deadlocked situation. So (Michelsen: Uh-huh) it isn't that I'm squeamish. (Michelsen: I know it isn't! I know) We'll (slight pause) put that one on the shelf, and I think, come the next meeting, xx / x —

[For some 15 minutes the exchange continues mainly between Michelsen and Mediator, discussing personnel versus industrial relations policies and practices, and the incalculability of worker sentiments toward both unions and employers. Mediator relates some of his mediation experiences in these matters.]

Michelsen: (Addressing Observer) Well, your operation's like panning for gold, isn't it, today? Get everything but mediation on that tape. (Laughs) And even that isn't what I would con — call a nugget. (Someone laughs slightly)

Union Caucus - F (4:33 P.M.)

Mediator: ... No, I was covering a few points that I thought, if developed, why, we might stay a little longer, but being there wasn't any enthusiasm there to (Gambon: H'm) follow it, so no use filling you in on a dead cow. Just didn't go over. So I'll call you Tuesday. Get in touch with you Tuesday. (Pause)

Gambon: All right.

Mediator: Have a Happy Easter.

Union Caucus - A (2:00 P.M.)

Gambon: I'm gonna take off on this. (Gives several sheets to Mediator) This is a bulletin they're puttin' out to all their foremen and supervisors, and they, in turn, of course, are givin' reports to our members before we even have a meeting. Take particular note to the very — almost the last paragraph in that letter (Saunders: Next to the last paragraph) about their firm position. (Long pause)

Saunders: And our — our unrealistic (Gambon: Yeah) against theirs — what, 4/10ths of a cent that they've been payin' for 2 months. [Extended period of miscellaneous conversations and laughing ensues among the group. None of the content refers directly to the negotiation. Tape changed meanwhile.]

Gambon: ... to force the negotiations before we even reported to our membership. They do that durin' (Mediator: Oh) negotiations (Saunders: This is the 2d time), but they use the bulletin for other purposes. I mean, / they x —

Mediator: (Over Gambon above) This B — this title.

Gambon: See, it's Bulletin 45. Yeah. They put it on this. See here Bulletin 45?

Mediator: Yeah. The —

Gambon: They put out information on all kind — kinds of things, but they only do this kind of thing during negotiation. They done it the last time. Christ, they were given a whole report on negotiations before we even went to a membership meeting and reported as a committee.

Mediator: Uh-huh. (Long pause) Well, I'll bring 'em in here. Gonna bring 'em in now.

Joint Meeting - A (2:35 P.M.)

[Michelsen and Gambon banter briefly about one of the local colleges, with Gambon commenting, "You guys should be wearin' this color" and "By the time we're done with ya you'll be wearin' black and blue."]

Gambon: I'm in a nasty mood today, believe me.

Michelsen: Are you?

Gambon: Yeah, I'm gettin' tired of your — oh, that's recorded. (Meyer and someone else laugh) I'd forgotten that.
[Michelsen addresses one of the girls with, "What'd you win?" bringing on an exchange of light remarks among several, including Meyer.]

Mediator: Well, at our last conference think we had discussed the union's issues, or went over them, and that we left it at a point where the

union had submitted a change in their position. The change was taken
to the company (pause), and I believe we recessed shortly after that.
Is that a brief — is that correct? (Slight pause)

Gambon: Uh-huh.

Mediator: Uh — today, before getting into the issues, or into the positions of the 2 parties, since we've had days of lapse between our last
meeting, I wanta give each side an opportunity to make a — a statement before we go into the issues, any statement that they feel might
be (pause) contributed to the negotiations here. Union first.

Gambon: Well, Number 1, George, I'd like to say that close of the last
meeting, 'course, we took the position of withdrawing the proposal
that we made — that is, in the meeting on (Mediator: For the x, yeah)
March 28th — and we went back to our original position. I'm at a loss
to know whether or not we're engaged in collective bargaining or what
we're engaged in here, because since March 28th the company issued
a — a bulletin — a la — industrial relations bulletin of some kind in
which they stated in part about the firmness of their position in regard
to the union's demands of any kind, I would interpret it — their firm
position on this issue of not doing anything more than 4/10ths-of-a-
cent increased cost as related to this (pause) increased cost for
hospitalization and so forth. I think we gotta get the air cleared here,
in my opinion. I mean, where are we? What are we doin' here? I
mean, I don't wanta waste your time or I'm not gonna waste my time
if all I'm gonna stay from now until m — membership meeting on April
12th, just listening to this same business. If it's a firm position, as
they put in writing, tell 'em to say so and I'll know where to go from
there. Now, if we're gonna bargain, that's one thing. But I wanta
know just what this firm position means when they start putting it in
writing after we met with 'em on March 28th. The date of that communication was April the 3d. (Rather long pause)

Michelsen: John (pause), whatever that firm position was that was in
that supervisory bulletin, it was no different than the firm position
which I thought was understood when we left the room here on Good
Friday, when (Gambon: Uh-huh) you asked me to make my language
evidently a little clearer and I thought that I had. I said at that point
that the company's position was that we would accept the 4/10ths' additional expense, and you said, "Is that what you want me to go and
report to my membership?" And I said that's a decision for you to
make (Gambon: Uh-huh) but that's the company's position. (Gambon:
Uh-huh) Now, I can add the other adjective, that that's the company's
firm position. (Gambon: Uh-huh) And that's / x.

Gambon: (Over Michelsen above) Well, look. That's — that's what I
wanta find out. How firm is that position? Is it so firm (Michelsen:
Well, firm is firm, John) that you're not gonna move away from it or
do we have to knock you off that spot?

Michelsen: That's the company's firm position! What I said in that bulletin and what I said to you was that we — our position is that we feel
that the union should pass up this reopening / except for this offer
that we —

Gambon: (Over Michelsen above) I don't care what you feel. I'm — I'm
tryin' to find out just how emphatic you're making this No, as you
called it the last meeting. (Pause)

Michelsen: End / quote, exclamation point.

Gambon: (Over Michelsen above) Are we wasting our time in these negotiations ? Are we wasting George's time sitting in here ?

Michelsen: John, I can make no evaluation as to what you consider to be a waste of time / xxxxx.

Gambon: (Over Michelsen above) A waste of time to me is sitting listening to you trying to justify your present position (Michelsen: I don't intend to spend any more time justifying [laughing slightly] it) and in effect saying, "We don't — we don't want to pay you anything. (Michelsen: Right) We don't feel that you should ask for anything." (Michelsen: Right) That — that's nice, the way ya feel and what you wanta do and don't wanta do. I wanta know whether or not you're sayin' emphatically No (Michelsen: Yes, I am saying emphatically) or whether we're bargaining.

Michelsen: I (laughs slightly) — this sounds like this program on Sunday night where the — What's My Line? — where they get the double affirmatives in the questions. (In rather loud voice) Yes, I am saying emphatically No. (Pause)

Gambon: Is there any particular use of going any further with this ? Because I won't wait for (Michelsen: I'm not the mediator, John. I'm —) April the 12th, believe me. (Pause)

Michelsen: That's a question which George Thomson decides. / I x.

Gambon: (Over Michelsen above) Well, you take the responsibility at this point. I'll go to the membership and recommend a strike. Now, what d'ya wanta do with it ? I'll be just as emphatic as you're trying to be. (Slight pause)

Mediator: Gentlemen, I wanta say this, that I think that the answers that both of you are seeking right at this moment could not be truly (pause) answered (pause), for this reason. (Pause) John, you're asking whether the company is taking an emphatic No and how firm is firm — their position. I — I don't think that the company, or myself, or yourself, can truly evaluate the genuineness of these negotiations until such time as the issues that are involved — till the parties — the realisticness of the positions of the parties is made clearer. I don't mean to take exception to your demands; you have a right to present any issue that you feel negotiatable. However, there are some guideposts, and you are familiar with those. I brought them out at the last meeting. I do believe that both of you at the present time are — are taking a wrong approach to find the answer to that that you seek. I believe it can't be truly evaluated until such time as the parties' positions are closer together. And I believe that it might be well for both sides to do a little considering, or reconsidering, of their positions. When both sides take a firm position (pause) stands to reason that you — the committees on both sides will dig in, and it's gonna — going to slow these negotiations down. I don't believe if I was sitting on the union's side that I could truly evaluate these present negotiations as to where they're going, with the positions of the parties both being where they are, and I don't think I could truly evaluate it wi — from — if I was sitting on the side of management. And I can't evaluate it sitting in the center as a mediator. So, suffice it or add it all up to say this. With positions where they are it's going to be extremely difficult to get the answer that both of you want, and there's only one

approach, and the approach — there's no time like the present to get
the right approach. I think both of you can save yourselves a lot of
time, a lot of thinking that is not conducive to good labor relations or
advance toward settlement, by going into a caucus and reconsidering
your positions. I don't think at this late stage of the game either of
you can afford to play footsie with one another at the bargaining table,
since you're well past your mark. I do believe that the sooner you get
down to that area, the sooner you're going to get your answer. Now,
I can put it blunter. Maybe sometimes bluntness is the thing that's
needed. I think that the problems that you have in your relations with
one another do belong on this table and any other table and should be
negotiated. It's the only way you are going to settle 'em. But I also
know that you can't do that until such time as you — a — a genuineness and sincerity is expressed, and it can't be expressed with your
positions where they are. You could jockey, you could (pause) f —
footwork with one another, but in the end you're not going to get the
answer. Now, that doesn't mean that you could even reach an agreement. But the answer that you're seeking is, can an agreement be
reached? And I say neither of you will know it until such time as
your positions are down to earth. I would suggest, without further
ado and without further discussion, unless this — both parties want
further discussion, that a recess be declared and that the company
committee and the union committee review their respective positions
and discuss their respective positions with me prior to a joint get-
together. (Pause) Any comments on those remarks?
Michelsen: No.
Mediator: John? I suggest a recess now, and if the company will retire
to the other room I'll join you there, later join the c — the union.
[Notwithstanding this latter remark, Mediator remains behind with the
union group.]

Union Caucus - B (2:45 P.M.)

Mediator: I meant every word that I said (Gambon: We understand that,
George), because you — you've gotta move (Gambon: Yeah), see.
They're — they're — if they're dug in you're not gonna get 'em out
until you make a (Gambon: H'm) — a — a re — recap your position,
and in the interests of — put 'em on the spot with a show of good
faith, "Let's see what they'll do." Because they're guarding their
position. It's — it's obvious. They're — they're afraid to move. Now,
if there is anything there, we'll never dig it out with you where you
are. (Gambon: Yeah) So you — you've gotta come down.
Gambon: Look. We're at least practical enough to admit that the position
that we have at the moment is not what we have any hope of attaining.
But it gets pretty objectionable when they start tryin' to justify themselves in written form to supervisin' foremen, who in turn tell it to
our members, that theirs is a realistic position. I don't wanta get to
the point, George, where I may have to go to the membership and
recommend a strike based on even an offer away from where they are
now and lessen the difference too much! I mean, you — 'course,
you're familiar with that. If it — if I'm gonna have to strike somethin'

I want a difference as far apart as possible. But I'm prepared to recommend to my committee very quickly, I mean, the position that I
wanta take with these guys now to — to move 'em.
Mediator: The — the closer ya get down to where you know the area —
an area of settlement is, the better. The closer ya get to that point,
the more you're going to weaken their position. Now, they — right
now they are in a good position to scream like they're screaming in
that letter (Gambon: H'm) because you are up where you are.
(Gambon: Uh-huh) Now, if you were in a realistic area — or maybe
that's an improper term. A better term would be a —
Gambon: Reasonable, huh?
Mediator: — reasonable area. (Gambon: H'm) Then you'd have them on
a spot. They couldn't crow like that because then the readers would
— would say — 'course, I don't believe in this. I mean, this (Gambon:
Yeah) is Lashley's method, and / that —
Gambon: (Over Mediator above) They're all doin' the same thing. Pre-
cision-Made, you know.
Mediator: That never, in my book, makes for good labor relations. But
that's a baby of the Taft-Hartley Act (Gambon: H'm), and some of
them are (Meyer: xx) using it.
Gambon: It's a — not the baby, George (laughing).
Mediator: I say it was born / of the —
Gambon: (Over Mediator above) It's a miscarriage, I mean. (Several
laugh)
Mediator: So, I'd suggest you do that. I'm going in and talk with them a
bit. But get this thing moving and call me before you —
Gambon: I think in about 5 or 10 minutes, George (Mediator: O.K.),
we'll be ready to tell you the position on xx.
Mediator: Right.

Management Caucus - A (2:50 P.M.)

Mediator: Why — (pause).
Michelsen: They gonna give (Mediator: Yeah) him a strike vote, George?
Mediator: (In low voice) No-o! (Michelsen and someone else laugh)
They're not gonna strike!
Michelsen: (Laughing) I wish I could get 'em to do it (One or 2 laugh),
frankly. (Laughter continues)
Mediator: Uh — I laid it — after you left the room I laid it down cold to
John. (Pause) I said, "Look," I said, "I meant every word that I
said while the company was here," I said. "Actually," I said (pause),
"you're not really trying to find out whether there's — this thing can
be resolved." I said, "Evidence of that is the position where you are,
up in the clouds." I said, "You leave yourself wide open." And I
said, "Anybody reading that bulletin would only take one glance at it."
Michelsen: Did you read it?
Mediator: Yeah! He showed it to me.
Michelsen: Yeah. I have a copy here for you.
Mediator: "Anybody reading it would — you put yourself on the spot."
And I said, "There's a reasonable area and you're far from it." I
said, "You would be in a better position — if you wanta find out

whether the company can settle this thing or not, would be to move
fast into that area, but don't jockey or footsie; it's too late for that.''
So, when I concluded — I said a lot more than that, but when I concluded he said, ''All right. We'll consider your remarks and call you
back in.'' So what he's gonna do now is move. He's gotta — we gotta
keep movin' him into the area if you're gonna find out whether the
thing can be resolved or not. But you couldn't take any other position.
(Michelsen: I know) You can't do it. You have 'em out there. And
even when he comes down, see.

Michelsen: I was tempted to — to say, and I restrained myself; maybe
it wasn't good in this — to say, ''Yes. I wish you'd go take a strike
vote.''

Mediator: Oh, no. That would've been bad (laughing).

Michelsen: Well, I have to, myself, get some gratification in my own
thoughts, George. (Laughs heartily, as do couple others)

Mediator: Just tell 'em to me! (Hearty laughter breaks out again)

Michelsen: I don't say 'em to the union, but at least I think 'em. Then I
come out and say 'em loud so I can hear 'em sound like a — sounds
good, doesn't it?

Mediator: You're like me. Sometimes I go home and bawl hell outa the
cat. (Couple laugh heartily)

Michelsen: I bawl hell outa the — bawl hell outa the kids. They hate to
see me come home after somepin' like this. Fact, they like these
night meetings. I sleep it off.

Loring: Do you think they will really move substantially this time,
George? If they don't, what does it mean to you?

Mediator: Well, if it — if — if they don't, it means that they don't want
to settle, definitely. But if I'm a judge of (slight pause) — of pace
(slight pause), I'm inclined to say that the way you have handled your
negotiations thus far under this high figure that they have placed
above you, I would say that your firm position in past meetings, coupled
with this letter, plus fact that part of your plant is moved — all those
things I think is going to (slight pause) reduce that lethargy on their
part, because I think they realize that they can't stay up in the clouds
too long, even if they have a plan. (Pause) Now, they've gotta move.
I think they will move, but I don't believe the move will be — will
bring them into the reasonable area. I think — after their move —
now, I may be pre-judging this thing. This is all speculation. (Slight
pause) I believe that after they do move (pause) they're gonna probably have to be moved again (Loring: Yes), to get in the area. I
question whether they'll come right down to where it oughta be.

Michelsen: (Laughs) So do I. (Laughs again)

Mediator: Pace is slow, and it might be that they have a plan. Keep mentioning April the 12th, April the 12th. That was mentioned again
(Michelsen: That's their meeting night) today. Now, I don't know why
they put so much importance on that meeting, because if it is I would
just as soon — I'm sure you would, too — wait for April the 12th.

Michelsen: Oh, yeah. We won't (Mediator: Uh-h-h —) agree to anything today.

Mediator: In the Aero negotiations, the fact that they had a meeting set
for this Sunday, or Saturday, just slowed them — those meetings down
to practically a stop. The company says, ''Hell, let 'em go to the

meeting first!'' Then the ABC this morning — they have a meeting set for Saturday. (Loring: Uh-huh) Now, I know the company is going to give more than 5¢ an hour, but that's all they offered today. And they won't offer any more until that meeting's over. (Slight pause) So, whether that meeting has any significance bearing on this thing or not, I think we'll bring that out sometime (?: H'm) this afternoon. / That —

Michelsen: (Over Mediator above) Well, George, you — you — you understand what — what's on this side of the table, don't you? I mean, we've got maybe (Mediator starts to speak) zero-plus to play with and that's —

Mediator: Well, here's — here's — / I —

Michelsen: (Over Mediator above) Not because we're commissioned by the company, but that's all I think we should do.

Mediator: Uh — let me put it this way. (Michelsen says something) I'm not interested at this time — I'm not interested particularly in what they'll settle for or (Michelsen: Uh) what you will settle for. And if it's (slight pause) whatever you say it is and it can be settled for that, fine and dandy. The important thing in these negotiations at this time is to get the — both parti — to close that gap into the (slight pause) position, or the area, where (slight pause) both sides will know whether that is their position or not. I don't think you can tell, or they can tell, at this (Michelsen: Uh-huh) time, and (pause) I wouldn't be satisfied until such time as the chips are down. Then when they're down and there isn't any more and it is that way, they should be satisfied, you should be satisfied, and I should be satisfied that everything was done to get into that area of at least finding out. This way, if you quit and got into a fight and left without having gotten down into that area (?: Yeah), you'd never know whether you really had a chance or not. Now, when I get down to (Phone rings) there, then I know everything has been done. It isn't that I'm trying to whittle you down into a position and then change your position. I don't know myself whether this thing could be resolved. It may be that it can't from the union side of the table, and that I have to find out. (Answering phone) Hello. O.K. Thank you. (Hangs up phone) Excuse me a minute. Another gentleman is here wants to see me. [Mediator leaves the room. He returns at 3:07 P.M. to say that he has been called back by the union group.]

Union Caucus - C (3:09 P.M.)

Mediator: Did you want me, or just the committee — / that is, the whole committee?

Gambon: (Over Mediator above) Yeah. Yeah. Uh-huh.

Meyer: Come on. You wanta (Gambon: Yeah) talk to George, don't / you?

Gambon: (Over Meyer above) Yeah. I wanted to give you our position, George — I mean, try to get this thing movin'. D'you have your copy of our proposals there?

Mediator: Yeah. (Long pause)

Gambon: I'm gonna come down as close as I can to my final position, George (pause), in order to try to move these guys, so that our

proposal to them at this point is Items 1 and 2, period — 35-hour
week and that 20% bonus for skilled trades and other day workers.
(Long pause, with Mediator writing)

Mediator: Uh-huh! Uh —

Gambon: Now, that, in our estimation — that cuts about 35¢ of their purported 65¢ right out of the picture. I'm still in a bargaining position
as far as you're concerned. (Mediator: Uh-huh) But I'm gonna stay
right where I am on those 2 points until they get off their can and
start moving here, because I'm willin' to fight on these issues right
now (Mediator: Uh —), if that's their position. If they continue to
say 4/10ths of a cent, I won't go no lower than this, George. I mean,
might as well tell you that much x, 'cause I don't think it would be
good sense for us to go below that if they're goin' to make it a proposition, "Well, do what you wanta." (Pause)

Mediator: The one thing I haven't talked with either of you has been
where are you actually going, and I have no intentions of talking about
it because the areas are — are too wide. (Gambon: H'm) I didn't
even bother with the company. I have practically ignored their 4/10ths-
of-a-cent position, and whenever they've discussed it or tried to discuss it in caucus, I (pause) wouldn't engage in conversation on it because I — I didn't wanta dignify it, because (Gambon: H'm) the more
I dignified it the harder it would be to — when the time comes to move
them on it. Bill is — appears (Gambon: Uh-huh) to be h — (pause)
even c — trying to convince me that (Gambon: Uh-huh) "This — this
is where I am, see." And that may well be! That may well be, see.
'Course, he's not the last say, I don't believe (Gambon: Uh-huh. No),
or — or has there been a change? I doubt it.

Gambon: Well, as I understand it, this committee they have has authority
to make a settlement. But I think if it gets to a position of where they
have to face the facts of life, they'll run back to the Board of Directors
and get guidance.

Mediator: Well, I do, too, and I think that the pace of the negotiations
are pretty clear, that you're really — we're not going to (pause) —
let me put it this way. As long as the union is too high or above
(Gambon: Uh-huh) anything that can be called a reasonable area they
don't have to report back to papa. (Gambon: Uh-huh) But when that
— the union's position starts to get down to where it's "Ya better
take another look, Joe, before you make a move," they're going to
have to decide 2 things: " (1), Can we make a settlement? Let's try."
They're gonna give it everything they got to try to make a settlement.
Failing in that, instead of saying No they're (Gambon: Uh-huh) gonna
have to go back (Gambon: Uh-huh) and report, where right now I
don't think they have to do any serious reporting while the positions
are as high as they do. / Uh —

Gambon: (Over Mediator above) I would say so, yeah. / xx.

Mediator: (Over Gambon above) Now, that's a — that's crystal ball gazing. But it looks — it looks — that's the way — and I guess what I'm
tryin' to say is, we still have a long hard road ahead of us.

Gambon: Oh, yeah! Uh-huh. I don't expect to see any settlement today
on the issues, but I do wanta find out one thing today. I wanta find
out whether they're — they're gonna take the attitude "You're still
out of this world," see, "and come down somewhere where we can

make a reasonable offer and bargain with you," or whether they're
gonna say 4/10ths of a cent again. If they say 4/10ths of a cent again
without givin' any indication that they're willing to engage in bargaining in good faith here, then I'm not moving away from there. I won't
go back to my original position, either. I'll stick with this and I'll
make that the issue.

Mediator: Uh-huh. Now, I'll tell you what I'd like to do. I'm gonna bring
them in here (Gambon: Uh-huh) and I want you to formally present
this. (Gambon: Uh-huh) Tell ya why, see. If I take this back it might
minimize your seriousness, and I don't wanta do that. (Gambon: Uh-
huh) Wanta bring them in there and let you give it to them. Following
that, I'll take 'em back there for discussions.

Gambon: All right.

Joint Meeting - B (3:15 P.M.)

Gambon: Well, gentlemens, I'd like to give you our position at this time.
I'm givin' ya this position and I want you to understand that I wanta
find out particularly whether we're engaging in bargaining in good
faith or not. (Rather long pause)

Michelsen: Well, I think we are. (One of boys laughs heartily)

Gambon: Item 1 and 2, Bill.

Michelsen: Mean that's your position?

Gambon: That's it.

Michelsen: On your letter of March 6?

Gambon: That's right.

Michelsen: Uh-huh. (Rather long pause)

Gambon: And I'll talk or fight on those issues, kid. Have it either way
you like. (Pause)

Michelsen: Well. (Rather long pause) D'you have any — I don't have
any questions about this. Uh —

Mediator: If not, then suppose we resume the caucus work.

Management Caucus - B (3:23 P.M.)

Michelsen: . . . to do that. The other would be to completely hold to our
planning with — to divert them completely from both of these. Well,
George, they come down to about what? 35¢?

Loring: 31¢. About 31¢.

Mediator: 31?

Loring: Uh-huh. (Pause)

Pranis: Ta —

Mediator: Well, that's better than last week.

Pranis: The thing that George should know, though, that of the 31, 26 is
in one item.

Loring: Yeah.

Mediator: 26 is in what?

Pranis: One item.

Loring: First / item.

Pranis: (Over Loring above) The 35-hour week is 26¢ – 25¢. (Slight pause)

Mediator: Interesting.

Michelsen: Well, that's out completely. (Pause)

Loring: That's the one that we'd be most against but not a money cost, George. (Pause)

Michelsen: Well, I was just discussing here some — 2 possible avenues down which this thing can go. (Slight pause) One is to assume that this business for fixed — skilled trades people — a fixed bonus, which is the Item No. 2 on their sheet — a 20% fixed bonus for all skilled trades and other day workers (slight pause) — is a real concern of theirs and that they'd — they'd go for it (slight pause) and feel that it's something that the membership would approve. I would reject it at this moment because it affects 100 people — 150 people — men. It is gonna do nothing for the 15, 1600 women who are working there, and I can't see them selling just that alone. So one strategy is to accept that as a legitimate demand and to work on it, but not to that extent, perhaps. Last time we gave — if you'll remember, we gave this group, skilled trades and day workers — we gave them an extra nickel (Mediator: Uh-huh), which was not 20%, and we could pursue it along that line by offering a nickel, which is 3/4ths of a cent, approximately, and going up to another nickel, maybe, maximum. And that would be all we'd be out of money — a cent and a half. The other thing is — to do is to do what I have originally hoped we could do, and that is to get them off every one of these demands (Mediator: Uh-huh) and to say that we're willin' to spend some money — it's not much money — [As tape is changed, Michelsen makes the point that he had hoped to be able eventually to get the union completely off their present set of demands and to say they are satisfied with the increase, in addition to which the company could do something for them on pensions and insurance. Mediator quickly replies that that is not for this point; that is for the much distant future.]

Mediator: ...uh — another move. (Pause) So you — they're still up in the sky. (Pause) They could've very well — if they'd been smart, they'da come in with — oh, if they wanted to come in with somethin' wild, 31¢. Start there; save themselves a hell of a lotta time. This way, we're wastin' a lotta time getting 'em down to where they have to get to, anyway, if (voice rising) there's a possibility of settling it. And they'll never know until they get down there. Uh — (slight pause).

Pranis: George, how do you accomplish the transfer? They have 2 items, now. One of the — one of them is the bulk, and one of them we're pretty well committed to not even considering it. / How do you get —

Mediator: (Over Pranis above) What was the first one? Bulk?

Pranis: Well, the — the bulk of the money is — that they're asking for at the present point (Mediator: Yeah) (Michelsen: The 35-hour week) isn't money. And this one item is the one that we don't even wanta consider. How do you get them to transfer to something else, something they haven't even mentioned yet?

Mediator: Well, this way. (Pause) They know, better than I (slight pause), that (slight pause) the t — th — 35, is it? — 35-hour week — they know better than I that a 35-hour week would just about cripple you.

Pranis: Huh-un.

Michelsen: Would like fun.

Mediator: Wouldn't it?

Michelsen: It would open our Rome plant. It would just about cripple them.

Mediator: Them. I'm — well (?: Yeah), whichever way it —

Michelsen: And I'm gonna tell 'em.

Pranis: Well, if we accepted it without the Rome plant, Bill, it would cripple us. I mean, this is — / we have a choice. They don't have any.

Mediator: (Over Pranis above) That's what I meant. You couldn't operate very well under it (Pranis: No), could you?

Espig: No.

Pranis: Not at all.

Mediator: Based on your prices, and (Espig: That's right) your market, and so (Michelsen: Yeah) forth. (Pranis: Yeah, it wouldn't — it wouldn't work out) They know that. Now, I feel (slight pause) that (slight pause) if you gave it to them — even if you gave it to them, they know it wouldn't be — it would really hurt them if the firm said, "Go ahead! But take the consequences," which would mean the firm'd have to make a certain adjustments that the union could feel. Uh (pause) — so, I don't believe (slight pause) that they really would hold out on that. And you say, "How do you get 'em to — to make a (Pranis: Some other item) transition?"

Pranis: Yeah. To something else.

Mediator: You gotta — it's got — they've gotta get down to the point where — and I think they're using that as a bargaining point — I think so. I'm not — I could be wrong, but right at this stage I think it — think it's a bargaining point — because they know this would hurt them. So they're gonna play with that as long as they can. Then when the time comes, they'll swap it off. (Slight pause) And when the time comes you say, "How will that happen?" They will probably — it'll happen this way. If I think they're serious, then, of course, I will have to go to work on them, to move them away from that. If they're not serious, it's a foregone c — conclusion that they will tell me (slight pause) what they're going to do on this. They have to. Either tell me or they'll tell you. (Slight pause) That's as near as I could answer it (slight pause) right now. (Pause)

Espig: (In low tone) Well, don't you think that we — don't (raising voice) you think the problem — don't you think that we could get something on this issue by stating to them that — some of the reasons why we can't accept a 35-hour week demand? Wouldn't that be one way of — of keeping the thing moving?

Mediator: Oh, it has to be! Yes. Yes, it has to be hammered, but I think more important than that 35-hour week, see — if you went in there now and started to talk about a 35-hour week, you're dealing with experienced negotiators and they'd m — immediately read something that might not be there. (Espig: That's right) See, they'd say, "Oh-oh. Talkin' about the 35-hour week, which means they're open somewhere else," see. Now, I think, if there was any discussion that the company would engage in, it should be the absurdity of their position (Espig: Uh-huh) — still up in the clouds! (Slight pause) Ya start to talk about one li — iota, with their — with them at 31 (slight pause), you weaken your position. (Espig: Yeah) But i — from — at / this point —

Espig: (Over Mediator above) In other words, they might — they might figure, well, they'll get a $37\frac{1}{2}$.

Mediator: U — up there where they are, they shouldn't be allowed to figure anything (Espig: Right [laughing slightly]) right now, you see, 'cause it would endanger it. Don't misunderstand me. I — I — I — I'm not trying to be the arbitrator who determines how much people should get. It's not that. But I know from settlements what is realistic and what isn't. (Espig: Sure) This is just a — well, I — I just have a — I don't know of any (Espig: Unrealistic as it may —) — anybody that ever got 30¢ — or 31¢ on a reopener.

Espig: Unrealistic as it may be (Mediator: Never heard of it! xxx), it's a dream — it's a dream which they would — which they would love to see come true, / without consequences.

Mediator: (Over Espig above) See, if you started to talk about anything at this time, it would indicate a — a show of seriousness on your part, see (Espig: Yeah) — interest. (Loring: Right) And you can't afford that at this stage of the bargaining. You've got to — we've got to take time and (slight pause) crack down on this — on this thing as — now — now, you might do this. One approach to it could be this, and I throw this out for your own thinking, that if we go in — when we go in — I — I think a right way to do it would be when we go in to joint session after you have s — considered their proposal, your reply should be that you have studied this thing b — but that (slight pause) it is still up in the clouds. It is (Loring: Yeah) (pause) — "We (slight pause) — we told you our position, and following the Mediator's recommendations, we can't see — we can't see — we — we followed his recommendations, and" —

Michelsen: What recommendations? You mean, just — just look at it.

Mediator: — "to look at it. And we've done that and we think that (pause) the area that he spoke of," or — or, no. "We just (slight pause) — all we can say to you that it's (Michelsen: Stinks) (slight pause) far over our heads. There's — there's nothing like it, and we can't see how anything could be worked out." I mean, you just gotta pound that one point home, put the onus there. Now (pause), if he's hoping for a counter-proposal — even if you were gonna give 10¢ (slight pause), or 15¢ — no, not 15; 10 — if you were gonna give 10 (pause), well, e — with them at 31 you couldn't even come back with (Loring: Uh-huh) a — and I know you're not giving anything. But that — that's how wide apart you are. (Loring: Yeah) Tryin' to show you how wide the — I don't want you — I'm — I'm very interested — I'm very concerned that you don't make a move that's going to make my job harder, see. And one wrong move here could really box this thing into a point where it'd be difficult getting out. He (pause) — he still evidentally has time on his hands. (Pause) (Loring: Yeah) I am a little concerned. The pace is slow; pace is slow. Uh —

Espig: Well, I think he's attempting to move the company, no matter how small the move.

Mediator: I do think this, that in these negotiations you're going to get this thing down to the crisis point. Uh — I don't know when that's going to be. The sooner, the better. Fact, that's what I — that's where I'm trying to steer it. So when it gets down to there, then you're going to know (slight pause) whether it can be settled or it can't be settled. Uh — but getting it in there — into there is going to be, I think, arduous

and long (slight pause) and time-consuming — uh (slight pause) —
unless these boys move — st — start to move faster than they're moving, which means they — they evidently have time.

Michelsen: Evidently. (Slight pause)

Espig: Yeah. I think that they have all next week. (Slight pause)

Mediator: And the one thing we — you — you can't afford is to bite on
that — on any kind of bait, if they have a timetable. (Slight pause)
Get ahead of the timetable, you're — you're in b — you're in trouble.
(Espig: Uh-huh) Uh — my suggestion would be to (pause) let them
know that you considered it. That's the first point. And, secondly,
let 'em know that it's (slight pause) <u>certainly</u> not a reasonable area.
It's a — or, instead of s — referring to that, that it's just out o — completely out of the reach of the company, unheard of. Make it as preposterous — use whatever words you want, but you have to m — you
have to <u>attack</u> that position as being — well, I won't use the word ridiculous, but a synonym to that would be — would serve.

Loring: Unreasonable?

Michelsen: Well (Mediator says something), suppose we do make it —
suppose I do make it a — bring the thing to a quick boil and John with
it, of course, which I'm very willing to do. Suppose I say that if he's
really serious about this position we're just wastin' our time. (Pause)
I mean, there're no — they're not — <u>can't</u> give consideration (Mediator: Well, that won't hurt) to an offer as — as (Mediator: Uh —)
preposterous as this, if he's really serious at this point.

Mediator: Uh — I might tell you this. The — the sooner he — he gets his
blood pre — pless — pressure up on this (slight pause), the better,
because he will then move. Uh (pause) — he (pause) — but all doubt
— or, all hope, rather, should be removed by the company. Any hope
they may have of getting a figure like this has first got to be attacked.
(Slight pause) But I do think that you ought to mention in your remarks that (laughs), "We're — we will say this — this can be said,
that from where you were to where you went is a sizeable jump, although it is — you have a lot to jump with" — something like that,
and you might mention (laughing slightly) that you're not saying they
didn't make a move, but to start with, they were — had plenty to move
with! That oughta be made clear. I've made it clear in the caucus.
I've cleared — pointed that out to them in caucus. (Long pause) He
would be very foolish to go back to the people to s — ask for a strike
vote at 31¢ on a reopener. (Loring: Yes [laughing]) If I was (Michelsen: [Laughing heartily] He'd —) the company I'd in — I'd (Michelsen:
[Laughing heartily] He'd be murdered! [Laughs]) welcome that. "G —
go right ahead and ask for it."

Loring: Yeah. Should Bill point out that they're asking for 31¢ at the
time when all these other people're taking reductions because of /
the —

Mediator: (Over Loring above) Yeah. That's — anything that can
(Michelsen: Sure) strengthen your position and minimize er — or
(pause) show how wild a figure that is, should be used.

Loring: I think — I feel that they have picked, if they really wanted to
get tough, 2 very poor issues, one at 26¢ — I mean, the membership
would <u>know</u> they couldn't get 26¢, and that one item is 26¢ here. Uh —
and the item i — i — is in — it's is — in — an item i — in itself, I mean.

Michelsen: Well, don't forget that they may be moving in the direction of half of that distance, to 37½ hour. (Slight pause)

Loring: Yeah, that's true.

Michelsen: Which is 13¢ or (Loring: Uh-huh) something less than that (slight pause), and which is not unheard of, because that's what our salaried employees work. (Pause)

Loring: Well, I guess you gotta bring him to a boil. And he will, too (laughing heartily).

?: Huh?

Loring: He will come to a boil, too, this time, I'll bet.

Michelsen: It's his blood pressure. (Pause)

Mediator: Whenever you're ready.

Loring: What are you gonna do if —

Michelsen: (At same time as Loring above) Well, I'll never be any better ready than I am now.

Loring: George, what i — would the strategy be if he really hits the ceiling and he (Someone laughs) — or m — makes believe he hits the ceiling and wants to call it off right there, / go to the membership?

Mediator: (Over Loring above) That's where I come in.

Loring: (In low tone) O.K.

Michelsen: Don't worry about it. Let George pick up the pieces. (Laughs heartily)

Mediator: Yeah. That's where I come in.

Michelsen: Gotta give this guy a little exercise. He's gonna get stale, sittin' in this kinda stuff.

Mediator: I had a vice-president at Aero's try that yesterday. It was in reverse; it was the company. (Slight pause) And he (slight pause) give me that business of, "Now, we're doin' nothin' here. We're wasting time." (Pause) So I said, well, we gotta sail into this fellow and straighten him out; so I did. "Look, this is your problem; it isn't mine. If you wanta walk outa here, you're gonna assume full responsibility for doing so. If you're d — doing this as pressure on me, then you're playing child games. If you're serious, that makes it worse." (Pause) And I said, "If a strike can be avoided by our staying here till any time, reasonable or unreasonable, it's worth it." And I said, "I don't wanta conduct a marathon, but I don't want — I got enough pressure on me without you putting it on me." So, he stayed. (Espig laughs) I said, "If you've got any pressure, apply it in there (Espig laughs) on the other side (laughing slightly), not me." (Espig continues laughing) But he was a new man in this area, had come in from the Midwest. So I guess he'll — I guess he figured, "Well, we'll show those country bumpkins how to negotiate." But I put an arm-lock on him. Then he went in there and this Hartman deflated him. (Phone rings) (Someone laughs) Hello.

Espig: I guess some of those boys that travel all over the country get some (slight pause) wild ideas.

Mediator: Would you give me 5 minutes to have a caucus with my secretary?

Michelsen: Certainly, George. (Pause) / You're —

Mediator: (Over Michelsen above) Well, I'll confess she brought me a cup of coffee. (Laughs)

[Brief period of laughing and talking at once about Mediator's coffee.]

Michelsen: (Over others above) Guess John can wait a — 5 more minutes for this 31¢.

[Mediator leaves the room a short while.]

Michelsen: Well, George (pause), let's go!

Mediator: Right..

Joint Meeting - C (4:00 P.M.)

Michelsen: Well, John, we have given consideration to your revised demands (pause), made a few quick calculations. This much seems certain, that you've come down out of the 65-cent area down into 31 — approximately what looks to us to be around 31¢, which is — (pause).

Gambon: How d'you break that / between the 2 items?

Michelsen: (Over Gambon above) Well, I think that you've got about — between 26 and 4 — something / like that.

Loring: (Over Michelsen above) 26 (Gambon: H'm?) and (Michelsen: 26 and 5) 5 would come nearer. (Pause)

Michelsen: The point (pause) — the arithmetic is quick, and not sayin' that — it's a movement as far as I'm concerned from one area in the stratosphere to another, and it's still way up there, / out of the question.

Gambon: (Over Michelsen above) Oh, hell — (1), I mean, look. Don't let's talk about the stratosphere. I mean, even if we talk about gettin' into clearer area, you get the hell out of the mines, will you?

Michelsen: Well (pause), we don't consider ourselves to be in the mines, John. We consider ourselves to be (Gambon: Realistic. I know that's what you say) on a very realistic position (Gambon: You're realistic), and (pause) this sort of thing is just out of the question. (Long pause) The only thing I can say, in addition to (pause) what I've already said in the past meetings, is that a (pause) — reading the newspapers, without even probing into industrial relations activities to find out what's going on, to read every day of workers who are taking reductions in pay —

Gambon: How unfortunate you wouldn't agree to put an escalator clause in the contract when we signed it. / You'd be happy now, wouldn't you?

Michelsen: (Over Gambon above) Unfortunate or not unfortunate, i — it's fortunate for you that we didn't. There's no question about that, because what you got is — is not on an escalator. But the point is that in this — this week there are 4 or 5 large companies that are going to be reducing the tag, not increasing it.

Gambon: Only because there is an automatic escalator clause in the contract (Michelsen: Correct) which works both ways. But don't forget, those same companies are going to have to go into negotiations with those same unions. (Michelsen: In 1955) In some of them they already have entered negotiations. I'm not concerned with just talking about Federal Leader and their union. How about Lashley? They've got an automatic escalator clause, too, haven't they? They're now in negotiations.

Michelsen: Yeah. (Gambon: xxx) What they do, John, I don't know.

Meyer: Yeah, but further back than that they've been reaping the harvest of that from the beginning of the 5 years which ends in '55. So from

1950 on and from 1950 on it took us until last year — this time (Gambon: Uh-huh) last year to get the $12\frac{1}{2}$¢ that we did get.

Michelsen: But, Bernice, in the 2-year period of time — I don't wanta get back into these (Meyer: Uh-huh) figures again or get my charts unwrapped, but the cost-of-living in the — since Korea's gone up 11%, as I remember it. Our rates of pay in that period of time have gone up something like 19%. (Meyer: Well —) We've more than matched any escalation (Gambon: Ah, no, you —) that would have taken care of / the cost-of-living.

Gambon: (Over Michelsen above) Only (Meyer: Huh?) in a couple of years' time. (Michelsen: Yeah!) And then it was only because we argued with you and pointed out how far behind the parade we were at that time!

Michelsen: Then we weren't far / behind at that time, John.

Gambon: (Over Michelsen above) Yes, you were. I mean, we showed you where you were, that people were 25 and 26 and as much as 30¢ in wage increases at that point, and we had the grand total of 10¢.

Michelsen: That's quite true, but at the same time that you had the grand total of 10¢ —

Gambon: All you did was narrow the differential that existed (Michelsen: Yeah. But at the same time —) between ourselves and some of these companies.

Michelsen: All right. At that time, in 1950 — and I go back to — to this chart and just read to you from it — in 1950 in January the industry average was $1.29, and at that time, where you say we were behind the parade, our average was $1.36, or 7¢ at that point — 7¢ ahead of the industry average, and I mean average for the electronics industry. We're taking out $1.29 in January of 1950. And that's after we've been behind the parade for a / couple years. We were taking out $1.36.

Gambon: (Over Michelsen above) And don't forget the average rate that you're talking about in Atlas is the result of increased effort and —
[Tape changed]
... the financial column, wasn't it? They even picked it up.

Michelsen: Well, they gotta write something, so they leaf through / the xxxxx.

Gambon: (Over Michelsen above) What do they do? They look in it and they say that Mr. Fuller says the — the future for profits is fine and "We're gonna give ya back the dime." He picked it right out of your financial report. (Michelsen: He did, indeed. He said —) Well, what the hell was Fuller makin' those statements for? (Michelsen: He said —) Just for publication? (Michelsen: He did —) To sell stock or somethin'?

Michelsen: He said that next year we expect — or this year we expect to be a good year. We do.

Gambon: We know it's gonna be a good year.

Meyer: Bill, what's that got to do with the company's ability to pay for the years that we recognized the company's ability not to pay when we were takin' $1\frac{1}{2}$¢ for females and $2\frac{1}{2}$¢ for males, for reopeners that went by before where we didn't take anything, for retroactive pay that we never fully collected? So today the company's in a position to pay. So what's the different? Who — who gets what? You never listened

to anything when we'd bring it up before. (Michelsen: Joh — uh —)
"We were not <u>able</u> to pay." Today you're able to pay!

Gambon: Hell, ya make that (Michelsen: Yeah!) very bluntly. Ya say
(Michelsen: Yeah!), "We're not arguin' on our ability to pay." But
we are! (Michelsen: O.K.) We are! (Michelsen: You — John —)
We're particularly arguing on that on the basis of the company's own
statements, "When we're doin' good, you'll do good." Let's see it!

Michelsen: You're doin' good. I've tried to have you (Gambon: Look)
see it.

Meyer: We can't see it.

Gambon: Look. Your opinion of us doing good ends at the point where
you think, "Ya've gotten all you're gonna get, guys. We want to do
something else. We wanta continue to decentralize. We wanta to —
to make — increase our profits. We / wanta increase our dividends."

Michelsen: (Over Gambon above) <u>We sure do</u>, and — and we've got to do
it, because the profits we're making now are not the kind of profits
that are needed for this business. And —

Gambon: Well, go find some other way of makin' — increasin' your
profits. Don't try to do it by not giving us our fair share of what's
coming to us, boy.

Michelsen: John, I'm not trying to take away from you your fair share.
I'm trying to convince you at this point that you have a fair share and
that it's not gonna be increased. (Pause)

Gambon: Now, will you please explain that for me, friend? I'm awful
<u>dense</u>. You know, "it's not going to be." Do you emphasize that?

Michelsen: I wrote this down before. I (Gambon: Emphasize it?) — I
said no, that our position was at — it was just as it was when I
(Gambon: Uh-huh) stated to you that we — our position at this point
is that we'll accept this additional cost of group insurance, / but that's
it!

Gambon: (Over Michelsen above) What kind of a position should I take
to make this at a bargainable proposition? Say to ya, "Bill, you're
at 4/10ths of a cent. Please come up and make — give us the other
6/10ths." Is that what you wanta bargain on?

Michelsen: John, I'd — no, it's not what I want you to say. I want you to
say what you people decide you w — are going to say. I'm not going
to do (Gambon: Uh-huh) your bargaining for you. I'm / telling you
what —

Gambon: (Over Michelsen above) Christ, don't do that, 'cause I <u>know</u> I
won't get nothin' if <u>you</u> bargain (One of girls laughs heartily) for
me.

Michelsen: Well (laughing), don't ask me to do it, then. I'm going to —
I'm saying to you just what I've said before, that this is the company's
position. This is it, period! (Pause) Now —

Gambon: Well, I'm trying to determine whether it's time for us to go out
and buy a shotgun. (Pause)

Michelsen: I — / I can't g — make that determination for ya, John.

Gambon: (Over Michelsen above) Or whether we're engaged in collective
bargaining in good faith.

Michelsen: Oh, we're engaging in collective bargaining and my faith
(Gambon: We're doin' a lot of talkin') is good and I'm <u>very</u> sincere,
/ believe me.

Gambon: (Over Michelsen above) We're doin' a lot of talking.

Michelsen: Well, I'm tryin' to, just by saying (Gambon: Uh-huh) No, avoid the / use of a lot of words.

Gambon: (Over Michelsen above) Well, don't get away from — don't get away from your financial report — your ability to pay — and don't keep tellin' me what you'd like to do. I'm quite aware of what / you'd like to do.

Michelsen: (Over Gambon above) I haven't said that for a — all day. You've been saying that. / This is what I'm —

Gambon: (Over Michelsen above) I'm only repeating what you've said durin' the course of these meetings.

Michelsen: During the course of (Gambon: Uh-huh) today's meeting I have said, in response to your questions, that the company's position is unchanged. Our position is 4/10ths of a cent, which is to be used for group insurance, period.

Gambon: Uh-huh.

Meyer: (At same time as Gambon above) Is that your way of convincing us that we have gotten a fair share, and we are getting a fair share? That's your method of / convincing us?

Michelsen: (Over Meyer above) My — my method is to try and supply you with the information which I have which will have you try and understand the company's position. We feel that it's a realistic position. It — it's the only / adjective that I can use. The —

Gambon: (Over Michelsen above) H'm, from the stockholders' standpoint, from the person who collects dividends, certainly (Michelsen: From a managerial point of view is that) it's realistic. "The only way I'm gonna get more is not give it to the workers."

Michelsen: It's not a question of — of —

Gambon: (In rather loud voice) Look, who are you kiddin'? If you get past this reopener without any benefits to this particular union, you're gonna increase your dividends the next quarter. Ya done it before! Who the hell do you think you're kiddin'?

Michelsen: I don't know that that's goin' to happen, / John.

Gambon: (Over Michelsen above) Wh — what are you doin'? Have you done anything to — to hold up the — the profit-sharin' plan durin' this period, in order to pay dividends? Oh, no! (Michelsen: We still have that and —) The same guys that collect the dividends got part of the profit sharing already. Then they got the gall to ask us to not take anything!

Michelsen: And we still pay d — we still pay incentive pay to workers / who are working on an incentive system.

Gambon: (Over Michelsen above) That's right. That's — you pay incentive pay and they (Michelsen: Yeah) work like hell to get it, / too.

Meyer: (Over Gambon above) You go up to the end of the line and you ship it out and get paid for it.

Michelsen: And we expect that the people who are getting paid under our profit-sharing plan are putting out extra effort / to — to get that compensation.

Gambon: (Over Michelsen above) Uh-huh. They're puttin' out extra effort. You're doin' a good job.

Michelsen: (In low voice) Yeah.

One of boys: (Laughs) Tryin' to.

Michelsen: Well (pause), I'm as much in — influenced by incentives as anybody. (Gambon: Uh-huh) You people are influenced by them. (Rather long pause)

Wollman: Don't know how you're gonna have a good year in '53 with your workers out on Oak Street. (Pause)

Michelsen: What d'you say, Stan?

Wollman: I said I don't know how you're gonna have such a good year in '53 with your workers out on Oak Street.

Michelsen: What's that mean?

Gambon: Let me interpret it for you. Do you want an incentive? (Pause)

Michelsen: Well, I don't understand it.

Gambon: (At same time as Michelsen above) Start talk — huh? D'you want an incentive? Ya believe in incentives? Let's (Michelsen: Yeah) do somepin' before April 12th. (Rather long pause) And when I say let's do somethin', I don't mean 4/10ths (Michelsen: Well, we've done something, John) of a cent, either. I want something realistic the way I read it out of the dictionary, not (laughing) your terminology.

Michelsen: Well, this is — this is realism as we see it, / and that's the company's position.

Gambon: (Over Michelsen above) Uh-huh. Realism to you is decentralization, too.

Michelsen: Yes (Gambon: Uh-huh), very real problem.

Gambon: This is the warm-blooded family group. H'm!

One of boys: Share the pie. (Pause)

Meyer: (Laughs) (Michelsen: Well —) Company'd get all the crust to eat. (Several, including Mediator, laugh very heartily) (Pause)

Denk: They had that pie in the ATLAS REPORTER. (One of girls laughs softly, again)

One of boys: Pie's gettin' moldy. (Pause)

Michelsen: Well, I don't know what else I can say. I can / re — review our —

Gambon: (Over Michelsen above) Why don't you say somepin' new, for a change? Been sayin' the same thing all along. (Pause)

Michelsen: I have nothing else to say, John. I don't know how else to say No, except to say that No means that's our position. (Pause) And I don't know how to say that I mean it any more sincerely, or it's realistic, than to say it's a realistic position on my part and on the company's part.

Gambon: O.K. I'll break off negotiations, George. To hell with it. (Sounds of chairs moving)

Mediator: Wait a minute. Just / a minute.

Gambon: (Over Mediator above) There's nothing bargainable here.

Mediator: When the negotiations are broken off, I'll have to break them off (Gambon: Uh-huh) because this meeting is called by the Service, and we'll adjourn it. The — so (pause) let's both sides remember that. (Pause) Breaking off isn't the answer, 'cause w — when you break off you're gonna have to come right back to the table one — sometime. I can understand how 2 people, not being able to get over a certain position can think of nothing but that. Now, while both of you have certainly tried to explore your positions and (pause) find a happy medium for — for the answer, it's evident that neither of you

have been successful, and I — I know that the answer is there. I — it
has to be there because y — neither of you can really at this time revert to the law of the jungle and settle it that way. Yo — it's one way
of doing it, but it's the hard way. No, I — I don't want any negotiations
broken off; right to the contrary. We're gonna have to — if we have
time to resolve this, we are going to use it. I know sometimes it's
going to be painful, but use it we will. As long as there's time left to
do it we're gonna explore and re-explore and negotiate and renegoti-
ate until we're all convinced that there's nothin' else to do but start
slugging. But that's a long way off, and I don't think we — I think
there's enough common sense among — amongst the 3 groups to
resolve this one. We certainly had tougher ones. So — I don't mean
to imply that I have the answer. Wish I did. But right now I wanta do
a little exploring with it. So, I want to talk to the union now. Like to
talk with your group, few minutes.

Union Caucus - D (4:20 P.M.)

Mediator: I — I still don't know what they're playing or what their movement is, but his reaction, or rather his reply to your counter-proposal
   didn't surprise me none. He — he hasn't indicated, in any way, shape,
   or form yet what the company is thinking about other than 4/10ths of
   a cent. Now, I don't believe that any more'n you do, / that that is —
Gambon: (Over Mediator above) I don't know, George. I — I think the
   guy's beginning to convince me that maybe he does wanta say, "That's
   our position. Go to your membership / and see what they'll do."
One of girls: (Over Gambon above) Yeah! That — that's the way it strikes
   me. It (One of boys says something) — it's the / way it strikes me.
Gambon: (Over girl above) And if he thinks I won't, he's nuts, because
   I won't — I said to you before I didn't set any deadline particularly in
   order to try to bargain the thing out with them first, and failing to do
   that, down here. But if he's gonna take that kind of a position and continue to take that position, I'll set a deadline. I won't wait for the 12th,
   as I mentioned before. Because if he thinks I'm kiddin' with him I'll
   call his bluff damn quick. (Pause)
Mediator: Uh —
Gambon: (At same time as Mediator above) Very true, I mean, what
   Bernice pointed out. These birds around here — they cried the blues
   on our shoulders for years. They — they do one decent thing once
   and then they're crowin' about it. (Pause)
Mediator: Your — your argument — the arg — yo — your argument based
   on the financial report is a very strong point and it would be hard —
   see, that alone, would be very difficult for me to believe that a Board
   of Directors for c — any company, in the light of a report like that,
   would actually stand on 4/10ths (Gambon: H'm) of a cent unless that
   Board of Directors have convinced or said to Michelsen, "You have
   4/10ths of a cent, or a cent, or a cent and a half, and that's all you
   have." Now, if they said that and he believes it or thinks that that's
   his limit, then, of course, other steps will have to be taken to find out
   (Gambon: Uh-huh) whether — and o — other steps, I don't mean strike
   — but other steps would have to be take — other strategical moves or

pressures would have to be made to flush them out, find out whether that is so. (Pause) Is there any reason — this may help clear up the air — is there any (rather long pause) — or <u>what</u> is the reason, is a better way to — the <u>pace</u> of these negotiations — is there any — the company seems to — while they haven't said so directly they seem to feel that — that these negotiations are taking a slow pace. Are these slower than your usual?

Gambon: I wouldn't say so, George. We've only had — when did we open up? — March 12th, and we've had — what, 4 meetings?

One of boys: 4.

Gambon: It's not particularly slow. If an — if anybody's doin' anything to make it slow, they are, because they were notified on January — in January about our intent. They know the reopener date as well as I do. We suggest <u>every</u> time we send 'em a notice, "Begin before-hand and far ahead so that you don't get into retroactivity, because you always cry about it," see. What do they do? They wait until March the 12th against an April 1st reopener date before they say, "Well, this is the date convenient to begin negotiations." It's curious that Standard Products, at this point, has not made any offers yet, either. Now, I — I'm in — we're not draggin' our feet. I think <u>they</u> are. I don't know just what — I know once, as far as relationship between Atlas and Standard Products is concerned, that at one time, back in 193 —

Mediator: Excuse me. Do they do subcontract work for Standard Products?

Meyer: Yeah.

Gambon: (At same time as Meyer above) Oh, definitely. / Yeah.

One of boys: (Over Gambon above) All Standard Products.

Gambon: Back in 1947 — about August of 1947.

Meyer: In the — on the insurance and all?

Gambon: Yeah, '49. That's right. Wasn't '47; '49. We were able to get a package involving all fringes out of Atlas for about 6½¢, whereas Standard Products, who had just concluded negotiations and were still faced with further negotiations with the union, had only agreed to 1¢ for fringes. Standard Products Corporation jumped down their throat for goin' out in front — small organization — because as soon as they gave us the 6½-cent package, 'course the union pressured the company in Standard Products. / The result was that —

Mediator: (Over Gambon above) I's just — I's just beginning to wonder. I wonder if we've got another Aero situation. In Aero negotiations yesterday I ran into this problem, that Aero wants to make a settlement (Gambon: Yeah) and can't b — till Federal Leader settles, and Ryckman is — just finished a meeting as of the day before yesterday — or not Ryckman, but his representative, Elliott Nielsen. (Pause) And they're — the — from their negotiations the pattern is always set, and the union fully realizes that it had a situation on their hand where the membership didn't realize it and they had to be convinced. I don't know whether they're convinced as yet. We still might have a strike there. / But it won't —

Gambon: (Over Mediator above) I heard that a week before it came off, George.

Mediator: Huh?

Gambon: I heard that was gonna happen a week before it come (Mediator: Yeah) up, but I didn't give too much credence / to it. The rank and file —

Mediator: (Over Gambon above) Yeah, I heard — I didn't hear it, but the company (Gambon: H'm) knew it was in the wind. I wonder if we have a situation here where Standard Products can be saying to Atlas, "Look, we're in negotiations. Watch yourself"?

Gambon: It's possible! They all belong to the N.M.E.A. It's National Manufacturers' Electrical (Saunders says something) / Association.

Meyer: (Over Gambon above) N.E.M.A.

Gambon: N.E.M.A., rather — National Association of Electrical / Manufacturers.

Mediator: (Over Gambon above) When's Standard Products expire?

Meyer: April 25th.

Gambon: (At same time as Meyer above) April 26th, I / think.

Meyer: (Over Gambon above) April (Gambon: Yeah) 26th.

Mediator: H'm. (Rather long pause) When you — when you're — on your last reopener (Gambon: Uh-huh), what was the status of Standard Products then? They were in contract —

Meyer: They were ahead. / They were followin' that —

Gambon: (Over Meyer above) They were — no, he / means wer — were they negotiating then?

Mediator: (Over Gambon above) No, I mean were they / negotiating then?

One of girls: (Over Mediator above but cannot be understood)

Meyer: They had that open- (Gambon: No) end con — thing. Come in any time / xx.

Mediator: (Over Meyer above) How about when your contract expired? (Meyer: They had a 2-year contract) Did you ever collide with their negotiations before?

Gambon: Oh, yeah. They're — they usually are either negotiating right before us or right after. See, they have a — they have an open-end contract there, and if they — 30 days' notice at any time, they can demand a reopener. (Saunders says something) We were involved with Viking in one of our reopeners.

Meyer: Last year we weren't / on that.

Gambon: (Over Meyer above) Not the reopeners on the contract (Meyer: Yeah) itself. That's right. It was Viking — we were — finished ours and they just got started right be — right before we finished ours. And all contracts, actually, in the radio-television-recorder industry and part shops we've been trying to get the termination dates to expire around the same time in order to try to establish some sort of industry-wide bargaining, least pressure industry-wide because of that very problem. We — we — we know that not too hard for them to develop policies through the National Association of Electrical Manufacturers — labor policies, definitely, wage policies — things of that type. I don't doubt it because — but I — 'cause I do know by their own statement to us that they caught hell from Standard Products.

Mediator: They never took this kind of an obstinate position before, did they?

Gambon: Not — not until the last time. We got the same sort of business as we're getting now, in October on the reopener, see. What they did,

they made that one contribution, see, in January with the new contract
— the 12-cent package and the 17 for day workers, and a couple of
those fringes that were in there. And ever since that time, every reopener they've been bellyachin' the same thing. They would — their
— their purpose actually — they don't wanta discuss anything with us
until the termination of this contract, and I know we're gonna have to
go through the same damn thing again in October of this year. Now,
they — they signed that in good faith, because that was an issue, if
you remember, about these reopeners. And they didn't wanta sign for
reopeners a'tall in the beginning, but yet, as a part of the settlement,
they said, "All right, 6-month reopeners." Now, in effect, they're
tryin' to renege on the reopeners. They're not bargaining in — on
reopeners in good faith. His attitude is, "Well, we're good faith that
we even talk to you on the reopeners. It doesn't guarantee you'll get
anything." As I told them before — I mean, we'da never settled for
the amount of money that we did settle for as against the total package
that we wanted if we had known that we were signing what in effect was
a 2-year contract with no further wage increases.

Mediator: Who's the pace-setter in this association of theirs? Is there
a pace-setter?

Gambon: Well, you'd have to take it industry-wide and get beyond the
recording industry and talk about the electronics industry generally;
and right now Lashley, Herculus — cules is setting the pattern for the
industry, that is, in terms of what's being done in the form of amount
of benefit. I don't think that Lashley, for instance, or Hercules may
— may not have the highest rates in the industry, but the way the
thing has been moving — I mean, this breakdown that I've given you,
it pretty clearly indicates that that's been the pattern. Standard Product's been following the Lashley pattern. Lashley pattern started to
follow the steel pattern in the very beginning. In fact, the 3 rounds of
increases (Mediator: Yeah), everybody went (Mediator: Yeah) that
way. And then the Lashley pattern began to develop on its own because
of that escalator clause. A good part of that wage increases that
they've gotten have been produced through that escalator clause.
Standard Products didn't have an escalator clause, but they got, in
terms of cents per hour, whatever the escalator clause produced for
Lashley workers, for instance, or Hercules. Now, we had no escalator
clause, as you — they refused that. They refused it on the reopener.
I didn't press for it because I didn't care too much about it. I'm not
interested so much in an escalator clause. And that was one of the
reasons we dropped the escalator clause, because we had the reopeners! (Pause)

Mediator: They'd been —

Gambon: (At same time as Mediator above) The last time — / h'm?

Mediator: (Over Gambon above) They'd been much better off to give it
to you.

Gambon: Today they would (Mediator: Yeah), sure. It very unfortunate.
They'd be happy. (Pause) But if they took it away from us and we
still had a reopener, it still (laughing) wouldn't mean that that would
be the end of it. We'd just take a wage cut and we wouldn't negotiate.
But if they hada given us an escalator clause and no reopeners, they'da
been in a nice position today. (Pause) I'm not too fond of those wage
— escalator clauses. I prefer to bang it across the table, depending

on what the company is makin' rather than depend on the cost-of-living entirely. I'm not just interested in existing. I mean, when I say "I," I'm the — not — I mean, I'm not exist — interested in just seein' my own people exist. I think they should get a fair share of what the hell the company's earning. (Pause)

Mediator: The comp — anyone in any company takin' a position like this can mean one of 2 things. (1), they probably feel that — they — they can feel that the gaps are too wide, that if they do have anything it's not enough, or it's too — too soon to put it out because of where they are; or, in this particular instance, the buyer, which would be Standard Products, could be influencing these negotiations and the progress of them. I don't know.

Gambon: Other than that there's only one other thing that I might suggest might be influencing the — the trend of the negotiations at this point and that is that he claims that they are definitely opposed to this idea of a 35-hour week. (Pause)

Mediator: Yeah.

Saunders: (At same time as Mediator above) They wanta save more money to move next year. (Slight pause)

Gambon: As he puts it, "We're opposed to that. We need all the production we can get." 35-hour week, in order to (Mediator: Approximately —) maintain the same production level, means more people, and certainly we're conscious of that. That's the reason it's an important bargaining point to us. We've lost 150 people right now; we know there's more of them to go by the end of the year. So the union's tryin' to meet a problem — an employment problem — security problem, from our standpoint. (Slight pause) But if that is not the kind of bargaining he wants to engage in, what the hell does he want? That's what I'm tryin' to find out. If he's gonna tell me something that he's willin' to bargain about and what form he wants it to take, at least we know what to consider. We know how to consider our own position. (Rather long pause)

Mediator: Well —

Gambon: (At same time as Mediator above) If he knows, for instance — here's a very unrealistic position. Here's this fixed bonus for skilled trades and other day workers, with emphasis on skilled trades. They can't hire men today for the rates of pay that we have for skilled help in our shop. Can't hire them, because the area rate's gone up. We got 2.27, and a guy can go out of this shop any place now and get two and a half for tool and die, I mean, without any trouble. They've lost 4 or 5 men. People down the line, even — the people w — directly supervising the — the people in those trades, for instance — are telling our peop — told Les right there what a — they wanta do somethin' — they'd like to do somethin'. I think the only reason they didn't make any offer was because they knew we were comin' into this reopener. They can't tell me, see, that he's not willing to move somewhere there, because if he's not thinking of that, he's nuts! He's only gonna lose more men, and he won't be able to replace them.

Mediator: Yeah, that's the skilled trades. (Gambon: That's right!) It's not all of 'em. / Yeah.

Gambon: (Over Mediator above) And if he'd — if he'd talk about what we'd like — "We'll just offer skilled trades" — again he's not bein' realistic, because the number of people left, if you took care of all

your skilled trades, would be so negligible it's not even funny. There's
not more than 100 and — well, the last time we wrangled about this
point I don't think there was more than about 117 total day workers in
the shop, which covered all the trades, and I think there's even less
than that today. (Pause) So, it's on that one point. Now, if that's the
kind of bargaining he wants to en — engage in and he wants to get away
from the 35-hour week, what form does he want these negotiations to
take? I do know he says, "We're utterly opposed to any idea of a
35-hour week. We need all the production we can get." 'Course, I
tell him, "Well, you can get production. All you need is more people,
which is what we're interested in. We want jobs for the people that
are losing out." So I'd like to know what is his bargaining area? Not
in terms of cost, at the moment, but the items in the area that's gonna
be bargainable from where he stands. Does he wanta talk fringes?
Cents-per-hour wage increases? What the hell does he wanta talk
about? That's what I wanta know. / If that's what's holdin' the thing
up, I think he should tell us that.

Mediator: (Over Gambon above) From — from what I can gather — from
what I — from — from what I can gather, and if my memory serves
me correctly, I — I believe he — he wants to talk about fringes.
(Slight pause)

Gambon: I was surprised, George. I said to Tom and Bernice — I said
if he comes in with anything, he'll come in with this holiday thing.
That'll be it — his first offer. I thought that's what he would pick up.
Instead of talkin' about the 2 points here I left all the fringes purposely
wide open to let him — give him room to come in with that kind of
proposition. He didn't do it.

Mediator: I'll tell you — I'll tell you what his thinking — or their collective thinkin' was. After they had their caucus they decided that (pause)
— without saying so (pause) it was evident when they come back here
and said you're — while you took a reasonable clip off your (Gambon:
Uh-huh) position — I forget what words he used, but / you're still —

Meyer: (Over Mediator above) Stratosphere.

Gambon: Yeah, the stratosphere. Well, I'm still in the stratosphere.
Yeah.

Mediator: (At same time as Gambon above) Stratosphere — still up in
the stratosphere — you're still in another stratosphere. (Gambon:
H'm) I think, without having to say so, that indicated what kind of
thinking went on in their caucus. Think that proves that what they're
saying is that, "If we do have something we can't reveal it at this
time while you're at — where you are." (Gambon: Uh) And I — I
think — the reasons. Now, I — I don't know, because he has — I have
not engaged in any talk with him on his financial position yet. (Gambon: Uh-huh) I've been letting him do the talking on it, expecting to
hear him say that, "We'll do this, that, or the other thing." The only
thing that I could get — as I say, I didn't try for it — was that he —
he ran over some of these fringes. Now, that doesn't necessarily
mean that he wanted to talk about (Gambon: Uh-huh) 'em, but I
gather that if and when he made a settlement he probably would like
to make it on fringes. Now, I may be guessing the whole thing wrong.
I've gotta have something more basic from him before I can even begin to patch the thing together, or reasoning — re — reason it. But I —

I can say this, that he fig — he — he no doubt feels he's still in dangerous bargaining territory. He probably feels that he doesn't have much
to work with. (Gambon: H'm) Whatever it is, I don't know. I have
my guess; you have yours. And guesses can be wrong, but I base my
guess on what has gone on in other industries and establish an average. Sometimes people even buck those averages, fight them. But if
my guess is right, I have an idea just like you and your whole committee, but — and maybe he has the same one; I don't know. But I believe,
if that is so — but I don't even know it to be true, but if it was so, he's
afraid to move, or afraid to reveal what he has at this time, probably
fig — figuring that he'd be stuck once he got there. Guess he figures
he's got X amount, "And when I get up to that point, I'm done. I
haven't got any more. And, hell, I may be this far away (Gambon:
Uh) from where they want, and I can't go any farther." Now, that's
what I think's running through his mind. I cannot believe — I can't
accept that he really means 4/10ths of a cent or fight. I — I just can't
buy that.
Gambon: H'm. Well, he's doin' a pretty damn good job of convincin' me
of it. The more he talks about it the more I'm beginnin' to wonder.
That's why I say, if he wants a — if he — if he's lookin' for somebody
to call his bluff, I'm willin' to do it.
Mediator: I've gotta go over this some more b — 'cause I — I, too, have to
get the answers. Now, if — if I'm convinced, or if I thought that the
man was actually playing it that way, I would reach this conclusion.
I would say to myself, well, then thing that's needed here is a crisis,
synthetic or not (Gambon: H'm), and that decision would be up to
you (Gambon: Uh-huh) and your committee. But I'm not sure yet
even that is in order until I know where he's going. So I gotta have
some more talk / with them on that.
Gambon: (Over Mediator above) Well, I think that he should be impressed with the proposition that up to this point, for a very good reason, that we wanta bargain the thing out. We've not set up any deadlines and said, " This is it."
[Tape changed]
Mediator: And the moving.
Gambon: And this moving business — the way they broke it to them, the
way they've refused to give anybody any transfer rights, which is
going to be continued in every move they make. Kind of t — lack of
consideration generally, regardless of how the hell long you been
here, see. We've got people — I mean, he claims this $1.71 for this
— people actually took pay cuts — the ones that are still working
there took pay cuts as a result of this move, people've been there
15, 17 years in the one department. Come — all the way from a
Grade E job down to A jobs or B jobs. That's an appreciable ra —
wage cut.
Saunders: $1.71's figuring incentive, too. (Gambon: H'm?) He got his
figure out of Department 5. Every 3rd day gives 'em a — a day at 96¢
an hour, figurin' on the incentive system. I was just figurin' out here.
They put out 43,000 units a day on each side of a — an S machine —
that's (Gambon: H'm) somethin' George don't understand, but it's
sort of — one of our main units — for $1.25. If they make their what
they call rate — bonus — for that day — it's 22,000 units extra, or

65,000 a day — they get an extra 32¢ an hour. So every 4th day they give the company a full day at 96¢ an hour. And he's still sayin' $1.71. That's when I (Meyer says something) got burned the other day when heard him (Gambon: H'm) say that. Every 4th day they get a day for nothin' / on that incentive system.

Meyer: (Over Saunders above) It's those x — it's the one department that has the high incentive earnings that inflates that 1.71 (Gambon: H'm), and the balance of the shop is very much lower, because I would be willing to bet that our average for females is closer to $1.52 and using (Saunders: Yes) that same department.

[For a period Meyer, Gambon, and Saunders, then one of girls, talk variously at once.]

Gambon: (Over others above) The interesting thing there, I think, was that the — the high incentive in this department was done in one way. The company speeded up the machines, period. Under the contract they — it wasn't a legitimate change of any kind, because it says specifically you can't change a rate simply because you speed up the machine. And that's — the (laughing slightly) — the company actually increased the earnings, and then — and just because they wanted more production, so that it's one of the departments where day in and day out they — it's about 155% bonus. (Saunders: Sure, and that — that shows that) But — as a result of speeding up the machines. Nothing more'n that.

Saunders: The chart he had in 1941 — those people were hand assembling that stuff.

Gambon: Yeah!

Saunders: And he went from '41 to '53, never mentioned the change in machinery.

Meyer: Or how many people he let go.

Saunders: Yeah.

Gambon: Back in those days practically everything / was x —

Saunders: (Over Gambon above) I — I — I'd love to some day get hold of that chart with him and take it apart good. (Laughs) From ni — I've been there since 1936, too, John since 1930. He's seen a lot. And Bernice since 1935. And we've seen the changes. He talks about $1.71; he's crazy. (Slight pause)

Gambon: Well, he could prob'ly justify $1.71 —

[Several, including Meyer and Gambon, talk at once.]

Meyer: I — I don't disagree with the weighted average, but (Gambon: H'm) I disagree with the number of people who get $1.71 (Gambon: H'm) (One of girls says something), because if 3 of us get $3.00 an hour here and the 10 people get $1.00 an hour, I can easily say their average is such and such. But 10 people are gonna say, "Yeah, but you got 3 bucks; I only got a buck." And he — / he knows what he's talkin' about.

Saunders: (Over Meyer above) No, I'm — I'm — I've (Gambon: Yeah) been takin' that same price index that he had and the wage index and then put in what he didn't have in, the predicted productivity increase (Meyer: Yeah), which we've <u>trebled</u> up there. We haven't trebled our wages. We've more than trebled the productivity in the 3 departments that I work in. (Pause)

Meyer: That's good management, Tom. It's what he said / the other day. (Laughs)

Saunders: (Over Meyer above) I think he left that out very — he — he knew / he couldn't x that one. Stone mentioned that in Department 3.

Gambon: (Over Saunders above) Well, it's a — i — it's one of the things that ya can't quarrel too much about — technological changes. That's what it's involved. But they are not passing along benefits (Meyer: And it's affectin' the profits in there) to the workers who — because of those technological advances that they've made, and all.

Mediator: Uh (pause) — you believe that they'll move that plant out entirely, eventually?

Gambon: George, I'm afraid of it. All I'm willin' to say to anybody in my union is this: "Look, I'm fairly certain that Atlas'll be at 1122 West Oak Street until April, 1956, period." They have an out in the (Mediator: Lease, uh?) clause that they can drop it in '56. If they don't pick that up — o — oppor — opportunity up then it runs till '62. But I can't, with any confidence, say that they're gonna be there after '56. We've got this plant up in Rome that they set up for the Navy (Mediator: Yeah) under a Navy contract. That thing could be — some way — I — I'm tryin' to find that out from them, whether there's anything in the contract givin' them the right t — to buy it from the government. As much as they'll tell me is that yes, they would get first crack at the equipment in there because it's electronic equipment that is peculiar to this company alone. But they haven't said that they can or can't buy the plant from the government. I don't see where the government would probably do anything different for Atlas than they're doin' for Lashley and a lot of these other places, sellin' 'em the plants. And if they did that, they wouldn't stay here, because Rome is a much lower paid area than the metropolitan area. And that would be — that would be the straw that would break the camel — camel's back, because the tape recorder less the amplifier is the biggest volume on any item we have. It would produce — I'd say, if that's all we had left in the metropolitan area, we'd prob'ly have, well, as a Local, maybe 500 members — 4 or 500.

Mediator: How many people could that plant in Rome hold?

Gambon: I don't know. (Meyer: I would say 900, if you just look at it xx on) I mean, there — you — you could — you could go 3 shifts. I — I don't know how many m — machines they have in there right now, offhand.

[Saunders, Meyer, and Gambon talk variously at once.]

Management Caucus - C (4:50 P.M.)

Michelsen: Good afternoon, Governor.

Mediator: Good afternoon. (Slight pause) He's talking strike now. (Michelsen: Uh-huh) He (slight pause) is getting steamed up. (Pause) Uh (rather long pause) — he's beginning to believe that the — he does have to take action now (slowly) to bring about a settlement between the 2 positions. He doesn't say where he's at isn't negotiable. (Someone laughs slightly) He says it is.

Michelsen: The only thing he said that made any sense to me was April 12th.

Mediator: Yeah. Now, that came up again. (Slight pause)

Michelsen: I'll see him on the 11th.

Mediator: Uh (rather long pause) — I (rather long pause) — I wish he wouldn't keep mentioning that because he throws me off. It throws me. I have to — I have to take cognizance of it, because it's important. (Pause) <u>Can</u> we get into the reasonable area of — and work out a settlement, or are we precluded by this April the 12th date, is the thoughts that keep goin' through m — my mind. If we <u>are</u>, all right, then we know where we're going and we know how to pace the conferences, set the dates, and so forth. On the other hand, I would hate to miss any opportunities. I would hate to be wrong, see, and (slight pause) miss the thing. I've gotta still f — work on that. Uh (pause) — he — he said, "I don't have to wait for April the 12th to meet again." He said, "I can strike before that." (Pause) And he made this clear. He said, "We will have no trouble pulling the people out, because they know very well that the company's contemplating moving the industry away, and if they're goin' to get anything, they may as well fight for it, they may as well hit 'em hard." He said, "They're in the mood to do so because of the fact that they know the company is moving." He said, "I'll have no trouble whatever there." (Slight pause) Uh —

?: (In rather low voice) Well, I think he's wrong, but — (rather long pause).

Mediator: So (slight pause), I just haven't made my mind up yet as to that April the 12th date, and I think the thing I have to establish now is a — a dead — what's the date today? / The 4th?

Loring: (Over Mediator above) Today's the 4th, George. It's a week from tomorrow, George.

Mediator: A week from tomorrow. (Slight pause)

Michelsen: Long time to go a short distance. (Pause)

Mediator: H'm. (Very long pause. Mediator is rhythmically hitting hands together) Geez, the time went fast.

Michelsen: Yeah. We quit at 5:00, you know.

Mediator: Maybe I'm getting (Michelsen laughs) punchy from (laughing slightly) bein' in the conference room too long. (Slight pause) (Raising voice) Yeah, we're union negotiators. (Michelsen laughs heartily, someone else slightly) (Slight pause)

Michelsen: (Still laughing slightly) I was thinking before we go — we go back in there I'll just say, "Well, look, I — it's gettin' (Someone laughs slightly) 5:00 o'clock, and we only work a $7\frac{1}{2}$-hour day (Someone laughs) — the salaried employees. We're gonna leave." (Laughs heartily)

Mediator: In the old days (Michelsen: It'd bring down the house) — in the old days when the union committee — when the union was in the — <u>unions</u> were in their (pause) early days when they were just growing, they were working day and night. Remember the organizers'd be out at night and, oh, they were putting in 16, 17 hours a day, and they'd come into the conference room and start negotiating and demanding overtime for over 8 hours. Quite often the employer would ask them, "How many hours do you work?" "Oh-h, we — we're never done." "D'ya get overtime? (One or 2 laugh slightly) That was a (laughs slightly) — that was a — the wrong thing to say. They'd hit the ceiling. So the unions got little more money, and then I think they tried to compensate 'em for it. But I don't think they have an hourly understanding on overtime for the organizers, even today. Well, I think we did enough for today. There actually isn't much more you can do today.

I'm (pause) — you've gotta have a little agitation here yet on their — on — they've gotta get a little more upset about this thing. And I'm — I — this figure 12 is staring me in the face. Now, I gave John an opportunity to make another move in this last conference. I said, "If you <u>were</u> going to go on strike, or you were contemplat — plating some action — any action like that, I would prefer being in a reasonable area and not where <u>you</u> are. I wouldn't wanta call any a strike for 31¢."

Loring: (In low voice) Nor does he.

Mediator: He evidently isn't ready to (Michelsen: No) move from there, see. (Michelsen: No, I think they're —) I gave him an opportunity to get in there (Michelsen: They're waiting for Friday, 12th), if he really wants a fight. Uh — now, look. (Pause) I think we're gonna have to give 'em a meeting next week. I mean (Michelsen: Uh-huh), you can't — can't let the thing get cold, because I had to jump him there when he started to talk about negotiat — uh — breaking off (Loring: Uh-huh) negotiations. (Slight pause) And (rather long pause) — <u>so</u>. (Rather long pause) I x to wrap this up, but, Bill, it isn't there. (Michelsen: You don't have to tell me) And if I could — there was a chance of doing — if I thought this was the right time, hell, I'd be in here Saturday with you. (Slight pause) (Michelsen: Yeah) But —

Michelsen: No. I — I think they're gonna / ride it out till the se —

Mediator: (Over Michelsen above) You've got a — see, you've got an outside problem to cope with, and that — that — that's that date. It's outside of your — you just can't do anything about it. And (pause) some thinking of theirs, too, is that Standard Products may have something to do with your (Michelsen: Yeah) position, too. They're (Michelsen: They won't be finished —) — they've taken that into —

Michelsen: — I don't think. They won't be finished by the 12th.

Mediator: No, they're not — they won't be finished until about the 25th (slight pause), if they're finished then.

Michelsen: Yeah. 'Liable to be down here, too. (Pause)

Mediator: I won't have that one. (Slight pause) I think Mediator Jones has it. (Michelsen: Uh-huh) I don't know; I think so. 'Course, you never know which one you're getting.

Loring: Well, outside of the fact that it's moving so slowly, are you satisfied with the progress — I mean, with the way it's going, George?

Mediator: Oh, yeah. I have the thing under control. I mean, it's not (Loring: Uh-huh) — it won't get away from me. Won't be any strike without me first exp — getting to the bottom of everything. That I'm sure of. (Pause) Uh (rather long pause) — I'm going in and talk with them about another date. I wanta make it sometime (slight pause) next week. What're you thinking about?

Michelsen: Oh, well, certainly not tomorrow or Saturday / with this —

Mediator: (Over Michelsen above) Oh, no. No. (Slight pause) Now, there's not a —

Michelsen: I think John would be very happy to let it go until the end of the week. So would I.

Mediator: End of next week?

Michelsen: Sure! I wanta just bang it up close to the 12th, if they want a photo finish. Least, if it's a date, / it'd —

Mediator: (Over Michelsen above) That's a good term, photo (laughing slightly) finish.

Michelsen: If they — if they wanta struggle into their meeting and tell
'em what a tough time they've had, why, I can fix that. Uh — (slight
pause).

Mediator: Well, I don't wanta — I don't wanta get it — I don't wanta get
— I don't wanta crowd myself too (Michelsen: Uh-huh) much. I
want a little spare time, in case I need it. / Uh-h-h-h —

Michelsen: (Over Mediator above) Well, Wednesday, Thursday, Friday.
Got 10th, 11th, 12th. (Slight pause) Thing that bothers me, George,
is — / is —

Mediator: (Over Michelsen above) Prob'ly one on Thursday?

Michelsen: Thursday? Yeah. That's what I mean. I didn't mean Friday.

Mediator: Oh.

Espig: Well, in all probability they may have a — an afternoon session
and an evening session on Friday (Michelsen: They don't have one
scheduled yet, but there could be one) unless — normally they do
that, don't they? If it's important enough. (Michelsen: Yeah. xx)
On the other hand — because, you see, / u —

Mediator: (Over Espig above) A session with who?

Espig: With their people.

Michelsen: See, they'd have a 2d-shift and a — and (Mediator: Oh) a
day-shift meeting. They'd have 2 meetings.

Espig: Their 2d shift —

Mediator: (At same time as Espig above) You said on a (?: Yeah)
Friday. (Espig: Yeah) This Friday?

Espig: No, next Friday (Pranis: The 12th), the 12th.

Mediator: Oh, is that the twelf (Pranis: They'd have one the —) — oh,
I was looking at the wrong month.

Pranis: They'd have one before 4:00 (Mediator: Oh, I see) o'clock,
George, and one after, / on the 12th.

Espig: (Over Pranis above) See, they have 2 meetings, to / accommodate their 2d shift —

Michelsen: (Over Espig above) Or they post — they postpone the 2d /
meeting until Saturday.

Mediator: (Over Michelsen above) Oh, wait a minute. I was lookin'
at — I was lookin' at March. Wait a minute. I'm all mixed up here.

Pranis: That's a Friday — next Friday.

Mediator: Oh, this — there we are, and I said Thursday, didn't I?

Pranis: Yeah.

Mediator: Thursday. (Pause) Does it — what is it, midnight of — oh,
no! No.

Michelsen: We're (Pranis: Afternoon and evening) past the deadline.

Mediator: We passed that. (Michelsen laughs) (Slight pause)

Michelsen: Yeah. I mean, they — they — their next regular meeting is
the 12th. According to the schedule, it would be a meeting only for
the day-shift people; it wouldn't be scheduled for all of their employees. It wouldn't include the 2d-shift people. Now, they just last meeting had their quarterly meeting, which (Espig: Oh, yeah) means that
they have a 2d-shift meeting. They start that at 2:00 o'clock and have
a meeting at night for the day shift. Now, they could do one of 3
things: they could submit this just to the day shift, which I think would
be very undiplomatic of 'em; they could have a double meeting on
Friday; or they could postpone the Friday meeting and have it Saturday and have it in time for everybody.

Espig: And that's prob'ly what they'd do, / Bill.

Michelsen: (Over Espig above) Yeah. (Slight pause)

Mediator: Uh-huh.

Michelsen: <u>So</u>, you may — the deadline may be Saturday. They love to have these things go on until 12:00 o'clock Saturday — you know, 15 minute — and then have a meeting at the union hall at 12:15 Saturday. 'Member the last time they all had to leave to go up to the meeting and they left somebody here to (Mediator: Oh, yeah) get the signed paper to ⌐

Mediator: That's right. / Yeah.

Michelsen: (Over Mediator above) Yeah. And they stroll in there and get up on the stage, you know, all sleepy-eyed from being up late that / night.

Mediator: (Over Michelsen above) Did we call 'em back at 9:00 in the morning?

Michelsen: Yeah. They were that — really pooped, and they looked worse than they were. And these people just ate it up. "Those stalwarts in there, strugglin' for us," ya know.

Mediator: This man doesn't apprec — appreciate all those / dramatics, does he?

Michelsen: (Over Mediator above) I understand good — I understand good theatre, George, and (Mediator laughs) I'm willing to do all I can to set the stage (laughing) as long as I don't tangle with the scenery. (Laughs)

Mediator: You know — you know, it might be said that (slight pause) we oughta have — we oughta be payin' dues to the Actors' Guild.

Michelsen: You're not kidding! (Espig laughs heartily) xxxx.

Mediator: One fellow put it that way. (Loring and Espig laugh)

Michelsen: They're doin' this over in Panmunjom right now, walkin' in and outa tents; we're walkin' in and outa offices. (Pause) But it's the same routine. It doesn't — it's a lot less painful than the other / xx.

Mediator: (Over Michelsen above) 'Course, you couldn't get your settlement till you went through these (laughing) / labor pains.

Michelsen: (Over Mediator above) I'm not — no. Oh, I — I'm not objecting. I / like it!

Mediator: (Over Michelsen above) I know. (Michelsen laughs heartily) This is the <u>easy</u> way.

Michelsen: Sure. I'm in f — favor of labor-saving / devices.

Mediator: (Over Michelsen above) Uh — he (pause) — I — I — I am inclined to agree with ya that he won't object to going into next week, either. (Pause) Then, too, they've got a lotta things on their mind <u>right</u> at this moment. They're thinking of the Roosevelt. (Michelsen: Uh-huh) See, the convention's on. (Michelsen: Yeah) And they will — they're all going to make a bee-line right over there. So that's another reason why we couldn't do much today or tomorrow.

<u>Union Caucus - E</u> (5:05 P.M.)

[While waiting for Gambon, who is absent from the room at the opening of the caucus, Mediator entertains the group for several minutes with an anecdote from the Aero case involving a union official whom some of them know.]

Mediator: Uh (long pause) — I would suggest we recess this conference, set another date; in the interim (rather long pause) your position's made a little clearer to the company. I feel at this time it will reflect itself in the next negotiations. (Pause)

Gambon: What do you mean, if our position is made a little clearer?

Mediator: Firmer. They / know —

Gambon: (Over Mediator above) Mean a deadline, and so forth? (Rather long pause) H'm. Will do! (Rather long pause)

Mediator: I —

Gambon: (At same time as Mediator above) I think we oughta give 'em a deadline now, them think about. (Rather long pause)

Mediator: I have a feeling — I have a — while I don't — while I don't recommend those things (Gambon: H'm), in this particular situation — we're speaking off the record (pause) — it will do more good than harm. (Gambon: H'm) With this understanding. You can set your — whatever deadline you want, see, but I wanta be on top of the situation all — in other words, don't want anything done — I don't want any action — any wildcats or quickies, or anything like that. Set your deadline; fine. I feel it will move these negotiations in the direction they oughta go and it will bring some outside pressure. Think you gotta have it at this time. I have analyzed the thing pretty thoroughly, and I feel quite certain / of it.

Gambon: (Over Mediator above) Uh — have they again reiterated their position at 4/10ths / to you?

Mediator: (Over Gambon above) No.

Gambon: No?

Mediator: No. (Pause) This thing needs a little push, and tell you why I'm thinking this way. I'll tell you my reasoning behind it. (Pause) You're over your April the 1st (Gambon: Uh-huh), and you're negotiating almost, we can say, when ya have no date, aimlessly (Gambon: Uh-huh), and there's no guidepost there for them to shoot at. I'm inclined to feel that until such time as they know they have to go along on a certain day they can't or won't put in their best efforts in this thing. I think it's just what the — the doctor would order.

Gambon: Uh-huh. Well, as far as I'm concerned — I think I've already said this to 'em, but I may not have; I may have just said it to you — but unless this committee can meet some sort of a — a satisfactory settlement with them that we can conscientiously recommend the members to accept, I'm goin' before that membership on the 12th and recommend a strike. And if he — if you want that kind of a date, I'll give it to ya that way, because I'll just lay it right to / 'em xx try to push me.

Mediator: (Over Gambon above) Now, let me ask you this. When your union recommends a strike vote (Gambon: Uh-huh) — each — different unions operate differently, and tha — in this respect, and that's why I have to ask (Gambon: Uh-huh) for clarification. When your union asks for a strike vote (Gambon: Uh-huh) and they get it (Gambon: Yeah) — some unions, it's — it's mandatory after that, or some unions give it — the power to the committee to call it whenever they see fit after that. There are various ways. What — is there any set procedure your union follows?

Gambon: No. The only thing that we have is that Hughes would have to be notified, 'course, of a pending strike. And if he thought that he could prevent a strike by personally involving himself in it he would probably do so. He's never had to do that with us. I mean, we've — durin' that last one we notified Al (laughing slightly) and told him we were — we gettin' to the point where these guys won't move, possible strike.

Mediator: Well, I / know —

Gambon: (Over Mediator above) I would say this to ya. If we were, for instance, to take a strike vote on the 12th, it wouldn't mean be on strike on the 13th. We would make an effort again to try to get these guys to do somethin' reasonable. But I would definitely ask for the committee to have the authority to call a strike (pause) (Mediator: Uh-huh) in the absence of being able to get any kind of a reasonable settlement out of 'em.

Mediator: Well, I think before we recess here and set another date (Gambon: Uh-huh) I'd want another meeting before anything like that — I'd want another whirl at it. And I also wanta allow myself time before that date, see.

Gambon: Thursday, the 11th, George.

Mediator: That's a good date. I'll buy that. That'd be a day before your / meeting. Your meeting at night ?

Gambon: (Over Mediator above) Membership meeting. I'm gonna meet with 'em on Friday. Yeah. 8:00 o'clock.

Mediator: 8:00 o'clock at night. Good. (Pause) I'll call 'em in here. Might be well for you to make your position quite strong and let 'em know that you're going to recommend a strike vote. (Gambon: Uh-huh) On — once that is done, between now and that meeting it's going to make my position a lot better, because I will be in touch with Bill between now and the next meeting —

Gambon: George, I — let me say this. It just flashed through my head. I'm not particularly anxious at this moment to tell him across this table that I'm gonna take a strike vote at that meeting because I'm gonna have a bulletin out in the shop.

Mediator: Oh, yeah.

Gambon: It's gonna confuse the hell out of our people before they even hear from their own committee. (Pause)

Mediator: Yeah. Gonna x / x —

Gambon: (Over Mediator above) I want them to hear the issues from us, not from some damn letter that they're puttin' out in the shop and have a bunch of foremen givin' all kinds of stories out on the situation.

Mediator: Yeah. Yeah, that could happen. (Pause) Put it this way. (Pause) I'll tell it. I won't say — I'll tell 'em that I'm certain they have a deadline by (Gambon: Uh-huh) the 12th, without going into detail. That (Gambon: Uh) way they can't write and say what I said. (Gambon: Uh-huh) But I think it oughta be established. (Pause)

Gambon: All right. (Other talking goes on in background among girls) The 11th is the date that I'd like to see / xx.

Mediator: (Over Gambon above) Hold yourself open on the 11th and the 12th.

Gambon: Well, the 12th, naturally we'll meet with 'em. (Pause)

Mediator: As long as this goes — see, as long as there's no date — now, I felt up till this last caucus — I thought, well, maybe there is a — an — an area where we can slip in here and start working, but I can see

now that this is a reporting job (Gambon: Uh-huh), see, back — back,
and as long as they've got nothing serious on in the line confronting
them, they're probably just sending in written reports as some negotiating teams do, or verbally reporting, but x —

Gambon: Well, they have what they call an Operating Committee meeting
every Friday. Michelsen participates in those meetings. Th — there's
no doubt that he makes his reports to the Operating Committee — his
personal and verbal report, as well as probably handin' in written reports and then broadening the program to include these bulletins that
they're giving out to all the supervising foremen who, in turn, as I
say, start word xx mouth the thing across to our people in there.
(Pause) / That isn't xxx —

Mediator: (Over Gambon above) Don't make any notes on my off-the-
record discussion. (Several laugh) You're going in the right direction, though. It's — w — w — ya gotta make the — you won't move
'em until you set that deadline. (Gambon: Uh-huh) They won't move.
I'm sure of it now. I'm (Gambon: H'm) certain of it. And (pause)
I think you're sound in not stating you're goin' to take a strike vote.
They would use that, I'm quite certain. (Gambon: Uh-huh) And with
you where you are in your bargaining position, it's not a good position
to be in to call a strike or even talk about it. So let me handle it my
way and I'll — he can't quote me. But I'll — what I give him he'll take
back and report to his people (Gambon: Uh-huh), and it'll be a deadline but it'll be from me. So, I think that now you've got some moving
material in on 'em and they're — they just needed it, because they
won't move. (Gambon: Uh-huh) I don't think Bill's the last word.

Gambon: No, he's not the last word. F — fact, I think Alexander, when he
was heading the negotiating commit — committee for the company had
more authority than — than Michelsen has at this time, and even
Alexander wasn't the last word. He used to very frankly admit that
he'd have to go back to the Board of Directors with some of the things,
so I know this guy don't have any more authority than that.

Mediator: Well, it's — it's necessary. It's needed. It'll (Gambon: Uh-
huh) — I — I think the next meeting'll have an entirely different color
— tone.

Gambon: O.K. Any — what're you gonna check on? I mean, there's no
sense of bringin' 'em in here, then. I mean, there's no reason for
me to (Mediator: No) make that kind of a statement, / is there?

Mediator: (Over Gambon above) No, I think we can recess now. You
can go (Gambon: H'm), and I might be in touch with ya, too, between
now and then (Gambon: Uh-huh), 'cause I'm — I — I know I'm going
to have a talk with Michelsen (Gambon: Uh-huh) before Thursday.
(Rather long pause)

Gambon: O.K. (Mediator: O.K.?), then. Yep.

Management Caucus - D (5:20 P.M.)

Mediator: Why (slight pause), there is a deadline. (Slight pause) Uh
(rather long pause) — I've recessed 'em, but I told 'em that you
(slight pause) — there'd been no change.

Michelsen: Then (Mediator: And —) you recessed 'em, sent them home?

Mediator: Yeah. And talked about March the 12th.

Michelsen: It's April 12th, George. (Mediator: April the 12th) That's just about a month from now.

Mediator: And he made it clear that (pause) come April the 12th, why, xxx. (Michelsen: Good) I said, "Well (pause), we'll bring the company in." He said, "Well, I gave that to you for your information. I'm not givin' it to the company (Michelsen: Uh-huh) here. But I don't want them going sending any letters out to the people before we (laughing) can report to 'em (laughs, as does Michelsen) xx." So, unofficially (Michelsen: Uh-huh) you have it. You can't use it, because they didn't give it (Michelsen: Yeah) to you, see. But / it —

Michelsen: (Over Mediator above) They said the April 12th (Mediator: Yes) is the deadline.

Mediator: And we have a meeting — I set a meeting on April the 11th (Michelsen: Yeah), which is Thursday.

Michelsen: All right.

Mediator: 'Course, there we really have to keep them going there, I mean, because by that time I think —

[Tape changed]

... uh (slight pause) — they could sell a strike if they wanted to. They could — that's easy, if you want to. Some unions just throw a picket line around and explain later. (?: H'm) That's been done. They won't do it that way, but if they — if they deve — if they — if they decide to strike, they will beat the drums in advance and give reasons, propaganda, as to why — now, it won't, probably, be 31¢. They'll prob'ly shy away from that (pause), but it's very important to both the union and the company that a line is established — a deadline. Very important. These negotiations would have gone on aimlessly (Loring: Yeah) and endlessly. You (pause) — you'd never know where you were gonna end. Now you know. And he made it clear that (?: Uh-huh) he would follow with a strike.

Michelsen: Uh-huh.

Loring: Do you gather that the rest of the committee feels as strongly, or is it John?

Mediator: I think John has — I — he does the talking, but I think that he has the majority of the committee (Loring: Uh-huh) thinking his way. I didn't see anyone that was opposed to him, but I — I'd prob'ly give him 80, 90%. I don't know the people well enough.

Loring: Uh-huh. (Rather long pause)

Michelsen: What time do we meet Thursday?

Mediator: 10:00 A.M. (Rather long pause) I don't usually operate this way, you know — this slow moving and — but this is a situation where it had me confused wh — why there wasn't movement. And was there a timetable, was there another plan that was on the — somethin' was (Michelsen: Any mention about —) — 12th seemed to loom up. Huh?

Michelsen: Any mention about me? (Slight pause)

Mediator: No. (Slight pause) Not a word. (Rather long pause. Espig laughs slightly)

Michelsen: I don't mean praise or condemnation.

Mediator: No, I know. (Michelsen laughs heartily) (Slight pause) Oh, they mentioned you. (Several, particularly Loring, laugh heartily)

Michelsen: (Laughing) No, I mean about my leaving.

Mediator: (Laughing) I know what you mean. No, they didn't mention that. No, they really didn't even mention you. (Slight pause) They — they didn't say too much <u>other</u> than that you were takin' a tough position. Nothing personal. (Michelsen laughs) They didn't get personal.

Michelsen: What'd they expect me to do, come in here and make 'em a daisy chain? (Laughs slightly)

Mediator: So — (slight pause).

Loring: That's it, George.

Michelsen: See you on Thursday, George.

[At 10:35 A.M. Mediator stops by the union caucus room long enough to say that he is going into caucus with the management group.]

Management Caucus - A (10:37 A.M.)

Mediator: Why, I was tied up. Start out there with an apology. Uh —
Michelsen: We have lots of time.
Mediator: Uh — I hear they moved up their meeting.
Michelsen: Yeah.
Mediator: That's Sunday, now.
Michelsen: Saturday, it was.
Mediator: It was Saturday, but they moved it to Sunday. / That it?
Michelsen: (Over Mediator above) Well, no. It was moved from Friday night to Saturday / afternoon.
Mediator: (Over Michelsen above) Oh! From <u>Friday</u> night to Saturday.
Michelsen: See, Friday night meeting would've got only the day-shift people, and it was a regular meeting. This meeting — so the bulletin board notice has been changed to Saturday at 1:00 o'clock in the afternoon so that both shifts can attend. I imagine that's the purpose of it. And they are urging — the announcement urges all employees to come out so that they can hear the report of the committee, which wouldn't have been possible with the Friday night meeting. There would've been maybe 3,400 people working on the 2d shift. (Mediator: Uh-huh) But now they're all in a position where they will be available to come out to the meeting. (Pause) No, there's been no change in that. I saw an announcement on the board this morning (slight pause), Saturday at 1:00 o'clock, union hall. (Rather long pause)
Mediator: O.K. Uh — what's the latest? Has there been any (slight pause) rumors flying as to —
Michelsen: This morning we heard the first one. Uh — been very quiet up to now. This morning we heard a statement which is reputed to have come from one of the members of the committee and an officer of the union that if there's no agreement by Friday night they're gonna padlock the place. / And —
Mediator: (Over Michelsen above) Padlock it.
Michelsen: Yeah. They're gonna padlock it on the way out Friday night when the shift's over. (Slight pause) But (slight pause) I would certainly expect they'd begin pretty soon to start talkin' like that. (Pause)
Mediator: 31¢ — my goodness. (Slight pause) Geez, we went into the ABC Association negotiations, and they're tough. They're generally considered tough. (Pause) In one day (pause) had 13 issues resolved and a wage settlement reached, and the whole package tied. 'Course, it was around midnight. But that was for one day!

337

Michelsen: Yeah.

Mediator: But those people were — I mean, they didn't come in with this 61¢ and — hell, they had a <u>wage termination</u> and came in with a <u>starter</u> of 25¢.

Michelsen: Well, George, they'll prob'ly add to their demands. They'll / prob'ly —

Mediator: (Over Michelsen above) Settled for just half of that. Now, / show —

Michelsen: (Over Mediator above) Prob'ly want 31¢ and want us to buy the padlock.

Mediator: It's — O.K. I'll — I'm gonna keep you separated pretty well today until I find (Michelsen: Yeah) out exactly what they're doing, unless you (Michelsen: No, that's all right) want it the other way.

Michelsen: We get along well together in here. (Laughs heartily, joined by couple others)

Mediator: I'm — I think I can move faster this / way.

Michelsen: (Over Mediator above) Yeah.

[Michelsen stops Mediator at door, saying he is going to wait for Mediator to give him a sign. As Observer moves to turn recorder back on, Michelsen acknowledges this with a good-natured question to the effect, Shall he wait for the machine so that his words can be preserved —]

Michelsen: ... for posterity? (Laughs)

Observer: Uh-huh.

Michelsen: These were the 3 channels. Fact, the 3 lines are still there. Uh — the 3rd one, and the one which I certainly would not recommend but which we could follow, would be to stand on 4/10ths of a cent till hell freezes over, and that's it. I mean, that's our final position. The other one is to accept the fact that they are honestly concerned with at least one of these 2 demands which are now on the table. That's the 35-hour week and the 20% fixed bonus for skilled trades and other day worker. We would eliminate absolutely the reduced work week except to say O.K. as — hoping that it would never even be accepted and wouldn't bargain past the initial statement, "O.K. We'll give ya a 35-hour week, but you'll get 35 hours' pay for it. If that's what you want, you can start Monday, and Tuesday we'll start openin' the local Rome plant and take care of the additional production up there." Well, that wouldn't do anything except if it scared 'em it would — we'd — certainly they'd retaliate with a hell of a lot of hard feelings. But it would make John a very unpopular guy to go back and say, O.K., the (laughing) company was accepting this 35-hour week and beginning this Monday have a reduced take-out, and that's what the company has agreed with the union it will do. Well, they wouldn't buy it. So it means that we would have to f — honestly and — stick at the position <u>no</u> reduced work week. That's — that's out, and accept the fact that that's — that's just a bargaining device to get us to move into the 2d area of (slight pause) 20% fixed bonus for skilled trades and day workers, which to me is a — is a — even if we would consider it, it's a trap. I mean, suppose we agreed on some portion of that and we did what we did the last time, if you remember — you sat in on that one — when they presented the same issue. We settled on 5¢ for those people. They got 5¢ more than the other incentive workers.

Let's assume we — we said for — just for purpose of illustration we'd
go along with the 20% fixed bonus and — for day workers and skilled
trades, but not all of it. We'd do it — treat it the way we did last
time. Let's assume we gave 'em 10¢, which would cost us maybe a
cent and a half, over-all — prorated over all employees — and the
union went back and presented to their membership the fact that O.K.,
the company's agreed to 10 perc — 10¢ an hour for skilled trades and
other day workers. And what — what's gonna c — happen when you
got 16 women — 1600 women who are gonna s — see the results of collective bargaining — of this long struggle gonna result in 50 or 60 tool
and die makers gettin' 10¢ an hour more and the women think they're
overpaid now? The union wouldn't be in a position to come back and
say, "We don't want that." They'd have to come back and say, "We
want that, but our membership tells us to go back and get us somepin'
for them." Which is what we'd have to wind up doin'. So I'm pretty
f — much forced to conclude that that's out, to — to be the only issue
on which we would agree.

Mediator: Uh-huh.

Michelsen: Which leaves me to — with the conclusion — I think this
group agree me — that we've got to turn this thing over into the area
where we're willing to do business. And that is, at some point somebody's gotta say, "Look! You people are just wastin' your time. But
the company is interested and will do something in the area of improving your pension and group insurance." But I don't see that until late
(laughing) tomorrow afternoon. But — I mean that — I want you to
know (Mediator: Yeah) what our — our strategy is and why I have
disregarded these other 2 things completely. This company would
never — they can walk the streets forever before we'd go to a 35-
hour week (Mediator: H'm); and after they walk 'em forever, maybe
then we'll have to work a 35-hour week. But that's the only way in
which we'd ever get it. That's the only way they'd get it, is to force
it on us because we wouldn't have enough customers to work longer.
(Slight pause)

Mediator: Uh-huh! All right, Bill, thanks for that. And I'll — I think we'll
st — start getting into that whole area probably (Michelsen: Yeah)
late today or tomorrow. I don't (Michelsen: All right) — I — although I haven't talked to them yet. (Michelsen: Uh-huh) So, good-
bye.

Michelsen: We'll see you later.

Mediator: Right.

[Mediator leaves the management group at 10:45 A.M.]

Union Caucus - A (12:20 P.M.)

Mediator: ... the company in caucus than it would here joint — in joint
session, although we'll come together jointly later. Now, Bill's thinking like this, that (pause) — think the sooner you get down to their
area the sooner you can understand what they're thinking about. He
hasn't mentioned a figure but what he has — what he talks about and
will talk about to you, and what he has talked about to me this morning
is, I gather he has in mind a very small amount. Now, I don't know

how much. He talks about probably the best that the company could move on would be some fringes. He don't say what they are; he doesn't say how much. At least he's thinking about other things that he didn't think about before, small as they may be or whatever they are. And I haven't asked him to find out. The important thing that — was for me to find out whether or not this company is takin' a flat stand at 4/10ths, and if they was I was gonna save myself some time. (Gambon: H'm) I am convinced now, for the first time, that he is not fixed at 4/10ths. How much he is fixed at and what it is I don't think we'll know until we get down to that point. However, I'm inclined to think that he — reading between the line — wants to, if he makes a settlement of any kind, make it on a fringe basis, and what the fringes are I don't know. I didn't d — discuss it with him yet. But that I have established, and that was what I wanted. Now, whether or not it can be developed into a settlement or not is unimportant at the mediate — it — it — right now the important thing was to know that his mind wasn't closed at 4/10ths of a cent. Now, there still may be an impasse or there still may be a disagreement, but at least there's — I — I feel that there is an area now that — here that existed — didn't exist before. Now, getting onto yours — your position, here — now, I haven't given you a chance to talk — to tell me what is on your mind, so (pause) overlook the haste, but (pause) I wanta say this. Your position at 31 is of course still way up in the clouds as far as a reopener settlement is concerned. More power to you if you can get it, and far be it from me to stand in your way. But I think you realize that that's a big bite for a — for a reopener, and I — I know why you have it and it's — a lot of it is for bargaining purposes and to protect your position. But I think this afternoon (pause) we've gotta get the company out on the table, and I've got to get them to commit themselves that their mind isn't closed at 4/10ths of a cent, to the benefit of you and your committee, and (pause) — then, of course, I — if we can get 'em out on the table and get discussion started in that direction and you're convinced that the door is open and it's not closed, or their minds are open and not closed, then, of course, you're goin' to have to get your figure down.

Gambon: Well, I don't know whether I'm gonna go down, George, to be very frank and honest with ya. I mean, he has between now and 1:00 o'clock on Saturday to start movin', because I'm either goin' to the membership with this 4/10ths of a cent or whatever he wants to go to by 1:00 o'clock on Saturday, plus the position that I've got at this point. I'm not gonna allow him to keep me comin' down and down and down and down till I get into the area where he — he wants to bargain. I'm gonna get into an area where I wanta bargain, see. And as far as I'm concerned the — the guy's fooled around too much, as f — from this — from way back in January when we first — first notified him. And I think it's about time he started movin'. We gave some evidence of good faith here. We moved once and they wouldn't do anything about it; we withdrew it. On your advice we made an appreciable cut and enut — for nothing more — no other reason than to get negotiations goin', and he turns around, takes a very firm stand, and he gets sarcastic as hell and prints a great big No, see. Well, I'm takin' that great big No and I'm lookin' at it, and I can't see another damn thing right now except that big No. And he's gonna have to eliminate that big 0 by doin' somethin' very concrete between now and 1:00 o'clock

on Saturday, because I'm not gonna move one damn inch away from
that position until I am convinced that he's honestly trying to negotiate here and to come in — come in here with something in a reasonable way. Now, he's not gonna giv — get any sympathy from me by
comin' in and throwin' me 2 holidays — somethin' like that. I want
the guy to really bargain because I'm not gonna go before a membership with a lower position than I have right now. Or if he wants to
call somebody's bluff, if that's what he thinks he's doin', see, I'm not
gonna fight with him on the pavement for less than the position that
we have now. This guy has created some maz — major issues. Now,
let him live with 'em.

Mediator: Uh-huh. Well, we'll do this. We'll get 'em in here right after
the lunch period. We'll get together jointly (Gambon: H'm) and find
that out. And that's exactly — I think — I think you're goin' to find out
that he's — his mind is open. At least I — if he says to you what he
says to me — said to me, you will find that he's not at 4/10ths. / Uh —

Gambon: (Over Mediator above) George, look at this (handing sheet to
Mediator). Read this.

Mediator: Another letter?

Gambon: Yeah. That's — that's the one we to — read this thing here.
(Pause) It's the last — that next to the last paragraph there.

Mediator: "With these in mind"?

Gambon: Y-yeah, and the ones —

Mediator: "With these in mind the company is quite firm in its position
that the reopener shall be limited to the maintenance of our group insurance benefits at their increased cost to the company. You will be
kept avi — advised of any further developments in our negotiations."
That's the hell of these letters in negotiations. (Gambon: Uh-huh)
They get out on a limb and you can't — when they come into mediation
it's tough to get 'em back off that limb and / xxxx.

Gambon: (Over Mediator above) George! That — that letter was given
out since they've been in mediation. (Slight pause)

Mediator: Because somebody has to — somebody has to eat these words.

Gambon: That's Bill Michelsen puttin' this out.

Mediator: Unless he means it, and if he means it, then I would personally
feel that I've been misled, because if he means it, h — there are ways
of letting people know that there's goin' (Gambon: Uh-huh) to be a
strike and you (Gambon: Well —) know that he can —

Gambon: R-right. Look. I personally recommended to the Executive
Board of this union and told 'em what I was gonna do. I was gonna go
before that membership in the face of the company's position and
recommend a strike. At this point I have unanimous support of this
committee and the unanimous support of the Local's Executive Board
on the — on recommending a strike. Now, from — I don't care whether
you tell 'em that or not or if you want me to tell 'em that, because I
don't want him in the dark about what my personal position's gonna be
or what the position this committee is gonna be or what the position
of the Executive Board's gonna be. If it'll help his thinking a little
bit and if he wants to find out whether his bluff has now reached the
point where it's no longer worth 2¢, I'll tell him that if you want me
to do it.

Mediator: All right, we'll do this. This afternoon — well, without planning (Gambon: Uh-huh) for this afternoon. First thing we'll do is
get here together jointly at the table. It's half-past 12:00. Ou — let's

get back about a quarter to 2:00 (Gambon: Uh-huh), 2:00 o'clock. Is
that — will that suffice? And I'll let them go. I still have (Gambon:
Uh-huh) them there.
[Mediator stops by the management caucus room at 12:32 P.M. to dismiss that group for lunch. He announces a joint meeting for 1:45.]

Management Caucus - B (2:15 P.M.)

Mediator: ... I was just sayin' to Bill that the temper of the committee
in there is warm, very warm, which — so I expect that they will be
— will be very vocal in making their positions clear. Uh — he's talking a lot tougher (Loring: Uh-huh) than he was last week, and he
said he was — wants to establish this today: find out if the company is really fixed at 4/10ths of a cent. (Loring: Uh-huh) And he
said, "We will take a strike on 4/10ths of a cent." He said, "We
will — that will be the strike issue." (Loring: Uh-huh) So I said,
"Well, I — I can say this, that you're way up above the clouds,"
I said, "at 31¢ with a reopener." I said, "I don't know how you
expect to get anywheres near where you — where you want to go
at 31¢." He says, "Well, I'm gonna stay at 31¢ for protective position so if I have to take a strike, it'll be there." (Michelsen laughs
very heartily) So I (Michelsen laughs again) said, "All right. We'll
have a joint session, and we'll see if you can bring those points out or
whether the joint session will bring about a change in thinking on your
31¢ or the company's 4/10ths of a cent. But right now the gap is very,
very wide." So, I think at this time we'll go in, hear them, and then
pick it up from / there.
Michelsen: (Over Mediator above) Uh-huh. Do they have somepin' to
say, or they (Mediator: Yeah) want me to —
Mediator: Oh, they have s — lots to / say.
Michelsen: (Over Mediator above) Or they want me to just — they're
gonna ask me whether we're gonna increase our offer?
Mediator: No, they'll do all the talking, I (Michelsen: All right) think.
Michelsen: 'Cause I don't think it's time yet for me to even indicate that
we will.
Mediator: So you can hold your position.
Michelsen: Yeah. I mean, what do you think?
Mediator: Well, I do — I — I — I don't think so at this time (Michelsen:
No), and certainly not at this (laughing slightly) joint session.
Michelsen: Too damn much time yet.
Mediator: That's right.
Michelsen: Yeah.
Mediator: Uh (pause) — but let's get this steam off (Michelsen: Yeah),
so — (pause).
Michelsen: O.K.!

Joint Meeting - A (2:25 P.M.)

Mediator: Uh (long pause) — today we open these negotiations at a point
where the company is at 4/10ths of a cent in monetary cost, the union

is at 31¢. Now, I open the conference that way to bring — make that
point as strong as possible. I know there are other things that are
just as important as that and probably more important to both the
committees, but I point that out to show that the gap between the 2
parties is pretty wide. Now, I know that the union and the company
both have other things to talk about. So, without further ado, I think
we oughta open this conference, call upon both sides for a statement
of position or anything else that they can c — contribute to the negotiations that has transpired since we met last. So, if the union wishes
to kick off, suppose you take it from there.

Gambon: I can be very brief, George. I'm in a listening mood from this
point until 1:00 o'clock on Saturday afternoon, period. (Rather long
pause)

Michelsen: Well (slight pause), I don't know what you wanta listen to,
John. I can —

Gambon: Anything, Bill, even 4/10ths of a cent.

Michelsen: Well, I can tell ya that again and I will, 'cause that's the
company's position. I can reinforce it with —

Gambon: Well, George stated our position when he said 31 — 31¢, or
whatever the approximate cost is that you — you talked about here.
Actually, for the record, our position is Point 1 and Point 2. (Rather
long pause)

Michelsen: Yeah. Well, for the record or for anything else, John, we
have come in here (pause) — this is the 4th meeting we've had with
the Mediation Service. Before that we had one, so it's the 5th meeting. During that time I have tried to be as clear and explicit as it's
possible for me to be with my (pause) — the facts that we have and
the feelings that we have, the reasons that we have for stating what
we have stated, and that is the company's condition being what it is.
And i — based on the performance of Atlas last year, based on the
(pause) — the future as we see it in terms of the need for the company to get in a better financial position, based on the (pause) — the
future of the company in terms that we can't forecast it accurately,
we feel that the offer we have made to absorb this additional group
insurance cost, small as it is, is the only one that we can make now
and for that reason we're suggesting that this reopener be passed up
except for that. Now, I'm quite sure that everybody understood my
remarks and there's no need to repeat them in terms of bringing out
these charts — and I'm — I'm not being funny about it — and having
you understand why we feel that the Atlas employee has done well,
compares very favorably with the — his counterpart in the electronics
industry, that in past, in terms of all the latest statistics, the one
which I mentioned just last week, which I've already forgotten pretty
much, was that the cost-of-living hasn't gone up in the last year,
Atlas wages has gone up far in excess of that rise. So that using all
of those bench marks, we feel that our employees are far and away
out in front. We feel that at — at this point that that position should
not be further increased. (Pause) The industry itself, as far as our
participation in it, is getting tougher, it's getting more competitive;
and you can only look around you in the paper and every day that
transpires in these negotiations you read of more and more agreements which were tied to the cost-of-living escalation movement and

the — the employees are taking reductions in rates of pay rather than getting increases. / And —

Gambon: (Over Michelsen above) Not all of 'em, Bill.

Michelsen: Well, not all. No, I'm saying generally / the ones that have gotten —

Gambon: (Over Michelsen above) Sure. One of the fact, of course, Federal has made an agreement with its union to leave the thing in status quo. There'll be no wage reductions in Federal.

Michelsen: I am not aware of the Federal Leader (Gambon: Well, I can read it to you) agreement at this point, but I'm aware of the fact that a great many employees who had wages tied to escalators are goin' to have the escalation downward. The fact that the cost-of-living is dropping, whether or not that there — there is escalator wage agreement, certainly results in an increase in consumer purchasing power as long as the purchasing power doesn't decrease along with the wage rates, and of course that was the theory of the escalator agreements, that is —

Meyer: Which we don't have (Michelsen: Which we don't have, so that ours —), and which you didn't subscribe x that you couldn't meet on cost- (Michelsen: Yeah. Yeah) of-living but ya could meet on what you could afford, and (Michelsen: Right!) today we say you can afford.

Michelsen: So that based on what we have done through collective bargaining, rather than through some automatic escalator clause, our rates have gone up faster and higher than they would have gone up had we had just an escalator agreement. So that the percentage of change in our wage rates has been greater than percentage change in Consumer's Price Index. But now that the Consumer's Price Index is dropping, not only is the purchasing power greater, but since it was greater from the beginning, since our rates went up faster than the cost-of-living, there is, in a sense, an — an additional inflation in the sense that — that you can now buy more with your dollar if the price of things had gone down. / So that —

Meyer: (Over Michelsen above) See, they went up faster than the cost-of-living and compared to the s — the starting-out base rate of 54¢, / ni —

Michelsen: (Over Meyer above) No, I — I'm talking j — I'm referring to / this —

Meyer: (Over Michelsen above) In 1939, 38¢.

Michelsen: I'm referring to this memo which / I had here the other day.

Meyer: (Over Michelsen above) Which was subnormal in 1939.

Gambon: Well, I'd like to follow that line for just a moment, since we talk a great deal about how well Atlas people have done. It's my information that the B.L.S. index, the old index that was used for a major portion of the time involving cost-of-living increases, accounted for about 13.56% increases from January, '50, till December, 1952. Now, let's examine that for a moment and what it meant to everybody concerned, particularly the companies that you have quoted — the rates you've quoted and increases in benefits that those companies received and so forth. 13.56 increase from J — January, 1950, until December, 1952, would have accounted approximately for, in Atlas, over the same period — for an increase of about $19\frac{1}{2}$¢ due directly to the cost-of-living at that 13.56% figure. Now, let's examine what Atlas actually did. As against the $19\frac{1}{2}$ which the percentage increase would have accounted for, we received $24\frac{1}{4}$ plus a fraction difference because of that (Michelsen: Yeah) inequity arrangement from 195 — January, 1950, to December, 1952. Hercules received 35.1 (Michelsen: Uh-huh); Lashley, 35.3; Standard Products, 32; big steel, 32; Monco System, $32\frac{1}{2}$; Precision-Made, 36.66; Dayco, 29. Let's examine that a little bit different. Let's take the 1946 to 1952 period (pause) — or, rather, let's take the 1951 — January, 1951, to December, 1952, period, which is something you've liked to (Michelsen: H'm) talk about. From January, '51, until December of '52, Atlas ran at $19\frac{1}{2}$; Standard Products, 22; Lashley, 25.3; Hercules, 25.1; Monco System slipped, I think — $17\frac{1}{2}$ — although there's no — there's some other things that have to be taken into consideration there; Precision-Made, 26.1. From 194 — and, by the way, I think that I should point out at this time that crediting all those companies with the benefits in terms of wage increases that they gave out as I read it, from January, '51, till December, '52, it left Atlas in this position in comparison with those companies as of December, '52: Standard Products had received 12¢ more than we had; Lashley, 15.3; Hercules, 15.1; Monco System, 6¢ plus whatever they got in '46 — figure that I don't have at this moment; Precision-Made, 16.1; Dayco, 9.3. Now we go back a little further and we examine that 1946 to 1951 picture entirely, and from 1946 until 1941 Atlas had granted $47\frac{1}{2}$¢; Standard Products, 61; Lashley, 67.3; Hercules, 67.1; Monco System, 46¢ plus whatever was done in '46 — again I say I don't have the figure; Precision-Made, $64\frac{1}{2}$; and Dayco, 57.7. Now, at the end of '51 that les — left us in this position in comparison with those companies: Standard Products is $13\frac{1}{2}$¢ ahead of us; Lashley, 20.3; Hercules, 20.1; Monco System was ahead of us to some extent — again I can't give ya a figure because of the absence of the 1946 increases; Precision-Made, however, was 17¢ ahead; Dayco, 10.7. Those are, to me, pretty significant figures, based on the kind of arguments you've been used about how <u>well</u> we did. Now, pointing out to you, Bill, that while you did a reasonable job in January, '52, let's say — I mean, I'm — that may no — not be the exact proposition. I think (Meyer: March 1st) it's April 1st.

Meyer: March 31st.

Gambon: March 31st — April 1st, 1952, when that 12¢-17¢ went into the picture, you were not doing nothing more, as far as I'm concerned, than catching up to a parade that left us back in 1950. And you didn't catch up all the way, because today those differentials of 12, 15, 15, 6, 16, and 9 still exist. Your suggestion about waiving the — the re-opener at this time or in October — well, to say the least, are very politely rejected — <u>completely</u> rejected. Get no consideration whatsoever. As I said before, I mean, in a very brief statement, we're in a very good listening mood. We'll listen to ya from now until 1:00 o'clock on Saturday, April the 13th, 1953. And I — I'm not particularly interested what you do about it, Bill. I'm perfectly willing to take 4/10ths of a cent or anything else that you can find your way clear to offer to this committee. But whatever you do, I'd suggest you do it between now and 1:00 o'clock on Saturday, April 13th, 1953. (Meyer:

You mean by taking you'll take it to the membership?) I don't care whether — take it back to the membership, I'm talking about. I — I'll be very frank with you, I mean, I'm as far as I'm gonna go. You can do the talkin' from now on. I don't care whether you take and write a bigger note than you wrote the last meeting. I don't care whether ya say it, print it, put it on a tape, telegraph it, any other way you want it. Just give it to me so I can take it back to my membership and tell 'em what it is.

Mediator: John, on your figures, what I didn't quite hear you say — or understand you to say, where did you get the 13.5?

Gambon: 13.5? (Pause) In the figures in terms of increases from '46 — 19 — January, 1946, until December, 1951, I said that in comparison with the amount of money that was given in forms of wages to the various companies, including Atlas, that at the end of '51 Standard Products was $13\frac{1}{2}$¢ ahead of the benefits we had (Mediator: Oh, I see) received. To give you a direct comparison, we had $47\frac{1}{2}$¢ at that time; they had 61. And —

Mediator: That's the part I missed.

Gambon: Yeah. No, I mean — take a look at those bottom figures. It may be a little clearer for ya. (Long pause)

Mediator: Uh-huh. (Pause)

Gambon: The other thing, George, the ones at the top are where we are today — the end of '5 — December, '52. The figures to the extreme right are the amounts of benefits ahead that these other companies are of anything we've been able to receive over that period of time.

Mediator: This / column.

Gambon: (Over Mediator above) That's right. (Pause)

Meyer: Bill, to get — this has been repeated and repeated, I think, but just to keep it clear so that I wanta know whether the company's position is still of saying, "Atlas feels at this time they have given their employees a very fair deal and asks the waiving of the reopener except for the 4/10ths of a cent so that Atlas can use those profits that they realized at the end of 1952 to the betterment of the company's financial position in any way that the company sees fit to better their financial position." Am I right?

Michelsen: No, that's not right, Bernice. If you want me to tell you — to give you a / statement, I —

Gambon: (Over Michelsen above) W-well, you state it.

Michelsen: Uh —

Gambon: That's what it sounded like to me, too.

Michelsen: I said this, that we felt that — that our employees, in terms of — of the past years — in terms of what has been happening to the employees in the electronics industry — and I'm not concerned as to what happens to the employees of Standard Products or some other / company. They're — they're —

Gambon: (Over Michelsen above) You're not? Well, then, why use it in your charts?

Michelsen: They're — they're customers of ours, and I've said that many times. We don't compete with them; we compete with the people in the radio-television-recorder industry; and — I said this, that we felt that this year, our sales dropping off in the way they did and the way our profits dropped off — and they dropped off sharply — 23% compared

to what they were the previous year — there isn't enough profits there
to begin with to use for anything; and I said this, that we are looking
forward to the time when our profits can increase —

Gambon: What, to the kind of thing that Wonder Brand Company does for
its stockholders, for instance?

Michelsen: I'm not aware of what they do.

Gambon: Well, then, let's take, for instance, Atlas would like to be in
the same position they're in (Michelsen: Well —) where they give
out the same amount of dividends for 6 months of 1952 as they did for
the entire year of 1951. I don't <u>blame</u> 'em! (Michelsen: No, I don't
xx) But I can assure you that Wonder Brand is not gonna continue
that kind of practice.

Michelsen: John, what the dividend policy of the company will be is a
problem for the Board of Directors. I (Gambon: Uh-huh) mean, I
don't think we can determine that here. / We do —

Gambon: (Over Michelsen above) Well, I wanta make it clear that we
don't intend to increase the dividends of the Board of Directors or
the — not the Board of Directors, but we don't intend to increase dividends of stockholders, nor do we intend to increase the profit-sharing
take of the officers of the company and the foremen and so forth who
participate in those plans at our expense.

Michelsen: We don't expect to ask you to increase it, John. It's something that the Board of Directors will make a decision on as to whether
/ or not xxx.

Gambon: (Over Michelsen above) Well, the Board of Directors bet —
better make some other decisions, / then.

Michelsen: (Over Gambon above) Uh — but we did say this, that we felt
that the dividend rate for this company — the earning rate, as evidenced by dividends — should be healthy enough to encourage the fle —
free flow of capital into the company, and we feel that the dividend
rate being cut as it was for the 2d half of last year has cut — been
cut below the point at which it <u>is</u> a proper dividend for a company of
our size and a — particularly in our industry. Our stock is — is —
is bought and sold across the counter, and we want it to be in a position so that in the event that we need capital — and we're always goin'
to need it. We're in the kind of industry in which research and development improvements have got to take place continuously. (Meyer:
Well, why —) They're only made as a result of either high profits or
reasonably good profits, which we certainly have not had up to this
point, reasonably good profits which in — which encourage the flow of
investing capital into the company in the form of additional stock purchase, should that be the way in which we get capital, or having had
such a good performance that we are a sound risk for a bank. And
whether or not we get additional funds from banks — private sources
— or from the public issue of stock is, of course, a question. The
one thing I don't think is a question is the fact that we are going to
<u>always</u> need additional capital coming into the company in order to
buy additional equipment, engage in research and development so that
we can continue to grow and — not only grow, which is almost a synonym for survival in this business; so that we can continue our position and improve our position, 'cause this is — this is a competitive
position. I've tried to have you emphasize that we do not monopolize

the recorder industry. We are not the only recorder manufacturer.
(Meyer: Well —) 'S a matter of fact, our position in the recorder industry has changed quite a bit since World War II, and I think you all
know that, not because of any deterioration of our product but because
of the great need which existed during World War II for electronic
products and the fact that the government actually expanded the facilities of a great many companies / who are —

Gambon: (Over Michelsen above) Mr. Fuller says all indications show
increased demand for our products in 1953.

Michelsen: That's true. That's true.

Meyer: Well, Bill, so that I won't misquote th — the company, or you
(Michelsen: Yeah) as representing the company, but your summation
to me — what I said was what I thought you said — considering everything that you have brought out (Michelsen: Uh-huh) about the company's profits and its decrease (Michelsen: Reduced profits) in profits (Michelsen: Yeah) and its sales maintaining a certain level but
the profits have dropped off, there is nothing been said that the company has not made any profit. / The profit had — no.

Michelsen: (Over Meyer above) Oh, heavens, no. There's evidence of
that / in our report.

Meyer: (Over Michelsen above) That's right. So, to keep the summation correct in my mind, if nobody else's, the company made 500 and
some thousand dollars' (Michelsen: Uh-huh) profit (Michelsen:
Which is not enough), and when the union asked for, a — as we put it,
a fair share of that, you said that the employees of Atlas, in the opinion of the company, have gotten a fair share of the profits (Michelsen:
Uh-huh), and the profits for 1952 — what're ya gonna do with 'em?
You answer me so I won't misquote you.

Michelsen: Well, what we're going to do with them I can't x but tell you
(Meyer: What do you wanta do with them? What do you wanta do?);
I don't know that Len Loring can. It — they're gonna be used for research and development, the expansion of our facilities, and other
uses for capital reserves.

Meyer: Uh-huh. Well, that's what I said for the first time, only the
words were changed. Well, I just wanted to be sure that I understood
it very / x.

Wollman: (Over Meyer above) Bill, I hate to keep harpin' on it but I
just heard you say that you don't expect us to pay for your profit-
sharing plan or any other plans that ya have. Now, you already cut
up a small little pie this year that was equal to 4.5¢ per hour for your
profit-sharing plan, but yet you come in here and you offer us, as our
fair share of that pie, 4/10ths of a cent. How d'you explain / that?

Michelsen: (Over Wollman above) But I didn't say that, Stan, to begin
with. I had the — I didn't say that. I said that I didn't expect you to
make any decision as to whether or not (Gambon: Oh) we would
have any profit-sharing plan. / That was John's statement.

Gambon: (Over Michelsen above) Well — well, we'll — we're gonna attempt to influence the decision which the Board of Directors (Michelsen: Yeah) will make. Now, Number 1, I mean, when you're talkin'
about less profits, let's remember you're talkin' about less profits
in '52 (Michelsen: Uh-huh!), and don't let's forget the fact that in
your financial report you say that the current sales volume in the
industry forecast for '53, together with strong emphasis on cost

reduction, point towards increased profits for 1953. I don't think
it's proper, when we're talkin' about wage increases, to talk about
profits after taxes and talk returns of $577,000.00 odd. I'd like to
point out that there were $1,241,694.00 profit before taxes in 1952.
It was less than '51, no doubt; but I (Michelsen: Uh-huh) think
it's a very comfortable profit, a profit at least comfortable enough
that the company can afford to do something for the employees who
helped to create that profit. I see no point in haggling too long over
this particular thing. We've hashed it and rehashed this situation.
What it boils down to, in my opinion, is exactly this. The company
says, "We want you to waive the reopener. We are not pleading inability to pay wage increases. However, we do like to have you waive
this particular reopener so that we can expand, so that we can continue research and development of new products, which we have told
you in our decentralization discussions may or may not be manufactured in the metropolitan area." And all indications, as far as we're
concerned, show that the likelihood is that they will not be manufactured in the metropolitan area. We take that position because the company has refused, or has been reluctant, to tell us exactly what will
remain in the metropolitan area. The union, on the other hand, says
that company should do something and must do something about this
situation because they entered in good faith into an agreement that
provided for reopeners in this contract with about approximately 6-
month period. We're engaged in bargaining with you on one of the
reopeners. We have another reopener before the expiration of this
contract. Now — and as far as we're concerned, Bill, the company
can't tell us to waive this reopener. Your suggestion again is rejected. No consideration whatsoever. Your position — your financial
position doesn't warrant it. Your outlook for '53 doesn't warrant it.
(Slight pause)

Michelsen: Well, John, what our outlook for '53 warrants is something
that can be determined at the close of 1953. I can't predict the
future. We certainly have made some attempt to look into the future. There is certainly plenty of evidence to support the fact that
business this year is gonna be better than it was last year, / and it
should be!

Gambon: (Over Michelsen above) I hardly think the president of any
company would go out in a financial report and indicate good prospects for 1953 if he thought he might have to eat his words later on,
particularly when you have so many new stockholders.

Michelsen: I agree with you. But I'm also saying that the very fact that
— that those statements are made now does not guarantee that because they're made the future is assured. Simply because Hal Fuller
and — and the people who advise him, particularly our Sales Department, feel that the prospects are good does not guarantee the fact that
they will be (Gambon: No, but I would say this, that —) good. It certainly indicates that in all probability they should be good.

Gambon: Being so close to the company's policies as they develop as I
happen to be at this time, I would say that the company's taken every
precaution to make certain that the advancement of the company will
continue and it will be done on a firm f — sound financial basis; and
I can't overlook the fact that when you talk about expansion and increasing your facilities and everything else, that you can't very well

ask us to overlook the fact that you're engaged in a very broad decentralization program. Now, we're not gonna pay for decentralization. We intend to ask for a fair share of every year's profit! (Michelsen: Uh-huh) We intend to get consideration when a year looks good ahead, as well as the one ya just completed, and I don't think that's any different position than we've ever taken with you. On the contrary, the company keeps changing its arguments as to why they shouldn't give wage increases. One time it's no money, one time it's a bad year; and at those times ya get considerations on those points. But when you get to the point where you can't ask for the union to waive anything because you've had a bad year, then you say, "We're not goin' to argue with you on the basis of our ability or our — or our inability to pay. We're simply saying you should waive this reopener so that we can do what we wanta do, which does not include increasing in — benefits to you people, because we think you've gotten about as much as you're entitled to get in comparison with other people." But you don't go back far enough and make your comparisons.

Denk: Bill, you mean to say what Hal Fuller said there in the papers — and we're quotin' him — don't mean a thing?

Michelsen: Oh, no, I didn't say that! I said that his statement that the future is going to be good (Meyer: Uh-huh) does not of itself guarantee the future. He (Wollman starts to speak) can't control the — the course of our business. He can certainly look at the facts which exist now and say the future ahead of us looks good, and that's what he's done. But he himself cannot tell you or anybody what are gonna be the conditions today, tomorrow, next week, 6 months. We can only forecast. The forecast is no guarantee of a — a — assurance that things are goin' to take place. (Gambon: Bill —) I can forecast what the weather's gonna be next week. Maybe I'll be right, maybe I'll be wrong. But nobody knows whether I'm right or wrong until next week.

Gambon: Well, you're not a weather man, but Hal Fuller's supposed to be a good businessman. (Michelsen: Right!) He's supposed to know what he's (Michelsen: So are good weather men, and they're often wrong) doin'. Otherwise he wouldn't be president of the company. But I'm pointing out that you're not a weather man (Michelsen: Oh, sure) but Hal Fuller is a good businessman (Michelsen: Sure), president of the company, member of the Board of Directors, one of the chief stockholders (Michelsen: Right), who is interested in dividends. (Michelsen: Uh-huh) On this question of reopener, it's always been understood by the company and the union that that works both ways. (Michelsen: Uh-huh) I'm curious as to what your reaction would be if ya had a bad financial report and came to us and said, "Look, here's justification. We've lost this much money. (Michelsen: We have had a bad financial —) We've lost this much money during the year's operations. Take a wage cut." (Michelsen: Uh-huh. Your tears —) You feel you have a right to do that, don't you?

Michelsen: Oh, I would think we would, / if we had to do it xxxx.

Gambon: (Over Michelsen above) Uh-huh. Well, then, please recognize the union's right on a reopener to say, "Look, ya made money. You're in no position to ask for a wage reduction." And we say to ya at this point, you're in no position to ask us to waive it. Ya made money, a million some odd dollars before taxes! That's what I'm interested in, not after taxes.

Michelsen: Uh-huh. John, don't get me wrong. I — / I —

Meyer: (Over Michelsen above) We're tax deductible, aren't we?

Michelsen: Yeah. (Saunders laughs quietly) Yeah.

Meyer: I just wanta be sure.

Gambon: (At same time as Meyer above) Oh, definitely. (Michelsen: Uh —) He's tryin' to make us expendable, too. (Several laugh)

Michelsen: I recognize very clearly your right to come in and — and ask for anything. (Meyer: Well, then, with $3\frac{1}{2}$ months under your belt, why can't you do somethin' for 6 months?) I also recognize my right to tell you what the company's goin' to do, / and I'm tellin' you!

Gambon: (Over Michelsen above) You have the right to tell us what you're goin' to do, and that's all I'm saying to you! I'm a good listener from this point on. You keep tellin' me from now until 1:00 o'clock on Saturday what the company's goin' to do. That's all I'm interested in hearing from you.

Michelsen: You mentioned our tac — our profits before taxes as being greater than our profits after taxes, which certainly they should be. (Gambon: H'm) Our profits before taxes this year are 43%, damn near half of what — less than what they were the year before! And one of the reasons that they're less is that we c — are now carrying such a terrific increase in our labor costs!

Meyer: Yeah, but, Bill, ya still have in the picture (Gambon: Labor —) which has not been given up by the Republican Party (Michelsen: The what?), of (Several laugh) — you still —listen closely. (Michelsen: Yeah) I mean, the one thing that Len Loring (laughs slightly) says that you didn't allow for in your report of 1951 — or January, 1953, you figured excess profit (Michelsen: Uh-huh) tax would be out at the end of June. Then (Michelsen: Yeah) in March you didn't think that it would be out, and now in April it looks like it will be out because they have the split in Congress / and I think —

Loring: (Over Meyer above) I hope you're right, Bernice. (Laughs, joined by Saunders and one or 2 others) xxx.

Meyer: Well, I mean, you know as much as I do that it will be out because they have to s — get their unity back in Republican ranks and it'll be your benefit and to our loss, as it always is.

[At approximately this point, Mediator quietly slips out of the room for 15 minutes. Tape changed meanwhile.]

Gambon: ... there, because looking at this financial report of yours, I look and I see that in 1951 you realized 16.2 profit before taxes on your total income, and I look at 1952 and I see that ya realized 10.2% profit on your 1952 income. Now, that's not 43% to me. It's a reduction of 6%.

Loring: On sales, John.

Gambon: Huh?

Loring: On sales / i —

Gambon: (Over Loring above) Income — total income. I'm — I'm reading your — your percentage figures here, which are based on percentage to the total income. (Loring starts to speak) And your profits before taxes in '51 were 16.2 of total income and in 1952 they were 10.3 of total / income.

Loring: (Over Gambon above) Well, Bill's statement was that the profit before taxes was 43% less, which I (Gambon: Well, that's true) think the point is right, John.

Gambon: I don't — look, I'm not disputing the fact that 43% might be the correct figure, but it's very misleading. I (Michelsen: But it's very accurate, too) mean, you imply that it might be — it might be implied that the company lost 43% / profit.

Michelsen: (Over Gambon above) 42%. I'm sorry. (Pause)

Gambon: 42?

Michelsen: 42%.

Gambon: Correction. I'm sorry. (Slight pause)

Michelsen: Yeah. (Slight pause) 23% after taxes.

Gambon: Uh-huh. (Pause)

Michelsen: And / xx —

Gambon: (Over Michelsen above) The way I look at — I look at your financial report after taxes, in 1951 it was 5.7 of your total income and in 1952 it was 4.8 in — against your total income, or less than 1%. (Pause) I think we could haggle about these figures. I mean, you can use 'em to try to make your point, I can use 'em to try to make my point. The cold facts are that the company had so much money that — termed in dollars and cents, and before taxes it was over a million dollars. You're in no position to say 4/10ths of a cent; you're in no position to say anything about crumbs in any way, shape, or form. (Michelsen: Well —) And you certainly are in no (laughing slightly) position at this time to ask this union to waive the reopener in order to keep and do the things that you wanta do which are not going to be directed in any form to benefits to the employees of the company.

Michelsen: Well, that — that's not true, John. Uh —

Gambon: Look, your letters on decentralization point up the fact that the company is in — i — interested in increased profits and efficiency and everything else. (Michelsen: Yeah) What am I to take from that? We waive a reopener. You will continue your profit-sharing plan for the people in the company. The fact that you did not increase your labor costs at this time to the union will automatically mean that they — those guys will get what we might have gotten durin' the year of 1953, up till at least October. It also means that the company has that money to use in whatever way it sees fit, whether it be decentralization or expansion of research or anything else. No matter what ya look at it or how you look at it, it's money which would normally and properly and justly and rightly go to the employees of this company. And when you do direct that particular thing, I am of the opinion, and I think you're quite aware of the fact, that research is not gonna stop in Atlas, decentralization will not stop in Atlas — nothing that will interfere with your particular policies and — and program in 1953 or '54 or '56.

Michelsen: Well, John, / re —

Gambon: (Over Michelsen above) You told us that.

Michelsen: Research is — is just not gonna continue automatically because we think it's a good idea. It's gonna continue if we can afford to pay for it.

Gambon: Have you ever gotten an answer to the question that I raised on decen — a decentralization meeting as to just how much y — your Research Department, that is, your engineers and so forth, are bein' covered by government subsidies, for instance?

Michelsen: Yeah. The only — and I don't remember the exact answer to the question, but I — I remember its general nature at this point. The only government contract we have for product development in our engineering and research is for miniaturization (Gambon: H'm), and that's all. And <u>that</u> is to develop it for the government — I mean, a miniaturized version of the tape recorder — as you know, and I can give you what I remember of it at this point — is to develop that product for the armed services. All of the equipment down there is owned by the government; it's not ours. We have a contract to develop it for them. It's theirs. They can take it out and use it wherever they wanta use it. We are / their —

Gambon: (Over Michelsen above) You certainly must have some sort of a gimmick in the contract which might give you buyer bids right — bid rights on the / equipment x.

Michelsen: (Over Gambon above) Oh, I suppose we (Loring: No, we — we don't act'ly own those, John) do. But I don't know that. But it's not our equipment.

Gambon: Well, wouldn't you say, with the connections that the company now has xxx and some of these agencies who happen to be personal friends of Hal Fuller's and so forth, that you will prob'ly have a pretty good in on that kind of business?

Michelsen: No, I wouldn't say that at all. I don't (Gambon: Well —) know. You can (pause) — / one can guess as to —

Gambon: (Over Michelsen above) Well, we're gettin' very influential down in Washington these days.

Meyer: Well, that's a businessman's government.

Gambon: Yeah (laughing slightly). (Meyer laughs twice)

Michelsen: Well —

Saunders: Has the (Meyer laughs again) 3d period for '53 ended?

Loring: No, it hasn't, Tom.

Meyer: It / ends Saturday.

Saunders: (Over Meyer above) The picture, I believe, is very good one, isn't it?

Meyer: It ends Saturday.

Loring: It ends Saturday. No, it's not — it's not as good as the first period. It — I mean, our — our indications of it it isn't.

Gambon: Is it as good as the 3d period of '52?

Loring: I don't know (Gambon: H'm), John. We have — we have very little indication just — (pause).

Michelsen: Well, Bernice, you raised this question of — of (Meyer: The profit tax, and the different —) the elimination of the excess profits tax. There's no assurance that that's gonna be done. / There's great — the only thing that that raise so far is that is that — that —

Meyer: (Over Michelsen above) There'll be — there'll be a cut in — in the corporate — in the corporate and excess profit (Loring: No) tax, and it'll be retroactive by the end of the year. They'll have to do it, Bill. You can look in the scenes. You know what kind of labor legislation will be put out during the (Michelsen: I don't) Democratic regime. I mean, it was being pushed forward. Well, you'll have the same things happening now. There's a split right in the Congress itself. Eisenhower won't be able to keep his promises to the people because he's governed by big business. You can see as far ahead as I can. / I'm no prophet. I know what you know.

Gambon: (Over Meyer above) Well, one thing I know that the company can see far ahead on and that is the fact that they're not gonna have an operating loss, based on what the going price was from component manufacturers, of 583,700 or 828 dollars which they lost, they say, on choke and power transformers generally. (Michelsen: Uh-huh) There's a loss item of over a half million dollars out of the picture right off the bat for 1953. (Michelsen: Certainly —) We'll say — we'll talk about that amount right now. We'll take it.

Michelsen: Certainly we hope it's gonna be eliminated.

Gambon: We'll take that half million bucks, suggesting how it be used.

Michelsen: Well, John, I've never criticized you for your generosity (Several laugh) in terms of accepting offers. (Someone laughs again) Nobody's (Gambon says something) a — criticized me for my generosity in extending it. (Slight pause)

Gambon: Well, you do it with your tongue in your cheek. (Pause)

Michelsen: No, I — my tongue's right in the middle of my mouth on this (Someone laughs quietly) situation. (Slight pause) Now, the — the fact that — that y — you feel that this $577,000.00 is a lot of money, that's a — that's — that's a very / small amount of money.

Gambon: (Over Michelsen above) Well, you said so, not me! You said so! I'm only usin' your figures to point out why there's going to be missing / from the scene xx —

Michelsen: (Over Gambon above) Yeah. I'm — I'm talking about (Meyer says something) now. You — you got the wrong — I'm talkin' / about this year's profits.

Gambon: (Over Michelsen and Meyer above) Oh! All right. I don't like about profits after taxes. I like to talk about that million-some odd dollars before taxes, because that's what's going (Saunders: Well, we're in —) to be affected, see.

Michelsen: Which is 42% less / than that we had the year before.

Gambon: (Over Michelsen above) Well, this 16.2 against total income in '51 (Michelsen: Uh-huh) of 10.3 against total income in — in '52 — that's what I like to look at. I don't like that 43%, because you're liable to confuse somebody. I just want you to understand you're not confusin' me on it.

Michelsen: Well, I'm not attempting to confuse (Gambon: No! I — I know. W — well, I — I don't want you to —) you. Trying to have you understand why the company's position is why it is.

Meyer: Well, Bill, we pay taxes on our gross income the same way the company does, and we are still tax exemptions. (Michelsen: Yeah) And there wouldn't be any such thing as an excess profit tax if you didn't have excess profits, whether it's in the picture or it's (Michelsen: Sure! That's true!) not in the picture. It's right? And that goes back — when does that go back to, '45 / or —

Loring: (Over Meyer above) '50, Bernice (Meyer: '50, is it?), I think it — incidentally, / we pay the —

Meyer: (Over Loring above) No, I mean the figure that's used to govern whether or not you have an excess profit.

Loring: Oh, that. (Meyer: Isn't that '45?) They use — they use '46 / on —

Meyer: (Over Loring above) '46. Well, they get end of the year '45 or the end of the year '46?

Loring: I think the end of the year '45. Yeah. Incidentally, we paid no excess profits tax last year. (Pause) We didn't get up to that bracket.

Gambon: Well, wouldn't the company rather pay that money to the employees of the company rather than pay it just drops to the government?

Michelsen: Well, we haven't paid it.

Gambon: Because then we (Several talk at once) have to pay taxes, so
what's the difference?

Loring: We didn't pay it.

Gambon: Huh?

Loring: We didn't pay it.

Meyer: (At same time as Loring above) Well, then why are you concerned (Gambon: Well!) about it? / You think you might pay it this
year?

Loring: (Over Meyer above) I say la — last year — that last year / we
pa — in talking about our figures —

Gambon: (Over Loring above) We feel for ya, Len. We don't want ya to
/ pay excess profit tax except xx.

Meyer: (Over Gambon above) H'm, yeah! Yeah, I —well, then — you
were the one brought up the excess profits in (Loring: N —) January,
that you hadn't allowed some $19,000.00.

Loring: That's — that's right. That's for this (Meyer: Yeah. That's
right) year. I mean, that's right. H'm.

Meyer: So that there wouldn't be any excess profit tax / in the picture,
with or without it.

Loring: (Over Meyer above) Well, I certainly hope we'll pay some,
Bernice, because we can't stand too many years when we're down in
the bracket like last year. (Rather long pause)

Meyer: But even with that, the excess profit tax, with just the corporate
tax, we're still tax deductible before you (Loring: Oh, yeah! Sure.
Sure) start thinkin' of taxes. And there'll still be corporation taxes.
There's no doubt about that.

Loring: Afraid that's right, Bernice. (Pause)

Michelsen: Yes. And —

Meyer: (Laughs) It better be or we won't be — we'll be better off on
relief. (Laughs, as does someone else)

Michelsen: I don't know (Meyer laughs again) about that. (Someone
else laughs)

One of boys: Think that be an x —

Meyer: (Laughing heartily) That's not taxable.

Michelsen: Depends on what kind of relief it (Meyer laughs again) would
be.

One of girls: (In low voice) That's what I say. It (Meyer: Prob'ly what
would —) wouldn't be relief if they —

Gambon: Well, friend, that sounds to me what you're tryin' to get relief.
(One girl and someone else laugh quietly) (Pause)

Michelsen: Well, we are tryin' to get relief in a sense, John, from increasing burdens of wage costs, / which we don't see at this point.

Gambon: (Over Michelsen above) Aw, look! My God, Bill! Increased
burdens! Uh! I feel for ya. But I wanta remind ya that we're helpin'
to carry your load — your burden. (Laughs slightly) We wanta get
paid for workin' and carryin' that burden along with it. We're worried about the company's well-being and everything else the same as
you are. We're even worryin' about them continuin' to have enough
money to pay you so you can sit across the table from us, talk to us

(Michelsen: [In low voice] They have enough money to pay me) and amuse us with your charts and so forth.

Meyer: (Laughing, says something but cannot be understood) (Pause)

Michelsen: Well, gentlemen, I'm —

Mediator: I was about to (Michelsen: Yeah) say, this wasn't settled in my absence, was it? (Several of girls laugh, one heartily)

Michelsen: (Over laughter above) I've heard no evidence —

Gambon: No. We just proved one thing, that the company made a $1,241,000.00 before taxes. I mean, it — it was hard — that's hard to refute, because it's in here in the financial report.

Michelsen: Which was 42% less than the same tax / figure or profit figure of the year before.

Gambon: (Over Michelsen above) It was — it was — it was 6% less profit against your total income.

Meyer: But you / say that co —

Gambon: (Over Meyer above) Not quite 6%.

Meyer: You say the cost-of-living is dropping so you don't need as big profits either as you've been tryin' to tell us we don't need wages.

Michelsen: Cost-of- (Gambon: Keep in mind that we're gonna help you carry your burdens by tryin' to make sure you could have no excess profit tax) living x. (Meyer: Uh-huh) Cost-of-living, to the consumer, is profit, and we see no evidence that it's dropping for the manufacturer. (Pause)

Gambon: (Michelsen starts to speak) The best investment you've got is your employees, not your stockholders. If ya ever brought your stockholders in to do your manufacturing processes you could forget that the word efficiency ever existed. They got the money, we've got the brawn. Now, let's talk about who gets what, and — and we say that we're not goin' to assure profits without sharing in the benefits. (Pause)

Michelsen: John, we're not, in a sense, asking you to assure us of profits. / We're x —

Gambon: (Over Michelsen above) You are saying that to me exactly, Bill, because I saw what happened before when t — in this business of dividends, for instance. I saw the company at one point durin' the year of '52, I believe it was, refrain from giving out a 10-cent (Meyer: [In low voice] '50) dividend — or was it (Michelsen: Yeah) '51?

Meyer: '50. It was (One of girls: Yeah) signed in October of '50 for '50 (Saunders: Uh-huh) in / January, '51. And then they gave xx, and they xx —

Gambon: (Over Meyer above) And you talked to us about it. You said to us, "Look! We didn't give the stockholders any dividends." But they wound up with 40¢ at the end of the year.

Meyer: Uh-huh.

Michelsen: All right.

Meyer: 3 (Gambon: Right!) days after we signed the (Michelsen: All right) contract.

Michelsen: And the year / following that —

Gambon: (Over Michelsen above) And — and during 1950 again, when the union — after the union was told what bad condition the company was in and you finally convinced us to take a 5-cent increase and then another 5 later on, what happened? Profit-sharing plan for all the

people in the — the company and the officers of the company and everything else. Not all the people in the company; a certain group of
people in the company. (Slight pause) Told us how (Meyer says
something) bad off ya were. You couldn't afford more than a nickel.
(Addressing Pranis) Bob, I don't (Meyer says something, then laughs)
blame ya for laughin'. Look, I don't blame you for laughin' (Pranis:
I'm laughing at — I'm laughing at you xxxxx), because, look, buddy,
here ya are. Here's where you are. 1950, $3,104.74 for each one of
the 66 people, or an average; 1951, 97 people averaged $2300.79;
1952, 114 people averaged $1534.00 per employee. I'd laugh like hell,
too, if I were you on that side of the table.

Pranis: I'm not laughing at them; I'm laughing (Gambon laughs slightly)
at your quick pick-up of all the people getting a portion of this thing.

Gambon: Oh-h!

Michelsen: Well, the point is (Gambon: Uh!) this, John, that that profit-
sharing plan, as far as the company's concerned, was a — a fair return to those individuals who contributed / to that profit.

Gambon: (Over Michelsen above) It's a matter of opinion. It's a matter
of opinion.

Meyer: That's all we want, is a fair / return.

Gambon: (Over Meyer above) Who the hell ever said that you have any
foremen or — I don't care who they are. You can't tell me that the
people that share in that plan contribute any way near as much as the
employee contributes to con — to building up profit for the company.

Michelsen: O-oh (laughing slightly), yes, I / can.

Gambon: (Over Michelsen above) Oh, no, you can't, either! Don't tell
me about that stuff when the same people are paid salaries and they
collect dividends, and then they have to go to an extent of setting up
a profit-sharing plan! (Michelsen: Well, let us be —) The hell we
raisin', hogs or makin' recorders? (Slight pause)

Michelsen: We're making recorders, / John, xx.

Gambon: (Over Michelsen above) O.K. Well, then let's get out of the
farming business. (Rather long pause)

Michelsen: Well, believe me, we're out of the farming business. We're
in the recorder business and / xxx —

Gambon: (Over Michelsen above) You certainly are! You certainly are,
and you're developing a new binaural recorder right now. (Michelsen:
We question —) But I'm tellin' you, that thing isn't gonna work!
(Long pause) It's unsound! It won't stand up to a test!

Michelsen: Uh-huh. Well — (rather long pause).

Gambon: We (Michelsen says something) can't sell it; there's no market for (laughs, joined by Meyer laughing heartily) that. That's the
important thing. (Laughs again) (Pause) We got a limited market
for it right now and no — no sale. (Rather long pause)

Michelsen: Well, / that xx —

Gambon: (Over Michelsen above) Very serious vein, let's start goin',
Bill. I'm gonna start listening to you from now until 1:00 o'clock on
Saturday. And very frankly I don't give a crap what you do. (Michel-
sen: Uh-huh) You can tell me from now until 1:00 o'clock on Satur-
day 4/10ths of a cent. That's your decision (Michelsen: Uh-huh.
Yeah. xx), see. That's yours.

Michelsen: O.K. Well, that's what I'm tellin' ya.

Gambon: O.K! Well, tell it to me from now until — I'm available between
now and 1:00 o'clock on Saturday afternoon. Keep tellin' it to me.
Meyer: At — at 12:45 / xx.
Gambon: (Over Meyer above) 12 — pardon me. 12 — oh, 15 minutes to
get there. / Well —
One of girls: (Over Gambon above) Let us — to get there. (Laughs
heartily) (Pause)
Mediator: Suppose we separate for a moment.
[As the group breaks up Gambon calls out, "It might be helpful if one
of us s — sat in their caucuses." This brings on general comments
and laughing, including Mediator and the management group.]

Management Caucus - C (3:15 P.M.)

Mediator: I hope it's nicer in here. (Someone laughs)
Loring: It didn't develop as much heat as I thought it might. / You —
Mediator: (Over Loring above) No! No. I thought — from what he was
tellin' me, I expected (pause) fire and brimstone.
Loring: Yeah.
Michelsen: He was exercising his — his rhetorical abilities there. He
was making very beautiful analogies between our — trying to make
this binaural recorder. We couldn't / sell it on the open market and
(laughs) — I'm gettin' good at it!
Loring: (Over Michelsen above) Well, why isn't it developing faster,
George? It — can you put your finger on it?
Mediator: What is what?
Loring: Why isn't the tempo developing faster? Is this —
Mediator: Because you have a problem that is different from the other
types of negotiations, and I think I can put my finger on the reason
why these negotiations are not progressing as fast as the — they
should under normal circumstances. I do not believe your circumstances are normal. You have this moving — this move that plant.
The (slight pause) prospect of more of your work going down South,
or West, or some other place, is there. It's (Michelsen: Well, it's
—) more pronounced.
Michelsen: It's certain. We've announced that it's gonna happen. / It's
definite.
Mediator: (Over Michelsen above) Well, there you are. That adds to it.
(Loring: Uh-huh) Now, you have a — tha — th — that creates (slight
pause) a different situation from the situations that are usual — that
we usually have under reopeners, for this reason. You've got a
tougher bunch now. You've got a bunch who are betwixt and between.
They have a problem. They ha — this is their problem: "(1), we
have 2 roads to go. We can — we can say, 'By gosh, you're not gonna
make us pay for your moving.' So how do we do it? We hit 'em while
the hitting's good, while we got 'em here and they're not in pieces.
Now, when we do that, we stand the chance of getting — forcing another amount, or the amount we want, that we feel is a fair share of
the profits. Too, we think that whatever it is it will appease our membership. Now, the other road is, well, if we strike, our people probably — some of the people may feel that, oh, our demands are the

cause of the company moving, and it might be unpopular to do this thing — take strike action." So there're the 2 roads that they have to decide. Which one they're going to take I'm not so sure. It — if their reactions are correct, then I would say they're — they've decided on taking action if necessary. So if tha — if that problem was removed — there wasn't such a problem, they would move faster. They're more jealous of their bargaining position in this reopener than they were during the termination when they were negotiating for a new contract. It's evident by the way they're bargaining. They're afraid they're going to be caught off base, and yet it's — i — i — they have so much to play with that it's a — it's almost a ridiculous bargaining position as bargaining goes — as we're used to it. Being in these things every day, we see the tempos, pace. This is very — this is a very different kind of negotiations from anything I have had in quite awhile. Here is a reopener where the p — plant is moving. That makes — it's different. So that makes the bar — I know — I know from the start the bargaining's going to be tough for that reason. But added to that, here comes a union in with a 61-cent package at a wage reopener. Well, I would expect that from a — a neophyte committee. But here is a committee whose labor relations have been good, whose habit pattern of behavior at a bargaining table is very good, relations with the company is good, comin' in with 61¢. After 4 long meetings they're down to 31¢, and the average settlement in the area for terminations — I don't know what the average is, but say — I'll tell you what the tops is. Tops, I'd say, would be around 14¢ — tops, terminations. I just s — settled one that had in it what I — about 14¢ — the ABC. 10¢ across-the-board and about 4¢ is in — 4¢ in fringes. However, they had — there was a lotta things they didn't have and were getting for the first time, such as h — Blue Cross and Blue Shield. They never had any of it, see (Loring: Uh-huh), and they were just getting it. So it — their case was a little unusual. But I'd say prob'ly it might strike an average of 10¢, might strike an average of 12½. Now, when you come in on a reopener, you do not come in at anything like that. Here is a union in at 31¢ right now! (Pause) So, the whole thing is helter-skelter, and you may have noticed that in these negotiations I haven't done a lot of steering or directing, because the thing is so up in the air. Now, I know when I have to move, and I know that any moves before that time would be more or less premature, because I still haven't got the real pulse beat of their po — but I know it's one of 2 things. They're betwixt and between. Which road are they going to go down? Are they gonna go down the "Well, we don't wanta chase the rest of the plant out"? Or, if they're convinced the plant's going to go, anyway, they'll fight. I think they'll take that road — "Well, we — we have more to gain by keepin' 'em — hittin' — hitting them here while we got 'em, even though some of our people will feel that this action is the kind of action that chased them away." (Slight pause) So after I weigh up the 2 I'm inclined to think that Gambon would probably go down the strike road if he had to. I don't think he wants to. So that's one of the reasons why this is a little different and the pace is slow. The pace is — pace is not only slow; it's irregular. It's up, it's down, it's over. It doesn't follow a — a line. And — and — and in talking to them in my caucuses (pause) there's just a (pause) — doesn't seem to be a desire to (pause) get the thing down where it should be. And I sort of get the feeling that, oh, they're saying to me, "Let us stay here, George. We know what we're doing." (Someone laughs shortly) (Pause)

Espig: I get the — I get the feeling that — I get the feeling, and maybe it isn't — I don't know whether you get it or not — that they're gonna leave this thing entirely up to the membership. May not even make a recommendation. (Pause)

Mediator: Yeah.

Michelsen: No. Well, I — I get this feeling, and in this sense I would say it's typical, George. They're go — they're gonna expect to do somepin' tomorrow and Saturday morning, I think.

Mediator: Ye-ah. I think they're —

Michelsen: I mean, if there's any — gonna be anything done, I think they recognize our position, that if we started now we'd — we'd — we'd be (Mediator: Ya'd have nothin' to work with) — we'd be s — we'd be in a position where we'd have to be moved and pushed and pushed over quite a few hours. / And —

Mediator: (Over Michelsen above) And, you see, I see that (Michelsen: Yeah), see, from the standpoint of mediation, and that's one of the reasons why I haven't been t — very active. Actually, the only reason I have called caucuses is more or less to just sort of break the strain of joint meeting.

Loring: Uh- / huh.

Michelsen: (Over Loring above) Of repetition.

Mediator: Repetition. At the same time, it's giving — it's — i — i — it's — it's performing a service. It's giving the union what it wants and needs, a meeting. I don't look for any real collective bargaining until tomorrow. Now, in the ABC negotiations (pause), Jim Westover, an attorney, represents the — does he represent the whole metal trades?

Michelsen: He may, George. I don't / know wh —

Mediator: (Over Michelsen above) I think he — I'm not sure that he does, but a good part of them — probably 75% of them. Well, he represents the ABC Association — not the union, the companies. Now, in those negotiations we had (pause) about 4 meetings. I said we settled it in one. It's true. The other 3 were like this (pause), but they performed a service in that the parties had to have those meetings. Now, lemme show you how they worked — give you a picture of it — and then you can understand that what you're doing isn't unorthodox. (Pause) They had one meeting, the union and the company. Westover called me. He says, "George, we — we need you." I don't even say any more to him, "How many meetings did ya have?" because it embarrasses him! But I found out they had one, and all they did was get together and say, "Let's get the mediator." (Someone laughs slightly) Now, there's a reason for that. See, they know (Michelsen: That's all we did), see — they know that to — they know that the thing isn't gonna s — be settled until the last day. They know that. And, see, they know the union couldn't settle before the last day for the reasons that I've mentioned before — political reasons. If there was a settlement made before, the "outs" would accuse the "ins" of s — selling them short. Westover knowing all that, he has to

have a yeoman service done. In other words, we have to baby-sit the
thing over the — to the day of action. They're very cooperative;
they're easy to handle. We'll hold a token meeting and we'll make a
few dry runs, or a few feints and passes which we know are not going
to be productive. But the committee on that union team, after all, are
not composed of union leaders. They're people who have a political
make-up, and a political make-up that affects the leaders. They have
to be given that service. If they didn't, they'd go back to their people
and criticize the union leader. So that has to be done. So we went
through that for 3 meetings. (Pause) Then (pause), night before —
day before yesterday — I'm losing track of time — what's today? —
Wednesday.
Loring: No, Thursday.
Michelsen: This is Thursday.
Mediator: Thursday. Tuesday (pause) — Tuesday was the last day.
   And you — see, I talked to you yesterday, didn't I ?
Michelsen: H'm.
Mediator: So that was Tuesday. Now, on that day the real bargaining
   started. (Pause) They had 12, 13 issues. They were tough! And the
   bargaining started, and it got rough, and it looked like there was going
   to be a strike! And there probably would have been, if we weren't
   able to, both Westover and I, neutralize a — one man on his committee.
   He really wanted a strike. I think he wanted a strike even if the company had given 'em a quarter an hour. But he was neutralized, and we
   had to stay with the situation until about 1:00 o'clock. Now, that is not
   an unusual situation. (Pause) Now, those people, in my opinion, are
   intelligent. If they, knowing they couldn't settle before that day, and
   if a settlement would embarrass one or the other, and knowing, also,
   that they must have meetings, they do it in the way that is the least
   offensive and the least chance of causing trouble with one another.
   And in those situations if you keep those people at the joint table under
   such circumstances when they know that it's — it's not time, you're
   bound to get into a fight. Personalities can spring up. Some member
   of the committee who isn't used to this thing can — well, he's tired by
   the strain and he'll blow his top and maybe say something that makes
   the negotiations more difficult to resolve. So — so this case is not unusual in that respect, but it is unusual in the respect that it — I mentioned earlier — the bargaining positions. (Loring: Uh-huh) See,
   now, with these — with this other union — they were at 25. Well, now,
   I — when — when I c — when I said to them, "Now, look. You're at
   25. You got a lotta debris here in these 13 issues. Now, you know
   they're debris, and I know you put 'em in there. You're not talkin' to
   the company; you're talkin' to me. Uh" —
[Tape changed]
   . . . See, now, I've made about 5 appeals to the union to get down to
   that area, and like I said to you, I've come away each time with that,
   "Well, let us alone, George. We — we'd like to stay here." So I'm
   lettin' 'em stay there. I'm letting them stay there because, like Bill
   just said, in this kind of a situation you're not going to know until you
   are up against the blade. In another situation I would know before-
   hand what it was going to be, but because of that one point that I mentioned, I think, at the — see, now, in your last — the last negotiations

that I handled with you — your company, which was 2 years ago
(Loring: Yeah) — and there I could pretty near tell you — tell about
where you were goin' to end, because of the movement on both sides
— the way they were going toward one another, and the pace. Here
you don't get that. There just is — there isn't a pulse beat there yet.
But what's gonna happen here, I predict, when that pulse beat starts
to beat, it's (beating on table) goin' to make up for all that time.
It's going to start moving fast, and so fast it's gonna be — we're
gonna have to ke — be right on our toes, catch it when it comes. I
think he's just holdin' back, and he's — he's changed his tack because
of this problem he has — this different situation of breaking away.
Now, he would be — this fellow couldn't settle if you wanted to give
him money today. If you wanted to give him 15¢ (pause) he couldn't
settle today because — particularly because of that moving away.
Loring: Yeah. You don't gather, i — in talking with him, that he's particularly anxious for a strike, George?
Mediator: No. I don't think so. I haven't seen it. Uh — I think a lot of
that is — a lot of that is bargaining strategy. I think he — I think this,
though. I think that if he's — feels he's been pushed into a corner,
and what has been offered to him he cannot — he'll d — like if he considers it a dishonorable — or — or not an honorable offel — offer,
one that he can save his face with or one that he can call a fair share
in the profit, or whatever term ya care to use, I think he'll fight that,
'cause then he has a lot more at stake. He has his reputation in the
community, and I've gathered that he is interested in a lot of other
union business and not just Atlas. So, for that reason if no other reason, he, when he feels that the thing is hopeless — he will get tough
and will probably feel it is better to strike in this situation than not
to strike.
Michelsen: Well, that — that may be so. I think John is today not the
guy we're gonna be talkin' to tomorrow, and I'm willing to let him
talk and smile when he says somethin'. I mean, he — he wasn't at all
excited today. I mean, he —
Mediator: No! He was more excited when I was there in the caucus than
he was / xx.
Michelsen: (Over Mediator above) Maybe you and I should change positions, George.
Mediator: And when I go — when I say to you, "Look out. You're gonna
get fireworks," and then it doesn't happen, I guess you (Espig laughs)
figure, "What's Thomson saying?" (Espig: We're satisfied. [Laughs
very heartily]) This went off like a wet shootin'-cracker. (Espig
laughs)
Espig: (Still laughing) We're satisfied. (Laughs)
Michelsen: No, we'd — I'd just as soon keep it that way, because I — I —
I'll listen to that tomorrow, I'm sure, and I'm prepared to listen to it
then, but I don't wanta play for fun. (Laughs)
Mediator: So, it's nice when we all know this. (Michelsen: Yeah) It removes that strain of not knowing what the moves are. And right today
— now, I'm not a bit concerned. I'm not a bit worried. / Uh —
[For several minutes Michelsen and Mediator exchange comments
about other negotiations in which they know Gambon to have been
involved.]

Michelsen: Well (pause), I don't know. I agree. I don't think John wants a strike. I think basically he — he just doesn't like strikes as — and who does? But I think he recognizes that this is not a time and the issues aren't great enough to get the people out on the street. (Pause) But —

Mediator: The inconsistency of — f — uh (laughs slightly) — the inconsistencies that have taken place here (laughs) are perplexing (pause), such as, "If I take a strike I wanta be at 31¢." (Someone laughs)

Michelsen: Ho-ly smoke!

Mediator: (Under breath) Cripes, t — t — to me (Loring: Th — that's xxx) that's the opposite that — what it should be.

Michelsen: You mean because he thinks he'll be — get a better settlement?

Mediator: I don't know what to think. / xxx.

Michelsen: (Over Mediator above) Ho-ly smoke.

Loring: Wouldn't that make him —

Mediator: (At same time as Loring above) He says, "I want them" — he said, "I want them at 4/10ths of a cent (Someone laughs), and I'll stay at 31¢ w — if I have to take a strike."

Loring: Wouldn't that make him look a little ridiculous in the face of the (Mediator: E —) union members?

Mediator: The way I would use it — or, analyze it, I would say it would.

Michelsen: Well, I don't think he'd ever get a strike.

Mediator: That's why I sometimes think John is figuring, "Well, I got lots of time. Maybe — let me stay up at 31¢ where I am and I'm safe up there until I have to start x."

Michelsen: Well, I agree with him. He can — he can stay there as long as — till 12:45 Saturday. (Laughs)

Mediator: Well, this Saturday business — I was gonna cut in once or twice and say, "No, gentlemen, you're wrong. That'll be (pause) — you have up until tomorrow." But I thought, no, I'd better not, because then I might have to eat those words and go in Saturday, so —

Michelsen: I think you would have to eat 'em, frankly.

Mediator: I just let it ride.

Michelsen: These people are gonna struggle up that road, George, again (Mediator: Observer), all tired out Saturday.

[Mediator and Observer, joined by Michelsen, engage in brief banter about working Saturday.]

Michelsen: Well, George, I don't know of any more pleasant company that we could have (Mediator: Thank you) — you and Observer. We (Mediator: You know —) — don't ever go — don't ever write a book (laughing slightly) exposing this process. (Laughs heartily) (Mediator: She x —) Everybody (still laughing) asks me — I — more people in this company — executive positions — are comin' up, you know, and tellin' me how tou — what a tough time this must be. (Laughs heartily) I hope nobody ever tells 'em.

Mediator: Well, in (Pranis: Keep quiet) — well, there are different — see, there — i — i — in mediation there are different (pause) patterns (Michelsen: Uh-huh) — no, no, no. That's not the word. There are different (pause) practices. Now, for instance, you're in one now. With this type of bargaining, see, it's — it's (Loring: H'm) pretty —

it's easy. But then there are others where you will have the company and the union in one room, and the me — they're — they're —
they've got it pretty easy, both of them. They only work about 50%
of the (Loring: H'm) time, each one. But the mediator's working
100, / see. He's going —

Michelsen: (Over Mediator above) Yeah! Well, it's tough on you.

Mediator: Well, not this t — kind isn't (Michelsen: Isn't it?), but that
kind is. (Michelsen: Yeah) See, there are — there are types of bargaining like — well, for instance, that ABC. That was one where I
never — never had a moment's slow-down, and it was move, move.
'Course, I'd — soon as I'd move f — out of one, out'd come the cards
and they'd start playin' cards, and they had a poker game, and
(Michelsen: Yeah) then when I come into the other they'd stop their
cards and we'd work.

Michelsen: Well, that's the way our first one was. / You were —

Mediator: (Over Michelsen above) And that's the way it is, see.
(Michelsen: You were xxx) But here it's a little different, see. We
all get a rest because I'm not — as you can see, I'm not pushing this
thing. But in those situations where we're pushing — but there's a
half-a — what I started to say was, there's a half-a-dozen different
practices. Like you said your friend asked you how — how it goes
and — or he felt sorry for you. Well, while we can be enjoying this
one, you may get another one next year (Loring: Yeah) may take an
entirely different twist.

Michelsen: Well, if I get it, I'm sure you will.

Mediator: Oh, I will. I'll get 'em before next week.

Michelsen: Yeah.

Mediator: Yeah.

[Michelsen and Mediator continue for about 4 minutes, mainly discussing current negotiations in several large national firms.]

Loring: Well, George, does this mean that we gonna, in using your words,
baby-sit today?

Mediator: Yea — yes. (Loring: Uh-huh) You might say that. (Pranis
starts to speak) In a sense; but, as I say, there's been a purpose
served. (Loring: Uh-huh) The union committee would have to have
a meeting. We had — see, we had a week (Loring: Yeah) — wasn't
it a week ago we met?

Loring: Yeah. Thursday.

Mediator: That's a pretty long time with a situation developing. See,
now, one of the reasons why I'm not too, too worried now, if — f — if
you remember 2 years ago, there were so many issues (Loring: Yes)
that I couldn't afford to sit (Loring: Uh-huh), see. Here we have
what you might call one issue, a reopener. (Michelsen: Yeah) And
there isn't — when people — when th — when they get down to business, if they are goin' to get down to business, there isn't that much —
see, I don't have to be — listen to hours of explanations, how this
works, how the other works, or what the conditions. It's just a cold,
clear-cut reopener (Michelsen: Yeah), which I'm very, very familiar
with, and I — I won't lose any time when it starts. So (pause), the
answer is yes, we — and I — I — I haven't any particular desire to
start moving. / Fact, I —

Espig: (Over Mediator above) We're never moderate. We had 31 or thirt — 31 issues with about 15 under each (laughing) 31 the other time; now we have one. (Laughs)

Loring: Well, you feel that one day will be enough to — to (Mediator: Sure! Yeah) start the fire and g — get it / over with?

Mediator: (Over Loring above) If they wanted to settle this thing, like if they were in the — in the frame of mind that settlin' people get in, this could be resolved in one hour.

Michelsen: Yeah. I'll bet you — I'll lay a bet with you you — we're in here on Saturday.

Mediator: Oh, I will, too.

Michelsen: I mean, their philosophy is this. I mean, I c —

Espig: And I'll lay a bet with you you don't settle.

Michelsen: With them? Well, I — I think — I don't know whether it will settle or not, but certainly they're gonna go back with a / recommendation to the membership.

Espig: (Over Michelsen above) They'll go back, but I — I'm — I'm — / I —

Michelsen: (Over Espig above) Well, their attitude's gonna be pretty much, "Well, hell, we're gonna have to come (laughing) in for a meeting on Saturday, so I'll get those birds in here, anyway." (Slight pause) Even if it's for only that reason.

[The caucus continues for a long time, branching off onto various topics all extraneous to the case at hand. Finally, as Mediator is leaving the room, he announces that everyone will be recessing in a half-hour.]

Union Caucus - B (4:25 P.M.)

Mediator: This thing's getting tougher and tougher. (Pause) But I had told you earlier that, reading between the lines of their conversation, I had felt that they were going to — in their joint — in the joint sessions let you — convey to you that they were going to do more than 4/10ths of a cent, but they chose not to, which at this time could be considered important or not important. (Pause) And we covered a lot of ground, and I probed and — wanted to find out where they're goin'. I think the thing boils down to this. I'm pretty well convinced that — I'm talking frankly, now — that (pause) it just isn't the time today. Now, I have made some openings that, under ordinary negotiations, they would have developed into talking material, and they didn't take those openings, which makes this a very un-usual bargaining sessions. One of their committee asked me if this pace of these negotiations are usual — uh — going as usual, and I said, "No, it's very unusual," and they asked why. I said, "It's unusual because in a — in another situation, where the relationship was different than the one you have — rela — relationship that you have with this union — had with this union last year is altogether different than it — than this year (pause) by virtue of the fact that you're moving your plant and your people." (Gambon: H'm) And I said, "That changed the whole picture. I can see it. The pace is slowed down because these people

feel as though they're — well," I said, "they've even told you they
don't wanta pay for your moving. Then there's a possibility of you
moving more out." So I said, "That has a tendency to make these
negotiations irregular. Union isn't moving; you aren't moving." I said,
"This is vintage 1937 — the — the — the movement — the movement.
Ordinarily they don't go that way." So (pause) I'm pretty well convinced after this last caucus that if there's any move or any real collective bargaining, and it has a chance to show itself, it'll be tomorrow.

Gambon: Uh-huh. (Pause) Under the circumstances, d'you think there's
any (slight pause) reason to bother with tomorrow? Maybe they
need to be convinced by a strike vote on Saturday, George.

Mediator: Uh-h —

Gambon: And that they'll get. (Rather long pause)

Mediator: Let me put it this way. (Pause) Yes, there's — yes. / There
— there's a need —

Gambon: (Over Mediator above) I prefer — I prefer to take his 4/10ths
of a cent in there.

Mediator: There's a need for further meeting, because I don't want to
close any door. Now, if they — if I am right in my analysis of this
thing, that if this thing has a chance to move, it'll move tomorrow —
reason I said tomorrow, tomorrow's the last of the week — I don't
wanta close that door. I wanta find out whether that's right. (Pause)
At this stage of the game I do believe that if they've got anything at
all they're still holding back for some 10-minute-to-12:00 deal. Again
I might be wrong, because these things are so irregular — this —
these particular negotiations. You can't — you can't (pause) — me
put it this way. In the 4 meetings that I have had — is it 4? 3. All
right. Well (Several talk at once), however many — 4 / today?

One of girls: (Over Mediator above) Today's the 4th. Uh-huh.

Mediator: I haven't had a chance to do any real mediating. Well, as you
know from the last time we met, I'm working altogether differently
(Gambon: H'm) because it isn't — th — the positions are entirely different. Now, eve — under normal circumstances, where you didn't
have this move to the South and some other factors, by this time
(pause) we'd be about there — that much of a gap. But I allow / for
the —

Gambon: (Over Mediator above) You wouldn't have the same kind of
issues involved, for one thing. You wouldn't have (Mediator: I
wouldn't have the same kind of issues) the same kind of — particularly the same major issue of (Mediator: That's right) the 35-hour
week involved if there were no decentralization proposition.

Mediator: That's right. So I'm allowing for all that and I'll allo — I
know this, that — pretty well convinced now if I am gonna break this
thing, the timing on it is going to be toward the end. Now, I've — I've
punched some pretty strong — or I made some pretty strong x — a
trial — put out some trial balloons, and I'm pretty well convinced myself that that's the way it's going to be. I think that he's playing his
cards very close to the vest. He's not showing anybody his cards
until he's — either the last day until he can say to the company,
"It's getting late. (Gambon says something) I have held the line up
to now, and I won't move until you tell me to." (Gambon: Uh-huh)
And I think that's e — I think we're — we're dead right about that. So —

Gambon: Well, maybe I oughta louse up the strategy. Maybe I oughta call a meeting for tomorrow at 1:00 o'clock instead of Saturday (pause), wants to play footsie.

Mediator: What would that mean? Let's see. Maybe that's good. Let's — let's examine it. Ya mean you call a meeting for tomorrow at 2:00?

Gambon: I mean a shutdown.

Mediator: Oh! No. Don't want that. (Pause) See — oh, you mean they'd go to the meeting?

Gambon: Yeah!

Mediator: Uh (rather long pause) — no, I'm not in favor of that. If I thought it would help, I'd say Yes. (Pause) Uh —

Gambon: Well, I'm in favor of it because I got a sneaky idea what he's attempting to do.

Mediator: Well, tell me, then. (Gambon: Huh?) Then (Meyer: He wants to send a letter x) maybe I'll / agree to it.

Gambon: (Over Mediator and Meyer above) He — he wants to — he wants to send (Meyer: Wants to send a letter) out another damn letter, I mean, and I (One of boys: I expect one tomorrow) wouldn't put it past him if he'd direct it to (Meyer and one of girls say something) the employees right before we have a chance to even report to — to our own membership. Now, by Christ, tell him this, if he does, I'll strike the Goddam plant, George! Bing! Right then and there, the minute he puts a letter out, tryin' to tell the people what goes on in these meetin's. I mean that. If he starts fussin' around any more, there's gonna be some fun around here. (Slight pause)

Mediator: Has he sent any more than this one?

Gambon: Not yet that I know (Meyer: He hasn't sent any xx) of. I don't care what he sends to his — to his foremen and supervisors, provided he don't instruct them to go out to hold meetings of the people in there, and most important, that he don't try sendin' out any letters to the employees, such as they've done in the past.

Mediator: Did they send 'em to the employee?

Gambon: Oh, definitely.

[Several talk at once.]

Gambon: On this decentralization proposition (Meyer: And on negotiations! xx), for one thing. (One of girls says something) And on negotiations. But on this decentralization thing (Meyer: Reopener) he — the night that he's gonna send and mail these things out to all the people, explaining what they're gonna do on this decentraliz — decentralization thing, he walks into my office at 12:00 o'clock noon to tell me what he's gonna do. (Slight pause) Practically ignores the union, even in their own letter. "If you want any further information, come to the Personnel Office. We'll tell ya about it." He better not pull that, because if he does they better count on the plant shuttin' down right — the minute — the first time I see one of them letters, bam! (Pause) He says, "We have a right to send letters." They got a high-priced attorney. You know Mattuck.

Mediator: Oh. Jack / Mattuck? Yeah, I know him.

Gambon: (Over Mediator above) They pulled Jack Mattuck in because they got themselves wrapped up in an unfair labor practice charge.

Mediator: With you?

Saunders: Ever since / then these 1 — letters x —

Gambon: (Over Saunders above) Sure! Hell, I filed unfair labor practice charge against 'em, the way they went about that.

Mediator: Oh, on the movement.

Gambon: Uh-huh!

Mediator: I'll — all right.
[Gambon and one of boys talk at once, with Gambon saying, "In — in October, George!"]

Mediator: (Over Gambon above) Well, I'm gonna — I'll — I'll tell them before they leave I don't want any letters. Uh —

Meyer: You might be too late. (Mediator: If I ask —) They're probably mailed this afternoon.

Mediator: Well, I'll find that out. (Meyer laughs) I'll find that out before you leave. I don't want any strikes while I'm handling this, if it can be settled. By the same token, I don't want any letters, either, on the company's side. So, s'pose we / xx —

Gambon: (Over Mediator above) Well, don't put me over a barrel, George.

Mediator: How?

Gambon: In allowin' this guy to drive too close to that 1:00 o'clock thing. (Slight pause)

Mediator: Oh, / no! I wanta get this thing —

Gambon: (Over Mediator above) If — if — if he can begin to bargain legitimately I say the same thing as I (Mediator: The way this thing —) said before. I'll listen to him up till 1:00 o'clock.

Mediator: The way this thing is set up, you don't have a list of issues. You don't have — you're down to 2 issues. (Gambon: Right) It isn't a situation where (Gambon: I'm down to fightin' territory right [laughing slightly] now) we got 10 or 12 issues and we need a lotta time. Actually, if the both parties were ready to do business, I see no reason why this thing couldn't be wrapped up in an hour to 2 hours. (Gambon: Uh-huh) So, as far as time goes, I don't think there's goin' to be any danger of you gettin' caught / too close.

Gambon: (Over Mediator above) Incidentally, Standard Products made no offers to their committee yesterday.

Mediator: Did not?

Gambon: No.

Mediator: When do they expi — oh, they have a / 30 —

Gambon: (Over Mediator above) Yeah. They're meeting again next Wednesday. Had a meeting yesterday.

Mediator: Well, how do — how do Standard Products — how do — how do they — they've got a 30-day — they — they've got a continuing (Gambon: They can open at any time, but we don't. 30 days' notice) contract with a 30-day notice. Now, when they give a 30-day notice, when's the deadline?

Gambon: Well, I suppose when they run out of patience. Well, m — / so far as the con — as I understand it —

Mediator: (Over Gambon above) They really don't know. They can continue the negotiations indefinitely.

Gambon: Yeah! (Pause)

Mediator: I / wondered. I asked that because I wondered whether —

Gambon: (Over Mediator above) Far as I understand, all they've done so far is that they've arrived at an estimated cost for an entirely-paid-by-the-company insurance plan — X cents per hour. I think they're talking in terms of 8 or n — or 9¢ for the cost, but they haven't — the company hasn't agreed to that yet, although they've been discussing the cost of such a plan, see. (Pause)

Mediator: Uh- / huh.

Gambon: (Over Mediator above) And I just mention that because (laughing slightly) of what you yourself said you suspected might be happening, you see.

Mediator: Yeah. I wondered about that (Gambon: H'm), but I (pause) — 'course, that's a termination, isn't it (Gambon: Huh-un) — Standard Products?

Meyer: (In fairly low voice) Yeah. / xx.

Gambon: (Over Meyer above) Oh, yeah, coming to a termination.

Mediator: That's termination (Meyer: 1st of May); this is reopener. (Gambon: 1st of May. Yeah) There is — there is a difference there. O.K., wait here for a few minutes till I talk to (Gambon: Uh-huh) them. I wanta find these things out. Then, if we get together for tomorrow's session, I think we can make it 11:00 o'clock.

Gambon: I was gonna suggest that. Bring us in about 11:00; you could bring 'em in at 8:00 o'clock and start talkin' to 'em. (Laughs shortly)

Mediator: Well, if they come in at 8:00, they'll have to wait for me. (Gambon and one of girls laugh)

Gambon: Well, that'll do 'em some good and maybe they'll sit around and toast their tootsies for awhile.

[Mediator brings up the ABC Association case just completed the night before. For a brief period he and Gambon compare the difference in pace of that negotiation with the Atlas one.]

Gambon: Well, George, I think that — I think that the company ought to understand that the — the proposition of fringes are not gonna resolve any — as you know, I've been making a very big point of the difference between the real wage benefits realized by Atlas people as against the same companies who they started out to make comparisons with. They've gotten away from that entirely since it's begun to backfire a little bit, see, because they only took a short period of time.

Management Caucus - D (4:40 P.M.)

Mediator: Well, xx should — like to know what happened.

Loring: Yes, sir.

Michelsen: Yeah.

Mediator: I was waitin' till ya asked me. (Several laugh heartily) Why —

Michelsen: Well, I'm just playing hard-to-get. (Laughs heartily)

Mediator: (Laughing) Yeah! Why, cutting it real short, why, they (pause) don't want ya to send any letters. If you send a letter, they'll strike the minute the letter is received.

Michelsen: Is that so?

Mediator: Any letter that goes out tonight. (Pause) I said — first he was talkin' about s — calling a meeting for 1:00 o'clock tomorrow afternoon.

Michelsen: Calling a meeting of — of the / x.

Mediator: (Over Michelsen above) Of the people, see. Yeah. And I (pause) — well, I said, "Well, I don't object to that." But I didn't know he meant take the people out of the plant. (Michelsen: Yeah) I wa — I was — I thought he meant those shifts that are not working. (Michelsen: H'm) And then later, when I found out it meant a shutdown, I said, "Well, I don't want that. Not as long as I'm handling the case." And then he said, "Well, George," he said, "we're gonna — we're gonna say this, that if there's any letters sent out — received tomorrow," he said, "we'll strike it tomorrow." (Pause) "Well," I said (pause), "I'll discuss that with the company and — however, I say to you, I don't want any strikes. And if sending no letters is the answer, well, I don't want any letters, either." So that's what —

Michelsen: Uh-huh.

Mediator: Uh-h (pause) — I told 'em that there was no change in the position; pretty much the same. I also told 'em that, same as I had just told you — I said, "These things are irregular. This — this — the pace here is (pause) — this is not a usual case." And I said I know why, and I told him the t — pretty much the same as I had told you. And he agreed! So I said, "This (pause) isn't a situation where we have 10, 11, 12 issues; we only have 2 now." I said, "If there were some — under ordinary circumstances," I said, "we'd probably have been a lot closer on this thing, and we'da been talking entirely different. The approach would've been different." He agreed to that. So, I set a conference for 11:00 o'clock tomorrow. (Slight pause)

Michelsen: Uh-huh. (Pause)

Mediator: I had a tough day. (Pause)

Loring: Worn out.

Mediator: But (rather long pause) he's talking about a strike, now. He wasn't talking about it before (?: Serious?), which I expect. Yeah (?: Yeah), I think he means it. I think he would have — I think if I had said on this meeting business — calling the meeting tomorrow (?: Uh-huh) — I think he would have done it. (Pause) Don't think he was (slight pause) playing around.

Michelsen: Why did he wanta have the meeting tomorrow? (Mediator: Well, just to show you —) Because they'd already advertised they were / gonna have one.

Mediator: (Over Michelsen above) Just to be mean — or — or to show you that he's serious. (Michelsen: Uh-huh) And I said, "Well, we don't have to prove that," I said (pause), " 'cause I know the company knows and I know that you've got economic strength if you wanta (?: Uh) use it. But," I said, "we're not here to do that. We're here to work this thing out." So (pause), he simmered down and we set it for 11:00 o'clock. Told him I's comin' in to talk to you people, so now I have and you people can now go home, if you wish. I'm going in there, have a few final words with them and send them home, call 'em back in here at 11:00 o'clock.

Loring: O.K., sir! (Pause) / Gonna get a night's sleep tonight, huh?

Michelsen: (Over Loring above) O.K., Colonel. (Pause) Or, Commander, I mean. (Laughs)

Union Caucus - C (4:50 P.M.)

Mediator: There'll be no letters. (Pause, then Saunders laughs)
Gambon: Didn't have any prepared, huh? That's what I / wanted to xx.
Mediator: (Over Gambon above) Well, I don't know whether he did or
not. I put it to him this way. I told him that — told him what you
said. I told him that (Gambon: H'm) the union was contemplating
holding a confer — uh — meeting and that I urged that they not do it,
and they pointed out to me that they didn't wanta be put in a position
of them cooperating with — with me and then only to receive letters
that aggravate the situation. And I told them that it's up to them;
that my recommendation to the company would be no letters, due to
the fact that the union is cooperating with me and I want the company
to do the same. Wasn't much talk about it. He said, "O.K.," and
that was it. So I set it up for 11:00 o'clock tomorrow, and we'll see
you then.
Gambon: O.K., George.

[At 11:10 A.M. Mediator enters the union caucus room. Since that
group has not all arrived, he moves on to the management caucus
room. He remains less than 10 minutes, conversing chiefly about another negotiation in which he has been involved. The Atlas case figures only briefly in comments on the inactivity; Michelsen concludes
the topic with: "Well, George, when you — if you ever are able to invite me down here to be an observer, you know, with Observer, don't
bring me in on one like this. I wanta see somethin'." Finally, with
the announcement "Well, I'm gonna leave you for awhile," Mediator
leaves the room. He stops by the union caucus room to say he will be
back soon, whereupon Gambon informs him that he has two meetings
scheduled for tomorrow and therefore must finish here today. Mediator replies that he is pleased to hear this, and departs.]

Management Caucus - A (11:50 A.M.)

Mediator: Well, you're well prepared today with reading material.
Michelsen: Yeah.
Mediator: Why, about the high point of (pause) little talk we had in
    there is this. There will be no meeting tomorrow.
Michelsen: (Says something brief but cannot be understood)
Mediator: They — John — let me get this straight — has one district
    meeting — what was the other meeting, Observer? Can you recall?
Observer: I can't.
Mediator: You can't either. Has 3 meetings — no, 2 meetings before the
    strike meeting.
Michelsen: 2 meetings of what?
Mediator: District — one is a district policy meeting (Michelsen: Yeah)
    with the union (Michelsen: Yeah); the other one I've forgotten. He'll
    probably tell you later. I don't know whether he means that or whether
    he doesn't mean it, but it was said. I / xx.
Michelsen: (Over Mediator above) You mean he wants to go to those 2
    meetings?
Mediator: Yeah. (Slight pause)
Michelsen: Rather than finish this stuff?
Mediator: Yeah. (Pause) Oh, he don't wanta go now!
Michelsen: No, I don't mean now.
Mediator: He wants to go tomorrow morning.
Michelsen: To those meetings.
Mediator: Yes. He says he cannot meet here tomorrow (Michelsen:
    Uh-huh) 'cause he has too much work (?: Oh, for cripes' sake!
    [Laughs]) in preparing the membership — or his ad — his report
    to the membership.

372

Michelsen: Well, how does he know he has a lotta work? He doesn't
know what his report to the membership's gonna be yet. (Pause)

Mediator: That's a good question. (Slight pause, then someone laughs
shortly)

Pranis: This I don't get.

Michelsen: Unless he's got a report / already figured out.

Mediator: (Over Michelsen above) Well, I do. He's moving the time up.

Pranis: To now.

Mediator: To today, see. He's moving it.

Michelsen: Oh, he wants to finish this today.

Mediator: That's the idea.

Michelsen: Oh! Oh. I thought you wanted to drag this over till next week.

Mediator: No-o! No, / sir.

Michelsen: (Over Mediator above) When're they gonna have their meeting, then?

Mediator: Huh? (Michelsen: When —) Tomorrow at 1:00 o'clock.
(Pause) What di — what did you ask?

Michelsen: You told me they — they weren't gonna have a meeting tomorrow.

Loring: No, we weren't. / x —

Mediator: (Over Loring above) No (Michelsen: Oh), I meant us!

Michelsen: Oh (Someone else talks at same time), oh, oh. I thought he
was putting (Mediator: Mediation) the union membership meeting
off tomorrow.

Mediator: Oh, no, no, no. (Michelsen: Oh) No, no. / That's —

Michelsen: (Over Mediator above) Oh, that's all right with me. / 'Course.

Mediator: (Over Michelsen above) I thought it would be. I wondered why
you (Michelsen: Well, I thought you —) objected.

Michelsen: Oh. I was going in the opposite direction. I thought this was
a (Mediator: Yeah) stall and we were gonna be here next week on
this business.

Mediator: Oh, no, no. He's moving it up. He's (Michelsen: Yeah) moving the date.

Michelsen: Yeah. (Pause) O.K. Well, that's — that's fine that I hear
what you say. Whether I believe what he's saying is another matter.
(Laughs heartily)

Mediator: Well, that's — that's — well, that's the way I / looked at it.
I don't know.

Michelsen: (Over Mediator above) (Laughing) You mean to tell me that
he's — that he's gonna drop off collective bargaining tomorrow to go
to some district meeting? Or he wants us to put all our cards on the
table tonight so we can print some new ones ton — tomorrow for it.
(Pause) O.K., George, let's go on from here. (Pause)

Mediator: Well, now that you're thoroughly th — frightened (laughing
slightly). (Michelsen laughs heartily) I thought you — (laughs shortly).

Michelsen: I'm more concerned with my personal problem. And th —
then you told me that this thing was gonna go into next week — or I
thought that's what you were saying. (Pause)

Mediator: I — I don't (pause) — I don't look for any genuine thinking on
the whole problem until after lunch. I think then we're gonna start.
(Loring: Uh-huh) (In low tone) xx and that, because (raising voice)
they really weren't in that union meeting unt — in that union r — that

r — room until — h'm-m, the last man, I don't think, got in there until about 11:30 (pause) (Loring: Uh-huh) — in and around there, so
(pause), the feet are still dragging, but — they're st — their feet are
still dragging there. So / I — I don't — I don't have —.

Michelsen: (Over Mediator above) D'you wanta make any bets on the
meeting tomorrow ?

Mediator: Huh ?

Michelsen: D'you wanta make those bets as to whether you'll be down
here tomorrow (laughing slightly) with us ?

Mediator: Uh — y — I bet that I will.

Michelsen: Yeah. Well, me, too.

Mediator: I bet that I will. That's why I say I took him lightly — unless
it is a situation that (pause) is more important than this, and I don't
know what it could be. It would have to be the Lashley (pause) strike,
and he's not on that committee.

Michelsen: Huh-un. (Pause) Well, I don't blame him for tryin' to get
us to (pause) put all our dough on the table as soon as he thinks
we're gonna do it. (Pause) Well — (pause).

Mediator: So, for the time being (pause), I don't have anything to talk
to you about as far (?: Yeah) as the case is concerned. I won't have
anything to talk to you about until after lunch.

Michelsen: Yeah. Do you — do you see — I made a note of one question
here which you mentioned yesterday and — do you see in your position as a mediator, not as George Thomson, my friend, John Gambon
really, with some degree of fatalism or sadistic delight, sort of getting
ready to play a Pontius Pilate in this thing ? I mean, going in front of
the membership and saying, "Here it is. I'm not gonna say pro or
con," but implying that he would be very happy if after all the years
we finally had a strike to show this company ?

Mediator: I've thought of — I — I've been thinking about (Michelsen:
Yeah) that, and / I'm not sure —

Michelsen: (Over Mediator above) Because I'd like to — if that's what
he's gonna do I'll — I'm gonna make him do it with practically nothing,
'cause we're not gonna come back again and (Mediator: Yeah. I'm
not sure) say that we'll pay more.

Mediator: I'll tell you why. My reasoning on that is this — or my thinking on it is this. I've thought about that and I th — in fact, I had an
experience in this ABC thing (Michelsen: Yeah) where even what
they received was — they still wouldn't recommend it (Loring: Uh-
huh), even though Smith said to me on the side, "It's a damn good
package." (Loring: Uh-huh) 'Course, it wasn't that — the size that
they blow it up to be. Uh — but he said, "It's a damn good package."
But it wasn't the package that they said they would recommend.
(Loring: Uh-huh) So what they did was go before the membership
and said — say, "Here are — here are the terms. This is what we
agreed upon. This is the best your committee could do, short of a
strike. (Loring: Uh-huh) Here it is. What d'you want us to do ?"
'Course, it was unanimously adopted. (Loring: Yeah) Now, that having taken place right on the heels of this — these negotiations, I was
prompted to think of that (Loring: Uh-huh), also. Now, I can't answer you — I — I — I don't have the f — the — my finger on the right
one, because of that m — your problem bein' different from the
others — this (Loring: Uh-huh) moving away (Michelsen: Yeah)

business. Now, John — under normal circumstances, I'd say, yes, John would do that. Uh — under these circumstances, I'm a little — I'm not certain, because —

Michelsen: Well, that's my reason for asking ya, George, does he wanta accomplish the same effect of really getting a strike but doing it without coming out and saying, "We recommend rejection and strike"?

Mediator: There's a good chance that he will go before the membership and say, "This is the company's position. It is 4/10ths of a cent. (Michelsen: Yeah) I, as your representative, could not agree at the bargaining table that that was a fair settlement in the (?: Yeah) light of these profits." And then he'd go into the expense — uh — the (Loring: Uh-huh) report — the company's financial report — or yearly report. "However, we know the company is moving. (Loring: Uh-huh) We know that we have a situation that is unusual from our regular problems or our — our everyday — or every-yearly problems in negotiations. So, these are the facts. They're — they offer you 4/10ths of a cent in the light of (1) these profits, (2) the cost-of-living in the last 6 months" — this (Loring: Yeah), that, the others. If he throws it out that way, he'll get a strike.

Michelsen: Uh-huh. Well, because — wait a minute. Yeah, maybe; but he's not gonna be talkin' 4/10ths of a cent when he gets to that point.

Mediator: Well, if he did. (?: Yeah) I mean, if it was that point, see, he would — he'd get a strike there. Now (pause), reverse the picture, he may do this — and I think before the afternoon we will know what — more about that. He may go in there and say, "This company, in my opinion, is going to move South anyway. (Loring: Uh-huh) Now, that being the case, and in the light of this report, where they look forward to a better year (?: Uh-huh), we, since th — long as they're going away we ought to get as much as we can out of them before they go. / We have them in a position" —

Michelsen: (Over Mediator above) Can he perjure himself by saying that? / xx —

Mediator: (Over Michelsen above) Can he what?

Michelsen: He can't — he can't actually say that, and as — it's on the record that that's not a fact. I mean, don't forget we've had 3 official meetings on — with the union on this Aiken situation. There are about 150 pages of stenographic notes, and Joe Messina and Jack Mattuck were both sitting in this thing. That's not a matter of hearsay any more, and he — I mean, he would put himself in a position to be — if a strike were precipitated and somebody said, "Let's go back and examine some of these things that Gambon said in the meeting," he would find himself in a position of — of having to take back some of his statements which he made to his membership, depending on how he made them, of course. But if he said absolutely that it definite that this company is moving away, that's a lie, because no one has said that. Fact, we said to the cont — we've made a statement to the contrary, that we are not moving away completely. (Pause) So that he might say those things and there are a lot of statements that would — can be made in a situation like this which maybe no one would ever check.

Mediator: Well, he would — they wouldn't check them, and he would use (Michelsen: Uh-huh) that as any other labor wo — leader would, to his benefit (Michelsen: Uh-huh) only — for his benefit only. Now,

there — that — that's a tack — now, he could take that tack. He could
(Michelsen: Yeah) say, ''Now, they're going. It's there. We can get
it. And we should get it. We're entitled to it. (Michelsen: Uh-huh)
Now is the time. It's the only time, because if they dismantle and''
(Michelsen: Yeah) — now, / I don't know the answer yet.

Michelsen: (Over Mediator above) But that's the biggest mistake he'll
ever make. (Laughs)

Mediator: I don't know the answer (Michelsen: Yeah) yet. (Michelsen:
Well, our latest —) I think we will have it before (Michelsen: Yeah)
this afternoon's over. We'll be able to tell just (Michelsen: Uh-huh)
exactly what John is going (Michelsen: Yeah) to do.

Michelsen: Well, our latest position is this. I got together our management this morning, or at least several of 'em — the president, and
vice-president — 2 vice-presidents, Len Loring, and Leland McDer-
mott, who is our general counsel — and we reviewed the whole thing.
In our opinion — I've told you how much money we're prepared to
spend here. We won't go much beyond that, and by much I mean a
fraction of a cent. Atlas is of the opinion, based on the things John
said, that our business is getting good. It's gonna get better. It's
gonna get better than — unless something happens that binaural sound
would drop the bottom out of it temporarily until the assemblers got
tooled up to produce it. Assuming those things didn't happen, we
rolled along the way we're going now, which is very good, then come
October we're gonna catch hell from this union in terms of a reopener.
Now, we're gonna catch hell in October regardless of what we do now.
We won't get credit for anything we give 'em, because it's gonna be
small. So that our opinion is that this might be a damn good time to
have a strike. I'm not saying we're gonna precipitate one. But if
they're gonna force a strike they're gonna get it now, rather than in
October. And they'll get it now because this company has never taken
a strike, and maybe in October we'd like to have 'em feel that we took
one in — in April and we'd take it again. So that the lines are gonna
be drawn very sharply at around 2¢ and not go beyond that. That's a
maximum. The — the management of the company told me, ''If you
can sell it around that, or reasonably close, fine. If ya can't, we'll
shut down. Let 'em — and let these people find out that we'' — we're
willing to do it, because we'd rather have them experienced it now than
to think next October that we won't do it. (Mediator: Uh-huh) So
that's — that's our strategy. It's pretty simple / xx.

Mediator: (Over Michelsen above) Well, that bein' the case, then I —
then we can say this to you. That bein' the case, you cannot afford,
then, to move away from 4/10ths of a cent (Michelsen: Yeah) until
the 1 — quarter to 12:00.

Michelsen: (Laughs slightly) I know that.

Mediator: That being the case. If you were to start to bargain for portions of that (Michelsen: Uh-huh) that you have (Michelsen: Well, I
xx. Yeah), you would — you would — the union would be (slight
pause) deceived. (?: Uh-huh) They would believe that that kind of
bargaining — they would accept that as a — a sign that bargaining was
just beginning. (?: Uh-huh) If you have a limited amount and your
people are fixed there and you mean that, and you (Loring: H'm)
have to stand on that, then it is my duty, or my jo — my job to tell

you how it can be best (Michelsen: Uh-huh) — the best chances that
it can have. And my experience with those limited m — amounts are
that there must not be any indication that there is even a s-s-s-
fraction there. Now, when the right time comes, which would be in
the last stretch, whatever the balance is looks better (?: Uh-huh)
(Loring: Uh-huh) in the end. Now, I'm not saying that it will do the
trick, but it has the best chance (Loring: Yeah) the last hour, always. You cannot — when you're — when you're bargaining — you're
negotiating with a small amount, you can't divide it up. Let me also
prove my — what I'm trying to say by using something — telling you
about something that happened, again in the ABC negotiations. We
were at 7¢. The company had offered first 5 and then 2. We (pause)
— the company called me into caucus, and they said, "George, we
think we oughta make a move. You know where we're going." See,
they had told me what their tops was before the first meeting. (Pause)
"We're going to 10. We're going no further than 10." And I know
these people. When they tell me that, that is it. (Pause) "Now,
we're at 7. We'll give you a counter-proposal. We'll give them 8
and some fringe." I said, "Jim, knowing that you're going to 10 I
advise against your throwing them a cent now, because when the chips
are down that 2¢ that's left isn't going to be big. I would rather you
hold at 7 (Loring: Uh-huh), and then when my right time comes,
that 3¢ is going to look a lot better than 2." So they went along on it.
And that's exactly what happened, because had I gone to 8, then I'da
had to get 11 (Loring: Uh-huh) — would have had to get 11. And it
wasn't there! (Loring: Uh-huh) Now, it isn't — don't misunderstand
me — it isn't that I try to keep the union from getting an increase or
anything that they're entitled to. But when I know that this is it and
then I take the company above that, I am responsible for the strike
that follows. (Loring: Uh-huh) So that's why I recommend that they
go this way and that way, because I want to get them to that point. So,
with this, where you have such a small amount — now, you have a
very small amount as (Loring: Uh-huh) — as amounts g — as compared to that ABC. They had (Loring: Yeah) so much more room.
They were in terminat (Loring: Yeah) — contract (Loring: Yeah)
negotiations; you're in a reopener. / Uh —
Michelsen: (Over Mediator above) Well, we gave 3¢ the last time.
Mediator: And you gave — yeah. Now, with that amount — if that amount
    has a chance to go over it — it is only going to go over after 1 —
    every thing has been sifted, shaken down, pressures applied from both
    sides, and then we're — a crisis developed, then we're on the 1-
    yard line and there it is. (Voice rising) Then we're gonna know
    (Loring: Uh-huh) whether it's going to go or whether it isn't going
    to go. But the job from now on is to make sure that we direct these
    negotiations to the point where it will have the best chance. So, we're
    a long way from that point, but everything I do from now until then will
    be in that particular direction. Uh — no doubt this afternoon when we
    get into joint sessions the union will probably reiterate what they said
    to me about tomorrow. Then, again, they may not; they may fool me
    like they did yesterday, where they were militant as all could be, and
    then when you came in they didn't say a word. But, anyway —
Michelsen: They like me, George. (Couple laugh slightly)

Mediator: Well, yeah (Michelsen laughs again), I think they do. (Michelsen: [Laughing] Well, you'll hear 'em this afternoon) They don't like your — they don't like your — they don't like your <u>bargaining position</u> (Michelsen: They don't?), but I — I don't think <u>they</u> dislike <u>you</u>.

Michelsen: They surprised by it? (Pause)

Mediator: Y — yeah, they've seemed to <u>register</u> surprise. They (Michelsen: Uh-huh) — they (pause) — but nowhere along the line of negotiations have they made this a personal issue that "Bill's holding back (Michelsen: Oh, I don't expect they would) this or that." I mean, it's the (Michelsen: Yeah. Yeah) <u>company</u> with them all throughout their negotiations, which is the way it should be. (Pause) But (slight pause) I can say this, your — your present bargaining position, they could push you out the window for that.

Michelsen: Could they? (Pause) (Someone laughs shortly)

Mediator: They don't <u>like</u> that. (Pause)

Michelsen: That wouldn't improve my position as a bargainer. (Laughs)

Mediator: No, you'd prob'ly (laughing) starve to death bouncing (Someone laughs) to the street. Uh (pause) — so, "Dem's (laughing) is da conditions (Michelsen laughs) dat (laughing) prevail." (Several laugh)

Michelsen: Dem sure is. (Pause) That's O.K. I — you frightened me to death when you came in here. I thought you were saying in effect this was postponed till next week. (Laughs heartily)

Mediator: No, I's wondering why you were objecting. I knew you were — (slight pause).

Michelsen: (In <u>very</u> low voice) Yeah. (<u>Long</u> pause)

Loring: Has John got himself in a position with the rest of the members there where he <u>can't</u> consider anything but this short — shorter work week, George?

Mediator: Uh — I haven't been talking about it. I've been avoiding discussion on it. You see, sometimes when a mediator singles out an issue and starts to talking about it, these people, being experienced bargainers, having been in negotiations so often (snaps fingers), they latch onto that very quickly. We have to watch, as mediators, many of the things we talk about because — and — and what items we select, because as soon as we start to dwell or talk about one subject they begin t — they say, "Oh-oh. That's the baby," see. "The company's worried about this one, or that one." So, in these negotiations I usually avoid talking about those things — any of the issues, or picking out one (Loring: Uh-huh) and saying — because I then give it too much importance (Loring: Yeah) and it misleads the union committee. They'll get onto a track that I don't want them on. Now, throughout these negotiations I have never discussed once money, other than to say, "Your position is ridiculously high. (Pause) You've got to narrow the gap." I have never said once, "What will you settle for?" To you, I have never even talked money with you. This is not the time. The time is when <u>I</u> am convinced that the gap is such that there is an area of agreement. Until that time I won't (Loring: Uh-huh) make any move. My job is to move it down to the point where I can first see that there <u>is</u> a chance of this thing being resolved (pause), and (pause) John (pause) has held at 31 and I have left him there now, because I have considered it that ridiculous that, "Well, you wanta stay there" — after that statement — that <u>confusing</u> statement that he made yesterday that if he takes a strike he wants to be there. So if I said s — now, from this point on s — say, "Now, look, John. You've gotta get down. You've gotta get down. You've gotta get down," he will agai — he will put too much importance on 31¢ or at his position (Loring: Uh-huh), and he'll hold. Now I'm gonna let him use <u>his</u> common sense and let him move away himself at the right time. He will, at the right time. It's not the right time.

Michelsen: Sure he will. I mean, he's got to. Otherwise — I can't imagine that I've been <u>so</u> convincing that he f — he really feels that this 4/10ths of a cent <u>is</u> an absolute figure, / xxxxx.

Mediator: (Over Michelsen above) Uh — that is true. He — he knows. And I haven't talked money to him one way or another, but he knows from experience, too, that a company would be very foolish to take a strike at 4/10ths. (Michelsen: Well, we'd be very foolish to consider —) <u>Unless</u> — unless they were (Michelsen: I would have refused to come down here xxx) really <u>sick</u> — ya know, a sick industry, like textile or (?: Yeah) something like that. Uh (pause) — so, from here on in we're just playing by ear and we're going to let — we're going to let the thing roll to the point where (pause) our persuasion and — and pressure will be effective. We just don't wanta waste any ammunition, and (Michelsen: Yeah. I xxx) to start applying pressure now would only confuse the situation. Actually, truthfully, I'm just sitting this one out. (Someone laughs slightly) Just sitting this one out. I'm not mediating. Because if I were to begin to mediate, I would have nothing to mediate at the right time. (Pause) So I — I — / I'm not mediating.

Michelsen: (Over Mediator above) George, there's no one we'd rather sit with.

Mediator: Well, the feeling's mutual. (Someone laughs slightly) Or should I say, Observer, the feeling's (Someone laughs again) mucilage, let's stick together? (Someone laughs again) Uh — uh —

Michelsen: The only thing I don't want, I wanta avoid the catastrophe of letting them get outa here with 4/10ths of a cent — / their membership think — that's ba — I — that would —

Mediator: (Over Michelsen above) Oh, that won't happen. I won't let that happen. No, I have control of this. I — I told the union — I said, "Don't wa — don't want any strikes as long as I'm handling this thing." (Michelsen: Uh-huh) I said, "If you do," I said (Michelsen: Yeah), "you're — you're working / against us."

Michelsen: (Over Mediator above) 'Cause I wouldn't want the membership to have to be presented with 4/10ths of a cent, believe me.

Mediator: No, I won't allow that. Don't worry. It won't happen.

Michelsen: But I want 'em to have heard 4/10ths of a cent long enough to think that what they're gonna hear about when they do get there is a / big movement.

Mediator: (Over Michelsen above) You — you — you can relax and rest assured that this thing is not going to get outa my hands. It's going to — we're going to play it right up to the right point where <u>whatever</u> you have will have the best chance. (?: Uh-huh) And we can't (pause) — art — from here on in it's timing. You gotta get the right time. It's not the right time now.

Michelsen: You think we're gonna meet tonight?

Mediator: There's a chance of that, if he is sincere (?: H'm) about tomorrow. But I don't — I'm not going to let him know that. I'm (?: Uh-huh) not going to tell him that I will meet tonight. I think we ought to hear the — this afternoon his reasons for not wanting to meet tomorrow, and then you, having worked with him before and knowing him much better than I do, I think you'll be able to evaluate, or sift (pause) — well, whether he's — means what he says, or whether it's just bargaining strategy. Now, you've — I think you'd be a better judge of that than I would.

Michelsen: Well, I — right at this moment, I don't believe it.

Mediator: I don't, either. (Michelsen: Yeah) And for that reason I would be very, very wary of applying mediation technique or action (?: Uh-huh) at the wrong time. But I'm very much interested in knowing (Michelsen: H'm) that we will not meet tomorrow, because, as I say, with the amount you are — you have to work with, you can't afford to shoot your — your gun tonight (Michelsen: Uh-huh) if we're going to meet tomorrow. We've gotta watch that. (Lowering voice) We've got — gotta be careful of it. (Pause) (Raising voice again) Now, at this afternoon's session, I'm — I'll probably make a speech, give a little — make some opening — or not a speech as much as some opening remarks. I'm gonna (pause) probably prod both sides. (Michelsen: Uh-huh) I'm gonna tell ya that the clock is running out. I'm going to also say that the positions of the parties are such that the gap — these are very unusual negotiations; pace is slow; I'm beginning to show concern about this because — and I feel that both sides ought to take a look at the positions — their positions. I'm gonna talk about the 31-cent position, I'm gonna talk about the 4/10ths (Michelsen: Uh-huh) position, and I'm going to sharply point out that (pause) it's later than you th — both think. And then, bingo — 'course, I won't use those words, but I'll open it up with that. And that will serve several purposes: (1), it'll show the union that we haven't been developing anything (Michelsen: Uh-huh), see; that the mediator is serious. He — and it's the truth! I mean, we're just not any — anywhere. They're at 31¢. So, that kind of a talk — that kinda opening remarks, I know, will stimulate the union, and the union will come out and really blow, I think. I (Michelsen: Uh-huh) might be wrong, but I think they'll (pause) say some things that we will wanta hear.

Michelsen: Yeah.

Mediator: So that you can be prepared for this afternoon. And the union will (pause) f — follow up, I'm sure, because I'll turn to them, and after that you can play it by ear (Michelsen: Yeah) for awhile until we — (pause).

Michelsen: Well, I'll think of some new ways to say No. (Laughs slightly)

Mediator: Uh-huh. (One or 2 laugh slightly) (Pause) They (rather long pause) — see, when it's — the time is right they will start to work with me and talk with me. They haven't done it yet. They will. I know they will. But when it's time I'll know. They'll talk to me. And I'll have the answers, buddy. We'll be getting the sweating period, and it's gonna be (pause) nip and tuck. (Pause)

[As tape is changed, Mediator explains that he does not usually talk as frankly as he is doing here. Loring counters that this is an education for him and that he is enjoying it.]

Michelsen: He hasn't begun to pay yet. That's why he's saying that.

Mediator: Huh?

Michelsen: He hasn't begun to pay yet. You know, these treasurers can be very (Mediator laughs) appreciative, but then you start talkin' money, he'll get very objective all of (Mediator laughs) a sudden (pause), and unhappy. (Rather long pause)

Loring: Well, until this time you've never given me much chance to be anything else but. (All laugh heartily)

Mediator: xxx? (Slight pause) That — that's a good statement, "but." (Hearty laughter continues) You (laughing) figure it out. (Loring, then Mediator, laugh again)

Loring: Well — (rather long pause).

Mediator: That's like the doctor that delivered a baby and the mother said to him, "Isn't that a beautiful baby, doctor?" And he looked at it and said, "Now, there is a baby." (Several, including Mediator, laugh) (Long pause)

[For several minutes Michelsen and Mediator discuss several other negotiating situations with which Mediator is particularly familiar.]

Loring: George, that raises a question in my mind. Now, we've been down — last 3 times, I guess, we've had openings or contract negotiations with the union we've ended up down here. The last time, right (snaps fingers) away, just like that. Once you get in the habit of that, I — do you ever break it off, or is this what we s — / x doin'? Huh?

Mediator: (Over Loring above) Well, yes. Now — now, here's an example. Take the Gadsen Furniture. Now, the Gadsen Furniture — whenever they got in trouble, we would have them. And they were in trouble quite often. Well, we haven't had Gadsen Furniture now for probably 3 years. They have settled their differences. They were able to. There are cycles that collective bargaining takes — that follows. For instance, you take your firm. Now, your firm never used mediation for probably 10, 12 years — or ever, until a coupla years ago. That is nothing to be alarmed at in this day and age that we're living in, with mediation, arbitration, and so forth. You couldn't have gone very much longer without it (Loring: Uh-huh), because a union lead — leader can have a good relationship with the company and go along for years and years, up to a point. That point — the reason he gets up to that point could be many. His union grows bigger, his opposition grows bigger. He will — no matter what settlement he will come in with, the longer the span is, the more the criticism — undercurrent, sometimes above. So he gets himself into a position sometimes, particularly at — when he reaches the — the end of this happy relationship, where he must have his face saved or strike the company, because the pressure is great — gets greater. That relationship that he has, sometimes he will be accused of not getting enough, too easy with the company (Someone laughs slightly), and this a — grows and grows and grows. Then he gets — has to show — he has to — he has to show everybody that that's not so, and he gets tough. "And this is gonna be a strike; this is gonna be this." Actually he doesn't want it. But he — in other words, it — it would be political suicide, after a certain span of time, if he doesn't do it. So that — then mediation comes in. Now, it'll come in. And what generally takes place is, for maybe 3, 4 years it'll be mediation, see, until they get back on that other track. Then they can look forward to a longer span. Now, my records — my personal records show just that. (Loring: Uh-huh) It's not a permanent (Michelsen: Well, there's gonna be a change — uh —) thing. It's a — it's not a permanent thing. And then there are other factors beside that union leader. The company has fact — problems that mediation fit in with and take them over this period. Then they get going again. Now, I can cite / more —

Michelsen: (Over Mediator above) Taft-Hartley Act requires it.

Mediator: Oh, yes. Mediation / is —

Michelsen: (Over Mediator above) There's a big change. / That's why you xx.

Mediator: (Over Michelsen above) Yeah. Mediation is a must under the law.

Michelsen: I mean, that's the only reason (Mediator: Yeah) we came down here the first time (Mediator: And —), so that our union could file termination of the contract.

Mediator: Uh — then, too, I — and I don't care how experienced you are as a — as a negotiator, there'll come that time when you're going to have a strike. Now, haven't you read in — in books or periodicals or labor magazines where Joe Doakes was awarded the p — a plaque (Michelsen laughs heartily) for the best labor relations? (Espig joins Michelsen in laughing)

[For a short period there are continued gales of laughter, particularly from Michelsen, who calls out intermittently, "Hey, buddy, you know who you're talkin' to? We won this the other year!" — then something about "Chamber of Commerce" and "annual Industrial Relations Award." Mediator remarks, on his way to answer the phone, "There ya are. The next year ya have a strike. It's the kiss of death." The management group continues to laugh, and Espig says, "Well, let's get it over with, then"; Michelsen answers, "We've been kissed"; someone else adds, "We're due."]

Michelsen: Who's that? John?

Mediator: No, your secretary.

[The recorder is turned off for Michelsen to place his call.]

Loring: ... undoubtedly go back to mediation in any settlement. We couldn't even begin to offer what we might have in the back of our mind, because we'd know that whatever it was, John, or — or whoever it would be would say, "Well, I have nothing to lose by goin' to mediation. I'll get that much, anyway, so we can end up in mediation (Michelsen continues on phone) maybe more." I mean, you'd always — how do you get back to the true principle of / really xx?

Mediator: (Over Loring above) Well, yeah. Now, several — several factors come into play there that take you back. One — the first one could be that your business — you may be expanding, or you may have come u — come — come into a windfall. You — or you're — you have an order — or you're — you're — yes, you do have an order and it means bigger things to come, and the company will evaluate that. They'll weigh one against the other, and they'll know that they can settle for a certain figure. They know the union will take that. They know that in advance, because they can tell by meeting with the union what the union will settle for. So what happens is, when they get into negotiations they pay a little more the first — the first step. The union buys it right away. They won't go to mediation, because they know how much they want. Now, they prefer doing this, getting it from the company without mediation. They prefer it that way (Loring: Uh-huh), because it shows their memberships that they're able statesmen, good bargainers. So ps — psy — psychologically they like to be able to come back and say, "We successfully got what you wanted." Now, that's one instance where — that will take ya back.

Loring: Uh-huh.

Mediator: Another one will be (pause) where you have a bad experience with mediation — the union leader or the company. You may get a mediocre 1 — mediator, or he may make a serious mistake in his handling of the case that will leave a bitter taste in the mouth of one or 2. So the actions of that — b — by the actions of that man the whole Service is adjudged. Comes next year, they might say, "Well, hell, we don't want to go into what we did before. Let's try to work this out ourselves." Now, that's — that's another reason may take you back. And then (pause), there (pause) can be this. There can be a change in leadership of the union. A new leader will take an entirely different approach, because he's new and he — he has a lot of leeway, see. There may be a change in the company's (slight pause) plans, and — if you go on and on. But (Loring: Uh-huh) they go back. (Loring: Uh-huh) They always go back. They just come into mediation about 3 years — an average about 3 times and they're back on the track again. If they didn't, we'd have to have a big staff.

Loring: Yeah!

Michelsen: But hasn't your case load gone up since Taft-Hartley, George?

Mediator: No. Now, I'll tell you what has gone up: notices. Our load has gone up in this (?: Uh) respect. The Taft-Hartley a — requires a 60-day notice (Michelsen: Uh-huh), where it didn't before. So thousands and thousands of companies that never used mediation, now, under the law must notify the Mediation (Michelsen: Uh-huh) Service when they are negotiating, or when they (Michelsen: Yeah) are contemplating changing or modifying their / contract.

Michelsen: (Over Mediator above) Well, do you notice any more of them coming in here?

Mediator: No — not — there — there isn't much (pause) (?: Uh-huh) difference in the — no! The answer (Michelsen: Uh-huh) — easiest way is to say to you No. See, I'm s — I'm thinking of active cases, now. (Michelsen: Yeah) We have more inactive cases due to the Taft-Hartley 60- (Michelsen: Yeah) day notice; but in actual disputes cases I'd say it's just (Michelsen: Yeah) about the same.

Michelsen: Uh-huh. Well, now, let me — let me — let me give you the reason for it. Let's assume that this is a case. I don't know, I'm not that —

Mediator: This is an open case — an (Michelsen: Yeah) active case.

Michelsen: I mean, le — let's assume that — that — that our situation at Atlas is — is as I'm gonna picture it. I mean, I haven't analyzed it yet enough to say that it is. But let's assume that suddenly the union discovers there is mediation service available to give some (pause) recognition to this collective bargaining process and make it look like a real tough, hard thing, and it also puts on a — a label they can go back and say, "We've been struggling, and the mediators have been in there." And so it's — it blesses it as a real stupendous

(Mediator: <u>Right</u>!) effort. And so they discovered that a year ago at
our first mediation, and <u>I</u> have the feeling that — that they're gonna
use it at every case they can in order to go back to the membership,
"Brother, we've been down there. The <u>mediator's</u> been tellin' these
people, and <u>we've</u> been tellin' 'em, and this is the best we can" —
Mediator: Up to a point they will. (Michelsen: Yeah) Up to a point.
Prob'ly (Michelsen: These people really <u>love</u> this stuff) 3 or 4
times — 3 or 4 times. Maybe someti — some instances, longer. Now,
there are exceptional cases. Now, Jim Westover — take him. He's
an exceptional case. With <u>all</u> his client, first thing he does is call
mediation. Some of our trouble with Jim is sayin', "Well, get in
there and bargain. We don't wanta come in when you're this far apart."
Uh — / but, by average —
Michelsen: (Over Mediator above) Well, that's because he's got a lotta
clients and he doesn't wanta take a lot of time / with each one.
Mediator: (Over Michelsen above) That's right. It's — i — it gives him
a — a — a real service. But the average times, you will find that our
records will show that they'll come down — they'll use it, but after
about the 3rd or the 4th time other things seep in, and they're able to
settle at the other level. And they <u>do</u>! (?: Yeah) They do not come
down regularly, or permanently. We don't have that kind of a — now,
you take the ABC that I just settled. While Westover brings us into
that quite regularly — and the union — sometimes we'll have them
for 2 years. 3rd and 4th year they settle by themselves; we don't
see them. 5th year we see them again. (Loring: Uh-huh) It depends
on the s — things that seep into the (Loring: Uh-huh) negotiations.
But, in answer to your question, thank God, no, they <u>do not adopt mediation as a permanent thing</u>. They don't. If they did we would have
probably 2,000 mediators, where we actually have far, far less than
that. No, it — it — it don't work out that way. They'll ride it along
— oh, I can cite cases. Now, even Precision-Made — there are periods where their conditions in the plant change, the political situation may change in the union. When it changes, they settle. That's
one factor in Precision-Made that's a problem. Well, now, when they
— when they get into a political fight, what can the company do?
Their hands are tied. (Loring: Uh-huh) They take that — take a
strike. All right, mediation does this. We get them down here, we
spot that right away — the political factions, and we go to work on
'em. And we put them in a s — in a position where — the 2 factions
— where we make — we put the spotlight on it and we tell them —
show them that we <u>know</u> what's going on here and we don't want this
to be the re — the — the reason for a strike, and we are not gonna
permit it! And when we say that, they know what we mean. And you
may say, "Well, what ca — could you do about it?" We could do this,
as an extreme measure: we could tell the union that our report, and
which <u>can</u> be made public — very seldom is — would be that this is
not an economic issue, this is not a — a collective bargaining problem; this is a political problem, and the union must get its house
in order before they can come down here and genuinely — something
like that would destroy the both of them. (Loring: Uh-huh) They
know what we mean. So when we say, "The responsibility is yours
and you — you've got to clean this thing up," they always do.

All right, now, the company couldn't do that. It would be <u>impossible</u>.
(Loring: Yeah. Yeah) Many companies get caught in that kind of a
situation. They have strikes that goes for days and days , and they're
— they're — they're in the middle, because the real problem they —
it would be suicide for them to try to adjust, or correct. They couldn't
do it. So there is a — there are — there are a thousand reasons why
mediation is the answer, but <u>each situation is different</u>. It's different.
You can't write a textbook on mediation. You just can't. You — you
couldn't do it, because what you'd — what I do in this case I can't do
in the next 10, 20, 30, 40. Every case will be different. Now, there's
another side to mediation; I'm not forgetting that. There are times
when a bad job of mediation has been done (pause), and a mediator
may get too — become, well, over-zealous and he may lose sight of
his objectives and start pushing one or pushing the other and making
it appear that he's, well, a partisan in the thing. And he — he may
say somethin' that may be misinterpreted, and one side or the other
side will blast him for him and destroy his effectiveness. (Loring:
Uh-huh) Uh — he may do — it's not a — I'm not painting ourselves as
a panacea — God's answer to all labor problems. No! We make mistakes (slight pause) in our Ser — but, by and large, as compared to
the (slight pause) number of disputes and the job that has been done,
the Mediation Service (slight pause) really doesn't get the credit —
public doesn't know what they do, because it's the kind of an agency
that <u>cannot</u> be in the newspapers continually and cannot be crowing
about the job they do, for a lot of reasons, because it's a confidential
work. (Loring: Uh-huh) It's — i — it's a — it's a thing that you must
do, and quietly get out of, and that's the end of it. Because if you advertised it you would have to reveal confidences, and if you did that
you'd be done. (Pause) Uh (rather long pause) — and that's about
the picture of the thing. (Pause) Well, now that you've had a lesson
in mediation (laughs), I think we'll adjourn / for lunch.
Loring: (Over Mediator above) Do we have a quiz after lunch?
Mediator: Uh — give me about 5 minutes with them. (Loring: Uh-huh)
I'll get them off for lunch.

<u>Union Caucus - A</u> (12:40 P.M.)

Mediator: I hear a radio — oh. (Pause) The game on? Who's playing?
One of boys: Not — that was just a news (Mediator: Oh) summary.
Gambon: Atlas and Local 89.
Mediator: That's been on for some time. It's about the 9th inning.
    (Several laugh)
One of boys: We hope. (Slight pause)
Gambon: What's the score, Ump?
Mediator: Nothin' to nothin'.
Gambon: Nothin'-nothin'?
Mediator: Uh-h-h — I conveyed to them first that — about tomorrow
    being tied up — you're going —
Gambon: H'm.
Mediator: It might be well that when we come into joint session, which
    will be immediately after lunch — might be well that you, somewhere

in your re — remarks, make that clear jointly. (Gambon: H'm) Think
that will be helpful. And you can make it as strong as you wish. Uh
(pause) — there doesn't appear to be any signs of move yet on the
part of the company, and we were talking a lot about their position
today that we — that we didn't talk before — their 4/10ths of a cent.
And we have started now to paint — to minimize their position, that
if they are serious about this 4/10ths of a cent, then the — that is one
thing; if it's for collective bargaining purposes, of course, we, as
mediators, can ride along on that. We can understand it; we can
(Gambon: H'm) understand the union's position. But if they are genuinely serious about this thing, then there is concern for all 3 of us
— the company, union, and mediators. So the general theme of all
our work this morning was trying to soften them up on this 4/10th
business. Now, we probably won't know yet or for the next hour or
2 whether we have (pause) made an impression, because I imagine
that during these meetings Bill or s — well, someone on their committee must contact their people and report these various things, and
I believe last night they've had some kind of a meeting with their top
people. He mentioned it. Now, as far as this morning was concerned,
I think we've — for the first time during these negotiations we're
starting to move into the positions and work on that theme, and w — we
didn't touch that up until now. So (pause), this afternoon, after lunch,
we'll come in in joint session, and I'll open the session up with my
remarks. I'll sum up to exactly where we are in this morning, and I
might raise a little hell with both sides about their position. Then
following that, the union will take off, and anywhere along the line you
can put in your remarks about tomorrow. And the clearer and stronger
that — that that is made, the faster the negotiations are going to move
this after — this afternoon.
Gambon: Uh-huh.
Mediator: So, it's 10 minutes of 1:00; let's get back here about 2:00
o'clock. (Slight pause) O.K.?

Management Caucus - B (12:50 P.M.)

Mediator: We've reached an agreement. / Unanimous —
Michelsen: (Over Mediator above) You're gonna tell us what time should
we be back from lunch. (Laughs heartily)
Mediator: Agree — the (laughing) agreement is that everyone's hungry.
On that we're agreed.
Michelsen: Well, I don't know whether I'll agree on that this (laughs) —
I don't want the record broken.
Mediator: Uh — how about 2:00 o'clock?
Michelsen: O.K.
Loring: All right.
Mediator: Joint meeting at 2:00. But come here first.
Michelsen: All right.
Mediator: O.K.
Michelsen: We'll be here.
[As Michelsen reaches the door, he inquires of Mediator how soon he
will know if the session will go on into the evening.]

Mediator: ... at about 4:30. If they mean what they say (Michelsen: Uh-huh), you're going to have to evaluate (Michelsen: Yeah) that, and I think you'll hear about it in the (Michelsen: Yeah) joint session. (Michelsen: Uh) If they — if they — if they mean what they say, you can look forward to a night session, because naturally if they mean it I'm not gonna let 'em get away without really finding out whether this can be settled or not. But I don't want a night session (Michelsen: Yeah) if I can help it. If they will meet tomorrow, I'd prefer that for psychological reasons and strategical reasons. (Michelsen: Yeah) I think it would be better (Michelsen: Yeah), since they have this 1:00 o'clock meeting, if we could meet tomorrow instead of tonight. I don't wanta be in a position where the best foot is put forward with time to spare and — see, the timing has to be (Michelsen: We won't be in that position) right. But if we know — if we — we — if we evaluate it and find out that — well, if in our own opinion we believe that tonight will be just as good as tomorrow, all right. But we — w — we — we haven't nailed that down yet.

Michelsen: Uh-huh. But in that event you'd never get me in here tomorrow. (Laughs)

Mediator: Well, I wouldn't do it to you. I wouldn't do it to any committee if I could avoid it.

Michelsen: Yeah. No, I mean if John (Mediator: Oh, if — if the —) — if he says (Mediator: Yeah) it's — this is the final thing and then / we xx.

Mediator: (Over Michelsen above) Oh, then we can all really — we — we can (?: Yeah) — then we'd all take — we'd say, well, we all did our best (Michelsen: Yeah) and that's where we are, and we'd be there tomorrow, anyway, and I think (?: H'm) we'd all sleep s — sounder.

Michelsen: Sure. (Rather long pause)

Joint Meeting - A (2:15 P.M.)

Mediator: Oh, you're not ready yet?

Meyer: Yeah, we are. Oh! There's another 3 missing.

Mediator: Shall we wait?

Meyer: (Says something but cannot be understood)

Gambon: Yeah, couple minutes.

Mediator: They have a couple girls still missin' — the rest of the committee. Their committee's not complete (Michelsen: Oh) yet.

Gambon: Sit down, boys, you can sit here! We won't / throw the hell out ya.

Michelsen: (Over Gambon above) xxx. I — I thought maybe they wanted to talk.

Gambon: No, sit down! The only thing we'd do is talk about ya, and I don't mind talkin' (Mediator laughs) about ya to your face.

Michelsen: I don't mind listenin'.

[For the few minutes which elapse before the arrival of the 3 union girls, light miscellaneous talk goes back and forth, mainly concerning the ball game.]

Mediator: Well, mo — most of the morning I spent with the company representatives and now I've asked you to come together in joint session.
(Pause) I want to say that the positions of the 2 parties have not
changed since our last conference, and before this joint conference
begins I — while I don't want to make a — or do I intend to make a
Pollyannic talk, I just wanta make a few remarks, remarks that I hope
will be strong reminders to both committees that the time is passing fastly and that the — if both parties haven't given their best thinking to the problem that is before us that they had better start doing so.
Time situations like this, where time is running out, the parties get a
late start and often fail to resolve their difference — differences in
time. I don't know whether that will happen, but I certainly hope it
doesn't. (Pause) I don't know that I could add any more to that that
hasn't been said. The remarks are made for a reminder to both of
you, and probably both of you don't need a reminder that the clock is
passing fastly. But it is; and at this particular time I'm sure the
both of you are concerned, and you can include me in that, too. I'm
beginning to get concerned because of the fact that neither of you have
really done any what can be called — haven't made what could be
called progress. Most of the work has been sort of reviewing and repeating one another's positions. Now, here we have a problem that is
a triple problem, or — or it needs triple attention. It needs the attention of the union, the company, and the mediator. And I think that
we've got to start reaching down to — into our best resources to find
it, if we're gonna have a — find the answer, if we're gonna have a
settlement. I know both of you can e — easily say, "Well, you know my
position, and (pause) that's how I feel about it." But that — that —
that won't settle it. The thing that's going to settle it is a — a thorough
look at the other fellow's position and then a move in the direction towards settlement. Now, there — there're my remarks for opening the
conference. At the opening of the conference you can talk about those
remarks, or you can use as a base some of the things that you wish to
say yourself. So, without further ado — you haven't met since yesterday. There may be some thinking that has developed overnight; there
may not be. There may be some points that you want to talk about that
developed yesterday or today or from my remarks. Use any base you
wish. So, at this point, maybe I should call on the union and get their
thinking. From that, I'll call on the company and see if we can't get
moving. So, John, if you will, suppose you take it from there. (Pause)
Gambon: Well, George, I quite agree with you that time's running out,
and I'm conscious of it. I think I might say at this particular point
that while I indicated that I was willing to sit and listen till 1:00 o'clock
tomorrow afternoon, despite the fact that I would probably still be willing to listen till 1:00 o'clock tomorrow afternoon, unfortunately that's
not gonna work that way. I've got a staff meeting to attend tomorrow
morning at the district office, and I'm — I want time enough to prepare my report for the membership meeting at 1:00 o'clock. Now, as
far as I'm concerned about today, I have a personal problem I'm gonna
be involved with, and I may as well make it clear right now that I'm
not gonna stay here after 6:30 tonight. My youngster's makin' his communion next week and I gotta take him to buy a — one of the white suits
that you pay money for and get nothing out of, but that's it. Now,

personally I don't think the company has engaged in collective bargaining up to this point. Perhaps they're following their own particular brand of strategy. I have no objections to find with that or anything else. I am not going to move from the position that the union has now! I think the moves are up to the company. We've moved twice in an effort to try to get the company to engage in collective bargaining, and I think it's up to them to do somethin' about it. I know that Bill Michelsen knows this union well enough, and he certainly knows me well enough, to know that he's not gonna sell 4/10ths of a cent nor anything like that to this union, and I think it's about time we stopped foolin' around and do some honest-to-God collective bargaining here. We'll review our position if the company shows and gives evidence of good faith that they're entering into collective bargaining in an effort to settle this thing in an amicable manner. (Pause) It's all right with me if we can't get anywhere by 6:30 tonight; I'm perfectly willin' to go back to the membership and state the company's position, if that's the way they want it. I mean, is this — it's just a question of tryin' to find out whether the union's calling somebody's bluff or whether they're tryin' to find out whether we'll call their bluff, we can do that at 1:00 o'clock tomorrow. (Pause) Now, that's about all I wanta say about it, George. I've been very disappointed about the way the things have gone because I thought that before this meeting, at least, we would have been engaged in some hagglin' about which — who's gonna move now and who's not gonna move, and so forth. (Pause) This is what? — the 6th meeting, I think, we've had. Company is still in the same position it was in in the first meeting. The union has moved <u>twice</u>. And I move no further, George, till the company convinces me that they're really tryin' to engage in collective bargaining. Collective bargaining doesn't mean to me the opportunity of telling the company what we want and have them establish as a matter of fact that they're good listeners. (Pause) That's about it, George! (Pause) Except that I wanta add one thing in closing here, and impress on the company — I wanta say again that we scrutinized very, very carefully the 8th, 9th, and 10th period of 1952 and the first period of '53, and you better look at 'em again, too, Bill. (Rather long pause)

Michelsen: Well, I've looked at them, I think, John, and I know where — what's there. Well, the only thing I can say, George, is that (pause) time is passing, there's no question about it. (Pause) I'm not as concerned with the passing of time as I am in impressing th — everybody here with the fact that the company's position at this point is the company's position. Whether it's 3:00 o'clock this afternoon or 6:00 o'clock to — tonight or 10:00 o'clock tomorrow morning, I don't think the passing of time is going to affect that position. In that respect it doesn't concern me too much. The problem of whether or not we've been engaging in collective bargaining, I — I — I call this collective bargaining. It's not — doesn't mean collective agreement to me. This time it's apparent we've reached a — a dispute and we're still in disagreement. As I said yesterday, I've said everything that I think that can be said about why the company's position is why it is. We are pressed with the fact that we've had fallen sales and with reduced profits, and I'm not gonna go into it again. I've said it enough. I think that everybody realizes that it's a genuine concern of ours. And we

feel very definite at this time that we are not goin' to add any more
ex — expenses, particularly labor costs, and that's the way we feel!
We're not gonna do it!

Gambon: If that's the company's position, George, I see no reason to go
ahead till 6:30. I'm perfectly willin' to break it off now. (Rather long
pause)

Mediator: Uh (rather long pause) — while I — I do not see any immediate daylight in the problem, nevertheless — and I can — I realize that
this situation is one that, using a term that mediators use, we usually
refer to a situation like this as a "dug-in" situation — I realize that
this is a "dug-in" situation and both parties are pretty fixed —
pretty well fixed in their thinking and their position, and each side is
— feels that they have right on their side. And I can say that after
hearing both of you state your positions, the average person would
say, "Well, what is there to talk about? And why not go home?"
Now, I have to say to both of you, while I don't have the answer and
we do not see the daylight, I cannot take this — that position — the
position that both of you may have that this is a situation that, "Since
we both feel the way we do, let us go home, or let's slug it out, or" —
so and so. Now, I have — again I must say that I have to take this position. I don't have to. There's no regulation or no order that tells
me I have to, but my common sense and my experience in these matters tells me that I must use every bit of time I have. When the time
comes that the 3rd man, myself, feels hopeless, well, I'll throw my
sponge in along with you. The only thing is I never throw mine in
until I'm certain, and I don't mean that I see any change in the situation, but I do know this. While we have explored and talked about your
positions for 4, 5, or 6 meetings — whatever it was, or is — there
still must be an answer to this, and I know the answer w — can be
found when the parties both begin to look at one another's position,
not their own. I know that's not an easy thing. I know it's easy to say
and I know it's not an easy thing to do. A lot of that is my department.
I think it might be well — I — I felt — I thought we could probably, at
this joint session, get into a vein that — that might give us a basis for
— for a continued joint session. However, in the interest of expediency, in the e — in the interests of exploring the thing further, I will
want to talk to both committees alone. When I find, or if I can have
or establish a basis wi — or joint discussion on this thing, I will certainly keep you together. It is not that I like to work with you separately; I would much rather have you both at the table working out the
problem in the way that you do work them out. But we first have to
find a basis if there is a basis there. So much of that work from here
on in will probably fall on my shoulders. So I'll look forward to both
of the committees' cooperations — uh — cooperation. So, I will —
well, would like to talk with the union committee now, so if the company has no further comments to make (Michelsen: No), or the union,
then I would suggest that the company committee retire to their caucus room and I'll be here with the union and join you later.

Union Caucus - B (2:30 P.M.)

Mediator: Has he, in the past, bargained this way? Has he held and —
Gambon: Yes. (Meyer: He would) He — he has taken more or less the
same position, George, in our — under our reopener back in September. The negotiations that took place in — I'd say in September of '52
on the October 1st reopener, we got the same kind of a — an attitude.
They waive it! Now, what they wanta do and what they've wanted to
do ever since they signed this contract is forget that there is any
such thing as reopeners in the contract and possibly we might walk
around with our hat in our hand, saying to them, "Well, look, we won't
demand anything of ya, but if you find you've got a little bit to spare,
why, don't forget us." Now, I think that's the kind of thing that — the
position they'd like us to take, which means not only did they want us
to do that in October, '52, not only do they want us to do that now, but
they'll want us to do that in October of '53. They don't like these reopeners! (Knock at door) The — (pause).
Mediator: 'Scuse me. (Confers at door) Mr. Saunders wanted on the
phone.
Gambon: The other thing that they're quite concerned with, I'm sure, is
the fact that they want to be able, as early as possible in 1953, to assure the stockholders that they're going to return to the 40-cent dividend level — at least the 40-cent dividend lel — level. The other —
another thing they want to be assured of is to have enough cash to do
the kind of things they want to do, which includes moving further than
they have moved now. I think we did mention to you that there are
several other operations to be moved out of the plant, according to
them, in November of this year: one, which is transformer potting
and winding; another, multiple coil winding; another one, an entire
new product which we're just beginning to get in production on —
binaural recorders; and another new product, some subcontract for
the Navy involving miniaturization. Now, the decentralization plans
go beyond that. We know that they go beyond that. They won't tell us
anything. They won't commit themselves as to what will remain in
the metropolitan area. We don't know yet! Since last November we've
been tryin' to get an answer to that. We don't know yet what's goin'
to remain in the metropolitan area. In the face of these uncertainties
and in the face of an absolute positive move on the part of the company, which is gonna result in less jobs in the metropolitan area, we
must do somethin' to protect ourselves in form of trying to create
jobs through this program we have, the 35-hour work week. Secondly,
we're not going to pay for their moving, which you put to 'em. We've
expressed it to you and you've told 'em very bluntly. They're aware
of that! We're not gonna pay for their moving out from under us and
having them go into low-paid areas. This company, as far as I'm
concerned — the financial report that they talk so much about in 1952
has to be looked at on the basis of their profits before taxes in '52,
which runs over $1,000,000.00. But the important thing to me is that
the trend — if the trend in '53 continues on the basis of what has happened in the first period of 1953 they're goin' to realize well over
$2,000,000.00 before taxes, almost probably more than double what
they had in '52. The 8th, 9th, and 10th period of 1952 and the first

period in '53 will bear that out, 'cause if ya look at their figures there
you'll find that there's been an appreciable increase from the 8th, 9th,
and 10th periods the company has.   That's the last 15 weeks, incidentally, of '52 and the first 5 weeks of '53.

Meyer: And they also said the 2d period, which we haven't seen.

Gambon: That's right. Now, the trend is evidently continuing. Now, in
the face of that, we had the president of the company's own optimistic
statements about dividends and profits and business outlook. We —
to support even that we have the industry outlook for '53, at least.
And we had not only the outlook, but the TV, radio, and recorder production for '53 is definitely up over '52 and has been continuing from
the first of the year on. They're — as far as I'm concerned they are
in an impossible position of trying to sell this union 4/10ths of a cent.
I don't honestly believe that Atlas wants to risk a strike. I'll b — I'm
very much surprised if they do, because the result would simply be
this. The m — no matter what the settlement might be, if a strike
lasted any length of time a'tall, it's certainly gonna be a factor in how
fast they're gonna be able to make these moves which they say they
already have on the drawing board.

Meyer: Well, one thing (Gambon: The —) add to that, George, about
Bill Michelsen's attitude. It — he has always been 2d man in position
up until last September, and it has been on — even grievances, he has
taken a very adamant stand against Alexander, where Alexander will
start to back down and see the light of day, even on questions like
seniority — I mean, he — Alexander would put forth a little bit of
fairness and put himself in the position of long service and what's
right and what's wrong morally, but Bill Michelsen — it's always been
"The industrial relations manager to make a name for yourself out
in the business world." And I don't think that his position is the position of the Board of Directors, because they can't afford to have any
kind of labor trouble as long as they can afford to pay a — a reasonable
amount that the union would ask. And I think it is personal prestige
with him, and I think you're gonna have a hard time breaking him
down. He's either gonna make or break himself in these negotiations.
And that's what you're interested in is what — has it always been like
this ? And it's not always been like this, but it always has been when
you deal directly with Bill Michelsen.

Gambon: That's correct. I mean, he has admitted very frankly to me
and to other members of this committee on occasion, on — that Alex
— Alexander was foolish for having agreed with us about certain
things that we had discussed with Alexander. Alexander's approach
was much more human. If you'll recall, Alexander, at the conclusion
of those negotiations, was practically a physical wreck. I mean, I
could hardly look the man in the face for fear he'd break down. If you
recall, he was on the verge of breaking right down then and there.

Mediator: He had to go away, didn't he, after the —

Gambon: Well, he had to go away for a couple of weeks when he — when
he finished these negotiations. Bill, I agree, is ambitious. I mean,
I've — I mentioned before he's been gotten — gotten an awful lot of
attention in the industry particularly because of his cold-blooded approach to these industrial relations problems, and that's exactly what
it is — a very cold-blooded approach. I don't attach that in any way

whatsoever to the guy as a personal individual — his make-up or anything else. He's just strictly a cold-blooded individual as far as his
job goes, and I do quite (laughing slightly) agree with Bernice that
he's ambitious. However (pause), there's a few things that I think
he overlooks, and that is, I think that he has, for a long period of time,
felt that he could call the union's bluff by virtue of the fact that he has
a sounding board (pause) in the shop through his First Aid Room.
Now, an awful lot of our pe — people / very —
Mediator: (Over Gambon above) Who is — what room?
Gambon: First Aid Room.
Meyer: Dispensary.
Gambon: Dispensary (Mediator: Uh-huh), or whatever you wanta call
it. An awful lot of our people go in there and they — they have the
nurses trained to be very confidential with the people and they blow
their guts in there and say a lot of things that they oughtn't to be saying. And I think he figures that his sounding board is so good that
nothing can happen in Atlas. Well, he overlooks one thing, see. Nobody in this union, and least of all myself, has stood up before the
membership yet and said, "This is it!" And I'll assure you, George,
if — if I put the chips on the line, this union's gonna move! I have
never gotten to the point where I've had to do that yet. The closest I
came to it, I think, was back in January when they were on the line,
and the company knew they were on the line. They found that out real
quick when we began to give them a little bit of taste of what can happen without an absolute shutdown in that the people refused to work
overtime and then the — the people themselves getting tired of the
length of the negotiations began to take a — as it comes. I mean, they
didn't get interested in making too much bonus any more. They made
bonus when they felt like it, and they didn't make it if they didn't feel
like it. And I think that particular negotiations in January for the new
contract pointed up that when the people in that shop realize that
they're fighting the company that then they take the bit in their teeth
and that something's gonna happen. Now, he — I think he's got an idea
that our people are complacent, and that's the biggest mistake that he
can ever make, because I'll pull all the stops, George! And if I
couldn't convince this membership, see, that the exact situation is as
I tell it to 'em, I think I'd resign, and I don't intend to resign. I have
no fear of having to resign, see. Now, Bill wants to be big about it,
let him go ahead, be big! (Mediator: What is the —) But he has to do
one thing. He has to convince himself, see, that if he's gonna maintain this position, he's gonna get a strike vote on Saturday at 1:00
o'clock, and Number 2, historically we have a very significant date
of April 30th, 1936, was when this union struck. I'll come back in
here Monday, Tuesday, any day you say, but he'll have a deadline of
April the 30th, 1953, to meet, because that's what I intend to recommend.
Meyer: Or if he gets off (pause) too much / it'll be xxx.
Gambon: (Over Meyer above) Well, if he goes off too much, I may even
go before that, but I'm willing to come back in here if he — if all —
what he needs is a strike threat, see, voted by the membership to
move him, he'll get that. But he's not gonna get a month to fool around
again. (Slight pause) The only reason that I'm goin' to go to the 30th

of April is to try to have it sink in in Atlas what happened in April 30th, 1936, and if they wanta try it again, it's all right with me. I thought they'd gotten a little bit intelligent over all these years, but maybe their greed is gettin' to be a little bit too much for their intelligence. If they want it that way they can have it that / way.

Mediator: (Over Gambon above) What is the — on that same subject of Bill and this that you have just talked about, what is the truth — the real sentiment or the activity or the (Knock on door) grapevine or the scuttle (pause) — 'scuse me.

Gambon: Uh-huh.

[Mediator confers at door, then leaves the room for the period of 2:45–3:12 P.M. Upon returning, he apologizes for the interruption, and checks the ball score coming in over the radio.]

Mediator: Well, as I was sayin', I started to — to ask you about, relative to the things that you had spoken about Bill and his thinking on this, what is the situation now — I just started to say, what is the situation in the plant? Is the — through the scuttlebutt and so forth, is there a indication of any kind that there is unrest or that there is dislike for the position of the company, or anything, or is it a situation where reports are not coming through and he could be interpreting that to mean that the membership is not supporting the bargaining committee, and — or just what — / what is the situation?

Gambon: (Over Mediator above) Well, I have to guess as to what kind of things are running through his mind. My guess would go along these lines, that they think that this decentralization problem has so put the fear of the Lord in these people that they're trembling and they wouldn't think of asking the company for anything. Now, I know that there are some (laughing slightly) people in the shop who talk like that and it's taken back to him. But, without bein' the least bit egotistical about this thing, I'd like to tell you exactly what happened this morning — as late as this morning. Before I came down here I was in the office, I'd say, for about — well, from 8:30 until about (slight pause) 10 minutes of 11:00, and during that time I think just about every steward in the place just so happened to call in with problems, and each one, as they finished their problem, I took the trouble to ask them what the sentiment was in their department, and I got this, George: "The people in the shop say that as John has never let us down and whatever John says is what we'll do. Period." Now, I said I'm saying that without bein' the least bit egotistical, but that's the way it stands! So this guy's not worrying me one bit. I know exactly what's gonna happen. I don't think those people in the shop are gonna let me down if I go for a strike vote, because I've never let them down. And I'm goin' for a strike vote. And I want you to know this. I picked my time for this kind of a showdown. I was inclined to go into a — locking horns with this guy in October, but nobody likes to walk picket lines in the wintertime. I was determined he wouldn't get away with nothing. He didn't. He came through with the additional holiday and the cost-of-living wage increase. I preferred, if I'm gonna fight with him, I'd do it in a nice time of the year. The time has come. The reopener in October is no time for me to fight, either, and I'm not gonna wait till April, 1954, to fight with him. I picked the time, I picked the place, and he can have the fight if he wants it. That's the

way — that's the position I'm in, George. Because he took exactly the
same kind of position — he rubbed the committee the wrong way the
last time, he rubbed me the wrong way with his attitude. And the only
thing that prevented me from making an issue over the whole mess
last year was because of the time of the year — October, November,
December — gettin' into that. Right now spring is here. That's the
reason I haven't set any deadlines! I'd like the end of April, George!
(Slight pause) Gets in the spring. (Mediator laughs) (Pause)
[Mediator requests that recorder be turned off. He explores with
Gambon the April 30 date just mentioned, and evaluates the effect of
using this as a deadline in the negotiation.]

Gambon: ... the union's position, a recommendation that will go to the
membership will be to give this committee the authority to call a
strike when and if it sees fit, depending on the — the negotiations with
the company from tomorrow on. That can be Monday, can be Tuesday, it can be any day. And I have no intentions of allowing him to
drag out these negotiations any more than he's done up to this point.
I use those words purposely because he did nothing from receiving
the letter in January 23 until February 20th. He wasted a whole
month before he even answered the union's request for negotiations
to begin as quickly as possible. On February 20th he sets a date for
March 12th. He al — he threw away almost a month and a half —
almost 2 months before we even started to negotiate, against an April
1st reopening date. I don't intend to have him go too far after Saturday. The only reason that I mention April 30th a'tall is from the
standpoint of the psychological effect it could have on the minds of
the older officials of that company up there who remember that on
April 30th, 1936, this union (laughing slightly) did hit the bricks,
and hit it good, and there was no question about whether or not there
was a 100% walkout. There'll be 100% walkout, George. I think you
know there's (Mediator: Oh, sure) — that's can be assured!

Mediator: In most instances you only have to throw a picket line around
there and they're out! (Gambon: Well —) Uh —

Gambon: I think maybe his problem is he doesn't think can be done. You
can assure him it's gonna be done! (Slight pause)

Mediator: Well, I think I still have my finger / xx —

Gambon: (Over Mediator above) And I'm — I'm — I'm hoping he calls
my bluff! Believe me, I hope he calls my bluff! Honest to Christ I do.

Mediator: Well, I think I have my finger on it. I believe that the more
pressure, the more talk, and the more firmness of your position relative to this meeting Saturday and contemplated action that may come
— may come Monday is the — will be the turning point in these negotiations. The fact that it isn't played up, I question very much whether
you would get a settlement. I feel very strongly — I'm speaking now
on the record of this (pointing to recorder) but off the record to you
— that the chances of breaking this depend 100% on your — your position relative to Monday, relative to the Saturday meeting, and so
forth. It's the only thing that's gonna move (Gambon: Uh-huh) him,
because it will do this. When I am able to convince him that this is
it, see — this is your — your — you're in trouble at this point on
here, then he will, I am certain, like any other industrial bargaining
team, pick the phone up and call Joe and say, "I've done my job. I've

taken it up to here. Here's the report. The mediator feels the same way. This is it. What d'you wanta do?'' (Gambon: Uh-huh) Now, sooner we can get him to that point, the sooner we're gonna find out whether he goes or not. Now, a lot of that is going to depend upon the kind of thinking and position rel — relative to your — your plans. (Gambon: Well —) I don't think any of your arguments — your economic arguments — let me put it this way — sound as they may be, will serve much of a purpose in convincing this company that you are entitled to more money.

Gambon: No, I'm — I'm — I agree with you there. (Mediator: Uh — the other —) Th — there's no reasonable kind of argument that they'll wanta listen / to.

Mediator: (Over Gambon above) That's right. Now, the other (pause) will be more effective. Now, I — of course, I don't care how deep ya o — off the deep end you go, because I can always pull you back. / And —

Gambon: (Over Mediator above) Uh-huh. Well, I don't go off the deep end, George. I mean, as far as I'm personally concerned, I'll bargain over this table as long as I think there's any reason for it or any — any good coming out of it. Th — if this guy's gonna take the attitude of saying, "I don't think ya can do it; go ahead and try," I'll prove it to him!

Mediator: Well, see, as — as far as / Bill's concerned —

Gambon: (Over Mediator above) Now, let me say one thing more to ya, George. Very significantly, we get a report while we're in here in this meeting, they call overtime for 3 very significant departments: Department 1, which is the place where they fabricate the chassis that they build the units on; Department 7, which is our Final Assembly and Packing — Tom works in there, and they're all men, very vocal; Department 52, which is <u>all the skilled trades</u>. <u>All</u> the skilled trades are in tomorrow, which is somethin' they haven't been doin' for <u>weeks</u>.

Mediator: Oh?

Gambon: And they — so they call overtime for tomorrow, and they'll probably all be scheduled for 8 days.

Meyer: 8-hour day, / it —

Gambon: (Over Meyer above) Or 8 hours, I mean. Not gonna be any work tomorrow, George.

Mediator: Oh, you've / knocked off?

Gambon: (Over Mediator above) Not gonna be any work tomorrow. (Pause)

Mediator: Well, that's (voice lowering) fine. (Slight pause) All right. Fine. Now, / xx —

Gambon: (Over Mediator above) If there is anybody works, they're (laughing slightly) not gonna work after 12:30. (Laughs shortly)

Mediator: Well, had they been working in the morning?

Saunders: No.

Gambon: No! They've been / working —

[Over Gambon above, one of boys and Mediator talk at once, Mediator saying, "On Saturday?" and later, "Oh."]

Gambon: (Over others above) — they've been workin' part of their skilled trades a few men each week, but now they call 'em all in tomorrow.

Saunders: Everybody! All the skilled tradesmen.

Mediator: Oh, they wouldn't work 12:00 t — oh, on account of the meeting?

Meyer: H'm?

Gambon: (At same time as Meyer above) No, that isn't. They try to pick the vocal groups, where they're liable to be vocal support of a committee's position.

Mediator: Oh! Oh! (Gambon: Uh! See!) Oh! Oh, I see.

Gambon: See, we have mostly women (Mediator says something), and both in this de — Final Assembly and Packing and the skilled trades are all men.

Mediator: So they couldn't go to the meeting?

Gambon: Yeah!

Mediator: Oh, I see.

Gambon: Why (Mediator says something) — why else? Hell, I mean, they don't suddenly get overtime out of the clear blue sky. They haven't had it for <u>weeks</u> around there.

Meyer: For months.

Gambon: Or months, for that matter.

Mediator: All right. Now, one more point. (Rather long pause) One thing, that when we get to the right place — the right place will be the place that I just mentioned, where this team has to call up Mr. Who-ever-he-is and say, "This is where I am. It looks pretty bad. What do I do?"

Gambon: I think that'll be done tomorrow afternoon when the union meeting is over and they get a report back from whatever stooges they've been able to get the report (laughing slightly) back.

Mediator: Well, I have a feeling that there may be an opportunity before that. I think that before this day is out you may get that opportunity. (Gambon: Well, look) As long as the company believes that, (1), you're not goin' to meet tomorrow, (2), you're havin' a meeting on Saturday, (3), there <u>may</u> be a strike on Monday. Now, with those 3 factors I'm of a mind to think ya have a good chance of getting that telephone call through to Mr. Atlas, whoever he is. Now, the sooner we get to that, the better. However, when we get to that you're goin' to be confronted| with this, and I wanta talk about it now. You have 2 points on the board: one is the 35-hour week and the other is the what?

One of boys: 20%.

Meyer: 20%.

[Several talk at once.]

Gambon: (Over others above) 20% for all the skilled trades and day workers.

Mediator: I believe (speaking very slowly and deliberately) — fact, I'm willing to wager that as long as the union is holding on a 35-hour week the company would take a strike. I believe that from what I've heard. I don't think they were playin' poker or playing cute with me on that. (Pause) The reasons you probably know better than I do. They — they could tell you why they couldn't operate with a 35-hour week better than I could. In fact, I've since forgotten why. But I do know this. The re — the statements that were made along with it were the ones that convinced me. I believe that if they call up Mr. Atlas, whoever he is, and say, "This is where we are. We've gone as far as we can, and the issue as it stands now — the union's demands is still 35-hour

week, 20% this," Mr. Atlas would say, "Take a strike." Sometime,
when the chips are down, the union committee is going to have to determine if — when it's the right time: (1), if you are serious about a
35-hour week at this plant, you're goin' to have to make a decision
on that, a decision that will determine whether the company can settle
with you or whether they can't.

Gambon: I can give ya a quick answer to that.

Mediator: All right. / What is it?

Gambon: (Over Mediator above) Well, this is off the record as far as
goin' back in there but for your information. I did mention to you
that the Points 1 and 2 were bargainable — that that was our position
at the moment. Somewhere along the line, when and if I'm convinced
they're ready to do some bargaining, I'm quite willing to drop the
37½-hour-work-week proposition. Now, knowing full well that they
had, at the very first meeting, stated their opposition to anything like
a 35-hour week, and I would assume that would probably go on the
37½-hour week, I would suggest that if they're so opposed to that that
they partic — they suggest what form the bargaining should take!
(Slight pause) Now, I'm not closing any doors (Mediator: Well, I — I
— I want us to —) to tryin' to reach a settlement. Certainly this is
our position, and this is what we're most interested in, the shorter
work week in order to create more jobs in the face of the problem /
we have in decentralization.

Mediator: (Over Gambon above) Good. 'Cause I don't want them to be
able, when they do talk to Mr. Chief, say (Gambon: Uh-huh) this is
a n — a situation that is not bargainable, because I'm inclined to feel
probably some thinking on that committee is they'd like it to go back
that way! (Slight pause) But I don't want it to go back (Gambon: Uh-
huh) that way because I feel this way, that if this company is convinced that you're going to take the steps that they think you're going
to take, they, not knowing about April 30th or anything else, that they
would be more prone (pause) to move — to move, and probably move
today. And I'm tryin' to steer this thing in that direction and I think
there is a chance of doing it, but first I have got to get them to the
point where they, in their own minds, believe we — believe they're
facing a crisis. Now, this is not a usual bargaining course we're
taking. It's unusual because of the things we've — we know that exist
in your problem. So that being the case, we have to handle it with unusual tactics. (Gambon: H'm) So, I believe (pause), probably, that
they want to get to where we want them to get to. But they don't know
how, and it's up to these negotiations here to develop a vehicle that's
goin' to carry them (Gambon: Uh-huh) to that point. (Gambon: Well,
a vehicle has to have more than just fringes for wheels xx) So I say
xxxxx for that vehicle is pretty much the position that you take relative to your meeting tomorrow and so forth. You know what I mean.

Gambon: H'm. (Slight pause)

Mediator: O.K.

Gambon: Well, I — I just want you to know that we — we have closed no
doors as to whether or not we — they want us to definitely get away
from the shorter work-week proposition. But in order to get us away
from that, they're gonna have to offer (Mediator: Right) some concrete suggestion. (Mediator: And I have no intentions —) And I'll

repeat again, they're not gonna settle this issue on a fringe issue alone.
Mediator: I have no intentions of using that until the right time (Gambon:
Uh-huh), because as long as i — as long as I need pressure, the 35-
hour will be a — also a pressure (Gambon: Uh-huh) move. And —
but I also want to know that when the time comes for removing it, I do
have another door to go through; and when you say it's — the door
isn't closed, that's — that's good enough (Gambon: Uh-huh) for me.
All right. Fine. That's what I wanted and (pause) we'll (pause)
play with it and —
Gambon: (Over Mediator above) Well, let me — let me suggest something, George, for what it may be worth. Would you — if you're going
back in with them, you might convey to them the desires of the union
committee to leave here unless they think they can come up with something that might start the ball rolling here, 'cause if they're gonna go
into a long caucus, we feel they've had lots of time to caucus and come
up with something. I don't see any reason for me to keep this committee here for 3 more hours until they come back and say No again.
So, tell them that we're quite interested in whether or not they're
gonna use the time to come back here before 6:30 with something or
whether it's O.K. for us to go home and let them think about it.
Mediator: Well, the bad — w — the bad part of that is that you're (pause)
— that wouldn't have the effect that you would like it to have, or I
would like it to have. They would — I think that would act more as a
detriment than a help, 'cause they might think that, "Well, the boys
are overdoing it." They know that —
Gambon: Well, we think they're overdoing it, / and —
Mediator: (Over Gambon above) No, I mean overdoing this — pressure.
(Gambon: Uh-huh) We've got pressure here to use, and we've —
you've got it on now.
Gambon: Yeah. But we agree, George, that the (Mediator: I say any
gain —) pressure at this moment isn't sufficient / to move 'em any.
Mediator: (Over Gambon above) Yeah. But any talk about, "Well, / we
won't come back until you" —
Gambon: (Over Mediator above) I mean, this isn't a xx. Don't misunderstand me. This — I'm not saying this at this moment for pressure.
I'm just sick and tired of sittin' around waitin' for them to play out
their string. Now, if they wanta play out the string till 6:30, come
back here and say No, he can just as well call me on the phone at
home and say the answer's No at 6:30. I don't wanta sit here waitin'
for him to develop a strategy. Let him develop it if he wants to.
Mediator: If it would work — if it would all work that easy, boy, we —
we'd all save a lot of hours (Gambon: Huh?), but it don't. It's like
havin' a baby. It takes 9 months, and ya have to go through every
month. (Gambon: How do you know ?) And anything short of 9 months
(Gambon: And how do you know ?) is an abortion. (Gambon: How do
you know ?) We don't want an abortion here. This is what we call
labor pains.
Gambon: Well, let me tell you (pause) — no, I won't, either. / W (laughing slightly) — we're on record. I won't.
Mediator: (Over Gambon above) Better not. Off the record. (Everyone
laughs riotously, including Gambon)
Gambon: Never mind. (Everyone continues laughing)

Management Caucus - C (3:35 P.M.)

[Before the machine has begun to record, Mediator is already saying, "Believe me, this time I was worried. We weren't just swapping stories."]

Mediator: ... startin' to — just like I expected — s — startin' to get a little active. (Pause) Uh (rather long pause) — the union (pause) talked a good bit about their strategy. Their talk about strategy came from a statement made by John. He says, "This company believes that we are — our people are complacent." He said, "We know that," and he says, "That has been brought" — he said, "We know that the company thinks that way." (Michelsen: Uh-huh) He said something about your sounding post is some first aid station. (Michelsen laughs) And he said, "Though some of our people," he said, "have gone in there and they have," he said, "made statements like 'We — we don't want a strike,' " see, he said, "But, George," he said, "we will strike that plant. We <u>have</u> to." (Michelsen: Uh-huh) He says, "If we can't get a settlement, that plant must be struck, because " — and then he listed most of the things that I listed (Loring: Uh-huh) — the going away — now, it's <u>evident now</u>, and I don't think he's playin' poker — we were concerned about which avenue he was going to go down. (1), would he be concerned about the pressure on the company and the moving away; would that — would that not put him in a bad position? Or would he take the other one? I think he's taken the other one. (Loring: Uh-huh) I think the whole committee has.

Michelsen: What ya mean by the other one?

Mediator: The other one bein' (Loring: He didn't want any x) that if the chips were down, he would strike instead of not striking. Uh — he continued, saying that (pause) he had a meeting (pause) — I don't know how it came about; I think it was today — with — somehow or another he met all his shop stewards. Now, how does he do that?

Michelsen: Well, he could've done it last night. (Pause)

Mediator: (In low tone) I'll just — I'll get this straight. Observer (pause), what did John say how — do you remember what — how he said he met the shop stewards (slight pause), and talked about them — about the sentiment in the plant?

Observer: Do you really want me to tell you?

Mediator: Yes! / Yeah.

Observer: (Over Mediator above) Over the phone.

Mediator: But he talked to each one. Oh, over the / phone.

Observer: (Over Mediator above) He talked to each one this morning / over the phone.

Mediator: (Over Observer above) Oh, that — that's what I thought.

Observer: Uh-huh.

Mediator: Uh — over the phone he talked to each one of these shop stewards, getting a feeler (Loring: Uh-huh), ya know. And he said that the shop stewards reported that the feeling in the departments as they saw it was that since the company is moving (pause), "Our best interests can be served" — now, I'm summing this up. This prob'ly (Loring: Uh-huh) wasn't each individual's (Loring: Uh-huh) way of saying it (Loring: Uh-huh), but — "Our best interests can be served by hitting them as hard as you can and getting everything you can."

(Slight pause) He said — then he continued, saying, "And the company is wrong if they think our people are complacent and that we can't strike and won't strike this place." He says, "We're now in a position where, when the time comes, and," he says, "that will be Monday morning," he said, "we (pounding on table) will strike that plant." And that's the first time he got that (pounding on table) positive. Now (long pause), I talked abou — I talked to him about his position. (Michelsen laughs slightly) (Pause) I said (pause), "Your position where you stand now is one where this company committee, even if they wanted to settle with you, couldn't." I said, "You've got 2 issues on the board." And I said, "Not only your 31% — uh, 31-cent position, but," I said, "you have 2 positions on the board, John, and you may as well know it, that this company will let you strike from hell to breakfast (Loring: Uh-huh) on — they can't buy that issue." "Well, what do you mean?" I said, "Well, the 31¢ is bad enough, but the application of it — the thirty — the 35-hour week" — I said, "you'll never get that." I said, "Here is a company — from what they have told me, and," I said, "I think you know it even better than I do — here is a company that would be crippled if they went on a 35-hour week. Now, the why and wherefore you know better than I do. I don't. I — I can't explain it as well as you do. I could give you a rough — but I know you know it better'n I. And on that, if there's any thought in the union — this committee's mind that this thing can be resolved around that," I said, "then you — you have got a strike." (Pause) I made that as strong as I could. (Michelsen: Uh-huh) I think it registered (Michelsen: Do they have any —) with the committee.
Michelsen: Do they have any conception, too, of the — of the fact that the Rome plant would have to be opened?
Mediator: We did talk about it.
Michelsen: You did?
Mediator: No (Michelsen: Oh), we didn't. No, we didn't talk (Michelsen: Uh-huh) about that. I — what you would do I didn't think was too important. I thought the point (Michelsen: Yeah) of "what (Michelsen: H'm) will happen if you insist on this," / see.
Michelsen: (Over Mediator above) Yeah. Well, that's better.
Loring: Yeah.
Mediator: And (pause) it (slight pause) — I think it registered. (Pause) I'm pretty sure it did, because he slowed down to pretty near a stop. He paused so long it was — could be called a stop. And I — I told him — I said, "Now, I don't know where you're going. I don't know where you're going yet. I don't even know whether there can be a settlement." (Pause) I said, "And I haven't learned a hell of a lot from either committee as far as the actual settlement, and I know why! The why is because you're too far apart. (1), how can this company think in terms of settlement with 35-hour week on the board — something — something they couldn't (pause) res — a — a — adopt (pause) under many circumstances, without (pause), as they put it, 'losing money'? Uh — your 20% for skilled trades — I haven't even gone into that. I haven't gone into any of the issues because I know it would be wasting my time while certain other obstacles are on the table." And I said, "The sooner we get those obstacles off the table, I think then the company's going to be in a position to know whether

they could do more than 4/10ths.'' I said, ''And I don't wanta ask
them, because (1), I know that they won't buy a 35-hour week. Till —
to ask them, or to — to r — even explore with them the possibility of
a settlement with those things on the question,'' I said, ''not even an
amateur mediator would try that.'' So I said, ''The sooner you start
thinking in that direction, the sooner we're going to know whether
we've got a settlement.'' Uh (pause) — again, I think I scored. We'll
know that later. They have to have time to talk this over (Michelsen
laughs slightly), as they're doing now. Uh —

Michelsen: Do you think he's serious with 'em?

Mediator: Yeah, I think he's getting serious. Yeah, I think he's startin'
to warm up. I think he's playing a l — he's still playing with time on
the tomorrow to buying the communion (?: [In low tone] Cheez) outfit for the girl. That, of course, don't — that don't (pause) hold with
me — that — somebody else could soon go shopping if —

Michelsen: Yeah. I mean, that — when I heard that — i — if I wasn't — if
it wasn't a danger of being hopelessly mis — being misrepresented
as — as —

[Tape changed]

... No. No. No, there's no real point by my arguing those issues
with him whether or not he's gonna decide things are important. He's
the guy accusing me of not (laughing) bargaining collectively. I'm
not (laughing) go — goin' out to buy any of my kids any clothes.

Mediator: Now, I'll tell you what I think we ought — I think we have to
start now talking about (pause) things to come before the day is
over. I believe (pause) that your — you as representatives of the —
of management are going to have to make a decision, and I think we
oughta talk about it now, even though the action from that decision
will come later. I think it ought — you oughta have time to start thinking about it, and it has nothing to do with the issues right at the moment. I think the time is going to come very shortly (pause), maybe
a couple hours, where you're gonna have to make a decision, and
that decision will be (pause): (1), whether you will want to play this
out past their union meeting (Michelsen: Uh-huh) (pause), or whether
you will not want to play it out before their union meeting. But I think
within a couple of hours you're going to be faced / with that decision.

Loring: (Over Mediator above) Well, what do you mean by that, John?

Mediator: I mean this, whether you believe that you stand a better chance
of reaching an agreement or being in a healthier bargaining area or
position by waiting until they have their meeting (Loring: Uh-huh)
or not waiting, see. That is something that —

Michelsen: You mean letting them go to the meeting with 4/10ths?

Mediator: Or — no, not necessarily that. Or anything else that you want
them to go with (Loring: Uh-huh), but letting them go. (Loring:
Yeah) I mean, that — that time will be coming.

Loring: Yeah. (Pause)

Mediator: Bear in mind, and don't lose sight of this, that (pause) —
and you sh — you know th — how these fellows operate m — better
than I do. I don't know how their proc — what their procedures are.
But some of these unions, you know, they can go to a union meeting
and they can postpone a situation as well as (?: Uh-huh) hit it.
They — so I don't know what they do. I don't know what this — how

this strike vote works. If they take a strike vote, some unions d —
now, for instance, in Aero — or — after all that hullabaloo in Aero
that ya heard last week, well, we were able to get a letter that satisfied John Jacobs and Dick H — Bo — Bob Hartman, and by getting that
letter they, instead of takin' a strike vote, they held the meeting and
did it this way. The membership voted to give the ex — executive
committee the right to call a strike vote in the event that they thought
one was needed. Well, that was (pause) (Loring: Yeah), you know,
around that way, which was nothing more than a face-saver. (Laughs
slightly) So, how thi — this union operates, I don't know. Now, do
they generally hold a meeting, take a strike vote, and strike, or move
the next day, or —
Michelsen: Well, they've never had a strike, George. Can't / answer it.
(Laughs)
Mediator: (Over Michelsen above) Oh (laughing), that's right. (Michelsen laughs heartily)
Michelsen: (Still laughing) They don't know how they move / xx.
Loring: (Over Michelsen above) This is the first for us, too, George
(laughing).
Michelsen: Well (Mediator: That's right), they have taken strike votes
and authorized the group to come back and bargain at one time, as I
recall, and with the power to call a strike. They've never gotten any
closer than that. (Pause)
Mediator: Well — now, let me put it to you this way. (Pause) Uh — if
you gamble (pause) — if you gambled this way (pause) — let us say
that you (pause) put your best foot forward today (Michelsen: Yeah)
or tomorrow (?: Yeah) and it was X amount (Michelsen: Yeah),
and they went to the union meeting and rejected X (Michelsen: Yeah)
(pause), then they would, no doubt, set a date (Michelsen: Yeah),
what time they would pull the switch, or they would strike (Michelsen:
Yeah) — one or the other. Now, you would be gambling right there
— all of us would (Michelsen: Uh-huh) — as to what they would do.
(Michelsen: Uh-huh) Now, as far as today is concerned, or tomorrow,
regardless of what they do, you would want them, when they leave
these negotiations, to take your best foot with 'em. (Michelsen: Huh!)
That's it, huh?
Michelsen: Yeah. (Rather long pause)
[Loring and Michelsen talk briefly at once.]
Mediator: (Over Loring above) Yeah! Yeah, because — 'course, there's
this gamble in it. There's this risk. (Loring: Uh-huh) When they —
if it's an amount that they're not satisfied with and feel they can't sell,
or won't sell, it may be enough to forestall an immediate strike. But
what they might do — what they generally do in situations like that is
vote to reject it and send the negotiating committee back and set a
date for another deadline (?: Yeah), see. Now, you may face that.
So you — you ought to know that, if you (Loring: Yeah) don't know it
already. That may take place. (Loring: Yeah) As against (rather
long pause) — as against not giving anything, letting them take a
strike vote and gambling that they wouldn't strike on the 4/10ths of a
cent but would send the committee back.
Michelsen: I wouldn't wanta take that / gamble.
Mediator: (Over Michelsen above) You'd have to make that decision.

Michelsen: Yeah. I have made that. (Mediator: Well, that — tha — it's pretty risky) That's too much of a — I — I would — I mean, I would only do that if I — if I were unconcerned — completely unconcerned about the possibility of a strike. I mean, if I — if I actually wanted to percipitate a strike I would take that kind of a action. 'Cause I think you could get one very easily that way. I mean, Atlas — we don't want a strike! But we don't wanta pay s — more than a certain amount of money, and we'll (Mediator: Yeah) take a strike rather than pay more than that. But we haven't reached that point at 4/10ths of a cent. (Pause) And I've told — the company is well aware of that and that — that if we go — for instance, let's assume we go up to 2¢ and it's rejected by the membership and the committee's instructed to come back and — and bargain further and to — with even the further blank check that, "You — you make the decision from that point on whether you come back to us with" — well, they would pretty much have to go back and then they'd take strike action. The company's aware of that, that probability of their holding at 2¢ — the company holding at 2¢ — is slight.

Mediator: Of course, you know — yo — you're — you — you realize that — you fully realize that when you make your t — if it's 2¢ and that comes out on the table right when the union leaves to go back to their (Michelsen: Yeah) people, you realize, then, that you — you are still gambling there. (Michelsen: Yeah) You still don't know whether they'll strike on Monday morning or not.

Michelsen: 'Course not. (Pause) No. I wouldn't know at — at the present time — I wouldn't know if that was 10¢ — I wouldn't know whether they'd strike on Monday morning. Likelihood is less that they would, but — I have the (Mediator: Uh —) feeling that this — that these negotiations are gonna be different than the previous ones. I don't think we're gonna go outa here with any signed agreement.

Mediator: Uh — I think you're right. Uh — I think because of your position being what it is — say 2¢ (Michelsen: Yeah), or whatever it is — they couldn't agree (Michelsen: Yeah) on that. If the membership wanted to agree on it, that's for the membership to do. So for that reason, they won't go outa here with an agreement (Michelsen: Uh-huh) across-the-table. It's gonna be a s — one of these situations where we ha — must go back to the membership, see what they'll say. O.K. I just — now we (Michelsen: Uh-huh) got the decks cleared for that.

Michelsen: Yeah. (Pause) Now, they may surprise me, and it would be a surprise if they would be willing to sign the agreement as a committee with the company on something like / this.

Mediator: (Over Michelsen above) I'd be very surprised.

Michelsen: But I don't expect 'em to.

Mediator: No, I don't expect it. (Pause)

Michelsen: But I don't expect 'em to go out with any more than 2¢, either. (Long pause)

Mediator: He confused this situation with his (slight pause) shopping trip and his / meeting tomorrow.

Michelsen: (Over Mediator above) Oh (laughing), gee. Confused it! He brought it to a new low level, in my opinion.

Mediator: He's wrecked my timing.

Michelsen: Well, I'm — I / would —

Mediator: (Over Michelsen above) Not that I can't have him change his plans if I really want to. Uh — it's just that it makes it a little harder to / figure out.

Michelsen: (Over Mediator above) I can only draw these conclusions, George, I mean as far as John personally is concerned. I mean, he's always operated — he's been pretty smart operator. Now, either this is a — either he's trying to make these things (pause) so (slight pause) funny on purpose, for some reason, or he's doing it unconsciously. But both of his reasons for not wanting to meet with the company on an issue which should be as serious as this one is after 4 mediation meetings, assuming that all of 'em have been held in good faith — now he's not gonna meet with us 'cause he's gotta go shopping tonight and a meeting tomorrow — gee! That oughta be written up in THE NEW YORKER.

Mediator: That's pressure that was applied in 1937. (Pause)

Michelsen: What was that?

Mediator: I mean, they used to do those tricks in 1937 (Espig laughs), / I think.

Espig: (Over Mediator above) George says that that's (Michelsen: But that's not a trick! [Laughs heartily]) — that — that's a little antedated. (Laughs heartily)

Michelsen: (Still laughing) I don't consider that very tricky.

Mediator: It isn't. It used to — it used to have an e — effect, but (pause) it's (Michelsen: If he wants to go shopping xx —) — it's as old-fashioned as management or the union jumping up and putting their hat and coat on during (Espig laughs) / xx.

Michelsen: (Over Mediator above) Why don't ya tell him, George, we'll recess for dinner and he can go out and do his shopping and we'll (Mediator laughs) be back at 7:00 o'clock?

Mediator: Observer, will you go out and do his shopping?

Observer: Uh-huh.

Mediator: Good! (Pause)

Michelsen: Tell him I'd be glad to have my wife come in and do it.
[Exchange continues briefly along the same lines, then drifts off onto a comic story by Mediator. Several laugh heartily, followed by pause.]

Loring: George, is there any possibility of John's strategy turning towards, if — if we assume that it would be best to go up to the deadline tomorrow, breaking — ending tonight, saying he'd be back tomorrow, and then not coming back so he could go in with the 4/10ths of a cent? / Do —

Mediator: (Over Loring above) That's a possibility there. Yeah. Yeah, we have to ascertain that before we leave here. See, we'd have to be sure of that before he (Loring: H'm) lift — leave — left here that he wouldn't — that he would be in. Now —

Michelsen: Well, he'd be in a bad position, wouldn't he (slight pause), if he did that?

Mediator: Well, he could say this to his people. He could say, "I've told them of my plan and they knew about it — of my appointments (pause), and we couldn't reach an agreement by then." (Michelsen: Uh-huh) He'd dress it up to make it sound logical, or (pause) right.

Michelsen: Yeah, but he doesn't come back to meet with us; he comes back here because you're coming back / xx.

Mediator: (Over Michelsen above) Oh, I wouldn't — I would never think
of lettin' him out here without knowing it. I would have to know that.
He — he couldn't leave here without us knowing that. We'd know that.
That's — we must find that out. (Loring: Uh-huh) No, we can't let
let him go there — there won't be a chance of letting him go there for
— at the (pause) — with 4/10ths.

Loring: No, my thought was that he might pull a fast one and say he
would be back but not come back.

Mediator: Oh, well, that we have no control of (Loring: Uh-huh), see.
He could do that. It's not very honorable or it's not done very often.
(Rather long pause) If he was thinking that way, I — I think that would
(pause) show. He's not very anxious to (pause) meet, or at least
he's playing good poker. I don't know which yet. He's talking about
recessing.

Michelsen: Now ?

Mediator: Uh — I have to call on my (pause) rememberer. What did
he say, Observer, about (pause) — oh, no. No. He said that jointly,
didn't he, when we were in joint session, "I see no reason for continue meeting" ?

Michelsen: Oh, / yeah.

Loring: (Over Michelsen above) Yeah.

Mediator: Oh, yeah, yeah. That was joint (?: Yeah) session.

Observer: (In low tone) Uh-huh.

Michelsen: (In low tone) Yeah.

Mediator: Uh — and then this shopping spree and this (Someone laughs
slightly) staff meeting, it all adds up to he — I think he's tryin' to
shorten the time. (Loring: Uh-huh) I think he's pretty well convinced
that your position is firm (Loring: Uh-huh) (rather long pause), but
I think (pause) 2¢ would never send him outa here in agreement with
you.

Michelsen: No, maybe not.

Mediator: It won't. He may do this. (Pause) It may be enough to have
him reject it at his meeting and come back into negotiations. (Rather
long pause) 'Course, before these meetings are over (pause), if the
opportunity (pause) comes (pause) — it's a little difficult, because
John doesn't leave his committee. See, some officers of unions have
— have no compunction about leaving their committee. But I think
John would be embarrassed if I pulled him away. But w — sometime
b — I hope, before the day is over, I'll be able to get him on the side,
and when I do, I hope to find out, at the right time, what this thing can
be settled for. (Loring: Uh-huh) If it's a figure that I believe can be
settled for, that you would be interested in — the kind of a figure that
you would be interested in, that would bring a complete agreement —
in other words, that they'd go back and recommend ratification, I
would then lay it on the table and have you examine it. (Michelsen:
Yeah. Well, we —) Uh — if it wasn't, then, of course, I'd tell you
that his sights were s — pretty high (?: Uh—huh) and that we might
have to take this other course, see.

Michelsen: Yeah. Well, the (pause) — we're prepared to — we are prepared for both of those (pause) results. I mean, when this (Mediator:
Sure) thing is really crystallized and it comes to either too much or
enough, we're willing to make slight adjustments in what's enough. I

mean, I'm not gonna recommend this company go out on strike for a difference of a half-cent, or even a cent, maybe. I don't know. It depends. But if it's a difference of between 3 and 6¢, I can tell you right now they're gonna get their opportunity. And Atlas, in a sense, while they're not determined to get it, are not gonna pay any more than that, 'cause they feel it.

Mediator: There's another thing I would also try to find out. (Rather long pause) I would also try to find out whether or not (pause) he was going to his meeting and recommen — or, reject and come back into negotiations. (Michelsen: Yeah) If he's goin' — then, if I know that, why, I'll know how to operate. Then I — then we'll know what to do — what to offer (Loring: Yeah) without getting hurt. (Loring: Uh-huh) See, I can't afford to get you out in front, because if I allowed you to go too far out in front I would destroy, or — or wreck the negotiations. Uh — and it's my job to see that you don't get out there too fast. At the same time, it's my job to see that nothing is done that would, well, cause a strike that could have been prevented. See? (Loring: Uh-huh) So that's my interest in this moving. What you 2 people agree on means nothing to me as long as you people agree on it, but the important thing is to not get you into a position where you can't agree on anything. See? That's the (Loring: Yeah) — (pause). So, I — those 2 things I have to work on. I believe that I will, before the day's over, have an opportunity to talk to John. (Long pause) Observer, I'm going to (pause) — into a — I'm going to try to get John out of that conference room (pause), so we can't be on machine. I'm going to have to talk to him alone. Later I'll report here. O.K.?

Michelsen: George, you — this is very unimportant to me, but you see this thing going into the night, don't you?

Mediator: I don't know yet. (Michelsen: Uh) I think I'll be able to tell you when I come back. (Michelsen: Uh-huh. O.K.) I'm gonna have the girl — and this is strictly off the record and you're not supposed to know this, and if you say I did, I'll probably deny it, but I'm gonna have the girl call John out and tell him (Michelsen: Uh-huh) he's wanted on the phone. (Michelsen: Uh-huh) See, there's no phone in that conference room, and that way it'll give me an opportunity to collar him. (Michelsen: Uh-huh) I think I oughta talk to him alone. I haven't had an opportunity, even on the phone, since these things begun. Because no use talkin' to him until it's the right time. I think it's the right time.

Loring: Good luck, George.

Mediator: Thank you. / I'll need it.

Observer: (Over Mediator above) I'll be here.

Mediator: All right, Observer.

[Mediator leaves at 4:10 P.M. for his "side-bar" conference with Gambon. A little later, Observer is called to another office where Mediator is waiting. He gives Observer a briefing on the encounter with Gambon.]

Management Caucus - D (4:55 P.M.)

Mediator: Well (pause), I learned more in that short time than I did all
  your meetings. (Laughs, followed by Michelsen laughing heartily)
Michelsen: Well, that's the way it goes (laughing), George.
Pranis: George said 6:00; it's only an hour off. (Pause)
Mediator: Yeah.
Michelsen: What time is it?
Loring: 5:00.
Mediator: 5:00.
Michelsen: Oh.
Mediator: Uh (rather long pause) — what does 20% of your skilled
  trades cost?
Loring: About 4½¢.
Mediator: (In rather low voice) That's just what I thought. (Rather long
  pause) Uh — gentlemen, what I'm going to say now — the reason I'm
  sayin' it is because you people haven't been in mediation too, too
  often and I want to caution you. It's very im — important that none of
  this — this particular conversation leaks. I'm not breaching any confidences, but (pause) sometimes irreparable damage can be done
  with a — a careless word. So I want to s — tell you that this particular part of our talk is strictly off the record — not (looking toward
  recorder) this record, but (?: Uh-huh) your record. (Pause) Now,
  I said to John — I got him out of the conference (pause) and I said,
  "Look, John. (Pause) The time has come — to go back into the room
  with you and the committee — the company committee and start to
  formally negotiate this thing would take a month of Sundays the way
  we're goin', and I haven't been too concerned about your 31¢ and the
  company's position, either, for that matter, but there is a problem,
  and I think the problem is that — don't know. I haven't talked to you
  yet, but I think the problem's going to be that even — that you (pause)
  — your sights may be too high. (Pause) So," I said, "I gotta find
  that out. Now, I can let ya leave here and I can let ya have your meeting and I can let — let you do it your way. In the end you're going to
  come back here and it's going to be settled here or at your plant or
  some other place, but it'll be over a table. So the time for formal
  negotiations have passed, far as I'm concerned. So, I'm gonna talk
  straight to you, and I want you to talk straight to me. And (pause)
  what will settle this?" (Pause) He says, "20% for the skilled trades,
  10¢ across-the-board."
Michelsen: What?
Mediator: 20% (laughing slightly) for skilled trades and 10¢ across-the-
  board.
Michelsen: (Loring speaks at same time) 10¢ across-the-board to who?
Mediator: All employees.
Michelsen: (In low voice) Oh, for heaven's sakes.
Mediator: Uh (pause) — I said, "John, maybe you didn't hear me correctly. If you're serious, you've got a strike, if you really mean that."
  And then he told me some of his problems, that (pause) — and just
  as I thought, the moving. (?: Uh-huh) See, it's — he said it's played
  hell with 'em in these negotiations. Certain people in his union are
  pretty well riled up — not all of them, but I guess the most vocal ones.

And (rather long pause) the close of our conversation, he was in favor of recessing so he could let it stay where it is. "Well," I said, "I can't do that, John, because I haven't explored the thing thoroughly with the company, and in all fairness to the company, I have to do that. And one of the reasons why I didn't do it with the company was I had to know where you were going, and if you're going here, now I know. But I do have to go back and talk this thing over with the company, and I certainly can't exp — say — promise you I'm gonna recess these conferences." Uh-h-h (pause) — he's pressing hard on the strike vote. (Loring: Uh-huh) He wants the strike vote, I'm sure. And he seems to feel that (pause) he has gotta take action this time. He's gotta build it up, get the support of the people, pull the pin in order to get what he wants because he s — knows how low you are thinking, see. He evidently knows that, although he didn't — he don't know it from me (Michelsen: Uh-huh) — the 4/10ths — but he knows there's more there (Michelsen: Uh-huh), but he does — he knows — he probably knows that whatever it is isn't enough, and he's preparing fighting machinery in the event he has to fight. I think he's — this $14\frac{1}{2}$ figure is still a joke, and I don't take that seriously. Uh (pause) — however, for everybody's information, he never offered to settle it for $14\frac{1}{2}$¢. You know what I mean. (Loring: Uh-huh) Because I'm going to leave him at 31, and the way I'm going to negotiate from now on is going to be this way, so that — and I'm going to leave you at 4/10ths of a cent, and whenever there is any developing of another position, it's going to be in a way that, in event that nothing can come of it, officially your position is going to be where ya left it, unless you want it on the table, see (?: Uh-huh) — or they want it on the table. But I'm gonna have to protect his 31¢. (Michelsen: Uh-huh) Why, I don't know — why he wants it that way, but — uh — so $14\frac{1}{2}$ is not official. (Pause) Anything else that comes won't be official, either. See, my — my — but, anyway, that's half of (laughing slightly) 31.

Michelsen: Uh-huh. (Laughs, then someone else also) I-yi-yi.

Mediator: Uh (long pause) — if he goes half of $14\frac{1}{2}$, again, that would be (pause) — half — what did I say? — $14\frac{1}{2}$?

Loring: Uh-huh. $7\frac{1}{4}$.

Mediator: $7\frac{1}{4}$. (Rather long pause)

Michelsen: Well, you split that again and then we're down where (Mediator laughs) we can talk.

Mediator: It's that next split.

Michelsen: He's makin' it awful hard for himself. Or else he's makin' it easy, to get these people out. (Rather long pause) Huh!

Mediator: Now, the thing that's on my mind is the — the — the problem is now determining (pause) whether we — I'm beginnin' to see daylight, by the way (Michelsen: Uh-huh. [Laughs shortly]), for the first time in this thing. (Pause) But it's a — it's a good way off. But I just have a — for the first time I — I (pause) see an opportunity for closing the gap. (Pause) What I have to determine now is (pause) when. Ya have to make a decision as to — and I think we have to talk out loud here. / Uh —

Michelsen: (Over Mediator above) You mean as tonight or tomorrow?

Mediator: Well, right now, I mean.

Michelsen: Uh-huh. No, I mean is that — that what you wanta talk about?

Mediator: Yeah. Uh (pause) — John does show (pause) — he — well, he seems to be — appear — he appears anxious <u>not</u> to continue the meetings and to recess them, and I think that's because he feels they're so — so far apart. (Michelsen: Uh-huh) I think what we have to think of is this: (1) (long pause), whether or not we <u>could</u> get (pause) that daylight clearer — whether we could bring it closer to-day or whether it would be best to give 'em the 2¢ and let him have his meeting. (Rather long pause)

Michelsen: I don't quite understand that.

Mediator: Well, what I mean is this. (Pause)

[As tape is changed, Mediator discusses his apprehension about asking the union to meet tonight because they will think he has something he is working on.]

... be the same thing. He said he wants to go to a meeting, and if I insist that he meet tomorrow, again he may feel that maybe I have developed a settlement of some kind, or I have something. (Pause) Now, we have to decide whether we wanta do that — and I'm open to it — or whether we want to (pause) put your 2¢ out (pause) — 'course, I must — I must say this. In doing that — holding a meeting tonight or one tomorrow morning — we would be workin' in the direction of a — getting him down from $14\frac{1}{2}$ into a realistic area. But what (pause) I really believe (pause), that if he comes down even half of that to $7\frac{1}{2}$¢, from that point on you're fighting with him (Michelsen: Uh-huh), as far as his thinking is concerned. I think he digs in around there. (Michelsen: Uh-huh) You got a fight on your hand at that point. The only thing is, which is best (pause) and what — is it the right time? Uh (rather long pause) — I'm inclined to think at the minute it may be best to throw your 2¢ on the table and let him have his meeting. (Pause)

Pranis: You mean throw it tonight?

Mediator: So, for his — yeah.

Pranis: There wouldn't be no / meeting tomorrow, then.

Michelsen: (Over Pranis above) But how are you gonna prevent us from meeting for 24 hours after that, or 10 hours after that? How are you gonna prevent us after that continuing to bargain from that point on and then be called back here tomorrow to do the same thing?

Mediator: Oh, no, no. No, no. I mean, throw the 2¢ on the board and let him have his meeting.

Michelsen: Yeah, but you can't stop him if he wants to stay here and keep haggling with —

Mediator: Oh, he <u>don't</u> want to.

Pranis: Yeah, but won't the 2¢ change his mind?

Mediator: (In low voice) Naw. (Rather long pause)

Pranis: Then he goes to the meeting with what, George? 2¢ (Mediator: 2¢) and 31.

Michelsen: Yeah.

Pranis: Or 2¢ and somepin'.

Mediator: Yeah.

Pranis: Point is you're not offering 2¢.

Mediator: Well, total.

Michelsen: Uh-huh.

Pranis: You're offerin' something xxx.

Mediator: Something, whatever it is, total 2¢. Now, uh-h (rather long
pause) — ssss — (pause) I don't like to make any s — guesses
(pause), unless ya want me to, because sometimes they're wrong.
Uh — let me put it this way. (Long pause; Mediator sighs) The way
I analyze this now, if you wanted to settle this thing before a strike
(rather long pause) — if John came down to 7½¢, I've said earlier
you'd have a fight — have to fight. The way it is now, as of this minute, I don't think (pause) — this is not allowing any bargaining latitude. This is — this figure that I'm about to throw out I — and I wanta
make a statement here. I don't have this from John. This is purely
George Thomson's analysis, nothing else. (Loring: Yeah) John is at
14½ as far as I'm concerned. He knows that I've been in the business
long enough to be able to read between the lines and knock 50% of that
off. But after that's knocked off, from there on in I have to — you
have to analyze, because there you're in hot water, from there on.
(Loring: Uh-huh) The way it stands now (pause) you can get, I think,
a settlement with a long meeting tonight, or tomorrow morning, or before the strike, but with a lotta hard work. (Rather long pause) It'd
cost you a nickel. (Loring: Uh-huh) (Pause) I (pause) — right now.
Now, that can change! (?: H'm) But (pause) he'll scream murder
when he gets down to 7½, if and when he gets there. So, what I'm tryin'
to say is this. You can give him 2¢, call the meetings off. (?: Uh-huh)
Let him have his meeting tomorrow. Let him report 2 and 31, or
whatever he wants to report, and take a strike vote. Will he strike on
Monday? I don't know. (Pause) Or (pause), can let him take his 2¢
to the meeting (pause), take his strike vote (pause), maybe get into
a session before Monday. I don't relish that, but it's another avenue.
3rd, you can try to wrap it up before the meeting; and if you do, you
may as well make up your mind you'd have to pay a nickel. (Pause)
Think there're your 3 avenues the way you stand now. (Pause)
?: Uh-huh. (Pause)
Mediator: This — he — oh, by the way, I think I have knocked out this
weekly business (Loring: What d'ya mean?) — 35-hour (Loring: Oh.
Uh-huh) week, 37½-hour week. I think that last meeting I had with him,
when I was so positive, said, "Yo — this — you're just wasting your
time here," I think I have completely shattered the — because in this
caucus with him he never mentioned it (Loring: Uh-huh), see. But
the skilled trades thing (pause) is a — a problem. He — I — I — I —
I'm inclined to think that whatever kind of a settlement is made, some
consideration has got to be made for this problem, whatever it is, and
I don't understand it too well. You might (pause) — you might be able
to (pause) wrap this thing up — or — r, anything that you settle on, I
th — I — I don't think will exclude consideration of these people.
Espig: Separately — / in addition to.
Mediator: (Over Espig above) Separately. I — I think that the total th —
whatever the total is, a portion of that total is going to have to go to
this problem (?: H'm), because he seems greatly bothered by it.
Now, whether that's justified or not, I — I haven't gone into it. You
people understand it more — better than I do. (Pause) And I guess,
too, some of his committeemen are in that department. Well, of
course, Baker (Espig: Baker) is. Is any / others?

Espig: (Over Mediator above) Well (Mediator: Oh, just the one?), xxx just Baker.

Mediator: Are they (Espig starts to speak) a vocal group (Espig: Yes) — skilled trades?

Espig: They've become so in the last — (pause).

Michelsen: Well, let's go through — do you mind giving me those 3 things again?

Mediator: Yes. I think it's — it adds up this way. (1), you can, at a joint meeting that I would call now, offer the union whatever you wish to offer them up to 2¢, or whatever you wish to offer them.

Michelsen: When would you call the meetin'? (Pause)

Mediator: Now, or whenever we go back in — the next joint meeting (Michelsen: Tonight) today. (Michelsen: Yeah) Now, reason I say that is because, (1), you said you — you do want them to have your offer. (Michelsen: Yeah) (2), he has said to me he won't meet tomorrow because he has a staff meeting. (Michelsen: Yeah) So because of those 2 things, I say we would go in in our next meeting and you would submit 2¢, or (Michelsen: Yeah) X amount, whatever it is. (Michelsen: All right) He would reject it, that's for sure. The meeting would recess and he would go before his membership tomorrow and ask for a strike vote. Then, I said, whether he would strike Monday morning or not I have not yet ascertained. I don't know yet. He's playing very cozy with that. Then I said the 2d one — the 2d avenue would be (pause) to (pause) offer the 2¢ (rather long pause) — I lost track of the 2d one. What was that?

Loring: And have a meeting before Monday.

Mediator: Oh, yeah. Offer the 2¢ and let him <u>have</u> his meeting and take a strike vote (pause), and then I could call a meeting before Monday if we thought he was gonna strike — going to strike. Thirdly — the 3rd one would be to try to settle the thing in its entirety, and by that I mean the union recommending s — to its membership a settlement. I said that <u>rock bottom</u>, and not a bargainable figure <u>as things stand now</u> — this was my personal analysis, as it stands now — would probably be a nickel. And the reason — my reasoning behind it, I said, was based on this. He's at $14\frac{1}{2}$. (Pause) I'm not — I don't take that figure serious at all and I believe that eventually, throughout the night, he would be brought down to half of that amount. (Michelsen: Yeah) When he got down h — to <u>half</u> of that amount, he'd prob'ly be at $7\frac{1}{4}$. Then, with the <u>extra</u> push that was left — the fight that I would put up, that you would put up, and all the arguments thrown in a hat, you could probably get a settlement around a nickel. And r — now, I don't know the cost of — or how — what would 10% — wha — what'd you say — $4\frac{1}{2}$ would be 20?

Loring: Uh-huh.

Mediator: 10% would be prob'ly around $2\frac{1}{4}$. If it was 5¢, and 2¢ went to skilled trade (pause), that'd only leave 3 for the —

Michelsen: Can't sell it.

Mediator: No. How would that work?

Michelsen: You could make a package up this way. You could give the skilled trades people 5¢ an hour, which is what we gave 'em before. That's 3/4 of a cent. (Pause)

Mediator: I don't follow you.

Michelsen: Instead of giving them — he's asking for 20% for the skilled trades (Mediator: Yeah), or you're — and you're talking in multiples of 10%. (Mediator: Yeah) I'm talking 5¢ an hour to the skilled trades, and 5¢ an hour'd cost us 3/4 of a cent, spreading it over our entire labor cost.

Mediator: Oh. Oh, I see. Well, then, in other words, whatever it — oh, yeah. Whatever he gave — what — whatever — / never would be a lot —

Michelsen: (Over Mediator above) In other words, it would cost you — would cost you a cent and a half to give 10¢ an hour to the skilled trades. In that area — 7/10ths, 8/10ths of a cent. I don't know exactly what.

Mediator: Oh, I — no, I was talkin' about percent.

Michelsen: Yeah. I'm not. I'm talkin' about cents per hour.

Mediator: Well — oh.

Michelsen: Spend too much money talkin' percent. Ya have to get down to too low a percent (Mediator: Oh) in order to / afford it.

Mediator: (Over Michelsen above) Oh. Oh, I see. Oh, I see. Yeah. That threw me off.

Michelsen: 5¢ an hour.

Mediator: So 10 — 10¢ an hour is a cent and 3/4?

Michelsen: What is it, Len? What / is —

Loring: (Over Michelsen above) Comes out 1.6, I think.

Mediator: 1 — 1.6?

Loring: I think that's right / x.

Michelsen: (Over Loring above) Yeah. It was 8/10ths, I think, last time.

Mediator: Has he ever made a settlement — yeah, he did (Michelsen: Sure. He's took 5¢ the last time) — where — where the skilled trades — do the skilled tra — well, lemme — here — here — here's what I'm tryin' — would these skilled trades, when — when — / do they get —

Michelsen: (Over Mediator above) Is he talkin' only skilled trades? Is that all he said to you?

Mediator: No.

Michelsen: His offer was skilled trades and other day workers.

Mediator: Oh, yeah. (Michelsen: Yeah) And that's what I mean. Now, these other day workers and the skilled trades, when he gives an offer, does the skilled trades get the day workers' offer and then this on top? Do they come out with more, or / do they come out even?

Michelsen: (Over Mediator above) No, they get the same. Skilled trades and day workers last time got 5¢ — all that group. In other words, everybody who was not participating in the incentive system got 5¢ an hour more. But what it resulted was with the — the 2 base rate system. You've got a rate for the day workers which is 5¢ higher than the incentive workers. If you gave another nickel, it would be 10¢.

Mediator: (Someone else starts to speak) But it all evens out.

Michelsen: Right.

Loring: Well, i — it would be (Michelsen: No, it doesn't even out. Even out in what respect, George?) over and above the incentive workers, George. It would be over and above the majority of the workers, because all your incentive workers would get a certain amount; the day workers would get that, also, plus / xx.

Mediator: (Over Loring above) Are the skills worker — are the skilled workers d — on incentive?

Loring: No.

Mediator: No. Well, let's say a man gets $1.80 an hour. (Loring: Yeah) He's skilled worker. Let's say that a nickel was granted. Let's say the company agreed on a nickel.

Michelsen: To everybody?

Mediator: To everybody.

Michelsen: All right.

Pranis: (At same time as Michelsen above) He'd have $1.85.

Mediator: Now, he'd have $1.85. (Michelsen: Right) Now, what is the union after for the skilled / workers?

Pranis: (Over Mediator above) 20% in addition / to that.

Mediator: (Over Pranis above) Aren't they aft — in addition to the (Pranis: Yes) whatever is (Pranis: Yeah) offered. / That's what I — that's what — yeah.

[Pranis and someone else talk intermittently over Mediator above.]

Mediator: So, in other words, when the negotiations are over, the union wants —

Pranis: They'd have 46¢ — forty — 30¢ (Michelsen: They want —) — 31¢.

Mediator: They want the skilled workers to have a higher settlement than the day worker.

Pranis: Right.

Loring: Yes.

Pranis: Right.

Mediator: That's the objective.

Loring: Uh-huh.

Mediator: That's what I thought. Well, that's the way I understood it, but I didn't (laughing slightly) / say anything.

Pranis: (Over Mediator above) Sure. They wanted a 35-hour week for everybody plus 20% more (Mediator: Yeah) for the skilled / worker.

Mediator: (Over Pranis above) Well, I think we can — about that, I think yo — you can forget about the 35-hour week. I think that's knocked in a — into (Someone laughs slightly) a cocked hat, but I think the — what you do have on the table now is the skilled (Loring: Yeah) problem. Uh — is it a problem?

Michelsen: (Someone else starts to speak at same time) With — not with me.

Loring: It's a problem (Mediator: In the shop?) with them, but I think he's gonna have a hard time (Michelsen: I don't think it's a problem with him, really) — I don't — the — with the people. I think the majority — you see, it's / a small group out of the xx.

Michelsen: (Over Loring above) I think the skilled trades people want more money, and certainly we would not be against actually giving it to them (pause), particularly because of the labor market conditions in the — in the skilled trade. But I don't see how he can sell that of itself as a settlement / xx.

Pranis: (Over Michelsen above) Bill, he couldn't go back with a couple, 3¢ to everybody in some form x just a lotta talk and a nickel to the skilled trades.

Michelsen: Well, I don't know —

Pranis: Even though it might be all right to us, how could he sell that?

Espig: By having the people there at the meetings to handle it.

Michelsen: Sure, he could sell that. He could. I — I would — I could see that (Espig: Sure) — selling the nickel plus some fringes to everybody (Espig: He could sell —), 'cause it's not just skilled trades; it's gonna be day workers. It's janitors, it's matrons.

Pranis: It's everybody. xxxxx.

?: Yeah. (Pause)

Pranis: This 3/4 of a cent you talked about — that's the same group you're talking about — not only skilled trades but everybody on (Michelsen: Uh-huh) day work.

Michelsen: Uh-huh. May be a little less than that now, but prob'ly about the same.

Mediator: Well, gentlemen (pause), there — there are the 3 roads. Suppose I leave you for awhile. (Michelsen: O.K.) You gentlemen think about 'em, talk about 'em, and when you're through, call me in and we'll look at it together.

Michelsen: O.K.

[Mediator withdraws from the management caucus room at 5:22 P.M. He stops by the union caucus room only long enough to report that the management group have gone into caucus and will let him know when they are ready for him again; then he leaves the union group, also. He is called back by the management caucus group at 6:10 P.M. Michelsen's opening remark, addressed to Observer — "You ready, disc jockey?" — sets off a short period of light exchange and laughter.]

Michelsen: Well, George, we've been kickin' around some numbers here. We — we are — we wanta get your thinking here. We're right at our original position, and now the question is, how do you present this — i — if we are gonna present it, and that raises the big question, and we're sorta torn between 2 approaches: Number 1, that we terminate the meetings tonight and take a long chance that they'll resume in the morning, at which time we'll spread out our 2¢; the other is to spread it out now, or sometime after — sometime this evening, with a pretty definite understanding that even though we were to continue meeting we wouldn't go beyond that point. In other words, if John suddenly found out that he didn't have to go shopping after he hears that we've got 2¢ on the table and suddenly decides he doesn't have a — the meeting tomorrow isn't important and he'll stick around and see what he can do with the 2¢.

Mediator: I can answer that right (Michelsen: Yeah) away. That one I can answer. I don't know what the next one is, but I can tell you the (Michelsen: Uh) answer to that one. (Michelsen: H'm) Uh — if you were gonna put 2¢ out and then spread it out — if you put t — 2¢ out tonight and c (Michelsen: Uh) — we called the meeting for tomorrow, that would be bad.

Michelsen: Oh, no. That's what I mean.

Mediator: That wouldn't be good.

Michelsen: No.

Mediator: Better —

Michelsen: (At same time as Mediator above) I don't want — I don't want / the meeting tomorrow.

Mediator: (Over Michelsen above) Better not to put (Michelsen: Yeah) 2¢ out, if you're going to meet tomorrow.

Michelsen: Right. Well, that's what I'm saying, that if we put it out now, we don't want a meeting tomorrow. (Pause)

Mediator: (Michelsen starts to speak at same time) If you put the 2 out.

Michelsen: Yeah.

Mediator: Oh, I / see.

Michelsen: (Over Mediator above) I mean, I'm concerned with the fact that we put the 2¢ out now, John says, "Oh, boy (clapping hands). Goody, goody. Collective bargaining." We stay here till 2:00 o'clock tonight, we get you to get us back here at 8:00 o'clock in the morning and he really tries to — to — to move that 2¢ into something. (Mediator: Oh) We don't wanta do that. We're not gonna move it (Mediator: Yeah), so there's no point in our — we — we question, for that reason, whether it's advisable to put it out now or to take the chance that they'll come back tomorrow morning, at which time we'll put it out. In other words, it would be out for such a long period of time that they'd sorta get used to depreciating 2¢ to the point where they'd — really would be appreciated. The other is to now go in and — and talk benefits: changing the group insurance coverage from (pause) \$7.50 a day — hospitalization — to \$9.00 a day; changing the scale of — of incidental expenses from \$75.00 at each illness to \$180.00 — all of that great change is gonna cost us a half-a-cent, and they're not asking us that; putting another cent in pension plan, which the union's pension committee, together with ours and the actuary's, can decide whether it will be funded, which would mean that the cent would go directly into our severance pay plan, or whether it — it would not be funded, it would go only for pension benefits. See, we have a — a severance feature in our plan so that a portion of the company's contribution — it's now $6\frac{1}{2}$¢ — be put into — $6\frac{1}{2}$¢ an hour for each employee goes into the pension fund. $4\frac{1}{2}$¢ of that $6\frac{1}{2}$ goes into an employee's individual account and if he leaves the company for any reason after 2 years of service, he t — he picks up that $4\frac{1}{2}$-cent fund and takes it with him as severance pay. (Mediator: Uh-huh) In other words, we're saving in a deferred saving, actually (Mediator: $4\frac{1}{2}$ an hour), about ninety — \$93.00 a year per employee, and it's compounded semi-annually — or, annually — interest. So that we would be willing to put a cent into this plan — another one — and it could go either into the funding — the vesting — which would mean we'd be saving a cent for them every hour, or it could be used to increase the pension benefits. See, when you put this into the severance pay fund, from an actuarial point of view you don't get much use of that cent for pension benefits. You just — because of the great frequency of severances it's — it's not there for pension benefits. You get the use of maybe 1/3 of the cent for the pension benefits, whereas 2/3 of it you wipe off as actually deferred savings. We have no feeling as to whether the cent should be funded or unfunded, and we would leave that to the discretion of the committee sitting with our actuary who would advise them, and they could decide on whether it would go in or out of the — the vesting. That's a cent and a half. And then additional 4¢ — 4/10ths of a cent which we are now paying for the group insurance, which takes us up to 1.9 — something like that. Now (pause), there are ways of changing that, or there are ways of even holding — even exceeding it by throwing in, either as a substitute for, let's say, the hospitalization improvement — changing the daily benefit from 7.50 to $9.00, which we think should be done, and changing the additional expense benefit from $75.00 to $180.00 — that's for additional expenses for anaesthesia and all the rest — X-rays, and stuff — not putting that in, but putting in 5¢ an hour improvement for the skilled trades people, which would cost us a half-a-cent. Just skilled trades. That excluded day — other day workers. In other words, we'd spend (Mediator: 5¢ an hour) for skilled trades — yeah. Skilled trades only. (Mediator: Uh-huh) Now, that would — that's exactly the same cost as the hospitalization improvement. The advantage of putting it in is — could be obvious, if that's something the union wants. The disadvantage is that it's the skilled trades people, and a great many of the female employees I don't think are gonna be interested in it, whereas the — may be more interested in — from my point of view, and I'm tryin' to be as unpaternalistic as possible, I'd rather see the company spend their money to improve the hospital — hospitalization, which gets far more usage than the skilled trades wage rates.

Mediator: Uh-huh.

Michelsen: Now, that's what I would wanta talk. I would wanta keep away until I was forced to mention that that costs 2¢. I'd wanta (Mediator: Sure!) talk $9.00 a day improvement in the group insurance, taking care of the additional cost — changing that from $75.00 to $180.00. And I'd want it presented that way to the membership. (Pause) Now, that's not an uncommon collective bargaining settlement these days. There are a great many reopeners that aren't touching wages (Mediator: Uh-huh); they're improving the pension plans, they're improving the group insurance plan. And this union, after having gotten a package — 15¢, the last one 3¢ — 18¢, as far as I'm concerned could go back with their hands pretty clean, saying, "We've improved the group insurance, and we've improved the (pause) pension plan, and we've got (pause) this additional improvement over and above the cost which the company is obligated to meet, and we're gonna get them to carry that, and we'll get those s.o.b.'s next October on wages." Now, I (pause) — my recommendation to the company has been that, and I'm — I'm —

Mediator: To go after the fringe.

Michelsen: For that reason.

Mediator: Uh-huh.

Michelsen: I mean (pause), right now our company would — u — unless I convened the company's Board of Directors or the ones who deal with me (Mediator: Uh-huh), they'd reject 5¢ quicker than the union would reject a cent.

Mediator: Uh-huh. (Rather long pause)

Michelsen: So I — I wanta — one of the reasons, not only from the — from the personnel administration point of view, I — I'd like to see these plans improved. Uh (pause) — I — I think that they take a lot of explanation in terms of — it's easy to say 2¢. That doesn't mean anything. But I'd rather talk about from 7.50 a day to $9.00 a day, and from $75.00 to — $190.00 — 80.00 in additional benefits, and improving the pension plan (pause) — carrying this additional cost. And (slight pause) that's it. I'd be willing to go, if pushed to the end, to throw in another nickel for skilled trades, which would take it to $2\frac{1}{2}$¢, but not tonight.

Mediator: Well, do I understand, then, that what you would like to do would be throw a total package of what amounts to 1.9 or 2¢ (Michelsen: Yeah), and that would cover these increased pension and hospital benefits? Right?

Michelsen: I'm suggesting that, or substituting for the hospitalization the skilled trades thing, if that's the hottest item. (Mediator: Uh —) See, one of the things that we're doing which is a little unorthodox is that we're giving the — everything we're giving the union they haven't asked for. None of these things are issues with them. None of these are their demands. (Mediator: Uh-huh) So that in effect I'm going in, which is the fact, and completely ignore their request and give 'em what I think I wanta give 'em. (Mediator: Uh-huh) And I'm not tryin' to be Sam Klinger about it. I mean, I'm tryin' to make 2¢ sound like 10¢. (Mediator: Uh-huh) Now, it may not sound like / 10¢ to you, but —

Mediator: (Over Michelsen above) Well, then, see — then, in order to — then your other objective — the one you mentioned earlier was to not let them go to the meeting at — with you at 4 — 4/10ths. You want to go (Michelsen: Oh, yes. That's right) — if they go to the meeting. Then, in that case, I would say that it would be best that you submit it now — your 2¢, because (pause), (1), you may have trouble getting them into a meeting tomorrow. I may have trouble if he's — if he's serious about this meeting of his. And if he wouldn't meet tomorrow you'd never have an opportunity to get the 2¢. (Michelsen: That's right) So it might be well to throw it out, but you may as well be prepared for — for this: it will be rejected. (Michelsen: Uh-huh) That I think you expect, though. Then, following that, we would have to have a — a brief separated meeting here (Michelsen: Uh-huh) to decide the next step, whether we're going to — what we're — well, the next step (Michelsen: Uh-huh) — you know, how we're going to adjourn, so forth. Now (pause), if I understand you right, summing up, you're saying this, that of the 3 avenues, or any avenues that are open, the one that you would prefer to follow now would be the one that — where you could talk about these pension in — or — or the hospital, or the tool — or do you intend to submit, in this, alternatives?

Michelsen: Huh-un.

Mediator: Just one — you decide on one.

Michelsen: Uh-huh.

Mediator: Well, then, if I were you, if you'll permit me to throw this thought out, I would s (Michelsen: I sure will) — I would stay away from the tool — skilled trades (Michelsen: Yeah. All right), because if he's going to push you on that later (Michelsen: Yeah) — if he is, and if he — what you would be doin' would be opening the door on that and (Michelsen: Yeah) he'd see an early wedge. So far you have only talked about the 4/10ths of a cent to take care of (pause) increased (pause) costs, wasn't it?

Michelsen: Uh- / huh.

Mediator: (Over Michelsen above) What was that 4 — whatever that 4/10ths was for. So you wouldn't be deviating; you would be following (Michelsen: Uh-huh) that same pattern by talking about (Michelsen: Uh-huh) health — increased health benefits, or whatever it is. Then, when the right time came — see, then (pause) when —
[Tape changed]

... That's what I would do. Then if ya had to shift later, which you
probably will, they would say, "Take it from there and put it here."
(Pause) (?: Uh-huh) But right now I'm afraid that if you even indicate that you're <u>thinking</u> about skilled trades — unless you <u>want</u> to.
Unless / you want —

Michelsen: (Over Mediator above) No. No. / No.

Mediator: (Over Michelsen above) But if you're n — if you don't want to,
I / think x —

Michelsen: (Over Mediator above) No, I think your reasoning's sound in
that.

Mediator: It would be best to stay away, because you'll open a door of
thought right there and (Michelsen: Yeah) they'll figure, "Well" —
and so far, all through these meetings, you have been standing pretty
firm and, aside from money, the application of what you have offered
has been for Blue Cross, or whatever it is, and here you come up with
another p — proposal, and this 2d proposal is in the <u>same vein</u> (pause),
and that's going to — then they're going to figure, "Well, by God, we
have to dislodge him from that kind of thinking." And any move that
you make they'll consider a vic — consider it a victory. And it really
won't be a victory in view of the fact that you're gonna — you're gonna
have to move there (laughing slightly), anyway, and it's one of your
alternatives (Michelsen: Uh-huh) <u>when</u> the right time comes. Now,
if you're in accord with that and you don't have 5¢ to wrap this up
(Michelsen: Uh-huh), then I would say you (Michelsen: Yeah) toss
out your 2. And about tomorrow — well, I don't think we can talk
about tomorrow until we see what kind of a reaction ya get from your
(Michelsen: Uh-huh) proposal. And I think we can talk about tomorrow
after we (Michelsen: Yeah) come back. What d'you think about this?
(Pause)

Michelsen: Oughta have dinner / now?

Mediator: (Over Michelsen above) It's half past 6:00 and I think we
oughta have somepin' to eat.

Michelsen: Yeah, I think that would be better.

Mediator: 'Cause if you throw this out on an empty stomach (?: Yeah)
right now (Michelsen laughs heartily, and one or 2 others), boom!

Michelsen: Well, that's what we want — our little boom.

Mediator: Yeah, but I want the <u>right</u> kind of a boom. (Espig laughs heartily) I don't want <u>that</u> kind of a boom. See, that kind of boom is without thinking. (Michelsen: Yeah) Aggravated people never do think
right, and hungry people are aggravated.

Pranis: Is <u>that</u> what's the matter, huh?

Michelsen: You're right.

Mediator: I — you got 2 of 'em up there walkin' up and down, pacin'.
And one (Michelsen: Yeah) guy said, "When the hell are we gonna
eat? Are we gonna get outa here? Are we gonna / eat?"

Pranis: (Over Mediator above) Stan Wollman and / Tom Saunders,
prob'ly.

Mediator: (Over Pranis above) And he was hungry, I could see. See,
these — we see it. It's a strange thing. Now, you people — business
people, industry people — you're trained. You're in these things at
your work. You're used to offices, and you're used to sitting for long
periods of time, working on problems.

Michelsen: We're used / to not eating.
Mediator: (Over Michelsen above) These — and (Michelsen laughs
slightly) sometimes not eating. But these fellows — the committees
— they're manual workers, and the strain of this in these conference
rooms — you'd be surprised how it physically wilts them — the biggest men! They — you see them a — after — when there's a test —
you'll see the union leaders; they're all right. They're on — they're
awake. They'll go all night long. But you see the others dropping
like flies. You'll see them with their head on the table; you'll see
them walkin' up and down; and toward the — I had the Smith Forge
case, and we had all those boilermakers and riveters and — we had
about 32, I think — I — in there. It was just a — ya — came 3:00
o'clock in the morning. If you ever saw! It looked like a — a (pause)
— a D.P. camp (Someone laughs slightly) the way they were all
layin' around, sitting on the floor (One or 2 laugh slightly) and playing cards, some with their heads on the table and others pacin' up
and down. They just can't take it — the — the manual workers — the
physical workers. And (pause) they're startin' to pace u — 'course,
ya c — Bernice and the other — Gambon — they're used to it. Well,
I think — I think it would be in order to get somepin' to eat. Even if
we didn't stay very late I think we oughta eat.
Michelsen: Yeah.
Mediator: Wait'll I talk to them.

Union Caucus - C (6:30 P.M.)

Gambon: I don't know. How are you?
Mediator: Fine. This is Observer. (Meyer laughs)
Gambon: Oh, xx, Observer. You've been away so damn long, but ya —
ya don't look very much older.
Mediator: I — I was — when I came in here I thought it was another conference I had (Gambon: Oh) scheduled. (Pause) That reminds me.
We had a si — we had a situation durin' the war where there was mass
production mediation. Durin' the war be one group right after another.
I — it was un — not unusual for — for us to hold 3 and 4 conferences
in one day, such as they were. I mean, you could just (Meyer: Uh-
huh) give 'em a lick and a promise and you were off to another place.
In the buildings where our offices were located there were just people
coming in and out rooms. Story goes, and it's true, and that one of
our mediators, having so many conferences he was confused and the
fellow that had the one conference scheduled for that day with the XYZ,
he was ill and he called up and said he wouldn't be in and the girl at
the desk forgot to make record of that. So one of the other mediators
who had another conference scheduled came and walked into the wrong
conference room. And he sat down and started the sessions going and
they started arguing their points, and he said — he said, Jesus, none
of it sounded familiar to him. (Someone laughs slightly) He had held
one meeting with this group that he had before, but he had forgotten
'em, because he had had so many conferences in between. The guy
had walked into the wrong conference. (Laughs, joined by Gambon)
He sat there all day. But the people that came to — he was to mediate

with was in another room (One of girls laughs) waiting, and they had
    nobody. (Laughs slightly)
Gambon: And they (Several laugh heartily) were cussin' him, I bet.
Mediator: Uh (rather long pause) — John, let me put it this way. I'm
    cognizant of the fact that you have an appointment tonight. Uh — I
    believe it may be well for you — you to stretch it a little. I would
    like to — I wanta get (rapping on table) them on the table, and I'm
    working on something, and I want a move of some kind. And while I
    don't wanta report out complete success — I'm not finished — I do
    think it would be well that we, if necessary, spend an extra hour or 2.
    So, I don't think I'd have time to do what I want to do before dinner,
    so I would recommend, if you could, call off your appointment, let us
    have a quick dinner and get back here, and I wanta bring 'em in here
    jointly. / He —
Gambon: (Over Mediator above) All right! They'll blame it on the gov-
    ernment. (Pause, then Meyer laughs slightly)
Mediator: I don't like the idea / xx —
Gambon: (Over Mediator above) Call my wife, will ya, and make an ex-
    cuse for me, will ya, George?
    [One girl and one boy, and Mediator, talk and laugh at once. Mediator
    says, "Who's gonna call mine?"]
Mediator: The only difference is, mine's pretty well — used to be a
    problem, but these days it's no problem. She's pretty well used to it.
    Sometimes / I go out —
Gambon: (Over Mediator above) Huh, my wife says, "Well, you home?
    When'd you come home?"
Mediator: Yeah. (One of boys laughs)
Gambon: All right. Will do.
    [Mediator continues briefly with the topic of absences from home
    while mediating during the war years. Laughter takes over in the
    group, including Meyer and Gambon.]

Management Caucus - E (6:35 P.M.)

Mediator: We'll go to dinner. (Michelsen: Yeah) We'll be back 20 min-
    utes of 8:00. I said to John, "I know you have — I'm cognizant of the
    fact that you have an appointment. (Michelsen laughs slightly) How-
    ever, I have been in session with the company and your — your com-
    mittee all afternoon, and I do not believe that I have time enough to
    continue the talks that I want to continue, so I would recommend that
    you cancel your appointment and let us go to dinner and get back here
    about 20 minutes to 8:00." He said, "All right. I'll blame it on the
    government. Will you call my wife?" I said, "All right. Will you call
    mine?" (Michelsen laughs) So (laughing) we left it that way. (Michel-
    sen continues laughing slightly) 20 minutes of 8:00. So, they're leaving
    now — startin' to leave. Now, let me — let me give you some good
    advice — real good advice. (Michelsen: Yeah) If you wanta get back
    here at 20 minutes of 8:00, don't go to Clark's. (Several laugh)
    [There are a few further comments about Clark's Restaurant. Then
    Mediator entertains group until 6:40 P.M. with a recounting of experi-
    ences with negotiators who have had ulcers.]

Management Caucus - F (8:00 P.M.)

Mediator: Uh — well, picking this up where we left it off — let's see, we were thinking about, (1), whether we would — oh! — that you would go in and talk on the basis of (pause) / x —

Michelsen: (Over Mediator above) Improving 2 of our benefits (Mediator: Yeah) and carrying this additional 4/10ths of a cent. I'm willing to say, Len, if (pause) — I would certainly prefer it, from my point of view, is that we would say we'd guarantee these benefits regardless of costs in the future. (Pause)

Loring: My question, George — I think we skirted around it a little bit. Do you feel that it wouldn't be a good risk to not make the offer tonight but to make it — try — assume we can meet tomorrow and make it tomorrow? (Rather long pause)

Mediator: This one here?

Loring: Yeah.

Mediator: Uh — no-o. See, I think this way. I think that if you make it tonight (pause) — if you make it toni — uh — as far as tomorrow is concerned — see, I don't want to — I think it would be wrong to say to him now that we want him to give up his staff meeting (rather long pause) — oh, you mean if you <u>didn't</u> make it tonight (Loring: Yeah) and give it tomorrow.

Loring: Uh-huh. (Mediator sighs deeply) I mean, i — is it a good risk to hope that we can give it tomorrow?

Mediator: The danger would be, see, he may (pause) go to that meeting, or he may say that he can't meet tomorrow.

Loring: All right, now. A — as against that, we give it tonight and then he crosses us up and tells us that he will <u>not</u> go to the meeting tomorrow but wants to meet with us. We've — we don't have any more to talk about.

Mediator: Well —

Michelsen: We don't talk / about it.

Mediator: (Over Michelsen above) Uh — you don't talk about it. See, I don't think it's much of a problem now as to when you submit this, whether it's tonight t — or tomorrow morning (pause), because (slight pause) evidently your thinking is that you're going to offer this and then see what is played back to you. (Pause) If they play back to you an indication that they're ready to do business, completely, that's all right. We know where we're going then. Then we'd know whether we'd want a meeting tomorrow. But if the play-back is, "To heck with this. We're going through with our meeting," and so forth, then I would say, let 'em have their meeting.

Loring: Uh-huh.

Michelsen: What meeting you talkin' about?

Loring: Member — / ship.

Mediator: (Over Loring above) Membership meeting.

Michelsen: Yeah. Oh, sure. Uh —

Mediator: Let 'em have their meeting, then. (Pause) But if you are (slight pause) — if you are — if you want to wrap this up, you're either going to wrap it up (long pause) — ya can't — see, it's spalu — there are a few if's and but's. The reaction that comes from this offer I think will tell you and me whether we would want a meeting tomorrow. (Pause) Now, assuming that the play-back is <u>good</u> (pause), then the rest — the next would be this. Does the company want to pay, or get up to the figure that it would take at this time to settle it? If so, then a meeting would be in order. If not, then your 2¢ is out and they go to their meeting. Then ya hold your breath.

Michelsen: What d'ya mean, the 2¢ is out?

Mediator: On the table.

Michelsen: Oh, it's out on the table. Yeah.

Mediator: Oh, I should've said that. Yes. I meant to say <u>out</u> on the table. Yeah. Then — then you hold your breath as to what they'll do, whether they'll strike Monday morning or <u>not</u> strike. See, we don't know what kinda — how they're gonna play this thing. Uh (rather long pause) — that's — that's — that's the best I can — without — I'll tell ya a lot more after this caucus — or, after this joint meeting. I think I'll be able to tell you a lot more that I can't tell you now. (Loring: Uh-huh) Because right now I have 2 — where there's alternatives. Prob'ly after that meeting we'll be able to just wipe one out and say, "This is where it's going." (Pause)

Michelsen: Uh-huh.

Mediator: Agree with that?

Michelsen: Yeah. (Pause)

Mediator: Are you (Michelsen: Yeah —) peop — are you — go ahead.

Michelsen: I think that — that (pause) — I think we oughta get the money out now, rather than take the long chance of / having —

Mediator: (Over Michelsen above) I don't think it makes much / difference.

Espig: (Over Mediator above) Well, you want it on the record to get it to the meeting.

Michelsen: Yeah.

Espig: As long as we want that, that's it.

Mediator: You may as well do it tonight as tomorrow morning (Michelsen: Yeah), see, and if there's any — if there's any indication — if there's a play-back that is healthy and I catch it there, I'm — I'm going to (pause) — regardless of what plans you may have, I'm gonna tell you about it. (Michelsen: Uh-huh) Then <u>you're</u> gonna make the decision. (Michelsen: Sure) (Pause) But if there's no play-back (pause), it's just, "Well, that'll never go over," or, "We won't take that," and then to me in c — when I'm in there with them alone and it's <u>still</u> that way, well, then we'll know that they (pause) — it might be well to let 'em have their meeting. <u>Or</u>, maybe (pause) after their meeting (pause) there may be (pause) something develop. You never know. (Pause) So it's — it's sorta if, and, or but right (?: Uh-huh) now until this session is over. (Rather long pause) But if you — y — you'd have to get it on the table, and I think tonight is as good as tomorrow, because if you put it out tomorrow we still have to get the play-back — the reaction. (Loring: Uh-huh) (Michelsen: Yeah) So we can get it tonight as well as tomorrow. In fact, it might even be better to put it out tonight. Then it'll give us more thinking time. (Pause) (Loring: O.K.!) Because, if it's 2¢ and then we're stopped there, the only thing is — a — well, they would go to their meeting after tomorrow morning's meeting with 2¢, if that were the case. So the only difference would be we just wouldn't have a meeting tomorrow, but they'd still have the 2¢ that they would've had if we had a meeting, unless you can throw in some reason that might change that that I am not aware of (Loring: Yeah), or not familiar with.

Loring: Uh-huh.

Michelsen: No, the only disadvantage of — in making the offer now is that they're gonna — it's gonna be around longer. That's all. (Mediator: Ye-ah) And since the probability of it not changing is very great, it's just gonna stick around at 2¢ for a long while. (Rather long pause)

Mediator: Well, x for a couple hours.

Michelsen: Yeah. It's a relatively short time (Mediator: Oh, yes. It's — it's —), depending on when you (Mediator: I don't think it's long enough to hurt you) recess tonight and when you reconvene in the morning.

Mediator: Uh — you see, bear in mind — see, you're in a good position here. Bear in mind — both of us are. When you put this 2¢ out (pause), if the meeting isn't held tomorrow it's not being held tomorrow because John Gambon said he (tapping on table) couldn't meet tomorrow (Michelsen: Yeah), and that is on his back. (Pause)

Michelsen: Don't forget when we offer 2¢ we're increasing our position by about 300%. (Someone laughs slightly)

Mediator: Never thought of it that way. (Someone laughs)

Michelsen: You don't get many offers go up 300%.

Mediator: 300%. (Pranis and someone else laugh)

Michelsen: The union's only reduced theirs 50. (Someone laughs slightly)

Mediator: That's right. / xx —

Michelsen: (Over Mediator above) I'm a great man for percentages when they're to my advantage. (Laughs)

Loring: John can agree to that. (One or 2 laugh slightly)

Mediator: Uh — are you prepared to make your (Michelsen: You bet!) address?

Michelsen: Yes, sir. I'm just gonna tell 'em we're gonna change — I — I'll tell ya just what I'm gonna say. We're prepared to — to make some proposals for changes in some of our employee benefits. I may preface it by saying that — that (pause) we still are not interested in any wage increases and we are recommending that this following — these following improvements.

Mediator: If — I — I would like to caution you not to say that this package is 1.9.

Michelsen: No, I'm not. I'm g — I'm not.

Mediator: If they / ask you —

Michelsen: (Over Mediator above) In fact, it's so close I'm gonna say (Mediator: If they ask you, let it —) it's close to 2¢.

Mediator: That's right.

Michelsen: Yeah. Oh, don't worry about that. I see enough of the grocery supermarket produce to not (Mediator laughs) wanta knock it down to 99¢ from $1.00. (Rather long pause)

Mediator: All right?

Joint Meeting - B (8:15 P.M.)

Mediator: Well (rather long pause), as both of you know, we've been in separate conferences here, and we have gone over and over the positions of both parties, and suffice it to say, s'pose I turn it over to Bill for purpose of his givin' his — givin' us his latest thinking on the position of the negotiations. So, Bill, motion's in — (voice dies out).

Michelsen: All right. Well (pause), here's what I'm gonna propose. We're proposing changes in some of our employee benefit plans (pause) of this kind. We're proposing that the group insurance program be modified: the — the daily hospitalization benefit is increased from $7.50 a day to $9.00 a day; we're proposing that the special services be changed from $75.00 to $180.00 in the hospitalization portion of our group insurance plan; we're proposing that the pension plan, terms of its cost to the company, be upped from $6\frac{1}{2}$¢ to $7\frac{1}{2}$ and that the Joint Retirement Committee meet with the actuary to determine how that additional 1¢ an hour shall be integrated into the plan of those — whether it has — will be vested or funded into the severance pay, thereby decreasing its value as a pension, for pension use, or whether it be used only for pension purposes — in other words, used in the contingent fund. At this point we have no opinion as to which of those 2 uses it be used for and believe it should be something worked out by the — the Retire — Joint Retirement Committee. In addition to that we propose, as we have in the past, that — past sessions here, that we will absorb this additional cost of approximately 4/10ths ¢ which this plan is now costing us over $6.00. I'm also willing to agree that the company will guarantee these benefits, regardless of increased cost. In other words, we would agree to these benefits as being available to the employee and that if the cost would go up in the future, that additional cost would automatically be borne by the company. In other words, the — the contract would specify the benefits rather than the cost to the company. (Rather long pause) And that's our suggestion. (Long pause)

Gambon: How many ya got — 2¢, Bill, here?

Michelsen: Just about, John.

Gambon: H'm. (Rather long pause) Well, buddy (throwing pencil onto table), for the time you spent gettin' to this point you certainly disappointed me. (Rather long pause) Committee — I'd like to meet with my own committee on this, although I don't want ya to be under any misapprehensions as to how I feel about it. I'm still looking at these financial reports. I'm lookin' very carefully at the 8th, 9th, and 10th periods, as I told you before, and I'm lookin' at the first period of '53. I'm looking at the fact that there's over $583,000.00 of lost items in recorders without amplifiers which you have out of here. I'm lookin' at the profit-sharing that's been goin' on since '50. I'm lookin' at the profit-sharing that went on the first quarter of this year, where you've already paid out the equivalent of $4\frac{1}{2}$¢ per hour for 1400 employees to about 114 of your employees. I'm looking at $160,000.00 which you quote over here in your figures that you would have had greater profit by $160,000.00 if you hadn't these lost items. That $160,000.00 is equivalent to about an 8-cent-an-hour increase for 114 employees. You're not makin' any offers yet, Bill, as far as I'm concerned. I think our people are goin' to tell you just as emphatically as I'm goin' — I — well, I'm not gonna even bother to try to tell you right now; I'm gonna let them tell you about it, if this is the kind of offer you want me to take back to the membership of Local 89. We

have a pretty good idea of what kind of an answer you're gonna get on it. (Rather long pause) That's all I got to say, George. (Pause)
Mediator: Well, suppose we then —
[Management group prepares to leave.]
Gambon: Oh — oh, Bill, I failed to ask you if this was a final offer. I assumed that since you went through to all this trouble and spent all this time on it that it probably is.
Michelsen: (Going out doorway) Yeah.
Gambon: It is? (Michelsen: Uh-huh) The final offer?
Michelsen: Yeah.
Gambon: For tonight?
Michelsen: The final —

Union Caucus - D (8:20 P.M.)

[Long pause, with Mediator strumming fingers up and down on table.]
Mediator: What does this add up to?
Gambon: I ma — I made a rough guess, 2¢. I mean, there's — those benefits that he threw in there in addition to the 4/10ths ¢ prob'ly equal about 6/10ths of a cent, makin' that a full cent, and he has a full cent in the pension.
[Very long pause, with Mediator strumming on table again.]
Meyer: In other words, before you can realize anything out of this you'd have to get sick. (Gambon: That's right) It's a health benefit.
Gambon: You'd have to get sick, or (Meyer: On pension. [Laughs]) — don't forget, George, that our pension plan — if we were to — to convince an actuary that we would rather have this 1¢ additional go into the severance pay feature, it would advance the 4½¢ in the severance angle to 5½. But you must be with the company 2 years before you're eligible to participate in that plan.
Mediator: Oh. (Pause)
Meyer: Then you'd have to quit to / get it.
Mediator: (Over Meyer above) And a (Gambon: H'm) good portion — y — y — 'bout 1/3rd of your people isn't — aren't qualified? (Slight pause)
Gambon: 1/3rd are?
Mediator: Aren't? Are not?
Gambon: Oh. I — I (Meyer: 'Bout that many) — I don't think we have that (One of girls: Yeah) many. Right now?
One of girls: Yeah.
Meyer: (At same time as girl above) About that.
Gambon: Yeah?
[Saunders, Gambon, and Meyer talk among themselves, sometimes at once, for short period.]
Mediator: Did you say you wanted to discuss this?
Gambon: Well, yes, I'd like to (Mediator: All right) hold a very (laughing slightly) short meeting.
Mediator: Call me, then, when you're x.
Gambon: All right, George.
[While waiting for the union group to call him back, Mediator puts in 5 minutes in the management caucus room. Michelsen prompts two

exchanges with him, though neither is sustained very long:

Michelsen: You don't seem tremendously happy, George.

Mediator: Well, I'm not disappointed. It — that I expected. I was a little disappointed in his saying, "Is this your final offer? Is this your final" — matter of fact, I mentioned — I said to him, "That's a hell of a question to ask anybody in negotiations. Maybe it is! But even if it isn't you make it more difficult by asking it."

Michelsen: Well, can only expect one answer. (Pause)

Then:

Michelsen: Did they seem surprised at the nature of the offer?

Mediator: Wasn't a comment from anybody but Gambon. (Pause) / Not a soul com —

Michelsen: (Over Mediator above) I don't mean the amount. I mean the way / in w —

Mediator: (Over Michelsen above) Bernice — oh. In / the what?

Michelsen: (Over Mediator above) The fact that it was in hospitalization we mentioned.

Mediator: Uh-h, no. But I'm — I can say now that I'm glad that you — that you stayed on hospital (Michelsen: Uh-huh) (pause), because the benefits of doing that, I think, will, on settlement day, if there is a settlement day, show up (slight pause) — pay off then. 'Cause he's — he's now gonna believe that this is where your sights are and he's then going to try to get off this tact or track. He's —

There is a knock at the door at 8:35 P.M., and Mediator is notified that the union caucus group is ready for him.]

Mediator: I thought it would be accepted.

Gambon: Huh? It's accepted as a prime (Meyer: x) example of the stupidity of some management — stupidity in the sense that when you're trying to buck a deadline and trying to reach a sensible agreement. It may not be stupidity from the standpoint of trying to take a strategic position. And I don't think it's even a good strategic position, because if I were him I'd have done a lot better than that before I let the union go to the membership, particularly when the union is contemplating a strike vote.

Meyer: Well, there's another little gimmick in that, too, George. In our contract, any dividends realized from the insurance (Gambon: H'm) policy revert back to the company so that by paying this additional cost, if there were dividends on the insurance they'd revert back to the company and the additional cost would be m — would not be as great as they estimate it right now.

Mediator: That's true. (Long pause)

Gambon: Well, based on what he had to say there a moment ago about the final offer, period, that seems to me about as far as we can go tonight, wouldn't you think? (Pause, with Mediator strumming on table)

Mediator: Yeah. Uh —

Gambon: (At same time as Mediator above) I still think the man has to be convinced. (Long pause)

Mediator: As for timing, in your next step I (long pause) — what d'you think he wants you to do? Think he wants you to take a strike vote? He have anything to gain from it?

Gambon: Does he have anything to gain? (Pause) Oh, he could, if he thought he was right. I assume he thought if — if he thought that the union — well, the committee went to the union and asked for a strike vote and didn't get it, he'd be in a beautiful position from now on out, and I think he may be counting on the fact that perhaps he's built up a fear complex in the minds of the people so far as job security goes. And that's where he's gonna find out he's made an awfully grave mistake. (Rather long pause)

Meyer: George, well, d'you know why h — his offer took this form, when we didn't even specify it in any of the things that we dropped?

Mediator: I thought of that, too. Evidently he's (pause) — his tact has been that, "If we're goin' to spend any money, why (Gambon: H'm. Well —), we'll spend it where we want to," and (Gambon: I — I'm not too surprised at his —) — o — or he's a strong supporter — I don't know, and only you would know that — of — is he a strong supporter of this kind of a program? Do they / x —

Gambon: (Over Mediator above) A — all I can say about this program, George, is (Mediator: I mean, how much x —) we had to battle like hell with 'em to get insurance and we had to battle like hell (Mediator: Oh) to get pension. They didn't hand it to us on a platter, believe me, and the only reason we got it was because tho — those things become — came into a trend there on the part of unions when it was mostly all fringe negotiations, if you recall. We took the in — we pushed the insurance program in first, and then — oh, couple of months — in fact, Standard Products wasn't done negotiating their pension plan when we slammed that one in. That was back in (slight pause) about '49.

Meyer: We always had the kind you pay for yourself.

Gambon: H'm. We did have the in — insurance plan in there — a group insurance plan which we paid for as well as the company. (Pause) / But —

Mediator: (Over Gambon above) Thinking out loud, what is your opinion of this? (Pause) In your opinion, do you believe that the company is more conciliatory before a strike vote or after?

Gambon: Well, I would say this. We've only had to resort to the strike vote situation for the first time in quite a number of years, back in January when you were (Mediator: Oh) on negotiations the last time.

Mediator: Ya didn't use it the last negotiations?

Gambon: We didn't (Meyer: No) use it in the last reopener, no. We didn't have to, although we were facing almost the same kind of a s — situation. Not quite as firm a position or as a take-it-or-leave-it attitude proposition that we're facing at this moment. We did have to do some — apply some pressures, I mean, through the mediator at that time, and I made it very clear to the mediator that there wasn't gonna be any — when it got down to the point where I figured we were goin' far enough with it, I told him as far as we were concerned they'd better not come back in again un — unless they had an offer that would lo — would at least meet the cost-of-living increase which existed at that time. And as I say, I didn't choose to make any fights then and it wasn't the right time, and decided, "If I'm gonna fight with you and I know I'm gonna run into the same attitude, I'll pick my time to do it." And I say the time has come. Now, he's asking for a fight. Very

frankly, George, I don't see what they hope to gain by it. They — they
may be relying on the fact that there hasn't been a strike since 1936.
Well, the only reason for that has been that we've been able to resolve
our differences. But it's significant to understand that we've been arbitration, now — or we've been in mediation, now, 3 times in a row,
and all s — from '52 on. (Mediator starts to speak) We're running
into arbitration cases for the first time in our bargaining relation-
ships with this company. We just finished one; we got 4 more cases
goin' into arbitration.
Mediator: Never happened before ?
Gambon: Never happened.
Mediator: (In low voice) H'm.
Gambon: So that it's definitely a new company policy, let's face it.
Mediator: Did that all come about with the change from Alexander —
    Alexander always handle your / labor relations ?
Gambon: (Over Mediator above) Yeah. Yeah.
Mediator: Then after he left this ch — or did it come before ?
Gambon: No. This — this particular attitude now is — well, it s — some-
    what began before. I mean, it — the company started taking on a new
    face, oh, I'd say, when Alexandria — Alex — Alexander first came
    there, but, I mean, it was very gradual and a very soft-tread propo-
    sition. They concentrated mostly on reducing costs and wastes
    throughout the plant, particularly up in the front — the offices. But
    it advanced from that to a proposition of w — of a — the union having
    to contend with for some time, now, the Time Study Department try-
    ing all ways and means of changing rates and in lots of — lots of in-
    stances getting around the contract to do it. We're still faced with
    some problems in that direction yet. We ran into a great deal of re-
    sistance and still have job evaluation problems. They had a plan that
    we had in existence at the time we signed the contract back in '49.
    That plan suddenly changed in — we know now around November of
    '49. (Saunders: That was part of the agreement we were here on xxxx)
    And — well, that — well, we didn't know. If you recall, we talked about
    job evaluation plan, and I made a major issue out of that in October.
    We still haven't resolved that completely. They have a completely
    different plan from what was originally put in here when jobs were
    originally evaluated. And whereas we had been getting jobs evaluated
    into higher wage grades, based on changes in job content, pretty
    steadily from 1948 on through '49 and into '50 we suddenly ran into a
    brick wall; and at this moment we're just about ready to begin trying
    to make comparisons between how they evaluated jobs under this plan
    and how they did it under the original plan that was in there. And one
    of the things I was able to force into the contract during the October
    reopener was a proposition that wherever disagreement existed on
    job evaluation disputes, it could go to arbitration. The contract didn't
    provide that until October, so that what we're goin' to do now is when
    we get a couple of good test cases, we're gonna take them to arbitra-
    tion on that and at the same time reopen this question of which job
    evaluation plan is the proper one to be used, hoping that we may be
    able, through arbich — tration, to establish the fact that they changed
    the plan, and in changing it they changed the — the weighted values of
    the various factors in there in order to keep the jobs from going upward.

So that, all in all, it's a big business policy proposition that we're facing up to now, as against a — a family group proposition — "one big happy family," as they used to put it. It's no (laughing slightly) longer a happy family. Hasn't been for quite a few years, now.

Mediator: Could very well be that under the specter of moving South / that —

Gambon: (Over Mediator above) Well, it wouldn't be so bad about that, George — I mean, we can realize the fact that any company has a right to do that kind of thing if they see fit, but the thing that gripes us so bad is the fact — the way they did it. They admit that while we were negotiating with them in October of '52 on a reopener they already had their plans down for the decentralization move. And then they cried the blues, and when they finally brought it out we rapped them about that. They said, "Well, we didn't wanta be accused by the union of trying to use that as a pressure durin' negotiations." But the — the whole thing stinks. And the fact, as I said to ya before, we still can't pin this company down as to what jobs are gonna remain in here. Ya got that plant up in Rome. If they ever put that in operation we may as well say we have nothing. All we know with any kind of degree of certainty in it a'tall is that they have a — a — a lease at 1122 West Oak Street which runs until 1962 with a privilege of the company getting out of the lease in '56. So '56 is as far as we can see anything staying there. (Pause) (Mediator: Uh-huh) I intend to try to make it very clear to the membership of this Local union that if they allow the company to do so, they're gonna pay for the company moving this place right out of the metropolitan area, and if — the least they take the faster they're gonna move out. (Pause) They're not going to lose themselves in Aiken, South Carolina, believe me. I mean, we've already been there; we intend to stay there, too, for that matter, keep after them there or any place else that they go. I don't mean just from the Local level, but I mean from the International union level, too. (Pause) But I have said before to this committee — many of the people on this committee have been on the committee, now, for the last 3 times we've been down here. And I've been saying all along that one of these days you people are gonna have to convince yourselves of one fact, you're gonna have to fight these people out on the bricks, and it's comin' just about to that point. And I was convinced of that back in January and I was more convinced of — of it in October. As I said, I didn't elect to pick that time as a time to fight about it. (Pause) Now, I'm — I'm gettin' to be a little bit fed up with this sort of arrogant attitude of Michelsen. I mean, he — he wants a little bringin' down. Whether he's expressing the feelings of the management generally I'm not quite sure. And as I say, I don't think that the — I can't (slight pause) — can't quite convince myself that Atlas — the Board of Directors — want a strike.

Mediator: Do you know anything about Bill's plans for his future?

Gambon: I know this. (Slight pause) / Uh —

Mediator: (Over Gambon above) Reason I ask, I heard a rumor.

Gambon: I know that he has been offered a job at a much higher salary. I haven't been able to tie down yet which — who the company is, but it wouldn't take me too much find — it wouldn't take too much for me to find out. (Pause)

Mediator: Well, 1 — last meeting (Gambon: Funny part of it is —) we were tryin' to explain his attitude. I was wonderin' whether that had somethin' to do with it.

Gambon: It might! It might! (Rather long pause) The only thing that I know about that is that it's quite a concern. I do think it's a concern in the Midville area. Could be Hercules. Could be any of those larger companies down the line. (Pause) If it's Hercules (Mediator: Well, we get all kind of rumors. We get here —) he's certainly — the kind of policies he's using is fixin' for the kind of labor relations they have with their people. (Slight pause)

Mediator: Is there — I was just wonderin' whether there's any connection between this firm and firm he's going with. Are they — this firm have any —

Gambon: No. I tell ya something very interesting that happened quite a number of years back. Not too long back, either. Alexander mentioned to me one time that they couldn't hope to hold Bill Michelsen too long. So I'm not surprised about this rumor about him mov — pardon me — moving to another company at a larger salary. (Pause) Bill is ambitious, there's no question about it. And —

[Gambon and Mediator continue this topic for several minutes, joined briefly by 3 others. Gambon fills Mediator in on Michelsen's job background. Mediator shifts subject onto an account of some educational conferences he has attended where "experts" on negotiation have mystified the people who actually do negotiating, whereupon Gambon contributes a definition of an expert which provokes widespread laughing.]

Gambon: Well, s — some of these people have some engagements. Some of 'em got — you gotta go to a veterans' meeting, you gotta go to a veterans' meeting, somebody else has to go somewhere else, so I'm gonna ask you to adjourn the meeting for the day, George, and I'll be in touch with you. You gonna be in here tomorrow?

Mediator: Not here. You — you can get me at MO 6-38 / 24.

Gambon: (Over Mediator above) I'll give you a call and let you know what the outcome of the meeting is. (Mediator: Yeah) What is it, George?

Mediator: MO 6-3824. (Pause)

Gambon: Uh-huh.

Mediator: Uh (rather long pause) — you — d'you feel that there's any (slight pause) advantage or disadvantage of meeting tomorrow?

Gambon: I won't meet with 'em tomorrow.

Mediator: Oh, you've got an appointment.

Gambon: Uh-huh. I have — I have a staff meeting over at the district, and I wanta get this report together, that membership meeting.

Mediator: All right. Let me talk to them before we adjourn. Uh — you give me a call. What time's your meeting?

Gambon: 1:00 o'clock.

Mediator: What time will it be over? Well, you can't tell, I guess.

Gambon: Can't tell that.

[Meyer and Saunders each add brief comments, but cannot be understood.]

Gambon: (Over Saunders above) Yeah, it's special meeting. Shouldn't take too long.

Mediator: Is it — where ya hold it?

Gambon: We're holdin' it out at the union hall.

Mediator: Right here — oh, at Oak and Eddy? (Rather long pause) Yeah, I'd appreciate a call and — (long pause). All right, let's do it that way. I was thinking of something else for the moment. And I'll — give me a few minutes with them before we recess.

Gambon: All right.

Management Caucus - G (8:50 P.M.)

Michelsen: Comes our messengers of light and truth. (Pause)

Mediator: Why (pause), he's very disappointed in you (pause) — your company.

Michelsen: Oh. / Oh.

Mediator: (Over Michelsen above) Not you personally. But, seriously, he (pause) — I could see that (pause) he wasn't too interested in following this thing up. He would be (pause) — oh, let me put it this way. If I wanted to twist his arm — let's put it that way — think we could stimulate an interest. Only I didn't, you see. I (pause) — I just listened. By that, I mean twist his arm into a — further meetings. (Michelsen: Uh-huh) Uh — so I — I said — or, he said that he had this staff meeting tomorrow and so on and he couldn't meet tomorrow. Gonna submit it to their membership meeting, so forth. Now, we're at this point. Your 2¢, of course, has been rejected. Now, they're going to have their meeting (Michelsen: Yeah) tomorrow at 1:00 o'clock. (Michelsen: Uh-huh) So that you thoroughly understood — so that we thoroughly understand what we're doing (Michelsen: Yeah), you feel, now, then (pause), to — no, before I put it that way, that you feel, I'd better say now we know we — the way this thing can go. Uh — I would say now, after coming from that meeting, that (pause) the (rather long pause) — the thing develops, or boils down to this. We just have a slight risk there, and that risk will be (pause) a strike order for Monday morning. (Michelsen: Uh-huh) (Rather long pause) I'm gonna get a call — he promised to call me immediately after the meeting. I asked him to. (Michelsen: Uh-huh) I say the same thing to you. After that meeting, call me, in case you hear something. (Michelsen: All right) Or let me put it this way. As soon as you hear something, call me.

Michelsen: Uh-huh. Where will you be? Home?

Mediator: Yeah. MO 6-3824. Now, what I'll do from there on would depend on the action they take. (Pause) So you now have this course: (1), let 'em have their meeting, and wait and see what happens. Or, the other course is, you're at 2¢, and if you want to move toward a settlement of the thing in its et — entirety, that would have to be done tonight, and then you would have to deter — decide whether or not that's feasible, or a lot would depend on whether you want it or not. So, there's your (Michelsen: We couldn't settle it, George, could we?) 2 courses. It would — (pause).

Michelsen: I mean, we're not gonna settle (Mediator: No) it for 5¢.

Mediator: You couldn't settle it less than (Michelsen: We can't settle, then) 5¢ tonight. That's — that I'm s (Michelsen: Yeah) — certain of.

Michelsen: Then we can't settle.

Mediator: So that being the case, we'll — it'll have to go (Michelsen: Uh-huh) this way, then. (Michelsen: Sure) So (pause), we'll adjourn (pause), put our earphones on tomorrow and see what it looks like (Michelsen: Uh-huh) after the meeting. Now you got your 2¢ on the table.

Michelsen: Yeah. That's what we want. (Rather long pause)

Mediator: Uh-h-h (long pause) — I think I've covered the field pretty well. I don't — I can't think of anything else. I'm (pause) — I expected it to go this way, so it's (pause) — the sooner we get there, the better (Michelsen: Uh-huh) we'll know. You just — short of 5¢ I don't think we could settle. Even at 5¢ you'd have a battle tonight. (Pause) (Michelsen laughs) Be a rough time.

Michelsen: (Laughing) We're gonna have a battle over less than 5¢.

Mediator: No, really, I'm serious. I mean (Michelsen: Yeah), even if you said 5¢ it'd probably be 2:00 o'clock in the morning.

Michelsen: Uh-huh. Well, I don't doubt that at all. (Mediator: Well —) And I don't know how else to convince 'em it's less than 5 except to not give 'em 5. (Pause) I don't know of any more obvious way than that. (Rather long pause) And it's very true, we may wind up there eventually.

Mediator: Wait — wait here till I have my final words with them and readjourn 'em. (Michelsen: Uh-huh) I wanta adjourn 'em, and then I want a few words with you.

Michelsen: All right.

Union Caucus - E (8:55 P.M.)

[Light, miscellaneous comments are exchanged by Mediator with the group regarding the definition of an expert which Gambon has now written out and presented to Mediator so he "won't have to play the tape" to get it. Mediator asks if this is from Shakespeare, but Gambon credits it to Confucius.]

Mediator: Uh — (pause).

Gambon: Did you tuck the little darlings in? (Meyer laughs and says something) Club it on the head with a wooden leg of a chair or somepin'? (Pause)

Mediator: The (rather long pause) — I'm pretty well convinced that (pause) there — there's no settlement here tonight. (Rather long pause) Wanta tell ya some is — something. Small as that offer was (pause), believe me (laughing slightly), if you don't think that wasn't like pulling teeth (Gambon says something) to x that. They were playing footsie and cute with the thing. (Pause) I'm inclined to think that (pause) they're probably taking a wait-see (pause) — a look-see.

Gambon: No, they won't have long to wait.

Mediator: So, I'm pretty well convinced now that it may be just as well for ya to go ahead and have the meeting. But I do think that when the meeting's over, give me a buzz. I'll probably be talking to them, and if there's any desire on their part — like if they think you're gonna pull the switch on Monday — if they do, they may show some concern.

If they as much as give me an opening, I'll move in quick. If they don't, all right. We'll pick it up in the usual manner in that we'll — you and I'll get together on the phone and talk about the next time we'll meet, and with the strike threat over their head (pause), it'll probably reflect itself at the bargaining table, and I think it'll prob'ly, at this stage, take something like that to reach the people in the white — or the ivory tower of the Atlas.

One of girls: (Laughing) The White Tower is like / they're another little hamburger.

Mediator: (Over girl above) I don't wanta see — no, that's hamburgers. (Several laugh heartily)

Meyer: (Laughing) You were right the first time.

Mediator: So (slight pause), I didn't think it was gonna be easy, even to start with, but / they're moving along, slow as it is.

Gambon: (Over Mediator above) Well, xx I, George. I'm not surprised at his attitude, tell you the truth, although I — I'm surprised that it's more an ar — an arrogant attitude than we faced in October. And I realize that the possibility for just this kind of thing existed, which is why I say I picked a time to — to get rough if they wanta play rough. Good weather. That's the reason I didn't wanta set up any / xxx.

Mediator: (Over Gambon above) Well, they're gonna certainly have their ear to the ground tomorrow at your meeting. (Saunders laughs)

Gambon: Oh-ho (laughing slightly).

Saunders: They'll hear / before you, George.

Gambon: (Over Saunders above) They'll have a few ears there / xx.

Mediator: (Over Gambon above) Oh, their people will be there like any other (Gambon: Yeah) plant (Gambon: We have our stooges in there, too), and what takes place there'll have a lot to do with how they're gonna negotiate (Gambon: Uh-huh) with you.

Gambon: Well, what will be said will be definitely intended to be carried back to 'em. (Laughs)

Mediator: All right. Thanks for your cooperation. You'll be in touch with me tomorrow.

Gambon: Right, George.

Management Caucus - H (9:00 P.M.)

Mediator: Why, I adjourned the conference. (Michelsen: Good) The boys are on their way home, puttin' their hats and coats on. (Pause) So, reviewing the day, I think we went slow. It was a slow day, but you couldn'ta went any faster (Michelsen: No, I don't think we could, either), short of a settlement, and you know what the settlement would cost you.

Michelsen: No. I — I was really planning to put this — make this over tomorrow morning.

Mediator: It's just as well, because I — I feel it's (pause) — might even be better / because, see —

Michelsen: (Over Mediator above) Well, I think it's better if we're not gonna meet / tomorrow.

Mediator: (Over Michelsen above) Uh — fact, comin' in tomorrow would be that (pause) — now that we're not meeting tomorrow — I mean,

it's just as well. The only difference is about 4 or 5 hours in which
c — / could stay.

Michelsen: (Over Mediator above) There's no difference in my mind as
long as there's no meeting tomorrow. (Mediator: Yeah) I was thinking of making it tonight and then meeting / tomorrow xx.

Mediator: (Over Michelsen above) Oh, no, we wouldn't do that. If we
were gonna meet tomorrow, I'd — I think I woulda held it there. But
(pause) — / uh —

Loring: (Over Mediator above) Well, he act'ly is going to his meeting
at $31\frac{1}{2}$-cent figure.

Mediator: Yeah.

Michelsen: (Laughing) Oh, gees, you're / x, George.

Mediator: (Over Michelsen above) (In low tone) Can't understand it.
What've they got?

Michelsen: He's crazy.

Mediator: 'Course, I think that he won't report out — he won't report
that out. I think what he'll do is say this, that, "We" (pause) —
he'll — if I don't miss my guess, he'll say this (rather long pause;
Mediator sighs): "The actual cost of our last offer is 31¢" — "our
proposal," I meant to say — "but (pause) it's a very high figure,
of course, but (pause) the reason we didn't move was that the company at no time throughout these negotiations showed that they wanted
to move in the direction of a settlement. So we just left that figure
there." I think that's how he'll get around that, and he'll (slight
pause) minimize the size of that. Think he'll play on that angle. He
won't — I don't think he'll go in there and —

Michelsen: Yeah, but he's gotta report 2¢.

Mediator: He's going after a strike. (Michelsen: Yeah) He's going
after a strike vote, and he — he made a s — he gave a — he made
some strong remarks. He says he really feels that — he's told about
the years that they never had a strike there and that he feels that the
policy of this company is such now that prob'ly the only way they can
(pause) come to terms would be by — when the people are on the outside. But he didn't say when. Now, that, I guess, will be determined
at their me — do they determine that at their meetings openly? Do
they? (Pause) Uh —

Espig: The strike vote they took 2 years a — last year was openly done.
It was o — it was (Michelsen: Yeah) done quite a long time before /
we came down here.

Michelsen: (Over Espig above) He's gonna get some motions for the —
from the floor tomorrow for a secret ballot.

Espig: See, last year when we came down here there was a — there was
a — there was (pause) — there was a strike vote, or, let's see,
there wasn't. I'm not sure now. I said there was. I — my impression
is that there was.

Michelsen: I don't think so.

Mediator: Well, he — he has never said once, nor have I asked him — I
wouldn't do it, because if I asked, "When are you goin' to strike, if
you are going to strike?" that would — that would be dignifying the
thing. I can't afford to dignify it. But reading between his lines, he
— he — without using words he makes it very plain that (pause)
there may be a strike Monday morning.

Michelsen: H'm. Well, we expect that that's a possibility.

Mediator: But we shall know. (?: Uh-huh) (Pause) And — I don't think you could do anything else under these circumstances, I'm certain. (Michelsen: Uh-huh) You people knowing how much you wanta spend, you know what they want, the pace of the negotiations, the positions of the parties — under all those circumstances, you couldn't have done anything in these negotiations that would've taken you away from where you are now. (Loring: Yeah) / Couldn't do it.

Michelsen: (Over Mediator above) No, I — I agree with you.

Mediator: So (pause), you be in touch with me tomorrow when you hear. If I hear first, I'll be in touch with you.

Michelsen: I'll prob'ly be up in the office.

Mediator: All right.

Michelsen: Maybe they'll lock me in, George.

[Mediator and Michelsen arrange to reach each other by outside phone. As tape is changed, Michelsen comments on getting packed to leave for Midville. Mediator, turning to Observer, asks, "I should tell him?"]

Mediator: ... They discussed you. (Michelsen: Uh-huh) Right at the very last! Just — they said you were ambitious. (Michelsen: Yeah) Now, they didn't say it in a — with any acrimony or (Michelsen: Yeah) bitterness. I mean, talkin' about you. First they were talkin' about the company's policy (Michelsen: Uh-huh), that it has changed (Michelsen: Uh-huh) — that — I said, "Well, when did it begin — when did it first see the change?" They said, "Oh — oh, before we came into mediation the first time." (Michelsen: Uh-huh) And then they said something about their having arbitration cases for the first time.

Michelsen: One.

Mediator: And —

Michelsen: With a man they didn't even wanta defend. (Laughs) (Mediator: And —) Never put him on the witness stand.

Mediator: Uh (pause) — so then they mentioned that last year there was a change in policy and you took over the labor relations policy and — or program. (Michelsen: Uh-huh) And they said that you were pretty ambitious.

[Mediator continues briefly in same vein, intercepted by Michelsen's occasional "Uh-huh."]

Loring: Wow! (Laughing continues)

Mediator: (Still laughing) Came right at the end, the last words (Loring continues to laugh) that were ta — talk (voice dies out). (Pause) So I said, "Well" — I said I had heard something. I said, "But we hear all sorts of things. But," I said, "you have (pause) — you're closer to the situation." (Pause) But that's — then they went on to somethin' else. (?: Uh-huh) Not too much time spent on it.

Michelsen: Yeah. (Laughs, followed by Espig also laughing) (Rather long pause)

Mediator: Came right at the end.

Michelsen: Uh. (Slight pause) Well (pause), then they won't be surprised when they don't see my happy, smiling face Monday. (Pause)

Mediator: Ya gonna leave Monday?

Michelsen: Yeah.

Mediator: Well, what's gonna happen here?

Michelsen: I don't — I don't know. (Pause) I've been resigning this company since March 1st, George!

Mediator: Uh-huh.

Michelsen: Those people down in Midville think I'm kiddin' 'em.

Mediator: Well, I'll tell ya what we'll do. We'll just move the ne — negotiations (laughing) to Midville. (Someone laughs heartily) We'll all go to Midville. Huh?

Michelsen: Well, if it looks like there's gonna be a strike I'd / like —

Mediator: (Over Michelsen above) You wanta go to Midville, Observer?

Observer: Uh-<u>huh</u>!

[Mediator and Michelsen continue their conversation for some 2 minutes, discussing Michelsen's new job set-up in Midville and other topics unrelated to the Atlas case. Mediator at last dismisses the group at 9:15 P.M.]

[Mediator, prior to joining the management group in caucus, puts in
an appearance with the union group. Gambon immediately raises the
question of Michelsen's purported withdrawal. When it is suggested
that a company attorney may replace Michelsen in the negotiation,
Gambon at once counters that perhaps the union should call in its attorney, also.]

Management Caucus - A (10:30 A.M.)

Mediator: So they're gonna throw the 3 of ya to the wolves, huh?
(Loring laughs heartily)
Pranis: Yeah.
Loring: I guess so. Well, I'm — I'm headin' up from here on out, George.
Mediator: All right.
Loring: I would certainly appreciate anything you can do to — to help me
along because this is entirely new to me. (Mediator: Well, I'll be
very happy to) Just take the thing and keep me on the ball. (Pause)
Mediator: I (slight pause) — yeah. I believe — oh, the union, by the
way, heard about it.
Loring: Did they?
Mediator: Yeah.
Loring: Yeah.
Mediator: They told me this morning. They'd just gotten in. They said
— they didn't know that it was a fact yet. They said the rumor's getting stronger that Bill was leaving. So I said, "Well, I don't think it's
any longer a rumor. I think it's a fact." He said, "Oh, did he leave?"
I said, "Yeah." And he said, "Well, who's going to represent the
company?" I said, "I don't know. Probably the treasurer, Len
Loring, and I don't know who else — whether there'll be any additions,
or" — (voice dies out). So (pause), he see — he said to the girl,
Bernice — he said, "Well, wonder if we oughta get Messina?" And
then we couldn't hear what's else he said. Now, I guess — I think he
— I think he must have felt that prob'ly you'd be represented by
counsel.
Espig: Yeah. I think that's — he prob'ly felt that Mattuck m — might.
Mediator: Yeah. They generally do that (Loring: Uh-huh) when a —
the company has an attorney. They run and get theirs for fear they'll
/ get —
Loring: (Over Mediator above) Yeah. Yeah. Well, we don't plan on
that, George. I mean, we will carry it just (Mediator: Fine) through
the committee.
Mediator: Fine and dandy. Now, we'll probably be about — we'll be
about 15 or 20 minutes late getting started today. I've got something
that I've gotta get off my mind before we (Loring: Uh-huh) start.
Has nothin' to do with (Loring: Uh-huh) your negotiations, and once
I finish this call —

Loring: Can we have a little briefing before we (Mediator: Sure) get together?

Mediator: Then we'll get together and we'll review and (Loring: All right) pick up exactly where we left off.

Loring: Uh-huh. Have you gotten very much from John about the meeting / Saturday?

Mediator: (Over Loring above) Uh — no, other than this. He said to me, when he called me, that — fact, he read to me the results of the meeting. I don't know whether it was a resolution or a release, but the gist of it was that the membership had voted by a majority vote, and I think he specified that all but 3 — there were only 3 dissenting votes — that the negotiating committee would be empowered to call a strike any time they s — deemed it necessary without going back to the membership or without calling a meeting. I said, "Well, s — going further into that, what does it mean? Now, that can have one meaning with one union and an entirely different meaning with another union. In your union does that mean you are going to set up a date — a deadline?" He said, "No." He says, "That means that if we don't reach an agreement on one day we <u>can</u> strike the next day." I said, "In other words, it's a 24-hour agreement." He said, "That's — that would be a good way of putting it." So I said, "It could be a day, it could be a week, it could be a month, then." He said, "It could be, but it won't be." So, that's the way he left it.

Loring: Uh-huh.

Mediator: Then I saw that there was something in the paper (Loring: I seen that, too. Yes) about their meeting. And (pause) that's about the gist of our call. And I didn't hear from him again after that until this morning.

Loring: So, I guess you'll have to keep your finger on it all the way now (Mediator laughs), won't you? Huh? (Laughs)

Mediator: Uh — I don't think it'll get away. If it gets to that point I'll surely (slight pause) — surely let ya know well in advance. I don't see it — I don't see any — I think they want to work out an agreement. Uh — the (pause) — the <u>pace</u> is the thing that I just can't put my finger on. I'm not quite satisfied that I have the answer to that (Loring: Uh-huh) — <u>why</u> the pace is slow.

Espig: Well, George, not <u>a word</u> has been said, in any way that we know, about money.

Mediator: To the membership?

Espig: Yeah! Or by the members. There's no expression from the members — from our employees about the fact that they think they oughta have more money. Or that they ought — how much money they think they oughta have. Or anything of that kind. It's — it's a — although they harangued the c — the — the meeting on F — on Saturday about 2 things w — and that was the — the very small amount of money involved in the offer made, and, Number 2, they harangued them about the executive bonus plan, which would indicate that money is a — is the factor. They still haven't talked to their membership about <u>money</u>, actually.

Mediator: Is that right? Didn't talk about the issues?

Espig: They talked about the 2 issues, 35-hour week and the (Mediator: Holiday) — and the 20% for the skilled / trades.

Pranis: (Over Espig above) It's not how much they were worth, or any magnitude of what (Espig: But they — they — they have no —) — I mean, but 2¢ an hour for the whole package. Then nobody —

Mediator: Stayed away from 31¢?

Pranis: H'm.

Espig: Stayed away from 31¢, stayed away from anything a'tall.

Mediator: Did they mention that you had offered 2¢?

Espig: Yes, they mentioned that — that the cost to the company was about 2¢, and they mentioned in what form it was made, too.

Mediator: Uh-huh.

Espig: And then, 'course, they went on to say that that was a very meager offer to make — to make at a time of reopening, and then they ha-rangued the committee — the group about Bill Michelsen, took a per-sonal crack at him here and there. Who did Bill Michelsen think he was to tell this committee that this was the final offer? John said, "I asked him as he was going out the room, 'Is this your final offer?' And he said, 'This is our final offer, period.'" And they took a crack at the fact that there were 66 members of the management sharing a profit distribution which amounted to <u>more</u> money than each employee earned during the cr — the course of a complete year. (Slight pause) Now, that is — the — the number 66 is inaccurate. That was true 3 years ago. And the amount — the amount distributed doesn't (Medi-ator: That so?) — doesn't equal anything that — anything that I know of. Our — our average employee earns about 1/3rd more, or maybe more than that, than the average that was distributed, plus the fact that this is in the — this is a — an incentive program, as Bill men-tioned casually. But (?: Well —) those were the points of haranguing.

Loring: That's something that sticks in their craw. Has, for the last couple years. And it <u>will</u> come to the fore continually.

Mediator: Uh-huh. Well, it's a good — it's a good point for the union to use. (Espig: 'Course) (Loring: Yes) And —

Espig: They had another point — they — they had another point that they make use of quite a bit whenever they get into these arguments and that is that several of the executives are stockholders in our — among the top stockholders in — in number of shares that they own. And that — that was the extent of the haranguing that we can get.

Mediator: Uh-huh.

Espig: All this took about 2 hours before they got around to a vote. Then they had 6 people against it, Bill told me y — told us yesterday they had 6 people or — originally against it, and they had 3 vote that — finally threw in the sponge and 3 held out.

Loring: Apparently they had about 250 there out of / the membership.

Espig: (Over Loring above) That's what the paper says, too.

Mediator: Uh-huh.

Espig: Now, this morning there's discussion both ways. (Slight pause) I mean, the — one department that we know that's very <u>definitely not</u> going to — not interested in having a strike. But that's Department 6, Subassembly. That's not a department that will carry a mass — uh — what would you say? — mass-production attitude. (Laughs)

Loring: Well, you'd get — you take care of your business and then let's have a little session (Mediator: All right. Yeah) here, and if you will, I'd appreciate it.

Mediator: Sure. We'll go over it and map out our next step (Loring: Fine), and take it from there.

[Mediator is absent from 10:40 to 11:00 A.M.]

Mediator: I can't get my man, so I'll take 15 minutes later.

Loring: All right, George. (Rather long pause)

Mediator: Uh (pause) — well, what were you thinking about this morning?

Loring: Well, it seems to me it — we're in a little awkward position right at the moment. I mean, a change in the committee and in this strike vote that they have. I wanted pretty much to discuss the whole thing with you, tell you what our position is, and be guided by you as to what we should do.

Mediator: All right.

Loring: We had a meeting yesterday with the negotiating committee — members that would decide. This whole thing was thrashed over pretty thoroughly. Feeling is we don't want a strike — definitely don't want it; doesn't do anybody any good, neither the company, the — or the employees. On the other hand, we feel that there's a point beyond which we can't be pushed. I mean, we'd be foolish to be pushed, and we — we have a position which is, as far as we're concerned, the final position, and that is that this committee can go to 4¢, tops.
Uh — we definitely would like to make a settlement and not have a strike. Now, how we go on from here is gonna be pretty much in your lap about what we should do. We (slight pause) — the feeling is that — that they'll — we'll do — abide by what suggestions you give us for strategy, but it almost felt as though — we almost felt as though maybe we should go very slowly today (pause), taking in view of the circumstances.

Mediator: I — I agree with that. (Pause) Unless, of course, we had posi — proof positive that they would settle for what we could settle for. But, again, I'm — I'd say I'm — I — I — I don't believe it would happen. (Loring: Uh-huh) Now that I know where you are I will steer the conferences in that direction, around that, and (pause) — and if they're — if they continue to show a slow pace you — you just have to let them have it (Loring: Uh-huh), see. Now, I can — I know this. They will not strike without telling me. And I know that in — I will know in advance when they really mean it. (Pause) Any move from your last position, 2¢, before knowing what they're going to do or what they would settle for, would be a wrong step at this time.

Loring: We — we have this definitely. We felt that 2¢ was as far as we should go. Now, because we don't want a strike, we — we are willing to make the added concession of 4. We would like to settle below it if we — we — we can, but that's tops. Now, also, if the time should come in this — we'd be guided by you — we aren't particularly anxious — or, I mean, we aren't set on the fact that the 4¢ has to be any particular way; it can be anything (Mediator: Uh-huh) except the shorter work week. That — (pause).

Mediator: Oh, there's my call.

Loring: O.K.

Mediator: So we'll just —

[Mediator leaves the room again at 11:02 A.M. On his way back to the management caucus room at 11:25 he puts his head in the door of the union caucus room, announcing to Gambon that he needs 20 minutes longer with the management people. He also reports that the company attorney is not with that group and that Len Loring will be their chairman for the rest of the negotiation. He begins again with the management group at 11:30.]

Loring: Just / in case —

Mediator: (Over Loring above) Yeah, I'm through, and that was a long 15 minutes (Loring: 'S all right), but I had to. Now I'm (pause) clear.

Loring: Well, just w — so you had a little more, George, as I — I told you, we have this definite top of 4¢. We're also concerned that — not only at this reopener, but we know we're gonna have a tough one in₁ October. Least we anticipate that we'll have a tough one. So we have both those problems in mind, and this has been given some very serious thought yesterday. We had quite a meeting. And while we definitely don't want a strike, we can be pushed to that point where we'll feel it would be the thing we'd have to do, much as we dislike it (Mediator: Uh-huh) — a thing like that. That's my limit (Mediator: Uh-huh) to work in. (Slight pause) And as I say, I'm — this is new to me, so I appreciate any thing ya can — things you can tell me about how I should conduct our part of the negotiations.

Mediator: Well, I certainly will do it, and will be glad to do it.

Loring: Thank you, George.

Mediator: The (pause) — the answer we want today is, (1), could we settle today; <u>could</u> we? Not <u>will</u> we, <u>could</u> we? We have to get that answer. We're only gonna get that answer after we've probed back and forth and even had a joint meeting (Loring: Uh-huh), you holding, and (pause) the <u>pace</u>, as I said earlier, has me a little disturbed. The union has too much time on their hands. (Loring: Uh-huh) They're taking this thing — well, they're not particularly anxious, and I know the reason why. They're not too, too anxious to get this settled. They have time. And why? You gave me the answer this morning — or you, Erv, when you said that they never even reported money, or there's no (slight pause) <u>real</u> push from your employees in the plant about money. That adds up to this, that the union has — doesn't <u>have</u> any <u>real</u> heat on 'em from the plant, from their membership. So they're comfortably safe in taking their time. (Loring: H'm) Now, <u>why</u> is the thing I don't know — <u>why</u> they're taking their time. But it might be — might be that maybe they knew that Len L — that Bill Michelsen — or had word that he might leave, and maybe they felt that they should wait. Maybe — that's — that <u>could</u> be an angle. The real angle I haven't found, if that — I — I'm not — I haven't been able to put my finger on it. Because unions, generally, want to get these things cleaned up. (Loring: H'm) They don't like them hanging around, especially if their people are keenly interested in it. But here they're not keenly interested in it or there would have been more than 300 people at that meeting. (Espig: Yeah!) But that doesn't mean that we can take any of their threats lightly. (Loring: Oh, sure) Doesn't mean that. They <u>can</u> use their economic strength whenever they want to. I don't think Gambon wants a strike. But he is, for some darn rease — reason, moving <u>slower</u> than a union —

Loring: Well, you — you definitely feel that he doesn't want one, George?

Mediator: I —

Loring: I had in the back of my mind that he might just like to see one.

Mediator: Well, you see, if he wanted a strike he would — I think he — he would have moved <u>faster</u> in that direction, whippin' the people up! But he has — you don't have any real strike sentiment in that plant. Now, if my memory serves me correctly, a year ago, when ya negotiated down here with me — well, that was a year ago. I've been saying 2 (Loring: Yeah, 2. It was a year ago) years, but a — a year ago. Did you recall — didn't they even have picket signs made?

Loring: Yes. Yes. / They did it.

Mediator: (Over Loring above) And the — they were <u>really</u> beating the drum. (Slight pause)

Pranis: Yeah. The people were for it. It was a (Mediator: Yeah) big adventure then.

Mediator: That's right. And <u>this</u> time a lot of that is missing. Now, that may not — that may be because it fits with whatever timetable he has. He may be deliberately <u>slowing</u> the pace, and he'll put it in <u>higher</u> gear when he gets closer to the time he wants to — all these are speculations, but we will — I think we'll get the answer today (Loring: Uh-huh) as to whether they want to go along on it. If they wanta go along and play this thing slow, if it's no disadvantage to you, let 'em go! Because if you're going to push for a settlement with them not wanting to settle, you're goin' to have to reveal everything ya have, and then you're gonna be stuck (Loring: Right) right where you are. So if it i — I — it would be better that if, by the close of today's sessions, the <u>union</u> shows no indication or no real desire to get this thing cleaned up, then we should just let it go for another time (Loring: Uh-huh) until it boils, till he s — he begins to show that — because you're not the petitioner; the union is the petitioner. Now, if <u>you</u> try to push you're going to weaken your (Loring: Yeah) position at this bar (Loring: Yeah. Uh-huh) — at this side of the table. So you just have to play it that way. He's got to show <u>me</u> — and he hasn't shown me yet any <u>real</u> — well, he has; I shouldn't say that. I mean, in our caucus he has indicated to me about where he go and he's not there on the — officially on the table. Unofficially, I think we have him at — what did I say, 14½ or 14?

Loring: About 14, I think.

Mediator: Something like that. / Uh —

Pranis: (Over Mediator above) There's only one catch, George. The longer it waits the — the worse this retroactive problem might be.

Espig: Well, that can bring it to a boil, if in some way — if in some way (Pranis: Yes) the word retroactivity gets in and we say, "Oh, no! None!" <u>That'll</u> bring it to a boil.

Mediator: That will! (Slight pause) That will speed it up. (Pause) And we might even today — if they're going too slow today we might even develop something on that, and (slight pause) one choice statement by the company, such as (rather long pause), "We feel it's our duty to remind you that" — and then your reasons why you won't and <u>cannot</u> permit retroactivity to come into this picture — "and if s — the union is thinking of it, well, then, you better start rehearsing your thinking or" — oh, words can be found (Loring: Uh-huh), but to get the general idea over that retroactivity is something that just can't

be — can't go on endlessly. (Pause) That would definitely stir them;
there's no question about it. (Pause) Now, I think later on — I'm
gonna have a talk with them. I haven't met with them yet. Later on,
when we come together jointly, which will probably be after the lunch
period (slight pause), you might prepare yourselves to (pause) give
a — an account of — a — a good start-out point would be an account of
Bill's absence (Loring: Uh-huh) from the committee and reasons
why, and then go into the company's position, reiterating a lot of things
that B — what have already been said but showing that even though
there's a change in leadership of the bargaining team, or chairmanship of the bargaining team, that (pause) — or spokesman, that thinking hasn't varied or there's (Loring: All right. Uh-huh) not — there
— see, you got to — in your opening remarks I think that point will
have to be made.
Loring: Yes. Yes. I think definitely, George.
Mediator: Then, of course, you'll get a rebuttal that you've heard before,
but that has to be done. They have to be shown that — because they're
going to be looking (pause) — well, they don't know. Sometimes a
change in spokesmens at a bargaining table can mean a completely
new proposal. They'll be looking for something like that. Now, until
that door is closed you're not gonna get their thinking in the direction
that we want them to, hence the reiteration of those p — / points.
Loring: (Over Mediator above) Right, George. Uh-huh. I'll be getting
ready for that. (Pause)
Mediator: I don't think we could th — talk about much more at this point.
A lot of our next steps will be dependent upon what (Loring: Yeah.
Uh-huh) takes place there. (Loring: Uh-huh) So we will go in and
spend the next 20 minutes or so with the union. (Pause) Or we might
do this. (Slight pause) On 2d thought, I think we ought to — if you
would like a few minutes to prepare your remarks, fine and dandy,
and then call me and then I think we'll go in jointly. It might be well
to get those remarks in now before the lunch period so that when we
come back they will have had time to discuss that and it'll (Loring:
Uh-huh) be that much more time saved.
Loring: All right, George.
[As tape is changed, Pranis explains to Mediator about a product
which is doing badly, necessitating a layoff. Espig adds that the layoff will affect about 25 on 2d shift. Pranis continues that the company
has to give a week's notice for the layoff and therefore should make
the announcement at once. He asks Mediator how the announcement
will affect the negotiations.]
Espig: ... the 2d shift was built up (Pranis: Sep —) rather recently.
Pranis: September last year. (Pause)
Mediator: And ya have to give a week's notice. I'd give it!
Loring: You think it would be all right to give it / today.
Mediator: (Over Loring above) I would give it, because what would happen would be this, that afterward, like if an agreement was reached,
they were laid off then (slight pause), the — that could be interpreted, "Well, ya knew it. Why in the heck didn't ya tell us? (Loring:
Uh-huh) And this way, why, we get an increase and a layoff to make
up for the increase," (Loring: Yeah) see. You'd be caught in that
switch there. They'd — the (Loring: Yeah) — so I have found in

these negotiations that I hold, when that problem comes up, that it always works out best that you tell the union so — and you tell them that it's not intended. It's a s — and they — they generally know that it's a production problem, or an order problem, and it — it just happened to coincide or come at this time, and "We felt that we should carry our business on with you as usual, as we <u>would</u> do — give you the notice." (Loring: Uh-huh. All right) And tell 'em, and — that's the best way. (Loring: O.K.) Then there's — then you don't get in any trouble.

Loring: Yeah.

Espig: Well, we wanted you to know before (Mediator: Yeah) we sent this notice (Mediator: I'm glad ya did) out, because in case of any — any fire that you knew we didn't — we could have considered something else, some way, somehow. (Mediator: Sure) Just what, I don't know. We've — we — if we don't do it now we'll certainly have — have to do it next week.

Mediator: I would / send them the notice.

Pranis: (Over Mediator above) Well, it'd be rough next week, Erv, because the people / wouldn't have anything to do.

Loring: (Over Pranis above but cannot be understood)

Espig: (Over Loring above) That's right. We'd have to start moving the people all over the place.

Pranis: Yeah. Then we'd —

[At 11:50 A.M. Mediator withdraws to give the management group some time alone, and while waiting he joins the union group. The conversation, to which numerous members of the group contribute, is almost entirely concerned with Michelsen's new job in a nonunionized plant. Gambon promises to look into the possibility of getting an organizational drive started there. Gambon declares that he has suspected all along that Michelsen's attitude in the negotiation was related to the fact this was his "swan song." After 10 minutes Mediator leaves the union group to return to pick up the management group for the joint meeting.]

Loring: O.K., George, I guess I'm —

Mediator: All set?

Loring: All set.

Mediator: All right. Shall we — (slight pause).

Loring: I would say you would — the strategy would be not to be too longwinded but just state our position.

Mediator: That's right.

Loring: Uh-huh.

Mediator: And then after they've had a brief discussion, I'm gonna recess for lunch. (Loring: Yeah) That'll give them a chance to (pause) (Loring: Uh-huh) see whether there's a change, discuss it or not — uh — to see whether the company — whether Bill's absence from this committee has changed the company's thinking. Then they will have a chance to discuss that. Then, in the afternoon I think we'll be in a better position to start negotiating.

Loring: All right.

Pranis: Can we wait a minute for Erv (Mediator: Sure), George?

Mediator: (In low voice) 'S right.

Loring: Was there any comment about <u>my</u> taking over?

Mediator: No.

Loring: Oh. I wondered.

Mediator: Uh — <u>Saturday</u> there was. Uh — Gambon said (pause) —
when he — he talked about — after he reported the — to me on the
union business, he said that the rumor was getting stronger that
Michelsen would leave. And I said, "Who do you think will handle the
company's negotiations?" He said, "Probably Len Loring." And he
said — he — he described you as a hell of a nice fellow (Someone
laughs slightly), and this and that. He said, "<u>But,</u>" he said, "he still
represents the company." He (laughing) says, "And he's" (laughs)
— he said, "He'd probably be no different than Bill Michelsen."
(Laughs, joined by Loring)

Pranis: Kind of the same brush. (Mediator and Loring continue laughing)

Mediator: But he — he spoke very highly of you. (Pause)

Pranis: Bet he's / x —

Mediator: (Over Pranis above) <u>Actually</u> I don't think there's <u>any</u> personal dislike, either, for Bill Michelsen.

Loring: I don't think there / is either, George.

Mediator: (Over Loring above) It's just business (Loring: Sure), and
— (slight pause).

Pranis: Well, you go in with a good reputation / xxxxx.

Espig: (Over Pranis above) No, Bill and — Bill and John got along very
well in their — even (?: Yeah) in their off moments.

Mediator: And, actually, I think they liked one another. (Espig: Right)
Like 2 lawyers, coming into court.

Pranis: (Laughing) Yeah.

Loring: That's right.

Pranis: That always amazed me. You come out of a very —

<u>Joint Meeting - A</u> (12:02 P.M.)

[As Loring enters the room, he first moves toward the chair he had
been occupying in the earlier joint meetings, then turns slightly to
sit down in the chair which had been Michelsen's.]

Gambon: My sympathy, friend.

Loring: (Laughs heartily) Thank you, John. (Rather long pause)

Mediator: At this session the representatives for the company have some
remarks to make, so we'll start this session off at that point, if you
will, Len.

Loring: Good. I don't know whether you know it yet or not, but Bill
Michelsen is separated from the company. He got an offer of a very
good job down in Midville, Christopher Air Conditioning Corporation,
and he has left, effective today. He hoped that he'd have the sessions
concluded by then, but hasn't worked out. I've been appointed as the
chairman of the negotiating committee. There'll be no other change;
there'll be just a 3-man committee, John.

Gambon: Uh-huh.

Loring: I'd like to present our position. We've given it considerable
thought over the week-end. I'd just like to point out a few things, tell
you where we stand. As we said before, our '52 operation has been
very disappointing to us. Sales were down 23%, and this after we got

an additional $1,250,000.00 of capital. The stock we sold in January
of 1952 gave us that much more operating funds, and yet our profits,
in spite of that, went down 23% after taxes. We find daily that our
competition is getting tougher and tougher. We have to spend more
to sell products. Sales Department is working as hard as they can
to find out how to get a better share of the market and keep what we
have. We find many more relatively small companies that give us
competition, and apparently they make a pretty good recorder because they're accepted in the trade. Many of them are selling at less
than we can sell our recorders for because they don't have the overhead problems that go with their short-range approach. That's the
type of thing that — it concerns us. We hope sincerely that 1953 will
be a good year, will be much better than '52, but here are a few of
the things that are in the horizon that — that give us concern. Ya see
every day more and more comment about changes in techniques in recording being just around the corner. Some of your recording industry committees seem determined to bring that out, cause a furor. We
don't think it is. But the mere fact that it's given publicity like that
can well make a lot of people hesitate about buying any kind of a recorder. We think that there is considerable possibility that recorder
sales will be hurt during the latter part of this year. And if they are,
of course you know that's a big part of our market. We s — read in
the papers about defense expenditures being cut — how they're tryin'
to prune the budget. A large part of our subcontract work is defense
work. If they're cut back we can expect a cutback, too. We see price
reductions in the paper, even in defense. Your automobile companies,
other companies are mak — announcing price reductions, which indicates the general softening, particularly in the hard goods industry,
which is the one we are most closely associated with. And last, we
notice the last couple of weeks a softening in our incoming order rate.
All of which points out that while we hope '53 will be a good year we
can't bank on it at this moment. Now, I'd like to point out our position at this time as we've given it to ya before. We would like to offer
some benefits along the hospitalization plan. We have now a daily
limit of 7.50 if you go to the hospital, and that is for a room. We think
that in line with conditions today that should be raised to $9.00 per
day. The services that our present plan pays for are 10 times the
daily rate, or $75.00. Those are for the hospital services that you
run into in the hospitals. We think that should be raised to 20 times
the daily rate, or $180.00. We think that is more in line with what it
costs today. We think those are things which will benefit every one
of the employees. Pension plan — we suggest an additional 1¢ an
hour be put into the pension plan, that the Joint Committee meet with
the actuaries and find the best way to get benefits out of that 1¢ an
hour. And we also feel that we should carry the additional cost of the
present group insurance, which is running over the $6.00-a-month
figure that we agreed to in the contract. We figure that offer amounts
to 2¢ an hour (slight pause), and we feel that in line with conditions
i — it's a fair offer. (Rather long pause)

Gambon: Well, Len, I think the union is already on record to the company's committee in regard to that particular offer. On Friday we
considered it and rejected it, and as you probably are now aware, that

particular offer was rejected by the membership of the Local on Saturday afternoon and a strike vote was taken, giving this committee the
authority to call a strike in its own sole judgment if such action becomes advisable, so that we're right now in a position of your offering again a proposal which has been doubly rejected, in a sense, both
by the union's committee and by the membership meeting on Saturday
last. (Pause) The union's position, of course, still remains where it
was on the point Number 1, dealing with the 35-hour week, and point
Number 2, dealing with the 20% fixed bonus for skilled trades and all
other day workers. (Pause) (Meyer: Uh —) Anything else that I
would say, I mean, in regard to the comments you made — I mean,
anything that I might offer in rebuttal would be only repetitious of
what I've already said, and I don't think that we should waste any time
in my going over that thing again. I think you're pretty familiar with
the position I take in regard to the company's financial position and
so forth, and anything a'tall is gonna be repetitious. I see no point in
goin' all over that again.

Meyer: May I ask a question here, though? Why did the company's proposal take this form when it — the union didn't request at this time
anything along these lines?

Loring: Well, Bernice, the reason for that was that we knew we had very
little to offer ya and we — we offered what we thought would be the
best way to spend it. I mean, there was no other purpose behind it.

Gambon: Well, I mean, the — I think Bernice's reason for raising the
question goes back to the very first meeting that we held in Atlas's
premises, when Mi — Bill Michelsen was asked whether or not he was
makin' a 4/10ths-of-a-cent-per-hour wage increase and he said, "No,
it's only in this particular form." And we assume, of course, that the
2-cent package that you're talkin' about here is in the form as you present it and it's not (Loring: Yes, that's —) to be considered in any
other form by the union. I think that was t — what gave rise to the
question as Bernice put it. One thing that I'd like to have for the record, George, since you raised the question and since it is not yet determined as an agreed-upon proposition, does the company agree that
the effective date of any settlement coming from these negotiations
shall be on April 1st, 1953?

Loring: No. At this point we do not (Gambon: Uh-huh), John.

Gambon: All right. I just wanted to make — have that clear in my
(Loring: Yeah) own mind whether we were / working —

Mediator: (Over Gambon above) I didn't quite get — was that retroactivity?

Gambon: Well, actually that's what it amounts to at <u>this</u> point, yes. I
was tryin' to establish for my own benefit, at least, and probably for
yours as to whether or not we have an agreement or disagreement
over the April 1st date (Mediator: I see), and Len indicates that
there is no agreement at this point on the company's part. I just
wanted to have that clear so we know what we're dealing with here.
(Pause)

Mediator: I think you're right, John, when you said that (pause) a rebuttal would be a reiteration, and I believe that it might be well at
this time for both parties to recess for lunch, and when we resume
negotiations I believe it may be well for us to explore with both

committees separately possibility of our next step — finding our next step, if there's a next step to be found.

Gambon: Well, I — just for the record and so that the company is quite clear on this situation, I wanta read the exact position adopted by the membership of Local 89 almost unanimously. Incidentally, the newspaper reports 3 No votes. That is an actual fact. However, the report — and this isn't defensive on my part, because you'll know why in a moment — the report of 250 people is incorrect; it was approximately 350 people present. The 3 No votes, I'd like for the record to mention here, were a gentleman and his wife and a friend, a gentleman who, incidentally, was offered a position as a foreman just recently by the company so that we weren't too surprised in having a vote of — a No vote against the strike from that particular individual and his spouse and friend.

Mediator: John, you're (Gambon: However — h'm?) — you're a perfectionist. (Several, including Loring and Mediator, laugh)

Gambon: Well, I — I always like to get E for effort, George, and I — I worked pretty hard / on Saturday to —

Mediator: (Over Gambon above) Well (laughing slightly), what — what I kept thinking of was this. My experiences have been with a strike vote, 99% of the unions, if they could get everybody but 3 (laughing), why, they'd consider that a big job (Gambon: Uh-huh), and you've done it! You — you've got 3 and you're complaining about / that, see.

Gambon: (Over Mediator above) Well, no, I'm not complaining. (Mediator laughs) I just wanted to make sure that I consider it to have been a unanimous (Meyer laughs heartily) vote of union members (Everyone laughs), see — of union members, see (laughing). (Several, including Mediator and Gambon, laugh further) Well, anyway, for the record, Len, and your committee, this is the (pause) actual (pause) action taken by the membership on Saturday: "That the negotiations committee of the Recording Equipment Workers' Union, Local 89, OPQ International, be empowered and have the right to call a strike of Atlas employees represented by the Recording Equipment Workers' Union, Local 89, OPQ International, at any time that a majority of said negotiating committee, in their sole judgment, deem such action advisable. Period." (Rather long pause)

Espig: My shorthand didn't do so / well.

Gambon: (Over Espig above) I'll give ya a copy / of that later on, if you want it, soon as I write it out for ya.

Espig: (Over Gambon above) Never — that's all right. I — I've got it all, I think. I got the 3 (Loring: Yeah) — the 3 items, but we'll appreciate a copy. (Rather long pause)

Mediator: Well, it's 12:20. (Pause) S'pose we get back between quarter of 2:00 and 2:00. And then I'll — I will wanta explore with both committees separately.

Gambon: Uh-huh.

Mediator: So we'll consider this session recessed until then.

Loring: O.K.

Meyer: Mr. Espig, are you the director of industrial reor — organization, or whatever (Espig: Manager) it might be?

Gambon: International representative?

Espig: (Says something but cannot be understood)

Meyer: Industrial relations.

Espig: Of the metropolitan area plant.

[Loud general laughing follows for sometime on this. Gambon asks, "Of the metropolitan area plant?" and shakes hands with Espig as he congratulates him. There is light exchange between Espig and the others, with Gambon saying, "We'll try to make it interesting for you, Mr. Espig," and Espig replying, "Ah, I'm sure you will, John."]

Mediator: I didn't — I didn't tell Len about our discussion — our early discussion. I was — mentioned to the union, wouldn't it be something if John went down there with his organizers and organized the Christopher Air Conditioning? (Laughs, joined by some others, including Loring heartily)

Gambon: I told George that if I can find out that it is within our union's jurisdiction, I'm going to certainly make certain (Several laugh) that there's a leaflet in that plant very shortly (laughing). (Several, including Meyer, laugh)

Management Caucus - B (2:05 P.M.)

[Just prior to joining the management group in their caucus room, Mediator has taken Gambon aside in another office, to speak privately with him.]

Mediator: Uh — I just had a session with John, away from his committee. (Loring: Uh-huh) I put it to him this way. I said, "John (pause), I've been spending a lot of time with Atlas — this case. Too much time. It should've been settled. Now," I said, "I don't know what your plans are, but I have a feeling, based on where you're standing, that this is going to be — take a lot more meetings, and I thought you and I had better talk about it, because where you are now indicates to me that there's — this thing's going to go on and on and on. (Loring: H'm) I cannot stay with you that long. I have too many other situations that need my attention. Now (pause), ju — just where are you going?" He said, "All right, George," he said, "I'll give it to you. Unofficial," he said, "and just for your own information" — well, of course, that's a guidepost for me to steer by — or steer to (pause) — "5¢ an hour and 20% (pause)" — is it 20? — 2 — 10%, I guess. Anyway, it comes to a total of — 10% for the skilled workers — whatever it is, 10 or 20, whichever comes to 7¢ — comes around 7¢. The 5 across-the-board and 2¢ for the skilled workers. I guess that would be — what would that be, 10%?

Loring: If it's (Pranis: Probab —) just the skilled workers that he's talking about, not day workers, it might be around there, George — 10%.

Mediator: He / figures it's —

Pranis: (Over Mediator above) Well, we said 20% was 2 — 4¢.

Espig: H'm?

Pranis: We said 20% was 4¢. 10% would be 2¢. This is the number (Loring: Yeah) here.

Mediator: Yeah.

Pranis: You remember we told you / only 6 and 5.

Loring: (Over Pranis above) Yeah. Well, he's figurin' on day workers.

Mediator: 7¢ he figured. So, now I said, "Look, John. Sooner you get the" — said, "You — sooner you get to know the facts, the sooner we're gonna get the thing resolved." I said, "I don't see 7¢. (Slight pause) I don't see it!" I said, "Then we'll have a strike." So he (laughing slightly) — he — I had to remind him that he wasn't bargaining with me. I said, "You're not — I — I'm not the company." I said, "Here I'm — we're — I'm tryin' to short-s —short-cut this — tryin' to make it easy for you by telling you exactly where you're going. And I know where you're going because I'm meeting with the company in separate meetings, I'm meeting with the union, and between the 2 I'm able to get a feel of where ya belong and where you would — and just where ya stand. And where you stand now I see too many more meetings ahead, too many ahead for my schedule. And I wanta remind you of that so that you're either gonna quicken your pace and get this thing resolved, or, if you've got a timetable you're workin' on, then I'm gonna let you — let you meet with the company or — without me, or let you wait your time out until the timetable." I said, "That's the reason of going over this with you." So, there's where he's thinking now. Uh (pause) — at least we're getting closer.

Loring: Yeah. (Pause)

Mediator: But — (rather long pause).

Loring: Well, that is not in the cards, George, definitely.

Espig: 10 per (Mediator: Now, here's one —) — 10% on top of the — on top of the skilled trades and other day workers would put us out in front of many of the jobbing shops.

Pranis: Yes, we'd be competitive at this point.

Espig: 10% on — we — we now pay $2.27 — would be 22¢ an hour increase for die makers alone. / 22 —

Mediator: (Over Espig above) 20¢ an hour?

Espig: Huh-un. 22¢ an hour.

Mediator: 10% would?

Espig: Uh-huh. (Pause)

Mediator: Well, now, / wait a minute.

Espig: (Over Mediator above) And that isn't our — that isn't our 4¢, George. 10¢ would be our 4¢. Now, I — if he's talking 10% or 10¢, that's a di — heck of a different thing. Because what we figured was — was 4¢ an hour for —

Pranis: 20%.

Loring: 20%.

Espig: Was it 20%? I'm sorry. / xx —

Pranis: (Over Espig above) Well, it's — it's close to 5. It's 5¢ an hour for 20%, but it's 8/10ths of a cent for (pause) (Espig: Per — per nickel) 10¢ for skilled trades.

Espig: Per nickel.

Pranis: We're talkin' xx, now.

Mediator: Now, here's — here's — here's what I think you're gonna have to do at this stage of the game — these negotiations. We're gonna have to (slight pause) — now, you remember I told you this morning that in order to get over what you want, if their pace is slow you have to let 'em be slow. Now, I think we're f — and I told we'd find that out this afternoon. Now, I think we've found that out. (Loring: Uh-huh) The pace is slow. Now we know where they are. Unofficially — and

by the way, I must caution your committee to be <u>extremely careful</u>
with any talk about 7¢ (Loring: Uh-huh), because it's <u>unofficial</u> and
you — you don't have it for <u>talking purposes</u>. (Loring: Right. Yes)
And if you were to drop it loosely it would impair our progress. So
(pause), I think we have to do this — ya have to do this. I'm going in
now with the union. I'm gonna try to have a <u>full</u> discussion on the —
oh, the futility of their position and the pace of these negotiations,
and — and I'm gonna lay it down hard that something's gotta happen
here; we've got to move. We're <u>not</u> moving! And also tell 'em that
I just have to take care of my other business and (slight pause) I
feel that if they want to move or keep this slow pace going, why, they'll
have to go it alone. We'll see what that does.

Loring: Uh-huh.

Mediator: And if they say, "All right. All right. Fine and dandy," then
that means they wanta go slow. And let 'em go slow! Now, they won't
pull any strike. And I won't meet with 'em before Thursday. (Slight
pause) Tuesday, tomorrow, I'm takin' — my time is taken up with a
meeting here. Following day I — I'm tied up. I wouldn't <u>have</u> to be
if there was daylight on this thing, but (Loring: Uh-huh) there isn't
at this stage.

Espig: But John intends to be in Plattsville Wednesday.

Mediator: And John intends to go to Plattsville. He said he could have
an early meeting. And I think we might just — just as well let him
go into next week (slight pause) if — and let 'em drag, if they wanta
drag, until they get noisy! (Loring: Uh-huh) And, then, of course,
we'll have another look at it, unless, of course, you're ready to pay
5 and 2. (Slight pause) But 5 and 2 is what it would cost you today.

Loring: Well, it's just not there, George.

Mediator: And — and — and — I was talkin' about 5¢ the other day, and
I told you, well, we'd prob'ly have to go till 2:00 or 4:00 in the morning, so that this'll give you an idea of (Loring: Uh-huh) how tough it
<u>would</u> have been (Loring: Yeah), because he thinks he's being very
generous now. (Loring laughs slightly) Very gentle with <u>me</u>! I mean,
his attitude, w — well, this oughta just — just be as simple — just come
in and tell you people and you'd be —

Pranis: Hoppin' right in.

Mediator: — hoppin' right in and very happy about the whole thing and it
would be all over. So, what we have to do with John, see, before today
is over — first, I'm going in there to soften him up, and the full committee. I tell (banging on table) him that this — your positions are
poles apart, I haven't anything to work on, and I'm getting to the point
where we're gonna have to use a little dynamite. "The company is at
2¢ and you're up in the air at 31, and (pause) I don't see any <u>real</u> interest or desire to settle this thing." If it was, why, I think we'd settle it. Then, following that, when we come in for joint sessions, I
think the company oughta be prepared again, when the opening — if
they give ya the opening, and they probably will — to tell 'em that —
again what you think about your figures. You'll have to just keep repeating (Loring: Uh-huh) that your position is there and you feel
that it's a <u>fair</u> one. But I wouldn't say, "This is my final offer."

Loring: H'm.

Espig: Well, do you think we ought to criticize the 2 pos — the 2 points
that they have made: **Number 1, the 35-hour** (Mediator: Yes, indeed)

week, and just — just tear that apart? And then the 20% — tear that apart, o — on the basis / that —

Mediator: (Over Espig above) Well, there's one — no, there's one gimmick in that 35-hour week. Might be all right to mention it's — that it would just <u>never</u> go over. <u>Never</u>!

Espig: Well, their newspaper article says that they're trying to make work.

Mediator: Well, then you can use that — the basis (Espig: That's what I mean), that newspaper thing. Say, "In the newspaper you mention a 35-hour week. Well, you may as well know it, that" —

Espig: We couldn't adjust our forces to include and — people on the basis of a 35-hour week; we couldn't adjust to our customers' requirements for a 35-hour week; we couldn't adjust to the cost problems involved; and so on. And then in the 20%, point out that 20% of the — of the — of the going rate at the moment would carry the — would carry this company far in excess of the area — the <u>top</u> of the area. (Mediator: Right) I mean, and we can take a — I — I don't know whether I have it here, but at some place, I — I think, among these papers I have a — a survey that was made in Oc — in October / of last year.

Loring: (Over Espig above) Well, d'you think this is the time to say that? I — I mean, here — here we're giving credence to what they want, if we pick at it right now.

Mediator: Uh —

Pranis: You're not giving credence; you're turning it <u>down</u>.

Mediator: You're turning it down. See, you'd be turning it down.

Espig: Then you'd go (Mediator: B — see —) on to say about, "Here's why we're offering you / 2¢ the way we are."

Mediator: (Over Espig above) Uh — yeah. In — see, that would be — that would come along in your <u>offer</u> of the 2¢. (Loring: Uh-huh) In other words, you would say, "<u>We</u> have submitted to you an offer which we think fair — is fair, based on the number — or — or the financial — or, rather, the number of increases we've had in the past," or whatever other reasons you line up to support your position. "You have asked for the 35-hour week; you've asked for 20 f — 20%. Earlier this morning you asked us why we were giving the offer that we gave — why we had specified that it be for hospital benefits" — or whatever they did say — "and we (slight pause) submitted that 2-cent offer to be applied to the health and welfare points because (pause) we felt that that's where the people would get the most benefit out, plus the fact that we couldn't even begin to <u>think</u> of an increase on the points that you have mentioned, such as the 35-hour week and the 20% for skilled workers." <u>Then</u> launch into what he has said about that. (Loring: Uh-huh) But your cue — your — your cue, or — to get into (Loring: Yes) that would be the 2-cent offer. (Loring: Uh-huh) The (Loring: Right) — you talkin' about it and then you lop into the (pause) — well, to their demands, as to the — the absurdity, almost, of their demand, see. So that would be the — the linking (Loring: Uh-huh) connection. That would give you an opportunity to say just that and then back to your 2¢ again.

Loring: Right.

Mediator: Now, we'll go in there with them for awhile.

Loring: All right, George.

Union Caucus - A (2:20 P.M.)

Mediator: Uh (pause) — I want to — I think it's time to give the union
committee — I've just given the company committee the same — my
views or summation of these negotiations, with the hope that (rather
long pause) — that the — both the union and the company can see my
point and then do something about it. These negotiations — I know
why they're unusual; I mentioned it already. They're unusual because of the circumstances of moving away to the South and a few
other things, but there comes a time in the — even these negotiations
where we have to take stock and find common ground. If we don't,
why, we're goin' to be playing footsie for months, and I know you don't
want that and I know the company doesn't want it and I don't want it. I
think the time has come where you have to know or get an idea — learn
as near as you can to where this company is going and what they will
do and what they won't do, and they, on the other hand, have to know
what you will do and what you will settle for and what you won't. Then
if it's an impossible situation, at least we will know it's that and that
we can both, or all 3 of us, go on doing the things that are more productive. Now, you have spent a lotta time in these negotiations and so
has the company and so have I. And I am — and I don't think the 3 of
us are very happy about the progress. The pace is so slow. Now, this
company, from what I can learn — and I have used all sorts of arguments of persuasion and all sorts of mild pressure and stiff pressure
to convince them that they ought to use X amount — just call it X for
the time being — to at least begin to consider as a common ground for
getting together. "X may not be satisfactory to the union, and it's
not satic — satisfactory to you. But your 2¢ isn't satisfactory to the
union and the union's figure isn't satisfactory to you, and since neither
of ya brought up an X figure, I'm bringin' it up and let's start walkin'
toward it." But they made it very clear (pause) and firm that anything like that figure was not in these negotiations. Now, he said he
didn't want a strike. This is Len Loring. He said, "But we cannot
pay more than (pause) we have to pay with or can pay with, and we
know what we have and we know what we can pay with, and we can't
go over it."
Gambon: The committee.
Mediator: Huh?
Gambon: The committee.
Mediator: No. What?
Gambon: The committee can't go over.
Mediator: Oh!
Gambon: That what he means?
Mediator: Well, I don't know. I guess he (Gambon: Oh) meant the com-
pany. He — maybe that's the way it is, but I took it that he meant the
company. I think he meant the company. In fact, I'm (Gambon: H'm)
quite sure he was speaking that — in that vein. (Pause) He must
have, because he says — said, "We would — we would then have to take
a strike," he said, / "and we don't want it."
Gambon: (Over Mediator above) Did he give any reasons why they had this
X amount that they could give — as to why that's all they could give?
Mediator: No. I presume that he felt that the reasons given during the negotiations explained that, and / I guess they —

Gambon: (Over Mediator above) Well, I'm — I'm thinking in terms of the statements made to us such as, "We want to expand our research; we wanta expand our facilities," and so forth, which to us means expand the decentralization program. Well, it's question of what they can afford to do; and I might remind ya, George, that they have not at any time pleaded inability to pay, here. The whole thing boils down to their offer at this moment, or any close offer to that, in my opinion, of bein' what they wanta do, and the — they wo — don't wanta do in excess of this particular amount that they're — may come out with during these — this particular session because it will then cause them to revise their plans somewhat to expend that particular money or that part of it which they forfeit to us (pause) — that they want to actually spend it some other way (Mediator: Well, that I —), which is not to our benefit, definitely.

Mediator: Well, that I don't know. (Gambon: H'm) W — I don't know the reasons behind that statement. Uh-h-h (pause) — I do know this, that — I figured — I figured that — I wasn't disappointed — let me put it this way — in these negotiations I wasn't disappointed when I saw them diggin' in at 2¢. When I say I wasn't disappointed, I don't mean that — I should explain that. (Gambon: H'm) I was disappointed in one way but not surprised would be another (Gambon: H'm) — would be the right way to say it, because I believe that on a wage reopener they have made checks and established averages and came at their figure that way, like all other (Gambon: H'm) in — indu — industry groups do. Now, the figure that they have arrived at is nothing like the figure you'd like to settle for. That I know. They would (pause) — unless they're damn good poker players or — or members of the Actors' Guild and I — and I am completely deceived by their acting ability. I don't believe that's the case. I really think that (pause) they — they've got a figure, like any other group — any other industry group. (Gambon: Uh-huh) And when they — they either settle at that figure or they (pause) — or they don't settle. Now, I don't think ya have to be a detective or an expert to reach this deduction, because 6-month reopener coming up in October, it doesn't surprise me that industry — this industry — this company takes the position that they take of digging in at 2 and fighting! Now, they figure this way. They must. Although these people have not said it, he did mention Oc — October to me in one of their discussions, but they did not say what I'm about to interpret. This is my own interpretation, and I think it will follow correctly that any company with a 6-month reopener coming up in October, as this one is, uh-h-h-h — can do it 2 ways. They can give an increase now, one above what they wanted to give or ever intended to give, and then fight it out in October for a lower figure that they would have settled for in October; or strike an average — try to hit a happy medium for this — these negotiations, the same in O — in — in October; or take a strike at this point, if, of course, it's better for them to have it at this time, so that come October the relations would be better and the chances of settlement be easier. Now, you don't have to be a detective to made those deductions. (Gambon: Uh-huh) They're — they're right in front of you. I don't know which way they're going, but I'm sure their thinking was — they arrived at their figures — when they arrived at their figures they took that kind of thinking into stock. (Rather long pause) I know there's more than

2¢ there. 'Course there is! (Gambon: I know it, too) How much more, I don't know. (Gambon: H'm) But I think they're at the point now where they're not going to make a settlement until they know a settlement can be made. And from where you are — the 2 positions — from where I stand — from what they tell me and what you tell me, you're apart, and I think you're apart at the point where you would take a strike and they would take one. I don't think that either of you have enough — I don't think you're near enough to a settlement, unless there can be a (pause) — some further thinking on your position. Now, I say all this because I have a personal problem — say all this with a hope that we can speed up this pace. I have a personal problem in that I have, like yourself, other cases, and I've been staying pretty close with this one and giving it a lot of time in the hope that we could polish — polish it off, but I knew, too, that it had to have a certain amount of time. But I think that time is — I think all 3 of us have given it a fair shake of the (Gambon: H'm) dice, and —

Gambon: Time's runnin' out. / That's the whole point.

Mediator: (Over Gambon above) — time's running out.

Gambon: H'm.

Mediator: I cannot meet tomorrow, I cannot meet Thursd — er — Thursday. Wait a minute, what's tomorrow?

Gambon: Tuesday.

Mediator: Tuesday. I can't meet Wednesday. (Pause) Might — I don't know / whether —

Gambon: (Over Mediator above) Well, wait a minute. Do I understand you to say you can't meet tomorrow, you can't meet Thursday, you can't meet Wednesday?

Mediator: I can't meet Wednesday. I can't meet tomorrow, I can't meet Wednesday.

Gambon: Yeah. But you could meet Thursday?

Mediator: I could meet Thursday.

Gambon: H'm.

Mediator: But I want to say before we even get into that, unless — unless there's some reason that you think stretching the negotiations out — if you feel that lengthening these negotiations enhances your position, well, that's all right. And you will — you'll get my cooperation there, because I have so many other things / to do.

Gambon: (Over Mediator above) Well — h'm. No. I — I don't wanta deliberately prolong these things, George. / xxx —

Mediator: (Over Gambon above) But I feel that — that both of you have a better chance of reaching an agreement (slight pause) today than you would next week.

Gambon: Well, I think that they should — that there's a problem of your time involved in here, while I wanta give you every opportunity to try to get the parties together on it. But if they're going to negotiate with us today and then possibly again on Thursday, I wanta know before we leave here today whether they're gonna stay with that position or whether they're gonna try to enter into some bargaining with the union in coming away from that position to an upward — in an upward move, with perhaps the union changing its position somewhat by the end of today. If they don't do that, then, despite the fact that we can't get together until Thursday, they'll have to take into consideration that it

may be my recommendation to this committee that we pull the shop
and negotiate with 'em while we're on the street, if that's the way
they want it. Now, if they're takin' that kind of a firm position to entrench themselves in back of 2¢, why, they better know that.

Mediator: Well, to further help you with your thinking, I would say —
again this is my personal (Gambon: H'm) observations — that unless
the 2 people start moving toward one another you're goin' to have to
strike that plant to move 'em.

Gambon: Uh-huh. I'm aware of it. (Pause) I'm aware of that and I
want them to be aware of it, that we're not goin' to drag out the negotiations. We think that the company, Number 1, delayed these things
and there probably might have been a settlement through honest-to-
God bargaining across the table on all these issues if they had started
early, as we suggested in the first place. But it seems to me — I
mean, in the face of the record — the union notifies them on January
23d. They wait until the 20th of February to acknowledge the letter,
and at that time they set up a meeting for March the 12th. Now, it
didn't seem to me as if they were too interested in trying to resolve
the thing. And in the face of the fact that Bill Michelsen insisted that
I give him something in writing as to what the union's demands were
before the meeting on the 12th and since he got those several days before the 12th and then came in here and had no cost estimates, I can't
see where they gave those demands any kind of consideration a'tall,
if they had no cost estimates on any items. You'll recall they said
that. And it was at subsequent meetings after that was first stated
that they came up with some cost figures. All in all, I think there's
been a deliberate delay on the part of the company playin' for time
for whatever reason they had for it, I don't know, perhaps thinking
that they were gonna place the union under pressure and perhaps
thinking that with that pressure that possibly they would get the kind
of a settlement at their figure that they're looking for. Well, that particular strategy is no good any more, as far (laughing slightly) as
I'm concerned, if that's what it was on their part. I'm not going to
delay it. I want them to begin to move.
[Tape changed]
. . . do something to give evidence that they really don't want the
strike and that they're gonna make some effort to — to (pause)
make some kind of offers which might get some serious consideration. I (pause) think that if they understand that, that maybe they
will do — begin to do some moving today. And, again, I might repeat
that if they don't move away from it today, and since we can't get together with you until Thursday, they're gonna have to face the possibility of the committee deciding that it's not in our interest to wait
until Thursday and continue the shop workin' while we try to bargain
with 'em again. I mean, up to this point there's nothing on the table
to show that they're really trying to get a settlement here, because,
as you say yourself, you know there's more than 2¢ there. I know it!
I'd be foolish to let them think they're givin' me a — a s — song and
dance here on the face of their financial report. That's all I'm arguing about here. They admit that they have money that they can expend and even imply expenditures beyond what they put out in '52 for
research, for instance, because they say, "We wanta use that money

to expand that research." And again they talk about — in their financial report and the newspaper reports, Fuller says, "We'll con —
we'll bring back the dividends normally pay" — which is 40¢ as
against 30 they paid in '52 — "as soon as we're in a sound financial
position." Again, that means to us that the — not so much the fact
that they won't put it back; I believe they will. But the timing as to
when they put it back evidently will depend a great deal on the kind
of settlement they make with the union at this time. There's been no
effort on the part of the company, in the face of all these claimed lost
profits and all that business, to in any way reduce the profit sharing
engaged in by officers and foremen and supervisors in all that company.
By taking less in the way of a wage benefit the union is doing one thing.
We're making it possible for the profit-sharing amounts per employee
to be increased! I mean, the evidence is there for the first period of
1953. And we're not willing to do that. And we're not willing — I mean,
lastly, we're not willing to provide funds that they can move out more
products other than what they have told us at this point are definitely
going to be moved. I think it might be interesting, George, if I got into
your hands, as quickly as possible, a copy of the letter that was issued
to the — all the employees of this company when they announced the decentralization program. And again I must repeat they they have never,
up to this time, gave us any consideration or any definite statement as
to what is going to remain in the metropolitan area. We only surmise
that we have some jobs — X number of jobs — until April of 1956, when
this company has an opportunity of getting out of their lease at 1122
West Oak Street, a lease which, incidentally, I think I've mentioned
runs until '62. But beyond April of '56 we can't see anything. And up
until April 15 — April 1st, '56 — or 15th, '56, I think it is, we don't
know what will remain here. All we know is that there are 2 items
which have been productive items and items which we were never told
before were considered loss items because they could be purchased
for less, power transformers and tuning condensers; mean a great
deal to us in term of the number — in terms of the number of jobs
that's represented in those 2 departments. These newer products, binaural recorders and that Navy miniaturization project, are brand new
products and could mean a great deal to us in terms of the number of
jobs that will eventually be involved as the company gets in more and
more into product — productivity on those 2 new items. Then we face
up to the proposition of many new items which are now in the Engineering Department in the development stage which, accordin' to the company's own letter, very likely will be moved out of the metropolitan
area. And when I say out of the metropolitan area, I'm talking about
the radius proposition in our contract, which says within this radius
of the metropolitan area we have jurisdiction. We have a very definite
statement from Mattuck, who's represented the company, that there
is nothing that the union can say or suggest or do that "will stop us
from moving" those 4 things I've just finished mentioning. Nothing!
Just as cold as that. We had to experience in trying to (pause) get
somewhere in this decentralization problem a very bad attitude on
the part of the company in that we had some people who were willing
to transfer to Aiken, South Carolina; and despite the fact that some
of those people had a good beal — deal of service with Atlas, they

absolutely refused to give them any consideration in the t — in terms
of continuing their seniority, their pensions and severance pay rights,
and that kind of thing, or other benefit rights such as vacation and all.
"Absolutely no," they said. "If you — your people wanta go down
there, Number 1, we'll take an application from them, but they must
resign from the metropolitan area — in the metropolitan area plant,
move to Aiken, and then we'll consider their application." They didn't
even guarantee to give 'em a job after they quit in the metropolitan
area and moved to Aiken. They'd take 'em on the same as they would
anybody else, and I suppose y — wouldn't take a detective, as you say,
to know that they'd be very reluctant to take somebody and hire them
in Aiken who came out of the metropolitan area plant, for fear of organization, which is exactly why they've been takin' the — a (pause)
— on setting up the kind of policy that they're applying toward the
Aiken plant and the metropolitan area employees. All in all, I mean,
the company has, accordin' to their own statements, increased the
stockholders up here by great deal. I mean, I believe — I think there's
4488 stockholders, whereas they had quite a few less than that the last
time, even in October when we negotiated with them. And of course
(pause) those people evidentally have invested their money on a basis
of expecting a sound return and a constant return. Now, that's all right
with us. We don't kick too much about a stockholder who gets 40¢ on
a share of stock as a dividend for the whole year. But we don't wanta
pay for it, particularly, George, when the majority of the dividends
that are paid out, see — they got 4488 stockholders, yes; but the majority of the stock in this company is owned by a small group of people!
And it's owned by guys like Hal and his wife, Clarence McGrath and
his wife, Dr. Hummel and his wife. It's a — they got — all their wives
are in this business, and their wives have almost as much stock as
they have! And I would s — I would venture to say that out of the total
amount of money that's paid out in dividends to all the stockholders,
probably better than 50% of the total amount of money goes to that
group of officers who are members of the Board of Directors or
actively working as officers in the company, drawing salaries! And
in addition to that they set up this profit-sharing plan for themselves
which, based on what's happening in '52, if the union doesn't get its
fair share out of this, is going to mean increased profit sharing for
those same people! We can't see it! That's why I used the term hogs,
and I wasn't kidding about it. I mean, they're drawing 3 ways! Yeah,
they gave us the old argument about, "Well, we're entitled to a fair
return for our money. We risk our money." And we don't argue with
anybody getting a fair return for their money. But I think they can
stand a little bit less much easier'n the people we represent can,
particularly when they're drawin' an in — they have 3 different avenues of reve — of income, whereas our people have one. I don't know
whether that covers sufficiently the — the things that we feel about
this entire situation, but I'm — I know this much, that slowly but
surely, for quite some time, now, they've been building themselves
a policy which is bound to — which was bound to and which is bound
to, if it's continued, result in a work stoppage. That comment's been
made by people outside of Atlas — I mean, union officials, of course,
that know this situation, have known it for years, and have — through

association with myself, know the way this thing has developed. And it's — I've known this for some time. If they're gonna continue, this is only one thing that they have to have happen to them in order to slow them up, pull 'em up short! (Pause) We have, as we see it now, very little to lose in the face of the policies and program that they've set themselves. They have, as we see it, a great deal to lose about it. And I think they are not goin' to take a strike (pause) unless the union, of course, retains a position which is real — unrealistic. I'm quite convinced that the union can realize a figure below what its present position is without any hardship on that company, without — as we usually put it to 'em, without puttin' 'em out of business or without puttin' 'em in a bad competitive situation or not. And again on that competitive proposition, they make a great deal about that; but, still in all, I mean, then you look at their financial report and you see the president of the company, Harold Fuller, stating that they are going to get their share of the — the demand that will exist during '53. And there's no doubt in my mind that they will, because despite the fact that Atlas makes claims of higher costs for their items than their competitors, it's also a matter of fact that that condition has existed for years and that they have been able to sell Atlas products on the basis of quality which has gotten the consideration from the customer because — even though the price is higher than some of their competitors. Their letter, incidentally, pointed out that what — or, why they were decentralizing was to become more efficient, to get more production, and to provide more profits, to the benefit of all. Now, we don't consider it's to the benefit of all, which would include us, when they move out of the (laughing slightly) metropolitan area, and if they make more profits, if we're not gonna share with 'em. That just about as I feel, and, anyhow, George, sums up the situation. These people can come up quite a bit above their present position without hurting 'em a'tall. We're dealing with — I'm — we have been mentioning 14 or 1500 people. Actually, now — I've checked with Bernice; we checked over the week-end — we don't have very many more than 1200 union members in that plant. And when you talk in terms of 2¢ an hour as applied to 1200 people, you're talking in terms of $45,000.00 an hour as applied to 1200 people, you're talking in terms of $45,000.00 roughly, in a lump sum, which would be spread out as a cost from April 1st, '53, throughout the rest of '53. And $45,000.00 to me is not — is nothing compared to what they can do, because I'm looking at a financial report which, based on the first period of 1953, gives evidence of Atlas winding up with better than $2\frac{1}{2}$ million dollars in profit before taxes at the end of '53. And 45,000.00, or even 450,000.00, isn't — isn't going to put them out of business. (Pause) And it's very ironic — very ironic and very distasteful to me to have them offer us 1-cent increase in pensions in the face of the decentralization program. That — that is terrific. I mean (laughs, joined by Meyer), you got to remember, first place, the people —

Mediator: D'you have a severance clause?

Gambon: We have a severance clause, but you must be in the c — you must be with the company (Meyer: You have to quit to get it) for 2 years in order to get the — to participate in the plan a'tall, and in order to get your sevance — severance pay you'll have to — well, you have to sever your connections with the company. You — you — you

can either die or quit or resign or be fired or anything else, you'd still
get it, but that's the only way you would get it. (One of girls laughs)
Meyer: And you have to go to the hospital to get that 7.50 to $9.00.
Gambon: Incidentally, that — I think I did mention to you — that's the
form of the bargaining goin' on in Standard Products. At least part
of the bargaining goin' on there is for a company-paid insurance plan.
And (laughs) it seems strange that they would direct their offer toward that kind of thing since we've never — didn't — it's not "never,"
but since we, for the first time, incidentally, in our wage demands
have not asked for increased insurance benefits or increased pension
benefits. We did that back in (Meyer: October) — durin' the new
contract, and we (Meyer: Oc —) did it again in October of '52, but
we did not ask for it this time. Both the demands that we presented
to them durin' the negotiations which were concluded in March of '52
— you remember; that contained a 2-cent request for pension severance and a 2-cent request for insurance. And that demand was repeated in October, but it was not part of the union's demands this
time. (Meyer: Huh-un) Yet they see fit to make their offers directed
to those kind of things, and, as I say, very ironically a — an offer to
increase pension severance benefits in the face of decentralization
program. (Rather long pause) / Well, that —
Mediator: (Over Gambon above) When you spoke of a — when you spoke
of a realistic figure, John, you said the union could come down to a
realistic figure. What were you thinking of? (Rather long pause)
Gambon: Well, George, a realistic figure to me may not be what they
would consider a realistic figure, because, after all, I'm a little bit
biased as to what my people oughta get. I — I don't think that the 35-
hour work week is unrealistic, see. They do. And I don't think that
20% fixed bonus proposition is unrealistic. Maybe they might agree
with me that the 20% fixed bonus in itself as a separate item may not
be unrealistic, but 35-hour work week certainly is, according to their
own statements and certainly lumped together with a 20% bonus demand is, in their opinion, unrealistic. I gave you some estimates on
the fixed bonus item, estimates which I think we c — were confronted
with back in — around March of '52, and I think the figure at that time
was $.04-some tenths. It was better than 4¢. It is my opinion that
there are less people involved than there were in March of '52, so
that I don't think that the — any estimated cost could exceed 4¢ by
any too great a figure and might possibly even be a little lower than
the actual 4¢. (Rather long pause) We have talked before about this
kind of a situation, and we have decided that in the event that the 35-
hour work week seemed impossible of am — attainment at this time
that we would be willing to accept the $37\frac{1}{2}$-hour work week, of course
with the same kind of provisions connected with the 35-hour work
week. (Mediator: Uh-huh) And I have no objection to offering the —
that as the union's position at this time, with, of course, the Item 2,
the 20% fixed bonus. Incidentally, reading the paper this morning,
we see an ad for a typist in the paper there, which I understand
Atlas's been running for a couple of weeks, now. And they're offering a job as a typist on a $37\frac{1}{2}$-hour work week. I wonder why? Now,
in regard to this $37\frac{1}{2}$-hour work week, if I haven't said it before I'd
like to call your attention again, George, that our contract provides

both a $37\frac{1}{2}$-hour work week and a 35-hour work week when we operate
3 shifts in any department. Immediately that a department goes on 3
shifts, the 2d shift works $7\frac{1}{2}$ hours and gets their 8 hours' pay, and
the 3rd shift works 7 hours a night, 35 hours a week, and gets their
8 hours', or 40 hours', pay. So that it isn't such a far step for this
company as it may appear to be. We have some departments operating on that $8 - 7\frac{1}{2}$ and 7-hour basis right now. And the production
warranted it in some departments, they wouldn't hesitate a minute to
go to it. And we've never heard any real beefs about that. We've had
that in our contract, now, I'd say, for about 4 years. It's one of the
few contracts in this city that has that kind of a clause in it. (Long
pause)

Mediator: What does $37\frac{1}{2}$ hours mean per hour — ¢ per hour? (Pause)

Gambon: Well, roughly, I'd say maybe about 12¢. (Very long pause)

Meyer: (In fairly low voice) 'Bout $11\frac{1}{2}$.

Gambon: Huh?

Meyer: (In fairly low voice) 'Bout $11\frac{1}{2}$. On their estimate I think
(Gambon: Yeah) it's lower. (Pause) On $1.71.

Gambon: That 12 c — 12 — 16-cent — 15 to 16-cent package'd run 'em
about, say — let's — between — as a total cost from April 1st through
'50 — '53, about $360,000.00. That would still leave them with better
than — over the $2,000,000.00 — before-taxes profit proposition in
'53 at the rate they're going, which is not peanuts. (Rather long pause)
But they're getting to the point where they're not satisfied with the
kind of profits that they've been making even in these several good
years that they've had recently. They want more of it! They wanta
get into the big stuff! I don't blame 'em (pause), 'cause the more
they get the more we'd want.

Mediator: What was the cost-of-living, John, from — in the pa — during
the last 6 months of your contract?

Gambon: I don't know. Our old contract? (Pause) I don't know. I had
some figure here I think I quoted the other day, about 13.5 — 6%. See
what that was.

Mediator: No, I mean since your last reopener.

Meyer: Since October.

Gambon: Since / October?

Mediator: (Over Gambon above) Since October.

Gambon: Oh, I think it's gone down, hasn't it?

Mediator: Yeah. That's right. It's goin' down.

Gambon: I'm not too concerned with that, even if it had gone up, because we still have this 12 to 16-cent wage differential existing with
the very companies that they started these negotiations — using comparisons with. You see, they started this wage comparison thing, and
then they don't like it when we go back and say, "Well, if you're gonna
use 'em for 3 years, let's do it right. Let's start where we all started
even — start goin' down here." (Pause) And their crowin' about having given greatest amount that they ever gave at one time means very
little to me because we've caught up a bit. We didn't get it from —
we never caught up entirely. (Long pause) Yeah, from '46 through
'52 we're still 12¢ behind Standard Products, 15.3 behind Lashley,
15.1 behind Hercules, we're 6¢ plus whatever they got in '49 behind
Monco System, we're 16.1 behind Precision-Made, 9.3 behind Dayco.

Dayco is negotiating now, Standard Products's negotiating, Lashley's
negotiating. We're gonna go further behind this — these people if we
can't try to close this differential up. (Long pause)

Mediator: Uh — (pause).

Gambon: Although we prefer to bargain on this reduced work-week proposition, though it might mean — in effect it would mean those same
wage differentials would exist, still our main concern was to try to
provide more jobs here in the face of a layoff which we've already
experienced and in the face of another one which is gonna result in
maybe a couple hundred more people being out of jobs by November
of this year. And then the other thing to take into consideration is
that they gave this — they gave these figures that they did here to us
and to you and then their own financial report, that despite the fact
that they got a million two hundred and some odd thousand dollars before taxes in profits in '52, they lost, they claimed, on these loss
items over $779,000.00, of which about 583,000.00 were volume con-
trols alone. Now, that's not a loss item any more. They can't lose
money on transformer production with the rates they're payin' down
in Aiken and the benefits that they're giving down there compared to
what they had up here. They got every job in that factory down there
is covered by a screwy kind of job calculation plan. We had scales
running from — anywhere from Grade A to Grade E in the department up here, which meant 63¢ was the incentive base rate for Grade
A and the incentive base rate on Grade E was 85¢. Now, people made
bonus on those figures plus the payroll add which is now around 62¢.
So you can see what is happening down there. That's gonna be a very
profitable item. And when it gets to be a profitable item, what they'll
prob'ly tell us, "Well, we're not — this plant's not in the metropolitan
area. We don't wanta have that counted in the financial statements of
the company when we bargain with you." They only wanta use it now
when it's to their benefit to use it, see. The minute it becomes a
profitable proposition, well, they're not gonna wanta count that.
(Rather long pause)

Mediator: Well, in the light of everything you said and in the light of
everything that they said (pause), I'm goin' to stick my proverbial
neck out, because I feel it's my duty and my responsibility to tell you
this. I think you know it, and I tell the same thing to the company.
Like to see you get together faster. Like to see you get to the point
where the both of you can reach an agreement that's satisfactory to
each other. But I do think that — and I'm — I never — I don't consider myself an expert economist or even an amateur economist, but
the figures where both of you are standing are so far apart from one
another that both of you are really fencing. Neither of you — you may
be sincere (Gambon: H'm), but you're not in your bargaining area,
and I don't wanta play games with the union and I don't wanta play
games with the company. I wanta tell both of you — and if the company was sitting here I'd tell it to them, and I — and I've told them a
lot stronger in my last caucus — that I feel that the time for footwork
is over and that both of you have a darn good idea of what you're gonna
settle for and you better get down to that area. If you don't get down
here you're gonna get down some place else (Gambon: H'm), but
I'll bet you a dollar to a doughnut it's goin' to be in that area. The

reopener settlements can be averaged out at a certain figure, and
that figure is — won't be far off from what you people are gonna work
out. Now, what I'm tryin' to say is — and I'm not tryin' to cheat you
out of anything; I want you to get as much as you can. I'm not paying
the bill; the company's going to pay the bill. But I — I know that they
can't pay the bill and you can't collect it until you get down there to
where they — where the both of you are no longer afraid of one another. Where you're standing now the both of you are afraid of one
another.

Gambon: Oh, I wouldn't put it on that basis. (Mediator: I mean — uh —
n-no. No. When I use the term, I'm not —) Not — / not afraid of
'em, but I don't intend to jeopardize my bargaining position. As long
as they —

Mediator: (Over Gambon above) That's what I — that's what I mean to
say. Both of you are jealous of your bargaining (Gambon: That's
right) positions, not afraid of one another economically. I don't
mean it that (Gambon: H'm) way. You're — you're jealously bar —
bar — guarding your positions. Now, so far I've done that for you,
too. I haven't let either side jeopardize their position, and I don't
want you to, because when you do that's exactly when it gets harder
for me. But even talkin' about 12¢, or whatever figure that was you
— you gave there, I — I would be very happy if this company would
pay you 12¢. / I wish they would. But you know —

Gambon: (Over Mediator above) Let me show you some interesting
figures, George. I mean, you'll — maybe you might understand why
I keep insisting about this company's ability-to-pay business. Back
in 1946 this company, according to their statements, lost $73,141.00,
and in '47 — no, I'm wrong. In '46 they — their net — net earnings
were $283,388.00. In '47 they lost $104,807.00. For the 2 years that
gives 'em net earnings of approximately $183,000.00 — 180,000.00,
roughly. Despite that kind of a financial record they were able to
grant, durin' '46 and '47, 28½¢ an hour in wage increases. In '48
they had net earnings —

Mediator: Is this some other company?

Gambon: This is Atlas.

Mediator: Oh, Atlas.

Gambon: In 1948 their net earnings were $132,719.00; in '48 we got 9¢
an hour. In '49 they come up with $320,060.00 net earnings; in '49
we got fringe packages that resulted in about 14½¢, all fringes. In
1950 they come up with $1,104,263.00 net earnings; in 1950 we got
5¢. But that's when they started their profit-sharing plan, see. In
'51 — well, they have their figures in '51.

[Tape is changed while Gambon is searching among his papers.]
... '51 (rather long pause), and their profits before taxes,
$2,134,675.00, although I would assume from this record here that
net earnings to them were profits after taxes. (Pause) Where's that
figure — here. (Rather long pause) Profit on activities during the
year, $754,675.00. Again, on the basis of that figure they come up
with only a nickel, and they expanded the profit sharing from 66 people
to 90-some people.

Mediator: Was that durin' a reopener?

Gambon: We negotiated this 5-and-5 business back in '50.

Mediator: Was that a termination?

Gambon: Uh (Meyer: No) — no. It was during the terms of the contract which expired on March of '52. The contract — the previous contract, the one we're now working with, ran from August of '49 until (Meyer: August of '51) — well, it run all the way till M — huh? (Saunders: Extension — extension of 6 months) — August of '51, and then we — yes, we did. We had an extension (Meyer: xx April) as part of that 5-and-5 business until April of '52, which was the expiration date of the contract previous to the one we now have. But their whole record here — they've been — they gave out some pretty nice increases over those years on — in the face of less operating profit and activities than they've been getting now since '50 and '51 and '52. But they don't wanta spend the money now for wage increases. I mean, they're blunt about it, and all their plans are indic — indictive of what the hell they're doin'. They wanta spend the money to p — to develop new products, and we know that those damn new products are not gonna be kept here in the metropolitan area. And they wanta — they want the money to — to — probably to push this decentralization program, to ac — accelerate it. Hell, we're not gonna pay for that kind of business. These people could — I — I gave you a figure — I said $360,000.00. Hell, based on what they got now, if they come up with 240 or 50 — or rather $2,500,000.00 — somethin' like that, they've still got over $2,000,000.00 before taxes. And their — their figures are — are indicating that to be a trend. The — the last 3 periods of 1952 follow right in back of the first period of '53. Take a look at it; you'll see it. It's not just the first period of '50 — '53, and that's why I kept repeating so many times that business about the — the last 3 periods of '52. (Rather long pause) (In low voice, while searching for something) Well, where've I got it? (Rather long pause) Well, anyway, I mean, they're — they're almost — those 4 periods are almost identical. And if you'll prorate that first period against 10 periods for '53 they're bound to come out with better than 2, $2\frac{1}{2}$ million dollars' profit before taxes.

Mediator: John, what d'you think they have b — short of a strike?

Gambon: Huh?

Mediator: What d'you — what d'you think they'd settle for? I'd like to / get your opinion, because i — either th — they're mis — they're misleading me or —

Gambon: (Over Mediator above) I don't know, George. I — I'm not in a position to make the kind of guesses that I used to in the face of this new policy business. (Mediator: — or —) All I want them to understand is, see, that they can get a strike! They can get one! I think, in the first place, they — through Bill Michelsen they didn't think that the union would take a strike vote — an approved one. That's an accomplished fact now. Whether or not they think we're — we'll make a cheap settlement rather than strike is your guess as well as mine, but I know this. There'll be no cheap settlement in the face of everything that we've gone through with this company since the signing of this new contract, particularly. (Pause) These people'll (Mediator: Uh —) probably try to bleed us to death on arbitration, for Christ's sake, for — if nothing else. We're — this guy Espig is not gonna 'prove labor relations in there because he's been the guy that i —

comes up with these screwball interpretations   (Mediator: Oh —)
which have caused a lot of arguments.

Mediator: What were you — what were you congratulating him / for?

Gambon: (Over Mediator above) He's probably tak — he's takin'
Michelsen's / place.

Meyer: (Over Gambon above) He's the new (One of girls says something) industrial relations manager.

[There are a few further comments about Espig's position in the company, with several speaking at once at one point.]

Mediator: Well, we're gonna get 'em in here and we're gonna lay the law
down, and if you wanta blast, start blasting, because it's time to.
They're — I'm reaching a point where I feel something's gotta be done
short of (pause) getting your positions out on the table. They're
standing pat at 2 and you're up above anything that they say they can
pay for. Now, I know both of you are closer than that. I know that.
And —

Gambon: George, I gave you a position — a changed position to take back
in there. I wouldn't bring 'em back in here with that 2-cent thing.
(Pause) I don't wanta listen to their 2¢. They're wastin' my time,
they're wastin' yours.

Mediator: Oh. (Pause) Wait, I didn't quite understand that. Say that
again.

Gambon: I gave you a — a new proposition to take in there: $37\frac{1}{2}$-hour
week instead of 35, and the 20%. (Pause)

Mediator: Well, I'll take it in. (Slight pause) That's why I asked you the
cost of it. When you told me the cost of it, I knew then that it's a —
I can take it in if you wanta waste time. / They won't buy that.

Gambon: (Over Mediator above) Now, wait a minute, see. I'm — I'm
sayin' this to you, in effect. I gave you a rounded-out figure, a lump
sum of $360,000.00, which I say represents the new position of the un-
ion, despite the fact / that it may run —

Mediator: (Over Gambon above) Which works out to about 12¢ an hour.

Gambon: 12 plus. I'm working that (Mediator: Uh — oh) $360,000.00
out on a 16-cent figure, not 12. I'm (Mediator: Uh —) including 4¢
additional cost in there for the 20% bonus. And I pointed out that by
even takin' $360,000.00 increased cost out of a potential $2\frac{1}{2}$ million
dollars, they're still in a good sound position.

Mediator: Well, you won't have to convince me on that. / You're gonna
have to convince them.

Gambon: (Over Mediator above) No, but I want them to know that.
We're doin' some / figuring in here, too, you know.

Mediator: (Over Gambon above) Uh — but they — they — if it adds up to
12¢ an hour (pause) —

Gambon: It adds to 16.

Mediator: — or 16, / they —

Gambon: (Over Mediator above) And that's what that $360,000.00 is. It
represents an increased cost to the company from April 1st, '53,
through '53. (Pause) 'Course, they'll have to face up to the propa —
probability (laughing slightly) of increased demands in October of '53,
but I'm — I don't cross my bridges until I get to them. (Slight pause)

Mediator: Well, John, we'll deliver it for you, but it's — you know, I almost feel as though I'm representing management when I'm trying to
tell you —

Gambon: I'm beginnin' to feel that (Mediator: Yeah) way, George.
(Laughs) / That's reason I'm bargaining with ya! (Laughs again)

Mediator: (Over Gambon above) I — well, I — I — I can't blame ya, but
it's more — it's more because I know where they stand, and I know
(Gambon: Well, Christ, I want them to understand where we stand)
— I'm trying to convey that to you so you'll get an idea that (Gambon:
H'm) 16¢ or 12¢ is — is not a figure that I believe the 2 of you could
get together at this table on. I really mean that. And you'll (pause)
— and if you were sinc — if you were serious at that point and meant
it, I don't think there's a mediator in the United States could bring
you together / at this — at this —

Gambon: (Over Mediator above) George, I'm not depending entirely on
you bringing us together. Let me be honest enough to say that, see.
/ I'm willing to —

Mediator: (Over Gambon above) If you've got somethin' else, then let
me / know.

Gambon: (Over Mediator above) Huh? No! What I'm saying is this, is
that I'm willing to try to have you get us together, but I'm not goin'
to try to get together with them at a figure that they wanta settle, see.
(Slight pause) If I have to — if (Mediator: Well, let me xxx) I convince myself that this company can pay a certain amount and this committee is convinced of that, then they'll either have to meet that particular thing, because that is what we'll fight on the bricks for, see.

Mediator: All right. Somewhere along / the line —

Gambon: (Over Mediator above) But I won't propose that particular figure — I mean — and you can understand why. I'm not gonna make a
proposal and then hit the bricks in order to try to make them meet it,
because if I hit the bricks I'm gonna hit the bricks with a proposition
with — of the union bein' in a higher position than what it's willing to
settle for. (Mediator: I can —) It's to my interest to have the difference between the 2 of us as wide as possible if they're gonna force us
to strike to get a kind of settlement that we're willing to get — / or
take.

Mediator: (Over Gambon above) Right. I can understand that. And when
you hit the bricks, as far as these negotiations are concerned I can
assure you your position is not going to be jeopardized, and when you
hit the bricks you can hit for the higher limit. However (pause),
some time, some day (Gambon: H'm), some hour I've gotta know
that (Gambon: Yeah. All right) figure. And when — when I learn that
figure and I know where they stand on it, then I can tell you whether
you've gotta hit the bricks (Gambon: H'm. All right) or not. But we
better soon get around to that point of telling me.

Gambon: George, I'm givin' ya an indication of movement possible by
the union. All right. So I say to you, not for publication to the company's team, that is not our final position. It is not a position which
I'm going to strike on, if the company begins to move, but I won't go
any lower than this new offer if they're not gonna move. That's as
low a position that I wanta take if I have to have it on the basis of a
strike. (Rather long pause) Again I'm attemptin' to get to the point
where I'm convinced that they're beginning to engage in some honest-
to-God b — bargaining here in an effort to reach a settlement without
a strike! And they're not convincing me or the committee of that
when they're talkin' in terms of 2¢

Meyer: On insurance, especially.

Gambon: Especially on insurance! Or 2¢ on a general wage increase basis is not acceptable. I mean, I was — I don't know why he — he did the thing that he did this morning in the face of an absolute rejection by the committee, knowing that we had to present the company's position to a — to the union membership on Saturday.

Mediator: He was instructed to do / that.

Gambon: (Over Mediator above) Well, he may have been instructed to do it, but, / hell —

Mediator: (Over Gambon above) That was evident. (Pause) And he m (Gambon: Yeah. x —) — he said they had a meeting yesterday, didn't he?

Gambon: I gather that there was (Mediator: He said — yeah. He said there was a meeting) a meeting somethin', somewhere, somebody.

Mediator: He said it here!

Wollman: He said they gave it careful consideration over the week-end.

Mediator: Yeah. I — no, I thought he mentioned the — the top people — their committee, I think he called it.

One of boys: Didn't hear him say that.

Gambon: Now might be a good time for you to raise this question of whether or not he should make a phone call, if you're convinced that he's acting under instructions.

One of boys: John, is there any —

Mediator: Well, I'll tell ya, the only time — or I think the time where he will do that is when he (slight pause) — when he's convinced that the union is goin' to strike at a certain figure.

Gambon: George, he's running out of time. Now, we're talking, let's say, fairly generally in terms of x. Maybe I haven't stated it clearly enough. If they don't change their position today, see, and in view of the fact that we can't get together with you and them before Thursday, this committee will then have to take into consideration whether or not we wanta sit on our can for 2 days and — with nothing more than the position that they have at this moment or whether we prefer to convince them that, "Ya've gone far enough in your delaying tactics, and we're going to hit the bricks and we'll talk to you while we're outside instead of doin' it while we're inside." In effect he's got a deadline to make some sort of movement today to convince us that it's worthwhile continuing to try to bargain this out and reach a settlement without a strike. And that's what it amounts to. Call it pressure if you want to. It's certainly pressure on my part tryin' to apply it to them. You know they can move and I know they can move, and I want them to move.

Mediator: Well, they're like you. They don't wanta move, they don't wanta get out on a — / in a position where —

Gambon: (Over Mediator above) Only I got a — I got a nice — nice poker hand here right now.

Denk: George, their position already has been rejected by our membership. So it's up to them to move. (Pause)

Mediator: (Addressing Denk) See, what I'm tryin' to say is this. They evidentally have a certain amount to spend, or ceiling, just like you have a certain amount to — below — to accept. You have your bottom and they have their ceiling. Neither of you know right now what will

settle this. They know what they'll take a strike on and you know
what you'll take a strike on. Now, what we're trying to do is establish
those 2 points. As for the — far as the company's concerned, and reading between the lines, most — they haven't committed themselves con-
cretely, but figures that they're — if I were to guess, make a deduction as to what they are thinking about, I h — o — I — let me say it
this way — it's nothing like that that you would settle for, and there is
where we have to — we have to put the spotlight on that. We have to
show a — we have to bring it out and stop the guesswork. And we've
got to, now, get it out in the open so both sides can see how far apart
they are. It appears like the only one that really sees it, as far as the
company and the union's concerned, is the mediator. Sometimes it
even looks like I'm the only one that's worrying. But I know that's not
true, because when you leave this conference room, responsibility belongs to the — what happened belongs to the union and company, and
with me it stops. But the gaps are so apart — so far apart, and both
of you are holding onto your positions — now, all this I've said to
them. Don't think that I haven't been talking this way to them. I've
been doing — using dynamite on them to try to blast them away to —
to even find <u>out</u> where they're going. They (pause) — I think I could
— I think I could write the ticket and not be wrong by fractions as to
where I think they're going. But I've gotta get that up on the table.
They've gotta come out and say so. And you're poles apart.

Wollman: They not only — they not only make us an offer that's not satisfactory; they tell us how to use it yet in the bargain, and then they tell
us they won't even consider April the 1st as a retroactive date this
time. They even tell us how to use the offer that isn't satisfactory in
the first place. (Pause)

Gambon: In effect what Stan is saying is that they're makin' it more difficult to get a s — settlement without a strike. (Pause) I mean, by their
approach to this thing! They're not makin' the right kind of approaches!
And I don't think it's fair to expect the union to do anything more than
I've done right as of this moment. We've made moves which we're
trying to indicate with, to the company, that, "We're in a bargainable
position and we wanta bargain. But we're not gonna come down into
your area and do the bargaining." And while we'd like 'em to come
all the way up to what we're asking for, we still recognize the fact
that that may not be, in their thinking, a realistic thing for them to do.
But they gotta get the hell out of the area that they're in now! And
they've gotta get far beyond that.

Mediator: Well, that's what they're afraid of, that / if they go beyond
that they —

Gambon: (Over Mediator above) Well, they're afraid of paying out any
more than they wanta pay out, George. That's all's the matter with
'em — I mean, the wh — the — what I've listened to. They've — they've
got the money, they're makin' the money, and they don't wanta give it
to us to any great extent because they have other plans for it! And
that's what we don't like! (Meyer: Well, we have other plans, too)
Their other plans — their other plans don't involve us! It's not to
our benefit. Nothing that they're plannin' to do is to our benefit. And
as long as they're gonna be here, they're gonna pay us a fair share of
what they make. Some day maybe we won't have them around. We're

— we're probably reconciled to that kind of a proposition eventually, but, by Christ, while they're here and while we're workin' for them, they'll never get us to come to 'em with our hat in our hands and say "Please, don't give us anything" in the hopes that they'll stay here, because they'd laugh in our face and not give us anything and move, anyhow. (Pause)

One of boys: Look —

Mediator: What we're tryin' to do — what we're tryin' to do here, and evidently without success, is not to interfere with — or, prevent the union from getting everything that the tariff or the traf — traffic will bear, but more or less to get the negotiations started. Now, they're — with where you are, see — here's — here's the way they look at it, and you — you can realize this. Their 2¢ — uh-h-h-h — you would be at 16, did you say?

Gambon: Yeah.

Mediator: You'd be at 16. (Gambon: Approximately 16 xx) You say they would have to make a move to show you good faith. They would say, / "Who" —

Gambon: (Over Mediator above) At this point the move — I mean, they gotta start moving away from 2¢ before (Mediator: That's what I mean) this meeting is over in order to convince us that there's any reason to wait until Thursday to bargain again without a strike! If they're gonna maintain the 2-cent position I can almost assure you that there'll be a strike before Thursday. (Pause)

Mediator: Well (rather long pause), I'm beginnin' to think that maybe that'll be a good idea.

Gambon: Well, I'm — I'm tryin' to find out, because (Mediator: See, as I —) I'll go along with 'em; I'll stay here as long as you think there's any possibility of getting them to do some moving. But if I'm gonna sit here all afternoon and possibly again into this evening the way we did the other day and they come out here and they repeat that 2¢ to me, that's it! (Slight pause) I'm gonna know then that they're — they're probably asking for a strike. Why they would do it, I don't know. I'm not convinced that they want it, because I don't see what they can benefit by it. They can n — they cannot only run into a cost involving a strike itself, but they're gonna lose some of their customers! They're gonna lose 'em. (Slight pause) And they'll have a hell of a time gettin' 'em back if they lost 'em.

Meyer: And if the weather stays nice they're gonna lose some employees for longer than the duration of the strike. (Pause)

Mediator: Well, some of these things we're gonna have to get over to them. (Gambon: Uh-huh) I'm gonna have to try to get 'em over and you're gonna have to try to get 'em over to 'em, because they've gotta be convinced and they evidently aren't.

Gambon: Well, my reason for saying that I didn't think it would be any good to bring 'em in here at this time because they'll walk in here with that 2% — or, 2¢ position. I've made a new proposition for you to relay to them, get 'em thinking again, so that if they do — if you do bring 'em in here again that they're beginning to indicate to us that they're moving away from 2¢. Because, by Christ, George, if they come in here after another bull session and say 2¢, I don't wanta meet any further with them. Not while we're still in that shop.

Mediator: Well, now, I oughta let them say this (Gambon: H'm) instead of me saying it, but this is what they're gonna say. If your position is where it is they <u>will</u> hold to 2¢, even / if ya strike.

Gambon: (Over Mediator above) Haven't I said we're in a bargainable position?

Mediator: Well, how do we / bargain?

Gambon: (Over Mediator above) But I'm not gonna — huh?

Mediator: How do we bargain?

Gambon: Get 'em start movin'! I've made a move now to indicate that we're in a bargainable / position.

Mediator: (Over Gambon above) Let me put it this way.

Meyer: Let 'em discuss the issues that <u>we</u> presented instead of the ones that they presented.

Mediator: Let me put it this way, in answer to your question. Here's — here's what any employer, or any union, would think. You — I would convey your proposal, which is tantamount to 16¢. (Gambon: Uh-huh) They're at 2. Now, let's say they had a limited amount to spend (Gambon: H'm), and let us say they moved another cent. (Gambon: All right) They'd be at 3. What would stop you from coming in and knocking 2¢ off your 16?

Gambon: What <u>will</u> stop / it?

Mediator: (Over Gambon above) Nothing.

Gambon: (In low voice) Yeah.

Mediator: So they figure those things out. (Gambon: Uh-huh) They know those positions are not realistic. They're in <u>danger</u> when they try to bargain, <u>so are you</u> when you try to bargain, in — in an unrealistic area. / Uh —

Gambon: (Over Mediator above) George, all I'm waiting for is th — those people to indicate that they're ready to try to resolve this issue without a strike by making a move that is somewhat substantial! (Mediator: But —) Not 2¢, <u>not</u> 3¢; tell 'em to move! We'll move, and we'll get into some God — honest God — honest-to-God bargaining here. (Pause)

Mediator: Well, I'm (laughing slightly) —

Gambon: But I'm not gonna make all the moves! I mean, if you wanta take it, all right. So we were in an unrealistic position. I don't look at it that way, on the face of what their potential is for '53. And I don't think I'm in an unrealistic position at this moment with the new offer that we're asking you to convey to them, because that represents a total cost to the company of some $360,000.00. Now, they gave out in profit sharing to about 114 people a couple a hundred thousand dollars! The hell are we gonna do? Let them keep givin' out a couple hundred thousand dollars to a 114 people or increasing it to 125, or 150, and we take the short end in order to provide that kind of thing? They're nuts!

Wollman: People that get that money pay most of it out in taxes, anyhow. (One of girls laughs quietly) Wilson got 581,000.00 (One of girls says something) and wound up with 100,000.00.

Healy: I think the fact remains when we left here on Friday it was a rejected offer. Our membership rejected it. I think the next move is up to them. (Pause)

Mediator: Well, I'll carry your proposal to them, have them discuss it.

Gambon: And ask them to please begin to bargain on the <u>union's</u> demands, not something that we didn't even offer here as for consideration.

Mediator: Yeah, I'll convey that to them. I'll take a piece of candy.

Gambon: Help yourself. Maybe you oughta take that in to sweeten them up a little bit, too, huh?

One of boys: (Says something but cannot be understood)

Mediator: They what?

Gambon: Say maybe you oughta take a couple pieces in and sweeten them up a little bit.

Mediator: They'd — they'd think it was a bribe.

Gambon: Huh? (Couple girls laugh)

Meyer: This stage of the game, / they prob'ly would.

Gambon: (Over Meyer above) They'd prob'ly look at the — they'd (laughing slightly) (One of girls talks at same time) prob'ly look at the —

Management Caucus - C (3:35 P.M.)

Mediator: ... in to management. I said, "They might think I'm tryin' to bribe 'em." (Loring, then Pranis, laugh) (Pause) Well, we had a session! We haven't stopped (laughing slightly) since we left here.

Loring: Is that so, George?

Mediator: She just (laughing) remarked about it in the hall. (Rather long pause) I kept right on top of John. (Pause) Fact, I got to one point where I told him — told <u>all</u> of 'em — I said, "It may appear that (slight pause) by the position that I'm taking that I represent management." I said, "It could be interpreted, because I'm taking such a strong position. But," I said, "in the absence of management I have to bring these points to you so that you can realize where you're going. As long as you're thinking where you are, this job of mediation isn't being <u>done</u>. I've got to get that gap down. And you — your — your sights are way up there." And I was trying to drive point — drive home the point (slowly, as though for emphasis) that the pace of these negotiations shows me that we do not have <u>realistic</u> bargaining. That's the point I was making. Then we got to talking about figures. So, they said, "Well, we're going to change our position and give you a proposal to take to management." They did: $37\frac{1}{2}$ hours a week, 20%, which amounts to about 16¢ an hour. (Long pause) I said, "I can take it in to them, but, again, we're gonna be wastin' time! What's the point of it? Particularly where we've been here for 6 meetings (pause) — 5, whatever it is." I said, "The time for footwork and fencing is over. Gotta get ya down to this area." See, I was tryin' to give him an opportunity to throw out officially what I'd had unofficially (Loring: Uh-huh), see. I was tryin' to make — open the door. (Pause) "Now," I said, "16¢ is — $37\frac{1}{2}$-hour week, 20%, is 16¢ or thereabouts, and I know and you know that won't go over." Well, John said that if the company sticks to 2¢ there could be a strike; they won't wait until the next meeting. They would strike sooner. "Well," I said, "maybe that's what you need! Maybe you need a good strike. I don't know." I said, "I'm beginning to think that something else — <u>something's</u> needed here to move the people —

you and them." I said, "And I'm also beginning to think" — and I
had to include the company also here; I had to say — I said, "I'm
beginnin' to think that I'm the only guy that's doin' any worrying here.
You're not, and neither is the company, as far as your positions are
concerned." So I said, "If you do strike, the responsibility will be
all yours and I'll just have to go right on to another case, so I, personally, after the strike takes place, wouldn't be hurt myself. But
you would." And I's layin' it on 'em quite heavy to blast 'em out of
his very, very foolish position. But he — finally I got the nub of it.
He came out. (Slight pause) He said, "The (emphatically) company
has to move from 2 ce — 2¢! They must move from it to show us that
they're bargaining in good faith." "All right, John," I said, "you're
at 16, officially — 37½-hour week, 20%. Let us say that the company
did move. Now they have a latitude, or a maximum, same as you have
a minimum. They have a maximum that they can pay, you have a minimum that you can accept. So let's say that their maximum is small.
It isn't — they don't have to play with that that they want to. And they
come back with an offer of a cent. (Slight pause) Then what would
prevent you from coming in as a counter-proposal and knocking 2¢
off your 16-cent package?" (Pause) He said, "Yes, that could happen. But" — then he went in — launched into your financial ability —
the profit-sharing plan, so on, so on, so on. So we concluded by agree-
ing to convey to you, officially, the proposal of the union, which is 37½
cent — (looking out of window) is that rain?
Pranis: I don't think — no! (Pause) Yes, it is. (Espig: Sure, it is)
    It is!
Mediator: Yeah.
Loring: Everything happens, eh? (Laughs, followed by Pranis and
    Mediator)
Mediator: 37½¢ an hour and 20% for the skilled trades. Now, that has
    been officially brought to you. (Pause)
Espig: You mean 37½-hour week?
Mediator: Oh. Didn't I — I —
Espig: You said 37½¢.
Mediator: Oh! 37½-hour week, and (Espig laughs quietly) they say, too,
    they object to the company not bargaining on the proposals that they
    submitted. Now (rather long pause), John, at this time, with all his
    toughness, I can't overlook the fact that we had a side-bar conference,
    he and I, and he told me 2 and 5. (Pause) But it is very, very evi-
    dent that even 2 and 5, if it was even acceptable to the company, John
    isn't ready for even that, based on what just took place here. He left
    no doors open other than this one that he gave me, which again indi-
    cated the — that this damn thing is going slower and slower. (Loring:
    H'm) Now, it could be that he's building up pressure to give you a
    strike threat if he doesn't get more than 2¢. (Slight pause) He says
    if he don't get more than 2¢, then he'll have to use the strike vote that
    he has. If he gets more than 2¢, then he'll continue negotiations. In
    other words, that would be a down payment on good faith. That's
    dangerous. I mean, that could lead to — I don't want — see, I can't
    afford to allow these negotiations to get into a (pause) untenable po-
    sition where you get in and can't get out. (Loring: Yeah) See, I don't
    wanta — I don't wanta get you — I wanta use what you have where it'll

do — be the most effective. And it's not e — it wouldn't be any good right now. It's not effective! It wouldn't — you could go in there right now and throw your 4¢ on the table and then they'd laugh at it! (Loring: Yeah. Yeah) It's — it'd die. I — it's — wouldn't have a chance. Now, they mi — they'd do this. They'd — they'd take your 4¢ and consider it a fairly good day's work today. "We'll meet to-morrow," or some other day. That's how that would be treated. So their sights are very high. However, high as they are, the other brings them down considerably lower. You're really at 7¢. (Pause) I believe now that you're going to be faced with a strike threat at this next joint meeting, when we get together. (Loring: Uh-huh) Now, I think that you're gonna have to be prepared to reply to it, and you're gonna have to take a position that you don't want one, but "If this is what we have to buy, why, we'll have one." (Slight pause) Unless you can pay 16¢.

Loring: (In low voice) No. No. (Someone laughs slightly)

Mediator: Then, of course, John will, I'm sure, move in for his (pause) — with his — with a suggestion that you (slight pause) move away from your 2¢ to show him that you're in a bargainable mood. (Pause) And, of course, the right thing to do is not answer (slight pause) jointly (Loring: Uh-huh) — in joint session. (Slight pause)

Loring: How would you get away from answering, George?

Mediator: Well, I think I would say that, "We have given you an offer that we think is fair, and we cannot see" — see, you gotta be careful. You can't say, "We cannot see where we could make any move, in the light of your position," which would immediately (clapping hands) indicate you had more. (Loring: Uh-huh) I think right now at this s — even at this hour you're gonna still have to hold to 2. Remember, you can always move at the — when you want to and when it's the right time. Y — but (rather long pause) the stiffer you are at this time on that point, the softer they're going to be in their relations with me, because they will have gotten it right from the horse's mouth that this is the way it is, see. (Loring: Uh-huh) They've gotten it from me. (Loring: Uh-huh) Now, if you did throw a cent out, you'd only have a cent left. (Loring: Right) And if you throw a cent out now you're goin' to go mo — have to go more than 4¢, because the — the jumps are such — and they're not moving! 'Course, with — off the record they are. They're at — they're at (Loring: Uh-huh) 7, and that's — for all practical purposes that's official (slight pause), because that was given to me and I would say so. And that —

Espig: Would this be a time to say to them, if they prefer to take the 2¢ in cash, in the e — pay envelope, that we'd consider it? Would that be a maneuver? Or is that not — are we not ready for anything like that, even?

Mediator: You mean, and continue bargaining? (Slight pause)

Espig: And continue bargaining. (Pause)

Mediator: Well, they wouldn't do that, to start with. I don't know of a union that ever did it. Do you?

Espig: Wait a minute. Maybe I haven't made myself clear. I'm — because I haven't followed your reaction. (Laughs)

Loring: This — this is the thing that came up, George, where we said this 2¢ is for specific things, none of which they've asked for. Erv

was saying, should we tell 'em at this time, "Well, you can take —
we'll give you 2¢ any way you want"?

Mediator: Oh, no. No. I'll tell you why. You see, this way you applied
this — ya know, on the Blue Cross — was the right thing to do because, see, there's where your bargaining power lays later on. That
is gonna be the thing that's going to move the whole (pause) problem.
It's gonna move it — that! (Loring: Uh-huh) Because you have to
hang that — onto that to the end. Then in the end you can agree. It'll
be that that'll settle it, agreeing to let it a — be applied as negotiated
(Loring: Uh-huh), other than your way. (Loring: Now —) That's
what ya need. Ya — ya (Loring: Yeah) need that for up — for just
turning the wheel at the right time.

Loring: One other question, George. You said some time ago don't at
any point say this is the final offer. How am I gonna get away from
it if John presses it as he did on Bill there?

Mediator: If he presses it, the reply should be that this — "As far
(Loring: Yeah) as we're concerned, this is the final offer." (Loring:
Uh) Now, that always leaves a door open (pause), see. (Loring: Uh-
huh) That means as far as you — you people are concerned. Now, if
your top echelon later decides that more should be paid, that's a different thing.

Loring: Uh-huh.

Pranis: You mean in theory, if John really threatens strike and we
would say, "Well, we don't know. We" — theory, we'll have to go
back and ask the top people are they willing to take strike? They may
come back with more. This is the opening we might have? (Pause)
We would go back for further instruction, in effect.

Mediator: Uh — well, if it — here —

[Tape changed]

" ... particularly in the light of where you stand. You're — you're
so, so far removed from the settlement area that even if we wanted
to consider more we couldn't, with you being out there. But where
you are now, that's wh — that's final (Loring: Uh-huh) as far as
we're concerned."

Loring: Now, one other question, George. Suppo — we don't know, as
you say. Suppose, then, they x and they say, "Well, O.K., we'll vote
on a strike right now." (Mediator: Yeah) Can you stop 'em if /
they —

Mediator: (Over Loring above) Sure. (Pause) They won't leave here /
tonight x.

Pranis: (Over Mediator above) Where — when, George, do we say that
we're not interested in a short work week, regardless?

Mediator: Right away! Now, when / I go back —

Pranis: (Over Mediator above) It's a big x and that's why I x.

Mediator: Oh, yeah. When you go back, see, / you —

Pranis: (Over Mediator above) Now that he's moved up to 37, and tell
him we aren't even interested in a / shorter work —

Mediator: (Over Pranis above) When I open up the conference I'll say
that I have conveyed to management the union's proposal, which was
a 37½-cent hour — wh (laughs slightly) — 37½-hour week and a 20%
increase for skilled workers. I've discussed this with management
and they have discussed the proposal amongst themselves, so at this

point, Len, you take it over, give your thinking on it, and then, bingo, you've got 'em. And then you can light right into that th (Loring: Right. Uh-huh) — 30¢ — 37½ hour and skilled trades. And then that will be your cue, as we said before, to go into — what was it? (Pause) What'd we say we'd use this 37½ hours to go into?

Pranis: Back to the 2¢. (Slight pause)

Mediator: Oh! To justifying the fairness of (Loring: Uh-huh) — or, rather, elaborating on the fair — fairness of your 2-cent offer. And then if he comes back and — t — that'd be his cue, then, to say, "Well, if you're gonna hold onto (pause) we're gonna strike you, and is that your final offer?" — then, of course, you'll have another opening: "Well, it's — as far as this committee's concerned, and particularly where you stand, in the position of your collective bargaining — your figure, far as this committee's concerned, yes, it is final. Far as this committee." (Loring: Uh-huh) But only make it clear / this committee.

Loring: (Over Mediator above) Yeah. Uh-huh.

Mediator: And he'll — he'll get that. He'll — he'll catch that. John isn't — he won't need to have a picture drawn from him, and he'll do one of 2 things. It'll tip him off, or it'll show him, that until he brings his — gets down into an area where ya can do business, you're gonna hold to 2¢ and he's going to have to strike. Now, before these negotiations are over you better p — you — you have to prepare (laughing slightly) yourself for this: we'll reach a crisis. We'll reach a time when it looks like (slight pause) — well, we're facing the blade. And (pause) the sooner the better (pause) (Loring: Uh-huh), because we're — we may move a little faster then. John may throw some daylight on this thing. Now, I hit him hard here in this meeting — the whole committee, as I say, all on the subject of "You're up there." Now, John is probably wondering to — wondering to himself, "Why in the heck is George pounding me when he knows that I'd settle for 5 and 2?" I's trying to draw him out to come out with a (Loring: Uh-huh) — open the door for him so he could officially get that 5 and 2 on the table. But he (slight pause) — he didn't want — he didn't accept any of the openings, which means he's (pause) dragging his feet with his committee. In other words, he's movin' way ahead with me and slower with his committee. (Loring: Yeah. Yeah) And I's tryin' to get his committee caught up to where I was. He evidently didn't want that. (Long pause) Well, how do you like it so far?

Loring: Well, I (Mediator laughs) don't think it would be my life's work, George. (Mediator and someone else laugh) (Rather long pause) Tell you better when we're finished. (Laughs) (Rather long pause)

Mediator: See, now, you couldn't come out — you couldn't come out (pause) and (slight pause) say to John (pause), even if ya had a figure — if you had a figure right now where both of you could agree on, you know, it would take about 4 hours to get there? (Pause)

Loring: It would even now, huh?

Mediator: See, he's way out ahead of his committee. Unless he can (snaps fingers) close that gap like that. But I think he'll need a long — when he says he wants a caucus, then we know we're getting somewhere. Until then (Loring: Yeah), we're doin' all the work. (Rather long pause) Well, what ya say we (pause) (Loring: O.K.) go in?

Loring: Now, the — the offer, now, is a $37\frac{1}{2}$-hour week and 20%?

Mediator: 20%.

Pranis: For the whole group, George? Whatever the Number 2 was didn't change at all. The Number 2 didn't — and as — is as written.

Mediator: On 20%.

Joint Meeting - B (3:55 P.M.)

Mediator: I conveyed the union's proposal or counter-proposal to management. The proposal was a $37\frac{1}{2}$-hour week and 20% for the skilled trades. Is that the proper / term?

Gambon: (Over Mediator above) And other day workers.

Mediator: Day workers. (Pause) The management discussed it shortly with me and then later amongst themselves, so at this point, why, management take it over and — (slight pause).

Loring: O.K. We've given a lot of thought to this shorter work week, John, committee. From the viewpoint of the company it's not a very workable thing. You keep in mind how we have built the business up. It's been mostly on prompt service, customer satisfaction. We've had higher prices on many things, and the way we've gotten business is to be able to give the customer something he wants when he wants it. A thirty-f — 7-hour week would mean that we'd be cutting production back. We — it wouldn't mean any more employees. We don't have room for more equipment; we wouldn't wanta buy more equipment. We couldn't have a 1-hour or $\frac{1}{2}$-hour shift to make up the difference; that wouldn't work. In the long run, it would mean that we'd give less service to our customers, we'd be producing less; and that, in turn, would prob'ly build up. We would gradually lose much of the special type of business we get now, which is based on service. On top of that, it would increase our costs tremendously in an area where we already are high, where our sales are — prices are higher than competition in many of our products. This would make the thing even worse. It would — it would hurt everybody. We don't feel that it's in the best interests of the employees or the company. We're not interested in — in a shorter work week. We want the present work week we have, as many employees as we can have. With regard to the 20% for day workers, our feeling is that that would put us way out of line with the area — competition. Just think of what it would mean in terms of an increase to a comparatively small group. A die maker now getting 2.27 would get a 45-cent-an-hour increase.

Gambon: That isn't our proposal, Len. (Loring: Well —) We would apply the fixed bonus the same as fixed bonuses are applied to other jobs in the plant, that is, to the incentive base rate, and the payroll add would be added afterward. In other words, instead of your 20% being applied to 2.27 it would be applied to $1.60 and your payroll add (Loring: I see) added to it. In other words, we don't want to apply this fixed bonus in any other way than what we normally do other fixed bonuses (Loring: Uh-huh) in the plant.

Loring: Well, in that case it would mean a 32-cent- (Gambon: Yeah) an-hour increase.

Gambon: Which would, in effect, give your tool and die maker a take-
out of about 2.59, which is not out of this world as far as the area
goes, because I think the area is approaching pretty much about 2.50
minimum. And I think your people connected with skilled trades are
aware of that situation, because you have, right at this moment, a lot
of difficulty — and I think Erwin probably knows that — difficulty in
tryin' to get men to come into that plant for 2.27 an hour. Ya've lost
quite a number of men already, and they haven't been replaced, as
far as I know, up to this point. And those men that left left for higher
wages. (Slight pause)

Espig: Most of the men who left, Len, and folks, in our examination of
the reasons that they left, left generally because of the fact that we
couldn't give them the number of hours of work that they could get in
other industries.

Gambon: Or the money.

Baker: Or the money.

Espig: Not generally the money.

Baker: Well, I talked with a good many of 'em that left on that / basis.
We —

Espig: (Over Baker above) Not generally the money. (Baker: Money is
the primary reason) Many of them — many of them left in the — now,
this is not the most recent survey, but several months ago, in looking
over the statements made by some of the men, they showed that they
left our plant to go to places where they got just exactly the same
money that they got with us. In one case there was a decrease. In
the one — in another case there was a sizable increase, but the man
was given a different job entirely. He was given a semi-leadership
job, and therefore he — his rate of pay was higher. Generally speaking, the — the real problem is the number of hours that they can work,
rather than the total amount of / money earned.

Gambon: (Over Espig above) Well, I don't think it's just because a
(Loring: Well —) man's interested in working more hours. He's interested in what kind of take-out (One of boys says something) pay
he can get.

Espig: That's true, John, but / it's re — you —

Gambon: (Over Espig above) So that I think that our — your guys'd be
very happy if they could take out in 40 hours what they may have to
work now 45 or — or, rather (Espig: They work —), 48 hours to get.

Espig: It's surprising, but they're willing to work and like to work up to
60 hours a week to get that double time.

Gambon: Well, don't forget that we're not basing our requests for the
fixed bonus entirely on the proposition of obtaining — obtaining a
wage increase. We feel pretty strongly that, with very few exceptions,
everybody in that plant contributes in some form to the general productivity of the entire plant. You can take skilled trades, for instance,
is a good example of that, where you have them working in Department 2, Bob — you're (Pranis: Yeah) conscious of that — where the
man actually maintains the machines run by productive operators.
He is directly related to the produc — production that those operators get out, and he —

[Tape changed]

... uh (pause) — degree to which they contribute to the general productivity in the entire plant. That's what it's, Number 1, aimed at. Number 2, insofar as skilled trades are concerned, it's directed to eliminating the kind of inequities that have crept into the picture over the years. And the only way, and the only proper way, that we can see to eliminate that inactivity — or ineq — equity is to tie them in directly to the bonus proposition in that plant. Otherwise you're never going to get around to the point of trying to eliminate the inequities that exist between skilled trades and production workers in Atlas. There may be some other way of doing it in some other plant, but not as we see it in Atlas — do it any other way. Now, we recognize this is making your estimates. We're willing that if the company applied that 20% to these day-work jobs and the skilled trades — and, incidentally, I don't think there's over 100 of those, Len — to remove the extra nickel that they get now, which was given in an attempt to try to correct some of that inequity. Now, that would mean that everybody would be on the same 62-cent payroll add basis and that their 20% would be applied to the incentive base wage rate the same as it is for other people, so that actually everything would then be on a uniform basis insofar as pay methods go. So you don't have a 45-cent figure, actually, and you don't have a 32-cent figure, actually, when you f — figure it out that way. (Pause) (Loring: Well, I —) Now, I would say generally we estimated — I think you people had estimated a cost on that 20% bonus of about 4-some-odd-tenths cents for all the people involved at that time, which I think w — was it (Meyer: 147) 172, or a hundred and somepin' like that?

Meyer: 147.

Loring: It was in that neighborhood. (Gambon: Was around 172, I think it —) It was — it was something over 4, but it wasn't 5 / x.

Gambon: (Over Loring above) But I don't think we have more'n 100 of those people left in that plant today in (Loring: H'm) that category. And since we're talking in terms of removing the 5-cent additional payroll add that they have, your over-all cost should be less than 4¢, Number 1, because of the number of people involved, and Number 2, because you've got to take into consideration that extra nickel coming away from those people would, in effect, result in — well (laughing slightly), 5¢ actually less to them than the 20% figure would indicate.

Loring: Well, I — i — in getting the — the demand from George (Gambon: H'm), I didn't have that thought / definite xx.

Gambon: (Over Loring above) Well, I d — I hadn't gone — developed that through with him, but I probably assumed too much, because I know that Erwin is aware of how we apply these fixed bonuses and I think Bob is, and they're applied to the — the incentive base wage rate, and all jobs in the plant have incentive base wage rates as well as the clock hourly rate.

Loring: Uh-huh. That's a little different understanding (Gambon: Uh-huh) than I had, but I — I have this feeling, John — and this is, I'm sure, the feeling of the committee as we discussed it — this would mean very sizable increases for a comparatively small group of the people. Now, if we don't have an awful lot to give, we'd like to give it to everybody so that i — they would all participate in this. When you're getting up in the area of 32¢ a — an hour for any one group, i — that — that's a big increase.

Gambon: Look, Len, pardon me for sayin' this, but will you, for Christ's
sake, let us start to worry how to — to portion this money out? Don't
be tellin' us how to use it. Let's get ya down to the point where ya
tell us what you're gonna do about it. Let us try to determine what's
needed here. Now, we know, and you people should know, that there
is an inequity that has to be recognized by both the company and the
union. We have a problem and — and <u>have</u> had a problem in trying to
get across to the production workers that something should be done
and has to be done in addition to whatever is done for people generally,
for this group of people who are determined as day workers. We had
no trouble in convincing our people that those people were entitled to
5¢ an hour more than people generally got before, and we don't have
that problem now. We have an inequity existing in the plant which you
people should be interested in clearing up as well as the union, because, regardless of what Erwin says, you're — you've lost men because of rates of pay. You're certainly not being able to replace 'em
because of the present rate of pay in that shop compared to, let's say,
Dayco, who has a $2.36 rate right now, and they're now in negotiations.
Meyer: And Precision-Made does.
Gambon: Precision-Made has a higher rate than us. The — in the area
— I'm not talkin' about jobbin' shops, now, particularly, because
jobbing shop rates are <u>way</u> above ours, but even the industrial plants,
the rates are advancing beyond what we have. Now, a couple of years
back we had a good rate comparative to what was being paid throughout the city here. But we're not in that position today. So that there's
2 things being corrected, as I see it, by having the company recognize
this fixed bonus thing. One is, we're correcting an inequity in our
<u>own</u> plant, and Number 2, we're correcting a — a differential between
our own plant and the area.
Loring: I didn't mean to indicate that I wanted to tell you how to spend
(laughing slightly) any money, John. (Gambon: Well —) That — I
was just pointing out to ya why we made the offer we did. We — we
feel we have very little to offer, and — and we wanta do the most
good with it. Our feeling is this, that in view of the uncertainties that
we've mentioned before — the prospect of new developments in recording techniques, the softening of our incoming order rate, the
price reductions that are coming about daily in the papers, the reduction in defense expenditures that's expected, the reduction in the cost-
of-living indexes, the large wage increase we gave in '52 — 18¢ —
toughening competition, and our poor showing in '52 — and it was a
poor showing, John, particularly when we got all this new money in
that should have been increasing the profits. Instead of that, it de-
creased it. We feel that we've made a very fair offer in the areas
that will be of the most value to the greatest number of the employees,
it's our feeling.
Gambon: Look, Number 1, if I didn't say it before let me say it now, and
if I said it before I wanta repeat it. It's rather ironical to have the
company offer us a 1-cent increase in the pension program in the
view of the decentralization move. Not only is it ironical but it's a
little bit distasteful to us, Len. Why the hell talk to us about a pension plan or a severance plan increase when the company is engaged
and <u>committed to</u> an all-out decentralization proposition?

Loring: John, as far as — as I know, and I think I'm as close to it as anybody, we have not made plans for an all-out decentralization / program.

Gambon: (Over Loring above) Len, we've engaged with the company in several meetings on decentralization, and as of this moment, this day, this date and year, we don't know what the company is goin' to retain in the way of jobs in the metropolitan area. Nobody has answered that to our satisfaction. Nobody has answered it to our dissatisfaction.

Loring: I think that's only from the viewpoint, John, that nobody can predict the future.

Gambon: Well, nobody (laughing very slightly) can predict the future, but I certainly think that the company knows if it has certain plans on the drawing board, as we've been told, involving decentralization. They must know how much stuff is gonna remain in the metropolitan area up to a given point — at least up to a given point. But the — the company, according to the statements we've listened to from Mattuck and from Bill Michelsen, doesn't wanta tell us that because they're afraid that if they tell us how long they're gonna have jobs in the company, they're gonna start losing employees who are going to be concerned about security somewhere else. So that all the company is interested in, from where we sit, is itself! They're not givin' one damn about the employees, see. It's a cold-blooded business proposition, and I can understand it. But we don't have to like it, and we certainly don't. (Pause) Len, it's our opinion that where we stand at this moment, on this 37½-hour-work-week proposition and this 20% bonus, the estimate that we have runs somewhere close to 16¢, probably closer to 15, involves about a 360,000.00 or $350,000.00 cost to the company from April 1st through '53. Now, despite all the things that you say about uncertainties and disc recorders and other items, the future for '53, at least, looks good. Contrary to the concern you feel about it and state here, we have statements in the newspapers by Hal Fuller and your financial reports showing something entirely different. Now, I don't think he makes those kind of statements just to make the stockholders happy. I'm not / disputing the —

Loring: (Over Gambon above) John, right on — right on that one point, I've heard you say that before and I have to tell you this. That was not given out by Hal Fuller. That has come back and plagued me so many times. Nobody gave that statement out that you saw in the paper.

Gambon: I've seen other statements, though — o — oh, lengthy newspaper items that I have in my files — I don't have 'em with me, but outlooks for '53. I don't know who gave 'em out, whether Ray Horton gave one (laughing very slightly) of those things out, which is (Loring: I don't —) his custom at times, or who gave it out, but it was a very glowing picture presented in the newspaper financial column — / uh —

Meyer: (Over Gambon above) At the same time you were movin'!

Gambon: Yeah, at the same (laughing) time you were movin', too. Now, those — those things a — add up to us — I mean, certainly the kind of thing you're talkin' about here can happen. But the — the industry reports don't show as much concern over the disc recorder problem as you people do. (Pause) Forget which one it was. I read a recent

N.E.M.A. (slight pause) report (rustling through papers) which talked about this disc recorder problem but did not indicate any great concern on the part of the distributors in their long-range buying plans, for one thing; and certainly if the distributors are not too concerned about it and continue to plan for a reasonably normal volume, I don't know why a manufacturer has to get all worked up over it.

Loring: We've had some expressions from some of the distributors, John, which indicate they are concerned.

[At about this point, Mediator slips out of the room, returning almost immediately.]

Gambon: Well, are they concerned because somebody else may get y — disc recorders out ahead of them? / Are they concerned about tape recorder sales?

Loring: (Over Gambon above) No, I don't think — I think they're concerned about this hiatus period be — between the potential advent of easily usable disc recorders and the — the dying out of tape recorders. (Gambon: H'm) Now, th — there will be — whenever it happens there's bound to be that period. Now, the fear seems to be that that period will come before they're ready.

Gambon: I don't know why the concern comes in here, because if they're gonna begin to worry about people not buying tape recorders because they're waiting for disc recorders (Loring: There's been quite a bit of this), well, those people are just not gonna wait for an indefinite period. I mean, they'll prob'ly be buyin' recorders the same as before. It didn't stop or limit sales of the old wire recorders for a long while when the tapes were brought out. And even today they're still buying some wire units. Somebody's got to make 'em.

Loring: Well, I'm not predicting this will happen, John. / I just point out that it's an area — it's an area that's xx.

Gambon: (Over Loring above) No, I know you're not predicting it, but I mean you're looking at the darker side of this picture where I can't — I can't ap — get over on your side of the table and look down the same alleys that you're lookin', Len. I'm lookin' at the brighter aspects. And I know this, that usually when Atlas looks forward to a good year they only make statements concerning the picture for the future after they've given a lot of careful consideration to their industry problems generally. And I — I feel — I've said this many times before — I have no fear about Atlas having a good year in '53, a good year that will exceed the year of '52. Uh —

Loring: Sure hope it does, John. / H'm.

Gambon: (Over Loring above) Well, Len, the last 3 periods — I keep repeating, this 8th, 9th, and 10th period of '52 and the first period of '53 show a pretty good trend to me, I mean. And I look at that last period of 1952 as more significant of the true picture of Atlas than I do the entire year of '52 because we — you did get off to a fairly slow start in '52, but you wound up that year in magnificent fashion, and it's continuing into '53. On the face of those prospects, I think we're entirely realistic in requesting a 37-hour week and the 20% bonus for skilled workers and other day workers, in terms of total cost to the company. Now, perhaps you have a right to ask us to consider the practical side of this 37½-hour question, and we will do that. But we're still talking in terms of what the company can afford to do as

against its financial standing at the present time, looking at both the
future business for '53 and what has happened during '52. And we
think that there is plenty of room for the company to come out of this
meeting today in a far more advanced position than you are at the moment. I think I've given you as much as I can. If you have any other
questions on this fixed bonus proposition, at least I've tried to give
you our thinking of the reasons why the union is pressing for these
things. I might say this. It's my opinion that on the basis of past
precedence of how we have established fixed bonuses for jobs in the
plant, particularly when you consider the relationship of the particular job with other jobs and its effect on productivity and earnings,
that in reviewing what has been done in the past and taking some of
these jobs in there now, that I could probably build a pretty damn
good arbitration case for many of these jobs. I don't wanta have to do
it that way and spend the union's money to do it, and at the same time,
of course, have the company to do it, if it can be brought to the attention of the company that here is a particular problem that solution
should be found for, to the interest of both the union and the company.
And I think it is a joint interest; I don't think it's a one-way street.
And it is definitely not directed to just producing a wage increase,
period. It is not directed for that reason. It's 2 things to eliminate:
Number 1, the inequities that exist between our skilled trades and day
workers against the production worker; and (2), particularly in skilled
trades, to bring the rates up to what is now happening in the area, and
that certainly should concern the company. On the $37\frac{1}{2}$-hour week, I
think it's easy for you to understand why we want to reach a settlement with you at least on a $37\frac{1}{2}$-hour basis. I'm conscious of the fact,
of course, that it would mean less production if you only retain the
same number of p — of employees on a sh — shorter work-week basis.
We had hoped that in order to maintain the same production that ya
have now that it would mean a — more jobs, more jobs in that we have
now some 150 people who were displaced because of the transformer
move with probably almost that same amount to be displaced, comes
maybe November or December of this year. We have no reason to
believe that it won't happen in November or December, as a date.
We have every reason to believe, by virtue of Mr. Mattuck's statement to us, that there's nothing that we can say or do or suggest that
will prevent the company from moving those products that ya've already told us they're gonna move. In view of that, I think it's understandable why we want the shorter work week, Len. I think the union
would be very remiss in its responsibilities to its members if it didn't
attempt to get some settlement with the company on this basis.
Loring: Well, I — I understand your reasoning behind it, John. The
thing that comes back to me, though, I don't see how that means more
jobs because we only have a certain amount of equipment. We don't
have room to put more equipment in, / John. It —
Gambon: (Over Loring above) We don't need more equipment, Len. We
might need more shifts. (Loring: Uh —) And we do have right now
in our contract provisions for shorter work weeks when you operate
3 shifts. / As you know —
Loring: (Over Gambon above) Th — that's true. That's true. But we
have the question of balance, John. We can't put more people on —

more shifts on in certain places and get the whole line out of balance. I mean, that — that's the problem we're up against. Isn't that true, Bob?

[At about this point Mediator again leaves the room.]

Pranis: That's true. Just to be specific, John, we have set up — I'll take a punch press, since that'll be the big item, or is the big item. We have set 2 shifts on everything but drawing. Draw press jobs have always been 3 shifts, so we'd be completely out. We did it purposely back in 1950 because of space. And th — there's no way of getting any more in. You'd have actually get more equipment. I don't know where you'd put it, if you could get it.

Gambon: I'd just thought you'd just heard of a good vacant space, Bob.

Pranis: Where?

Gambon: Recorder (laughing slightly) assembly.

Pranis: Oh, yes (Gambon laughs), that's true. But it would certainly be outa line to put any m — to buy more equipment, put it down there, John. You just couldn't afford at this time to buy equipment. It's rather expensive, of course.

One of boys: Plenty of space left in our shop, Bob.

Pranis: I know. 942 in the Department 20.

One of girls: (Says something but cannot be understood)

Pranis: And to put equipment there, which we don't have — first of all, ya gotta get the equipment. It comes kinda high, of course. And it would be very much out of line to — to break your line up. You'd have an aw — an awful messy flow to put it — stuck — stick it in corners. I remember we put Department 9 where it was because it was not dependent on anybody. We moved it purposely for that reason. (Long pause)

[Mediator returns at about this point.]

Loring: Well, we've given this a lot of consideration, John. We're not just being arbitrary on this. (Gambon: H'm) We're tryin' to be just as fair as we possibly can. But we are seriously concerned about many of these things we've / xx.

Gambon: (Over Loring above) Len, I think the company has every right to be concerned about the situation, because we don't quite agree that the company is being as fair as they should be about this situation. We've listened during these meetings with you in these offices here to statements that the company wants to do other things with the money that they might be paying out to us. Now, we know — of course, it's an assumption on our part, the same as it's an assumption on your part to predict a good year for '53 — we know that if that assumption becomes a fact that the company stands to show better than $2\frac{1}{2}$ million dollars' profit for — before taxes in '53. And we don't consider an item of $360,000.00 increased cost to be an unrealistic position in the face of that kind of a possibility. I can recall, and I just took the trouble to show George here — I remember back, Len, in '46, when you had net earnings of $283,000.00 and you lost in '47 $104,000.00, and yet in those 2 years we got $28\frac{1}{2}$¢ per hour in wage increases. And ya get down to '48 where you only had 132,000.00-and-some-odd dollars in net earnings, and in '48 we came up with a 9-cent-an-hour wage increase. In '49 ya had $329,000.00 net earnings, and we came out of there in '49 with a $14\frac{1}{2}$-cent fringe package, which included the

pension, severance plan, the insurance plan, and other items. And ya
get down to the '50 and you had $1,000,000.00 — 104,000.00 net earn-
ings, and in '50 we got less than we did in those proceeding years
when you made less money and even lost money, and at the same time
when we were sold a bill of goods for 5¢ and 5¢ — 5 which we got in
'50 and 5 which we got in '51 — the company doesn't tell us a damn
thing about it. We just discover in the inner — intervening period between the 2 increases that the company started a — a profit-sharing
plan which produced, in effect, for the — would have produced, in
terms of the amount of money, more than 5¢ an hour for our 1400
people. If I — my memory serves me right, the amount of money that
you gave out in profit sharing in 1950 would have produced at least 7¢
an hour. We got a nickel. And you had about 66 people that shared
that amount of money. In 1951 you again gave out what was equivalent
to an 8-cent-an-hour increase for our 1400 people, and in '51 we still
only had a nickel which we negotiated in '50. And now only 97 people
got that money. Again in 1952 your profit sharing produced at least
— I think it was 6 and 2¢ — 6.2¢ for a small group of 114 people as
against a — the big amount that you people talk about of 18¢. What ya
fail to recognize is the fact that that 18¢ was not something that we
weren't entitled to. We were far behind our own industry in this area.
We were back 15 and 16¢ when that increase was granted — those 2
increases were granted during 1952. And we're still back anywhere
from 12 to 16¢ behind the companies which you people used in your
charts to try to show comparisons in wage benefits. You people only
went back 3 years. We went back to when we all started even in '46,
and we can show you the exact differences there. We're still 12 to
16¢ behind. Standard Products at this moment is in negotiations, and
certainly it's not gonna be a zero situation; Lashley is certainly not
gonna be a zero situation; Dayco is in negotiations, or about to go into
negotiations; Hercules very shortly. All of these companies are now
in nego — negotiations again, and we're still 12 to 16¢ behind. Now,
it's interesting to note — at least, it was interesting to me to note —
that this 8th, 9th, and 10th period of '52 and the first one of '53 showed
these nice figures, particularly profits before taxes, despite the fact
that you realized the full effect of both increases in '52 during those
4 periods (Loring: Uh-huh); and yet those 4 periods, on the average,
were better th — much better than the entire year of '52 (Loring:
Well, that —), even when you didn't have the full effect / of these
increases.

Loring: (Over Gambon above) That — that's true, John, but we also had
5 poor periods in '52, and we need more than 4 or 5 good periods /
to xx —

Gambon: (Over Loring above) I understand that, Len. But I'm pointing
up the fact that you had the full weight of those in — increased labor
costs to us — right (Loring: Right)? — plus whatever other labor
costs you put into effect for non-union people during those 3 months,
and with that full effect you were still able to show a much better picture for those 4 periods than you did for the year of '52 itself. And
that trend evidentally is continuing, and it's looked for to continue
through '53 with some finger-crossing, I suppose, that something that
you're not actually lookin' for can happen. Now, we've faced this kind

of situation with you people before, the fact that things look good and possibly something can happen and everybody looks for boogey man, but it — they never seemed to really develop in recent years. It's been — 1947 was the last year that this company actually lost money i — for a year's operation. Since that time, and particularly since 1950, you've been — you've been way above anything that ya've ever experienced, goin' back to '41. The first time ya ever made a million dollars in net earnings was in 1950. (Loring: That's right) You repeated that in '51; you've repeated it in '52. So I — I think that Atlas has gotten to the point where they don't start now, when they're becomin' more prosperous than they've ever been in their life, to try to — to tell us (Loring: Yeah) that there's a li — we should take just little bits so that the company can use the money which they might give to us, to do other things, such as expanding research. Research for what? New products that may (laughing slightly) not and probably won't be manufactured in the metropolitan area? That's no benefit to us, Len. I mean, we're being realistic as hell about this thing. We intend that as long as ya stay in the metropolitan area we're not gonna take some crumbs, or come to ya with a hat in our hand and say, "Please do somethin' for us" or "Please don't give us anything" because you're afraid you'll move out. Because, from the way Atlas goes today, Atlas would prob'ly say, "All right, we won't give ya nothin'," and then they'd laugh like hell at us and move, anyhow, because they're bein' very cold-blooded and business-like about this proposition, as we have been told across the table. We're bein' just as cold-blooded and realistic about this, too. And I suppose you can sum it up and say, well, as long as you're here, damn it, you're gonna pay. You're not gonna give us any Aiken business. Down there maybe they'll take that for awhile; I don't know. We're not concerned with that. We're concerned with what happens in the metropolitan area here now. And we can't help but recognize that in taking into consideration what's gonna happen in '52 that there's close to $600,000.00 that were lost on recorders with amplifiers alone last year that are not in the picture now.

Loring: John, with regard to our profits you know we've — we've continually gone out to the public, get more money to put into the company. That in itself makes it a bigger company (Gambon: H'm), if it's used right. Take 1950. That was our first good year. We had $1,000,000.00 after taxes. 1951, that dropped to $750,000.00 (Gambon: Uh-huh); 1952, it dropped to $570,000.00. You can't say that the trend has been that we're making more and more money; we're making / less money.

Gambon: (Over Loring above) I'm talkin' about in — in comparison to what you used to do in years past. I mean, the — Jesus, when you got the 400-and-some-thousand dollars, I think it was, you were havin' good years in those days. The — the — the highest year you had up until — up until 1949, in profits after taxes, which I interpret this net earnings to be, $318,535.00 in 1941. You didn't touch $300,000.00 again until 1949 when you c — come up with 320,000.00. From '49 — after '49, from — from — into '50, ya've never gotten back down to anywhere near that figure after taxes. But I keep repeating your figures of profits before taxes, which I think I have a right to do since

we're deductible, as it were. And I look at it from the standpoint of
sayin' to you, all right, we're — we have a $360,000.00 item layin' on
the table here, Len, and all evidence that we can find, based on your
own financial reports, statements of the company a — appears very
likely that the company is going to realize some $2\frac{1}{2}$ million dollars'
profit before taxes in 1953.

Loring: I sure hope you're right, / John. It'll save me some gray hairs.

Gambon: (Over Loring above) Well, I know you do! And we hope so. I
hope it's higher than that. (Loring: Would save me some gray hairs)
I hope it's higher than that. And I hope ya produce $2\frac{1}{2}$ million before
October of '52 (Loring laughs) (?: 3) — or '53, I mean. (Someone,
then another, laugh slightly) (Pause) But we — we're not bargaining
with you people on any different basis. In fact, the company was the
one (pause) some time ago that started us into this kind of a bargaining (pause) procedure, let's call it, in that they used to say,
"Don't let's look at what we did last year; let's look at the year
ahead." And then when we wanta look at the year ahead they say,
"Don't look at the year ahead; look what we done last year." Well,
now we're lookin' both ways. We say, "Look at what you did here
and look what you're doin' here," see.

Loring: Well, I think we have to look both ways, / John. In fact —

Gambon: (Over Loring above) N'h? Well, we're — we're lookin' both
ways, and I'm particularly lookin' at the fact that while you — in
statements that Michelsen made he points out 9% less sales, he overlooks to point out that in the last 3 quarters — or last 3 periods there
was a 14% increase. In some — I read it somewhere there was a 20%
increase for — I don't know what that — period it was but I read that
in the newspaper report. But I know from your own financial report
the statements are a 14% increase in the latter part of '52. So — and
that's continuing in '53 for the first period, and I think, from what ya
said the other day, that first period trend has gone into the 2d period.
I don't know what the 3rd is (Loring: I don't either, John), but I
would say that if you're goin' to get hit with any problem on disc recorders — I don't think it's gonna happen myself, but if it does happen I don't think it'll happen before the late fall. And I don't think it
would have the effect that you people fear, because in the late fall,
particularly as far as that kind of product goes, the production increases that take place usually take place right before Christmas
time, so that if there were any —
[Tape changed]

Loring: We don't say they're gonna happen, John. They're (Gambon:
Huh?) things on the horizon that disturb us greatly.

Gambon: Well (laughing slightly), Len, there're certainly things on the
horizon that disturb us greatly, too. (Laughs) In fact, we're havin' a
hell of a time locating the horizon sometimes. (Pause) Well, I still
claim that the union's position — tossing the $360,000.00 item on the
table for your consideration — is not unrealistic, even though you —
the projected figure of $2\frac{1}{2}$ — better than $2\frac{1}{2}$ million dollars' profit before — before taxes may not develop to that extent. I think that what
probably might happen is that the company's plans for expanding research or expanding their decentralization program at this time might
be deterred a bit. And while I'm not trying to do that particularly,

I'm not gonna worry about deterring the company's plans that mean
nothing to us in the form of benefits in the long range view (pause),
'cause I — I — I still —I'm firmly convinced that it wouldn't matter
if we were to say, well, we won't take anything on this reopener; we
won't take anything on the October reopener. That wouldn't have any
effect on what Atlas has planned to do both in '53 or '54, '55, or '56.
They've convinced me of that much. (Rather long pause) I have decided, as far as I'm concerned, Len, that for some time, now, Atlas
has gotten away from this old business that they used to give us,
"This is one big family." Well, there's a hell of a lot of brawls goin'
on inside the family, I suppose you could call it that right now. And
I'm not particularly happy with the expressions of policy and programs
advanced by the company, and I'm not particularly happy about the
trends that I run into where we're forced more and more to arbitration proceedings — the things of that kind. It's been my studied opinion and judgment that Atlas has been asking for some trouble for a
long while and that they've gotten a little bit arrogant about things
generally and getting a little bit thoughtless about their employees as
represented by the union. I can still remember when Len Fuller went
out of his way to make a lot of pleas to us when this company could've
been put out of business entirely by this union ex — exercising some
very unresponsible actions. And we listened to him! And we listened,
among other things, to a promise from Len Fuller — er, Ha — Hal
Fuller — that when the company was doin' good we wouldn't have to
come to them, that he'd come to us. I have yet to see that happen. I
don't expect them to ever do that and I'm not particularly interested
in whether he does or not, because I think we will come runnin' to you
when we think you're doin' good and we won't have to wait to have Len
— Hal do it for us. But I'd like to have him, when he starts considerin'
this whole situation, try to remember that, and try to remember that
this union coulda put him outa business at one time and went along
with him in the hard times, and that we still expect that what he said
to us about "when things are good" still means something around
here and that we're not going to listen in any way, shape, or form to
"Please, that we don't wanta do this, that, and the other thing, because we have other plans for that money," when we know that that
other plan proposition runs directly or indirectly to a decentralization program. All I can say is if that's what's been decided on and if
it's in — in its entirety means Atlas won't exist in the metropolitan
area, that's up to them to decide, and they probably will do it without
the union having anything to say about it. But I do say this, that while
they're here, by Christ, they're gonna give us our fair share of what's
coming to us, because we're helping to produce these profits, and
we're not helping to produce 'em so that they c — can be used to take
jobs away from us. (Pause) And I think right now that Atlas better
start thinking in these kind of terms that they are now facing a pretty
serious situation. They bucked into a pretty serious situation when
we signed this contract. They're now facing the same kind of a serious situation. I may be wrong, but I think that Bill Michelsen had a
funny idea in the back of his mind that this union would never take a
strike vote because of this decentralization problem. I think the Local
union has answered that question in the back of his mind or in the back

of anybody else's mind that may have had that idea. And I think that
it's important that the Board of Directors of this company get it
through their noodle that we're goin' to get what is a fair settlement
here, or else! And the "or else" isn't gonna wait too damn long
(Loring: John —), because it's my conviction, Len, that there's been
(Loring: Yeah) too much delay, delay which I consider to be pretty
deliberate. Now, we wrote a letter to the company on January 23d.
I got no answer to that letter from Bill Michelsen until February 20th.
That's almost a month. And when I got the letter, he waits until
March the 12th to set up the first meeting. That's a delay of almost
2 months and leaves only a few days before the reopening date of
April the 1st, despite the fact that time after time we've always asked
the company to get started far ahead so that the matter of retroactivity would not become involved. / You're in here bargainin' now —
Loring: (Over Gambon above) But we — we're not taking this lightly.
We — we take these very seriously, just as you are. We wanta be
fair with the employees. We feel that we've made, in view of all the
things we've pointed out to ya when we began — I think you have them
in mind — that we've made a fair offer.
Gambon: Well, I'm sorry I can't agree with ya, Len. I mean, that's as
it stands. The thing that I wanta get resolved here this afternoon is
whether or not we have reached a stalemate, whether or not the company has any intentions of going any further in your present position
or if there's going to be a continuation of bargaining between the positions of the company and the union. We'll give serious consideration to the questions of practicality that you raise in regard to the reduced work week, but it will not change our cost proposals at this
time. Now, I'd like the company to get away from the proposition of
what they think is best for us and take the union's demands, as presented at Bill Michelsen's request, and begin giving them serious consideration, both in the matter of increased costs for fringes contained
in those demands and increased costs in terms of wages, if the shorter
work week is an objectionable one to you people because of the practical problems involved. Now, I think if we can get some determination
of what your position is (slight pause) — or perhaps you were prepared to tell me that your position and final position is where you are
at the moment, then we can save some time there, too. (Loring: Well
[laughing slightly], John, that —) But I want you to understand, Len,
and I don't wanta kid you about it, if the company takes a position as of
the end of today's sessions that the 2¢ figure, whether it be in the form
of wages or whether it be in the form of the fringes you're now talking
about or other type fringes, but as a total cost in one form or another
to the company, as your final position, then I must tell you that this
committee will immediately go into session on the advisability of calling a strike in the plant.
Loring: John, I've never taken anything you've said very lightly. (Gambon: If —) I know you mean it (Gambon: Uh-huh) when you say it. I
figure that the proposal you made — your — your last proposal, the
37½-hour (Gambon: H'm) week and the 20% for day workers, comes
between 17½ and 18¢ an hour to us. Now, it's the opinion of this committee, particularly in view of your high position, that we can't go any
further than 2¢. (Rather long pause)

Gambon: What — you estimated what, 17¢ ?

Loring: 17 / ½ or 18.

Meyer: (Over Loring above) Only bec — I think it's because he was using the / over-all guaranteed —

Gambon: (Over Meyer above) Are you talkin' about the 2 items now, or just the one / item?

Loring: (Over Gambon above) 2 items, John.

Gambon: 2 items.

Loring: 2 items.

Gambon: Are you — you're figurin' your 17¢ — this inflated business on the 20% (Meyer: Yeah) angle?

One of girls: The clock-hour wage, yeah. Huh?

Loring: (At same time as girl above) Well, I — I may be a little higher — a little high on that, but not (Meyer: Huh-un) — it isn't a great deal high. (Gambon: H'm) But I mean it's — it's in that area.

Gambon: Well, I — I (Meyer: 16 to sev — 15 to 16) had — I had estimated somewhere around 15 to 16.

Loring: I get (Gambon: [In low voice] For — yeah) about 13½¢ on the 37½- / hour week.

Gambon: (Over Loring above) Well, what do you think is a reasonable position for the union to take?

Loring: John, I — I can't answer that for you. I —

Gambon: I know you can't. (Laughs)

Loring: In the first (Several laugh) in — in the first place (laughing), this is new to me. I mean, you have the advantage of me. / You'd xxx.

Gambon: (Over Loring above) Well, I — I — well, I wouldn't take the advantage of you for the world, Len. I'm (Loring laughs heartily) not directin' my (Several laugh) — I'm not directing my attack against you personally or any member of the committee (Loring: I appreciate that) personally. I'm attacking the company's financial ability to pay (Meyer: Wouldn't —) very directly.

Meyer: Wouldn't 11½ be more than 13½? That'd be that — more the figure than 13½?

Loring: I don't think so, Bernice, not the way / I figured.

Pranis: (Over Loring above) You figured / there were about 60 people.

Meyer: (Over Pranis above) Usin' that 6.7% (Loring: Well, I — I —) on a 1.71 weighted / average?

Loring: (Over Meyer above) I figured all of the — we fi — made a rather detailed calculation on the 35-hour week (Gambon: H'm) (Meyer: Uh-huh), and that came to just over 27¢ an hour. Now, I'm just cutting that (Meyer: Uh-huh) in half (Gambon: Uh-huh) because it's 37½. (Rather long pause)

Meyer: These are soft chocolate, if somebody (Gambon: Well —) wants some candy.

Loring: No, thank you.

Gambon: Don't bribe him, Bernice. Uh — (long pause). Do I interpret what you've s — just said to me to mean that you believe that possibly we can reach agreement on some figure between the present positions of the company and the union? (Pause)

Loring: I don't know, John.

Gambon: Uh-huh. (Long pause)

Loring: But I certainly think we should explore it. The action that you speak is something that wouldn't be good for either of us. You can see that. (Pause)

Gambon: Uh (pause) — will the company commit itself to the 20% fixed bonus at this point and then see if we can reach an area of bargaining on the question of a general wage increase?

Loring: No, I can't commit the company to that, John.

Gambon: H'm. (Rather long pause)

Meyer: Len, didn't you say, "Because of" — in the summation, I mean — this isn't all he said, I know, but the final sentence was, "Because of the high figure of the union the company cannot go higher than 2¢ offered"?

Loring: I said that this committee, Bernice, cannot go higher than we are, particularly in view of the —

Meyer: The union's / high —

Loring: (Over Meyer above) — the union's high position. Yes, I did. (Rather long pause)

Gambon: Can we have a short caucus here — a short recess?

Management Caucus - D (4:50 P.M.)

Mediator: Could I have — could I have called it any closer?

Espig: (Laughing) No.

Loring: No.

Mediator: Didn't I tell ya he was gonna say that?

Loring: Yeah.

Mediator: And your answers was perfect. (Espig: Question!) (Pause) And I said on re — when he calls for a caucus we're in business.

Pranis: Yeah, but we gotta have an offer now. Soon. Or ready for one.

Mediator: Well, you — no, you don't have to — you don't have to do much until you see what comes out of / the caucus.

Pranis: (Over Mediator above) That's true. And then we can caucus / and discuss —

Espig: (Over Pranis above) Then we can go out and caucus quick.

Pranis: That's right.

Mediator: See, I (laughs) — see, I x that he would — that he would eventually come to that point of, "Is this your final position?"

Loring: Uh-huh.

Pranis: It seems awfully early, though, George. Why is he doing it so soon? You needled him too much?

Mediator: I — I pressed him very hard. (Espig: I felt —) In fact — in fact, Observer said to me in the hall — first thing she said — sa — mentioned how much pressure I'd put on in — in that session. That was a gruelling session. And all the things that you people were talking about, we had gone over every one of those in that other session.

Loring: Uh-huh. I (Mediator says one word in low voice) — just from a viewpoint of bargaining, I'm interested. I felt a few times w — while he was talking along, saying all these things, butt in and — and rebut them a little bit, but I felt maybe it was better for him to — to keep going.

Mediator: Oh, it is. (Phone rings) (Loring: Uh-huh) It is. The only time it pays to rebut is when you're with an arbitrator. (Loring: Uh-huh) (Answering phone) Hello. Oh, that's fine. That's the best news I've heard today. I'll be right out there. (Hangs up phone) The girls brought me a cup of coffee.

Loring: (Laughing) Oh, boy! (One or 2 others laugh)

Mediator: We're making progress. (Laughs, joined by Loring)

Observer: Very good, Mediator Thomson.

Loring: (Mediator starts to speak at same time) So you thought it went all right, George?

Mediator: Oh, that was perfect! (Slight pause) Couldn'ta been better. I couldn'ta asked for anything more. Your answers were right (snaps fingers) and (pause) convincing, too. (Pranis: Uh-huh) Because — see, you — you had prepared; you — you had prepared your answer. (Slight pause) (Loring: H'm) And when the question was fired ya had your answer, which made it all the better. (Pause) He (pause) — he showed, for the first time (slight pause), by these 2 counter-proposals he made that he's looking for an area. (Loring: H'm) And what will turn the trick, the whole works, is one thing that you said (slight pause), and that was, "You're too high. As far as this committee is concerned, it's 2¢, and we have to be there as long as you're where you are." That — that'll turn the whole thing. That one question will reverse the whole pace from now on. Now, you wait and see.

Loring: Bernice picked that up pretty quickly, / didn't she?

Pranis: (Over Loring above) Yeah, she wanted a rehash.

Mediator: See, that's — that — and that was the one I wanted you to get over, because I knew that that will turn. It always does! It always turns it when you — see, your — your — your bargaining position is so important, and often negotiators — labor unions and companies — make it difficult for themselves and for us by not properly dividing what they have in their proposals. Some of them will come in — let's say they're gonna use 6¢ and they know that's their maximum. They'll start off with 2, and may jump to 3. That's wrong, particulalry where the union is still way, way up. Lot of 'em say, "What do we care how far they're up? We know how much we have to give." Well, they should care, because — they don't know it but they're making it difficult for the union! Now, John wants to come down! I know that! But if you made it easy for him, you — he'd have to stay up! (Loring: H'm) You're making him come down, and he wants ya to do that because he's already said to me 7, and he has to come down there. Now, evidentally, he's wh — he's wh — whatwe call "grand-standing" for the committee. He's — he — he has to show that, "We've got to reach down to the bottom of the barrel before we make our move." Now I think all this has got him to that point where he can now turn the wheel. And particularly based on what you said, "No, we're at 2¢. As long as" — see, there was a difference in the way you said it and the way Bill said it the other day. Bill — Bill would have said it, if he (slight pause) — probably another way if he had had time, but the thing (snaps fingers) came like that, I think as he was going out the door, / wasn't it?

Loring: (Over Mediator above) Yeah. Yeah.

Mediator: Well, the difference between the 2 points was — and, f — and
I wished he hadn't asked that question, because a real sharp negotiator never asks that question. It's like, as I said before, asking some-
one, "Are you an illit — illegitimate child?" (Someone laughs
shortly) It's a question that, once you ask it, you're in trouble!
(Loring: Uh-huh) And a good negotiator never asks it, 'cause he don't
wanta force a company to say Yes and No until he's really at the end!
And even at the end they don't ask it! They know, without asking. So,
it puts you on a spot. And Bill has — "That is final!" I think he —
Loring: Period.
?: Period.
Mediator: Period (Loring: Yeah), see. Well, the difference between
the way he said it and you said it just turned that wheel, see. And,
as I said, we expected he would ask him. But then when you said,
"Yes, as far as this committee," see, you opened another door. See,
you didn — you didn't hog-tie yourself. This committee. "Far as
this committee's concerned, we're at 2¢ because of your position."
Now he'll say to his committee, see — I know just — I — I could write
the minutes of what's going on in there. (Espig laughs) Here's what
he's gonna say — and every other union committee will do it! He will
say, "Now, look. Now we've got what we want, an indication that the
company's mind is open. Now that that's the case, we're all satisfied, let's get down to the realistic area. Now, how to do it? Are we
gonna do it in one step or 2 steps?" That's what they're talkin' about
now (slight pause), I'm pretty certain.
Observer: Would you throw me out if I said something? (Slight pause)
Mediator: Uh — no! I'd never throw you out, under any circumstances.
Observer: Well, did you have a feeling that there was a change in there
from the beginning to the end in the general atmosphere?
Mediator: This last meeting?
Observer: Yeah.
Mediator: At the conclusion of this talk?
Observer: Yeah.
Mediator: Yes.
Pranis: Yeah, definitely.
Observer: (At same time as Pranis above) Well, I thought it had some-
thing to do with the way Len Loring talks. You couldn't pick a fight
with him, you know? (Loring laughs heartily)
Pranis: Yeah, I find it difficult. (Mediator and Loring laugh heartily)
Observer: Well, I thought (Mediator: Well —), sitting back in that cor-
ner in there —
Mediator: Let me put it this way, Observer. That, of course, is always
helpful in negotiations. Always. A man who is calm and deliberate
and stabilizing is al — can always — like Westover, for instance —
they can always go farther — further in this game than the others.
(Pause) But when the score is counted (pause) — when noses are
counted, you will find this, that (phone rings) — there's yo — my
coffee, I'll bet. (Answering phone) Hello. Oh, Mr. Espig.
Espig: O.K.
Pranis: They bought your coffee up at the plant. Thought you / were
xx.

Mediator: (Over Pranis above) You will find that, as settlements go, he won't get too much — or, too many more than the other fellow, but his will be more peaceful. Now, what I'm tryin' to say is, the unions have to get certain things, regardless of how well composed (Pranis: Uh-huh) the company's bargaining team is or how well they like them — no matter what it is. Does that answer your question, or have I confused it?

Observer: No!

Mediator: No. Now, Jim Westover — we mentioned Jim Westover. Do you know him?

Loring: No, I don't know him, George.

Mediator: Jim is a lawyer. He represents industry, partic'arly the metal trades. He is — he has a very easy-going disposition. And in every conference he sits in, he leaves the shingle outside. In other words, he's the human being, not the lawyer. More unions like him. Well, they just think he's swell (pause) as a person. (Loring: Uh-huh) He — he has a way of saying No that is firm but not aggravating. He has — he treats everyone the same on the committee. He's just a swell guy all around, and his relations with the unions are the best. Now, somebody — some people may say to you, "Well, maybe that's because he gives the unions more." Naw! Records will show that's not true. However (pause), if you will look at all the settlements and the costs of them, you will find that his is right up there with the others (Loring: Uh-huh), not lower, not above. And he gets his strikes, too. But even in a strike they — they have great respect for him, and — in fact, I can tell you this, that he has a waiting list, I'm told, for clients, because it's a personalized business and he can't hire anyone, because Westover is known for his capable handling of his clients' labor business, so naturally they don't want Westover's assistant. They want Westover. So because of that — and he can only spread himself so far, and I don't know how he does it. He's a human dynamo. He's bouncing all the time. He's on the train, he's on a plane, he's here, he's there, and he's — he's all over.

[There is a loud knock at the door at 5:00 P.M. Mediator answers it and encounters Stan Wollman from the union caucus, who announces, "We got a bouquet for you. Come on in." Mediator intercepts him with "O.K. All right," then closes the door and turns back into the room.]

Because of (pause) — oh, this one union — I know one union went to him and said, "Look, Jim. There's a s — X company that's on your list waiting for you to take the ca — the account. How about takin' it? We can't get along with these people! They don't know how to handle theirs. We — we don't — we're havin' strikes up there, and there's no reason for them." He took it. They went in negotiations and settled it. Now, you'd think there was collusion there, if you heard the story without knowing the facts. That's a pretty good relationship to have. (Loring: Yes, sir) But, even with Jim Westover with all those human assets (slight pause), when there's — noses are counted, he had to give just as much as the fellow who fought. But it is, definitely, that (pause) I prefer negotiators to handle themselves the way you do and the way Jim Westover does. I think you get fur — further; and if you have to fight and it comes to that, well, you can agree like gentlemen to fight. There is a difference. You — you oughta see some of the others. Then you'd — then you'd really know what I meant. (Loring: Uh-huh) Uh — I guess he wanted all of us.

Joint Meeting - C (5:03 P.M.)

Gambon: Well, Len (speaking haltingly), the committee — well, we discussed this particular problem of trying to sort of break what amounts to a deadlock at the moment, and we have been developing a feeling and have pretty much been convinced that one of the things that seems to be preventing negotiations from advancing is this question of a shorter work week, and at this point we're gonna leave that particular type of negotiation provision. We're gonna propose to the company that they put into effect, effective April 1st, 1953, 10-cent-per-hour general wage increase and also in effect April 1st, 1953, the 20% fixed bonus for all skilled trades and other day workers, and that the 20% fixed bonus shall be applied to the incentive base wage rates / of the —

Loring: (Over Gambon above) That's as you explained it / before, John.

Gambon: (Over Loring above) As we explained it before, with the provision included that the present existing 5-cent differential plate — pay to those people would be taken out of the picture. (Pause)

Loring: This 10¢ an hour — that's pay add, John?

Gambon: Well, we prefer it in the incentive base wage rates, Len, but since it's a question here of trying to reach agreement on a figure that the company thinks it can meet, we'd only be adding to the total cost by insisting that it go into the incentive base wage rate. One of our points, of course, in our demands was to eliminate the payroll adds altogether, which'd be 62-cent figure in itself, I think, far in excess of a 10-cent wage general increase. But (pause) at this point we're talking in terms now of payroll add. (Pause) I don't know whether there's gonna be enough time left to ever have Atlas and Local 89 eliminate that problem. (Pause) But that's where we are on this particular (Loring says something) issue. We think, by the way, that we have earned the right to ask the company to begin approachin' the problems here on the table in a more realistic way than they have up to this point. I'm pointing out that we have moved away from a maximum position in several instances, now, without the company having made any too many moves. There are — there isn't any room left, from the union's standpoint. We make the present offer just stated with full conviction that the company can meet that increased cost since we have removed the problematic shorter work week, which involves not only additional cost but a product — production problem, and we think now that you people can get down to some serious consideration of what we're proposing here, with a — in our opinion, the ability to meet that kind of a increased cost problem. I might ask, Len, does the committee, as it's now constituted, have the authority to make a settlement with the union's committee?

Loring: (In fairly low voice) N-no.

[Mediator rises from the table, makes some remark, and leads the management group out.]

Management Caucus - E (5:10 P.M.)

Mediator: How much is this 20% fixed bonus ? / That would —
Loring: (Over Mediator above) I'm gonna have to figure that, George.
I had / figured it, I mean —
Mediator: (Over Loring above) I think it runs about 4¢, doesn't it ?
(Slight pause) Well —
Loring: It — it — well, it prob'ly won't run that much on their basis, but
I can / figure that one.
Espig: (Over Loring above) Yeah, this was figured on that basis, Len.
Loring: Was it ?
Espig: Yeah.
Loring: As we were figuring (pause) — no, we figured on the average
base rate of $1.21½. That would be the total, wouldn't it ?
Pranis: Of a x ?
Espig: No (Loring: Huh ?), couldn't possibly be.
Loring: Oh.
Espig: Couldn't possibly be. (Pause) Because your $1.14 is for your
— your $1.14 is the base rate for the — the — that — that's your av-
erage rate — base incentive wage rate (Loring: Well, are —) fig-
ured in accordance with their — / with their —
Loring: (Over Espig above) That's the average base rate (Espig: Uh-
huh. Uh-huh) xxx all into this 4¢.
Espig: Uh-huh. (Rather long pause)
[While Loring is busy with some calculations, Mediator leaves the
room briefly. Pranis places a telephone call to advise his wife not
to expect him for dinner. Mediator, returning in time to hear Pranis
say over the phone "I haven't the vaguest notion," provokes general
laughter with his comment, "I know just what she's askin' (pause):
'How's it look ?'"]
Loring: Well (laughs slightly) (long pause), that's 14¢, George, where
they are now. (Sighs deeply)
Mediator: Say, ya know what he's done ? He's knocked a cent off.
(Slight pause)
Loring: Huh ?
Mediator: He's knocked 1¢ off. Didn't he say, by his own (Loring: Yes.
Yes. Yes) words — his figures, the other thing was 15¢ ?
Loring: Uh-huh. (Rather long pause)
Mediator: This pace is terrifically slow. I've never seen anything like
it. (Pause)
Pranis: You think he wants to settle tonight, George ?
Mediator: At the rate he's going, he doesn't.
Pranis: That's what I was thinking. He wants to (Espig: I don't think
he wants to) — wants to recess till Thursday, or something like that.
(Pause)
Loring: Well, we'd be just throwin' our pennies away, I would think, to
do much now, at this point. (Pause)
Pranis: Incidentally, remember the retroactivity business, effective
April 1.
Loring: Uh-huh. (Long pause)
Mediator: See, these figures, he's lookin' for an 8-cent settlement.
(Pause)
Loring: 8¢. Yeah.

Pranis: Well, they said what before, George? 5 and 2.

Mediator: Yeah. So he's 1¢ above that with this counter-proposal. Here's the way you work that out. You're at 2 (Pranis: Uh-huh), they're at 14; the difference between the 2 is 12. (Pranis: Uh-huh) Half of 12 is 6. Add the 12 to the 2 that you have and you get 8¢.

Pranis: Does it always work out this / way?

Mediator: (Over Pranis above) Oh-h! Pretty near always that way.

Pranis: Let's remember that formula. (Slight pause)

Mediator: It very seldom misses.

Pranis: Uh-huh. (Pause)

Mediator: Now, he's actually 1¢ above what he told me. (Loring: Uh-huh) Now, what he may be doing, too, is this, as I look at this. Uh (long pause) — what was his other proposal? Oh, $37\frac{1}{2}$.

Loring: Yeah.

Mediator: Now, this $37\frac{1}{2}$ amounted to —

Pranis: $13\frac{1}{2}$.

Loring: Not $13\frac{1}{2}$ / x.

Mediator: (Over Loring above) $13\frac{1}{2}$, and then he — he had 20%.

Pranis: That's 4¢.

Mediator: Which was 4¢, and you figured it came to 7¢? How did he get 15?

Pranis: Well, Len adds the salaried people / xx.

Loring: (Over Pranis above) They — they — I don't know how they figured that in, but —

Mediator: Would we be in a safe position to say to him, in our remarks — or your remarks, that, "Your $37\frac{1}{2}$-cent-hour proposal, plus the other — the 20%, by your own words, costs 15¢"?

Loring: Well, he said that, but I don't — I think it's nearer the $17\frac{1}{2}$.

Mediator: Oh. Well, then, actually, he dropped 3¢. (Slight pause) Is it — would that — (slight pause)?

Loring: Yes. Yeah. (Slight pause) Although he still is figuring it was 15¢. It — I mean, that — that was their figuring.

Mediator: Ye-ah. (Long pause)

Pranis: Well, he was figurin' what? 15 and 4 are 19. (Pause)

Loring: Huh?

Pranis: No, 15 for the package.

Loring: That's what he was figurin'. Yes.

Pranis: So he came down a penny, just about. (Pause)

Mediator: Uh (rather long pause) — now, this may be — this offer here may be his way of going — trying to get to the 5 and 2 that I mentioned. He (pause) — 14¢. See, another way could be if you apply the 50% — see, if you cut that in half, you got 7.

Loring: Uh-huh. (Slight pause)

Pranis: What do you imply or infer from his statement, George, that it's time that w (slight pause) — we got off the "fixed position of 2¢," as he said?

Mediator: He wants a proposal.

Pranis: He apparently does want something, / or some movement.

Mediator: (Over Pranis above) He wants something. Yeah. Uh — now, you're at 2. (Pause) / If we mo —

Pranis: (Over Mediator above) Before you go further, George, may I ask a question?

Mediator: Sure.

Pranis: We're at 2, tied up in certain things. (Mediator: Yeah) Would
a movement from this tie be a movement?

Mediator: No.

Pranis: Wouldn't consider anything a / movement.

Mediator: (Over Pranis above) It would be at the right time, which
(Pranis: Oh, I see) will be later.

Pranis: We're still to consider we're at (Mediator: It'll be a concession)
2% of — 2¢ worth of something we're giving, not / 2¢.

Mediator: (Over Pranis above) That's right. See, right now we just figure costs. (Pranis: H'm) Now — then, at the end, after you agree on
costs, then come — always comes applications. Now, applications
sometimes — sometimes can prevent cost agreements from going /
over.

Pranis: (Over Mediator above) Oh, we always battle over it.

Mediator: Now, here you have 2 bargaining points, 2 things on your side:
(1), the question of retroactivity; (2), the — the way you're applying
these things. (Loring: Uh-huh) Now, they — at the right time, if the
bargaining goes right and you're not forced, through a turn in the bargaining, to move away from your present position (pause), you'll
have that to bargain with — that is, the application of it. And (pause)
as long as you can hold onto benefits — if ya haveta make an offer
later, any be — if it still could be tied in — the benefits — you've still
got a wonderful bargaining point for when the time comes to wrap this
thing up. (Loring: Uh-huh) They'll pressure like the devil for "Let
us spend it!"

Espig: Well, the one point — the one point that they have made, and I
think it's a good point and I think we oughta consider it carefully, is
the 1¢ in the pension plan. I don't know why we overlooked the — the
point. It's good for bargaining at this point. It isn't — it hasn't done
us any harm. But propagandilize is no damn good!

Mediator: You're / right!

Pranis: (Over Mediator above) You mean the fact that now there're —
are gonna get so many people —

Espig: As a matter of fact, it's — as a matter of fact, it (pause) — I —
I don't — I — I — I — I don't know why he doesn't use it against us as
much as possible, because it's something which isn't even a permanent
advance!

Loring: Well, whether they will lose, they'll get that cent if they terminate.
(Espig: Yes!) It's a — it's a savings account's / wha —

Pranis: (Over Loring above) Yes, but the idea of pension is security,
Len, and he hammers home that what security do they have if (Loring:
Uh-huh) 1/3rd of their members disappear?

Mediator: Not (Espig: Not only that) only that. Not only that. He puts
it this way, also, that 1/3rd of the present (pause) employees — of
the present employees wouldn't come — wouldn't be eligible for severance pay because they haven't been in the employ of the company
more than 2 years. (Pause)

Espig: 1/3rd is a f — a high figure, George. But there is s — there are
some. / There are s —

Mediator: (Over Espig above) But I wasn't worryin' about that part of
it — where you stuck that cent. You can always pull / that cent out.

Espig: (Over Mediator above) Yeah! Yeah. But, now, it seems to me
— it seems to me that — that if there's to be any footwork at this

point, that is certainly not — that is certainly not something that's
hard to <u>take</u>, to shift that penny.

Mediator: <u>Where</u> would you shift it?

Espig: I don't know. I don't know. I suppose the only / thing you can do
is —

Mediator: (Over Espig above) On Blue Cross?

Espig: No. The Blue Cross is adequately (Mediator: Covered) covered.
Yeah.

Pranis: You think what we've offered is — what we've agreed is — suggested so far is an adequate coverage, then — the $9.00 and the
180.00.

Espig: Oh, yes.

[As tape is changed, Pranis asks Mediator what they should do, in
his opinion. Shall they move? Mediator answers No, then says,
"I'll show you."]

Mediator: ... but your 2 — you've got 4, so you put up a cent. Certainly
you wouldn't offer $\frac{1}{2}$¢. (Pranis: Hardly) So you put up a cent. All
right. There you'd be at 3. You've got 1¢ left. You're at 3 and
they're at 14. Now, when you up a penny, compared to what you have
to spend and compared to what they have to <u>bargain</u> with, there's a big
ratio. They have 4¢ to every cent you have.

Pranis: Uh-huh. (Slight pause)

Loring: Well —

Mediator: They have 4¢ on paper.

Pranis: Excuse me.

Mediator: Sure, go ahead.

Espig: Oh! I was thinking in terms of something like this. They gave
us a counter-proposal, steamed us all up for "Th — this is the big
thing." Stan knocked on the door and said, "We got a gift for ya,"
and all that. Now, we got the cent in the pension fund. Suppose we
pull that cent out of the pension fund. Let — do a — think — just ins
— I'm asking for your thought, not that we should do it. We take the
cent out of the pension fund and we say, "We'll give you 5¢ an hour
for all the skilled trades." (Mediator: Can you do that with a —)
Skilled trades —

Mediator: Can you do that with a cent?

Espig: No. We can do it for less than that. (Mediator: Uh-huh) We can
do it for less than that. "We'll give you (Pranis: But you — you —)
5¢ an hour for the / skilled trades."

Pranis: (Over Espig above) O.K. Well, you've pulled the pension penny.

Espig: Yeah.

Pranis: That's out.

Espig: Yeah. / Now —

Pranis: (Over Espig above) But skilled trades as such, not just mass of
/ anything.

Espig: (Over Pranis above) That's right.

Pranis: Uh-huh. This is x 1$\frac{1}{2}$¢ so far, if you put it back in.

Espig: Now, what'll we do with the rest? / I —

Mediator: (Over Espig above) With — with what, $\frac{1}{2}$¢?

Espig: Yeah.

Mediator: I see. Well, that's a good point, because (Espig: Well, they
— they —) you've got some skilled tradesmen on that committee.

Espig: We got / one.

Pranis: (Over Espig above) One.

Mediator: Just one?

Espig: Just —

Pranis: One.

> [The exchange concentrates for a few minutes on the skilled trades representative on the union committee. Pranis commends his skill and points out that having him on the other side of the table is a "novelty for us, 'cause usually we're arguing <u>with</u> him."]

Loring: Well, aren't we gonna be in an awkward position if we get a little firm, George? Are they gonna get (Mediator: Uh — well —) the bit in their mouths?

Mediator: Now, let's look at it this way. Let us say that you make an offer. S (pause) — if you — let us say you took the penny out and you put 50% or $\frac{1}{2}$¢ — did you say $\frac{1}{2}$¢? (Pause)

Espig: A half —

Mediator: (At same time as Espig above) A half —

Espig: Say 5¢ an hour to the skilled trades.

Pranis: That's worth $\frac{1}{2}$¢.

Espig: That's worth <u>about</u> $\frac{1}{2}$¢.

Mediator: Oh. 5¢ an hour to the skilled trades is worth $\frac{1}{2}$¢.

Pranis: Now, George, remember, the skilled trades is not what they asked for.

Espig: They're asking for / <u>all</u> day workers.

Pranis: (Over Espig above) Asked for all day work. We (Mediator: Yes) — we take half that group and say No. (Pause)

Mediator: Yeah. Now, that leaves you with $\frac{1}{2}$¢ there. Now, let's say you put up another cent of the one ya have. That would be $1\frac{1}{2}$¢. (Loring: Uh-huh) Now, that would leave you with 1¢. Now, I — I will say this. That would be a (pause) — that would be a (slight pause) — as <u>these</u> negotiations have been progressing, that would be a step forward — a <u>big</u> step forward in these kind of negotiations where you're — you have a — such a limited amount. Now (slight pause), if that was going to go over and your 1¢ still be protected — the one that ya have left — if it were, it could only go over <u>providing you were able to thoroughly convince this group</u> that that was it. Not — not — that you had reached a point where you were scraping the bottom of the barrel. A lot would depend on the effectiveness of your presentation. If they thought — now, ordinarily, ya wouldn't — with so little you wouldn't make a move until they were down to a point. However, you <u>know</u> where they are, off the record. You're at a — they're at 7, but <u>not</u> officially — 5¢ f — across-the-board and 2¢ for (slight pause) — and you know the formula; I don't.

Espig: 10%.

Mediator: 10%. Well, what's that? Day workers, too?

Espig: Uh-huh.

Pranis: It's everybody.

Mediator: Oh. Well, now, wait a minute. That sho — that throws a little daylight. Did they ever get, in any of your past negotiations, a percentage increase like they're asking for for day workers?

Espig: No.

?: No.

Mediator: So — oh. So this is new. That'll help.

Pranis: Not in negotiations.

Mediator: So then there's a <u>possibility</u> of getting a settlement for X amount per hour. (Pause) Oh, no. Whatever you get per hour must (pause) be reflected into the skilled trades. Are they piece workers (Pranis: No) — skilled people?

Espig: No.

Mediator: Oh! (Loring: No) Oh! Oh, / well, that changes it.

Pranis: (Over Mediator above) They would — they would get per — the cents per hour, though, George.

Mediator: They'd get cents per hour?

Pranis: Definitely. (Slight pause) Of the same cents per hour plus, under his proposal. (Slight pause)

Mediator: Oh — oh, I see. / Oh, I see. Yeah.

Pranis: (Over Mediator above) See, they would get 10¢ plus 20%. Can I pursue a thought that he put up?

Mediator: Sure!

Pranis: Remember, he — he said several times — 3 or 4, at least — that there are inequities in our set-up for the skilled trades. He played the skilled trades. He made no mention of these other people who are not skilled tradesmen. Could it be possible that he was looking for the kind of a thing <u>we're</u> suggesting, that we give the skilled trades people something and <u>not</u> the others? Now, this — i — if this were so, we would be in agreement with the guy, because we don't wanta give the (Espig: No) unskilled people monies.

Espig: For this reason. You overlook the fact that he <u>did</u> drag in the machine adjustor (Pranis: Well, he dragged the whole batch in), and his arbitration — his arbitration program. (Pranis: True. But remember, Erv, he said —) Now, his arbitration program has no meaning.

Pranis: Yes. But we are n — we have no inequities on the unskilled peoples; we have inequities (Espig: No) in the skilled peoples.

Espig: He's talking about the inequity between the earnings of the skilled people as compared to the earnings of the <u>unskilled</u> people.

Pranis: To which we sub — pretty much agree. We think there should be a bigger gap. So that, is he — is he offering that we come back with the skilled tradesmen, period, increase change?

Espig: Well, that's what I had in mind!

Pranis: Now, if we pull the penny out for pension and we put the skilled tradesmen in only, you'd be back at a penny and a half.

Espig: Well, suppose we — suppose we look at it this way. Suppose that we pulled out $\frac{1}{2}$¢ from the pension and gave it to the skilled trades and left the other $\frac{1}{2}$¢ <u>in</u> the pension.

Pranis: Is that possible under whatever plan's been proposed by xx? Can you / cut this thing in half?

Loring: (Over Pranis above) You can do anything you want.

Espig: Sure. (Slight pause)

Loring: You wouldn't take out anything that's in there now. Erv was / saying —

Pranis: (Over Loring above) No, I'm thinking of this. You would increase it (?: Yeah) by 7.50 to $9.00 and then maybe, instead of 20 times the base, / give 'em 10 times the base?

Espig: (Over Pranis above) No. No. No, no. (Mediator: You might do this) $7\frac{1}{2}$¢ would go to <u>7</u>¢ per hour for the pension. You are talking insurance.

Loring: I think at this point we oughta listen pretty closely to George's strategy (Espig: Oh, sure!) about this here.

Mediator: One thing that you said there, you might be defeating your — your purpose by takin' $\frac{1}{2}$¢ out and leavin' $\frac{1}{2}$¢ in. If you recall, the very reason he raised that point was — the point about pensions was that, "What the heck good is security when you're moving? Our people have no security." So, if you let that $\frac{1}{2}$¢ in, it would really — would not have the — the worth that you're want — that — that you want to give to it, if ya left the half in. I think if you're going to take that cent out you better leave it out and stay away from pension, since they would not — in other words, you'd lose 50% of your strategy right there (?: Uh-huh), by leaving it in there. If you were goin' to make any offer, I would suggest that you think about, if you're going to take that penny out, if you'll apply one-half of that penny to the skilled trades, ya take that other half and put it on the — with the other. Oh, no. You — you haven't got <u>anything</u> on the hourly rate. (Pranis: No) Uh — what <u>could</u> ya do with that and not put it on the hourly rate?

Pranis: More hospitalization benefits — something like that. It's the only thing we're offering other than that. (Slight pause)

Espig: I hate to open that subject any further, because you can bet that's gonna become a — something we'll get tossed at us in October. We've <u>admitted</u> that we ought to improve our program to this extent.

Mediator: How about a — have ya (pause) — you're speaking of inequities. (Pranis: Right) Can you take the $\frac{1}{2}$¢, throw it into a pool (slight pause), or would you be opening a door on ineq — inequity negotiations that you don't have now? / Are ya —

Loring: (Over Mediator above) I think we'd open a door / on that one.

Mediator: (Over Loring above) You'd open a door. Well, that's out. Some — some firms have / a —

Espig: (Over Mediator above) You could — yes, you could do it, but I don't see us backing away from it later. That's the point.

Mediator: Yeah, you couldn't get off it.

Espig: Much as — I — I can tell you this. I think we're gonna have some inequity adjustment regardless of <u>any</u> settlement we make.

Mediator: Then we'd better wait —

Espig: But that — that's one of the / things that's —

Pranis: (Over Espig above) You plan to take it up later, huh?

Mediator: Yeah. Uh — see, what I'm tryin' to do is keep that $\frac{1}{2}$¢ on benefits more than per hour if (Espig: Yeah) — to get them thinking — <u>pushing,</u> see. (Espig: Well —) They'll appreciate when a settlement is made — they'll appreciate more fully the settlement if they can win the concession of having (Espig: Uh-huh) <u>diverted you</u> from benefits to cents per hour. If you tip your hand at this time that you're going in that direction, the door is open, then, and the effectiveness of the move is destroyed.

Espig: Well, then, what do you think of adding — of adding just to the offer as it stands now 5¢ an hour for the skilled trades? (Pause)

Mediator: What was that?

Espig: What do you think of adding to the 2-cent package as it's now added — as it's now — exists 5¢ an hour for the skilled trades?

Mediator: Well, that's what I was thinking about.

Espig: In other words, / leave the penny in the pension.

Mediator: (Over Espig above but cannot be understood)

Espig: Leave (Mediator: No) the — leave the — leave the penny in the pensions, leave the insurance as it stands, but add to the offer 5¢ an hour for the skilled trades. / x — that would cost us $\frac{1}{2}$¢ of our 3 — of our 2.

Mediator: (Over Espig above) Well, here's what you're doing, now, you see. $\frac{1}{2}$¢ — he'd get his — he'd get his pencil out (Espig: 2) and see $\frac{1}{2}$¢. (Espig: Uh-huh) But in your presentation, see, you'd — he — he'd note that you were paying heed to what he was saying, and he would appreciate this, if you would, in your presentation when you go back, if you would say, "We — w — we listened and discussed your remarks on the question of pension, and we have decided to take the cent that we have offered out of the pension. We think there's merit to what you say, if" — or without saying that, saying there's merit to it. "We — we decided, on the basis of your remarks, to remove that cent and (pause) take — and add 5¢ to the skilled workers." (Pause) Now, the other $\frac{1}{2}$¢ I think you'll have — we'll have to find a place for it. But it will have a lot of effect. You're showing them that — but, see, they've used an argument and you have reversed your position to comply with their proposal — their pr — or, their argument. Their argument was, "What good is this?" So you're takin' something and making it good. The only thing is, ya have an end hanging over. What (Espig: Uh-huh) are ya gonna do with it?

Espig: Well, you could — it might not be a very good suggestion, but you certainly could say, "We'll let you apply the $\frac{1}{2}$¢ the way you want it." (Pause) And they may come up with an extra holiday.

Mediator: Is that good?

Espig: I don't know.

Loring: No.

Pranis: Extra holiday at $\frac{1}{2}$¢?

Loring: No, I think it would be more / than that.

Espig: (Over Loring above) 7/10ths of a cent.

Mediator: How many d'you have now?

Loring: 8.

Espig: 8. We / have —

Mediator: (Over Espig above) Oh-ho!

Espig: We have enough.

Mediator: Yeah.

Pranis: (Says something but cannot be understood) (Pause)

Espig: (In low voice) I don't know.

Mediator: And you don't put half-cents on hours, do you?

Pranis: We / got 'em now.

?: (Over Pranis above) Got 'em now.

Mediator: Do (Espig: So —) you have it now?

Espig: Oh, / yes! Yes!

Pranis: (Over Espig above but cannot be understood)

Espig: Uh-huh.

Loring: That — that (laughs shortly) — that's so small, though (slight pause) (Pranis: Well, you add that to this —) — $\frac{1}{2}$¢ an hour. (Pause)

Mediator: It's so important that you — if you can keep this thing steered in the direction of benefits. (Pause) It'll strengthen —

Espig: Well, let's think a minute. (Rather long pause)

[Loring and Pranis exchange short comments about a letter which
Pranis is holding.]

Pranis: He's got his benefits listed out here. You (Loring: Yeah) divide it out and see what you can get. I'd rather stick the ½¢ in there.
(Pause)

Loring: Uh-huh-huh-um. That would — we could raise — what you
could do would be to say we'll make a $10.00 daily benefit and
(Pranis: $200.00) $200.00 special services. That would just about
be another ½¢. (Long pause)

Pranis: (In low voice) I think 20 divided by it'd get it.

Loring: Uh — well, you multiply that by 12 and divide by 19.36.

Pranis: (In low voice) Oh, yeah?

Mediator: That would (?: [In low voice] Sure) take another cent — ½¢?

Loring: Yeah.

Pranis: (In low voice) Do it this —

Mediator: And then you'd take — and then you'd have the other ½¢ for —

Loring: Your — your 5¢ an hour.

Mediator: — your 5¢ an hour —

Loring: — for skilled —

Mediator: — for skilled trade. (Slight pause) And then you would —
that would be (long pause) — that would take care of the penny from
the pension.

Loring: Uh-huh.

Mediator: Then (rather long pause) — now. Then, the next thing to do,
you would have to (pause) — you would have to attack the figure 14,
make an ex — very, very clear that the company isn't thinking of 14¢.
They can't think of it. (Pause) See, the lase — the — the least you
say about that, the worse it is.

Loring: Yeah.

Mediator: You've got to — you've got to make clear to that whole committee that — that 14¢ isn't there and, ''We don't want any strikes,
but when you're out of a bargaining area and we're forced into it, we
have no choice. However'' — and if that isn't a true statement, don't
make it.

Loring: Uh-huh. (Pause) Well, 14¢ (laughing slightly) is certainly —
it's — it's in that area.

Mediator: Uh — because if they — see, they watch how you present.
Both bar — company and union bargaining teams are — watch the —
the way a thing is presented and what things you put emphasis on
(Loring: Uh-huh), and which things you treat lightly. The ones you
treat lightly indicate that that's where an opening is. (Loring: Uh-
huh) Now, if you went in there — well, knowing yourself that you
couldn't — your company couldn't pay this 14¢ but not saying much
about it, you'd be making your job doubly hard. (Loring: Uh-huh)
Got to hit that 14 — that — their bargaining figure. (Pause) And
then I think you ought to — here is the thing that is most important in
this next presentation, at the right time. I think you would — you
should again follow up with the first cousin of the last opening you
made. (Loring: Uh-huh) The last opening you made was, ''Your figure is too high and — for this committee and that's why we're at 2¢.''
Now, the first cousin to that — the follow-up should be, ''Your figure
is too, too high. It's out of a bargaining area. (Pause) We wanta see
this thing settled, and this committee has the authority to reach an

agreement with you" — repeat what you have already said. (Loring:
Uh-huh) "But we <u>cannot</u>, from our position (pause), <u>begin</u> to bargain with you at a package like this because" — and then give 'em all
the becauses why you can't go at 14¢. You've got to keep punching
that 14. (Loring: H'm) And before ya — and John will, again, catch
onto this. Then I think I can predict what he will do. He will then
call <u>me</u> into a caucus (pause) with their committee, if it goes that
way. But —

Pranis: Purpose of t — that will be what, George? (Mediator: To —)
Find out what, in your opinion, is (Mediator: Yeah) the neighborhood?

Mediator: What is in the neighborhood, <u>or</u> he will say, "Look. At this
point we'd like to protect our bargaining position. Suppose you handle
it unofficially (Pranis: Uh-huh), work between the 2 points unofficially so that if we <u>can't</u> reach an agreement, we're here and they're
there where they were."

Pranis: Officially.

Mediator: Yeah. (Pause)

Pranis: (In rather low voice) Like a bunch of Chinese.

Mediator: Well, see, they have to do that sometimes.

Pranis: Face — I never s — considered face to be so important.

Mediator: It <u>isn't</u> face! It's — no. It's —

Pranis: Well, bargaining / position.

Mediator: (Over Pranis above) No. Politics is tied up (Pranis: Oh,
there's a lot of things, but —); uh-h — union prestige (Pranis: Especially with John) amongst other organizers; uh — oh, there's a —
I could name dozens of reasons <u>why</u> they have to — now, up to a point.
<u>Once he gets near</u> you and <u>sees</u> a settlement, then he no longer needs
the mediator. <u>Then</u> he'll roll, see. They'll come right out from the
— that side of the table, I'm sure, and make a — to close the deal, if
it can be closed. 'Course, this is all crystal-ball gazing and prognosticating, but he — they generally follow that s — steps — those steps.
Now — and, then, too, they have a committee, and it <u>is</u> difficult for
them to make statements in front of the committee — or, in front of
a <u>company</u> committee and their full committee the — where they <u>may</u>
— that <u>could</u> be <u>misinterpreted</u> easily or they could be <u>quoted</u> in the
letter, we'll say, see. They — they're bargainin' against those things.
(Loring: Uh-huh) That's why they will use the intermediary to protect their position. The companies do the same thing — exactly the
same thing. (Rather long pause)

Pranis: Let's see, where were we, now? You were gonna pull a penny
from the pension. Right? We had what? .0047 originally, Len?
(Slight pause)

Loring: Uh —

Pranis: What are we carryin', the 60¢? .0047.

Loring: What d'you mean?

Pranis: Well, the thing that we said we would continue to carry — our
first position.

Loring: It's about ½¢ — <u>about</u>, or 4/10ths of a cent, Bill said. (Rather
long pause)

Pranis: Got a penny and 6/10ths of this package again — the next step up.
(Pause)

Loring: Uh —

Espig: No additional!

Pranis: That's what I said. Look. No, I'm saying th — that's the — the $10.00 daily benefit plus the 20 times it, you go up from 8/10ths to (pause) 1.12 — something like that. (Slight pause) Increase 4/10ths of a cent, which is a total of a penny and 6/10ths x total benefit ya give 'em now, as against ½¢ before. Now you take your penny from your pension —

Espig: Well, you like the idea of 5¢ (Pranis: All right) for the skilled trades? If you don't —

Pranis: I — I like it. I like it for a lot of reasons. Doesn't cost much and it looks good. Gets him off the hook and us.

[A long interval follows, during which Mediator carries on a personal conversation on phone. Espig and Pranis continue their estimations, with Loring silent until Pranis calls on him for comment.]

Mediator: I think we better knock 'em off to dinner. (Pause)

Loring: Uh-huh.

Mediator: Don't ya think so?

Loring: I think it might be a good idea, George, and — (pause).

Mediator: We'll have a fresher start, with somethin'.

Loring: With something. Yeah.

Mediator: (Mumbles word or 2) (Slight pause) (Addressing Observer) Do you agree with that (pause) — dinner? (Slight pause) That — that motion's always in order. (Pranis and Espig laugh)

Pranis: Nobody ever argues, did they? (Espig continues laughing)

[Mediator goes to the union caucus room at 5:50 P.M. to dismiss that group for dinner. Gambon calls out, "Looks like they're goin' to dinner," then asks Mediator, "The boys healthy, are they? Havin' a movement?" One of the girls asks, "Are they buyin' dinner?" which brings on several remarks from Mediator, such as, "I think that — that's negotiable," "May endanger your bargaining position," and "They could send a letter out. They'll say they bought your dinner." Meanwhile, one of the boys suggests, "They're gonna get some All-Bran" and "Some All-Bran will move them." The amount of time to be taken becomes the last topic of discussion, eliciting these general points:

Mediator: Let's make it as sh — as short as possible. How long does your group need to have dinner? 45 minutes?

Gambon: Look. What's — what's the difference how long we take? I mean, it depends on how long they're gonna take and how long it —

Mediator: Well, I — it — I think they'll be about ready. They — they're workin' on some figures and calling up and getting —

Gambon: Why I say that, we usually get back here and then they're still in caucus for another couple of hours.

Mediator: No. Oh, I see. Oh, they'll be ready. I'm quite sure they'll be ready at that time. Maybe 10 minutes or so longer.

Gambon: About an hour at the outside?

Mediator: No, make it an hour at the most.

Gambon: All right. 7:00. At the latest, 7:00 o'clock.

Mediator leaves the union group to return to the management caucus room at 6:00 P.M.]

Mediator: . . . back by 7:00?

Loring: Gee, I guess so.

Mediator: See, well, I told them to be back at 7:00.

Loring: Yeah. Does this look like it might go for awhile, now, to-night?

Mediator: Uh — a lot will depend on how they treat this. (Rather long pause) Let me put it this way. If we start to make — if it looks like we can wrap it up, I'll stay right with it. But if it looks like about 8:00 o'clock — when we get up around 8:00 or 9:00, quarter to 9:00, and they're (drawling slowly) still moving slow, then I'm convinced that it'll still take a little more time. (Loring: Yeah) That's why I don't want to get ya out too far without knowing (Loring: Yeah) what the pace is goin' to be.

Loring: Uh-huh. Well, I — I'll rely on you to keep the thing in hand. I mean, that's the only part that bothers me, George, if we (Espig: George —) push 'em over the brink there (Espig: Bill said yester-day —) on a strike vote.

Espig: Excuse me. Bill said yesterday that Standard Products was going to lay their offer on the table on a particular day. Did he say Wednes-day?

Pranis: Wednesday.

Espig: I — I'm wondering (Pranis: Mattuck said Wednesday) — I'm wondering whether / x —

Mediator: (Over Espig above) Does the union know that?

Espig: I wonder whether the — th — whether the union knows that?

Mediator: Well, even if they did (pause), what — it wouldn't make a lotta difference in — because of the 2 different dates — or, the 2 dif-ferent (Espig: Oh, that would have no —) negotiations, one / being a reopener —

Espig: (Over Mediator above) That wouldn't have any meaning to John.

Pranis: That wouldn't mean anything to John. He compares us with Standard Products always. Remember?

Mediator: Well, I — I can understand them comparing you on a termina-tion negotiation, but here they're terminating and you're in 6-month reopener.

Pranis: To John it's money in the hand, I think. He doesn't give a hoot what it'd —

Espig: Huh-un!

Mediator: Yeah, but he can — that may be bluffin'. That may / be pussy —

Pranis: (Over Mediator above) Oh, it probably is.

Mediator: But when the chips are down, he can't run away from <u>facts</u>. Uh-h —

Pranis: He might be looking for more points, George.

Mediator: No, I'll watch that close. I'll — and if we do disband, I'll have a clear-cut understanding as to what the status of (Loring: Uh-huh) the negotiations will be. If we disband, it'll be — or, recess it would be until probably Thursday (pause), 'course with an understanding that there'd be no striking. (Pause) No, I'll (slight pause) sit right on it (slight pause) <u>unless</u> it develops into a situation where they say, "We won't wait." But I <u>doubt</u> that that would — doubt it very much. (Rather long pause)

Loring: O.K.!

Mediator: See, these are the — these negotiat — when this thing is settled, I know what — you can't help but <u>think</u> — you're gonna say, "Well,
hell, why couldn't they done that in the first place?" (Pause) But —
(slight pause).

Pranis: I'll probably ask you that.

Mediator: Yeah. (Pranis talks at same time) And I'll — I'll give ya the
answer now. (Laughs) The answer is that (pause) the smaller the
figures are the longer the negotiations must take (pause), because
they have to show me —

Pranis: (Making sound of exhaustion) I guess so. It's hard on an efficiency expert —

[As the group prepares to break up, Pranis, in continuation of his
point, adds: "I don't like to see that tape go by with nothing on it as
many times as it has in the past. The transcriber must have a tough
time sitting there waiting while foot after foot goes by."]

Mediator: Observer, are you gonna put the feed bag on?

Observer: If you're through. Are you?

Management Caucus - F (7:10 P.M.)

Mediator: Well, let's see. Where were we?

Loring: Well, we were just discussing, when we left, strategy in this
session, that we'll go in and make a to-do about the 14¢ that they're
now at, tell 'em why we can't consider any such cost. Company can't
possibly consider it. Go into that a little bit, then point out we've
thought over their comments about our previous offer and we're willing to revise it along these lines. Instead of offering the cent in the
pension plan, which they don't seem to care about, we'll give them —
we'll offer 5¢ an hour to the skilled trades and use the balance of that
cent to increase the hospitalization benefits to $10.00 a day and
$200.00 for services. (Pause) Then go back again at, we think this
is a fair offer because, with the things that's g — bothering us, we
can't possibly consider a 14-cent position, that we have the <u>authority</u>
to settle this but, as far as this committee's concerned, we <u>can't</u> do
any more than this now, they're so far apart — <u>we're</u> so far apart.

Mediator: And then h — he's going to come back, see — now, here's what's
gonna happen. When he rebuts he's going to (pause) say a lotta things
that ya've heard before. But watch for the high point. The high point
is going to be (rather long pause), "If — if that's the way you feel,
we — our — our people will never accept this and we're going to have
to report back to them," or "We're goin' to" — see, he's going to hit
on that vein of strike. That should be your cue. At that point, when
he pauses, or when he finishes, be well for you to then make this kind
of a statement, "We don't want a strike," even though you've said this
before. And I think you should make this statement on a personal basis.
You oughta say, "John, we don't want a strike! <u>But</u> we have our limits.
We would like to work this thing out with you, and even tonight if we
could. <u>But</u> we <u>never</u> could do so with your thinking where it is." You
do that and watch what happens. (Pause) Now, that should come at the
end, after —

Loring: Uh-huh. (Pause)

Mediator: And he'll — he'll latch onto that, and then we'll start to move. That's just what he'll need — just that. And he'll go to town. I'm s — I'll — I'll — I'll wager you he'll start walking in your direction fast. And if he <u>doesn't</u> we'll all go home, because that will be positive proof that he — <u>he's</u> playing footsie. (Pause) So if you — if you're ready, I am.

Loring: Just about 2 minutes, George. I'll just (Mediator: All right) get this out here.

[Mediator leaves, remaining in another office until notified by the management group that they are ready for the joint meeting.]

Joint Meeting - D (7:20 P.M.)

Mediator: Go ahead.

Loring: O.K. Well, we've gone over very carefully the union's latest proposal. John, we've — appreciate that you've moved from your previous position. We figure that the new offer is a cost to us of about 14¢ an hour through calculated x and that's as against the previous position of just slightly more than that. We'd like to get this settled, but we can't consider such a high cost, particularly because of the things that — that we've told you about before. The various costs of 15¢ an hour would pretty nearly ruin us. We're faced with this uncertainties this year that, while we can't put our finger on them and say they're gonna happen, they — in our mind they're re — very real uncertainties, doubts. I've pointed out to ya that even at this moment we're having a softening in the incoming order rates; competition is building up, particularly the lower-price competition; and, on top of it all, we had a pretty poor year in '52. 14¢, in the c — in the opinion of this committee, is — is pretty much something we can't even consider. We've also given some consideration to your comments about our previous offer. You didn't like the way in which we offered it, so we've discussed that and we're prepared to revise that along these lines. You had given us comments that you didn't like the 1¢ in the pension plan. In place of the 1¢ we're prepared to offer you 5¢ an hour to the skilled trades and use the balance of that cent to increase the hospitalization from 7.50 a day to $10.00 a day and $200.00 in special services, in case of hospitalization. We feel again — I can't stress too seriously — too — too strongly from our viewpoint that this 14¢ an hour is just <u>completely</u> out of question. We have the authority, as you've asked, to settle this thing if it's at all possible to settle it, but, in the opinion of this committee, we're at our top — I mean, as long as your position is so out of the world for us, John. And we've given it a <u>lot</u> of consideration.

Gambon: Well, let — let me get this. What's this, 5¢ to skilled trades and balance of the 1¢ to what?

Loring: Into the hospitalization plan to increase it to $10.00 per day and $200.00 in the special benefits. (Espig whispers to "stress the skilled trades") And we mean that skilled trades, John, not / all day workers.

Gambon: (Over Loring above) Yeah, I understand that. (Pause) Increase the benefits from 7.50 to (Meyer: Yeah) $10.00?

Loring: Yes.

Meyer: From 75.00 to 200.00. (Pause)

Loring: And from 75.00 to 200.00. (Pause)

Gambon: Uh-huh. (Pause) That still remains a 2-cent total (Loring: Yes, it does, John) cost to the company. Yeah. Uh-huh.

Loring: It's just —

Gambon: Well, let me ask you a question, Len. Since you've been complaining here about the company — the union's high figure, and assuming, of course, that there is a figure above what your present position is that the company would like to have a settlement on, would you mind stating what the figure is?

Loring: I'd — I don't have a figure in mind that I would state, John. I'd just say that we're — in — in my opinion, we're not in a bargaining area at this point.

Gambon: What is your bargaining area?

Loring: I don't (Gambon: I understand it's 2¢ at the moment) have a particular bargaining area. John, I — I'm waiting for you to get down into a bargaining area.

Gambon: Well, I'm not gonna come down to 3¢, Len (Loring laughs, joined by Gambon), if that's what you want (Loring: I didn't expect that you would, John, not right away) me to go to, because I don't think that would be realistic on the union's part to consider that that's all the company can pay. (Pause) Dealing with first things first (slight pause), can we get an agreement from the company involving the 20% fixed bonus item?

Loring: In what — what d'you mean, John?

Gambon: Uh (pause) — in this — let's put it this way. Can we reach an agreement on that with the understanding that the union would expect that, in addition to the 20% fixed bonus item, there would be X cents per hour in terms of a general wage increase?

Loring: I would say No, John.

Gambon: Well, that's the general area that I'm willing to get into at the moment. (Long pause)

Loring: No, I'd say no, we can't concede that.

Gambon: Are you, in a sense, telling me that the company is not prepared to try and to come up with a settlement that is equal at least to — let's approximate the cost on skilled trades, 20% fixed bonus item, and other day workers of approximately 4¢ — are you tellin' me, in effect, that 4¢ is out of your field of bargaining?

Loring: I'm — I'm not telling you anything about what our / field of bargaining is.

Gambon: (Over Loring above) Well, ya — I'm tryin' to find this area that you're talking about, Len, without coming down and goin' in the cellar, see. Now, I've expressed as clearly as I know how our interest in this fixed bonus item and our reasons for wanting to have it in effect in the plant. I'm saying to you, again in effect, that the union, in order to reach an amicable settlement with the company, will expect in addition to that item X cents per hour in terms of a general increase, if there's going to be a settlement without a strike. Now, without coming down to specifics on a general increase, I don't know how to try to reach your area.

Loring: Well, John, nobody wants a strike (Gambon: H'm) less than I do, or the company. It's something that would hurt us (Gambon: H'm),

would hurt you people. We don't want that. We certainly want to work
out an agreement if it's at all possible, and we will try hard. On the
other hand, we have a limited amount we feel that we can spend. We
can be pushed too hard on it. Now, I hope that doesn't happen but at
the moment, you at 14¢ an hour and we at 2¢ an hour, w — we're just
not bargaining. We're / not in that bargaining area.

Gambon: (Over Loring above) Well, I'm trying to give you a — I'm
tryin' — tryin' to give you a bargaining springboard, as it were. I'm
talking in terms of placing first things first, now. I'm saying to you,
in effect, let's reach an agreement on the 20% fixed bonus item and
go on from there, and I'll wrangle out with you the position of the company in terms of zero in general increase and a 10-cent increase on
the part of the union.

Loring: John, I don't think we can reach an agreement on any one part
of it. It's gotta be a whole package that we reach / an agreement on.

Gambon: (Over Loring above) Well, I understand that. I mean, it will
eventually be a whole package, but I'm making — tryin' to make the
point that this one part is a very important part of the entire package.
It's represented by certain cents-per-hour cost to the company, no
doubt. Your estimates are available as well as ours are available.

Espig: Well, we have tried to show our position on the matter of the
skilled trades / by this particular statement.

Gambon: (Over Espig above) H'm. Well, that — that is not adequate.
(Espig: Eh — that may be true, but at this —) Let's put it that way.
This does not answer the problem that we have in Atlas. This business of continuing to give additional cents-per-hour increases in a
plant that is almost entirely on incentives is not going to eliminate
the inequities that exist. I don't think anybody can deny that, to some
degree, greater in some cases, less in others, every employee in that
company who is now determined as a day worker contributes in some
form to the over-all productivity of the entire plant. (Pause) Our
plan and our suggestion, in our opinion, will eliminate once and for
all this question of inequity. The — it only points up that this 5-cent
business now, as well as the 5¢ we had in March of '52, is something
which ya keep chopping at, and it doesn't eliminate the prob — it
doesn't answer your own problems, because all the effect that this
would have at the moment would be to raise your rate to $2.32, which
is not going to meet the area rate for tool and die maker! (Pause)
Now, that's one problem, and that's why I'm putting it first, because
we both share an interest in that and we both realize benefits from it.
There — it may — let's — we can differ about why these fellows left,
if you wish, but it's a matter of (Espig: Wait a minute, John) fact
that you're not — you're not havin' too much success in hiring men
to replace the men who already left!

Espig: Well, I merely point out that — that here is the position of the
company in what we think will help to alleviate that problem. (Slight
pause)

Gambon: It's not adequate, Erwin. (Rather long pause)

Loring: Well (Gambon: I'm —), as — as Erwin said, John, we attempted
to give some effect to what you're asking by s — offering this 5¢. Now,
that would be, since the last time, 10¢ an / hour xxxxx.

Gambon: (Over Loring above) Well, look, Len, I'm talking about — I'm
talking about an over-all cost here, too. (Slight pause) You're

limiting this, of course, to just skilled trades, and that's not the answer to our entire problem. (Slight pause) Talking about this area of
bargaining again, I don't know how I can go any further than I have,
trying to get somewhere near your area of bargaining, because I'm
beginning with the first-thing-first proposition which is less than 2¢
away from your present position. I make it clear, however, that I
wanta go beyond that. (Loring: Yes, you've made it clear) Now, how
else can I do it? I begin with a s — specific figure of, let's say, 3¢
plus — 3 to 4¢, whatever that figure may / be.

Loring: (Over Gambon above) We're figurin' 4¢, / John.

Gambon: (Over Loring above) Huh?

Loring: We figure it 4¢.

Gambon: Well, I — I might quarrel with that, but I'm not going to. I'll
leave it at a 4-cent proposition for the purpose of discussion. But
I'm coming away from a 4-cent position there at the moment and trying to explore this area, and where is it? And I'm starting and I'm
saying 4¢ plus, and I'm putting myself in a position of tryin' to bargain you above the 4-cent figure. (Pause) Now, I mean, can't we get
that part of it out of the road?

Loring: No, I'd say we can't, John. I mean, our — our position — the
position of this committee at this time is that we have a top / xxx.

Gambon: (Over Loring above) Well, let me ask this question. Is the
company opposed to the principle —

[Tape changed]

... That's important, it's terribly important (pause), because the
form that you're presenting here as an answer to the inequities is
not the kind of form that we would like to see develop. I don't know
how to get into your area, Len. (Long pause) I might suggest this to
you, that you have partly answered our request in directing your proposals towards — more towards the items the union had in its program submitted to the company, and I would suggest that you get away
from this hospitalization thing entirely, because we have not expressed
at any time durin' this reopener a desire to increase benefits that are
now available to the people und — under the plan that we now have.
And I would appreciate your directing yourself towards the union's
position and its form, that is, the question of a general wage increase
plus the method of correcting the inequities in the skilled trades and
other day workers. (Pause) Seems to me that if you were to direct
the total cost to the company toward those 2 things that you should be
coming outa here, after your next caucus, with a proposal directed
towards the fixed bonus question, if the principle of fixed bonus is not
opposed by the company, as well as a proposal directed towards the
problem of general wage increases, because it should be clear by now
that any settlement that is reached will be along those lines, that is,
any settlement acceptable to the union has got to follow those 2 lines.
Uh (rather long pause) —I don't know how to reach your area, Len.
I think the proposition of trying to get us to reach your area depends
on the company's recognition of the union's position and the form of
its demands at this point; and until you begin to direct yourself to the
question of a general wage increase and the s — proposition of fixed
bonus for skilled trades and day workers, I'm quite convinced we're
not gonna get anywhere. And in — included in directing yourself to

those 2 things, of course, comes the big item of moving away from your total 2-cent cost position, which is certainly a deterrent to trying to have any settlement reach a — across this table. Despite the fact that you claim our figure is too high, yours is too low, much too low, to have any hope of reachin' a settlement. (Pause) George, I — I'm afraid I'll have to turn this back to you. It's about the way I see it at this moment.

Mediator: All right. (Pause) I'll — I wanta talk with management, and then I'll wanta talk with you.

Management Caucus - G (7:40 P.M.)

Mediator: That was all right. (Rather long pause) Oh! (Rather long pause) Very good! I think you — 'course, you can see that he was tryin' to punch a hole here. He was tryin' to punch a hole when he says, "You must start speaking of the application and then we'll bargain the (Loring: H'm) amount." Well, now, he's putting the cart before the horse, see. (Loring: Yeah. Yeah.) If you did that (Espig: First things first), be backwards. It's backwards. (Espig: George, first things first!) And (rather long pause) — see, I told you that that would eventually disturb him, see. He wants that — he wants to get you away from that — the way you're thinking of application. (Loring: Uh-huh. Uh-huh) Now, if you had given that up earlier, see, he would a — he would have been much more difficult to work with. Uh — I'm afraid to say — I'm afraid to — that — not afraid to say; I mean, I'm af — I regret that our — that our friend John is still moving slow, unless he's going to fold up, all at one time. He's still playing footsie with his figure. Uh (pause) — now, this area of agreement (rather long pause) — he is — appears to me to be, f — from the way he's bargaining, his sights are set on 7. (Slight pause) He says that's where his sight is.

Loring: That's just not there, George. I mean, that's definite.

Mediator: Yeah, he's set on 7, as ya can see the way he's bargaining. He's holding right on, see. Now, it — i — b — because, see, he's at 14. He wants a move from you to protect the balance of this, which is 7. I can see what he's — how he's bargaining. Another move from him (pause), see, would put him in a position where he might have to settle for less than 7 at this particular time, and he's holdin' onto that. (Pause) But we're — we're moving along. I mean, we're — we're going along. Not as fast as I'd like to, but (rather long pause) John seems to want it that way. Does he — he — how's he fare with his committee? I mean, is — does he — (slight pause)?

Pranis: He's the committee.

Espig: He's —

Mediator: Yeah, I can see that he does all the talking, but (Espig: Well, he manages all —) does he have to put a show on? Does he / have to put a demonstration on?

Loring: (Over Mediator above) I think he does. I (?: Yeah) think he does.

?: Yeah.

?: (At same time as person above) He must.

Espig: And I think — I think now that we've got — I think now that you — that we've been as broad as we are, I think now there might even be some doubt whether he could shove us into a strike (slight pause) (Loring: H'm) quickly — quickly. (Pause)

Loring: That — / that x —

Espig: (Over Loring above) They — they know there's something more there, and — and they — they'll be a little hesitant about pulling out their fellows. (Slight pause)

Mediator: Yeah. I don't see any immediate danger of a strike overnight, although I do believe that you could get one if he believes he's stopped where he is. If he thought he was stopped where he is, you'd get one.

Espig: Well, he gave us an out (pause): do we believe in t — in the fixed bonus for these jobs?

Pranis: (Under his breath) Yeah, / but x —

Mediator: (Over Pranis above) Now, just what does that mean? I'm gonna have to ask you / what that would mean.

Espig: (Over Mediator above) Well, there's — there — now, this can be used in the negotiating program; it can also be used otherwise. Up to this point what we have done is this, George. We had an incentive system in the plant, and during the war we couldn't get people to take the day-work jobs. So what we did, we compensated for the lack of an incentive system by placing a fixed 20% bonus —

Mediator: For day work?

Espig: — for day workers in many of the jobs and, in addition to that, production workers. It started with production workers who couldn't work against an incentive rate because none was there. Then it got — the next step was to include inspectors, for whom an incentive rate, at that time, was thought not to be proper. Then from there it traveled to a group of people who service incentive workers and who are considered to work harder because they must ser — service incentive workers, people who have to carry the materials to them, people who have to carry the materials away, people who have to take particular items to these people w — w — within a given length of time so that they are continuously busy on their incentive job. Those were the 3 kinds of jobs that grew into this fixed bonus area. That right?

Pranis: Uh-huh.

Espig: Now, in the last 2 years he has come to us and said, "Look. Here are certain of these jobs that ought to be incentive jobs on a fixed bonus basis. Material handlers" —

Mediator: Day jobs.

Espig: P — / p —

Mediator: (Over Espig above) Day workers.

Espig: Yeah. Material handlers and machine adjustors. Material handlers who carry material from one to the other, machine adjustors, many who go out and while the girls are working on these machines keep them in adjustment, in alignment. These machines are sensitive. The girls are not prepared to make the adjustments. So we have a machine adjustor. Depending upon the type of operation is, we may have a machine adjustor to every 2 machines, or every 4 machines, or maybe to every dozen machines. But we have a man there who is in the nature of a set-up man. Actually he doesn't set it up, he just does the adjusting. Now, that's — there — that's the group they're

interested in. In addition to that, they're using this, of course, for
the entire group. This is a — a sweeping motion on their part. Now,
up to — up to about a year ago we used to expand this group of people,
one at a time, as the union came in and said, "Now, look. They're
servicing incentive workers. You oughta give them the 20%." So we
said, "O.K., we'll go along." But they got a little bit on the piggish
side and they wrote a letter. And they said, "We want 20% for all
machine adjustors. And we want 20% for this group and that group."
So, Bill and I looked at the contract and said, "You can only set —
you can only get 20% for these people by mutual agreement of the 2
parties, the union and the company." So we said No! And it's been a
battleground ever since. So when John says, "We'll go to arbitration
on it," he knows damn well (laughing slightly) why he isn't goin' to
arbitration on this point, because the arbitrator will throw it out! It
takes a d — it takes an agreement between the company and the union.
T — the arbitrator can't make that agreement. And that's where we
stand. Now, 20% for people who service these people — well, it has
been endorsed. That theory has been endorsed. We go back there and
say, "We don't agree with it," he'll say, "Well, you did agree with
that ti — kind of a program, piecemeal." On the other hand, we have
never agreed that 20% for maintainence workers is good, bad, or indifferent. For instance, a machinist, or a die maker, or a plumber,
or a carpenter, or someone of that character, we have never said that
we would agree to a 20% bonus. And this is the first time that this
group — these — these 3 fellows here have had to decide whether they
believe 20% fixed bonus is a proper thing for a maintainence worker.
Now, I don't know how these / men —

Pranis: (Over Espig above) Well, that's the question he asked (Espig:
That's — well —): do we believe in / 20% for —

Espig: (Over Pranis above) That's — that — but we have to confine ourselves to — to the skilled groups, because we are in a — in a — in a
controversial area on the rest of the people.

Mediator: Now, let me ask you this. You s — t — I wanta reconstruct it.
Do I understand you to say that the 20% was for day people — day
(Pranis: Yeah) workers?

Espig: That's right.

Pranis: All / this xx —

Mediator: (Over Pranis above) During the war is where it au (Espig:
Is where it originated) — it's been x and then it has been supplemented —

Espig: It originated on other production jobs (Pranis: That were not
incentive rated) that could (Mediator: That were not incentive rates)
— that could not be incentive rated at / that time.

Mediator: (Over Espig above) x. Right. Then after the war / you supplemented it.

Espig: (Over Mediator above) Then it spread — then it — no. Then it
spread during the war to inspectors. They were the first class / of —

Mediator: (Over Espig above) Now, are inspectors incentive people?

Pranis: No.

Espig: Generally no. Generally no. And (Pranis: They were day — they
were day workers at that time) at that time — at that time it was —
at that time they were conceived of as day workers.

Mediator: All right. Now, have at any time s — a — have you at any time since the war extended that — this principle to incentive people?

Espig: To other day workers.

Mediator: That were on incentive?

Espig: Yeah.

Pranis: No!

Mediator: (At same time as Pranis above) You have?

Pranis: Not / people who are on incentive.

Espig: (Over Pranis above) Well, wait a minute. I — I — not — not to people who are on incentive.

Mediator: That's what I mean. You haven't (Espig: N — u —), ever!

Espig: People who were on incentive would never have this. (Slight pause) This is only for people who'd like incentive (Mediator: Oh) operation.

Mediator: Now, his —

Pranis: (At same time as Mediator above) Conceive of 2 groups, George: people on incentive and those not on incentive. This principle only h — has anything to do with the people who are not on incentive. These are known as day workers to us. It originally started out with whole departments i — productive workers (Mediator: I see) being paid day work. They were not considered to be ratable, as we call / it, which means they have no incentive.

Mediator: (Over Pranis above) Oh. So they'd have to — then John is talking only of — (slight pause).

Pranis: Day workers.

Mediator: Day work.

Pranis: Pure day work. What's left of the day work group he thinks oughta have flat / x —

Mediator: (Over Pranis above) But, then, beside that he wants attention for the skilled group, also.
[Several talk briefly at once.]

Pranis: (Over others above) Well, he says that — he says that his 20% will straighten out the inequities of the skilled groups. He uses this to s — to st — get rid of / the inequities.

Loring: (Over Pranis above) See, the skilled group is non-incentive as well as th — the regular (Mediator: Like x — yeah) xx. So (Mediator says something) it's really one group, George.

Mediator: I see. They're one group.

Espig: You have 3 groups (Mediator: Uh —) within this group. Ya have the skilled tradesmen —

Mediator: Well, you, at the offset — or at the outset of your remarks seemed to indicate that you saw daylight on this. Now, where do you see the daylight? (Slight pause)

Espig: No. I don't see the daylight — oh, other than this. He said — he asks us whether or not we agree that 20% for these day workers is proper. My answer to that would be, un the — in the area of the skilled tradesmen, no, it is not proper because there is nothing to indicate any increased production for that 20%. There is something to increase the production of the average person to whom this 20% has been given, theoretically. Theoretically, this 20% replaces a normal incentive earning for the average operator, and we expect, theoretically, normal incentive activity from the operator who receives it. For the service people who receive it, we say that the incentive worker, working at a faster pace than the day worker, requires that service person to work at a faster pace and therefore they're — she's en — entitled to the 20%. Now, this ignores the historical approach. I wanted you to know the historical approach. Now you can take the theoretical approach. But for the incentive worker, for the person who is alli — allied with an incentive worker, th — we get some extra production, some extra effort for this 20%. But for the skilled trades-men we get nothing!

Mediator: Well, now, let me come right to the point on this. Are you say-ing, then — is the gist of your remarks this, that there might be some parts of his pro — his proposal of this 20% for day workers that you could talk about and probably agree on? Is that what you're saying?

Espig: We could talk about it; I don't say we could agree on it. But there are several men in the material handling group that they have been attempting to get this 20% for (Pranis: They aren't comparable xx) who are somewhat comparable to others who have it!

Mediator: Well, now, I have to — now, I have to ask this question. You know John; you've been in negotiations with him, particularly at the plant level, where you — many of your nego — more negotiations take place than here. Can John live with a settlement in his shop where he can get more for one group and not another? (Slight pause)

Espig: He could in this case.

Mediator: He could?

Espig: Yes. He can explain it.

Mediator: Uh-huh. (Slight pause)

Espig: For instance, he could — he could say to these people, "Look. I have done nothing excepting get for these people what they were en-titled to a long time ago. Over here's Joe Doakes getting 20% and here's Bill Smith doing practically the same job and not getting 20%. So I got him 20%." Now, whether he — I say that he could explain that and the skilled tradesmen might agree. But we — we don't think that we ought to pay these other people — th — the machine adjustor. We have compensated those people in the past by a fudged rate within the evaluation system, which is another thing that w — happened during the war. Now we pay for something that we did in the past and didn't do properly, that's all, if we do this. (Slight pause)

Loring: Well, I think I — I mean, my feeling on this is that the answer to John's question, if we do answer it, is that we feel that the company doesn't oppose, as such, the principle, but we don't think it applies to everybody. The — the — the selection —

Pranis: Well, all right. You don't wanta bargain any of this group.

Loring: No. No! I mean / that that xxx.

Espig: (Over Loring above) No. I think we do oppose the principle.

Pranis: We oppose the principle / x —

Espig: (Over Pranis above) Excepting as it — as it has been applied in the past.

Pranis: Remember what he said: does — does this committee — we should find out whether or not we oppose the principle of the 20% bonus for the skilled trades. He said specifically that. And if you talk about skilled trades, I would say we are opposed. (Slight pause)

Espig: To the skilled trades (Pranis: To the skilled trades) and to the machine adjustor?

Pranis: And to the machine adjustor and to these people (Espig: And —)
    still left in the group who don't get it / we are in xx.
Espig: (Over Pranis above) And to those people unrelated to the — to
    the servicing of incentive operators.
Pranis: And presumably the people who are left are those with whom we
    don't agree (Espig: That's right!), so we would have to be opposed,
    Len, just based on previous history. And we also are opposed in the
    skilled trades, definitely. (Loring: Yeah) The answer to his question
    is, we are opposed to a flat incentive rate.
Espig: And n — an incentive bonus which gets us no incentive effort.
Pranis: Well, we're opposed to 20% for these people mentioned.
Espig: This 20% is a <u>normal, average operator's expected normal earn-
    ings.</u> (Pranis: Right) This cannot be applied, in theory or practice,
    to a day worker.
Pranis: May I ask a question? Could this be John's method of getting
    off the hook and accepting a flat hou — cents-per-hour increase for
    (Espig: I don't know) these people, d'you think, George?
Espig: I don't know.
Pranis: Think he's pushing for a percentage, remember, based on an
    incentive — an <u>incentive theory.</u> We have tentatively offered a cents
    per hour. He has previously said there are inequities in the relation-
    ship between the normal worker and the skilled tradesmen. We ten-
    tatively recognize that there are inequities in <u>our</u> plant. We say, as
    an area, that it's not <u>too</u> bad. But we recognize some inequity here,
    so we've (Espig: Well, let's — let's —) — we've offered cents per
    hour rather than a percentage / increase.
Espig: (Over Pranis above) Let's justify our approach for a minute.
    We have said we're willing to pay 5¢ an hour to skilled workmen.
    (Pranis: All right) <u>Why</u>? (Pranis starts to speak) Because we've
    recognized an inequity! (Pranis: All right. So we say —) But we
    didn't offer 5¢ to other people who have no incentive program, be-
    cause we don't recognize an incentive for the general laborer. Our
    general material handlers, warehousemen, and otherwise are well
    paid, in comparison in this area — to other (Pranis says something)
    people in this area and in the industry. Our skilled people — well,
    there's something to be said for them, so we're going out for another
    nickel for them.
Pranis: But we are opposed to a flat incentive bonus for this group.
Espig: We are in — we are opposed to a percentage which is supposedly
    an incentive which cannot, either practically or theoretically, be ap-
    plied as an incentive.
Pranis: (In low voice) Right.
Espig: It's 20% given away, that's all it is. It's not an incentive.
Mediator: I think that was — in direct answer to your question, I think
    a lot of this is for an across-the-board increase.
Pranis: I — I'm (Mediator: [In low voice] Inclined —) beginning to
    think so, that / he wants all —
Mediator: (Over Pranis above) I figured it all the way from the beginning
    that this is — he's putting the heat on this for bargaining purposes.
    When the flag goes down, I think he — he'll toss that aside.
Pranis: Yeah. Well, he's tryin' to make it big now, isn't he, George, to
    build it up so / that he think he got a big thing, like that —

Mediator: (Over Pranis above) Just like — just like you are building up
    this Blue Cross and other benefits. So while you're hammering on
    that, he's picked one up and he's hammerin' on there. Uh — (pause).
Pranis: George, how d'you answer this business about area bargaining,
    or do you?
Mediator: That — there's another word (slight pause) that you — I'm
    sure you'd understand what area bargaining means if I give ya the
    other real title. It's — the other real title is jockeying.
Pranis: Oh (laughs shortly), that's what he means?
Mediator: That's all. You're jockeying. He means — see, the area of
    bargaining — there i — there — there is no such thing as an estab-
    lished area of bargaining. There are established rates in a — in an
    area and there are established patterns, but there — there are —
    there are — there just is no such thing as a — an area of bargaining,
    because in my mind it might be one thing and in yours another and
    yours another, so there's — there isn't any such thing! Now, it's just
    a figure of speech. What he's trying to say is (pause) he — what he's
    speaking of — area of bargaining — is probably a range within 3¢.
    (Pranis: Uh-huh) Now — now, you noticed he said, "Give us the 20%,
    which is 4¢, and then we'll talk about a general increase from there."
    (Pause) So, that gives you an insight as to the kind of figure he's
    think — he's thinking about. You're at 2. (Rather long pause) If he
    gets 4 there, he's got 6. (Pause) Then he doesn't have far to push
    after that. Then he can apply the strike and maybe take ya up to 8.
    (Loring: Yeah, that's the trou — that's the danger) That's the —
    that's the way he's thinking. But this area of agreement is — or
    rather area — bargaining area is — can mean anything. In this par-
    ticular instance it's just — depends on how he's — his area of bar-
    gaining, I think we would say, is — I would say what he considers his
    to be would be over-all 10¢ area. Then he could drop off (Pranis:
    Uh-huh) 3¢. Now, you're at 2 and he figures, well, maybe you need
    3 or 4, so that oughta put you at about 5 or 6. (Pause) It's — ya can
    read right — I can — well, you g — it's just like reading a newspaper
    as to how — now, where they — how they wind up, of course, is an-
    other (?: H'm) question. But their directions — you can read them
    and see how they're shooting by throwing away the window dressing
    and getting down to the meat. And he's — those figures I gave you
    before still stand. He got a 7-cent target. (Pause) And he's jockeyin'
    for position. If he can get into a position, then the next move — he's
    standing pat. He can hold, then. If he can get — if he can get you up
    to 4¢ (pause) and no settlement (Pranis: Then he puts the squeeze
    on), then he's in — he's on good ground. (Pause) So (pause) I tried
    to get him to put it in my hands, in that long caucus we had. Gave him
    the opportunity to do it. But I saw that he didn't wanta, and (pause) —
    'course, that doesn't mean he's not cooperatin'. He is cooperating or
    we wouldn't have had those side-bar conferences. (Loring: Yeah) But
    he wasn't ready! And when I saw that I pulled away. Now, this — the
    position that you have taken in this — with this committee has done
    exactly what I think we need. It has — and what he needs, that is, to
    show his committee that the company is firm on this and that they will
    soon have to start thinking about a strike or a change of position. I
    think he needed that to get him to move. But he's hoping, see, that

you'll come back with a 4-cent proposal. And he — he'd like to see 4¢ on the board as the next proposal. (Pause) He's playing — he's playing this difficult. If he (pause) — and I'm letting him do it, because I think he needs it. It's always been a policy of mine to let either the management or the union — always allow them to play their positions to the end, because I know, from experience, that they have to. Even management — not your particular team, but other managements' teams — have reasons why they have to play along certain lines. But he's played with his position there so long. (Pause) (Espig: George, xx —) And yet in the end he's going to —
[Espig comments at length on experiences with Gambon in grievance handling.]

Loring: Well, what — what do we do at this point, George?

Mediator: It's too soon to — to go in there with anything yet, I think, that — w — well, then again, it isn't. But (slight pause) at this point I have to go back and talk with them. See, I said I would talk to you and then talk (Loring: Uh-huh) to them. And again, my move will be toward more softening up (pause) moves — discussions; and probably from them I may get my — an opening that we can explore. He may now, from the results of the 2 joint sessions and the one that I had with him — the long one — be in a position to be in confidence — act in confidence with me. Now, he has, but I mean officially. See, we'll be all right when he says, "All right, look," in front of the whole committee, "we're gonna tell ya where we'll go. We'll go at s — 7¢." Now, when he puts that on the table, see, then we're really going to move, see. Then we're getting — then we're in that area. (Pranis: Uh-huh) We get 'em down there, see, then we — we're s — we're s — officially. Now, I know we're there. We're there of — unofficially; and unofficially, while it helps us all —
[Tape changed]
... and although we were gonna, when he comes out on the table — now, this may take place here, or he may stop, play cute with this 20% business. (Pause)

Pranis: Should we answer him, George, on the — whether or not we —

Mediator: Oh, you must always / answer.

Pranis: (Over Mediator above) Have to answer that, don't we?

Mediator: Yeah. Even if ya disagree — even is ya disagree, ya haveta answer. (Pause) That's on the 20%?

Pranis: Yeah. Whether or not we agree to the principle of the 20 — that's the question he asked.

Espig: Well, I think we should — I think we should / tell 'em —

Mediator: (Over Espig above) You don't have to say anything you want about it u — unless — if you feel it's — it shouldn't be said, I think that one answer could be that, "Agreeing on a principle — whether we're agreed on the p — principle or not, we — we couldn't answer that until we knew what the cost was." (Pranis: Well—) Cost would determine, wouldn't it, whether or not you're agreed on p — even the principle?

Pranis: Well, he has done 2 things, George. He asked us a specific request and then asked later whether or not we agreed to the principle — the — in — to which the specific request applied. Sort of backward here. He asked for the 20%, then he says, "Do you agree to 20% for these jobs that I've just asked you for 20% for?" Doesn't seem to

make too much sense. But I — I have a feeling — and, again, I'm a
neophyte — that he's lookin' for somethin' to get off this hook of 20%
incentive as for a <u>flat</u> so much / an hour. I don't know! xx.

Espig: (Over Pranis above) No. I don't — I don't — I don't think he is.
I think he's pressing for 20%.

Mediator: Oh, he's <u>pressing</u>.

Espig: Now, the reason I say / that —

Pranis: (Over Espig above) But what I'm thinking of now is a permanent (Mediator talks at same time) thing. I'm thinking quite / a way
off.

Espig: (Over Pranis above) Wait a minute, Pran. No. No! Tom — Tom
Saunders has been in my office in the last — while we were down here
he came in, and other stewards came in and asked the secretary
whether Tom Saunders and I had agreed to pay 20% to this particular
material handler and that particular material handler, and one or 2
others. Department 25's one; so on. Now, we had quite a battle over
this a — a year ago. You remember, I'm sure (Mediator: That's
right), when we discussed this. I think he's serious about this! I
may be all wrong.

Mediator: The 20%?

Espig: Uh-huh.

Pranis: I think he's usin' it as a point. That's what I'm tryin' to get
around. If — if (Mediator: Uh —) — if my theory is right that he's
using it as a point, I think he's lookin' for a way off / or — or —

Mediator: (Over Pranis above) I think he wants something. (Slight
pause)

Espig: I think he'll settle for less, / but I think he's serious.

Mediator: (Over Espig above) Oh, yes. The principle he may — he'll
even scrap that if he can get a good enough <u>other</u> settlement. But if
he can't, I think he'll f — he'll hold to the principle; but 20, never.

Espig: Well, he's already come out — a — a — a — agreed to take 5%
— 5¢ off the 20 (pause) — the 5¢ which we gave (Mediator: Well —)
a year ago!

Mediator: The very — the very thing he told me, if — if it holds true, 5
and 2 would be 10%.

Pranis: Yeah, he said —

Espig: (At same time as Pranis above) Uh-huh. That's right!

Mediator: There ya are right there. (Pause)

Pranis: See, that's half of it.

Mediator: And then when the flag goes down it might even be less.

Espig: Well, sure!

Mediator: If ya had to work on the principle. So, I agree with you, this
far he's — right now he's thinking strongly about that principle. And
then that principle, too, comes into play often in these situations
where the most <u>vocal</u> of the shop — departments or the individuals
are located. They'll press for s — individual increases to pacify /
those groups.

Espig: (Over Mediator above) I don't think that's the case here. I think
what hap — <u>I</u> think what he's after here is an expression of principle.
You go in and say No, he'll say, "Well, what in the hell's wrong with
you? You've agreed to this case and that case and this case and that
case. Now, why did you do that?" <u>Then</u> he's got ya for an arbitration
case in that group of cases that you said that you agreed to, <u>or</u> he can

drive his bargain for that group of cases here, if he sees fit to do it. Or he can wait, later drive his bargain with you. But, in some way — in some ways — in some way, it's not good to say just how we <u>did</u> arrive at that. I say, let's — let's ignore it if we can. But if we <u>gotta</u> face it, let's deny that we like the principle, because it's no good so far as the skilled trades is concerned.

Pranis: No, that's true.

Espig: If anything, it's the worst thing we could have (Pranis: In our relations), because if we ever <u>did</u> get an incentive — an indirect labor incentive down there, we'd then have som — a base to — a false base to start with. (Rather long pause)

Mediator: Well, we'll go in and — let us work with them a little while and see how they feel about / this x.

Loring: (Over Mediator above) O.K., George. (Pause)

Union Caucus - B (8:10 P.M.)

Mediator: Uh (pause) — you know, when this case opened, I figured a reopener wouldn't be too much doin'. Ya — ya just have to get an agreement on the wages — one thing, wage rates, get it over with. This thing's developing into a — proportion of — well, the kind of negotiations ya have at a termination. I don't think you've made too much headway with them on the 20% angle. Espig did a lot of talking on that. (Gambon: Uh-huh) Seems as though that's probably his department or he's in this thing more — he's affected more by that, I believe, than (pause) (Gambon: No more than generally) Len. (Rather long pause) The (pause) — they're still worried about getting out on a limb and not having enough to buy themselves back off. (Slight pause) Your position, 14, is too high. The bargaining area ya speak about is good discussion, but getting into it is another question. The bargaining area that you have they feel is — even the minimum of that area is something they couldn't pay, they say, and would be in the category of his — using his words, his limit. Uh-h (pause) — he has said to me — he's gone this far this time. He said, "We have a limit, and we're afraid that that limit — from the way the union is talking, it couldn't settle it and that the union wouldn't buy it." And he says, "We're very concerned about it because we" — the — his people — and when he said people, I presume he meant Board of Directors — have told 'em that that — that that's where he stops. (Gambon: H'm) And he said, "And it doesn't mean that we go back at that point."

Gambon: Doesn't mean what?

Mediator: That he — that that's the point where he goes back to his Board of / Directors.

Meyer: (Over Mediator above) That (Gambon: Oh) means the end.

Gambon: That m — that means the company which the — er, the point at which the company's willing to take / a strike?

Mediator: (Over Gambon above) That's right.

Gambon: Tell him to get it on the table; I'll give him a quick answer.

Mediator: Well, I think we oughta do that (Gambon: I think so) soon. And —

Gambon: 'Cause if he wants to know whether he's gonna have a strike or not, he might as well find out tonight — get our statement.

Mediator: So, the direction you're tryin' to — I — I — I saw how you were — the tack you were taking. And knowing what I know from being in there, I'm afraid it'd take ya a month of Sundays to get down to where you wanta get that area ya speak of, because they're just standing on this position / that they don't have too much.

Gambon: (Over Mediator above) Well, I'm not gonna come down into his area which is indicated by a maximum / figure.

Mediator: (Over Gambon above) I don't think it would do any good at this point, John, to come — to — to — it wouldn't be a hell of a lot of help if we were in the area (Gambon: H'm), because —

Gambon: Evidentally not. It doesn't sound like to me that they have a bargainable situation a'tall. It seems as if they've been told by the Board of Directors of Atlas that this is the maximum figure and that's it. Now, he can either tell us what that maximum figure is and find out whether or not it's an acceptable proposition (Mediator: Well, the one — he hasn't —) or he can stay with 2¢. He can get the same result.

Mediator: Yeah. Well, that's — that's what I was just comin' to. He hasn't said this, but from the way the — these negotiations (Gambon: H'm) have been — have been goin', his fear, timidity in coming out and getting out on the — his limb, as he put it, I think is based on tha — on — on this, that if they find they can't reach an agreement and they take a strike, they'll take it probably at 2¢. I — now, that — that's a guess. I don't know. He hasn't said that. He'll probably — you'll know it before the night's over (pause) the — if a settlement can be reached. Now, I'm not payin' too much concern — or I'm not too concerned about their position (pause) on these benefits and (Gambon: H'm) — ya know, givin' it to you the way i — I believe it's simply a question of how much, and when that how much is established, either you can, or I can, knock them out of that tack they're going (Gambon: H'm) into and get it negotiated into the places that you want it in. But it — it — it's (pause) — it — the big question is how much. I'm not too worried about the other. I haven't — they have been very, very careful to — any — any changes they made, to steer it in that direction.

Gambon: Are they making any effort to find out what the Board of Directors' feeling is towards the principle of the fixed bonus for skilled trades and day workers?

Mediator: They discussed it, but they didn't make any telephone calls. (Gambon: Uh-huh) Not to my knowledge. / Not while I was there. Now, I don't — maybe he did.

Gambon: (Over Mediator above) Well. I wasn't sure whether he said that they were gonna talk it over among themselves to (Meyer: He wants the committee first) determine company policy (Mediator: Yeah) or whether he was gonna make / a phone call.

Mediator: (Over Gambon above) Now, one thing he — one thing — o — one part of their discussion on that went along these lines, that — I asked 'em a question. I said, "Have you ever done this before?" And they said — they gave me a little history on it, history that began during the war where certain jobs were given a 20 — 20%?

Gambon: Yeah.

Meyer: (At same time as Gambon above) H'm. That's right.

Mediator: — bonus for those jobs, and I think they were s — peop — service people, weren't they?

One of girls: Yeah.

Mediator: Service people.

Gambon: Lot of them. Not all of 'em.

Mediator: Not all of 'em, but majority of 'em was service people, and he said something about the pri — your principle couldn't apply (pause) in, for instance, the skilled trades, where they <u>don't</u> work on an incentive. I don't know; I get — have I got that straight? Uh — (rather long pause).

Gambon: No. It's / just that they —

Mediator: (Over Gambon above) But it — that there would be certain jobs that that principle — well, precedent has a — has established it on some of these jobs (Gambon: H'm), but it couldn't be applied on — but he wasn't saying he was agreeing to that but (Gambon: H'm) he was — he was giving me the history of / this.

Gambon: (Over Mediator above) Well, that's why I particularly mentioned that, following the principle that we used to (pause) institute fixed bonuses on many of these jobs — the relationship of that particular job to other jobs directly connected with it or indirectly connected with it (pause) — well, how shall I put it? — depending on the effect that the individual in this job can have on the production or the earnings of people in other jobs. Now, there — there's where your service people come into the picture. Service people who are bringing work to or taking work from production operators can certainly have an effect, both on production and on the earnings of the individual operators by the degree of efficiency that they apply in doin' their own x. And I tried to point out a few moments ago that we could apply that same principle to the job of machine adjusting, for instance, where a man has t — to care for 4 or 5 machines on which there are maybe 2 crews to a machine, all productive operators. And in b — b — keeping those machines in maximum running order, he has control, to some degree, over the production and, of course, earnings, which tie right in with production, for those operators and machines. The same thing goes for some of the skilled trades where they maintain the machines and keep them producing at a — at a level which will be high produc — highly productive to the company and, of course, earnings effective for the operators. It doesn't apply to all of 'em. Ya can't get that kind of a direct tie-in with a tool and die maker workin' on the bench. But you can get an indirect tie-in by virtue of the effect that he may have on productivity in the terms of how soon does he get a die back into production, let's say. I mean, o — over-all there — there are very few jobs, if any, that don't play some part in producing the over-all production in that plant. (Pause)

Mediator: Well (Gambon: Uh —), he will — he will answer you, I'm certain. You asked him for an answer (Gambon: Uh-huh), and when he answers you, he'll — he'll no doubt tell you what I've been unable to tell you. He — when he gave me the history I didn't pay too much attention to the technical explanation of the thing. And I guess you know it from A to Z, and when he tell — when he brings back his reply

to you on that, you'll understand what it means. I gathered from it
that there were spots in which it was done, but there are spots it —
in which they would never agree to / it.

Gambon: (Over Mediator above) Oh, look, we had this question of machine adjustors — I have been hanging that for (Mediator: And he
mentioned that. He mentioned that) quite some months with a possibility of still goin' to arbitration. That's the reason I mentioned it.
Because although there's nothin' written, even in the form of a guide,
to say how you apply these fixed bonuses, our contract says clearly
that the fixed bonuses may be applied by mutual agreement between
the company and the union. We've set our own guideposts. The company puts fixed bonuses on jobs, for instance, which they would determine are not ratable at this moment, and they pay a fixed bonus
until such time as they can apply an incentive rate. Now, that pretty
much is the situation on all our fixed bonus jobs of — pretty much of
an understanding that whenever they can develop an incentive rate
which is fair under the terms of our contract, the fixed bonus would
be taken out and the incentive rate applied, which should produce at
least 20%, according to the contract. So that — there's several different guides which we ourselves have established by practice and
among which is this relationship of the day worker to the production
worker. Now, there are some jobs in skilled trades and some jobs in
other day-work jobs which I think are in a minority as against the
total of all such jobs where you can't get a very direct association.

Saunders: The — there're 3 jobs in Department 5, Assembly Department:
spot checker, 20%; wirer, department average; and utility operator,
line average (Gambon: H'm), on the / xxxxx.

Gambon: (Over Saunders above) Well, there're — there're variations of
the fixed bonus idea where we have some people who get what we would
determine more or less to be a fixed bonus despite the fact that it's a
variable, depending on the product — production of other operators.
(Pause) Well, I don't know. (Pause) I think that if we're going to
(pause) hassle around here on the basis that he has one final offer
and he's gonna try to get me down to that offer, he's wasting his time
and my time and your time, because it's very apparent to me that that
particular offer is very likely gonna be unsatisfactory to the union,
and in order to — to save time, I think he oughta throw that thing on
the table and get his answer to it, if that's his final offer.

Mediator: Well, I'm b — I'm —

Gambon: Because if he doesn't do that and I leave here with 2¢, he's got
it, anyhow.

Mediator: Well, that's the thing. I don't know whether he'll take a strike
at 2¢ or / whether he'll throw his offer out.

Gambon: (Over Mediator above) Well, I mean, he may as well. What
the hell's the difference if he takes one at 2¢ or 3¢, George?

Mediator: Well (Gambon, then one of girls, laughs), they — you're —
t — that's right, but they — some of them have the idea that if ya take
a strike at 2¢ you're in a better position than if (Gambon: H'm) you
were at 4¢. (Gambon: Yes) They — they do think that way, and I don't
know whether these people think that way, but we have 'em in here
that do think that way. They think their po — position is a — better,
but (rather long pause) I think we're gonna have to do this. We're

gonna have to make our minds up — both — all of us — within the
next half-hour. (Gambon: I'd appreciate it) Uh-h-h — I'm starting
to lose a little patience with the — not with the people on your — but
with the — more or less the <u>positions</u>. I'm — I'm slowly, now, becoming — coming to the conclusion that (pause) if we can't find out
from both sides what will settle it, we're gonna have to let 'em go
home. And if we find out what will settle it and we know it <u>won't</u> settle it, gonna have to let 'em go home, anyway. (Gambon: H'm)
(Pause) There — there hasn't — there hasn't been enough plain talk,
and (pause) the heck of it is I could write the settlement. I could
write it and put it in an envelope, and I wouldn't be off more than a
cent. Yet I'll be darned if I can get either side down to that figure.
(Pause)

Gambon: Well, it — at this point I don't know how ya could write that,
George, if he's talking about having a final figure which he's reluctant to divulge. (Pause) I would hazard a guess and say that the maximum figure which he would represent would not meet the minimum
figure which we would be willing to accept as a settlement.

Mediator: Right there you put your finger on it. I don't know what that
maximum is. I have an idea (Gambon: Uh-huh), same as you do, by
— from what they've said and where they are. I don't know what your
minimum is. But that's when we'll know whether you go home or not.
(Gambon: H'm) Because even if he gives — remember, we haven't
gone to work yet. We haven't had anything to work on. When he gives
us his m — maximum and that maximum isn't enough but there is a
chance of pushin' him harder, we will push him <u>if we think it can be</u>
<u>settled</u>. If (Gambon: H'm) it can't, we won't push him. (Pause)
There's the — you put your finger right on where we wanta go (Gambon: It's where <u>I</u> wanta go), and when we get there, that's where we'll
— when we'll move! Now (pause), you won't be jeopardizing your
bargaining position if we start to discuss that. Let me — / let me
put it this way. I'm gonna x —

Gambon: (Over Mediator above) Well, you don't expect me to give him
a minimum position in the face of their general attitude at this point,
do you?

Mediator: Well, let me put / it this way, by —

Gambon: (Over Mediator above) I don't think I'd give <u>you</u> that right now,
George.

Mediator: Well, then, until that time comes (Gambon: H'm) we're
really gonna do nothing, because —

Gambon: Well, he — look. From what you have said, you say they have
a maximum position and beyond that they're — they'll have to take a
strike.

Mediator: That's what <u>they</u> said.

Gambon: All right. That's what they say. Now, if that is an actual fact,
then I say he should throw that on the table and we will then determine
then and there whether or not there is any possible settlement depending on his maximum and our minimum. We know our own minimum.
Now, if it appears that there's some possibility of haggling the thing
up to our minimum from a point which he says is a maximum, all well
and good, but if he takes a hard and fast position and says, "This is
it; we'll take a strike beyond this point," we oughta know about it!

I mean, I think he oughta throw it out here. (Mediator: Well, he's gonna throw it out. He's gonna throw it out —) Because if I were in his position — if I was saying, "This is it," I'd throw it on the table unless I was telling you that it was a maximum with the idea of bargaining beyond that point (Mediator: But I don't think —) with holding it back.

Mediator: I don't think this committee has any bargainable room after they reach their point. I don't think — I — I — I believe you know that from past experience. (Pause) (Gambon: Well —) I do think, though, from what he said they have full authority. He touched on s — on their meeting yesterday in the caucus, and he told me that he does have the authority and he knows that — how far the Board will go. (Gambon: H'm) And (pause) I really think Len Loring wants a settlement.

Gambon: I really think Atlas wanta a settlement, but they want a settlement at their terms, which is something that we'll have to determine whether or not we wanta accept. (Pause) I don't doubt that. I don't think they're particularly anxious to have a strike, 'cause come — when you come right down to it, a strike is gonna cost them a hell of a lot more money than it will to pay it out in terms of a — a difference in 2 positions that may develop here as a result of a minimum and a maximum position. And I can't see Atlas (Mediator: Well, I gave — I gave Len Loring —) saying to me across this table, "This is our maximum position; go ahead and strike." That don't make sense.

Mediator: I gave Len a figure, and he told me — and I believe him — he said, "George, we will take a strike (Gambon: Yeah. We oughta know —) at that figure."

Gambon: Tell him to — tell him to give us a maximum on / which he says, "Go ahead, we'll take a strike."

Mediator: (Over Gambon above) Oh, no, I gave him a figure. And on it he said, "George, we will have to strike on that one." Was a figure that I thought would be acceptable to the union. (Pause) Uh-h-h — so —

Gambon: Well, I would interpret that to mean, then, you've take a guess between where we are now and what you assume might be our minimum position and presented that to him, and he in effect has turned down what you may have been estimating to be our minimum position. So then (laughs), if your (laughing slightly) minimum guess was anything near what our actual minimum is, I think that's just about it. (Slight pause) And if he says he'll take a strike, then I can assure ya that's what he'll get, if that's the terms that we have to confront here — that we're confronted with, rather. (Pause)

Mediator: That's why I'm worryin' about this one.

Gambon: Well, I don't blame you. I mean, I'm a little bit surprised at the — the (pause) form these negotiations have taken, particularly because it is a reopener proposition, and I'm more than ever convinced that they probably made up their mind to hold out as long as possible in order to do what the hell they damn well please with this dough, and it's just not gonna go that way! As adamant as they are about this thing, I'm just as adamant about it.

Meyer: Our people would never accept that, even if we were simple enough to.

Mediator: What was — what?

Meyer: This thing here!

Mediator: Oh, well, I don't <u>blame</u> / you.

Meyer: (Over Mediator above) The form it takes, even. (Mediator: I don't blame you) If it was $75.00 a day to be in the hospital, they wouldn't accept it. (Pause)

Mediator: As I say, that — that I — the application doesn't worry me. Now, they're — I haven't even talked to them about it. I heard your remark about your dislike for the way they had it form — formulated, but in the caucus I have never touched on it because I'm not particularly interested in (Gambon: Uh-huh) it. <u>I'm</u> not, as a <u>mediator</u>. I — when the c — time comes, I will be. (Gambon: Uh-huh) But I'm more concerned about the <u>bigger</u> thing. I know what's holding this thing up / is how much.

Gambon: (Over Mediator above) How many skilled trades have we got at the minute, Les? Do you know? (One of boys: About 50) How many skilled tradesmen would ya estimate we have at the moment? (Rather long pause, with Gambon figuring on paper) Roughly. It may not be exact.

Meyer: How many you got in your department?

Baker: We got 13, electricians got about 13; that's 26. There's 3 in sheet metal (Meyer: Model Shop has 8 and —), 5 in the Carpenter Shop, / 2 painters.

[Over Baker above, Meyer adds other information, and Gambon and Meyer continue for awhile to run over various categories and numbers, sometimes assisted by Saunders and Baker and others of the committee. Finally, Gambon calculates to self as rather long pause ensues.]

Gambon: Roughly, we prob'ly have about 90, then.

Baker: 90 — between 90 / and a 100.

Meyer: (Over Baker above) Top would be 100. That would be the <u>very</u> top.

Baker: I figured about 40 tool and die makers.

Meyer: Yeah, there's 42. (Very long pause)

Gambon: Hell, that 5¢ an hour is (pause), oh-h (Mediator: What're ya lookin' for, cost of it?), about 3/10ths of a cent, / isn't it?

Mediator: (Over Gambon above) A half a cent.

Gambon: Huh?

Mediator: Half a cent.

Gambon: I / don't agree with that.

Meyer: (Over Gambon above) He said a cent.

Gambon: No, he said they'd (One of boys: The 5¢ for skilled — the skilled —) — he offered that and the balance of 1¢ (Meyer: Oh) / to the hospital.

One of boys: (Over Gambon above) That's a h — he — he said it was a half- / cent.

Gambon: (Over boy above) Yeah. Oh, I — I don't even get a half-cent on it. (Long pause) Huh-un. That's th — 3 to 4/10ths of a cent I get, George. (Slight pause) Don't know where he gets his figures from. (Pause) That's the only real concession he's made to the question — 2 questions that we have. (Rather long pause) My suggestion is, George, ya tell 'em to get this figure on the table that he says he'll take a strike on.

Mediator: Well, I'm beginnin' to agree with you. Not beginning; I am agreed with you on that, and whether he'll do it or not, of course, be up to him. (Gambon: Well, that's —) Uh — the (pause) — the (pause) — it's still a bargaining position. He's afraid to get out there and (Gambon: H'm) get sawed off. Uh-h-h (slight pause) — so, we can't work it out, we'll go home.

Gambon: Well (slight pause), I think it not a question gettin' sawed off right now, because if I — if his maximum figure were anyway near the minimum position of the union there would be some / xxx —

Mediator: (Over Gambon above) What d'ya call — what d'ya call near?

Gambon: Huh? What?

Mediator: Wh — what would you call near your figure?

Gambon: I'd say within a cent or 2¢. I think if we were only 2¢ apart we could still bargain it and probably settle the damn thing. (Pause)

Mediator: I figure, from what they've said, and reading betwe — you can — you can read the — their bargaining pattern. (Gambon: H'm) And as I said, I wouldn't be wrong if I put it in a sealed envelope. I think I could — I think I could put the figure where they are — or what their maximum is — right now, without them having tell me — told me, and put it in an envelope and wager ya I'd hit it on the no — I'd miss it by probably 3/10ths of a cent. I figure that you're about 3¢ away. (Pause) [Mediator announces that he is leaving to get the management group for a joint meeting.]

Management Caucus -H (8:40 P.M.)

Mediator: D'ya ever hear 2 people speak without using words? (Pranis: [Laughs shortly] Yeah) Or without using (slight pause) — I was negotiating in there with — 2 of us were talking, John and I. We were talking about your position and their position but using no figures. (Loring laughs) (Pause) / And it wasn't —

Espig: (Over Mediator above) What were you doing, going this way? (Pranis and someone else laugh)

Mediator: Well, I — I'll show you ju (Espig breaks into very hearty laughter) — I'll — I'll show you just what we did. (Espig laughs again) (Pause) I said to John, "Look." I said, "It's a question of bargaining position. The company doesn't want to get out — get into a position with their bargaining and then have you saw the limb. In other words, if they put their best foot forward and you say that's not enough, they're stuck! Where're they going after that, especially if that's their maximum?" (Pause) He said (pause), "Well, George" — now, remember, we haven't used any figures so far; we're speaking of minimums and maximums. He said, "Well, John" — or, "George (rather long pause), we — we think they oughta put it out on the table so we'd know where we're goin', so we either can accept it or can strike!" "Well," I said, "maybe they don't wanta put it on the table. Maybe they'd rather take a strike at 2¢." (Pause) No, I didn't even say 2¢; I said, "take a strike at where they're at." "Well," he said, "that's rather ridiculous. It wouldn't have much bearing. We know what we want, and (slight pause) we had a strike, we'd certainly go out for all of it." And up — still up to this point we hadn't talked figures. And he says, "If I knew," he said, "what

that maximum figure was and we weren't too f — and our minimum
figure wasn't too far away from it, well, I wouldn't take a strike on
something like that." (Loring laughs shortly, then Mediator, then
someone else riotously — but all under their breath, so to speak)

Pranis: So far ya haven't said anything.

Mediator: (Still laughing slightly) Well, I was followin' him close! I
knew everything — and I knew what he meant. I said, "Well, if you
wouldn't take a strike on that," I said, "then (rather long pause)
what would be the area of difference that you would be willing to negotiate — the difference between a minimum position, yours, and the
maximum, theirs?" (Slight pause) "Well," he said, "if it was
probably" — and this was the first mention — he said, "a couple of
cents' difference between us, I probably wouldn't strike <u>there</u>. Might
do a lot of thinking about it." "Well," I said, "they haven't told me,
but reading between the lines, I would say (pause) their thinking is
more than 2¢ between the 2 positions." "Oh, well," he said, "that
wouldn't be good." It reminded me of a conversation between 2 fellas.
I'm lookin' down the street and one of 'em had a watch and both these
boys were illiterate, and o — one boy knew he had the watch and he
said, "What time is it?" The other boy pulled it out. He said, "There
she is!" First (laughing) boy looked at it. He said, "Damned if she
ain't!" (Everybody laughs heartily) That's what that conversation reminded — (laughs again). But I got a lot out of it! Now, <u>I</u> was working
on the premise — see, 7 — I had the figure 7. I <u>hope</u> he wasn't
(laughing heartily) talking about 14, see. But if <u>he</u> was talkin' about
7, see — and I think he was — then that puts him at 6¢ for a fighting
figure. Here's the way I add it up. Now — now, I'll spell it out. I
said — he said, "If the company would put their maximum figure on
the table, I would know how far it was from my minimum." Then I
said to him, "<u>And</u> (pause) what would be needed to prevent a strike
or have a strike?" "Well," he said, "couple of cents." Well, I
know you're at 4. I know he's at <u>7</u>. (?: H'm) 2 — a couple of cents
would be <u>6</u> (rather long pause), see. Now, if — if that holds, <u>indi-
rectly</u> he's come down a cent! (Pause) See, this is the way he bar-
gains. Now, everybody don't bargain his way. Lotta people are more
to the point. But ya have to keep reading him in between the lines.
But he's moving! He is moving. And even if it's by innuendo or otherwise, he's — he — he had — he had feelers out, see. He <u>still</u> doesn't
know where you are. I said I could write where you are — the company — put it in an envelope, and I said I wouldn't be wrong by maybe
more than 4/10ths of a cent. And I said, "I could write where you
are and I could put it down and I think it would be right. And the hell
of it is I could write the settlement figure (Pranis laughs quietly)
and I wouldn't be wrong by no <u>more</u> than a cent!" And I said, "My
job is to try to get you there, and I — yet <u>I know</u> what it's going to be,
within a cent." (Someone seems to laugh quietly) I said, "It sounds
a little ridiculous, but it (pause) — that's it!" So I think that shook
him up a bit. He would like very much now — in fact, he even makes
a recommendation that we get it on the table. Now, we're startin' to
get in close quarters. We're startin' — the negotiations are startin'
to move into tight corner. You've got to — first you have to get ready
to answer that principle business — uh (Loring: Uh-huh) — this 20%.

Then you can follow up and you can say that (pause) I conveyed to you the union's recommendation that the company put its best offer on the table. (Long pause) At this time (rather long pause) you're going to have to make your mind up now, and we'll talk about it, whether you're gonna hold at 2, whether you're gonna put out 3, or whether you're gonna put out 4. Now, if ya hold at 2 you can aggravate the situation this far. (Loring: Uh-huh) If you put out 3 you've only got one left, and they're still at 14. (Slight pause) (Loring: Yeah) If you put out 4 you're — you're done! They won't buy it. 4 won't — can't be bought. That's for sure because of the bargaining positions. Uh — before you make any recommen — any — a — a — before you think about anything relative to makin' an offer, you should try to swing the negotiations by putting the union on the defense. (Loring: [In low voice] Yeah) I think it can be done, or at least it can be tried by the company saying to the union at this point, "We would like very much to know, we've been unable to find out; we've been unable to read between the lines; even the mediator doesn't know — we've asked him — where we're going, what a minimum is. You asked us for your — to put our best offer out. Now, we say to you, 'What i — where do you' — your offer where you stand, it — it's just prevents us from doing any thinking on the matter. And when you ask us for our best offer, we — we — we would have to return and say to you, 'What is yours? Can we meet it?' And where you are now we certainly can't." Try to swing the thing back, see. They — you — you can't afford at — at 2¢ to be put — put on the defensive. You've (Loring: H'm) gotta reverse this thing. (Slight pause) And if you do that, why (pause) — and then you — then you might even come out and say, "Maybe we're not too far apart or maybe we're miles apart. But we'll — we don't know!" This thing'll break with that kind of talk. The 2 suggestions that you've followed — both of them are drawing him out. Both of them are responsible for drawing him out (Loring: Uh-huh), where you s — indicated that you do wanta settle. And — but when you got to a certain point you'd be pushed and — and you'd have to take a strike. You also showed firmness there. So, both those suggestions, and the one that turned the wheel — one before that — are all drawing him out, and he's hard to draw out, but they're doing it. Now, you — you come — come out this time, reverse the situation! And then add that for all ya know, "We may not be too far apart, but how are we gonna get there? How're we gonna know what you — how far apart we are? We don't even know at this stage whether we're — sure, we're at 2¢. But we — we don't have much more." I think now's the time where you can talk this way. "But we certainly have to know where you are. And you're a — for all practical purposes you're up in the air. And we — we would like to know as well as you do what would settle it! Or whether we could settle it. But (rather long pause) you've got a minimum and I've got a maximum. Now, where — where do we stand?" And then he'll start. See, there'll be x, and when you feel yourself in a tight spot, call for a caucus. See, you have a right, too, to (Loring: Uh-huh) — when you — you can just say to me, "Well, Mediator, suppose we have a caucus," any time you feel that (Loring: H'm) you're getting boxed in.
Loring: Uh-huh.

Mediator: O.K. ?

Loring: O.K.

Mediator: D'you want a little time to rehearse this ?

Loring: Just on this question that we wanta answer. I think we've pretty much made up our mind how we want to answer it, but along these lines, Erv, that they asked us if we recognize the principle of fixed bonus for day workers. And I'm gonna indicate that we — we don't believe that there's any one answer to that question. In some cases it might be Yes, and other cases, particularly skilled workers, it would be No. If it's a bonus it's supposed to be an incentive bonus, and there's no way of measuring or getting an incentive out of it. We believe, as the contract says, that i — it's a question of mutual agreement whether a fixed bonus should be placed on any job and we're willin' to go along on that principle, and then drop it right there. Then get into the other things.

Mediator: My recommendat — or, rather the union's recommend — the union asked me to ask you (Loring: Yeah) to put your best (Loring: Uh-huh) offer out. That recommendation thing made that start talkin'. (Prepares to leave room for union group) Oh, they're to call — they're to see me.

Loring: Yeah —

Joint Meeting - E (8:55 P.M.)

[Several of the union group, including Gambon and Meyer, engage Espig in a brief exchange about his promotion. This ends in widespread laughter when Gambon inquires of Espig if he, too, lacks a contract with the company.]

Mediator: Go ahead.

Loring: Well, John, 2 things. One was the question you asked us about whether we recognize the rightness of principle of a fixed bonus for day workers (Gambon: H'm), s — skilled workers. We've discussed this pretty thoroughly and we're in agreement this way. We don't believe that you can give an unqualified Yes or No answer in all cases to a thing like that. It's conceivable that in some cases it — it's the thing to do, but in other cases a — the fixed bonus like that which is intended to represent equivalent of an incentive, certain areas of workers we don't believe that applies to. Now, we believe we should go along as the contract says and that is, by mutual agreement you would consider jobs as they come up a — and on that basis you would decide whether the principle was right. The 2d thing, the mediator has communicated to us the — your request that — that we place our best offer on the table. We're awfully anxious to get this thing settled; we want to. We wanta do everything we can, but we — we are disturbed at this point, too. We have a maximum position. We're at 2¢ now. We don't have an awful lot more to go, but we haven't any idea where you people are, John. I mean, you're up at 14¢. If it's 14¢ is your minimum position, that's out of our reach entirely. We're interested at this point in — in your putting on the table for us what's your minimum position. It's conceivable that we're not too far apart, but we don't know. We have no idea. We've asked the mediator can

he tell us. He says No. We'd like to know your position — your minimum position.

Gambon: Well, on the basis of what you've just said, Number 1, I'm not
willing to leave the proposition of fixed bonus to a matter of trying to
reach mutual agreement as to what jobs should be placed on the fixed
bonus, because I have, up to this point, unsuccessfully attempted to
get the company to recognize in some instances — the — a direct —
very direct, in some instances — a connection between this particular
type of day worker such as a die setter or a machine adjustor to the
production worker. When I can't get an agreement on something as
direct as that, I'm gonna have very little chance of getting agreements
for jobs which are more indirectly connected with it. This isn't just,
as I mentioned before, a proposition of applying a fixed bonus for the
purpose of getting a wage increase alone, but it does — it is the union's
approach to resolving the pro — problem of inequities between skilled
trades and day workers generally and other production workers; and
I don't listen to your having considered that angle as much as you do
the problem of fixed bonus as such, and how it should be applied. The
question you raise about the union putting its minimum position on the
table, from what you've said the last couple of times we've been together here, Len, I don't think you are prepared to meet the union's
minimum position. Very frankly, I'm not inclined to place a minimum
position on this table and then be forced to strike the plant in order to
obtain a minimum position. The minimum position is a bargainable
proposition as far as the union goes in attempting to settle — or reach
a settlement with the company in an amicable way, but it is not the
kind of a position that I would take and then have to strike on it. And
I think you are more or less possibly in the same position and that
you don't wanta throw your maximum position on the table and then be
faced with a strike on the part of the union because we find it an —
unacceptable. (Pause) Since the company, however, takes a position
that the maximum amount involved here is one which they can't afford
to go f — further than that, I think it's more in order for the company to
place that position on the table and let the union decide from that point
on whether there is a possibility of reaching a settlement or whether
it's a — a thing where we'll very necessarily have to say to ya frankly,
"Well, we can't accept it. We know our members won't accept it,"
and that's gonna be it. Now, that — that's the way I feel about it, Len.

Loring: Well —

Gambon: Mean, because in a sense you're implying that we — we have a
figure that — well, even in the event of a strike, you should be supporting that maximum position. (Pause)

Loring: I appreciate how you feel, John. I think you can appreciate my
position, too. Suppose we threw our best foot forward and threw everything we had on the table. We've — we've lost all bargaining from
that point on. You can say, "No, it's not enough." I mean, just re-
versing the logic ya gave me. (Gambon: That's right) I mean, / it's —

Gambon: (Over Loring above) That's — how do you resolve it, Len?

Loring: Well, I don't know. I think the mediator's gonna have to help us
on this one.

Mediator: Well, I's just gonna stick my oar in at that point and say as
long as both sides have recog — have — have so <u>clearly</u> stated what

you just stated, it <u>can</u> be resolved when both sides uh-h — produce more confidence in the mediator. When that is done we'll find out whether the latitude is too great, or the area is too different — too far — the p — the parties are too far apart. If it is, neither side's position will be endangered. You will leave here and do it your way. If not, and the area is found to be one where discussion can follow and negotiation on that difference, that's the answer. Suppose — (pause).

Gambon: Well, I think there should be one thing understood, without quoting figures at this point — one thing cleared, for the benefit of the union's committee, and that is whether or not the company is going to continue to make its offers along the lines that it has been making them up to this point, or whether they're gonna make a maximum offers — offer in terms of increased cost to the company which can be directed in other — towards other items than the ones that they're proposing here. I — I say that, because if the — the maximum offer of the company is directed toward the same kind of — of objects here that you've been presenting up to this point, we're not going to reach any kind of an understanding a'tall. (Rather long pause) So that in effect I would say that if you have a maximum position that the union's committee certainly would like to know what that maximum position is, but the maximum position that you present should be directed towards the 2 items of request that we have on the table at the moment, namely, the general wage increase item and the question of fixed bonus. Dis — regardless of what your maximum figure may be, it would not be an acceptable proposition so long as it's directed to things that we did not indicate any interest in, such as the insurance.

Loring: Well, I would like at this point, John, to take the mediator's recommendation that we — we, as he says, show more confidence in him as a negotiator, and I'd like to have a caucus with my people on what you just asked.

Gambon: Uh-huh.

Loring: And I'm s — we will do everything possible to cooperate with the mediator, and I know you will, and prob'ly we can break this log jam. I certainly hope so.

Gambon: Uh-huh. (Pause) All right, let's try it.

Mediator: You'll call me when you're through? / You —

Loring: (Over Mediator above) All right, George. Yes.

[As the management group leaves the room, Meyer makes a reference to "caucus." Mediator immediately inquires, "You wanta caucus?" Gambon replies, "Yeah, for a minute. Sure." Thereupon Mediator leaves the union caucus room at 9:10 P.M., putting in time in the management caucus room until called back by the union group.]

Union Caucus - C (9:17 P.M.)

Gambon: What d'ya want me to make? Minimums? (Laughs shortly, along with Mediator)

One of boys: (Laughing) Let's go.

Mediator: Let's go. (Several laugh heartily) I know a joke but I can't tell it, on minimums and maximums. Not because we're on the air. (Saunders laughs)

Gambon: 'Cause there's ladies present? (Pause)

Mediator: Yeah.

Gambon: O.K.

Mediator: A gentleman never mentions a joke he can't tell. I'm sorry.
I'm not a gentleman. (Pause)

Gambon: You're a lousy joke teller, too. (Laughs heartily, along with
one or 2 others) All right, George, I got a minimum for ya, but it's
not a bargainable proposition. I mean (slight pause), I'm tryin' to
get them into the same kind of a position. (Pause) You can even —
after you s — see where they're comin', I would appreciate you do this.
You have this in confidence at the moment, till you get their maximum
figure. If their maximum figure doesn't reach it, tell 'em what our
minimum is and tell 'em if they can't meet it they're wastin' time,
and that's a 10% fixed bonus and 5-cent general increase. Now, if
they start guffin' off about what this means, this means in increased
costs to the company for our some 1200-odd members, a period of 6
months, about $84,000.00. And even if we were to double that — see,
this figure that they're bellyachin' about, that 14% — or 14¢ still runs
about — 'bout only $168,000.00. And on the basis of the business
they're doin' it's entirely conceivable and realistic and everything
else that goes with it. Now, this is no — this is not bargainable,
George, as far as I'm concerned. If they want a settlement without a
strike, they can do it on that basis and nothing less. Ask their maximum, and I have no doubt but what their maximum will not meet this
minimum. But if ya hear their maximum and it's less than that, tell
'em what our minimum is. (Mediator: All right) Give 'em a little
time to think it over and then tell 'em to come back and tell us what
they're gonna do (Mediator: Now we're workin'), or how much further they're gonna come to that minimum. (Rather long pause) O.K.?

Mediator: Yep.

Management Caucus - I (9:22 P.M.)

Mediator: Why, I have their irreducible minimum. (Pause) Can you
guess what it is?

Loring: 7¢?

Pranis: (At same time as Loring above) 9¢. Let's go home.

Mediator: 5 and 2.

Loring: Uh-huh.

Mediator: 5 and 10%.

Pranis: 10%. (Long pause)

Mediator: He said (slight pause) — in line with your recommendation,
he said, "We are going to let you know." Now I know what it is, see;
he's been playin' the grandstand here. Now, you know how long I've
had that 5 and 2. When did I get that 5 and 2?

Loring: You got that last (rather long pause) Thursday, wasn't it?

Mediator: You're right! I am confused. I said to her I got it this morning.

Pranis: No. You got 14¢ last Thursday and you guessed 5 and 2 this
morning — you guessed 5 and 2 on Thursday. You actually got it from
John in a side-bar conversation today.

Espig: Right.

Loring: (At same time as Espig above) Right. / xx —

Pranis: (Over Loring above) This side-bar — this — 'cause today was the first side-bar conversation ya had with him xx.

Mediator: That's what I thought — how much / he was x.

Pranis: (Over Mediator above) But you guessed at — you guessed at 7 (Mediator laughs), previously, George, with saying 14. He cuts it in half; he wants —

Mediator: 7.

Pranis: This / was Thursday.

Mediator: (Over Pranis above) And today he gave me (Pranis: That's right) the application, 5 and 2. Now he's on the table. He'll — he's — he's practically official. He — well, he is officially, because he told me after I found your maximum, and if your maximum didn't meet this minimum I was to officially tell you that it was 5 and 2. Uh! I keep sayin' 5 and 2. 5 and 10%, which I believe amounts to 2¢ an hour.

Pranis: Presumably retroactive date on the 1st, George?

Mediator: Yes. (Rather long pause) Now your gap is 3.

Espig: (In low voice) Yeah. (Very long pause)

Mediator: Think I'm gonna have a shot of coffee. This is getting (laughing slightly) too much. (Laughs)

[Mediator offers to divide his container of coffee with the others. 6 or so minutes are consumed in miscellaneous conversations: Loring and Observer discussing Observer's earlier point about his effective negotiating manner; distribution of coffee; Mediator's recital of 2 previous case experiences, in one of which each call by the union for a caucus turned out to be a rendezvous at the hotel bar, in the other, Mediator had to move the sessions out of the hotel to the Mediation Service offices because management's hospitality with alcoholic refreshments had induced serious discussion among the negotiators about moving the case to Bermuda. Pranis and Mediator, later joined by Loring and Observer, then contemplate in light vein the advantages of convening the Atlas case a year hence at some resort spot or at the Aiken, South Carolina, plant. Very long pause closes out this interlude.]

Mediator: Uh (long pause) — there's no use kiddin' 'em at this point. Uh (rather long pause) — ya see. Sometimes in these negotiations, if you show good faith with your bargaining position, after you've got into an area — ya know, a — a (Loring: Uh-huh) — a reasonable area. (Pause) They wou — will know — they will be in a good position to know whether it's your maximum. They do one of 2 things: they reject it and try to bargain for more; or they accept it, with modifications or revisions of X, Y, or Z — little crumbs here and there. They do one of 2 things. This union will, in all probability, go after more. The question now is, and is coming up, if you put out 3¢ as your best position, it wouldn't — it would be better, I believe, at this stage of the negotiations not to play with a cent and say "This is my bottom position" when it wasn't (Loring: Uh-huh), because they have a pretty good idea of what you would like to settle this for without me having e — ever discussed it with 'em, based on your last year's settlement — uh — 6 months ago, I mean. (Loring: Yeah. Yeah) Uh — they don't know whether your bottom figure is a — 4¢ or a nickel. But they're thinking it's one or the other. I'm sure of that. Uh — if you were to put out 3¢ — another cent now I'm certain they would know that that was not your figure. Now, you can take 2 roads. You can do it that way — and I'm gonna give you your choice there, because there may be some factors with your economic position that I am not familiar with and you wou — y — only you people could be the best judge, in this instance. So I'm gonna give you the 2 roads. (1), y — they will be official — officially, within a few minutes, or when we leave this room to go in there, they will be at 7'd (pause) — 7¢; 5¢ and 10%. (Pause) You can go in there, and one proposition could be, you will get away from their — from the benefits that they want you to get away for the application of it, call that a concession (pause), and throw another cent in, making it 3¢. I don't think you would be fooling them. I think they would know. See, they've been in the business long (Loring: Uh-huh) enough to know that that wouldn't be, because they knew you settled for that before, and other factors, such as the moving and some of the other things that have come into this — they — they would know that that wasn't it and it might upset the negotiations, where, in the end, before you got out of the building, you'd wanta give them 4, in all probability, if they were gonna strike. So that's the one road. You could do it that way. The other road is to give 'em 4¢, with a very, very (hitting table) strong pres — convincing presentation. "This is our — (bangs table). This is it! This is — if you — you asked for our rock bottom, and we are giving it to you." (Pause)

[Tape changed]

... a 4-cent package away from the application, your best chances for survival is to get away from benefit application, see, and get it onto where they want it. (Loring: Yeah) Especially if it's to be your la — you know, your m — maximum. (Pause) Now, you — you've gotta go from — within about the next 15 minutes, I think you've got to, when you meet them, be prepared to present one or the other. (Pause)

Loring: Suppose we decided on the 4¢, George. Would you split it 3½ across-the-board and a half a cent for 5¢ an hour to the skilled trades, or just say, "Here's 4¢ we'll spend"?

Mediator: I think that — that could be all right. The — but (slight pause) I think you might — you might be in a better position, if you don't mind, if it won't affect your operations too much, to say that — that it be X amount (pause) with no strings on the application — in other words, that you're willing to negotiate, with how it will be applied to be negotiated. (Loring: Uh-huh) See, and that's not committing yourself, see. They would prefer, I think, it that way, because they may have a pet somewhere (pause) and you might be blocking (pause) something that you could digest, anyway. It wouldn't hurt you, whatever it is, see. It might be well to say, "We're — we're — we'll — we'll give this; the application we'll negotiate. Our minds are open on certain things, but" — and (pause) that'll take a lot of the heat away — if, of course, this doesn't — the appli — the application doesn't bother you.

Loring: No, I can't see that it — how it would bother us, George. It x / x —

Mediator: (Over Loring above) Well, then, if that's the case, I would — s — I would present it that way. Say, "We've considered your (pause)

— and in the interest of reaching an agreement we <u>have</u> re — we <u>will</u> reverse our position and <u>not</u> request this be applied to the benefits, as earlier stated. But we will submit to you our position, which is X (bangs table), and the application of it can be negotiated between us." (Pause) But (pause), see, if you go out at this stage — if you go out at 2¢ and take a strike, John is right. You're not protecting your bargaining position, if there's a strike taken, because he knows, (1), 2¢, if he's gonna take a strike, helps <u>him</u> (Loring: Uh-huh), see. And he <u>knows</u> that durin' a strike, when he gets negotiating with you aft — during the strike, he's gonna get ya up to where you — the area, anyway. He's not gonna lose anything. See, if it was a question of whether you could hold back 2¢, let him take a strike, and then have more to sit down with him to negotiate with, that would be one thing. It doesn't work that way. In reverse ya can put it this way. Let us say you, here at the bargaining table, said — went in there and said, "Look, gentlemen. That being your attitude, we're taking back the 2¢. We're withdrawing it." Well, ya know how much effect that — you know how much that would really (Loring: Uh-huh) — as far — for all practical purposes, that 2¢ is in their pocket, even though you withdraw it. (Loring: Sure) See? Well, the same with taking a strike. If you took a strike at 2, John wouldn't be worried about the part — the money that's missing. He knows that he'd get that back at the bargaining table because he knows he's entitled, by, oh-h-h, standards of the kind he's brought in here, to X amount — some figure, some agreeable figure or some standard or norm, whether it's 2¢, or 3¢ or 4¢ or 5¢ — whatever it w — is, he knows that with economic pressure he can get a certain amount. (Pause) So, if you went outa here at 2¢ and he took a strike on that, it would strengthen his position with — with his people. He could get a strike very easily. Now, if ya hit him with 4¢ and he took a strike on f — at 4¢, well (pause), I think he'd do a <u>hell</u> <u>of a lot</u> of talking before he struck at 4. (Pause) I think he'd do an awful lot of trying before he struck. And then if he struck at 4 (pause) on a wage reopener, he's — he has a problem on his hands. He's got — got a membership there that may not think it's too bad! (Pause) / I know so.

Espig: (Over Mediator above) George, do you think — do you think that if we put 4 on the table he'll reject it?

Mediator: Oh, yes.

Espig: To all intents and purposes tomorrow and Wednesday there'll be a sounding out of the employees, and Thursday will depend upon their reaction, as stated to their committee tomorrow in the plant. Think that could be possible?

Mediator: Yes. Stands a very good chance. Then he might — he'll do this. (Pause) If he can't reach an a — complete agreement with ya tonight, he'll follow that, and then — and then he will (pause) call for a meeting — whether it will be Thursday or some other day, I don't know — for the purposes — for the purpose of telling you that it won't do the trick and he's — has to have more. Now, that's one way it could go. The <u>other</u> way is, make — if ya got that <u>close</u>, 4 and 7, he may try to wind it up tonight. (Pause) There's <u>that</u> chance, too. One way or the other, Herb — Erv, it'll — it'll go (pause) — see, if he doesn't want to — if he gets the 4 and doesn't want to settle tonight, he can play it cute and say, "Well" —

Espig: Well, you don't see any <u>real</u> chance of a strike tomorrow / morning?

Mediator: (Over Espig above) No. I don't think / so.

Espig: (Over Mediator above) This would eliminate a great percentage, not all of it.

Mediator: That's right.

Espig: But a great percentage.

Mediator: That would definitely hold it.

Loring: What position would we be in, George, if we put the 4¢ on the table and they <u>did</u> take a strike? Then we're kinda / licked —

Mediator: (Over Loring above) Ya mean tomorrow morning?

Loring: No, I mean at <u>any</u> time.

Mediator: Any time?

Loring: Then we're faced with considerably more to get 'em back, prob'ly.

Mediator: Yeah. Yes. In order to get 'em back you would have to — you would have to negotiate above 4¢. You'd go <u>in</u> — you'd start at 4. Now, what you have to weigh up is (long pause), (1) (pause) — (1), there's a <u>chance</u> they may say, "Well, we'll take this 4 with a (long pause)" — and then throw in maybe something on that hospital benefit — something extra. They may! It's a chance. You never know. I've seen — but it's not very — I wouldn't <u>bet</u> on it."

Espig: But they wouldn't take a strike on it.

Mediator: They wouldn't take a strike on it. (Slight pause) They would be more prone to say, "No, that won't do it. Well, let's call it a night." Now, when they do, you wanta be careful not to ask, "Well, does this mean strike?" I don't think you should do that. If you do that, that's just what they want. <u>I'll</u> do the askin'. I'll find out when I'm with 'em alone, see. Because if <u>you</u> do it, it's gonna danger your bargain — weaken your bargaining position. No, just take it in your stride.

Loring: Uh-huh.

Mediator: Uh (rather long pause) — <u>or</u> he will — he will figure, "Hell, if they're up to 4, if I strike 'em I'll probably settle at 6 or 7." This is arithmetic he may be thinking of. (Slight pause) And then he'll put some <u>real</u> pressure on here tonight for a — some kind of a settlement above 4. It <u>must</u> go into one of those slots; it has to. Either he'll take the 4 with a fringe, he'll reject the 4 and wait till Thursday, he'll take the 4 tonight and shoot for a complete settlement tonight. Go (1), (2), (3) — one of those. (Rather long pause) But I think at this stage you don't — I — I — I'm personally — I don't want to influence you, because I told you it was a — a money question and it was yo — it's your department there, but the 3¢'s — offering 3 — I'd be not in favor of — of holding a cent (Loring: Uh-huh) and being forced to put it, because it could more damage than good. He might even <u>hold</u> ya at 3, not let ya get the other cent out, which wouldn't be too good, either. So I think you're in the position in these negotiations where you have got to decide which one of those courses you wanta take. See, there's certain things I can't advise you on (Loring: Right, George. Yeah); I have to follow you on. (Loring: Uh-huh) And this is one of those times. Now, if you want to discuss it —

Loring: I'd like to (Mediator: All right. We'll —) discuss it a few minutes with my group.

Mediator: And then you call us back.

Loring: Fine, George.

[Mediator waits in another office from 9:50 to 10:00 P.M., when he is called back by the management group.]

Loring: If this is in line with your thinking that we will throw the 4¢ on the table, we would like to throw it as 3½¢ across-the-board and a half-cent to go into 5¢ an hour extra for the skilled trades. We want, if possible, to keep away from a percentage increase with that group. (Mediator: Uh-huh) And if we state it this way, rather than sayin', "Well, we'll negotiate," we might have a better chance.

Mediator: Good enough. (Slight pause) Uh (pause) — now, I think what we'll do is this. (Pause) Uh — we'll go back into joint session, and (speaking slowly, as though planning aloud) I will pick it up. I'll open up by telling both committees exactly what John Gambon told me, and that was that he gave me his position and informed me that if the company's position was not — did not meet it that I was to then inform the company wh — officially what the union's position was. And the union's position, as reported to the company by me, was and is 5¢ an hour plus 10% for the — what ya call that ? xx / x —

Espig: (Over Mediator above) Day workers.

Mediator: Day workers. (Pause) I — I've (still slowly) given the company — when I learned that the company's maximum did not meet it, I officially gave it to the company. There's been discussion on it. I've asked the company to come out here and submit to you their max — maximum figure, a figure which they have also told me before I've — came into this joint session. That's where I will lead 'em. Now, here you better really be convincing, as convincing as you can be, that — and don't forget that you're making a concession in getting away from all these benefits — ya know, the application (Loring: Uh-huh) there, and you're perfectly willing to apply this, and s — so on. Build it up as much as you can and as firmly as you can without being tough, and drop 'er there. Then we'll be — from that point on, we're gonna know the things you ask: (1), will they go till Thursday, or will they continue tonight ? I think we'll know. This part you — we've been waiting for, and here it is. I mean, now we know where we're going. We'll know, rather. But that application is O.K. with me — the 3½. That's fine. I think that (rather long pause) is all right.

Loring: O.K., George.

Pranis: Well, do we say 3½ and ½, George, or we say 4¢ applied this way ?

Mediator: That's right.

Pranis: We say 4¢ / but we will apply it —

Mediator: (Over Pranis above) Make it big (Loring: Yeah): "4¢, but we wanta apply it this way." No. And before you say — I think it's very important that before you say, "We want to apply it this way," I think you oughta say, "4¢. And we've given serious consideration to your opposition to the way — to our ap — our — our previo — our application toward benefits, and, after consideration, we have agreed to withdraw the applications we've made — or the directions that we were applying our other proposals, and the 4¢ — we'll apply it this way." (Pause)

Joint Meeting - F (10:04 P.M.)

Gambon: You guys keep comin' in, interruptin' my story all the time. (One of girls laughs heartily) I'll never finish it.

Mediator: Before the last 2 separate conferences, I had asked both committees (pause) — because of the bargaining stalemate, I appealed to both of you to express more confidence in the mediator in order that we could safely establish, or get to, the points that both parties wanted to get to. I wanta say that both the union and the company has cooperated fully on the — on my request. In meeting with the union, the union gave me their figure and informed me that if the union's maximum — or the company's maximum figure did not meet their figure, that I was at liberty to reveal their figure. The company's maximum did not meet the union's figure, so I informed the company, following that, of the union's figure, which was, or is, 5¢ an hour·plus 10¢ — or, 10% for the day workers — and you understand what that is, both of you. The company acted in good faith by giving me, before they knew your position, their position. They have held a meeting — caucus, and at this point they'll submit theirs, so, Len.

Loring: Well, I've done just as Mediator Thomson asked, John. I'm not holding a thing back. I'm — I'm throwing our bag on the table. At this point — and this is — this is it. This is all we have. We're willing to offer 4¢ an hour. We've taken great deal of consideration to the objections you had to our applications, or suggested applications, and we're willing to withdraw our applications that we have heretofore insisted upon. We offer this 4¢ as a $3\frac{1}{2}$-cent-an-hour across-the-board increase and a 5-cent-an-hour increase to the skilled trades, in addition, which makes the 4¢. Now, we've gone all out on it. We're not holding back, as the mediator asked us to do, and we ask that you give serious consideration to it. (Long pause)

Gambon: $3\frac{1}{2}$-cent general across-the-board and 5¢ additional to skilled trades. That's your (pause) (Loring: Yes, John) — just skilled trades. You're not talkin' about other day workers, now?

Loring: Just skilled trades, / George.

Gambon: (Over Loring above) Uh-huh. (Rather long pause) Well (pause), we'll give ya an answer as soon as we can caucus, Len.

Loring: All right, then.

[As the management group withdraws, Gambon calls out to Mediator to remain behind with the union group.]

Union Caucus - D (10:10 P.M.)

[At Gambon's request, Observer cuts the recorder off for several minutes during an initial exchange between Gambon and Mediator. Primarily, Gambon checks his current estimate of the real management position against Mediator's judgment, disclosing some of the cues and the process by which he arrives at his estimate. At the end he informs Mediator he is going to reject the present management offer.]

Gambon: We had been in a position for quite a long time, now, in these
meetings of havin' the company tell us about a — what they consider
to be a very unrealistic position, and we get to a point where we say,
"This is our minimum position and we — we're not gonna make it a
bargainable re — prop — proposition," and that minimum position
represents in total cost to the company, in round figures, around
$84,000.00 away from a position which they claimed was unrealistic,
of something like $360,000.00. I tried to convince them of the reason-
ableness, from our point of view, of the $360,000.00 increased cost to
the company based on an estimated $2\frac{1}{2}$ million dollars' profit before
taxes for 1953. We've got — we get away completely from the thing
that we thought was making the negotiations impossible from the
standpoint of the company, because they consider the shorter work
week an impracticable operative proposition. I can't see, for the life
of me, where the hell they come off with this business of trying to tell
somebody that their maximum position is 4¢ and imply that it's a maximum position because this is all they can do!

Mediator: It might be, John.

Gambon: I don't believe that, George. I mean, / on the face of their
reports —

Mediator: (Over Gambon above) I might be — be wrong in my deduction.
Now, I — I'm basing my — my thinking on pretty much the same way
you are, that if their last position is 4 and they have to weigh up between taking a strike (Gambon: Uh-huh) and your position (pause),
I — I (Gambon: Look, x —) — logical reasoning would be that they'd
give a hell of a lot of thought to that, but sometimes, too, as you have
found out, the straw — the extra straw sometimes drives 'em to take
a strike.

Gambon: Uh-huh. (Pause) Well, let's take a look at this picture for a
minute. (Rather long pause) You know what that 3¢ an hour represents? $36,000.00. You mean to tell me this company's gonna take
a strike for the sake of $36,000.00?

Mediator: I don't know.

Gambon: Jesus Christ, they'll lose $36,000.00 in — in no time. In a day,
or 2 days.

Mediator: I've seem 'em take a strike (Gambon: Uh) — I've seen 'em
take a strike for 84 bucks and (Gambon: xx) 10,000 people.

Gambon: I'm talkin' — I'm talkin' about people who are pretty realistic
when it comes down to dealing with very tangible figures.

Mediator: But I — I feel, like you do, that they certainly oughta give it
another look before they / take a strike.

Gambon: (Over Mediator above) I think they better. I think they'd better
take a damn good look at it. (Mediator: Well, I don't know how far
they're —) Because now they're startin' to get down and quibblin'
about pennies here. I mean, at your urging I wrapped the minimum
figure into the picture, principally because I thought, Number 1, as I
indicated to you, I had a good idea of what their offer might be — I
mean, on the basis of the trend their offers have been taking here —
and I thought that once you knew the maximum and being certain that
it wouldn't be our minimum, if they knew the — our — our minimum
they would give thought to the difference that existed between the 2
and weigh everything involved in this situation as to what can possibly

happen in the probable — probable cost to the company involved in the dispute as against the difference that exists between what they said was a maximum and what we're saying is the minimum. And in round figures it totals 36,000 bucks. Now, any company that's going to face up to a probable strike in the face of a (pause) very likely $2\frac{1}{2}$-million-dollar-profit-before-taxes proposition for the sake of $36,000.00 is nuts, and I don't believe they're nuts. I mean, all indications are that they're pretty shrewd apples and they know what they want. But it also happens that we have a pretty good idea as to what we want. I think you oughta tell 'em a few of the facts of life along those lines, George, and let them do some hard thinking about it. (Pause) I still think they're bargaining, and I've tried to get that out of the picture here (pause, during which Mediator rises), / in interest — in the hope that we could reach a settlement.

Mediator: (Over Gambon above) Well, I hope you're right. I don't think they are. They may later (Gambon: Uh-huh), after they make a telephone call, or — or whether they go back to their plant and talk it over. But I don't think this committee's bargaining. Now, I — I hope I'm wrong. (Pause)

Gambon: Well, if they're not bargaining, they oughta call somebody and find out if they can bargain up to what happens to be the minimum position that the union has set up for itself now. Now, I've come a long / way away from the thing that I said I was gonna fight about, George.

Mediator: (Over Gambon above) All right. Now, you asked me a question, John. You asked — you asked me a question and I answered it. Now, I'm gonna ask you one. (Gambon: H'm) Uh-h-h (pause) — you asked me whether I thought there was anything more in it, and I gave you an honest deduction based on (Gambon: Yeah, I think I agree with you at this — this time) — on experience in how the — in — in other situations.

Gambon: Well, I think I agree with you at this time that this committee without a phone call would probably up the total of 4 to 5 without too much trouble.

Mediator: No, I don't think they could.

Gambon: Well, I — I'm / inclined to think that they might.

Mediator: (Over Gambon above) I dou — I question that, without — I think they would have to make a phone call (Gambon: Uh-huh) on it. Uh-h —

Saunders: Len Loring got a lotta power up there.

Mediator: Has he? (Slight pause)

Gambon: Well, I was particularly interested in getting his answer to the question of whether he had the authority to settle this thing.

Mediator: Well, now, he might! He might, now. See — see (Gambon: Well, he said he did), this is my thinking. He said this — now, he — he — he said — he also said, "This is my maximum."

Gambon: H'm. Well, I can't / xxx.

Mediator: (Over Gambon above) Now, if — if that is his maximum, he has to be taken off a hook, doesn't he?

Gambon: Well, i — if it is, if that's his maximum as the s — as a position for the company, he is the chairman of the committee, all well and good. If he's committed to that by order, that's something else again. If he's only set up a momentary maximum for himself as the chairman

of the committee, he can take himself off the hook. I think the thing
regarded here is whether or not he's working under orders from the
Board of Directors and that this is the figure that he's to go to without further instructions.

Mediator: Well, we'll find that out (pause) and I'll give ya every opportunity to get all you can from him. You will (pause) — you can apply
any (pause) — any and all reasoning that ya can bring to bear into
the situation and (pause) — but that's — those are the things that —
in answer to your question, as I see them from — benefiting from my
contact with 'em in there. Now, I might be entirely wrong. They may
play a different type of poker or they may, as I've seen 'em, too,
sometimes where they're so naive that — in — in negotiations that
you think they're real smart. I don't know whether this is one of
those cases, but — (pause).

[A brief exchange on the negotiating competence of the management
team is turned by Mediator onto himself in a fashion that produces
laughter from everyone.]

Mediator: I feel better. (All laugh heartily) (Rather long pause) Well,
I think you're gonna have to do some work on him, John.

Gambon: Uh-huh. (Pause) Well, I would ask you to present our (pause)
few items of discussion we've had with ya here to them and tell 'em
to do some more thinking and (pause) / xxxxx.

Mediator: (Over Gambon above) Well, John, at this stage of the game,
I think you're gonna have to face this, too. At this stage of the game,
when you say "do more thinking" without bein' definite, it's gonna
be, o-oh, extremely / hard —

Gambon: (Over Mediator above) Do more thinking about meeting the
minimum, I mean, to be very / specific.

Mediator: (Over Gambon above) Oh! Well, now, if that's it, then
(Gambon: That's — that's the point) we know what ya mean, but if
(Gambon: All right!) you were to — if you were to say, in between
the 2 points do some more thinking, / you'd never get an answer.

Gambon: (Over Mediator above) Oh! O-oh, look! No, I'm still talkin'
about the f — fact that I've a minimum position which I stated in the
first place was not a bargainable proposition, a thing which is entirely realistic, as far as I'm concerned, even in their book, because
you can add things up and you can't get more'n $84,000.00 total cost
to the company on it. If they didn't do any better than they did last
year, $84,000.00 wouldn't take a hell of a lot of a bite out of a million
dollars' profit before taxes. (Pause) And keep in mind what they've
been doing here. I mean, they've got that power transformer loss
completely out of the picture. They said themselves (Mediator: Well,
are — are you thinking —) if they hadn't had had those losses it would
have produced $160,000.00 more profit, George.

Mediator: O.K. I — I — I — I have to — I — I can't argue with you there.
/ I mean, you got good —

Gambon: (Over Mediator above) That — that $160,000.00 extra would —
would result in an 8-cent per hour figure for 1400 members. It would
produce more than that, since we're down around the 1200 level. Would
probably produce at least another cent — a 9-cent figure. We're
talkin' about a 7-cent minimum! They could pay that increase, and
on the basis of nothing better that they done in '52, still come up with
at least $577,000.00 profit after taxes. And that — all indications are

it's gonna be better than that. They've absorbed the full shock of this
damn total cost that they gave out in March and October of '52. That's
what they can't — well, I mean, I don't think they keep forgetting it.
They're just being hard-headed about this situation, and they wanta
use the money for something else. / And we're determined that they're
not gonna use it.

Mediator: (Over Gambon above) John, if your — if your sights are on
your minimum (pause) / tonight —

Gambon: (Over Mediator above) Dead set! Bull's eye. Ringer.

Mediator: Then we'd better to home.

Gambon: Well —

Mediator: I've got endurance and patience, but I've also got common
sense, and I know when — and the target's there and when it isn't. I
wanta give ya every opportunity to soften 'em up all you want before
the night's over (Gambon: H'm), but I w — I would be kidding myself and kidding you if I thought for a minute you could get it. Now,
you won't get it xx. You — you may be able to get it later, with a
threat of a strike or something like that, / but you'll never get it.

Gambon: (Over Mediator above) Well, that's on the table now.

Saunders: George, during negotiations in October they already were
buildin' a place in Aiken.

Mediator: Yeah.

Saunders: They're liable to be buildin' some place in Aiken right now!
(Slight pause)

Mediator: Possible.

Saunders: They're gonna move those other 2 places.

Mediator: That's not the point I'm making. See, if it was there —

Saunders: Well, if we can get the rest of the — we can (Gambon: We say
it's the —) at least keep the roof off it for awhile, that's all.

Gambon: They're not sayin' that (Mediator: Do what?) they can't / do —

Saunders: (Over Gambon above) We're tryin' to keep the roof off it for
a little while longer, that's all. We're — try to hold this.

Mediator: Oh.

Saunders: Get the walls up, and if we can keep the roof here —

Mediator: Well, don't — look, don't misunderstand me.

Saunders: No, I don't. I don't.

Mediator: See, I'm not saying you're not entitled to it. I'm saying —
I'm tryin' to point out to you whether you can get it or not tonight
(Saunders: No, I know. I know what you mean), see. If you could,
I'd be — / I'd stay here.

Saunders: (Over Mediator above) What was that? One week after we've
settled, and they x / xx?

Gambon: (Over Saunders above) That's right. Right after we settled.
Yeah.

Meyer: Uh-huh.

Saunders: And they already have broke ground?

Mediator: Yeah. Uh-h — (pause).

Gambon: And that's what — one of the things that we're concerned
(Mediator: There's a chance that —) about. The minute this settlement is made, I wouldn't be a bit surprised to see the dividends reach —
[Tape changed]
. . . hopin' he gets it for nothin', huh?

Meyer: Yeah, it's his chance.

Saunders: It's his chance at profits / they made in '46.

One of girls: (Over Saunders above) It's his chance at profits.

Gambon: Yeah. Cheap chance — 36,000.00 bucks. (Saunders laughs)

Mediator: All right! I'll convey your thinking to them and (pause) — and —

Gambon: Look. I'm — I'm very sympathetic to your running out of patience, because, by Christ, I am, too. (Pause)

Mediator: Well, I wouldn't run out — common sense comes into play some time during my handling (Gambon: I know. Look —) of these cases, and if there was an end hanging out that long, a Chinaman's chance of you gettin' sss — gees, I'm thinkin' (Gambon: 7¢?) of 7.50, now (Someone laughs slightly) — 7¢ (Gambon: Uh-huh), I'd be here till 4:00 o'clock in the morning. But I never knock myself out when I'm convinced it just isn't there. (Pause) For that reason, I'm telling you that, not to throw you off. Maybe another day'll soften 'em up. Maybe it will; I don't know. I know tonight it isn't there. Know — and when I know that I'd be a darn fool to keep everybody, including myself, in session. (Gambon: Uh-huh. Well, I'm — I appreciate that, and I don't wanta stay here if it's not possibility, but I wanta —) And, as I said, I'll give ya every opportunity (Gambon: H'm) to soften 'em up or work on 'em or do what you want. I'm convinced it isn't there. I wished I was wrong. (Gambon: Uh-huh) But there comes a time where I have to give it to you, tell you! I'd do it with them, if I thought there wasn't a chance of settling it. That doesn't mean it isn't there, but it isn't there tonight! (Gambon: Well, that's 2 different things) And then again, it may still be the same position next week; I don't know. But as it stands right now, as I can analyze, having the benefit of being with them separately, having heard their position here and heard yours and so forth, I add / up the —

Gambon: (Over Mediator above) Is there any possibility of your meeting before Thursday, then?

Mediator: No, John. I (Gambon: Uh-huh) — I've got this meeting tomorrow. (Pause) It — I don't know how I could get out of that. Wednesday — I'm committed Wednesday. (Rather long pause) I don't know how I could, John.

Gambon: H'm. (Pause)

Mediator: I'd like very much to get out of tomorrow's meeting. (Pause)

Gambon: Well, if it's — only takes a request from us, we can get ya out of it. (Laughs, joined by several others)

Mediator: Take (laughing) more than a request from (Gambon laughs) — ta — (laughing) take more'n a request from you or (pause) — it's a —

Gambon: Frankly, I think the request should be comin' from the company rather than us because they're the ones that have a decision to make here (pause), as I see it. I think our approach has been — to this whole problem has been more directed to tryin' to get an amicable settlement here than the company's has, considering the length of time involved and everything else.

Mediator: (In very low voice) Uh-huh. (Pause)

Gambon: And this particular kind of thing they're doing here is just about the same kind of thing we were confronted with in October last year. Try to get by as little as ya can. Well, how about givin' the boys a

little stir and see what can be (Someone arises from table) x on top
of the mess ?
Mediator: Right.

Management Caucus - J (10:35 P.M.)

[Mediator and Loring engage in preliminary period of exchange about
the turn of events in the negotiations going on concurrently at Lashley
Equipment. Mediator bestirs everyone into trying to locate on their
charts the figure for Lashley's average hourly rate.]
Mediator: Well, here's where we are. (Rather long pause) John said to
me (pause) — uh (rather long pause) — he said, "George (pause),
we're apart 3¢. (Pause) Do you think there's more there?" (Pause)
I said, "You heard the man." (Slight pause) And (pause) we then
talked about whether — he then talked about whether that was your
final position. And (pause) I tol — he said that he had to have his
minimum, 7¢. (Pause) "Well," I said, "John, it would be wrong
for me to even slightly indicate to you, or insinuate in any way, that
you could get 7¢. You won't get it tonight, I know that! And I only
live 24 hours a day. And you may not get it next week. Then, again,
you might. So that's how — that's the best answer I can give you.
But from where I sit I think I have to give you the benefit of my being
in the conferences — in the separate conferences with the company
and yourself so that you can (pause) correctly take your next step.
And the benefit — my ben — the benefit that I can give you is this: it
isn't there. (Slight pause) And if you want to — an opportunity to try
to get it, you can have it! I'll bring the company in and you can say
anything to you wan — you want to them that you believe will change
their mind. But you asked me a question; I gave you my answer."
(Long pause) I thought he was going to say (pause), "Don't you
think we can split the difference?" But he didn't! He went whole
hog, which, I think, is strictly a bargaining gesture. (Pause) Now,
one thing he said that (pause) interested me more than any of the
figures was, "Can't you meet any sooner than next week?", see.
(Addressing Observer) S — s — did he say next week, or Thursday?
Observer: Thursday.
Mediator: Thursday! Thursday. (Pause) I said No. (Pause) I said,
"No, I'm committed tomorrow and Thursday." (Slight pause) So
the very fact that he mentioned that (pause) was the first good sign
I've had since the negotiations began. (Pause) But he's at 7¢ right
now. (Loring: Uh-huh) He wants me to convey to you that that's
where he is, and he would like very much to have you give him 7¢.
So I have conveyed it. (Rather long pause) Uh (long pause) — now
I think we oughta do some out-loud thinking on the next step. The
blade's getting closer and closer. (Laughs)
Loring: Yes, it is, George.
Mediator: Uh (long pause) — he has, for the first time, showed an interest in time. So far — I mean, up to now he didn't care when I may
set the next meeting. This is the first time. That I like, for this reason. (Rather long pause) They won't strike so easily. (Loring: Uh-
huh) Got 'em at 4, now, and he's afraid of the strike, I think, at 4

without raisin' a lot of hell before he pulls the pin. (Pause) I think
the monkey's on his back, now. See, the — I think he's going to
(pause) make all the passes from here on in, where we were making
them, pushin' and tryin' to dislodge him. (Loring: Uh-huh) I think
now he's going to (pause) have to take the next step. Now. Getting
right down to cases (pause), it may be very well for us to find out
whether or not he wants to do anything for completely settling this,
and only by listening (pause) — only by listening. (Loring: Uh-huh)
Right now he's 7¢. Later we're goin' to have to go back in there and
you're going to have to give the union the answer to this that I have
conveyed to you. I have — they have asked me — now, it's almost
silly, because you've rejected it, by your — r — offer. If you were
goin' to accept 7¢ you wouldn't have came out and said your last position was 4¢, which, again, shows that John is holding these negotiations. (Pause) However, the only thing you can do is stand pat and
stand pat hard (slight pause), right now.

Loring: Uh-huh. (Pause) Gonna have to.

Mediator: And (pause) if John has any thinking may come up next
    couple of days — how do you feel about a delay of t — a couple of days ?

Loring: It's all right with me, George (Mediator: As long as there's no
    strike), xx.

Mediator: And I don't think there will be. (Pause) Uh (pause) — well,
    here's what I think. I think that soon we ought to go in there and you
    answer that that I told you in any way that you want to. And if he
    wants to keep these negotiations going, I'll listen, if for no other rea-
    son to find out where he — just where he's going. Uh — I told him
    that if there was a Chinaman's chance of resolving this thing tonight
    I would be here, stay here with it. But I said, "As I see it, there
    isn't that much of an end hanging out, and I have no intentions of sit-
    ting up all night nursing a dead duck." (Pause) "Now," I said, "I'll
    convey your message, and then anything that you want to say to the
    company later to strengthen your position or to (pause) bolster it or
    convince, persuade — do whatever you want to do to the company,
    you'll have the opportunity in joint session. But I," I said, "— 7¢ is
    your figure." I said, "They've told you their maximum, and I — I
    can't see any daylight. (Pause) Now (pause)" — then we ought to
    adjourn. (Pause) (Loring: Uh-huh) We oughta adjourn and let it go
    till Thursday. Let it sit for awhile. See what he does! (Pause) I
    would have much rather left it — like to have left it subject to call
    and not committed myself to Thursday, even, but sometimes that's
    bad, because when you don't set a meeting they think that that's the
    end.

Loring: Yeah. Yeah.

Mediator: So (long pause) — so we'll do just that. I can't — I — I've
    been — the reason I've been hesitating, I was tryin' to explore all the
    angles. I don't see anything else you can do unless you want to do
    something else. (Loring: O.K. xx —) But I — I think your best po-
    sition is to just do just that. And (pause) I think you oughta force
    the issue tonight. You gotta — you gotta hold your hand. (Long pause)

Loring: (Mediator starts to speak at same time) He didn't show any in-
    tention of budging, you say ?

Mediator: Oh, well, his position — no. He didn't show any in — intentions of — of budging at all. But (pause), see, he knows, just like
you do, that (slight pause) he's in the tightest spot of these negotiations right now. He knows what the difference is. He knows that if
he has to go down there and call a strike at 4¢, that's an unpopular
strike (pause), and I don't think he wants to be in that position. So
for that reason he would be a damn fool, in my opinion, to go to that
ef — to go up and call a meeting and a strike at 4¢. Understand, he
could do it! I've seen strikes for 1¢ — the difference between the
parties (Loring: Uh-huh) is 1¢. (Loring: Uh-huh) Fact, I know one
that went something like 9 weeks! (Pause) It was ridiculous! There
was one in here, ½¢! But when they get down there it's — it's usually
some other reason other than (Loring: Yeah) money.
Loring: Well, we — we have hit our top, George. I mean, that's our
authorization. It's — that's it.
Mediator: Good! And we'll let 'em know that as quickly as po — the
only thing I can't — I'm not quite sure of whether I should — no. I
think we should go in together. I was gonna go in and play with it,
but then they might think we're — we're jockeying. Be — it may —
may as well go in and (long pause) — yeah. Yeah, that — that will
be the best move.
?: O.K.

Joint Meeting - G (10:55 P.M.)

Mediator: Well, gentlemen an — or, ladies. (Meyer laughs) I'm so
used to —
One of girls: Just don't forget us. (Laughs)
Mediator: So many of the committees don't have ladies on them that —
a majority of them — say it without thinking. Ladies and gentlemen,
why, I — after the last 2 — or, the last joint meeting that both of you
had — now, I've talked it out and did some exploring with the union,
did some exploring with the company. (Pause) I have conveyed to
the company the union's (pause) reiteration of where they want to
go, namely, the last figure that the union spoke about, namely, 7 —
what is it? — 7¢. (Pause) Now, at this time I think the — I'll call on
the company's and cut all the corn — I'll cut all the corner short by
not repeating. So, Len, s'pose you take it. *
Loring: All right. Well, we're very anxious to settle this. We wanta
settle it. But I honestly tell you, we — we did just what Mediator
Thomson asked us to do, what — what is our maximum position, and
we've thrown it on the table. We're not holding anything back. We've
given it to you — I mean, 4¢. (Pause) That's all we have. (Pause)
Gambon: Not all ya have, Len. You mean that's all you're willin' to
offer, / let's put it.
Loring: (Over Gambon above) That's (laughing) all we feel is all we
have, John. (Pause)
Gambon: Well, as I see it at the moment, then, the union has 2 choices
(pause) — 3 choices: Number 1, accept your offer; Number 2, maintain our minimum position and strike; or Number 3, introduce

something different into this particular position. And I think, of the
3, I prefer to introduce something different into this situation in an
effort to try and reach an amicable settlement without a strike. But
when I do, I'm going to do it with a request to the company that they
give very serious consideration to it, because there's gonna be a
time limit on this proposition, and it's gonna be a position from which
I'm not going to do any retreating. I'm conscious of the fact that
we're gonna go through this crap all over again in October of 1953,
and I think you are, too. (Loring: Sure am, John) I'm gonna propose
a settlement that will take us to the expiration of this contract, Len,
and I'm gonna fight about it now, in the spring of the year. I'd rather
do it with sneaks on than I would with snow shoes. We'll reiterate
our offer — our proposal, rather — that we had previous to taking this
minimum position, and we think it's a reasonable proposition when
you consider the fact that you're talking about a settlement that takes
you right up into April 1st, 1954. That proposal, of course, goes back
to the cent — 10-cent general increase and the 20% (Loring: Uh-huh)
fixed bonus. (Pause) Now, I don't know whether you're prepared tonight to give that consideration or whether that involves discussion
with the Board of Directors or whoever else is guiding the particular
negotiations, but if it can be worked on tonight, fine. If it can't without any hope of settlement tonight, then I would suggest that we set up
a meeting as quickly as possible to get at that angle. It doesn't seem
to me, in the face of what we went through in October of '52 and what
we're going through now, to be sensible in trying to think that something different than this situation is gonna exist in October of '53.
Maybe everybody'd be happy if we can have the company in a position
where they know what their cost is going to be, from the standpoint
of the union, from now until the expiration of our contract, as well as
to have us pretty certain of what the benefits are gonna be for us the
balance of '53 and, for that matter, into the first few months of '54.
(Loring: Well, as you say, John —) I'm saying that because I've become pretty convinced that even though the company entered into the
contract containing all these reopeners, I thought in good faith, we
had expressions from Michelsen during October, '52, reopener and
again during this, that the company dislikes very much this proposition of all these reopeners, and I think that holds as much for October,
'53, as it does for this — w — with the previous ones. I think our best
bet, to avoid a dispute which involves a strike in the plant, is to try
and approach this on that basis.

Loring: Well, as you say, of course, that — that's a — a new issue that
(Gambon: H'm) you inject, John, and I'm not prepared on it. I, at
this point, would like to have a caucus with my committee and decide
what to — how to answer you on that.

Gambon: All right.

Mediator: Now, you'd — y — a point of clarification. (Gambon: Yeah)
You didn't submit your proposal; you just submitted the principle.
Or did I —

Gambon: I just submitted a proposal (Mediator: A figure?) of a 10-
cent general (Mediator: Oh) wage increase and the 20% fixed bonus
for skilled trades and all other day workers, which would take us —
which would be a settlement writing out the October, '53, reopener,

in effect, a settlement which would take us through to April 1st, 1954, which is the expiration date of the contract. It's understood, of course, that I'm talking about an effective date of April 1st, 1953, which is a settlement based on an entire year.

Mediator: Uh-huh. (Pause)

Loring: All right, George.

Management Caucus - K (11:05 P.M.)

Mediator: I didn't even _hear_ it, even when he said it! I had (laughs) — I — I thought he was just talkin' about the _principle_ of the thing. xx 10¢ general increase, 20%. Well, I must — I'm gettin' foggy, or it might have been when I's winding my watch. (Someone else, and then Mediator, laugh)

[Tape changed]

Pranis: ... do we wanta consider it in principle?

Loring: I would love not to have another reopener this year, but not at that price. (Pause) What's the purpose in throwing that out, George?

Mediator: Uh (pause) — I can see through that one. (Pause) Uh (long pause) — (1) (pause), you're (slight pause) — come October, they feel they might be in a different bargaining position than they are to-day. More of your work may go South. That's one thought. (Pause) (?: Yeah) And then come October, they wouldn't be able to (pause) bargain as strongly as they could now. Secondly, it's as much a nui-sance to them, in many instances — the negotiators — the union — as it is to the companies, and it's not an unusual thing to swap 'em off. They've been bought off before, and (Loring: Uh-huh) they're done — they do every day. That's another reason. Another one could be that (rather long pause) he feels that if he can strike a price (slight pause) that — he's probably satisfied that the cost-of-living leveling off the way it has, that he couldn't get too, too _hurt_ by giving up his reopener. These are some of the things I think (Loring: Uh-huh) — now, which one it — it is, but I think it might be a little bit of each. (Rather long pause)

Pranis: Bill pounded before that, while we have reopeners, as he inti-mated — he said the intent of reopeners was to talk about more money, and Bill has said several times that while we may have re-openers, it isn't necessarily true that we will give money each time. Now, it was during several meetings here — a couple meetings here, repeated he didn't think he would _ever_ give up the reopener. Now suddenly he reverses his field!

Espig: Well, my God! Figure it out for yourself! Even if we give him 7¢ _now_, we got 6 months to go to pay 7¢ more. _This_ is no bargain.

Pranis: Well, I don't say it's a bargain. I was tryin' to figure what — would there be an additional angle?

Mediator: I don't think there's — a — a — 'course, the last — see, I mentioned 3. The one I didn't mention was the 4th, _his_ — the one _he_ just mentioned. (Slight pause) (Loring: H'm) Now, there's a — there's _another_ reason why it would be a darn good settlement.

Loring: Yes, it would be, for him.

Mediator: So that's another reason. (Slight pause) Uh — (pause).

Pranis: George, d — he intimated when he said this — he said there were 3 courses, the latter of which he preferred, being the one we now have. The other 2 was — the other 2 were, as I remember, gonna either take our 4¢ or he would strike. These were / his 3 offers.

Loring: (Over Pranis above) Well, no. (Pranis: No ?) Another one that we'd set up another meeting.

Mediator: Yeah.

Pranis: (At same time as Mediator above) No. Now, wait a minute. He said there were 3 courses he could pursue. He could take the 4¢ — this is prior to any / further meeting discussion.

Espig: (Over Pranis above) 3 courses. 3 courses.

Pranis: 3 courses. Take our 4¢, strike for the difference between 4 to 7, or take this 3rd alternate.

Loring: He also mentioned setting up another / meeting.

Pranis: (Over Loring above) Only if we took this 3rd alternate and you couldn't answer tonight — if you / came out of this caucus and said xx of it.

Loring: (Over Pranis above) No, I didn't — I didn't — I didn't xxx. No.

Mediator: No, I didn't get it that way, either. I (Loring: Yeah) thought he said, "(1), we can accept it; (2), we can reject it and set up another conference; (3), we can talk about a new proposal, which is" — and then he shot it out. (Addressing Observer) Do you remember that ?

Espig: Yeah. Your — they — excepting for the fact that the 2d / was —

Mediator: (Over Espig above) Was it the way I said it, or the way —

Observer: It was my impression he talked about another meeting before he hit this new proposal.

Loring: Yes, that was true. (Espig: Rejected —) He wants a strike, / rejected a strike —

Espig: (Over Loring above) Rejected and strike, accepted, or introduce a new idea.

Pranis: Well, that's / what I said.

Loring: (Over Pranis above) No. See, he — he had one of (Mediator: That's the way he said it) each. He (Pranis: That's what I said) — he said — he — he also s — he / said —

Espig: (Over Loring above) x, I made a note on it!

Pranis: He gave himself 3 courses (Espig: Sure!): accept, reject to the strike, or the 3rd alternate, the 3rd alternate (Loring: No. There was one more in between) being what we're talkin' about. Further along that, he said in accepting it, he didn't know whether you were in a position at this moment to accept this 3rd alternate or whether you wanted a further meeting for acception / or rejection of the 3rd alternate.

Loring: (Over Pranis above) No. Bob, he — he mentioned another meeting before he mentioned his new idea.

Pranis: Mr. Espig and I concur that you are wrong!

Mediator: Uh —

Observer: (At same time as Mediator above) We'll run the tape, Mr. Loring, if they don't believe us. (Laughs slightly, as does Loring)

Espig: Well, maybe he spoke about it — another meeting and 2 positions.

Pranis: Well, I'm pretty — I know he spoke about a meeting as to your acceptance of this 3rd / proposal.

Espig: (Over Pranis above) Well, he — he said — he said (Pranis: He didn't know x —) we could either talk about it tonight, and i — but if you're not prepared, we'll have to talk about (Pranis: Yeah) it at a little later date.

Pranis: And then meeting as soon as possible. Now, that's the time I remember the meeting. Other than that, I remember him saying he had 3 choices, 2 of which were take what we offered or reject and strike, and then there was a 3rd alternate. I don't — specifically, I don't remember him saying anything about a meeting prior to that time. (Espig: Yeah) But he certainly did say that maybe you, Len, or the committee were not in a position to accept this 3rd alternate, in which case we should recess and have another meeting very shortly in order to discuss this 3rd / x.

Loring: (Over Pranis above) He said that, but also before that he mentioned, I think, he —

Pranis: You're probably right, except that I don't remember.

Mediator: I'm not sure, now, myself.

Pranis: Naw, / xx.

Mediator: (Over Pranis above) If it's important, I could ask him.

Loring: I don't think it is, at this point.

Pranis: Well, no, Len! Maybe it is important.

Mediator: Well, how? (Espig: In what way?) Maybe — / let's hear it.

Pranis: (Over Mediator above) Well, let's assume you have 3 alternates: yeah, nay, or maybe. Let's say we reject the maybe. We are not interested in this point of buying off no reopener in October for the price he mentions. We give him the alternate of — we then — then have the alternate of saying the price is too high but we will buy for less money, or we're just not interested.

Espig: Well, that's the thing we have to canvass.

Pranis: All right. But we are not in a position to say that now (Espig: Naw), in any case. (Espig: No!) So the only thing we can do tonight is go back and say, "We can't answer your thing. We need further time (Espig: Well, sure!) to study." Mean a further meeting.

Espig: We can certainly say to him that — that we don't see ourselves sitting here till 5:00 o'clock tomorrow morning and even then getting an a — an agreement and —

Pranis: We don't see an agreement on this basis (Espig: No!) tonight! (Pause) But we wanta pursue / the subject thoroughly.

Espig: (Over Pranis above) Let's — let's think about it. Let's — let's think about the — the avenues that he's a — that he's traveling here.

Pranis: We don't wanta be / xx.

Espig: (Over Pranis above) We don't have to rush into this thing like that!

Pranis: He's apparently not in a hurry. (Pause)

Espig: Let's look at it from — / from —

Loring: (Over Espig above) I — I think, from many angles, George, that we wouldn't be interested in buying it at all, one of which is we — we're not sure that even if we bought it off him, couldn't have trouble, it come October, if we had a good picture, 'cause they have the right to strike at any time. (Pause)

Pranis: It isn't possible to — to write an addendum in the contract, / saying that —

Espig: (Over Pranis above) Well, you're not — you're not rejecting the idea at this point.

Loring: I'm saying it has little appeal to me.

Espig: Well, right! Right! (Pause) For any further negotiations tonight, I think it's past that stage.

Loring: I would rather —

Mediator: It would be well, though, to do — to consider this, that in reporting <u>back</u> to them on this, be well to put it this way, that you have — your committee has discussed this latest proposal. (Rather long pause) "We (rather long pause)" — s — then say, just as you said then, "We — it doesn't have too much appeal to us. But we're perfectly willing to (pause) take it back for a further look, but we can't — we can say now that it prob'ly — it d — well, we don't want to raise your hopes on it." I think, (1), you're dignifying it. But you're also making it clear that you, the committee, are not sold on it. And then, if he has any other ideas tonight that he wants to get over, it'll give him an opportunity to shoot them over. If not, then you know there's no use to — (rather long pause). See, to say to him flatly, "Well, we'll take this back and consider it (long pause)," you may get his thinking embedded. We'll have a hell of a time dislodgin' him.

Espig: This'll be embedded tomorrow by noon in the plant. (Laughs shortly)

Mediator: What?

Espig: This kind of an offer. This'll get a great deal of publicity tomorrow. (Slight pause)

Mediator: (In low voice) Huh-un, that wouldn't hurt, I don't think. It — that won't bother nego — it's a new proposal. But if you — if he shows you're inter — if you show you're interested, I think, i — Number 1, you should dignify it. (Loring: Uh-huh) But not too — but add that, "But in all fairness to you we think we oughta tell ya that it — we, ourselves" — or "it — it doesn't hold much appeal to us, but we're perfectly willing to give it a further look, but it's not attractive." (Pause) Then he might wanta talk tonight! But you may be wastin' a lotta time! But if he thinks you're dignifying it, or that you're going to make a big deal out of it by taking it back to your Board of Directors and then reporting back into another meeting (Loring: H'm), I wouldn't want ya to raise it or have him raise his hopes on it. Where, if — if he — if he gets the feeling that you're not too, too sold on the thing — uh-h-h-h — he'll keep thinking. But if he thinks you're sold on it he'll <u>stop</u> thinking. (Loring: Uh-huh) I don't think ya can afford to have him stop thinking! (Loring: Huh-un) (Long pause) And <u>then</u> if he doesn't come — if he doesn't show any signs after this pitch, we're all going home. It's getting late, and if he doesn't show any bright spots, we'll know it now. (Rather long pause) So, whenever you're ready!

Pranis: Take your pipe with you. You've got a rough opponent. (Espig laughs)

Joint Meeting - H (11:15 P.M.)

Loring: Well, we've just discussed this new thought, John — the committee. As we told you before, we had a certain amount of money which we threw on the table. This is way and above beyond anything that we had to play with. It's a new idea. At this moment we, as the committee, feel not a great amount of appeal — it doesn't have a great of amount of appeal for us. We would prefer to take the reopeners as they come. However, because it is a new thought, there are some things about it that might be good. We're willing to take it back to the company, but I don't want, in saying that, to raise your hopes on it, because (Gambon: Uh) the committee itself doesn't feel too strongly towards it.

Gambon: (Laughs) Len (laughing slightly), this isn't a hopeful proposition. This is the — a — an exploratory proposition of tryin' to find some way of reaching a satisfactory settlement with the company.

Loring: Well, I appreciate (Gambon: And I would —) your motives in that, too, and that's — that's one reason that we (Gambon: H'm) say that we'll take it back to the company. We ourselves don't like it as well (Gambon: Uh-huh) as — (pause).

Gambon: Well, we would like to make this particular point clear, that — that this point. In view of all that's gone before, the union's position will be for a settlement that — that will cover everything between now and April 1st, 1954. (Pause)

Mediator: What was that, John ? I don't quite understand it.

Gambon: I say, the union's position now, in view of everything that's happened up to this point, will be to press for a settlement covering April 1st, 1953, to April 1st, 1954, and we'll direct our negotiations to that objective. (Pause)

Pranis: See if I understand you. You're saying that your / efforts now — there'll be no October —

Gambon: (Over Pranis above) I'm saying go back and tell the Board of Directors that, Bob. (Laughs slightly)

Pranis: Well, you're saying that you would prefer no October reopeners at this point.

Gambon: I prefer not to go through this damn (Pranis: Well, that's what xx —) thing all over again the same as we (Pranis: O.K.) did once before, and I'm — I'm being very frank with ya and tell ya if I'm gonna fight with ya, I'm gonna do it now. I'm not gonna do it on snow shoes in October, 1953. (Pranis: Now I —) I can't be any franker than that.

Pranis: Now I understand you. (Rather long pause)

Gambon: So ?

Mediator: So, we've had a long day.

Gambon: Yes.

Mediator: I think the day has come to an end.

Gambon: I would say that it's been a little more productive than the previous days have been. (Slight pause)

Mediator: So (pause), we'll adjourn the conference, and because — now, I — I hope we can meet Thursday. I — I don't see why — right now at the moment why we can't. (Pause) So you can tentatively set it

for Thursday, and if there is any change — and I hope there won't
be — why, I'll get in touch with you, both the union and the company.
Loring: What time will it be Thursday, / George?
Mediator: (Over Loring above) Uh — 10:30? (Pause)
Gambon: I would prefer an earlier starting time, George, because I will
not be able to meet for any great length of time —
Mediator: Yeah, you mentioned that you were — / had some appointment
on Thursday.
Gambon: (Over Mediator above) Uh — I would wanta set up a 5:00 o'clock
deadline. (Rather long pause)
Mediator: Uh-h-h-h (pause) — 9:30?
Gambon: It's satisfactory to me.
Loring: All right. 9:30. (Rather long pause)
Mediator: All right, we'll (slight pause) meet then — set that — now,
reason I say tentatively, I have one situation that I must postpone
(pause), and if there was a delay, it wouldn't be (pause) — or, leave
it that way. 9:30.
Gambon: W — when you say leave it that way, you mean you're makin'
it a definite (Mediator: Meeting) meeting, or is it (Mediator: Yeah)
still a —
Mediator: x. (Rather long pause) Like some of your appointments, you
know. You (Gambon: Yeah. Yeah) can't — you're — it — it looks
all right as — as of — a — as of tonight. I believe it's — but let me
confirm it / tomorrow.
Gambon: (Over Mediator above) Well, I'm — I'm concerned because of
the time involved, George. I mean, if we don't meet on Thursday,
that runs us into next week, see. (Pause)
Mediator: Yes. (Rather long pause) Let — I — I — I — I wanta discuss
a matter with the union (Loring: All right, George) and then I'll discuss it with you.
Loring: Well, you're makin' my maiden effort a long one, John.
Gambon: Huh?
Loring: You're making my (laughing) maiden effort a long one today.
(Several laugh heartily)

Union Caucus - E (11:21 P.M.)

Mediator: Uh (rather long pause) — does — is time of great — great
importance to you?
Gambon: Yeah. (Rather long pause) And as I mentioned before — I
mean, in — this time, in all sincerity and all honesty, time is running
out, because I'm not going to take chances of having our people subject to a lot of propaganda and all that crap.
Mediator: Well, now, look. I'll tell ya what — I'll tell ya what w — we
might be able to arrange. We might be able to do this. Now, we have
a meeting scheduled here tomorrow. (Gambon: Uh-huh) I told you
about it. (Pause) Also told you that I'm not too, too happy about it.
(Rather long pause) They oughta have some time.
Gambon: Yeah. I don't think a meeting tomorrow would give them time
to discuss this particular switch here / to —
Mediator: (Over Gambon above) What I was thinking about was, instead
of Thursday, givin' ya tomorrow afternoon, if time was of the essence
to you. (Gambon: Uh-huh) Uh-h-h-h (pause) — I'd —

Gambon: I — I don't know about tomorrow afternoon. Again I'm saying,
I don't know whether this — this proposal is going to take — they'll
prob'ly go into session practically all day tomorrow on this proposal.
Now, I mean, his saying that it doesn't appeal to them is eyewash to
me, because I think that's — from the way they've been talkin' about
these reopeners and bellyachin' about 'em, that appears to me to
be what they'd rather have. Now, on the basis of the way the thing's
been goin' here and the way the thing is bound to go in October, I
see no point in striking the plant on the minimum position of 5 — 7¢
here, against a 4-cent wage offer when I'm probably gonna have to
take the same kind of action in October. My particular thinking is,
do it all at once and get it over with. (Pause)
Mediator: Uh-huh. / Well —
Gambon: (Over Mediator above) I think I could gain my objective in —
in very short time — I mean, by havin' the people out on the bricks
while I'm talkin' to 'em. I'm talkin' about the — the 7-cent minimum.
(Slight pause) But rather than do that and then have to go through it
again in October, which is not a desirable time from the standpoint
of the union as to season of the year and all in which to pull a strike.
The — the shoe gets on the — the other foot a little bit in October;
the advantage's in theirs — favor. I prefer to make use of what advantages I may have at this particular time.
Mediator: Well (pause) — well, we'll — we can let it go till Thursday,
then (Gambon: H'm), if you want.
Gambon: I think that it would be best to give them sufficient time to
give a lot of serious consideration to this proposition.
Mediator: The only reason I mentioned it was I thought it would (Gambon: Uh-huh) — you'd be in / a better x.
Gambon: (Over Mediator above) Well, if we started in the afternoon I'm
afraid, George, that they'd come up with a pr — the story that they —
they have no — haven't had time to thoroughly look into it, and we'd
probably be sittin' here all afternoon and possibly again tomorrow
night without getting any real results. If you can possibly make that
on Thursday, they've had 2 days in which to give this the kind of serious consideration which I say it deserves. Now, if they come in here
Thursday and tell us that they can't — haven't had time enough to talk
about it, why, I know we're gonna start movin' real quick, / that —
Mediator: (Over Gambon above) O.K., Thursday. I'll call you. I'll c —
I'll have to confirm it (Gambon: Uh-huh) and (pause) — my — my
book is crowded — crowding up, because I have spent more times
with this case than another one I have which been usual. / Uh —
Gambon: (Over Mediator above) Uh-huh. Well, if you'll recall — I
mean, I may have gone off a little bit on this thing here, but, I mean,
when I began to see what was developing here (pause) — I waited
until now, this late today, to throw this proposal out, knowing that we
had this probability — I mean, as far as I was concerned, I thought we
were committed to a meeting on Thursday. I mean, I didn't know you
had gotten yourself / in the meantime involved in somepin' else.
Mediator: (Over Gambon above) Well, there's a 90% chance that it will
be set (Gambon: H'm) that way. I just have one thing to take care
of, and (pause) I think it can be taken care of, but I — I — I wanta —
I'm not hanging ya in the air (Gambon: Uh-huh) when I give ya 90-
10. And if — if I did have to do the other, it might take an hour or

2 hours at the most. (Gambon: Uh-huh) But I might — I think I can handle it.

Gambon: All right.

Mediator: What I have to do is stall someone off, and I've stalled the fellow off twice, and this time I wanta do it in person. I don't wanta do it on the telephone. (Gambon: H'm) And he's coming in from another city, and I wanta hang him up here for another day. Now, if I can keep him on ice on Thursday until Friday, that's the objective. [The group prepares to leave, and Mediator departs with "All right, see you later." Gambon's reply is "Yep."]

Management Caucus - L (11:30 P.M.)

Mediator: (Sighs) I called for that caucus to find out just how anxious they were to get together. Now, I would have been willing to give up gladly this meeting I have tomorrow.
[Mediator continues about his reaction to the meeting scheduled for the following day. Espig and Observer exchange light remarks about the fact the tape has recorded Mediator's comments.]
Uh (rather long pause) — however, John felt that now, since he submitted a new proposal, maybe the company oughta have time — it might be crowding them too much. They oughta have a little time to think it over. So he didn't wanta pursue it after that. So I said, "O.K. (Pause) We'll leave it this way. Set it tentatively for Thursday. I have another fellow that I have to postpone, and I have to talk to him. I have — at this stage, it's not final. It's 90-10 I will, but there is that 10%. So," I said, "This fellow's coming in from another city and (pause) I have to postpone him till Friday." (Pause) So we left it for tentatively — a — a tentative meeting for Thursday — wh — did I say what time?

Espig: 9:30.

Observer: 9:30.

Mediator: (At same time as Observer above) 9:30. Yeah, I'm getting tired. (Someone laughs very quietly) 9:30. However, I'll have to call him to confirm it. I'll call you, too, but (Loring: All right. Uh-huh) I think it's 90-10. So, there won't be a strike. I think ya got him in position where that 4-cent offer has done — now, see, if you had put 3 out — see, ya held that one back — I don't think ya would have got the results that ya got in there tonight — the kind of thinking that was stimulated and the position they're in. Think they can — much better chance of getting a strike at 3 than 4. (Loring: Uh-huh) That penny would make a world of difference. (Pause) So, gentlemen, I think —

Loring: Well, what is your — I mean, are you (slight pause) happy with the way this — this last offer came out? I mean, that could cloud the whole thing up again.

Mediator: Uh-h-h-h — I (Loring starts to speak again) didn't expect it. I'm not — I'm not too concerned about it. It's not unusual for unions to make an offer like that, and it's not unusual for companies to reject 'em.

Loring: As I got it — now, maybe I'm wrong — that his very last comment was that everything else has been withdrawn and that is their / position now.

Mediator: (Over Loring above) I thought he did that, too, and that's why I asked (Loring: Uh-huh) what did he mean by that. But (pause) — uh-h-h (rather long pause) — again, I think that's just a switch to new angle, and he's using it, too, as — for pressure. (Rather long pause) Now, he sprung that one. He prob'ly had it in reserve, but he sprung that one as brand new. All he was talking about was money. (Pause) But it wasn't surprising, because I've heard it — I've seen it and heard it done in many, many instances, and if it's an attractive figure, I've seen companies buy it. (Pause)

Loring: That — (slight pause).

Espig: Well, i — if it can be made attractive we at least oughta — we — we might at least talk about it, anyway.

Mediator: And (pause) it's worth while if — if — if ya — if the both parties can agree on a figure, they think they're both satisfied with the deal, it's worth it! But (slight pause) I wasn't sure, either, as to how he put that, as to whether he was s — saying, "All bets are off. This is a — it, and anything we get will have to be now from" — and I don't know whether he can do that, to start with. You have a contract that calls for a 6-month wage reopener, and there's nothing in there that could legally give him — and his attorneys would straighten him out, I'm sure, when the chips were down on that one — a right to come in and say, "We insist on you waiving the October reopener." You think you got him there, legally. His union would be in a bad spot. I don't think his — I think his lawyer would so advise him if he didn't know, and I think he would consult his lawyer before he did it and took any action. So I'm inclined to think that — that — that's my curbstone opinion that that's a (pause) little piece of strategy. I think he would have been much better off to say explore this, period. (Pause) If he meant it, fine, and if he didn't, maybe we misunderstand — stood him. I hope we did. (Loring: H'm) But it did sound a little like a veiled threat. But (pause) think 2 days of sober re — reflection may change the thing.

Loring: O.K., George. Well, at least we're a little closer together now.

Mediator: Yeah. I — I think this. I think the threat of a strike immediately has been removed by the — your action and your handling of the thing today. (Rather long pause)

Loring: Well, I thank you for your help — your hints. I (Mediator says something) needed 'em.

[As the group is breaking up at 11:35 P.M. someone emits a strong sigh on getting up, as though stiff from sitting.]

Management Caucus - A (9:42 A.M.)

Mediator: ... Or is it a good morning?

Pranis: Why, it's a fine / morning.

Espig: (Over Pranis above) Oh, sure.

Loring: Tell ya better around 5:00 o'clock (Mediator laughs) xx. (Pause)

Mediator: Uh — (rather long pause).

Loring: Anything happen at Standard Products, George? Did you hear anything?

Mediator: No, I haven't.

[Mediator, Pranis, and Espig continue the exchange for some time, mainly about two other negotiation cases concurrent with the Atlas one.]

Mediator: H'm. (Pause) Well, how's the Atlas thinking this morning?

Loring: Well, I'll give you the whole picture of our thinking, George, and — just so you'll have it. We — I've been authorized to move a little bit to prevent a strike. I mean, we don't want a strike. I can m — move a cent, up to 5. We have hashed over John's other proposal, that is, to negotiate now for the next reopener — might as well with this one. The idea is attractive, but we don't — we — we know we can't pay what John will want to buy it off. Unofficially — it's strictly to you — we could go to 7¢ if we could get the whole thing wrapped up on that basis, but I doubt that he would buy that, and I wouldn't want him to know it, because I have the feeling it might be a trap to stick us now.

Mediator: I think you're very, very right! I think you're right in this respect. (1), John would never buy the 7¢ for 2 years — or a (snaps fingers) —

Loring: 2 reopeners.

Mediator: — 2 reopeners (Loring: Uh-huh) now. Secondly, if ya indicated that — and if that was your top and you indicated that you wanted to do business on that principle, he would — he could very well move you into a long sessions, 'cause then he'd have 2 issues. (Loring: Yeah) See, he could play with 'em. He could play one against the wage in — one against the other. (Loring: Uh-huh) And you might be in negotiations for a month of Sundays. Uh (pause) — I — I — I think your best bet would be to — when we go into joint session, let him know that the company gave serious thought to his proposal but they're not interested in a (slight pause) extension (pause) — or a (snaps fingers) — a year's / contract.

Loring: (Over Mediator above) Reo — yeah. (Slight pause)

Mediator: See, you're gonna have to say it, to close it off. (Loring: Yeah) If you indicate that you're not opposed to the principle of it, it's still open! (Pause)

Espig: Well, is there any way that we could find out before we go into joint session (Loring: Well —) his — his se — the seriousness of his position?

Mediator: Y — you're going to find that out before the day's over. Well, now here's how you're goin' to find it out. If you go in and take a position that you're not interested in the — well, you talked it over and your people feel that — uh-h-h (slight pause) — they would rather stay within the purview of the contract, which calls for the 6-month reopener in October, and let it go at that, he will do this. After w — the — after I go into session with him, if he really wants to do business on that he will then talk to me. He will say, "Well, d'you think it's a matter of money or do you think they're really opposed to the principle?", or he'll put feelers out some (?: Uh-huh) way. Now, that's my curbstone or immediate thinking on it, unless you — unless you would like to approach him in some other way, why, my mind is open, too.

Loring: I think that's a good way, George. We can't evidence interest in it or we'll never get the 6-months' reopener sewed up.

Mediator: If ya — now, I'd like to see ya get a year contract —

Loring: (Laughing) I can appreciate why you would (Mediator laughs), George! (Laughs heartily, and one or 2 others laugh, also)

Mediator: I'd like to see ya get it, but I doubt — now, I was at coffee with Observer. We were discussing that and I gave her what I thought would — he would — probably be his rock bottom on a year's contract, and I figure 10¢. I figure 5 for this year and fi — or, this period, 5 for the next period. So I said to Observer, "I think he's s — / x" —

Espig: (Over Mediator above) You mean split it? Take 5 now?
[Several talk at once. There are a number of "No's," including one from Mediator. Pranis says, "No. It costs a dime for no reopener."]

Espig: You mean a dime (Mediator: Dime) for — for the full year?

Mediator: Yeah. That's what he's thinking of. (Pause) That's what I believe. Now (pause), here's — here — here's what I wanta point out. What you want to know you're going to find out, but you couldn't find out in this session. You want to know and I want to know whether he would be interested in a year's contract without you appearing that you're at all interested in it. Now, that will come out! I know it will come out before 5:00 o'clock. (Pause) And the how much would come out, because if he is really interested in it he is going to try to sell me. He's gonna try to convince me (Loring: Uh-huh) that you, the company, should buy it. Now, if that was only a feeler, see — which could be very bad if it was. Could be bad for our negotiations because it will s — s — if it's just a feeler, he may have been drawing you out this direction to move in here and up this p — price. If he (Loring: Yeah) thought ya had more for a year's contract (Loring: Yeah. That's — that's what I'm afraid of, George), he might up there, see. And ya don't know! Now, the only way to avoid being mouse-trapped is to just say, "No. We've considered it but we prefer to continue under the terms of the contract, which are — call for a 6-month reopener." Then, later, if the thing doe — has a real value and it wasn't intended just for a trap, he will come out and start selling to me. I know it! If it — if it has a real value. Now, then, i — if he and I talk, it's — it's — it's him talkin' to me without the company being committed. They don't know anything about it! In other words, we're devel — he's developing, and I can, as I often do, give him my opinions, opinions that I haven't even discussed with you! For instance, the 7¢.

I said, "You'll never get it, John. It isn't there!" Something like
that, I've said something without even asking you (Loring: H'm)
whether you wanted to or not because — and wi — likewise, with this,
I would say to him, "You'd never get that 14¢ — 7¢ for this or that.
They're — I don't think they're interested, to start with, and if you
— i — if we did have the chance of getting the company interested,
you'd have to have something — you'd have to give me something to
work with. 14¢ isn't a working tool." Then if he said, "Well, look.
I'll tell you what we'll do, George. We'll do this, that, or the other
thing" — whatever it is. And if it was worthwhile bringin' back to ya,
I'd bring it back! But that's how it would develop! But if he never
mentions it after we've had a joint session, well, then you can bet
your life that it was just a feeler. He wanted to find out just what you
had in mind. Then don't lose sight of this. He's thinking, too, of this.
He's not so sure — he said so — about the company's plans — future
plans. Well, this would be one way of finding out. He'd offer you a
year's deal; then if you discussed it and adopted it, well, least he
knows he's good for a year. Now (Loring: H'm), that could be a
feeler that way!

?: H'm.

Espig: I don't understand.

Mediator: Well, he has said that he doesn't know. He put it to me this
way. He — they don't know from day to day what the company's going
to do about moving South and taking more work out, and (slight pause)
your plant in Rome — some of these other things.

Pranis: What he says is he's a little scared.

Mediator: That's right! Now, he's a little concerned. Now —

Pranis: So if he / gets a year's — if he gets a year's contract, in effect
xx —

Espig: (Over Pranis above) Yeah. But he has — but — you remem —
uh — I'm not reading into your words something which I could have, I
think, and that is that if he were to get a year's contract on money that
that in some way would alter his thinking about whether we're moving
or not?

Mediator: Well, it would — it would do this. He has said that the company — in some of his arguments that, in his opinion, the company
wants the union, or the workers, to pay for the tr — for the transition
— or the trans (slight pause) —

Pranis: For the move — the / Aiken transfer.

Mediator: (Over Pranis above) — the move — transfer. Uh-h (slight
pause) — if he could negotiate a year's contract with you now, waive
a reopener, it would allay a lot of fear (Espig: Yes!) in that plant.
(Espig: Yeah) Just the psychological aspects of it are attractive to
John right (Espig: I think that's true) now. So if he could get a
year's contract, he — it would be sort of a psychological guarantee
that you're not moving the whole plant out tomorrow. It doesn't mean
that you can't! I don't mean / that. That's —

Espig: (Over Mediator above) That's right. O.K. That's all I — now,
one other thing. There are 2 things that — that strike me. Number 1,
are you aware of the fact that there's an Executive Board meeting tonight of the union?

Mediator: No.

Espig: Uh — all right. Well, there is, and in addition tonight it has been planted, possibly, that tonight is the night of decision (slight pause) and that if there — if there is not a settlement there will be a work stoppage tomorrow, after the people receive their pay checks. That's the rumor. Number 2, the skilled trades have expressed an opinion concerning their — their status. They feel that they could get a better break —

Loring: This, too, is rumor. I mean —

Espig: Yeah. This is — this is a statement from the men. This is not rumor. This is a statement on the basis of their / feeling.

Loring: (Over Espig above) To whom, Erv?

Espig: To some of the people.
[As tape is changed, Espig continues that his third point is that Gambon may be trying to avoid "a nasty situation in October," that is, the emotional aspect involved in the reopener. He speculates on possible motivations for Gambon's actions.]

Loring: Still in all, I don't think much of that last one with John. One other thing, George, after discussing with Pran and Erv, we feel that we would like something done for the skilled trades. We think that's an area that — that's worthy, but we feel that it isn't justified for the whole day-work group as a group. Now, his proposal in every case up to now is a percentage increase for the whole group — day workers, including skilled workers. We are receptive to an increase for skilled workers, but we are s — set against an equal increase for the day workers. We don't think it's justified.

Mediator: All right. Now —

Pranis: Another thing, George. None of the membership know about the 4-cent offer.

Mediator: They don't?

Espig: No!

Pranis: Has not been so handled. So one of the things the Executive Committee may have to decide tonight is what to tell the people. (Mediator: Yeah) I mean, I think the time is come — they've met long enough, now, with very general statements. They (laughing slightly) have to tell the people something! One of the things, I think, on the — on the agenda tonight will prob'ly be, "What do we tell these people?"

Mediator: Well, if we're goin' to have an opportunity to settle this, my counsel to you would be to, at no time during today, regardless of what pressure is applied in these negotiations, at no time should you show any indication that you are frightened (slight pause) (Loring: Well, we're not really frightened. No) at the aspect of a strike, because John, if this meeting's — now that you've mentioned this meeting to me, John is gonna play that up sometime during today's negotiations and he's going to use it as a — as a bargaining pressure, and (?: H'm) he'll apply it hard and heavy. Now, if this thing is going to have a chance to fall into its proper slot — and I think there's a good chance of it doing it today — if it is, it's only going to have that chance if the company, Number 1, is polite but firm on the 6-month business. Play that as not interested. Well, g — well, yes. You've looked it over. You've — the company considered it thoroughly and they would prefer to ca — continue on under the terms of the contract, which call for a 6-months' reopener in October and no more than that. And hang on

that, no matter how stormy it gets. If you do that, then I will have the
opportunity, later — in other words, you will make an opening for me
that I will need later. (Loring: Uh-huh) I ju — I — I can — I can almost call the shot. I — I have a st — I'm of the conviction that John
will then turn to me and say, "George, what d'ya think of this, that,
and the other thing?" Until we get to that spot, we're nowhere until
we get there. We can get there when — if it's — you're — you're at
4¢. You're not at — y — y — it's your — it was your bottom-of-the-
barrel deal, you've looked over the other and you've consulted with
your people on it — your Board of Directors, or whoever (pause) —
and you gave it serious consideration but you prefer it to continue under the terms of the contract. Then we'll take it from there.

[Mediator leaves room momentarily to find a cushion for Loring.]

Loring: Well, I hope we make real progress, Observer. (Pause)

Observer: I hope you finish it off today, for your sakes. (Slight pause)

Loring: I'd like to finish it off before lunch. (Laughs, as does Observer)
Thank you, George.

Mediator: Right. (Pause) So, if you're ready (Loring: We'll go in now?),
or d'you want — d'you want / time —

Loring: (Over Mediator above) No, I'm ready.

Mediator: O.K.

Joint Meeting - A (10:03 A.M.)

Mediator: When we recessed last the union had submitted a proposal to
the company, a proposal that called for the company's considerating
— consideration of a — of waiving the next October's reopener, and
the company said that they would consider that and report back to this
meeting. Prior to that, negotiations were being conducted or approached on a basis of — well, where we last left it, the union had
proposed 7¢ and the company had proposed 4¢. Following that proposal came the new proposal, the waiving of the next October reopener. So, the company's was to consider that, so at this point we'll
pick it up there and, Len, you take it from there.

Loring: Well, we've gone back to the company with your proposal and
given very serious — very thorough discussion and consideration.
We've come to the conclusion that we prefer to negotiate on a basis
of the contract — wind up this 6-months' reopener and then worry
about the October one when it comes. There've been one or 2 things
that I would like to throw out on the table. I have talked to ya about
the things that we're concerned about — the uncertainties this year.
Now, these 2 things strike me as bearing out somewhat the things
that I've talked to you about. I just today got the billing for the last
period, and it's down to a million and three-quarters. Well, that's
some 2 or $250,000.00 less than the first period. The trend has
started. Our incoming order rate, particularly on standard recorders, which is the one we use as a — more as a bellwether of the incoming orders, was down last week considerably and this week is
running down from what it has been. I just mention this to point out
that we see these uncertainties. We certainly don't say they're gonna
happen, but there are some — some little indi — in — indications that

we might well be right. In view of that, I'd like to restate the company's position as we gave it last, that is, that we offer $3\frac{1}{2}$¢ per hour across-the-board and a nickel an hour to the skilled trades. We feel that, in view of all the indications, all the conditions, is a fairly good offer. (Pause)

Gambon: Well, in effect you are offerin' me, as you put it, 4-cent package, then?

Loring: Yes, John.

Gambon: Uh-huh. Accordin' to your estimates. Well, Number 1, I'm not too surprised and — about this business of incoming orders perhaps dropping off a bit because I think those kind of things do occur where there's a possibility of a strike situation. For your information, of course, the Navy people have been calling me — they've prob'ly been calling you (Loring smiles and nods) — wanting — wanting to know when the strike will occur, if it will occur, and I've had to tell 'em exactly what the situation is, that at this point there has been no decision made to call a strike although it can be called at any time. You mentioned quite a number of things at one of our last meetings, Len, about the concern you've had about business and so forth, and it's interesting to note that the N.E.M.A. industry report dated April 15th, 1953, to me, at least, points a very — points up a very optimistic picture, and I'd like to comment on a couple of 'em for y — for you, and you prob'ly have seen this, and I'd like to quote a — from a speech that a Mr. Mentor made. He made a speech for the president of the N.E.M.A. xxxxx (Loring: Uh-huh. Uh-huh) business. And he said in part here: "Looking to the future," Mr. Mentor said, "the growth of our industry during the past decade has been phenomenal and there is every reason to believe that it will continue in the years ahead. While the current high rate of military spending probably will decline somewhat as we near our rearmament goals, it is certain that it will continue at a high level and not in our lifetime return to the low point it reached immediately after World War II, and the percentage of military expenditure on electronics will increase as we move further into the field of robot — robot-controlled planes and guided missiles." (Pause) We have another statement credited to Peterson, who, I believe, is the general counsel for N.E.-M.A., in (Loring says something) which he predicts that the "Industrial electronics is on the threshold of a tremendous development and the small manufacturer will be just as vital in this field as he has been in the growth of radio, television, and other communications devices." I don't know whether you still consider yourselves a small manufacturers. I — I don't. Peterson also stated in his speech, in part here — at least I'm quoting from him — "One has only to look into the history of the big industrial corporations today to realize that most of them were small business yesterday." I think this applies pretty much to Atlas. "This is particularly true of the recorder industry where practically all of the old and well-established manufacturers began operations on a small scale." Then he continues during his speech that, "While there are no doubt many gaps in the government and industry programs for aiding small business, complaints and fears of small electronic manufacturers, so far as defense production is concerns, have practically disappeared. No doubt this has been due, in part, to the gradual increase in sub-contract and the maintainence of substantial civilian production which together have kept the small manufacturer busy even though he may have had no price contracts.''

[Tape changed]

... Recorder production for the week ending April 5th amounted to 154,860 units compared with 149,735 the week of March 29th. I mean, it's constantly recorder production is going upward, and I don't see any indications in these reports of any kind of a black picture which seems to be concerning you people at Atlas. (Slight pause)

Loring: John, I — even I — let's put it that way — even I feel that the long range prospects for all electronics is excellent. I think it's — the prospects are as good as for any industry in the country. When you're talking long range you're talking anywhere from now to 5 or 10 years from now. (Gambon: Uh-huh) I — I s — I agree they — they look good. Now, with regard to production and the reports ya have there, that is exactly the same situation that occurred in 1951 the first part of the year, and everybody was optimistic. Production kept increasing each week, and then it fell on its face the last half. Now, with regard to Peterson, with apologies to Erv — maybe George, I don't know — he's an attorney, and I don't know what your experience with attorneys has been but I've found that they aren't businessmen for the most part. They — they put up a case. Excuse me, Erv. (Espig laughs heartily, then one of girls laughs) I can't disagree with what's in there, John. I just say that we think there are uncertainties / in —

Gambon: (Over Loring above) Confucianists. (Loring laughs, as does someone else) Experts. (Pause) Well, I wanted to point out that the fears that you people have been expressing here don't seem to be general in the industry. (Pause) You see (slight pause), here's this chap, Ty Hennigan, who is chairman of the N.E.M.A. Home Appliances Divisions. He reports that home recorder manufacturers are enjoying good business conditions. (Rather long pause) H'm! I mean that — that everything that I read in here from your own organizational reports indicate a good year and particularly a — a very bright outlook on the long-range program. / Uh —

Loring: (Over Gambon above) Well, long range, I agree, and up till now it is a good year. Thing I'm pointing out is these uncertainties (Gambon: Uh-huh), John. And keep — and — and I think you realize that (Gambon: Well, there's uncertainty in anything. Life itself is uncertain these days) there's a certain amount of propaganda so they don't — they don't wanta discourage people in these reports, either.

Gambon: Well, I don't think that they publish reports — at least I would hope that they wouldn't publish reports which were not — would not be factual information. (Loring: I would certainly hope so, too) I think you would — gettin' in reports like that, if it wasn't factual information you'd pretty quickly withdraw your membership there, to which I understand you have to pay a certain amount of money as a membership —

Meyer: Dues.

Gambon: — dues.

Loring: That's right.

Gambon: But I would feel the same way if I were getting reports from
my International union which weren't factual. But I can't — I can't
find, in the industry generally, any — anything that would indicate the
type of thing that you're worrying about here, particularly in the face
of a trend that's moving upward in ra — in recorder production. The
production of the deluxe units is off a little bit every once in a while,
according to these reports, one week against the other, but it's keeping pace pretty generally with the over-all recorder trend, particularly in smaller units — lightweight portables and things like that —
indicating a increased production in those items. (Loring: Well —)
We — since you have restated your position, of course, I think I should
restate our position at this point in that we are requesting the 10-cent-
per-hour general wage increase and 20% fixed bonus for skilled trades
and other day workers, with the understanding that the union will waive
the October 1st, 1953, reopener. Now, I can appreciate the company's
wanting to let October 1st, 1953, take care of itself. (Rather long
pause) I — under some circumstances I might agree with ya that I
would be willing to do that. But I think that both of us ought to face up
to realities here, and I think that you may be able to see my position,
Len, in that this is the 3rd time in — since this contract that we have
listened to the company, in effect, complain about the reopeners themselves. And it's strange to me that when we talk about waiving a reopener, which I thought would be received with open arms by the company, that we find that they say, "Well, we — we wanta continue to let
the reopening in October take care of itself." Now, if that's a bargaining — bargaining position, all well and good. But think that, from
the union's standpoint, since the company has complained, as it were,
about these reopeners that we ought to try to settle up this question of
increased benefits for the duration of this contract, in order that
there'll be no question of any possible stoppages again in October,
'53, and particularly since I think it would put the company in a position of making their plans on a much more certain basis than they can
if they still have to face up to a October 1st reopener. I'm talking now
from the company's standpoint as I see it. From the standpoint of the
— the union's position, we're interested, of course, in settling on that
basis, because I don't want to have to, during the same year, possibly
have 2 stoppages, if that's what it's goin' to amount to. Now, I recognize, as well as the company, of course, that October 1st, 1953, may
not be a desirable time of the year to go on strike, but I can assure
you that we (laughing slightly) would press much harder in August
and September, let's say, of '53 to get negotiations started before
October 1st than we allowed to happen this time. I think there's —
there was too much delay in this particular thing, getting these negotiations started. We should never have been up to the point we are
now, where we're up to April 18th. We should have been into this long
while ago. (Pause) I want to make it clear that sooner or later we're
gonna have to say to you something that we haven't said to this point,
because I'm still hopeful that we can get these negotiations settled in
an amicable way across this table. But sooner or later — I mean, Len,
time is running out and we're gonna have to set up a deadline here and
start working against it, if that's what's gonna be — it's — that's what's
needed to — to bring these things to a conclusion. Now, as I look at

this particular situation, I see nothing wrong in talking about the — waiving the reopener and approaching negotiations on that point, because (pause) I think the company would be up against the same pressures in October 1st, '53, that they're up against right now, and I think it would be good from both sides if wha — that pressure were removed until the expiration of this contract, at which time we could review the entire year of '53 with very certain things hav — having occurred rather than these suppositions that both of us may have at the time, one of which, in your case, is a sort of a fear complex of certain things happening, the other, on our part — I suppose company calls that an optimistic view of what's gonna happen in '53. I think we're in a better position, of course, to defend our optimistic position, based on the company's financial position and the trends, than the company is to support its position about these fears in the face of existing trends. I don't know much else I can say about it, Len. (Pause) If it is a bargainable proposition of saying that "We would rather let October 1st take care of itself," I would appreciate your committee again going back into session and approach — trying to approach this problem on winding up these negotiations until the e — expiration of the contract on April 1st, '54, at which time we can fight again.

Loring: John, there's no question but what the company is extremely anxious to settle this amicably and no question but what that nobody in the company that wants to settle 'em any quicker than I do, right at this point. (Laughs) Uh — (slight pause).

Gambon: Well, do you have the / authority, now, to settle this thing?

Loring: (Over Gambon above) Yes. Yes, we do, John.

Gambon: Uh-huh.

Loring: We have had, right along.

Gambon: Are you in a position to bargain on the basis of waiving a reopener or are you under instructions to reject that entirely?

Loring: We have — as I pointed out, John, the company has discussed that very thoroughly, and they prefer to bargain on the 6-months' reopener.

Gambon: You prefer it. But I'm askin' you, are you limited as to whether you can bargain / on that?

Loring: (Over Gambon above) Yes. We've decided that we want to stick to the contract (Gambon: Uh-huh) and bargain on the 6-months' reopener.

Gambon: Well, then I suppose that would take a decision of the Board of Directors to decide whether they wanta bargain on this proposition or not. (Loring: Uh —) That is, a — a reconsideration of the issue, if — let us suppose, for the moment, that retaining the 2 positions we have now that you have forced the union into a position of sayin', "Len, this is it. Here's a deadline. Now, we wanta bargain on our basis." That would then take, I think, on your part a call to find out whether they wanta change it or whether they wanta leave us in a position of saying, "Your offer at this point is — is rejected. This is what we wanta bargain with. This is what we want and what we're willing to bargain with." And in the face of the company's refusing to bargain on that basis, we'd be forced to take a strike. Now, I wanta find that out. I mean, I think if we can't find that out you're forcing me to take a position here.

Loring: John, when I say the company has considered this it hasn't been the Board of Directors, but the people that made the decision would be the majority of the Board of Directors. (Gambon: Uh-huh) I mean, the decision would be the same.

Gambon: Well, in effect it would be the same. Yeah.

Loring: Uh-huh. (Pause) We feel that we agreed that we would look at the problem every 6 months. We wanta do that. / And —

Gambon: (Over Loring above) Yeah, but looking at it doesn't mean anything in the face of our experiences, Len. I mean, we've sat down and wrote out a contract with these r — reopen — reopeners speci — cifically spelled out. And at least — I said 3 before; I should c — correct that and say at least twice, now. In October, '52, we got the story, I mean, from the company, "We don't wanta do anything. We wanta use the money some other way." And we got into quite a hassle then. We finally reached a — a — a settlement at that time which, if my memory serves me right, was in — somewhere around the figure of 3¢, and the union went along with that reopener and that kind of a settlement because we <u>had</u> taken a pretty good bite out of you in the early part of '52. Despite the fact that we took a good (Someone laughs quietly) bite outa you, it did not make up the differentials for us that existed between the other plants around this area that you've used in your comparisons in these discussions. And we are still behind that parade. Again this time we have listened to the same kind of thing. Now, I mean, the — the attitude that we usually get is that, "Well, we have no objections to discussing these things with you," but it's always, "We don't wanta do anything about it!" Now, I know and you know we're gonna get the same kind of a story in October 1st, 1953! And it seems senseless to me to be developin' these things — th — these crises where you — nobody knows what's gonna happen and everybody is on the verge of nervous breakdown, I suppose — on the part of the union people, "When are we gonna go out?", on the part of the company, "<u>Are</u> they gonna go out or are they not?", and then you got your customers all upset and everything else. I think it's a sensible proposition! I think it's not only a sensible proposition, but one of the things that have been — more or less influenced <u>my</u> particular opinions about this is that I find that a great many of our unions now are closing out the negotiations on the basis of a year, and I think that it would be very much in keeping for us to try to do this in order to maintain at least some sort of good relationship with the company for the balance of the contract, without any further crisis bein' developed in October of 1953. (Pause) I don't know what to say beyond that point, and I think I'm in a position to have to turn this back to George, with only the repetition of what I said before on the point of, you're forcing us into a position here — taking a position of setting up a deadline (pause) — well, a deadline, as (laughing slightly) far as that goes, of <u>any</u> time a'tall if that's what it's gonna take to move us out of the proposition of 3½ and 5 additional for skilled trades <u>and</u> the reopener in October 1st, '51. (Pause)

Loring: Well, I think we prob'ly have to turn it over to you, George.

Mediator: Very well, I would like to meet with the union committee, so, if you'll retire to the other room, I'll join you over there.

Union Caucus - A (10:31 A.M.)

Gambon: Will you turn it off just a minute, Observer, please?
[The recorder is turned off. Gambon, referring to a slip he is holding in his hand, asks, "Who wrote this note?" He reads the note,
and Meyer points out the answer she has written on the bottom. Gambon then signals for the recorder to go back on. Rather long pause
follows.]

Mediator: It's evident that (pause) they're not interested in the 6-month
— waiving 6-month. This may sound like a foolish question, but in
your opinion, why? (Slight pause)

Gambon: Well (Mediator: Is there any —), they — they feel, as I am
honestly admitting, that they feel that it would be much more difficult
for us to strike the plant in October, '53, because, Number 1, of the
— the time of the year involved in here, see. (Meyer says something)
And Number 2, they probably feel that if there's a settlement now on
the — with the 6-month reopener in the picture that their position will
be that much more stronger in October in saying to us, "We don't
wanta do anything." In fact, it's my opinion that they'll say very flatly,
"We will not (hitting the table) do anything," and say, "Go ahead and
try to get the people to strike." I mean, it's a bargaining position, as
I see it, George. It's very strict bargaining position on their part. It's
damn good strategy, I might (laughing slightly) say. However, I think
they're entirely wrong if they assume that — that we couldn't develop
the same situation we have today. That's where they're entirely wrong,
because they only judge these things on the basis of what they hear, and
they hear it from the wrong sources. (Slight pause) Now, I'm — I'm
particularly interested in cleaning the thing up, because I don't wanta
have to develop this thing again to a point where there's a strike hangin'
up in the air, see. I'd rather close it out, and if I'm gonna have any
fights with 'em, I'll have a damn good fight with 'em on the expiration
of this contract, and it won't be all over money matters, either. But the
— at this point, as I pointed out to him, and I mean it very sincerely, if
he's gonna continue this position and if they refuse to bargain for the
balance of this contract, then they're gonna force me to take — go into
session with this committee and set up a deadline which c — depending
on their attitude, of bein' to — today, tomorrow, or real damn quick, because I'm not gonna drag this out too much any more. I don't see any
point in draggin' it out any further. And the only way he could get me to
drop this question of one year is to meet the minimum demands of
the union for a reopener, now, see — the 7-cent package proposition.
If he wants to go ahead — go along on that basis, O.K. I'll — I'll —
I'll go ahead and make a settlement with him for the union's minimum
position and take my chances that I have defeated my own purposes
as far as the reopener goes in February of '53. Because the higher
he comes at this particular reopener, the more difficult he makes it
for the union to get anything on the reopener in '53, if that's what he's
tryin' to do. But he's not gonna get that kind of a position with this
4-cent proposition he has. (Pause)

Meyer: There's a correction. You meant reopener October, '53, not
February, / '53.

Gambon: (Over Meyer above) Did I say February? (Meyer: Yeah) I meant October 1st, '53. (Rather long pause) In other words — it may be simplified. If he wants to buy (pause) a position, a strong position, that will enable him on October 1st, 1953, to say No and leave me with the problem of, "What d'we do about it?", he can't buy it for 4¢. He can buy it for 7¢, and I'll take my chances with that No that I know I'm gonna get on October 1st, 1953. It won't be a question i — in '53 — October, '53, of sayin', "Well, we don't wanta do anything. We'd like to use the money elsewhere." It'll be a flat refusal to do anything. That I can foresee right now because of the way these things have been developing. This position on this reopener is a little stronger than the position that they took on October, '52. And I know — I'm — I — I bet money on it / that —

Mediator: (Over Gambon above) You didn't have this many meetings, did you?

Gambon: No-o-o! Hell, no. As I point out, the only reason I didn't fight with 'em as strong as we're stickin' our backs up at this point, in October of '52 was, Number 1, we done all right in '52, as a year, despite the fact that we were still behind. Number 2, I didn't feel as if it was the time and the place to do it — that time of the year, particularly — 'cause we had gotten into October and almost up into November by that time. Hell, we didn't wanta fight in snow shoes.

Meyer: Well, you wouldn't have an Oc — you'd have an October 1 deadline, and that would be Indian summer, / see. (Laughs very slightly)

Gambon: (Over Meyer above) Oh, yeah. Oh, I see. I mean (Meyer says something), that's what I say. If he wants — if he wants to buy this thing, leaving us and himself in a position to take our chances on October 1st, 1953, he can't do it for 4¢. (Pause) I'm — I'm tryin' to assure the membership of this union of getting a fair shake (slight pause) of what's goin' to be done in this company for 1953, and I'm not willing to settle for 4¢ and then tell them — have them tell me to go — go ahead and pound sand on October 1st, '53. I'm willin' to take my chances on it for 7¢ (laughing slightly). (Meyer: Uh-huh) And if I do take my chances on 7¢, as I told him, he could rest assured that they're — we're gonna tie them down to bargaining much before October 1st, because I wouldn't allow myself to get into November on that basis. (Pause) So that, in effect, George, if he wants to continue this — the reopener in the picture, we have reached the minimum position from which we are not going to move. In effect, that's what it is. (Rather long pause) Because I know doggone well that they can afford to do this. I know I'm not puttin' 'em in any position of being strapped or anything else. And they know it. They have not once — again I repeat this — not once have they pleaded about their inability to pay anything here. Always it's this fear complex that they seem to be developing which the industry does — doesn't support! I've been reading these reports. I get 'em every week! It's their own particular organization. And there isn't any of that fear complex involved in this in any section of the — of the industry. (Rather long pause) On the contrary, I mean, we hear their ne — negotiation committee expressing these fears to us, and the president of the company and the chairman of the Board of Directors of the company make very glowing statements in their financial report which indicates just the opposite! Fuller, in effect, says, "We're gonna get our share of this work around here." And the — ya listen to these guys and they're afraid they're not gonna get anything. (Long pause)

Mediator: He's worse than the — Glickman in the last contract negotiation.

Gambon: Well, in effect I would say in — in lots of respects they are, and I think the positions are — at least on the part of the union, is just as firm as we were then. If you recall, the only difference that existed then that doesn't exist at this very moment is that we set a deadline and we reached the minimum position and we didn't budge. We said, "It's up to you to start moving." And in effect that's what I'm telling him. If he's gonna maintain this position, the next caucus that's gonna be held is gonna be a caucus of this committee to set a deadline, you see. Now, if he's gonna — if he wants to — to — to have us do that in order to ha — convince him that he's gotta come up to that 7-cent minimum package of ours with the reopener in the picture, we'll do it for him. I'll do that very quickly. If he wants to bargain for — on the basis of closing out the reopener and finishing the bargaining on this question of wages and fringes until the cons — expiration of the contract, I'm willin' to do that. In fact, I'm saying, in effect, we have a minimum position for 6 months; we have a bargainable proposition of 10 plus the 20% fixed bonus for the closing o — until the closing of the contract. (Rather long pause)

Mediator: As early as this morning — take this for what it's worth (pause), coming from Loring — Len Loring who is, in my opinion, a neophyte negotiator. (Pause)

Gambon: No, don't get the opinion that he's naive. / Huh-un.

Mediator: (Over Gambon above) No? Well (Gambon: As I said before, I never saw a New Englander that didn't know how to take care of money), I felt that as far as leading negotiations, he's a newcomer.

Gambon: He's been in negotiations —

Mediator: Oh, / has he?

One of boys: (Over Mediator above) Almost / every year.

Gambon: (Over boy above) Oh, yeah. He's been in in every negotiations we've had with the company for quite a few years, now. / He's not a novitiate.

Mediator: (Over Gambon above) Well, then I'd better take some of that back.

Gambon: H'm. (Mediator: Uh —) He has — this is the first time, of course, that he has led the negotiating committee. But he has taken a very active part for the company, particularly on the question of finances. (Mediator: Uh-huh) That's one of the principal reasons I believe that he's always been a member of the company's negotiating team.

Mediator: Well, then, I'll lay that aside and not rate him as a neophyte. But coming from him the way it has, this morning — as early as this morning — I feel you oughta know this because the sooner ya know it the sooner (Gambon: Uh-huh) we're going to not have an agreement or have an agreement. Now, he said that on your minimum demands that there can be no settlement at 7¢. (Gambon: Uh-huh) (Pause) On the other, he's expressed himself. I, personally, would like to see and had hoped that they came in with their mind open on a year contract (Gambon: Uh-huh), because I think it's going to be better for the — th — both the union (Gambon: H'm) and the company.

Gambon: So do I! I honestly feel that, George.

Mediator: So I waited until this morning and I had some thinking on it that I would have expressed if they had been amenable to the principle of the thing (Gambon: Uh), but since they aren't, there was just no need of talking about it. I prefer it very much because — before these negotiations would have concluded I would have proposed it before the — however — if the union hadn't or the company hadn't, eventually I'da got to it, as I usually do in these things. I try to get rid of re-openers because — especially in state (pause) of economics that we have now — you know, the index (Gambon: H'm) and so forth. (Pause) So, he's practically closed that door. About the only thing that's — that I have in front of me to work on is the positions of the 2 parties — the 4 and the 7. You, on one hand, say, "If he's — doesn't consider our proposals for a year, 7¢ is the price." He, on the other hand, says that can never be. And there's where we stand. Now, I would like very much — I'm repeating myself again, but it's wishful thinking — I don't even think it's the — your price that scared them, / or —

Gambon: (Over Mediator above) H'm?

Mediator: I don't think your price for a year's contract had much to do with it. Maybe it did, but I'm inclined to think, if reading between his lines this morning, that they were discussing the thing from an entirely different position (Gambon: H'm) than price.

Gambon: That's correct. I think so, too. Very strongly.

Mediator: I don't imply — I don't mean to (Gambon: Uh-huh) imply that even if they were agreed in principle that they would buy at your price. I don't mean that. I don't mean that they — I — I should say this. They probably have enough money to do it but wouldn't. (Gambon: Uh-huh) But I had ideas for that, but they were dashed when he came in. / Uh —

Gambon: (Over Mediator above) But I — I don — I'm not convinced that he has (pause) taken a position so firmly against this 7-cent thing that he's willin' to take a strike. I'm not convinced of that.

Mediator: Well, we're gonna have to find out (Gambon: Uh-huh) soon. I — uh-h-h- / h — if he's playin' — if he's playin' —

Gambon: (Over Mediator above) Well, I — I wanta find out soon, George, so I can tell him, "O.K., you're tellin' me this is it. Now, I'm gonna give ya a deadline, and this is it." / I mean, somepin's gonna have to give.

Mediator: (Over Gambon above) Well, you're gonna be able to get there today because (Gambon: Oh, yes! I wanta get there today) I'm tied up tomorrow in the Aero situation. (Gambon: Uh-huh) I think we'll have the Aero people in here if it doesn't develop into a jurisdictional dispute.

Gambon: And I'm buckin' a straight (Mediator: Uh —) deadline in Plattsville tomorrow. (Laughs slightly) (Pause) May as well buck 2 at the same time. (Rather long pause)

Meyer: Can exchange pickets.

Gambon: H'm?

Meyer: We can exchange pickets.

Gambon: Yeah, set up a shuttle line.

Mediator: Where? Aero and here?

Meyer: No. Plattsville and here. (Slight pause) Change of scenery while we're at it.

Gambon: Bring a couple of Advance Design signs down. They cry the blues about Advance's bein' a competitor. Advance's a little company like that. Christ, we're turnin' down a 3-to-17-cent-an-hour increase up there. It averages out about anywhere from 8 to 9¢.

Mediator: Contract (Gambon: Yeah!) termination?

Gambon: Yeah. (Pause)

Saunders: (In low voice) Same thing.

Gambon: Same thing. I mean, it's protect the dividends and stockholders. Same old cry. I mean, they don't come out and say it that way, but that's what the hell they're tryin' to do in Advance's. And th — these people are tryin' to do the same thing. I — I bet anybody any kind of money that the minute we made a settlement that's way lower than what we think we're entitled to, we assure, right off the bat, the return of the 1951 dividends for the stockholders in Atlas. And we insure very likely a higher profit-sharing proposition for these 114 (Meyer: Here) people, or at least we provide maybe _more_ profit sharing for more people — or, not more profit sharing but more people involved in the profit sharing, because they've been moving that up every year. They haven't done a doggone thing about that. I mean, that's one of the things that burns us up. He's offerin' us 4¢, and they've already given out — f — for the first period of 1953 they've given out the equivalent of a $4\frac{1}{2}$¢ increase for all of our members. Even more than that, George, because we actually have, as of yesterday, about 1250 members. And all those figures that I gave to the company while you were here, of course — for instance, this $4\frac{1}{2}$¢ that I said would — was equal to an increase for 1400 of our people, as against the total amount of money they gave to 114 of their people, that would be higher than $4\frac{1}{2}$¢ for 1250 people. They've already given that to these 114 people. They're not doin' —

[Tape changed]

"... these non-union people will take care of them, and that's none of your business."

Mediator: How long has that profit sharing been in?

Gambon: It started in '50. (One of boys: In '5 —) In '50, the average was over $3,000.00 for 66 people; in '51, it was an average of over $2300.00 for 97 people; in '52, it was an average of over $1500.00 for 114 people. And now they've continued the 114 people, and they've already received an average of somepin' like $900.00 for the first period of 1953.

Meyer: We don't know what they got for the 2d and 3rd. (Gambon: Huhun) The 3rd period's over.

Gambon: See, they get — they'll get their profit on each period. They get theirs! If the company was to lose money (Meyer: Yeah) for a couple of periods, they wouldn't get anything, see.

Meyer: They don't give it / back, either.

Gambon: (Over Meyer above) But they wouldn't have to give it back. But if the company loses money in a p — couple of periods and we come in for a wage increase, then they start tellin' us, "Oh, we can't give you anything. Look, we lost some money." In effect, he started to try to bring out that this 3rd period, which would be the — from the (Meyer: To the 13th of April) — from the (One of boys says something) 11th to the 15th week the 3rd period would pay. See, each one of their

accounting periods is for 5 weeks, so that they have 10 periods per year. Now, he's talkin' about things — sales and orders droppin' down a little bit. Well, that's not — that's understandable! Christ, they got a publicized strike situation on their hands! Guy from the Navy called me the other day. He's all hot and bothered about it. He wants (laughing slightly) to know if there's gonna be a strike. I told him — I said, "You better call Atlas and ask 'em." I says, "As far as I'm concerned there isn't any necessity for a strike if Atlas can see the light. But," I said, "if they're gonna continue to — to take the same position they're takin' now, it looks to me as if they're gonna get themselves a strike." (Pause) At the same time — same thing last time when we had the — the strike vote up. All — all of a sudden the — the Defense Procurement Agency start gettin' all interested. "What's gonna happen in here?", see. I asked the guy — I said, "What are you tryin' to do? Pressure me?" "Oh, no, no, Mr. Gambon." I said, "Well, don't bother," I said, "because I'm not gonna subject myself to that kind of pressure." (Pause)
[For the balance of the caucus Gambon and Mediator swap stories about their experiences with government agencies which try to intercept industrial negotiations. Discussion brings out the fact that Atlas was formerly on the government's "critical list," while manufacturing sensitized tape for use in fire control recorders in Korea. After a pause, the topic shifts back abruptly to the Atlas case.]
Mediator: Wait a minute.
Gambon: All right.
[The recorder goes back on to catch Gambon's parting message to Mediator on the way out.]
... in the — I'm gonna be prepared, see. I'm gonna c — have a caucus with my committee here on this question of setting a deadline. You can tell 'em that in there.
Mediator: Yeah.

Management Caucus - B (10:57 A.M.)

Mediator: Len, that was well done. That — that was well done, and it — it was the right tact. D'you notice the pressure (Loring: H'm) that came back for the —
Loring: Yeah.
Mediator: And he wants that, see. He wants a year's contract.
Pranis: Why, George? / xx?
Mediator: (Over Pranis above) Uh — he wants a year's contract at — and — and there could be 2 reasons, I think: (1) (pause), I think he's sincere when he says he don't wanta be bothered with it (Pranis: H'm) in 6 months. I think you or someone here talks about his outside activities. (Pranis: Uh-huh) I think he has a lot of other work. (Slight pause) I think he knows about how much he can get next year, he knows about how much he can get this year, and he — or he thinks he knows and is approximating — and he'd like to wrap it all up so that he wouldn't have to come back. And I think that's one. And I think the other is the one I mentioned, that psychologically it will be an advantage to him is to be — to know that they're not gonna have another

situation 6 months from now. And it's — it's — it's a mild or psychological form of security which he can enjoy right now, if he has it. Now, I think for — for these — I don't know if there are any others.

Pranis: He mentioned pressure on both of us. D'you think that indicated he had pressures on him?

Mediator: Well, I think he meant, when he used the word pressures, bargaining pressures — the (Pranis: Oh) going through the throes of this and you not knowing whether you're gonna have a strike and him not knowing whether he has to pull his people out. I think that's what he meant by pressure. (Pause) Are you people caucusing?

Loring: No. No. No.

Mediator: But, you see, if you had opened your mind to that subject this morning you — you would have <u>killed</u> the effectiveness of this meetings today (Loring: Yeah. That's right) — the meetings. Now, you can't afford — soon as he finishes I'll give ya a (Loring: Yeah) full report (Loring: Uh-huh) on what took our discussion here and how I think the thing had to go. And it's going all right. He showed disappointment. Now, a man that shows disappointment, his mind is open on that question. What's <u>in</u> his mind or how far he'll go to buy that we have to find out. (Loring: Yeah) But you're not gonna find out now, immediately.

Loring: I could see what you said was — worked out, because you — as you said, he couldn't possibly evidence <u>any</u> interest or else we might just as well quit and come back.

Mediator: That's right! Now, he knows, too — and you have an out. He even touched on it. He t — he said something about, "I might have to call back the people to reconsider," or something like that. Well, you're firm right now, and you — you're standing there. Now, there's nothing in the book says that if he gave you an attractive offer that you wouldn't have the right to reconsider. That stands in <u>any</u> negotiations! So your door is open. (Loring: Uh-huh) Well (pause), he (slight pause) reiterated to me, after you people left, that he wants a year's contract. If he can't get it — if the company won't bargain — bargain on those terms, then his <u>minimum</u> is 7¢ for settlement of <u>this</u>. So I said, "Well, John, if that's the case, you'd better prepare for a strike. If your mind is closed at 7¢, you're gonna <u>have</u> a strike. Might be wrong that you could have a strike." I said, "Now, personally, I'm in favor of a year's contract in <u>any</u> situation. I'm not one that favors 6-month reopeners. They're a nuisance. And," I said, "I would have been very happy if the company had said to you, 'All right, we'll go along on your proposition.' But" — and I said, "I had some thoughts on it that I would have thrown into this meeting but they were dashed when the company said they didn't want to talk about it" — er — "that they had talked about it and were satisfied to continue under the contract." I wanted John to know that it — see, I wanta get from John his real thinking. That's all I'm after. I'm not tryin' to short-change him; I'm tryin' to (Loring: Yeah) draw him <u>out</u> so that he'd lay his <u>real</u> thinking on the board. And if his <u>real</u> thinking is good and attractive, we want it! You wanta look at it, anyway. (Loring: Sure) That's what I wanta do. I want ya to (Loring: Uh-huh) — and <u>I</u> wanta look at it. May be the answer! <u>Then</u> if we see that it's not an interesting or attractive proposal and an impossible one, well, then you know then that you're gonna have to center your guns on the other

kind of negotiations — the reopener. And — now, here's the way
we're shaping up now. John is startin' to talk tough in here at this
caucus, which is fine, and I think we're gonna have a crisis on our
hands today, which I want. I'm very much in favor of it. Well, I
wisht it would come soon! The sooner the better for these meetings.

Espig: I hate to dash it, but a member of the Executive Board, who isn't
in here, has said that there can't be any strike till May the 1st.
(Laughs slightly)

Loring: Well, that's rumor. Ya can't (Espig continues to laugh quietly)
(Mediator: Uh —) — I discount all those x.

Espig: (Still laughing) I just (Mediator: Well, May 1) men — I — I just
wanted to see — see what — see / xxx.

Mediator: (Over Espig above) Oh, I think I — I — he mentioned that date.
Isn't that the anniversary date of a strike ya had? (Slight pause)

Espig: I think it is.

Loring: The only strike they ever had was an organizational / strike.

Mediator: (Over Loring above) Was that on May 1?

Loring: I don't know. That's back in '33, I think.

Mediator: Well, I don't know why — what significance is attached to May
1, but I heard that date.

Espig: This is the 3rd time. Now, I'm gonna give you — / I mean, telling it to you because it comes from a member of the —

Mediator: (Over Espig above) Uh — ordinarily in these negotiations or
somewhere along the line, but (rather long pause) — here's what you
have to do from here on in, as you do in any negotiations. You —
you're — f — from — from here on in you're going into a cold war. Y —
you're — you're really — this — this is goin' to be the test. (Loring:
Uh-huh) (Pause) I say to you, don't — don't show any signs of crack-
ing, no matter how rough it goes, because I know I have the situation
in hand. (Loring: Uh-huh) I won't let their — the meeting break up
without knowing well in advance — now, I may even — I may even, if
we can't get it resolved, let 'em go, because I'm — I'm quite sure that
they still have a few motions to go through yet. Now, the sooner they
get through those and the sooner John expends those, the sooner John
is going to talk business. But there is still an opportunity — now,
John would like to avoid that, so because of that, see, we have a bargaining point, or we have an area where he might make an agreement
today, to avoid getting into this (Loring: Yeah) cold war. As he said,
ya could h — ya — we could both get ner — nervous breakdown. I
think he means that! But I'd — by the same token, I'm inclined to
agree that there is time somewhere. How much I don't know yet! Now,
he said, "We're gonna set a deadline if they don't move." "Well,"
I said, "that's up to you." He said, "Well, we're gonna caucus now
while you're talking to the company." So don't be surprised that —
when we go back if they say to you, "Well, we've talked this over and
we're goin' to do X, Y, and Z on th — on a certain date." Now, whatever date that will be or whatever he's going to say, I don't know, but
what — the sooner he gets to that point, the better, because we're
gonna be here all (Loring: Uh-huh) day, anyway.

Loring: Well, you don't see any early settlement?

Mediator: See, John is in a frame of mind where — if this was — if he
was handling this differently, as it should be handled, this would have
been settled a long time ago. But John is making it difficult for

himself by playing games — bargaining games. Now, if he was another u — another leader — a union leader would do this. He'da
called me on the phone in a situation like this and say, "All right,
George, we threw 14¢ out" — isn't that what he threw out for a 2-
year — / a year contract?

Loring: (Over Mediator above) Yeah. Yeah.

Mediator: — "but in order that you can know where we're going, in order
that you don't break off the meetings thinking we're stuck there, we're
nego — we can negotiate. Now, we think that there's a figure there
that the company and us will agree on." All right, then I know how to
operate. Now, John hasn't done that. Now, John plays — well, I had
no idea he was shooting out that proposal — that 1-year the other
night. (Loring: Uh-huh) That came right out of (Loring: H'm) the
sky, which was good it did, but I had no inkling or idea that it was
coming. And, in order to direct these negotiations I should know a
lot of those things. But then, on the other hand, I can't complain, because when I call him in side-bar he <u>does</u> cooperate. You know, he
let me know about the 7, days <u>before</u>. Now, before the day is out I'll
have to have another side-bar with him, if I — we can't get it outa
there. But I want — I think it would be healthy for them to go through
these tough statements, and I think you'll haveta ride through it.
(Loring: Uh-huh. And not move) The sooner the better.

Loring: We don't move at — at this point at all.

Mediator: No. I don't think you should. I don't think there's a — any
move here, you just make it tougher for yourselves (Loring: Yeah)
and the — the negotiations because, see, don't — don't lose sight of
this. John knows that — that he's in an area now where it's nip and
tuck. It can be a settlement, it can be a strike. He knows he's in the
danger area. (Pause) (Loring: Yeah) If there was any indication
that there was a crack in your bargaining defense you would als —
you would be making it difficult for John, because then John would
have to go after that, where, if your line is held right now, you're
gonna make it easier for John when it comes times today — late today
— for John to say to his committee, if we have developed something,
"Look, I'm pretty well convinced that they won't go for any more
than this." So will the committee be. It'll be easier for John to <u>sell</u>
whatever kind of a settlement can be arranged if this kind of a bargaining position is taken. Many times employers make it difficult for
the union leaders by indicating to the full committee early that their
minds are open to a c — certain thing. Now, you know how much you
have to give. Now, it's just a question of timing — getting the time
— right time when <u>that</u> that you have will have the best chance. That's
simply what we're doing today. John, on the other hand, has another
proposition that <u>he has not laid</u> on the table completely. Now, what —
he <u>will</u> when <u>you</u> — when he sees there's no crack in your de — the
bargaining defenses. In order to crack through them, he'll either
throw a new proposal out to you or he will, in side-bar, say to me,
"Look. We wanta wrap this thing up. We'll do this, that, or the
other thing." Somethin's goin' to happen some time today — <u>one</u> of
those things. Now, it's just riding it through. (Loring: Uh-huh) See,
I wanta give you a little preview so that you'll (Loring: Yeah) be able
to follow it. (Loring: Uh-huh) It's goin' to go that way, but of course
it's gonna look pretty dark at times, so be prepared for that.

Loring: O.K. You just keep your finger on it. That's all, George.

Mediator: It's on there.

Loring: O.K.

Mediator: But it's gotta go through that way. Well, I'm gonna kill a little time, prob'ly for about another 15 minutes. I'm gonna take a little recess, because I've said to you all I could (Loring says something) say at this caucus, and later — we'll go back then.

[At 11:12 A.M. Mediator leaves the management caucus room and goes alone to his own office. Shortly afterward he sends for Observer, to whom he outlines his next step. He intends, he says, to call Gambon out of the union caucus room and to put to him the question of his deadline.]

Management Caucus - C (12:02 P.M.)

Mediator: Eh! We were just in a huddle, Observer and I (pause). We had our heads together tryin' to work out some math here. We think we have the answer but we wanta check it thoroughly with you. (Rather long pause) You're — I got — I was able to get John out. I called John out of the room and went into a side-bar with him. I said, "John, I've gotta know the timing on this thing." See, this May 1 thing you mentioned bothered me a little. And I said (pause), "If you have to go through some motions yet and you feel you haven't used them and you want to use them, fine and dandy, but I wanta be in on it so that I don't seriously push for a settlement that couldn't be accepted." "Well," he said, "I've got the answer for ya." He said, "When the company comes back, we're givin' 'em their notice. We're going to strike the plant Mon — Saturday morning."

Loring: Saturday morning?

Mediator: Saturday morning. (Pause) "Well," I said, "that answers that!" I said (pause), "All right," I said, "now we're comin' to the point where I'm going to have to recess these conferences if I don't see some daylight there. Now, they're — company's fixed at 4¢ and you're fixed at 7. Now," I said, "I haven't even tried for a settlement nor am I going to try, at this stage of the negotiations, unless I know that a settlement will be bought." I said, "Remember, the company has the money; and if I go in to the company and say, 'Look. I don't think you should have a strike. You should settle this thing. And you should move away from your position,' and the company would say to me, 'What would settle?', then I couldn't answer them! And," I said, "I am not going to try to settle this unless I know I have a buyer. And you have got to tell me what you're going to buy. And if you think it's 7¢, go ahead and strike. You won't get it! Or maybe I've been exposed too long to the company caucuses. But they tell me 7¢ is not there. Now, I say to you, if you want a settlement you gotta tell me." He said, "Well, what d'ya think is there?" I said, "I don't know and I'm not goin' to even try to find out until I know you're gonna buy. You tell me what!" Then he switched back onto the 1-year, without answering. And he said, "We — we feel as though if they — we want the year — we wanta get rid of these negotiations in October." He said, "George, they're a general pain in the neck." And he said, "They oughta be all wrapped up together." I

said, " Well, what do you — what will wrap 'em up? Even that," I
said, "the company has t — given you their answer, but even there I
don't know!" I said, "Let us s — assume that I could persuade the
company to change its position. What would I persuade them on?
Just a change? I got to know, John!" (Pause) So we got — then
got — we — he — he — we — he gave me his position. Now, we got
into a maze of figures which are not clear to me, and I'm sure they're
not accurate. We're tried to work them out. Now, he said any settlement that is made has to include the 20% for the day workers. I think
he said 183 people is involved. And he said that is a must. (?: H'm)
(Rather long pause) I said, "Look, before ya go into the details, the
cost is one of the things I am pre — I'm primarily interested so I can
follow you. It's difficult for me, an outsider, to be able to follow you
— when you start talkin' about percentages for day workers, I don't
know the cost of that, so when you tell me what you'll settle for, tell
me in cash. I can follow that better. You're at 14¢ for a 1-year contract. What will you settle for?" "Well," he said, "I'm going to
prove to you and to the company that their cost — total cost for the
20% — or their estimated cost is not accurate. They say it cost $4\frac{1}{2}$¢."
He said, "I'm gonna prove it cost $2\frac{1}{2}$¢." "Well," I said, "I don't
know. If you can prove it to the satisfaction of the company, fine!
That lowers the package." So he says, "Actually I'm at $12\frac{1}{2}$."
"Well," I said, "all right, assuming you are. What's gonna settle it
for a year and a — what's gonna settle it for a year?" Now, I'm goin'
to give you a picture — I'm gonna give you the whole thing as he gave
it to me. It may be more and it may be less, but I actually think it's
his fighting position. As I figured it out it comes to around 9¢ for a
year. I think so. It may be more, may be less, and may be a lot
more, if our figures aren't right. So will you mathematicians get
your pencils ready (Loring: O.K., George), see if we can't figure
this thing out. Now, here's what he says he would settle for. Now,
generally, when he meets me in side-bar and gives this to me, it's —
it's generally his fighting position, as it was with the 7. Now, I
(Loring: Uh-huh) don't think he's kidding on this. I think he's — it's
his fixed position, but I think with you he's goin' to argue higher
(Loring: Uh-huh) than 9¢. You're gonna get that for a couple of
hours, I'm sure. (Pause) 5 c — 5¢ an hour for your people — for
everybody (Loring: Uh-huh), now — 5¢ across-the-board (Loring:
Uh-huh) (pause); for a final settlement, 10% for the day workers —
or that proposition, whatever it is — you understand it, don't ya?
Loring: Yeah. Yeah.
Mediator: — which he says costs a cent and a quarter (pause); 5¢ more
across-the-board in October. (Pause)
Pranis: For who, George?
Mediator: Everybody. Across-the-board. And 10 more % in October
for the day workers, or same propo — (voice dies). Now, what does
that average out for a month, taking — having his figures — using his
figures, not your — not the correct figures, if there are correct fig-
ures, but using his?
Loring: Well, see. That's in — the first one is a nickel, of course.
(Mediator: Uh-huh) (Pause) The — forget the day workers, now.
The 2d nickel is equal to $2\frac{1}{2}$ right now, isn't it? (Slight pause)

Pranis: Why?

Loring: Because it's 6 months away.

Mediator: That's right.

Pranis: Oh! All right. Then, on the — (pause).

Loring: Now, the 10% for day workers (slight pause) — he says $2\frac{1}{2}$¢?

Mediator: Uh (Loring: No) — 20 — for 20%, it's $2\frac{1}{2}$; for 10%, he says $1\frac{1}{4}$. Now, let's use his figures. (Loring: Uh-huh. Well —) Let's use his.

Loring: Well, the 20% — let's see. 10% would be $1\frac{1}{4}$ (slight pause), and then —

Mediator: For 6 months.

Loring: For 6 — for the — for this one now, and for the 2d one would be half that, or .062 on his figuring. (Mediator: It's gonna be lower) Be .0937, I think.

?: (In very low voice) That's right. (Slight pause)

Loring: Well, his figures are wrong.

Espig: Take 5¢ / out of there.

Mediator: (Over Espig above) Yeah. I — I don't even think he's right on his figures — / his own figures.

Pranis: (Over Mediator above) Wait a minute. Is he still taking the 5¢ out (Espig: Yeah. That's — that's —) that we gave in April to the skilled trades — I mean (Mediator: Yeah), wo — e — for the percentage?

Espig: Yeah.

Mediator: Yeah.

Espig: Because that would create another inequity which he don't wanta live with.

Mediator: Yeah. He wants that out. He takes that out. / Now —

Pranis: (Over Mediator above) Because he got 5¢ an hour, Len, which is $\frac{1}{2}$¢ for a year.

Loring: Now, taking his figures, Bob (Espig: He's takin' —), which presumably (Pranis: Yeah. But —) he's taken 'em out, see?

Pranis: Yeah. But you're saying his figures are low (pause) (Loring: Yeah) because you're comparing them with yours where (Loring: No) you got the nickel in.

Loring: George said to use his figures.

Mediator: No. I said to use (Pranis: Oh) his own figures as — as he gave them to me. (Pranis: H'm) Now, these are the figures he gave me. Now, I said to him — no. Now, what do you get for a total / cost x here?

Loring: (Over Mediator above) .0937.

Mediator: Well, that's about right! See, I did it a different way, and I wasn't sure of my arithmetic. I took 5 — I took $6\frac{1}{4}$ (Loring: Uh-huh) and $12\frac{1}{2}$ (pause). See, you got $12\frac{1}{2}$ for the 2d period.

Loring: $12\frac{1}{2}$?

Mediator: Altogether, see.

Loring: Oh! Oh! / All right.

Mediator: (Over Loring above) And then I got 18 3/4, and (?: Yeah) I divided 18 3/4 by 2 and I got 9.3 (slight pause) — got 9.3.

Loring: Well, that's what I got — .0937 (Mediator: Yeah) — .094.

Mediator: I just did it a different way, but this didn't seem right to me (Loring: Uh-huh) and I wanted to check. Now, we checked — we did it another way, and it came out pretty near the same. (Rather long pause) Well, it's good that they both jibe. Now, I don't say that his figures are correct — I mean, whether $2\frac{1}{2}$ is right for 20% or not. But, anyway, this is giving you an inside look of what he's thinking about, and you (Loring: Yeah) probably won't get anywheres near that till around 3:00 or 4:00 o'clock.

Loring: Uh-huh. (Slight pause)

Mediator: But that's his thinking. Whether it's good, bad, or indifferent, we'll know later. Now, when we go into the joint session you're going to get the strike ultimatum. Now, following that he will probably hammer on this 20% thing. Then we'll go to lunch. (Pause)

Loring: Uh-huh.

Mediator: And we'll — so (pause) I — this thinking I don't think he has even discussed with his (Loring: H'm. Well, this is beyond us now) committee. He couldn't have discussed it with his committee the way he was changing it (Loring: Uh-huh) in my presence.

Loring: Yeah. This is still way beyond anything we could — could even consider for a year.

Mediator: The 9.3?

Loring: Yeah. Definitely. There's (Mediator: Uh —) n — no hold-backs on that.

Mediator: Well, we'll — we know — we know where his sights are (Loring: Uh-huh), and we didn't know that. (Loring: Uh-huh) Now we know it. And it's a lot more encouraging. I mean, he was 14 when we last took a look at him; now he's down around 9 for a year. Uh —

Pranis: You think he's really serious about the year, George.

Mediator: Yeah! He wants a year.

Pranis: Definitely wants it.

Mediator: Yeah! He really wants it. (Pause) Yeah. That's — that I'm certain of. (Rather long pause)

Joint Meeting - B (12:15 P.M.)

Mediator: Uh (pause) — I've been going over several points with the company that — getting near lunch time, and then, too, when we recessed the u — union had gone into a caucus, so before we recess, does the union — I'm not finished yet, but does the union want to report, before we recess, the results of your / caucus?

Gambon: (Over Mediator above) Well, we've already had a caucus, if you — you're thinking of us holdin' a caucus.

Mediator: Yeah. I (Gambon: We've already had —) (Meyer: Report to him) mean, you've had it, so d'you wish to —

Gambon: Yeah! I could report that as far as we're concerned the committee is unanimous. We've set up a strike to be called at 8:00 A.M. on Saturday — this coming Saturday. What's the date? April —

One of girls: 20th.

Gambon: — 20th. (Long pause)

Mediator: Well (pause), we'll recess for lunch, unless there are any co — comments on the part of the company, if you have any questions.

Loring: No, I guess not. (Pause)

Mediator: How about quarter to 2:00?

[Both parties agree to this time, and the meeting breaks up at 12:20 P.M. Mediator goes briefly to the management caucus room but dismisses that group almost at once.]

Management Caucus - D (1:50 P.M.)

Mediator: Well, how'd the luncheon go?

Loring: Pretty good.

Mediator: And how did your thinking go?

Loring: Well —

Espig: (At same time as Loring above) Well, that isn't as good. (Laughs)

Mediator: Not as good as the lunch.

Espig: (Still laughing) I'm — I'm only kidding. I — I xx — (continues laughing).

Pranis: Lunch was much better. (Long pause)

Loring: Uh (pause) — I've just been doin' some rap — rough calculations here, George, on the basis of this day work — 20% for day workers. I get .0975, or pretty close to 10¢ on — on his basis, as against his .0937. Now, that is assuming that the nickel that's already been given is eliminated from here. (Pause) That's above our ceiling. (Mediator: Uh-huh) I mean (rather long pause), what do you think are our chances of settling for the 6 months?

Mediator: I think that (slight pause) toward the end of the afternoon you'll know (slight pause) whether — I think what he's goin' to try to do is — i — he knows it — now that he knows you would rather have 6 months than a year (pause), he's playin' it cute by saying, "7¢ is my minimum; I don't move! If you want to buy a 6-months' settlement, it'll cost ya 7¢. If you wanta buy mine, it'll be" — whatever it is. I don't know the answer to that and won't know it until — I think — I don't think you'll get the answer to that until the end, until he really (Loring: Uh-huh) has to make a decision. I don't think he's — I — I think ya got to wait until he's convinced that you're not goin' to do anything on the year business. Only then will he begin to think in terms of a 6-month settlement. He's still shooting hard for a year. So, the answer to that would be I don't think you can — we would know.

Loring: Now, if he's so anxious for a year, then he really isn't — s — s — say — say he really is anxious for a year (pause), on the basis of his position which, let's say, is .0975 — I think our figure is better than his — I mean (Mediator: H'm), been calculated pretty accurately — in what area do you think his final settlement would be possible? If he's sa — if he's told you .0975, do you think that is his minimum?

Mediator: I imagine — no. I think that — now — now I'm splitting hairs now. I'm down to the point where my guessing can be wrong one way or another, but as near as I could come to it I'd say that (pause), at the final stages of your negotiations, if he has decide between a strike on Saturday and accepting something less than the 9-cent package —

Loring: Really a 10 — / cent —

Mediator: (Over Loring above) — or a 10-cent package (Loring: Yeah), I think he would take less and that less could be between 8 and 10. It could be 8, it could be $8\frac{1}{2}$, it could be 9, it could be $9\frac{1}{2}$. But I — I

imagine that his minimum would probably be a — around 8¢. Thinking — and the reason I get that figure is, you've offered 4, and I think
his rock bottom minimum would probably be 4 and 4. Ya'd never get
4 and 3, or 4 and $3\frac{1}{2}$. (Loring: H'm) I don't think you could get it.
Now, that's if you could get him down there. But I do believe that it's
in that area between 8, $8\frac{1}{2}$, 9, $9\frac{1}{2}$ — somewhere in there.

Loring: Uh-huh. Well, we've got to go about tryin' to find out what it is.
(Mediator: Yeah) Now, the one thing concerns me a little bit, suppose
we get no place today — Lord forbid it turns out (laughing slightly)
that way — I don't suppose you can meet with us tomorrow. You've
probably got this Aero thing. Where does that leave us with his
strike authorization / for on Saturday?

Mediator: (Over Loring above) Well, the Aero thing is a little up in the
air. (Pause) It's developing now into a jurisdictional dispute. Now,
if it becomes jurisdictional the — there's no mediation.
[Mediator continues for several minutes to elaborate on the position
of his agency in jurisdictional strikes and its particular application
to the Aero situation.]
Well, I think we should go in there. I'm gonna start the ball rolling
by (rather long pause) briefly summing up the position of the parties and telling ya something that both of you already know, that the
stalemate exists and that we have to know where we're going soon,
and (pause) let him take it from there. See, there's nothing to work
separately with ya — with — with either party, because he still has
that committee, and I know — here's what I'm — see, he gave me that
figure, see. Now, he — I — I — I — I'm quite certain I've — I've got
that before the union committee. Now, he'll probably take a position
at $12\frac{1}{2}$ or 14¢ in there with us, and he'll hold on that damn position
for maybe 2 hours before he even (tapping table) gets down to this
point, like he did with that 5 and 2. Well, then again, if 5:30 is the
deadline tonight, why (pause) — oh, wait a minute! Isn't he going to
Mockton tonight?

Loring: I don't know.

Mediator: Plattsville?

Pranis: (At same time as Mediator above) There's an Exes — Executive
Committee meeting tonight.

Mediator: Oh, is that what it is?

Pranis: Maybe he's goin' to Mockton; I don't know. But (Mediator:
Maybe he's been there) — but our story is Executive Committee
meeting.

Mediator: Oh!

Pranis: That's the hour of decision that we hear about.

Mediator: Oh.

Loring: We're not sure of that, are we? / We don't —

Mediator: (Over Loring above) Well, I think it's certain now because he
has said strike at 8:00 A.M. in the morning — uh (Loring: Yeah) —
Saturday morning. So I guess he feels certain he could get their — I
guess he's the Executive Board, isn't he?

Pranis: Well, no. They're a committee, and / they're not unanimous.

Espig: (Over Pranis above) No, but the group goin' — the group in there
constitutes a majority (Mediator: Oh) of the Executive Committee.

Pranis: But he — he would keep the pretense, at least, George, of making
it legal according to the constitution (Mediator: Yeah), and he

wouldn't x sure. And, beside (Espig: Well —), there'd be an awful lot of planning to do if ya — if he thinks there's gonna be a strike there's a lotta work to be done.

Loring: George, why the strategy of a strike Saturday morning, when they don't work? Is that to give us Saturday and Sunday to get it straightened out?

Mediator: Oh, don't they work?

Pranis: No! No Saturday work. (Slight pause) (Mediator: Oh-h-h-h!) Skilled trades only, and repair maintainence. That's all. (Slight pause)

Mediator: I thought ya had — you were on overtime.

Pranis: Look! We can't move the stuff out. Can't ship it out in a box car. All the friends! They — that's what's —

Loring: Yeah. But I mean from their viewpoint they could have a 2-day strike without costin' 'em anything. I mean, it might —

Mediator: Yeah. (Pause) True! Possible. But, now, he's takin' a chance, because he hasn't found out whether I'm available (rather long pause), if that was his strategy. (Long pause)

Espig: What do you think would happen if you indicated to them that you thought you could get $3\frac{1}{2}$ plus 5 and $3\frac{1}{2}$ plus 5, in an off-the-record approach to John?

Pranis: Plus 5¢ an hour — is that what you're sayin'?

Espig: D'you think he'd make a more — take a more adamant position on this 5 plus 10 and 5 plus 10 position of his? You think he would. (Pause)

Mediator: See, I've — I've watched John's style of bargaining. (Espig: Yes. That wo — that's —) Now, with another f — man that would've — that would click beautifully. With John, his style of bargaining indicates that he has to reach a stone wall before he starts throwing out ideas. He has to be convinced that he's up against the blade. (Pause) And as soon as he's convinced — and that's why I was saying, hold onto your position (?: Yeah), because only until then —

Espig: Well, I just wanted to get sure — clear in my mind whether that would be your reaction.

Mediator: $3\frac{1}{2}$ and 5 and $3\frac{1}{2}$ and 5 (pause), you'd haveta — that would be knocking out those day w — that day worker. Now, there's your — there's where your big job is coming. (Slight pause) He is going to — w — why is it — by the — let me — I didn't ask ya this question. What's the importance of this 20% for the day workers, or any % for the — why the day workers? Is it — is he getting a — is it a block of workers who are pushing this thing, or (Espig: Could be) (Pranis: All males —) what is behind it?

Pranis: They're all males, George.

Mediator: They're all males! / xx?

Pranis: (Over Mediator above) They're the only males (Mediator: Oh, I see) left.

Espig: And they have made the remark that the company will not give them that because of the fact that they do not swing enough votes in the meeting as a whole, which indicates that they have — that they may have been rather a — a pressure group on John. (Pranis: I think that) I certainly know that some of them are! (Pranis: They're a very valuable minority xx) They're the — I know — I know very well that the — that the warehousemen have been thinking in this — in these

terms for a year. That's a fair — fair-sized group of people. I've
argued their — their base rate of pay under the evaluation system
with them several times over the course of the year. The same thing
goes for several of as — for m — some minor repairmen. And the
set-up men have been <u>extremely</u> voluble on this subject. They've
been so voluble about it, because they see minor repairmen getting
20%, and result of that 20% on their particular pay creates an inequity
problem, if you're looking at it strictly from an evaluation point of
view. The take-out pay — the evaluated — the evaluated rate is <u>not</u>
the take-out rate, you see. The result is that this — this is a fairly
<u>good</u> situation to talk about an inequity in pay! That's what it is!
Ever since we built this 20% into our — into our system, it <u>had</u> to
some day come to this effect, because then —

Mediator: He wants 20% of the base?

Espig: He wants 20% of what we term a base incentive wage rate. / That —

Mediator: (Over Espig above) For day workers.

Espig: That's right. Now, that base incentive wage rate is the old wage
rate that was in existence in 1946, prior —

Mediator: That's — that's the one you explained / the other day.

Espig: (Over Mediator above) Yeah — prior to the granting of the first
major increase, which was — which was not in — figured into that but
was made what is known as a payroll add. (Slight pause) And that's
where you get your incentive base wage rate from. Now, the incentive
base wage rates are in pr — in — are in proportion in an — in —
in proper evaluated position, but the take-out pay is not. A D-grade
minor repairman, with 20% added to his rate, is practically equal to
a G-grade set-up man. And I don't think anyone in this room would
argue that the set-up man has the — has the — the greater job content, by far. (Pause) So that there is — there — the — th — you j —
you can't — you can't knock yourself out by — when you start — when
you start arguing inequities. You can't knock yourself out of the picture. It's there! (Long pause) Now. If you get 20% built into <u>those</u>
rates and you don't build it into the skilled trades rates, then you get
the set-up man who is not a skilled tradesman at G plus 20 equaling
and taking out as much as the machinists are taking in — in I grade.
(Laughs shortly) So you see w — how it goes? It — it's just a — it's
— whenever — when it was first built in it began at a — a dis — dis —
dismemberment of the — of the evaluation system. And it will continue! (Pause) If we could get — I — I'd — I question they would buy
it. If I were spending the company's money I personally would buy it
if I thought that the base rates of pay could be frozen. (Pause) But
that — that, nevertheless, it — it — nevertheless, it's — it's a — it's
a cost issue which does not benefit all employees, and that's why we
think we oughta take it in bites. (Rather long pause) Plus the fact
that it breaks down the true meaning of an incentive system in that it
builds and — i — it builds what was termed to be a fixed bonus incentive into a picture on a job that can't be made an incentive job! (Slight
pause) That's the <u>greatest</u> objection to it. (Slight pause)

Mediator: (In low voice) Uh-huh. Well, suppose we —

Espig: Suppose we — suppose we <u>talked</u> about that?

Mediator: Well, see, if you bring it up — I think <u>he'll</u> bring it up. Let
<u>him</u> bring it up.

Espig: All right.

Mediator: If you raise the question, see, it'll indicate that you were considering it. It's gotta be brought up by him. I'm sure he'll bring it out this time. He was supposed to bring it out there before we recessed. So I'm gonna try to flush it out by my opening — by announcing that a stalemate exists and what are we gonna do about it, and go through a u — a few other lines to stimulate the — the discussion. I'm sure that when he'll — he'll prob'ly start with your profits or something else, but he'll get to that. Then when he gets to that, let him do the talking and then argue back, and he'll — but I think he oughta open it because the first sign of the — of a — of interest in any of these things — see, he has got to, right now — see, he — he f — he sees no interest in any of the things that he's talking about coming from the company's side. Company has said, "We've given 4¢. That's our settlement figure. We want ya to buy it. That's it." He's made a proposal for a year contract. The company has replied they're not interested in it. Now, to me he been talking 20%. That's a must. Any settlement, it must be in there. The company — if they begin to discuss that he'll see that they're interested in that. They still — you still have to be disinterested in order to get him — see, you can't show any cracks yet in your bargaining defenses, and if (Espig: Yeah. Sure!) — it would be a crack! Right now you've got to just be in a position of, "Well, here we are, and" —

Espig: Too bad, huh?

Mediator: — "too bad." And it's — it's — just has to go that way for a lit — because John will come out! He's just a — a very difficult bargainer in these negotiations. (Espig: Yeah) And when he does, don't be surprised if he hurls something brand new. I won't (Espig laughs quietly), after what he did the other night. Might — he might have several ideas on that, but you'll (pounding on table) not get those ideas out until he's convinced that your position is firm. Oh, we'll have bargaining time! We'll have ba — because in the — in — once he indicates movement (pause) openly, see, in this thing we can start moving real fast. But he (slight pause) — he's holding. Now, if you go in there — if you went in there now and start talkin' about anything (pause), you'd have a good 3 hours of back and forth and joint, and back and forth and — he'd hit ya for — he'd hit it with everything he has, to — to make the crack wider. (Espig: Oh, yes!) Now, he said to me here — he said to me in our — in our side-bar conference he says, "George, anything ya get from them," he said, "if you can get the company to give us more than where they are at, we'll agree to bargain further." (Pause) "Well," I said, "you're generous!" (Espig laughs quietly) I said, "Gees, you're a big help!" I said, "What d'ya think I would do, go in to the company and say to the company, 'Give me another cent! If you will, John will continue negotiations with you'?" I said, "Now, that's exactly what it amounts to!" See, when a man's thinking like that, he's not ready! You've got to sh — you've gotta just hold tight. That's xx. (Loring: Yeah) And he meant that! He wasn't joking. He — he felt that (Espig: John is —) this here — the strike threat — if you wanta buy off his strike threat, put a cent on the table; then we'll bargain from there between there and 7¢!

Espig: John is — John is — sincerely believes that when he asks for something and gives up a point, he's really doing (laughing slightly) you a favor. (Laughs)

Loring: Well, we hold firm this session, George.

Mediator: I think you oughta say to him, though, that, "We've considered your strike ultimatum and we regret that it's had to be that way but — and (pause) we're (rather long pause)" — I'll tell ya what ya could say if you consider this, and I think it would (slight pause) — you're gonna have to use your judgment as to (pause) what you would do about it, but at least you could say it and I know darn well it would — it would help your position. I think my reply to John, if I was sitting on your side of the table, would be something like this, that, "Well, we've discussed your strike ultimatum and regret that you had to do that and that there would be a strike. But we've told you where — what we can do and (pause)" — somewhere along the line of discussion you could weave in that (slight pause), "Our people intend to report our position to our employees." See, that has a bargaining pressure. That has an effect. They don't like that, because when you said they didn't report the 4¢, they'll know that you're going to. And it's gonna put a bonfire under the — under them. They're gonna move.

Espig: Could it be a bonfire to the extent that we would (slight pause) go out tomorrow morning?

Mediator: No. (Pause) See, you — you would just have to (pause) — because what are ya saying? All you're saying is — after all, they served the ultimatum, see. Say, "We're sorry it happened but we'll have to prepare our people for it, and in the preparation we'll have to honestly tell our people what we did offer. And we regret that it's — has to happen. We certainly want to (rather long pause) maintain our relations with everyone, the union and the people, and feel we owe it to them" — somethin' like that. Now, that doesn't say ya have to do it if you don't want to, but I know that it will work on John. It will give them somethin' to think about. Now, psychologically, no union likes their people to receive a report from anybody else than themselves. But in some situations where they, the union leaders, do not report out to the people, many employers use that method and with good results. I don't advocate or recommend that an employer should do it in situations where a union is reporting out to its people; but where an offer — when an offer gets up to the — into the fair area and it's not reported out, then — well, the employer should. Fact, the union is foolish for not, in my opinion, reporting it. So, I think the mere mention of that would aid this — these negotiations. (Rather long pause)

Loring: Uh-huh! Well, we'll see if we can't / get a way to work it in.

Mediator: (Over Loring above) S — see, John has been applying pressure on these negotiations here. Now, in return, a little should be applied there, because John needs some to move, to blow his top, and that's what we want. Sooner John blows his top or the sooner there's talk about that, the sooner he's going to move. Now, see, he's — he's handed you an ultimatum. You have a perfect right to say, "John, we're sorry that it had to reach that stage and sorry we couldn't reach an agreement. But since that's the way it is and we can't reach one, we do wanta tell you that we have to — we feel that we're gonna have to report our offer to our people. We think it's a fair offer. We're sorry there's a strike going to take place but we have no other choice in the matter at this stage of the negotiations." I don't know what he'll say, but whatever he says is all right. But you oughta weave it in there somewhere. (Loring: Uh-huh) Make it as x —

[For a few minutes Espig and Mediator discuss the pro's and con's involved in confronting the union with a certain point. Mediator argues against using it, suggesting another tack "where it can't be interpreted as a pressure move or a threat, because they watch that! They watch tone, they watch facial expression, they watch everything. It's a part of bargaining. And soon as you up any — it can be in — i — a — they'll see right through that, and I don't want 'em to get that idea, see, 'cause I don't want any cracks in the wall at this time. So far there isn't."]

Mediator: (Concluding above) When he knows that, you watch these negotiations start moving.

Loring: O.K. Fireworks, too. (Laughs)

Mediator: Yeah. That xxx. So, if you're ready —

Joint Meeting - C (2:20 P.M.)

Mediator: I — I wanta say to both committees that I brought you together here more or less to sum up, make a report, because I feel that after meeting with both of you separately a — a report is in order. Your negotiations — the status of them — are unchanged. The union has set a deadline. I've talked with management, I've talked with the union. Parties are still — company at 4¢, the union at 7¢ in one proposal; in another proposal the union leaves open the door for a — proposes a year contract, waiving the October reopener. Both these proposals have been thoroughly explored and discussed and counter-proposed, but without result. Now, the afternoon is waning; there isn't a lot of time. I felt that it was necessary to tell both of you, instead of continuing as I were, that you're still in stalemate and the stalemate has got to be broken if you're going to get an a — get a contract. So far I have been unable to break it. The — so I think it's some ti — time now that we oughta have discussion, at least on the report that I have just made. Now, if I'm incorrect in my summation of the position of the 2 parties in the last proposal, well, either side can correct me immediately. If there are no corrections, then I'd like to see some discussion here on the over-all picture. Now, I understand that — fully aware that we have a deadline to meet, but the problems are unresolved and it doesn't look as though that deadline or any other deadline's going to be met until such times as we get some more thinking out on the table here. It's not a very optimistic report, but, nevertheless, those are the facts, and the sooner we — both sides, or all 3 of us, know and are aware of the facts, it's only then that we're goin' to — something's goin' to come out of these negotiations. That's my report. John, any comments?

Gambon: Not one!

Mediator: Len —

Gambon: Except to say that we're goin' ahead. (Pause) If you (Loring: Well —) — if it's any interest to anybody, we prepared our strike signs, 'cause I assume that if they're as firm about their position, they may as well know we're just as firm in ours. There's gonna be a strike at 8:00 o'clock Saturday morning. (Pause)

Loring: Well, I'm _genuinely_ concerned, sorry that we seem to be at this stalemate, John, committee. It's something that the company and I personally hate to look forward to — a strike of that kind. We've presented to ya, to the best of our ability — perhaps if I could talk a little more fluently or eloquently I — I might get the ideas I have in my mind across better, but traditionally, you know, I don't talk too much. But I've tried to make you see the picture as I sincerely see it — things we're concerned about. The company would love to give you what you want — sincerely that, John. However, we've spent a lot of time, a lot of discussion, a lot of consideration. We've come up with what we feel is a very fair offer and most that we should go to.

Gambon: Well, Len, if you say the company would like to give us what they want — what we want and you _don't_ plead inability to pay, why don't they do it?

Loring: John, when you talk inability to pay, you're getting into an area that ya can argue about. We say that _this_ is a fair offer in — considering the things that are happening, that we think _might_ happen this year, we — we feel it's a fair offer. Uh (pause) (Gambon: It's only a difference of opinion. That's all it amounts to) — we're going as far — as far as we can, John. I mean, the company doesn't want any trouble, _certainly_ doesn't want a strike. But there comes a point at which we have to take any consequences that it — that come at that point. Now, I'm sorry that you feel that ya have to give us a strike ultimatum, that you have given it to us and that i — if it's irrevocable, I — I'm awfully sorry about that. I can only say that we'll have to do all the things that we'd have to do in a condition like this. We'll have to notify our people of our offer, which we think is a fair one, and present our side of the case. (Gambon: We'll present it to our people) Sorry, but (slight pause) — I wish it could be different.

Gambon: So do I, but unfortunately that's it. Just happens to be a difference of opinion about whether or not the company can afford to do it. Now, you people repeatedly have said to us that, "This is all we think we should do. We wanta use the money for other things" — other things which, repeatedly, we're tellin' you, are of no benefit to us either at this moment or in the long-range view of the situation, particularly in the long-range view of the situation. Now, I think we've haggled just about as far as we _can_ haggle in view of the company's position, and I think, frankly, that this union has made _much_ more effort to prevent a strike than the company has made, because we've tried to get these things on the table and discuss 'em with you since January of this year. We have tried by repeatedly reducing our position and particularly in removing as a — a bar to the proposition of tryin' to get a settlement here, the question of a shorter work week. We tried everything that we know how, reduced our wage increase positions and everything else. And the company, I think, has moved very little from its original position when you look at the whole picture of these negotiations. Unfortunately, Len — I think you have stated the

position pretty clearly when ya say it's unfortunate but we're up
against the proposition of the company's saying, "This is as far as
we're gonna go," and we've said ya haven't gone far enough, and under those circumstances we set up a strike deadline for you. You
mention — is it — u — proposition on the union's part of being the
v — irrevocable position. I don't say that and I haven't said that yet.
But I do say it in the face of the union's firm po — or the company's
firm position. We've offered 2 — 2 different propositions here for
consideration, one which I think is to the u — company's benefit as
well as to the union's, in trying to iron out the situation on a basis of
making an agreement that'll cover the balance of this contract. I
don't think the company has given enough s — consideration to that. I
don't think they gave it <u>serious</u> consideration.

Loring: It was given serious consideration, / John.

Gambon: (Over Loring above) No. I — I don't think they have, because
I think the company is not trying to meet the union's demands and trying to give them a fair offer. I think the company is bargaining for a
stronger position in October of '53. I'm no — suffering no disillusions
about the fact that I'm dealing with businessmen and not a bunch of
people who are concerned about the employees who happen to be members of our union. They proved that to me and to the members of our
union not too long ago. So we — we don't think that we're dealing with
people who are doing something for us out of the goodness of their
heart. They're only gonna do as much as they can do and as — do as
much as they're <u>forced</u> to do by the union, not as much as they can
do, because they haven't given evidence of that up to this point. And
that's no reflection on your chairmanship, Len, 'cause I'm quite convinced that you're operating under orders here. (Pause) I have seen
developing in this company, now, for the last couple of years just exactly this situation. And I think Atlas has, through its policies and
changes — has been slowly gathering together its strength to call for
a showdown with the union. And if that's what they want, they've got
it, and we'll engage in a showdown with the company / on this or any
other kind of issue.

Loring: (Over Gambon above) Certainly what — not what the company
wants, John. (Gambon: Huh?) I can assure you that. It's not what
the company wants.

Gambon: Well, they're not givin' any evidence that they don't want it,
Len. (Pause) Not to us, they're not. (Pause) We're just as conscious
of the seriousness of the situation as the company is, perhaps more
so. (Long pause)

Mediator: I would like to have some words with the union.

Loring: All right, George.

<u>Union Caucus - B</u> (2:35 P.M.)

Mediator: Uh (long pause) — I have explored 3 or 4 approaches to settling this with the company, and I felt it best to talk about them here in
caucus rather than in joint session. The — instead of giving you a detailed report on their thinking, it can be summed up quickly by saying
that (rather long pause) the gap, again, between the 2 of you is one

where both of you are pretty firm. And the things that you are thinking about and would like to have are the things that are just standing
in the way, and then the things that they would like to have, <u>they</u> can't
get. (Rather long pause) I don't think it's a question of how <u>much</u>
this — it <u>is</u> a question of <u>how much</u> it will cost, but there's ano —
there are other questions involved: how it will be applied and whether
it will be a 6-month proposition or a 1-year proposition. So there's
3 questions — cost, how it will be applied, and length of contract —
and that's without even discussing the figures. And it seems to me
as we go along we've got to get some kind of an agreement first on —
in principle, and instead of getting it we're adding to it. I think we
started off with one; now we have 3. First it was how much, and then
it got to the point where application became involved — if an agreement was reached, how would it be applied? Then it — then termination — the length of the contract — came into the play. (Slight pause)

Gambon: Who raised <u>these</u> questions? Company?

Mediator: No. These negotiations (Gambon: Oh) raised 'em. (Pause)
The comp — oh, yes, the company talked about each one of them, but
to you (Gambon: H'm), and you know their position. They talked
about the — they offered 2¢. They were talking about a 6-month contract then, reopener.

Gambon: Well, I misunderstood you. (Mediator: You were just — you
were —) When I — well, when you said length of the contract I thought
maybe they had been exploring the possibility of extending the <u>present</u>
contract.

Mediator: I have gone over that (Gambon: Uh-huh) with them.

Gambon: What, an extension after April 1st (Mediator: No, no, no, no.
The —), 195 —? Oh! Well, that's why I say I misunderstood what ya
meant by length of the contract.

Mediator: Oh! No. No. I meant, by length of contract, 6 months or a
(Gambon: H'm) year — whether a reopener would be waived. (Pause)
Seems to me that on a reopener like this, for these negotia — it's very
unusual, and, of course, I can understand, again, why it's unusual for
negotiations like this to get into such a (pause) inflexible position,
unusual because of the factors involved — the ones I've already mentioned — the moving out — moving South. So, under ordinary circumstances, reopeners are not this tough. (Pause) But (rather long
pause) I think you're gonna have to decide, or we're gonna have to
work out first, whether this thing is goin' to be a 6-month proposition
or whether it's goin' to be a year proposition. I don't know how we
can start talking about costs until we know which direction we're
going in.

Meyer: Well, why, George? I mean, you're stuck with it for a year unless <u>they</u> reopen in October.

Mediator: What?

Meyer: They're stuck for a year unless <u>they</u> reopen in October.

Mediator: How are they stuck?

Meyer: 'Cause it's part of the contract.

Gambon: H'm.

Mediator: Oh, / yeah.

Meyer: (Over Mediator above) That doesn't (Gambon: Question is
whether it's **a reopener**) **end in October 1st.**

Mediator: No (Gambon: H'm), you — me — what I mean is, we started these negotiations talking about — or <u>you</u> started them (Meyer: Uh-huh) talking about (Meyer: The reopener) a reopener. (Meyer: Yeah) Then later a proposal came from you — a counter-proposal (Meyer: Yeah) to the effect that you would <u>waive</u> your reopener.

Meyer: Yeah. But they won't even consider / xx.

Mediator: (Over Meyer above) And they won't consider it. (Gambon: Uh-huh) Then you said, "We won't give up that thought unless — and if we — if we <u>have</u> to give up that thought our minimum is 7."

Meyer: That's right.

Gambon: That's — uh-huh.

Mediator: See?

Gambon: Uh-huh.

Mediator: So <u>they</u> say, "We can <u>never</u> pay 7 but (Meyer: At this time) we don't wanta go for a year."

Meyer: Uh-huh.

Gambon: But they'll pay 4 for a year is the point Bernice's making: I mean, the 4¢ doesn't (Mediator: No!) go out of the picture on October 1st. / That continues.

Meyer: (Over Gambon above) Just a minute, John. They'll pay 4 till October 1st / and then come what may.

Mediator: (Over Meyer above) They'll pay 4 to — well, any (Gambon: Uh-huh) contract would (Meyer: Uh-huh) (Gambon: Yeah) until you reopen it, negotiate more. But in outlining this I'm tryin' to s — show the — the (pause) — how the — how the whole thing is (pause) being immov — can't move.

Meyer: Well, we dropped that 1-year thing, as long as they won't buy that, and we say we're (?: Yeah) striking on the position of 7 (Mediator: 7¢) versus 4.

Mediator: Now, that — well, then there's where we are. (Meyer: Uh-huh) We're pinning that down. There's where / we are.

Gambon: (Over Mediator above) Well, are they willing to move away from their position? I don't get that. I mean, I'm not gonna move any further! I think — I honestly believe that we've made more moves than the — than — in this whole situation than the situation itself warrants us movin'. We started out in an attempt to try to eliminate a problem which we have by virtue of a company policy of decentralization, and when we find that is not a practical thing from the way they view it, we switch over to their <u>field</u> of bargaining, in a sense, and we find them reluctant to move away from the kind of increase that they wanta give us, until eventually they do that. Then when they've gotten us down to what we say is our minimum position they set themselves up in a maximum position and come out with a lot of regrets about a strike and all. Well, they're gonna get their regrets unless they show some evidence of the fact they they really don't want a strike! They're not convincin' me that they don't want a strike when they say, "We're — we're not gonna go any further than 4¢. We think that's fair." And then he comes out and — and he's — he's sorry, he hopes it's not a — an irrevocable situation on the union's part. What's he want us to do? Withdraw from the 7¢ and accept his 4? (Mediator: Yes!) Because if that's what he wants he's got a strike at 8:00 o'clock Saturday morning.

Meyer: From where I'm sitting, if we dropped to 4 they'd withdraw the 4 and offer us 3. (Pause)

Gambon: And if he thinks he's worryin' anybody by tellin' us, "We think we'll go — we'll tell our people"! They happen to be our people. We'll do some tellin', too. But while we're tellin' 'em they'll be out on the Goddam street. (Pause) (In quiet voice) I think he's kiddin' — I mean, to come up with that pressure stuff. (Addressing Observer) I'm sorry that I let loose on you. But I'm gettin' a little bit fed up with these tactics here, and I think the only way we're gonna convince these guys that we're not kidding with 'em is to tell 'em to go to hell as quickly as possible and to get out of this particular room and start doin' our work and lining things up for 8:00 o'clock Saturday morning.

Meyer: Well, we could change till 8:00 o'clock Friday, too.

One of boys: Maybe we oughta make it Friday. (Long pause)

Mediator: I'm gonna have what may be the last caucus with them. / In the meantime —

Gambon: (Over Mediator above) Uh-huh. Well, tell 'em this. It's a — our position at this moment is not irrevoc — irrevocable, that it's just been suggested here we may take a position in p — because of the attitude that was just expressed in there a minute ago, of changing the deadline for this damn strike. They think they're gonna capitalize on their rights under the Taft-Hartley Law, they got another think comin'. (Rather long pause) I'm runnin' out of patience with these jerks. You can tell 'em that for me, too. (Rather long pause) I'd like to see Len Fuller come down here and sit across (Meyer: Harold Fuller) from that table for — Hal Fuller (One of girls: Hal Fuller) — and tell me, "We're givin' ya a fair shake." (Pause) One guy I wanta get my teeth into. (Rather long pause) I almost settled it — give us back that $350,000.00 they borrowed from us, in effect, to get into a position where they could spit in our eye, or think they could spit in our eye, and we'll withdraw our present position. Just give us what they owe us from back in 1949. (Rather long pause)

Mediator: What was the last offer you made, as you have it?

Gambon: The last offer we had? We had the — on the 6-month reopener we had the — uh —

Meyer: 5¢.

Mediator: Well, that —

Gambon: (At same time as Mediator above) — 5-cent general wage increase and the 10% fixed bonus.

Meyer: For all day workers.

Gambon: For all day workers, not just skilled trades. And we estimated that, based on their estimate of 4¢ — we estimated that at 7. (Slight pause) As against that position, they have offered 3½-cent general increase and 5¢ additional for skilled trades only, which means a total of about 71 employees out of a total of 183. It's a rather high figure on the basis of what I've been saying of not being much over 100%, but that is a — a current figure. Surprising to me as it may be, that was checked just yesterday. But they're willing to do something additional for 71 people out of 183, whereas —

[Tape changed]

... bar monetary fringes for the balance of the contract, and we set our figure at the 1-cent general wage increase and the 20% fixed bonus

for all day workers, which includes skilled trades, and we said that
was a bargainable position. They have refused to accept the proposition of bargaining with the union for a settlement covering the balance of the contract (pause), and as much as they bleed about tryin'
to prevent a strike, they make no further effort to meet the union's
minimum for the 6-month period. (Rather long pause) What, if any,
is their position? Has it changed on this question of recognizing the
principle of a fixed bonus for these day-work people?

Mediator: No, it hasn't changed, John. They're — when I said — when
I said that the application of any increase was (Gambon: Uh) another
problem, that's one of the things I had in mind. I covered that 20% —
or the principle of % without (Gambon: Uh-huh) mentionin' 20 or 10,
and the resistance there was pretty strong on that particular question.
Skilled workers / they don't ob — object.

Gambon: (Over Mediator above) Despite the fact, George, that they —
they say to us in one of their meetings here that they were willing to
straighten out some of these fixed bonus problems for these groups
(pause), following more or less the yardsticks that we set up for ourselves in the past. But they've refused to do that, as I pointed out!
They've refused absolutely to go any / further than they are, and
there's a lot —

Mediator: (Over Gambon above) Oh, what did they — what did they mean
by that? Did they mean that in the past — I didn't — never asked 'em
for a clarification on that, but I — I took it that they meant that in the
past there were certain classifications in which they had made exceptions to that rule and did grant a percentage increase for / day workers. Is that correct?

Gambon: (Over Mediator above) Uh-huh. There's no exception to the
rule, George. The contract states in very broad terms that the company and the union, by mutual agreement, can a — can agree to place
fixed bonuses (Mediator: Oh. Oh. x —) on any job. And what we've
set up for ourselves in lots of cases, see, is that where we have a job
— let's say any — any day-work job where there — the individuals on
that job are directly or indirectly connected with the — the production
workers to the extent that by their application to — toward their own
job they can affect either the production or earnings, or production
and/or earnings of the group that they're directly or indirectly connected with — now, where that's been established, they've come
across with the 20% increases. But, like everything else, the union
had been too successful in establishing the connection between day
workers and production workers, and they are not recognizing that
and they will not recognize it! They're not kidding me on that score,
because we have a couple of instances where we can show even better
factual information about the connection between the day-work and
production — production workers on jobs not yet given fixed bonuses
than we've had on some jobs in the — in the past! And in some instances, if it's to their benefit they'll throw 20% bonus on there without any urging from the union a'tall, for only one reason, because it's
a bottleneck, see! And they don't concern themselves with the — the
relationship of the day worker to the production workers in those instances. Or if they wanta get away from the contract provisions, in
lots of cases they'll define the job as an incentive job and be unobligated

to pay an individual average earnings until the time they issue a rate.
They won't define it as an incentive job; they'll throw a 20% fix —
fixed bonus out there only to save money. This is a chiselin' outfit,
George! Don't let them sell you any ideas that they're fair-minded
individuals. They're a bunch of damn chiselers! Because every increase we've ever had, we've had to fight with 'em to keep their other
hand out of our pocket to the — operation of this incentive system.

Meyer: And at the same time they're saying that this extra 5¢ costs a $\frac{1}{2}$¢.
If they would go through with this 10% they could drop the 5¢ on 100-
and-some people and the total cost would not be 7¢.

Gambon: We (One of boys starts to speak) dispute their 4-cent figure,
George.

Meyer: It would be closer to 6$\frac{1}{2}$!

Gambon: We keep on the table this — this moment the fact that they're
offering 4¢. If it's a 4-cent figure, we want 4¢! Not that I'm sayin'
we — we were accepting it, but I'm using this as a point for il — illustration here. We want 4¢. We don't want it to result in 3.3¢. Now,
we dispute their evaluation of a $\frac{1}{2}$¢ for skilled trades as they have it
here. According to my figures, this 5¢ to skilled trades, which they
claim is a $\frac{1}{2}$-cent cost to them, is .00284, which is less than 3/10ths
of a cent, not a $\frac{1}{2}$¢. And that's for 1250 people.

Meyer: Yeah, but if they continue in their contention it's a $\frac{1}{2}$¢ on the
other end of the picture and you raise the — if you get the 10% — if
they'll pay the 10% (Gambon: H'm), then that will drop it from 7 to
below 6$\frac{1}{2}$¢-an-hour (Gambon: Correct) total package! And on top of
that, on the principle of 10% or any kind of a bonus or incentive, if
you recall the flowery speech that was given out, is it the principle
of incentive it's — they don't agree with the principle of incentive
that people who are not actively engaged in production. But yet when
you mention this profit-sharing plan they tell ya, "Well (Gambon:
H'm), we need that for an incentive for these people who aren't making incentives like your people are under the contract." So how can
you say 2 things at one time? It doesn't make any sense to me.

Gambon: It's all right for an officer of the company or a foreman or
supervisors to receive a profit or an amount (Meyer: x) of money
from a profit-sharing plan as an incentive although he's not required
to work against an incentive standard, but it's not all right for a tool
and die maker or a minor repairman or other day workers in the
plant to receive a bonus as an incentive to more efficiently perform
his work. And if — I think if you'd measure it, anybody in God's
world will agree that the person out in that shop is much more connected with the production that comes out of that plant than anybody
'at sits in the front office! That's a gravy train! They know we don't
like it. We certainly don't like it when the result was back in 1950 in
the very beginning that they sold us a bunch of crap that they couldn't
afford this, that, and the other thing. And then they stuck behind their
backs, as it were. They k — kept it very quiet that they had started a
profit-sharing plan which produced that same year that we got a nickel
— it produced on the average for our people around 8¢ an hour!

Meyer: Which they never even told us / about, but we suspected — suspected that they —

Gambon: (Over Meyer above) They never told us. We found that out to —
through a big argument. And we found it out when they issued something

that had to be made public. They didn't even have guts enough to tell
the union, "Well, we have to save some of this money because we
wanta give it to X number of people." It was a — would have been
very embarrassing to try to tell us to take a nickel, "because we
wanta give the officers of the company a crack in the profit-sharing
plan in addition to their dividends and in addition to the salaries they
receive as officers of this company." And then they did it again to
us in '51! They did it to us actually in '50 when they got an agreement from us for 5¢ in '50 — October of '50 and 5¢ in April of '51,
which was moved up a couple of months, I believe.
Meyer: January, / '51.
Gambon: (Over Meyer above) But — up to January, '51. But, in the
    meantime, while we got 5¢ and 5¢ they got this tremendous profit-
    sharing proposition which would have resulted, in addition to the
    nickel, of 8¢ in '50 for us and 7¢-and-some-odd in '51! And then they
    try to give us the business that they're givin' us a fair share of the
    profits of this company! These people are nuts! (Pause) They're
    not nuts; they're just — they've just made up their mind that they're
    goin' to tell us from this point on, "This is what we consider to be
    your fair share." And I think they've gotten around to the thinking
    that, "Well, they'll take what's offered to 'em in the long run." I've
    been watchin' this, and it's been concerning me for a couple of years,
    now, see. And I've known, God, George, for the last 2 years, that,
    Christ, come one of these particular things before this contract was
    out, we were gonna have to strike this company in order to get their
    feet back in the ground! And I've said that repeatedly to the people
    on this committee; I've said it at union meetings; I've said it at Exec-
    utive Board meetings. And here it is! Now, I think they're lookin'
    for a showdown and they're gonna get it, because this company is not
    gonna hand us a financial report and ask us to believe that this is all
    they can give us as a fair sha — our fair share of this business! It
    is not our fair share, and we're not gonna allow them to hand this kind
    of thing out to us so that they can assure the stockholders of their in-
    creased dividends for '53 and so they can assure the people in that
    profit-sharing plan the same amount, or even a greater amount, in
    '53 than they got in the preceding 3 years. To hell with it![1]
Meyer: And we don't —
Gambon: And I can assure you one thing, if they got any ideas that
    they're gonna come back after we hit the bricks and settle the strike
    for a piddlin' cent or 2¢, I'll do my damndest to keep that union fightin'
    the hell out of the company till hell freezes over, because what have
    we got to lose with a lousy outfit like this that's been movin' out from
    under our nose and intends to continue to do it? Get big ideas maybe
    reduced to smaller ones before we get done with 'em. (Pause)
Mediator: On that 10% application, I want a point of information. If you
    have a man making $1.50 an hour in your plant now, would that man
    get a 15-cent increase?
Gambon: Not necessarily, if he's makin' $1.50. I mean, if the $1.50
    would be what we would call his incentive base wage rate, the answer

---

[1]During this vigorous speech by Gambon, Comeau and Healy called
each other's attention to the volume needle flicking back and forth
violently on the recorder.

would be Yes; but if his take-out hourly rate — his clock-hour rate
was $1.50, the answer would be No, because we have —

Mediator: You'll have to explain what a / clock-hour rate is.

Gambon: (Over Mediator above) Well, that's what I was just gonna try
to do, George. We have a payroll add, as you know. The payroll add
in our shop means this, that for the incentive worker there is no bonus
paid on 62¢ an hour, which amounts to the payroll add. To give you
an — as more specific example of what I'm talkin' about, our lowest
labor grade is Grade A. The incentive base wage rate on which bonus
is paid in Grade A is 63¢. Any bonus earned by the individual is calculated on that figure. In / addition —

Mediator: (Over Gambon above) May I ask — may I interject?

Gambon: Yeah.

Mediator: I just have an illustration here, and I wonder if — if a man
made $1.62 an hour (Gambon: Yeah), his payroll add is 62¢.
(Gambon: Yeah) (Meyer: Uh-huh) Subtract that from $1.62 (Meyer:
That's it) and ya have $1.00. (Meyer: That's it) He would get 10¢?

Meyer: That's right. / That's it.

Gambon: (Over Meyer above) No. Oh, oh!

Meyer: Yeah! For 10%.

Gambon: Wait a minute.

[Gambon, one of boys, and Meyer talk at once. Gambon is saying,
"You're talkin' about his $1.62 bein' the take-out figure?"]

One of boys: Yeah.

Saunders: No.

Meyer: Yeah.

Mediator: If a man earned $1.62 (Gambon: Yeah) / an (Gambon: Yeah)
hour —

Meyer: (Over Mediator above) Take-out. Straight / day work.

Mediator: (Over Meyer above) When — when — when ya use the term
take-out, d'you mean take-home?

Gambon: Yes.

Mediator: His —

Gambon: Hourly take-out.

[Gambon, Meyer, and one of boys talk at once.]

Gambon: (Over Meyer above) Talkin' of the day worker, now. Right?

Mediator: Yeah. So 62¢ from that would leave $1.00. (Gambon: Right)
(Meyer: That's right) And you're sayin' that this 10% would be 10%
of $1.00 (Meyer and Gambon talk at once, chorusing "That's right"
several times), which would mean he'd get a dime.

[Several, including Gambon, Meyer, and one of girls, again chorus
"That's right."]

Mediator: That —

Gambon: (At same time as Mediator above) Look — well, let's be more
specific about it, I mean, particularly since we're talkin' about skilled
trades. We'll take our top rate, which has a take-home pay of $2.27.
Now, that take-up pay is comprised of an incentive base wage rate
despite the fact that it's a day-work job. All of our plant — all our
jobs have incentive base wage rates of $1.60, and the other (Meyer:
6 —) balance of that 2.27 is made up by a payroll add of 67¢, which
is 5 cent higher — 5¢ higher than the incentive worker's payroll add
of 62¢ as a result of that 5-cent differential we got back in March of

'52. (Mediator: Uh-huh) If that man were to get 10% bonus, we say
the company would re — take away 5¢ of the 67¢ which was given in
the first place to try to correct the inequities. (Mediator: Uh-huh)
After ya take away the 5¢ you would then apply 10% to his incentive
base wage rate of $1.60, which would give him 16¢ but in effect actually
only 11.

Meyer: 'Cause he's got a nickel / in his pocket right now.

Gambon: (Over Meyer above) Because you took away the 5, see.

Mediator: Are they clear on that?

Meyer: Yeah, they know it!

Gambon: I explained that to 'em. (Meyer starts to speak) Because, if
you recall, he started to talk about 20% on 2.27 and I corrected him
at that point.

Meyer: George, what it boils down to, the (One of boys starts to speak)
top grade is 2.27 right now. It would be 2.38 with the 10%. (Gambon:
Let me give you s —) It'd be $1.60 (One of boys: You know why,
George, it's —), 15, and 62.

Gambon: Here's some rates I picked up —

One of boys: Day workers now get 5¢ an hour more. There would be no
more day workers under this plan. Everybody'd be on incentive.
There'd be no 5-cent added payroll add. It wouldn't be 67; it'd be
everybody, whatever c — amount it / is.

Gambon: (Over boy above) 62 (Meyer: Be —) plus whatever the general wage / increase would be.

Meyer: (Over Gambon above) Well, that — well, that's over and above.
I'm (Gambon: Yeah) talkin' about what the increased cost, presenting the general wage increase.

Gambon: Here's some rates, George, that I picked up just yesterday —
the tool and die makers: Dayco Company, 2.36; Monco System, 2.32;
Hercules, 2.47; Precision-Made, 2.36½; Aristocrat, 2.30 (?: H'm);
the Hamilton Arsenal, 2.43 to a top of 2.54. Now, our rate of 2.27 is
below that. Many of these companies are in negotiations. Aristocrat
start negotiations this week, as I understand it; Standard Products is
now in negotiations; Precision-Made — I don't know when they have a
reopener, but still they're — they're almost a dime ahead of us right
now; Dayco is almost — well, they're 9¢ ahead of our rate, and they're
now entering negotiations, too. The 16¢ that we talked about here, as
Bernice pointed out, would bring our rate from 2.27 — it would bring
it to 2.25 — would be 2.41, wouldn't it?

Meyer: Well, if (One of boys: 2.38) you count — 2.38. Plus (One of
boys says something) whatever — plus whatever across-the-board
increase is resolved.

Mediator: Uh-huh.

Gambon: That's right that way. But (Meyer starts to speak) let me
take these things — and you can't overlook your jobbing shop rates.
And the Metropolitan Area ABC Association, which is made up of 12
shops covering about 558 employees, I believe (Mediator: I had those
negotiations) — they have a minimum of 2.15 for tool and die makers,
a weighted average of 2.41, and a maximum of $3.08. Then you've got
some of these companies around here who are doin' jobbing stuff, like
Ace Manufacturing, 2.66; Metropolitan Metal Stamping has a top rate
of 2.80; Ames Brothers, 2.70; X-Cel Precision Manufacturing, 2.55;

Consolidated Machine and Manufacturing, 2.60 (pause); what's this? — Forge, or Ferguson Machine Company, 2.60; Knapp Tool Company, 2.60; Dawson Tool and Die Works, 2.50 — 2.55; Frontier Machine Company, 2.50. Now, who the hell are they kiddin'? I mean, even with the increases that we're tryin' to put in here on the 10% as a minimum figure, they're not gonna be at the top rate for the area! (Long pause)

Mediator: Now, on the cost, you — I believe you said, Bernice, that —

Meyer: That if they use their $\frac{1}{2}$¢, 7¢ is too high.

Gambon: Yeah. Our figure is not — doesn't agree with theirs by a long shot.

One of boys: You fellows —

Mediator: Now — / yeah.

Gambon: (Over Mediator above) Given the full / 20%, George, what we —

Meyer: (Over Gambon above) Yeah. But now if we use their figures, John, he's askin'. Now, wait.

Gambon: Using their figures, they come up with 4¢.

Meyer: Uh-huh.

Mediator: Are you sayin' —

Gambon: (At same time as Mediator above) They estimate the fi — here's what they say. They say that the 5¢ for <u>skilled trades only</u> (Meyer: Is a $\frac{1}{2}$¢) is a $\frac{1}{2}$¢. And we say that is not correct, that that 5¢ for skilled trades only represents .00284. (Pause) Now, according to our figures, we take 183 day workers at the full 20 percep — 20% proposition, and without disturbing the present additional 5-cent differential for all of those people, we estimate the actual cost to the company for the 20% fixed bonus 3.24¢ an hour. Now, taking away the nickel, which we say we're willing to do in order to put the 20% in there, the total cost to the company then becomes 2.51¢ per hour. (Pause) So if they were to say to us $3\frac{1}{2}$ plus the 20% for all day workers, according to our figures they would be then offering a proposition of about 6¢ total.

Meyer: And we're also asking for 10 right now to make up, and they're sayin' that 7¢.

Mediator: You're only what?

Meyer: 10%.

Gambon: (At same time as Meyer above) We — we're sayin' that our minimum position — we're willing to take — we're not asking them to give us the full $2\frac{1}{2}$¢ that 20% represents to us. We, in effect, are saying give us 1-2-5 for skilled trades and 5, which is $6\frac{1}{4}$¢.

Meyer: (In fairly low voice) That's the point. (Pause)

Gambon: So theirs — their — we — we're keep — we say 7 when we state our minimum position, because that's the figures they're using. In reality they're claiming they're givin' us a 4-cent package, so right now, from what we really want, they're $2\frac{1}{4}$¢ away, not 3¢. (Pause)

Mediator: Well, then you estimate their 4-cent package to be $3\frac{1}{4}$?

Gambon: I — I estimate their package to be (emphatically) 3.50284. (Laughs, as does one of boys heartily) It's slightly less — or, over $3\frac{1}{2}$¢, not 4. (Pause)

Meyer: (In low voice) Over about 3-5-2, it'd be about. (Pause)

Mediator: That's a — that's a —

Gambon: (At same time as Mediator above) Yeah. Would be — actually it'd be .0350284. That's really draggin' it honest.

[After a rather long pause, Mediator gets up from his chair and leaves the room.]

Management Caucus - E (3:10 P.M.)

Mediator: Why, pretty good. I survived that one. (Pause) Again, congratulations! (Loring laughs slightly) Well done! (Laughs very slightly) I think it's working perfectly. (Loring: Oh, do you?) I think that the (slight pause) — mentioning the letter gave me exactly what I wanted.

Pranis: He made no comment, George, other than a very short one.

Mediator: He certainly did when ya left the room.

Pranis: Oh, did he?

Mediator: (In low voice) Yes, he did.

Pranis: (Laughs) O.K. That's what we wanted.

Mediator: And, in fact he even apologized to Observer. (Loring laughs)

Pranis: Oh, you've heard him now! Ah-h!

Mediator: For some of the French he used. (Espig laughs quietly) Yeah, made him sizzle. I figured that was the chink in his armor. And I think it's going to do what I want it to do a little later on. I waited till he — I gave him all the time to get it all off. I let him blow for better part of 15 minutes. Then when he ran down I began to question him about the — his arithmetic. I said, "We have 3 problems here. See, we started out with one. The one problem we had was how much for 6 months — the reopener." I said, "That's all we had when we started. Now we have that — how much; we also have, how will it be applied; and now we also have the length of the contract (laughing slightly) — whether it'll be 6 months or a year — another proposal which embodies that." So I said, "As we're going along we're pickin' up more disputes. Now," I said, "before we can get anything settled, which direction are we going to go? Is it — are we goin' to stop and talk about 6 months? If so, can we talk about a figure without getting into the dispute of how the 6-months' settlement can be ap — whether some question of application — 20%? Or do we talk about a 1-year contract (pause) with the other details?" I said, "It's getting confusing — confusing. I don't know where we're goin'." Well, that got him started. Then I said, "You say on one hand — you made a statement, John, and I'd like to — you to say some more about it. You challenged the cost of the company's — you — you — you — you challenged the computation of the company's cost estimate." He said, "We do! The 4¢ that they're offering us is not 4¢. It's 3½¢." So I got him talking about that. He just poured forth with a lot of arithmetic here, ably supported by Bernice, and, anyway, it has done this. I've left them. I let 'em talk this thing over and then I said, "Well, I'm going in and talk with the company for awhile." When we go back later — not right away; we will not go back for at least t — till about 20 minutes of 4:00. The reason for that is, Bernice said, "How long d'ya think you're goin' to be in there?" And I said — she said, "Will you be 20 minutes?" I said, "I believe so." She said, "I have an errand to do." I said, "Go ahead." And she went out to do the errand, so we'll take at least till 20 minutes of 4:00.

Espig: She just wanted to get a couple of new signs made. (Mediator laughs shortly)

Mediator: So, when we go back, see, you're at a stalemate. You're still at a stalemate. Then I'm going to say — I'll announce again that you're both at a stalemate. However, "A serious question was raised by the union and I feel that it's serious enough, <u>even though ya can't agree</u> on a <u>final</u> settlement — serious enough to get the <u>air</u> cleared of the smoke even <u>before</u> ya strike, if ya have to strike! So, here it is. The company has submitted a package which they say is a 4-cent offer. The union, to me, has said, 'That is not a 4-cent offer; that is a $3\frac{1}{2}$-cent offer.' <u>I</u> think in <u>any</u> negotiations — not think; I <u>know</u> — that that's a <u>very important thing</u> to get clear. So I've brought ya together to clear that." That's all I need — that opening. The groundwork has been done. Your remarks about you're holding the line, see — no cracks — is there. As far as they know there's going to be a strike, which is fine. Far as they know — and the letter — they know that you're going to send a report to your people, and they don't want that. Now, those things they know. So all we're doin' now is comin' in to challenge one another's arithmetic — or not challenge, but discuss it. From <u>that</u> we should <u>get</u> the — the next step. This should be a spring-board to get to where we wanta go. Then <u>they'll</u> make the next opening, I'm certain.

Loring: Have you any idea which way it's going — I mean, the 1-year or the / s — 6-months'?

Mediator: (Over Loring above) No, I don't. Tha — the — I still would bet on the 1-year. I — I think I favor — I think if I were asked, just like you asked me, "Which way d'ya — which has the most chance (pause) — which would they <u>rather</u> settle for?", I'd say a year. I think they'll <u>hold</u> at 7 just to make you go the <u>other</u> way. They'll probably take <u>less</u> for a year than they're — where they're at now to <u>get</u> a year, but they charge ya more and <u>hold</u> to it for the 6-month deal. I think they'll fight ya on the — on the 6-month, see. I can see — they can — they can <u>hold</u> at 7 on the 6-month and go back to their people and — and take a strike on it <u>maybe</u>. I don't know. 4¢ may be a little hard to take a strike on, too, but I — I don't doubt that they couldn't get it! (Pause) They could get a strike at 4. They can get it at <u>8</u>, if they wanted it, by — but (pause) I think they're keeping that 7¢ up there just to get you away from a 6-month contract and get you thinkin' about the other. Price is <u>high</u> on the little one; it's a <u>bargain</u> rate on the other. That's the way they're tryin' to make it appear, only they don't know what price tag to put on the other to call it a bargain. I think they favor the other. (Loring: Uh-huh) But we're on schedule! (Loring laughs)

Loring: So John sounded off for the first time, huh?

Mediator: It went <u>just the way</u> I figured it would. Just the way. He didn't like that letter business. Yet, ya had him in a position, see, where it was good. See, you didn't raise the question until he said "Strike." And all you said was, "Well, we feel it's a fair offer and we wanta — we think we ought to report it." And he — he can't quarrel with that because he knows that you didn't use it as a pressure move, because <u>he</u> raised the strike question first. And he knows that all throughout the negotiations you **have never** used that until he said "Strike," and

this is the end! Puts ya in a perfect position. (Loring: H'm) All
this to make him do what I know he's going to do — almost know he's
going to do seems ridiculous, but that's the way it's gotta go! (Slight
pause) It's gotta go that way.

Loring: I suppose that's one of the disadvantages of a <u>large</u> negotiating
committee, George — a certain amount of forensics have to be gone
(laughing slightly) through.

Mediator: Well, with large committees, Len, it's difficult for another
reason. You — you have to mediate so many people. (Loring: Yes)
See, on some of these committees — see, you're lucky. Your committee is all together; they're controlled by one man. These other
unions that come in here — they're not. And 3 will be with this faction, 3 will be with that faction, 3 will be the other faction. Then I
have to go around bringing the 3 together before I can get them to
agree on what I want. After I've worked on the company and get it, I
have to <u>then</u> go in and — and mediate their differences, and it's difficult. (Loring: H'm) That's the Precision-Made problem (Loring:
Yeah) — one of 'em.

Loring: One thing about this that hits me is — I mean, it's interesting
as a problem. I presume that because I don't talk too much I make
your job as mediator more difficult because we come to a stopping
point. On the other hand, I think it bothers John a little bit, sizing
him up from the previous negotiations. He's an opportunist, and
<u>much</u> of his argument is things that you say. I mean, <u>not</u> prepared
material but anything you say he picks up. He doesn't have too much
opportunity, or he hasn't the last couple of sessions. I think that has
stymied him a little bit. I mean, not stymied him, but slowed it down,
I — I'm afraid, but I just <u>don't</u> talk too much.

Mediator: Well, that's good! (Loring laughs slightly) In some instances
that's good. This one, it's not doing any harm. If he had — if you
gave him more material, we'd be there longer. The faster we get
outa there and then in here and then back there again and in here again,
the faster we're movin'! But if you got into long harangues of — we'd
just be there that much longer. You're crampin' his style a little, is
what you're saying. (Loring: Um-hum) You're not bothering mine.

Loring: Well, I didn't know (Mediator: No) whether I's making it harder
for you in this.

Mediator: No, the other way around is more bother to me. The long-
winded harangues over positions that have been repeated and repeated
and talked over — that wastes my time more than — this I prefer!
(Loring: Uh-huh) See, it enables me to work more directly with 'em.
You've said your piece, you bolstered my position, you're out, and
then I move in. See, now, from what you did there he had an opportunity to blow his head, and then we explored the — see, I have a talking issue, a dispute between the parties' computation. It's a good
talking issue. So I'm going to use it. He knows that my bringing you
together for that is to clear the air. He'll <u>know</u> that, although he
doesn't know I'm going to bring you in there to discuss that. He'll
<u>know</u>, when I do, that that's what it's for. Now, I know that that'll
just open the talking door and move ya in to the channels I want ya to
get into, which will be — and I'll ask questions that will <u>get</u> us into
the channel. Now, the channel I wanta get into is the — the year

proposition — this 20%. <u>Again</u> he hasn't brought it up to you. See, I have to flush that out because he has some talking to do on that — a <u>lotta</u> talking — and I know we've gotta talk about that before he will give it up or compromise it or — or throw it out or — it's gotta be talked about. It's still a problem. And until he gets it off his chest — if he's going to drop it he has to be shown he doesn't have a chance, <u>or</u> if he's going to modify it in agreement with you he's gonna have to talk about it. We've gotta get those 2 points talked about: (1), the difference in your thinking on the computation; (2), the 20%. (Loring: Uh-huh) I'll get him into that later. (Loring: H'm) <u>Then</u> doors will open! Doors will open then and we'll — and we'll get to that point where we'll know whether he'll — how much he'll — he wants to settle for for a year we'll know, and then <u>he'll</u> know whether he <u>can</u> settle for a year or not. And when he find out he <u>can't</u> settle for a year, if that's the way it is, then he knows he — he's got to do one of 2 things: hold onto his 7¢ and strike you, or s — stop thinking about the year and concentrate on the other. There's where we have to get it. (Very long pause)

Loring: I imagine you don't have many that go along like this, George.
Mediator: Not on reopeners. Well, we have some worse ones than this, but generally no — not on a reopener. But as I explained, your reopener is in a different — it's in an unusual position because of the company's moving some of its work away. (Loring: Yes) Weren't for that, John would have been talking about an increase, and that's all. (Rather long pause)
Pranis: Very thankful it went on. Look at all the work I got done today!
Mediator: Uh-huh! (Pause)
[For a brief period Mediator and Pranis exchange light comments unrelated to the Atlas case.]
Mediator: What time's this Executive Board meeting?
Espig: I don't know anything / about it.
Pranis: (Over Espig above) I would imagine 7:30. (Pause) John'll wanta go out and get dinner, have a couple of drinks at Coppla's, have a sidebar conference with x.
[Mediator, Pranis, and Espig get into discussion of governmental agencies, with Mediator detailing some wartime experiences with uniformed defense personnel who insisted on sitting in on mediation cases. After more than 5 minutes of this, Mediator announces, "I gotta make a call," and leaves the room. It is 3:33 P.M. While Mediator is in the main office away from both groups, Gambon comes out of the union caucus room and corners him for a short while. Mediator, after going out for coffee, returns to the management caucus room at 3:55 P.M.]
Mediator: (Laughing) Ye-ah! I (pause) — takin' care of another client.
Pranis: So soon? Boy, that was quick.
Mediator: Gees, I have to call Aero's. They'll prob'ly be wondering why I — (rather long pause, while humming and drumming on table). Why, I think we'll go in now, reviewing that — I'm going to — I'm gonna raise the question that there seemed to be some doubt. Even though neither party can agree on any figure, that it's always my policy to make certain that people are <u>clear</u> about these proposals. <u>I</u> was not — <u>I</u> was on the — <u>I</u> believed that there was no dispute about the estimate

cost of the package proposal. The union has disputed it, and it's my
policy always, even though the people are — can't agree on the package, but it's always been my policy to clar — clarify it in the event
there is any doubt. And I brought you together, if for no other reason
but — than that, to get it clear. Then I'll tell you what the union says.
You can be prepared to answer (Loring: Uh-huh), or I may turn it
over to the union, since they're disputing it (Loring: Uh-huh), and
let them make s — statements. From there I'm going to ask them a lot
of more questions about — later about the cost of this — the — the
whole subject of 20%, or d — or the whole subject of day workers.
I'll make it clear that I'm exploring this, see. And if he's goin' to
drop that, or if he's — like I said, or he's gonna modify it, he — he —
he'll wanta talk about it. And he hasn't had the chance. He didn't
bring it out yet. Bernice's back; she just came back. So (pause)
let's try to give it another whirl. Soon we're gonna really get into /
negotiations.

Pranis: (Over Mediator above) George, the fact that we're checking the
costs — will it lead us into the trap that maybe we're saying we can
afford something?

Mediator: No. I'm gonna make that clear, see. I'll make that in my remarks. See, we're at a position now where I came in and told you
they disputed your (Pranis: Oh, I'm sorry. So now we can talk about
it) figures, see. And we — th — they raised it. We didn't.

[Out in the hall, on the way in to the joint meeting, Mediator comments
to Observer that this is the "beginning of the end": either a settlement or a stalemate, now.]

Joint Meeting - D (3:58 P.M.)

Mediator: In talking with the union I learned one thing — I was told one
thing that I felt sh — should be discussed with the company. When I
went into the separate meeting with the company I discussed it with
them. The reason I discussed it was this. Even though it is not a
part of the proposal for settling this that was made by the company —
the 4-cent package — I meant to say it — it was a part of the 4-cent
package and because of that I feel it important to talk about it. Now,
the unio — the company submitted a proposal of $3\frac{1}{2}$¢ and 5¢ for the
skilled workers, which the estimated cost was 4¢ an hour. In a talk
with the union the union disputed that cost figure, and I believe — I
might be a fraction wrong — they said that the cost was $3\frac{1}{2}$¢. Now,
even though neither of you at this time, or the — particularly the
union, is interested in a settlement of that figure, I feel that when a
— a cost is disputed it is very important to clear the clouds of — and
shadows of doubt, because if the union is right in the contention, well,
that's one thing; then we'll know where we're going. And if the union
isn't right in their contention, well, they themselves would be glad to
have that clarified. And I don't think that we could get to the problems that we have before us without removing all the shadows of doubt,
no matter what they are. So, John, in talking with you you raised this
point with me. I would appreciate it if you would, at this time, state
your thinking to Len and let's hear from him on it.

Gambon: Well, the cost figures we dispute — that portion of the 4-cent figure that we dispute is this $\frac{1}{2}$¢ that the company credits to the 5¢ for skilled trades which they offered. Now, Number 1, we say that the actual cost to the company, using the present membership that <u>we</u> have of 1250 people, is an actual cost of .00284 for that 5¢ and not a $\frac{1}{2}$¢ as you contend. Further than that, Len, we point out that the total cost for this 20% proposition which the union is requesting for skilled and other day workers would be a cost of 3.24¢ to the company without disturbing the present 5-cent differential; but based on the union's proposal to remove the 5-cent differential and to apply the 20% to the incentive base wage rates of all day workers and not to the total (Loring: Uh-huh) clock-hour rate, that the actual cost to the company for the full 20%, calculated on that basis, would be 2.51¢. Now, there — I mention those last 2 figures because I — I wanted to get them into the picture so that if there's any estimates that you people have — I mean, on this question of the 20% — for instance, our reason for giving you that at this point was that you had estimated the cost of 20% to all day workers to be a figure of 4¢. (Loring: Yes) Now, we dispute that figure by offering here our figures of 3.24 without the 5¢ being involved, and a figure of 2.51 by removing the present 5-cent differential. Now, we've arrived at that by taking all these jobs involved in day work, 183 in number, and we broke 'em down into wage grades and applied the percentages to the incentive base wage rates for each one of these jobs in the wage grade, multiplied by the number of people involved in each grade, and we can't figure anything other than the figures I mentioned here. I don't know how you can arrive at the 4-cent figure on the basis of the specific information which we collected as late as yesterday. (Loring: Uh-huh) I don't know whether we had made it clear the other day as to how we wanted to apply this 20%. I thought (Loring: I think you did, John) I did, but George wasn't — didn't — wasn't too sure in his mind, and that's why I've just repeated it again in the connection with the application of the 20% to the incentive base wage rate, which would, in effect, produce 16 (whistles) — 32¢ on $1.60 incentive base wage rate, less the removal of 5¢ (Loring: Right), or a (Loring: Uh-huh) total of the 27¢ there instead of 32. Now, that's using the full 20% figure. But when you consider all of 'em, the tot — actual total cost to the company prorated against tw — 1250 members is about 2.51¢ per hour actual cost with the 5¢ removed.

Mediator: And that's for 20%?

Gambon: That's for the full 20%. Yes. The t — the full 20%, according to our cost figures, would cost the company $2\frac{1}{2}$¢, in effect.

Loring: 2 and a — yeah.

Gambon: $2\frac{1}{2}$¢, as against your / estimate of 4¢.

Loring: (Over Gambon above) Yeah. 4¢, yeah. Well, all I can say on that, John, I had a x party work this up for me. He used the week of March 31st, which would — at that time was the latest we had (Gambon: Uh-huh), and he went down by departments — the incentive workers, the day workers, and all that — and he — he figured the average pay for the week and all that, just, I presume, much as you did it. / And he thinks that —

Gambon: (Over Loring above) Well, we — we approached it from a much more simpler basis. We simply took each wage grade (Loring: Yeah)

and we applied the 20% to the incentive base wage rate of that wage
grade (Loring: Uh-huh), multiplied by the number of people — day-
work people in that wage grade. For instance, we began here with
Grade H on our sheet here. We have one employee in Grade H, which
would give him — 20% on $1.25 incentive base wage rate would be 25¢.
In Grade I, where the incentive base wage rate is $1.35, the 20% appli-
cation there results in 27¢ for 22 employees; and so on down the line
for all of them. 10 employees in Grade J, .05; 10 in K; 28 in Grade
L, which is a top rate, $1.60 incentive rate, producing 32¢; and fol-
lowing all down the line for every day worker that way. And averaged
out and applied against the — actually against 1253 employees — that
is, union members — we come up with the 2.51¢ per hour, taking into
account removing the present 5-cent differential. How else you can
figure it, I don't know, Len. (Loring: Well —) This is taking the
exact wage grades involved (Loring: Uh-huh), the exact number of
employees involved as of yesterday.

Loring: As I say, John, that was a calculation made for me by a party
who is usually very good at this stuff, and he — he gave me the figure that I've been using with you, which was .041. (Gambon: Uh-huh)
That was for everybody, including all day workers. Now, if we're
wrong on that we certainly wanta / recalculate it and know it's x.

Gambon: (Over Loring above) Well, I — I'd be perfectly willing to submit these calculations of ours to you for p — for perusal. They're all
marked down here: the number of employees, the wage grade, the
amount of money the 20% would produce on — in each wage grade,
multiplied by the number of people, total cost per hour for all the people in each individual wage grade. This is skilled trades, apprentices,
all other day workers.

Loring: Well, i — if it were for no other reason than what George says,
that we know where we stand and what we're talking about, I would like
to get agreement with you on what — what these things cost. (Gambon:
Uh-huh) I'd like to state again, John, that our 4-cent offer was 4¢. It
was 3½¢ per hour, and the balance, whatever it is, would go into this
skilled trade. I mean, that was — I mean, that was what I meant our
offer to be. I (Gambon: Well, that wasn't —) — I said a nickel, which
I thought was a ½¢, but I was thinking in terms of a ½¢ to go to the
skilled trades. I mean, there was no intention (Gambon: Well —) to
make the offer less than 4¢.

Gambon: There has been at no time, as far as I know, anything different
than the fact that we were dealing with what amounted to a 4-cent offer.
Now, when you —

[Tape changed]

Mediator: ... the other one of low value on it, and it's (Gambon: Well —)
very important that we (Gambon: I —) close that gap before we —

Gambon: A — as of yesterday we had 71 skilled journeymen going through
all the trades, and takin' their 5¢ an hour, that would produce a round
figure for 1048 hours — that's / these —

Loring: (Over Gambon above) You only had 71 journeyers?

Gambon: Huh?

Loring: You only had 71?

Gambon: That's all we have! (Pause) Well, how many do you have?

Loring: I had — I — I believe I had some — some 80-odd. / (?: Yeah)
Yeah, it was —

Gambon: (Over Loring above) Oh, but we're — you pro — somebody prob'ly threw in the apprentices on ya, then. (One of boys: Yeah) There's 13 apprentices. They're not journeymen.

Mediator: But do they — would they come into this?

Gambon: Huh? Not — not the way they p — not the way the offer interp — the interpretation that we have on that offer would be skilled trades. They're talkin' about journeymen, not apprentices.

Loring: I don't know, John. I'll have to / xx that.

Gambon: (Over Loring above) Now, if ya add the number of apprentices to the number of journeymen, you'd get 84. (Pause)

Mediator: Is that what you had? 84?

Loring: I don't — no, mine was a little higher than that, but mine was taken back on March 31st, George, which would make a difference from John's figures. I had something like 89, I think it was. (Mediator: Uh-huh) But I don't know what it was composed of; I'll have to find that out (Gambon: H'm), John. This was done for me. (Gambon: Well —) I think we can find that out / xx.

Gambon: (Over Loring above) As of yesterday, taking the remaining number of hours — work hours — that is, straight time work hours between yesterday and October 1st, we had about 1048 hours. And using your 5¢ applied to 71 skilled journeymen, it represented a total cost of $3,720.40 to the company. / Uh —

Loring: (Over Gambon above) Well, I — I can see one difference right away, John. When we calculate a wage cost, I mean, it's there from — from now on. We figure (Gambon: It's tw —) it on a basis of a year; you're figurin' on a basis of / 6 months.

Gambon: (Over Loring above) Well, I'm — well, it doesn't matter to me — I mean, if — if I do it for one hour or 1048 (Loring: All right. O.K. All right) or for a year. So the only reason I'm using this is (Meyer: This is —) because I was interested in the remaining hours and so forth. And then I took the — I took and applied that cost of $3,720.40 to 1250 employees for the same period, and you get a figure of .00284.

Loring: Do you wanta get those down, Erv, so we can (Espig: Yes, I have that) — can see (?: Uh-huh) if we can agree on these? I (?: Well —) certainly want them to be in agreement.

Denk: Well, you (Gambon: Now, let's — let's —) usin' 1250 people, Len?

Loring: I — I had 1223, Walt, as the number of people / x —

Gambon: (Over Loring above) 1223?

Loring: Yeah.

Gambon: Well, we have 1253 on our records.

Loring: Uh-huh.

Gambon: Some of 'em, of course, are on the —

Mediator: (At same time as Gambon above) Now, are the apprentices — are the apprentices (One of boys says something) in your / union?

Meyer: (Over Mediator above) No. It was the week (One of boys: Yeah) of (Gambon: Oh, yeah) March 31st. (Gambon: Huh?) May have been some people out because it was that tran — transition. There was some laid off and then (Gambon: H'm) recalled.

[Loring and Pranis talk at once. Loring says, "This was March 31st. Yeah," which Meyer confirms.]

Gambon: This — this is our check as of yesterday, 1253.

Meyer: That's how many people paid dues during the month of April.

Loring: Uh-huh.

Meyer: As of yesterday.

Loring: Well, I — I certainly think it's a thing we should get straightened out, George (Mediator: Definitely), and we can quite easily. And if we have made an error here we'll certainly be / glad —

Mediator: (Over Loring above) Are you in a position to work on that now? I (Loring: I think so) — c — can you get that from your plant?

Loring: I think we can get it in a matter of / half an hour.

Mediator: (Over Loring above) It might be well — I offer this as a suggestion — when you're talking to your people you're — that do this work, if at any time there is a — a question on John's figures, I offer this as a suggestion. It might be well to put John on another phone, if — if it would help the fellow that's doin' the computing, so that they could exchange their arithmetic (Loring: Could do that) and / one could straighten the other out.

Gambon: (Over Mediator above) Well, what — what — what is this supposed to accomplish?

Mediator: It's supposed to accomplish this.

Gambon: Enlighten me, will you?

Mediator: I certainly will. I'll certainly try. In — in any negotiations that I've been in, when people are negotiating they're both concerned about the costs. (Gambon: H'm) One side wants to get for his people what it calls — decides is a fair share of the profit. (Gambon: Uh-huh) On the other side they want to d — know the costs so that they can report to their Board of Directors. Now, if one side thinks it's 4¢ and the other side thinks it's 2 or $2\frac{1}{2}$, I, as a mediator — as — I'm goin' to have one <u>heck</u> of a job ever getting that those people into the agreement on the <u>principle</u> with (Gambon: H'm) both their minds separated by 2¢. Now, that's why — why I'd like to get that cleared, because if I can get that cleared, then I think I can talk about somethin' else, but I can't talk about <u>anything</u> else while people are thinking in 2 different veins. (Gambon: Uh) First job is to find out where the discrepancy is, and if the company's wrong, fine; if the union's wrong, fine. Then both know how to straighten out the wrong. Then, i — if you were wrong, for instance, I'm (Gambon: Uh-huh) sure you'd want to be — you'd want to know where you're going.

Gambon: Yeah, I want somebody to prove it to me! (Mediator: That's right) I mean, I'm — I'm just taking (Mediator starts to speak) figures as I see them, simple arithmetic.

Mediator: And you may be right. (Gambon: H'm. May be) And if you're right, I'm sure the company wants to know (Loring: That's right. Certainly), because then the company couldn't sit there and say, "We have offered you" whatever it is.

Gambon: Well, I'd like to — since they wanta check these things, here's what we have. This — this is a breakdown on the number of people involved. Now, look, suppose you take these figures and then I won't have to ask you to copy them down. We can save some time.

Loring: All right.

Gambon: Now, this is — this is your incentive base wage rate in the first column (Loring: Uh-huh); this is your g — wage grade; this is the amount of money — ¢-per-hour increase — that 20% will produce on this incentive base wage rate; this is the number of people in each of these wage grades; and these wage grades here, from H to L, represent the grades in which our skilled journeymen exist. Down here we have our apprentice set-up, and this is the amount of money now being earned by each apprentice — each one of the 13. This is the result of a — this is the wage increase that will result by the application of 20% on this figure; this is the number of apprentices receiving this amount of money; and these, of course, are the total amounts per hour when they're multiplied by the number of individuals (Loring: Uh-huh) in there. Same thing over here: again ya have the incentive base wage rate, the wage grade, the number of people in each grade, the result — resulting increase of 20% applied to this incentive base wage rate, and again the total. You have the total hourly increase here and the total hourly increase here, which, added together — gether, give you this total hourly increase here for 183 employees, which is all of 'em. This is the figure we say — 3.24¢ per hour — that would be the cost to the company for applying the full 20% to these 183 people without affecting the 5-cent differential that now exists a'tall. And this 2.51¢ per hour is the figure we say will be the actual cost to the company by applying the 20% to all these 183 people in the various wage grades and removing the existing 5-cent-per-hour wage differential that they now have (Loring: Uh-huh), and substituting, of course, this 20%.

Mediator: So there's a cent-and-a-half difference.

Gambon: Huh?

?: Uh-huh.

Loring: Cent / and a half.

Gambon: (Over Loring above) It — according / to our figures, yes.

Loring: (Over Gambon above) Well, but not (Gambon: There's a cent —) — our 4 didn't — our 4¢ didn't include that 5-cent adjustment, George. I mean (Gambon: Uh-huh), that — we — we figured (Mediator: And what does that amount to?) that before we knew what John meant. I don't know what that amounts to, but that's part of the difference. (Mediator: Well —) Our 4¢ compares with John's 3-2-4.

Mediator: Oh. (Pause)

Meyer: It's just the nickel that's in question right now, costing 5 — uh — $\frac{1}{2}$¢.

Gambon: Yeah. We're (Meyer: No — yeah) questioning — this — this (Loring: xx) is our estimate against your 4-cent / estimate.

Loring: (Over Gambon above) That's right, John. I understand that.

Gambon: And the — on the other, you have our figure as to what the 5¢ for skilled journeymen alone. Now, we say — we only figured our estimate of .00284 against the 71 journeymen. Now, you said it was a $\frac{1}{2}$¢, and I don't know whether ya applied it to 71 or 89 or what it was. You mentioned / 89.

Loring: (Over Gambon above) It was — I think it was the higher figure, John.

Gambon: But as of yesterday we can only find 71 of 'em to count, whether they were workin' (laughing slightly) or not (Loring: Well, we can —), and that includes all the skilled journeymen.

Loring: We'll check that. We'll check / on that.

Gambon: (Over Loring above) And along with the skilled journeymen, of course, there are 13 apprentices which you may have gotten in the figure that you have there.

Loring: May well be, John.

Mediator: Well, I would suggest that if you could do that now that you would work on that immediately. (Loring: All right. I think —) Then we'll get together and come back in here, and let's see what it looks like after you've made your check.

Loring: Uh-huh. A list.

Management Caucus - F (4:20 P.M.)

Mediator: From what I could gather there, was that the real difference there is about 7/10ths of a cent.

Loring: Uh (pause) — it's — yeah. I mean, that's the difference (Mediator: Yeah) — that area.

Espig: Well (Mediator: Uh —), that — that's made up by a calculation on — on apprentices that's false, Number / 1.

Mediator: (Over Espig above) See, I want to minimize (Pranis: See, he — he put apprentices in that —) this as much as possible. He had it up around 2¢ there one time. (Loring: H'm) And already this discussion has revealed, for the first time to me, that it's 7/10ths.

Loring: H'm. (Rather long pause) There were several things that enter into it. We have the date of March 31st, for instance. He's using the current date.

[Espig begins talking on the phone with the Atlas offices about the cost of 20% for day workers. Mediator leaves the room. He is called back by the management caucus group at 6:35 P.M.]

Espig: This has come out exactly as John has 'em.

Loring: Uh-huh. We finally got it, George. They — we don't keep our records in such a manner to get the breakdown that John had, easily. So they've been working on it, and now here's how we come out. On the — and — and Erwin has the details, I guess, of the calculations. On 20% for all day workers we had .0411, and now, on this basis, we get .0363. That's — (pause).

Mediator: Almost 4, but —

Loring: I — it's — it's less than 4 but not greatly less. Now, on / x —

Mediator: (Over Loring above) 3 — wait a minute. .003 s — / .0 —

Loring: (Over Mediator above) .0363.

Mediator: .0363.

Loring: H'm. (Pause) Taking credit for the 5¢ that was given last time, it's .0286. We hadn't figured that before.

Mediator: Oh, .03.

Loring: .03.

Mediator: Oh!

Espig: 3¢. (Mediator: Yeah) 3 and 6/10ths / cents.

Mediator: (Over Espig above) Yeah. 3 and 6/10ths cents.

Loring: It's just about ½¢ different (Mediator: Yeah) from what we had. (Slight pause)

Espig: But this bears out our — our — our nickel estimation. .0363 — 20%. Take 5¢ out of the picture and what d'you get? .028, or 8/10ths of a cent. Almost 8/10ths of a cent (slight pause) instead of the ½¢.

Loring: Well, except (Espig: We said —) that's for the whole group, / Erv.

Espig: (Over Loring above) Yeah. And we said the ½¢ — it would cost about ½¢ for the skilled trades.

Loring: This looks as though it's about 3/10ths of a cent for the skilled
    trades alone, $3\frac{1}{2}$ tenths —
Espig: .0149 and —
Loring: We were a little high on our estimates, George.
Espig: (In low voice) Yeah.
Mediator: Well, the best thing to do under those circumstances is to
    admit that.
Loring: Oh, yes, I think we should.
Mediator: And (Espig: 3/10ths of a cent) then, if you want to follow it
    up and say that, "While we were wrong, we will and intend to live up
    to our offer. If we said 4¢, it'll be 4¢."
Loring: H'm. Well, I told 'em that, and I wanted to get that across.
Mediator: Well, are you ready to go in?
Loring: I guess so!
Mediator: Uh (Loring: Now —) — following that — go / ahead.
Loring: (Over Mediator above) Excuse me. I mean, we give 'em this,
    they either disagree or we will agree on it; then he's gonna come
    back to this question, I'm sure, of what this — where does this get us?
    I mean (Mediator: Yeah), we — i — we gotta pick it up there some /
    place.
Mediator: (Over Loring above) Yeah. I'll pick it up. We might go to
    — oh, it's 20 minutes of 7:00!
Loring: Yeah.
Mediator: We've gotta get somethin' to eat. We'll take a quick break.
Loring: All right.
Mediator: We got him over his (pause) 5:30.
Loring: H'm.
Mediator: We'll take — take a quick break. Then when we come back
    there'll be no more stalling for time. Then we're gonna start work.
    I'm gonna start to work fast, because (slight pause) now we are in
    that area of (slight pause) ne — we'll need time, now. So the move-
    ment is goin' to be faster this evening. We're gonna get — we're
    gonna be more direct. (Slight pause)
Loring: O.K., sir. (Long pause)

Joint Meeting - E (6:38 P.M.)

Loring: Our people have been working on this all this time. We haven't
    been stalling, John. (Someone laughs slightly) Our records aren't
    kept in such a way we could get those breakdowns easily, so they've
    been working on that. We've just, a minute ago, got this call, and
    here's how our figures come out. We were high, but we still aren't
    in complete agreement with your figures, but I don't think the area's
    too great now. We said before that 20% of the day-work group would
    be .0411 — that is, 4.1¢. New calculation, based on taking the exact
    rates and working 'em out as you did, and which I think is — is p —
    undoubtedly the better way to do it, comes to .0363. This is not too
    greatly above your figure and it's below ours. Taking credit for the
    5¢, it looks as though, on our calculation, we get .0286. (Pause) Now,
    that's the entire group.
Gambon: Uh-huh. (Pause)

Loring: That is not a great deal different from yours, but it is a little higher. And those are the late — those are the latest figures we have, Erv, as to people and grades, isn't it?

Espig: Yes. These are taken right off the records as of today, I guess. (Loring: Uh-huh) Way it looks. (Pause) There's some discrepancy in numbers, but they pr — probably average out a great deal. (Pause)

Mediator: Well, even though this is not acceptable to the union, and by my — me asking this question I don't mean to jeopardize the union's bargaining position, but one point I wanta ask is that in your offer, assuming that the union had accepted it and this discrepancy was made, when you made (slight pause) — or rather, when you presented this, you presented it as 4¢.

Loring: As a 4-cent package we (Gambon: H'm) intended right along, George. (Pause)

Mediator: All right. I (pause) — I — I want to say this, now. You people — both of you — both committees are fixed pretty well in your thinking and — at this time, and this evening is — or right now is — could be the last time that we could be with you before your time runs out. I'm going to suggest to both the committees that every bit of time be used. I don't think either committee, regardless of your respective positions, should, at this time, break off negotiations. I will want to hold further meetings tonight. Uh —

Gambon: Tonight?

Mediator: Yes. I would suggest that we recess, take as short as period as possible for dinner or a sandwich, and get back here as quick as we can. (Pause) Uh —

Gambon: Well, what (pause) — what's wrong with a separate caucus for the moment, to find out whether there's any reason to come back — uh — break and come back, George? I'm thinking particularly of a personal schedule.

Mediator: There's this. The answer that you want — what is the reason for comin' back? — is one that could never be found. (Gambon: Uh —) These things are too complicated; there's too many variables in them to answer that question. We — there are some things that I haven't talked about yet that I wanta talk about with the company and some with the union, and I want to use every moment of time I have. If I didn't have this Aero situation, or we had time, why, I'd feel better about it. Not that you haven't, both of you, put in lots of time. You have. But as far as tonight is concerned I want to satisfy myself and for the Service that everything was tried before you did hit the bricks, and everything hasn't been covered. So, that's the best answer I can give you, John.

Gambon: H'm. (Pause)

Mediator: It's a quarter to 7:00. (Pause) If you can — the sooner you can get back, the better — let me put it that way.

Gambon: Well, I would say so, because we are now debating and probably will make some d — decision, based on what you're saying here now, after we come back from getting a bite to eat as to whether we're gonna move up this shutdown from 8:00 o'clock Saturday to 12:00 o'clock midnight tonight. That's the way we're beginning to think around here right now.

Mediator: Well, I — that's a — your de — that's your department there.

Gambon: That's my department.

Mediator: My department is from now until then. So you —

Gambon: All right, let's break.

Mediator: We'll be back — (calling out over noise of group breaking up) be back as soon as — 7:30 at the latest.

[Upon returning from dinner at 7:50 P.M., Mediator stops by the management caucus room to announce that he is going in for a caucus with the union: "I'm goin' to go in with them. I'm going to (pause) feel him out for the last time on the year business or the other. And we get — well, we're gonna have some real plain talk with him now, because he'll — if he's goin' to move he'll wanta move now."]

Union Caucus - C (7:52 P.M.)

Gambon: Well, George, are they sayin' anything / worthwhile listenin' to?

Mediator: (Over Gambon above) They just got back from dinner.

Gambon: Huh?

Mediator: No, not yet.

Gambon: Except that they enjoyed their sandwich and coffee?

Mediator: Something like that. (Saunders prompts Gambon with "Why don't you call Bernice?") I — I — they're in one —

Gambon: She — she'll be in in a minute. That's all right.

Mediator: Shall I wait, or go — (pause)?

Gambon: Go ahead.

Mediator: Uh (pause) — th — the way this thing shapes up now, the way I see it as far as your problem with them is, we're gonna start talking frank now, because there's no time for anything else, and I expect you fellows to do the sa — girls, too — to do the same. (Gambon: H'm) Uh —

Gambon: Incidentally, I forgot to ask this. They did not dispute our estimate of their 5¢ for the skilled trades. I don't know whether they made comparisons. I'm talking about the / $\frac{1}{2}$¢ —

Mediator: (Over Gambon above) What was yours, 3 —

Gambon: .002 / 84.

Mediator: (Over Gambon above) I think — I think they agreed with you.

Gambon: They did?

Mediator: I think so.

Saunders: They come out with .00 — / .0286.

One of boys: (Over Saunders above) .0285, wasn't it, / or 6?

Gambon: (Over boy above) Huh?

[Boy above, saying "5 or 6?", Gambon, saying "I don't know," and Meyer, "They never did —" all speak at once.]

Gambon: No, no. (Meyer: That, now —) This — their .02 — .0286 (Meyer: Means 20%) compares with our (One of boys: Yeah) .0251 (One of boys: Oh) (Meyer: Uh-huh), or the 10%.

Mediator: Oh.

Meyer: They didn't talk about the 4-cent / package.

Gambon: (Over Meyer above) They didn't talk — I meant to ask about that.

Meyer: Huh-un.

Gambon: Not the 4-cent package — the —

Mediator: Well, I think I could —

Meyer: (At same time as Mediator above) The half a cent x / x.

Gambon: (Over Meyer above) — the $\frac{1}{2}$¢. / Yeah.

Mediator: (Over Gambon above) I think I can tell you. (Meyer: Huh!
  It's gonna be a mess) You ha — you — you were at 3-point-something?

Gambon: No.

Meyer: 0 —

Gambon: .003 — less than 3/10ths of a cent. .00284 (Mediator: Oh) for
  the 5¢ for skilled trades that they have offered, which 5¢ they estimate
  is $\frac{1}{2}$¢, see.

Mediator: Yeah. Well, I think — I think that they agree that — they did
  in a — in to — with me, and (Gambon: All right! And —) you can
  bring it up and remind me of it. I think they agree that it's a little
  less than what / they said it was.

Meyer: (Over Mediator above) Did you say it does — from what I understand, he (Gambon: Well —) says it's less than the 4¢ "but we want
  you to understand that this is a 4-cent package. Whatever's over and
  above (Mediator: Right) $3\frac{1}{2}$¢ (One of girls: Yeah) go to the skilled
  trades." / Right?

Mediator: (Over Meyer above) That's correct. (Pause) Yeah, he did
  say that. / Uh —

Gambon: (Over Mediator above) Well, their actual figure, based on our
  m — estimates, is not 4¢. It's .03784 (laughing slightly).

Meyer: Uh-huh.

Mediator: Well, whatever it — whatever figure it (Meyer: We might
  maybe get —) is (Gambon: Yeah), / the balance —

Meyer: (Over Mediator above, says something but cannot be understood)

Gambon: They say the other (Meyer: Goes to skilled trades) .003 or
  .002, whatever — goes to skilled trades. But they're confining it to
  skilled / trades.

Meyer: (Over Gambon above) That's right.

Gambon: Right?

Meyer: That's — that's what he said.

Mediator: I believe / so.

Saunders: (Over Mediator above) Uh-huh.

Gambon: Well, I mean, that may (Meyer: Uh-huh) result in maybe 6
  or 7¢ instead of a 5. I'm not worrying about that at the moment; I'm
  not interested. Go ahead, George, I'm sorry to interrupt / you.

Mediator: (Over Gambon above) Uh — what I was gonna say was this.
  (Pause) I wanta — I wanta reconstruct again. (Rather long pause)
  You're in this position. When I say "you" I mean you and the company. The (rather long pause) — the company right now, from what
  they say in the caucus, they aren't sure — they — as they see it,
  there's 2 pro — 2 proposals on the table, one that they want and one
  that you want. (Gambon: Yeah) You want a settlement based on waiving the reopener and a year contract.

Meyer: Huh-un. Huh-un.

Mediator: You would prefer it.

Gambon: I'd prefer that. Yes.

Mediator: If not, you will take the other, based on your terms — your
  minimum. (Gambon: Yeah) They said they w — can't meet your

minimum, so they said that precludes 'em from thinking — thinking <u>any</u> further about / that.

Gambon: (Over Mediator above) Well, I'm not quite sure that they have said to me in effect, or specifically, that they <u>can't</u> meet our premiums. They have said to me in effect, "We think this is a fair offer." (Meyer: That's right) They have <u>never</u>, at this <u>point</u>, even tonight, pleaded inability to pay, see.

Mediator: Well, I don't think they have ev — no, I don't think they've ever (Gambon: Uh) plead <u>inability</u> / to pay.

Gambon: (Over Mediator above) Yeah. Well, they — they haven't said, "This is <u>all</u> we can pay." They (Meyer: But —) have said, "We think this is a fair offer."

Mediator: That's true.

Gambon: I wanta keep — keep your (Mediator: Well, you're just — you're just dealing with words) thinking straight on this. I mean, maybe I'm wrong, George.

Mediator: They have said to me — and I'll have them — or we can bring it out on the table (Gambon: Uh-huh), say — use the same words they said to me — "7¢ is too much! We won't pay it!"

Meyer: That's right. (Gambon: That's different. That's different) That's what they said, "7¢ is too much. We won't pay it." But they didn't say, "7¢ is more than we can afford / to pay."

Mediator: (Over Meyer above) Oh! No, / I see what you mean. Oh!

Gambon: (Over Mediator above) Uh-huh. See, I'm tryin' to make the point that they have <u>never yet</u>, up to this very moment, pleaded inability to pay. They keep repeating the fact that their offer (Mediator: Well, I see what you mean. Well, that's true) is a fair settlement, the same as they said 4/10ths of a cent was a fair offer in the beginning.

Mediator: So (Gambon: xx) — so we leave that for the moment and go to the other prop — po — proposal. (Gambon: Uh-huh) Now, on the other proposal, I covered that pretty well. I've been pushing that hard — the — doing it because I would like to see a settlement without next October. If you can get that waived and get a satisfactory agreement, I would like to see it. I have spoke about its virtues and its good points in the caucuses. I've been selling it all afternoon. (Gambon: Uh-huh) One of your toughest blocks on that thing, in my opinion, is the 20% business for the day workers. I believe that if that wasn't a problem I would have a good chance of pushing them into a year contract. Wh — now, wh — on — into the principle. Whether we could get an agreement on the <u>cost</u> of it would have to — would be determined later. But as far as the principle is concerned, it's my opinion that the day-worker business is the road-block on a year's contract. Now —

Gambon: Are you saying to me, George, that you think you could get them on a year's contract basis to agree to the principle of a 20% fixed bonus for skilled workers? (Rather long pause) I'm explorin'.

Mediator: I have to stop and think so I don't get confused.

Gambon: That's what I interpreted you were / saying. Uh-huh.

Mediator: (Over Gambon above) Uh — no. 20% for day workers. Now (Gambon: For all day workers?), your proposal — the 20% proposal that <u>you</u> made — how did <u>you</u> make?

Gambon: Yeah. There's 183 people.

Mediator: That's right. Now, does that include skilled workers?

Gambon: Yes (Meyer: Yeah), definitely.

Meyer: And I / x —

Mediator: (Over Meyer above) Before I an — before I answer that for you, I have to get a couple —

Gambon: (At same time as Mediator above) In other words, let's — let's — for your — for your information, our — our n — our figures — I don't know what they've got. We may have to match this later on if we start hagglin' over tenths of a cent. As of the 17th, yesterday, our count is 71 skilled journeymen. That includes tool and die makers, machinists, electricians, electronic instrument men, carpenters, plumbers (pause) (One of boys: Sheet metal) (Another boy: Sheet metal), painters, sheet metal men. 71. I don't know what their count is. 13 apprentices in all those trades. Some trades we don't have any apprentices, but we have 13 apprentices. Now, we — we took their offer — when they say skilled trades to us, we consider just the journeymen, and that's what our estimates were based on.

Mediator: Well, they offered a nickel, didn't they, to skilled trades? (Meyer: Right. Yeah. / Skilled people) Now, who did they offer that to?

Gambon: (Over Meyer and Mediator above) Skilled trades. Right.

Meyer: 71 people.

Mediator: Seventy —

Gambon: That was sev — we counted that as 71 people. Now, it sounded to me as if what Len was talkin' about was not only this journeymen but the apprentices, because we can get a figure of 84. And when he talks about 89 I think he's a little bit wild, but it sounds to me like he's including the apprentices there.

Mediator: Uh-huh.

Gambon: But our estimate was only based on the 5¢ for 71 journeymen in the shop. Now, if he can count more, he's good. I don't know where he's gonna get 'em.

Mediator: Well, now I'm gonna have to ask you to e — explain that. What had that to do with what I was talking about, the 20%?

Gambon: Uh —

Meyer: We want it for a hundred and —

Gambon: We want it for a hundred — I'm tryin' to keep straight on this. When you said you think you can get 20% (Meyer: Huh-un) on a year's basis — / didn't you?

Mediator: (Over Gambon above) I — no, no.

Saunders: No.

Meyer: (At same time as Saunders above) No. (Mediator: No!) That's the stumbling block.

Mediator: No, / you misunderstood me.

Saunders: (Over Mediator above) For day workers, he said then. / And you asked for the skilled.

Mediator: (Over Saunders above) See, I said that the 20% was the stumbling block, that th — that's the thing that stands between you and them, I believe (Gambon: Yeah), and a year's contract — the principle of it. I said (Gambon: Oh, I see. Uh-huh) if that stumbling block was removed (Gambon: Yeah) I believe that I would be in a prosi — po —

position to <u>persuade</u> them on the <u>principle</u> of a year's contract. Then
I added, for how mu — th — then the question of <u>how</u> (Gambon: Uh-
huh) <u>much</u> would be an entirely — would (Gambon: Uh-huh) be something where you'd have to negotiate. (Gambon: I see) See, I can't say
at this time, if — if we c — if I could <u>persuade</u> 'em on the principle,
what it would (Gambon: H'm) cost. I don't know at this time. That
would be something else. One step at a time. (Gambon: Uh-huh)
But their biggest objection, when I've discussed it with 'em, has been
the applying this 20% to all the day workers. (Gambon: Yeah) /
That's —

Meyer: (Over Mediator above) Or to anybody at all. It / would —
Mediator: (Over Meyer above) Well, that I don't know, Bernice.
Meyer: I mean, including skilled trades.
Mediator: Uh — / I don't —
Gambon: (Over Mediator above) That's the thing I'm tryin' to get clear
in my mind.
Mediator: Well, why don't I get it clear? I may as well get it clear
(Gambon: Yeah) now. I can ask / 'em for a clarification.
Gambon: (Over Mediator above) Well, Number 1, I — I'd like to know if
they have opposition to the principle of 20% fixed bonus, or <u>any</u> fixed
bonus, and if so, <u>what is the objection</u>? If they have — if, as they already have, I should say, said across this table that, "We're willing
to continue to negotiate with you whether or not any job in the plant
now on day work shall have a fixed bonus attached as our contract
provides." The contract provides that the union and the company can
do that by mutual agreement. It's a very broad statement, see. Now,
following our yardsticks, George, I can show some just cause for <u>some</u>
skilled tradesmen who are servicing and maintaining productive machines, see, as to using <u>that</u> as a — an argument as to why <u>those</u> particular tool and die makers should have a fixed bonus of 20%. I can
show some good arguments why a die setter in our Punch Press Department should have a fixed bonus of 20%, again following our own
yardsticks. I can show some good justification for all the set-up men
to receive a fixed bonus of 20%. In that particular case and in the die
setters' case, we can show where the company, particularly with set-
up men, pays the operators on the machines that he maintains in good
working order to keep the production level up — the company pays
those operator their average earnings. If through some default of the
machine and the inability of the set-up man to get it back into full productive capacity quickly, they lose out.
Mediator: Well, are you saying to me that where, on one hand, the company — the road-block is the 20% for day workers — now, are you
saying / to me —
Gambon: (Over Mediator above) George, I'm not gonna put no road-blocks
in your way!
[Meyer taps Gambon's arm, as though suggesting he wait.]
Mediator: Well, let me / finish.
Gambon: (Over Mediator above) Go ahead.
Mediator: Are you saying to me — and we're just exploring (Gambon:
H'm) this. I wanta find out what you're saying, and if you've got
something there that I can develop, I wanta develop it. Are you saying
to me, "Well, if they're opposed to t — the 20% for the day workers"

(Gambon: Yeah) — are you saying to me, "Well, w — would they be receptive to looking at this classification, that classification, the other classification?" Are you pickin' out spots (Meyer: They've already said that) where you say you / can show that —

Gambon: (Over Mediator above) They've already said they're willing to do that.

Mediator: Well, then what — what was (Meyer: But it wouldn't —) your point in making it?

Meyer: But when you get into negotiations with it, they / won't agree to ya. They said it wasn't xx.

Gambon: (Over Meyer above) They won't do it. I mean, soon as they leave this room they'll be done with it, see.

Meyer: They said across this table, "We wanta continue to do it the way we have in the past." We've been trying for 7 months / on some of these jobs.

Mediator: (Over Meyer above) Oh, s — oh, I see. (Gambon: More'n 7 months) So y — what you're saying (Meyer: Yeah. But it —) is, the way in the past isn't any good.

Gambon: That's right. / The way in the past —

Meyer: (Over Gambon above) Uh-huh. Uh — well, the principle is but won't agree to it.

Gambon: The yardsticks and principles are all right, but the (Mediator: Oh, I see. I —) company says No, period.

Mediator: I see.

Gambon: And once you're past the reopener period you can't strike unless you want to violate your contract, so you have to go to arbitration with it. And the arbitrator will look at the (laughing) contract, and the contract, because of the broad terms, says, "The company and the union may mutually agree to apply a fixed bonus to any job in the plant."

Meyer: Well, George, on this stumbling block of 20%, the way you see it, do you mean that they may have in mind a flat cent per hour for skilled trades only and (Mediator: It could be) that day workers (Gambon: Of 10¢, for instance?) stay in the same one?

Mediator: Yeah. Whatever way they were (Gambon: Uh-huh) — whatever way you've been (Meyer: Uh-huh) operating. Now, I believe that if — now, I don't know. I — I — that — that's possibly the way they would want it, but the — the point I'm trying to make is that in order to — for — in order for me to — I — I can see that in order for me to get at the principle of this thing and sell them, if I can, I know that I'll — the difficult problem is goin' to be selling them with that 20% in there, because that is the thing they're objectin'. They have never once said to me, in these caucuses, that they object — now, they said to you that they won't go for a year contract. (Gambon: Yeah) Now, I have been s — pointing out the good points of it. (Gambon: H'm) I've been hammering on it most of the afternoon. And in rebuttals they have never said to me, "We won't" (Gambon: H'm), but they continually talk about this 20%. (Gambon: Uh-huh) Now, that's where I get my cue.

Gambon: All right. I think we have to find out from them whether or not they are definitely opposed to the principle of the fixed bonus idea regardless of the amount involved. (Pause) And I think they should be

more specific in this sanctimonious statement they made here about
continuing the practice that we have in the past, which, as far as
we're concerned, is no good. Practice and the principle involved is
all right, but I mean their attitude stinks on that proposition. We'd
have to go to arbitration on everyone of those cases, and there's nothing in writing to support the yardstick that we ourselves set up. Now,
I — I think you oughta find that out, George, because it's important to
us whether it's a 6-month proposition or whether it's a year proposition, and I think they oughta tell us why they're opposed to the fixed
bonus idea in a plant which, out of 1253 members of the union, at least,
everybody but a hundred and thr — 183 people are on a — on incentive,
either fixed bonuses or incentive rates on which the average incentive
earnings is better'n 135%. (Pause) I don't get their opposition / to
the principle!

Mediator: (Over Gambon above) Well, I don — one thing — one thing I
might ask. They didn't raise this, but I did. I — when you went over
some of those rates this afternoon (Gambon: H'm) as to what a man
would get with the 20% in (Gambon: H'm) — I think in H, for instance,
wasn't that one of the high classifications?

Meyer: It's in the middle.

Gambon: (At same time as Meyer above) No, H is one of the / small.

Mediator: (Over Gambon above) Well, which one was the high?

Meyer: L.

Gambon: The L.

Mediator: L?

One of girls: L.

Gambon: Yeah. Uh —

Mediator: I believe you said it came to 32¢.

Gambon: That's right.

Meyer: That's (Mediator: Now —) for 20%.

Gambon: 20%. / Full 20 per — right.

Mediator: (Over Gambon above) Yes. 20%. The full 20%. Now, when
that man got 32¢ an hour, wouldn't that throw that rate out of line?

Meyer: No, 'cause it's a bonus.

Gambon: (At same time as Meyer above) No, why would it? It's a payroll add. It's bonus. (Mediator: Oh) It's got nothin' to do — here's
your — see, as far as our job evaluation goes, this is the (Mediator:
Yeah) rate, George — this do — $1.60. Bonus has nothing to do with
it, see. This is still the evaluated rate here, and this is what we
would call our incentive base wage rates. Now, despite the fact that
none of these people earned any bonus from the time we put in a job
evaluation system, we've always carried in our wage schedule these
rates here as the incentive base wage rate, and the — the difference
between this and 2.27 is listed as a payroll add, and the total of those
2, the payroll add and the incentive base wage rate, is listed s — as
a clock-hour wage rate.

[Tape changed]

We would take away the s — 5 of the 67, which would make that 62. If
you gave her 10%, as we're suggesting here, she would get — take
away the nickel, she'd get 6.3¢. That's the low wage grades! It's not
all the high people! (Meyer: Not that many high) Incidentally, 71 out
of 183, see, are in the high wage grades — the very high wage grades.
(Slight pause) Here's (Meyer: And they wanta give all the people —)

99 people in grades — well, all the way from I to B, that out of the —
the most of those people — actually there's only one guy in I — Grade
I. That — that means that there are 98 people in Grade B to G. And
you can see here, George — here's the — the total cost per hour to
the company for 99 people is $17.476. For 84 people —

Mediator: What is this figure?

Gambon: 7 — this is (Mediator: 6/10ths) cost per hour for all of 'em
— $17.47 and a — and 6/10ths ¢ per hour. For the skilled trades
alone, 71 men, it's $21.05. It's 71, 21.05, and 99, and 17.476. (Pause)
So the — the — certainly the amount of increase is gonna be higher up
in here because of the existing rates, but this is where it's needed!
And on the basis of the wage rates I quoted for you this afternoon —
I mean, area rates here — the same shops that they've been throwing
at us for comparisons — even with 10%, or 16¢, we get $1.60 — we
get 16¢ bonus; we would then get 62¢, would give us 8 — $2.38 for a
top rate! And that's still lower than some of the — the wage rates in
this area! Now, that company, if they're interested in eliminating inequities, is never going to do it within a reasonable time by applying
5¢ now and 5¢ again and 5¢ some other time. Christ, it'll take $2\frac{1}{2}$
years to do it, and it's — look what happened in Aero's. I got the
same problem! Believe me, the day that Aero's walked out — their
skilled trades — what happened in our place? "That's what we oughta
do," see. So then we gotta sit on the guys, but how long's anybody
gonna sit on 'em with these rates around the place? If that shop of
ours walked the hell out of there we'd be tied (?: H'm) up, too, because it's — it's (Meyer: Nobody'd work) — basically it's a maintainence group. We buil — build very few new stuff. Maybe 5 or / 6
men in that plant —

Mediator: (Over Gambon above) All right. Let me ask you this. Why,
then — why do you suppose that h — that they would object so strenu-
ously to this / 20%?

Gambon: (Over Mediator above) You know what I (One of boys: Yeah.
I think I can answer that, John) — you know what I personally think?
I think that they'll — if they can get a cheap settlement here they'd
willin' to go around and do somethin' about the skilled trades on an
individual basis (One of boys: Yeah), 'cause they've been indicatin'
/ that all along.

[Over Gambon above, Baker talks, then Gambon and one or 2 others
of boys briefly at once.]

Baker: (Over others above) I have from Leo Gibson — we've — the —
he told me that the company is tryin' to resist do anything for everybody but they are willin' to do somepin' for skilled trades in the
neighborhood of $2.50 an hour.

Gambon: H'm.

Meyer: And this wouldn't even give 'em two and a half.

Baker: (At same time as Meyer above) That's — is 23¢. And this man
keeps askin' me how we makin' out. I said I haven't heard nothin'
over the table yet.

Gambon: Well, the full 20% would take 'em up to 2.54.

Mediator: Yeah, but is that scuttlebutt or is that from an authority?

Baker: That's from a man — a responsible person in the company. In
fact, the 3 responsible people in the skilled trades have been tellin'
us in the skilled trades meetings that we have that, "We would like

to do somepin' for skilled trades.'' They made a sign of it and they
paraded through the front office. Here's another man that just left.
Grossman made a (Gambon: H'm) sign up and paraded it in front of
office. (Pause)

Mediator: So your thought is that what they would like to do is make a
settlement less than what this would cost and then up the skilled trades?

Gambon: Yeah! But you know what they're gonna do if they do that?

Meyer: Merit increases.

Gambon: It'll be a merit proposition, because they've been throwin' in
there estimated times in there for some time, now. I mean, sp —
actually it's a speed-up proposition. They're tryin' to institute jobbing shop practices. So it'd be a merit increase proposition, and the
only thing they'll do is they'll — they'll offer these merit increases
to the younger men who perform a lot faster than our older guys, and
that'll upset the works! (Pause)

Mediator: Be back.

Management Caucus - G (8:15 P.M.)

Pranis: Home! Guess it's (laughing heartily) that place I (Mediator
says something) came from a long time (Espig laughs quietly) ago.
(Still laughing) xx, I think.

Mediator: Look, in another week you'll be able to vote in the primaries
from our office building here.
[A short period of miscellaneous conversation, unrelated to the Atlas
case, follows.]
I was discussing 20¢ — uh — 20% with 'em — this fixed rate — and
feeling them out x it, asking a lot of questions, and — (pause). They're
pretty well set on that! I do think that you're goin' to get a terrific
struggle on that. They want this — whatever they get distributed s —
on that basis. (Rather long pause) Now (slight pause), I put it to
them this way. I said, ''Here's where these negotiations are. Your
negotiations are really in a dilemma. The company has 2 problems,
not one — 2 proposals, not one. (?: H'm) They have the difference
between 4¢ and 7¢. That is one — the 6 months. On the other hand,
there's a year proposition with a 20% involved, not to say the least
about another problem, the total cost of the package. We're jumping
from hither to yon and hither to yon because we don't know just what
will do this. On one hand, you want — we know you want a year's contract! I know you want a year contract, and company knows you want
a year contract. You've stated so! But there are gimmicks that are
in that thing. I don't know how we can approach one without dropping
the other first, so we know we have no other avenue to go up or down.''
(Slight pause) That led into our discussion of the year bonus. I said,
''Now'' — uh — year proposal. I said, ''Now, y — you're — you favor
that. The company has told you that they're not too, too anxious about
it. But it might be well for us to talk about some of the gimmicks,
and if the gimmicks could be — or the objections to it could be resolved, maybe the principle could be adopted. I don't know. But I
know that I can't do it until such time as we reach this point.'' (Pause)
Now, I — I broke off there. 'Course, I — that's just the gist of what

we said. It's not the detailed report. Now, I came in here with a thought in my mind that I wanted to talk to you about. I <u>haven't</u> talked to — to them. (Slight pause) I'm pretty certain that they're going to stand <u>hard</u> and strong against any settlement based w — on a 6-month period, and I think they're in a cozy, comfortable position of saying, "7¢ is our rock bottom on that deal, if ya want it." (Rather long pause) Now, if that is a fact (slight pause), then you would have to explore the other, see whether <u>it</u> had any merit — the <u>year</u> business — and what the gimmicks were — road-blocks. Now, I got this thought, based on the way they proposed this thing — the year deal. What kind of a proposition could you develop here with me along the terms that they have outlined, putting your own cost, not their figure — a figure that you could live with but under their proposal? In other words, the way they have proposed the 10%, 20, 5, 5; but never mind their 5's, or never mind their figures. But, first of all, could you go along on the principle of their proposal?

Loring: We could go along to some extent, George. Yes.

Mediator: Now, what I'm asking you to do now is to develop a package under those terms for <u>me</u> and <u>you</u>. Just between us (Loring: Uh-huh); not — not to be used <u>yet</u>. (Pause) Now, let's get a look at it and see what ya could do — what ya — something you could live with but with your — your prices in there — your costs. (Pause)

Loring: All right. I've been thinking along the lines — seein' what we could do within the limits of — I — in some ways I — I hate the year's contract whereby — whereby the contract itself, we have a chance to look at it 6 months from now. It's very conceivable they'll get a much better deal now than if we have 2 reopeners. (Pause) I mean, if — I — I wasn't just putting <u>on</u> the things that we're concerned about. Each day they become more <u>in</u> the realm of real, rather (Mediator: H'm) than just speculation. We would like — as I say, we would like to take 'em as they're set up. On the other hand, if we <u>can</u> work it out, well, O.K., we won't say we won't turn it down if it can be worked out, but we will not buy it at an exorbitant price (Mediator: That's right), definitely.

Mediator: You give me what you think you can do on that.

Loring: Now, d'you want the — the top figure, or somethin' that we will <u>bargain</u> with?

Mediator: Give me your top. That's the one I want, because, when that is sold, I have to know what it is, see. Now, it doesn't mean that you'll get short-changed, but if I know what your top is or your bottom, however you wanta (Loring: Uh-huh) put it — your top, rather — top that you would go, it's a foregone conclusion that that's going to be lower than their 10-cent package, or whatever their cost was. (Loring: Uh-huh) I think we better approach it there. Give me your top one when ya write it.

Loring: O. / K.

Mediator: (Over Loring above) O.K. Yeah.

Loring: Well, we'll work on that now.

Mediator: All right. Why don't you do that? As soon as you get it set, call me in. (Loring: Uh-huh) Let's take / a look at it.

Loring: (Over Mediator above) How serious is this midnight tonight threat that we got last?

Mediator: I haven't heard it.

Loring: Yeah.

Mediator: Haven't heard it mentioned again, and I didn't dignify it. I
didn't follow it up. See, when you dignify those things, even if they're
true, why, you (Loring: Yeah, I see) x 'em. I a — I think that the
way these negotiations so far are moving — it's a little difficult for
you who are here in the caucus room and don't have the benefit of
being in there when we're talking (Loring: Yeah) to them — it's a
little difficult for you to appreciate it as we do. We can see if you
hadn't done some of the things you did, the positions you've taken
(snaps fingers), they'd been on top of those, and with each one they'd
dig in. Soon as they think — now, I know what kind of a bargainer he
is — negotiator he is. Soon as they think — soon as you — they watch
every move you make, every word you say, and as soon as they think
there's an opening there, their bargaining is gonna tighten right up.
Now, he's pretty loose now. He's loose because you're — there hasn't
been a crack in that wall. (Pause) And he wouldn't be in a receptive
mood this early if it hadn't been for that. And I's — he — I think that
(pause) one of the reasons is because we haven't been dignifying any
of his threats, or followin' him up on it. He doesn't know whether
you're worried about 'em or whether you aren't. (Espig: Good. That's
where we'd like to have him) He doesn't know that. (Loring: H'm)
And I can't afford to let him know it (Loring: Yeah) because, see,
he's the petitioner. So I have to work from that angle (Loring: Right),
always figuring him out there. (Loring: Uh-huh) So you do that.

Loring: It won't take us long, / George.

Mediator: (Over Loring above) All right. Fine. Call me in as soon as
you get it done, because I wanta work on that as quickly / as possible.

Loring: (Over Mediator above) Fine. Uh-huh.

[Mediator leaves the room at 8:25 P.M. At 8:33 he is called back by
the management caucus group.]

Loring: Well, we played around with some figures here, George. We
feel that we can live with this. We feel that it should be our top.
Right — now, this is along the lines of John's proposal, but a little
different: 4¢ an hour across-the-board, April 1st; 10¢ an hour to the
skilled trades, in addition, April 1st; and 5¢ an hour to the other day
workers, April 1st; and in October — October 1st, another 4¢ an hour
across-the-board. (Rather long pause)

Mediator: Repeat that.

Loring: 4¢ an hour across-the-board, April 1st, everybody; in addition,
10¢ an hour to the skilled trades — skilled trades / only —

Mediator: (Over Loring above) In addition to the 4 (Loring: In addition),
making it 14.

Loring: — for the skilled trades; and 5¢ an hour to the other day workers, which would mean 9¢ an hour to them, rather than 14. Other
words, in your day-work group you got the skilled trades and the
others. Skilled trades would get an extra dime, the others would get
an extra nickel.

Espig: Janitors, for instance.

Mediator: Uh-huh. Uh-huh.

Loring: Then in October another 4¢ an hour across-the-board to everybody.

Mediator: And what do you figure the cost of that package?

Loring: The cost of the April 1st comes to .0512.

Mediator: And the other?

Loring: The other is 4¢ an hour, dependin' on how you figure it. If you say it's from now to the end, it would be 2¢; but it's 4¢ at that time.

Mediator: So your total is exactly n — what is it?

Loring: It's — well, if you're gonna figure from April (Mediator: A year — for a year. Yeah) 1st to April 1st, then (Pranis: [In rather low voice] See —) it's only .0712.

Mediator: .0712.

Loring: But, actually, it's another 4¢ at the next (Mediator: Yeah) re-opener, without any argument. (Slight pause)

Pranis: This assumes, George, no reopener in October, I guess. (Slight pause)

Mediator: Yeah! It's an automatic inc — increase.

Pranis: That's right. We — we don't like the 20%, as you've gathered. I mean, / as a percentage we don't like it.

Loring: (Over Pranis above) That — that's — that's gonna be a stumbling block, George, because my — our people here don't think it's fair. We feel there is merit to give the skilled trades more, but there's not nearly as much merit to give the other day workers more, / generally.

Pranis: (Over Loring above) No. We don't — we don't wanta give the skilled trades a _percentage_, either. We agree there are inequities, but we figure a percentage is not the way to do it. (Loring: Uh-huh) An _incentive percentage_ is not the way to do / it.

Espig: (Over Pranis above) We feel there's an adjustment necessary for basic rate inequities but not a matter of incentive fixed bonus, which can't _possibly_ be attached to the job, anyway. Bonu — figu — these fixed bonuses — you can say this to them. These fixed bonuses started out to be substitutes for incentive rates _until_ ra — incentive rates could be established. There's no possibility of incentive rates _being_ estab — established on these jobs. These are what are known — commonly known as day-work jobs. How are we gonna esta — establish an incentive on — on a — an — a janitor's work, for instance?

Pranis: Or a matron.

Mediator: Uh-huh.

Espig: (At same time as Mediator above) Or a man who ser — who handles out brushes, or collects wastepaper, or somepin'. We don't think that that — we don't think that those people should get a 20% increase. We're already paying _far_ and above what this area pays for janitors and matrons. (Rather long pause, with Mediator drumming on table)

Mediator: I don't wanta make any notes on that. I want it in my head. (Pause) 4¢ now, April 1; 10¢ to the skilled workers, making it 14 for the skilled workers; 5¢ for — what title were they?

Espig: Other day workers.

Mediator: — other (Pranis: Rest of the day worker) day workers, making a total of 9 (pause); April 1 (pause) — or, October — come October, 4¢ across-the-board, _everybody_. (Loring: Uh-huh) That would make, for the skilled workers, 18¢ in October altogether, counting the increase they would get (Loring: Uh-huh. Uh-huh) now. That would make — for the _hourly_ day workers that would make 13¢.

Pranis: Yep.

Loring: Right. (Rather long pause)

Mediator: (In whisper) 13. (In natural voice) Didn't miss anything, did I?

Espig: No, that's right.

Pranis: (At same time as Espig above) And 8¢ for the other people (Loring: 8 c —), come the day in October / for the rest.

Loring: (Over Pranis above) 8 for all the other people.

Mediator: Uh —

Pranis: (At same time as Mediator above) A total of 8 for all the rest of the people.

Mediator: Well, what other people are there?

Pranis: All the incentive workers (Loring: All the incentive workers) — all women. Practically all of 'em are.

Mediator: Oh, now, wait a minute. Wait a minute. 4¢ for everyone across-the-board.

Loring: Right.

Pranis: (At same time as Loring above) April and October, / too.

Mediator: (Over Pranis above) Oh, I see. On the incentive workers, they just get 4¢ now and 4¢ in October, which would — now, would that go into their (Pranis: Pay add) a —

Pranis: Pay add.

Mediator: (At same time as Pranis above) Oh, with the pay add.

Pranis: All this is pay / add.

Mediator: (Over Pranis above) All this is pay add.

Loring: Uh- / huh.

Pranis: (Over Loring above) On incentive.

Mediator: Doesn't go into the incentive system / at all. Doesn't touch it. [Over Mediator above, 2 or 3, including Pranis and Loring, answer "No" in quick succession.]

Pranis: That's right. More / pay.

Mediator: (Over Pranis above) So now, how many of your people are — the majority of 'em in — incentive workers?

Loring: Yes.

Mediator: Uh —

Loring: I can give ya a rough (Pranis: Well, they're —) estimate.

Pranis: All right. They're incentive.

Espig: Well, I have the exact figure here.

Loring: There's 1000 out of 1200 and — there's a — 1042 out of 1223 / xx.

Mediator: (Over Loring above) Are incentive workers. So the bulk of 'em would really get (Loring: 8¢), for a year, 8¢. (Pause)

Loring: Not as — yeah, that's right. (Slight pause)

Pranis: No, I — wait a minute. (Slight pause) In October —

Loring: During the year they / would get 8¢.

Pranis: (Over Loring above) In October they would have gotten a total of 8¢ more.

Loring: Uh-huh. (Long pause)

Pranis: Incidentally, we wanta say October 1, or the first Monday?

Mediator: Now, tell me this. This is important. (Slight pause) Now, how strong are you — how sticky are you on this 20%?

Loring: Well, we feel very strongly, George, that we wouldn't — if we could meet the cost, I mean, depending on how they'd wanta split what we can offer. We wouldn't wanta take a strike on account of it, but we do feel strongly about it. I mean, it's up to that point. (Rather long pause) Isn't that right, Erv?

Espig: Yes, sir!

Loring: Bob, you feel that / way?

Pranis: (Over Loring above) Right! Not worth a strike. To him either, for / that matter.

Espig: (Over Pranis above) Yeah. I would hate to spoil it and I'd hate like hell to have it — have it sent to them, but (Pranis: Question. October 1 is a W —) we said we're gonna do everything we can to put an inc — an indirect incentive program in there.

Pranis: October 1 is a Tuesday. D'you still wanta say October 1? (Pause)

Espig: No.

Pranis: Fine point?

Espig: No.

Pranis: (Says something but cannot be understood)

Espig: (Over Pranis above) But let's — let's — let's leave that for the 11th hour plus.

Pranis: Well, what are we talkin' about, so George knows what xx made?

Espig: If it's a Tuesday, we're talkin' about / September —

Pranis: (Over Espig above) Is it October 7th, or you talkin' about September (Espig: Na-ah!) 30?

Espig: Yeah. / To get it settled —

Pranis: (Over Espig above) xxx September 30th was the fir — last Monday. 'Cause April 1's a Monday, as it is. (Slight pause)

Mediator: All right. That helps me with my thinking. 'Course, I'm not using any of it. Now, what I wanta do now is go back and strengthen — hit hard again the 20% thing. See, I have to neutralize that, if I can. Now, that's what I've been doing in the last meeting. Now I have to go back and <u>hit</u> it again. (Loring: Uh-huh) Now, if I can get that thing knocked out, then I think we can move. And I've told them that. I said, "I think that if you knocked that thing out you will then give me something to p — persuade the company with, to get them onto the <u>principle</u> of a year's incre — uh — contract." So, I wanta go back and finish the job.

Loring: O.K., George. Good / luck.

Espig: (Over Loring above) Well, George, look. We could — we — we had no way of putting janitors and matrons, and there are 31 of them, out of this group of people involved there on incentives. There's no way that we can honestly say they're entitled to 20%, the same as an in — production worker who <u>can't</u> work on incentive, because we can't find a way to put it on — or haven't got time to put it on. The kind of people we have on matrons' and janitors' jobs don't lend them to the incentive program. And the same thing can be said for the skilled trades. Now, we're willing to — we're willing to recognize the inequity <u>in earnings</u> but not through some screwball incentive program that we're — we're already stuck with <u>part</u> of, let's put it that way. Let's not — we don't wanta expand (Mediator: H'm) that which is already a — a poor set-up. (Pause)

Mediator: (In low tone) Uh-huh.

Espig: I mean, i — if — if there's any — and John'll understand you.

Mediator: D'you have a shift working tonight?

Espig: Yes.

?: (At same time as Espig above) Uh-huh.

Mediator: What — or how many people?

Pranis: Couple hundred.

Mediator: Do you — twa — well, you work 3 shifts?

Pranis: 2. We have a 3rd on (Espig: We have a 3rd small shift) of about 20 or 30 people.

Mediator: Oh.

Pranis: After / midnight.

Mediator: (Over Pranis above) 3rd shift would be after midnight.

Pranis: After 1:00.

Mediator: 20 people. (Pause)

Pranis: All is quiet in the 2d shift so far.

Espig: Yeah (Pranis talks at same time), there's been no — there's been wondering. I just talked to one of the girls that's talking to employees all the time. She's up there making transfers, and sh — these people talk in front of her without — without thinking too much about it. There's groups of 'em there. She doesn't ask 'em. She doesn't try to get things from them. But she says there's wondering about a strike date but there's no — been no strike date mentioned up there. That could change easily. (Pause)

Pranis: 'Course, the chief steward of the night shift is down here, the fellow with the big W on his tie.

Mediator: Oh. Yeah, we had to give him a couple anacins.

Pranis: You did? Well, good for them.

Loring: Our hopes go with ya, George.

Union Caucus - D (8:50 P.M.)

Mediator: John, they're (rather long pause) — that 20% is the road-block (slight pause) — that application. / They're —

Gambon: (Over Mediator above) Did he say why? (Pause)

Mediator: Yes, they said that (pause) — one illustration — they said there's 31 people — janitors and some other people — that would be involved here, and he said you certainly can't set up an incentive rate for people like that. And — (pause).

Gambon: All right. I buy that for the moment, and tell me some more th — if they have it. I got a breakdown of the jobs involved. There are 31 janitors and matrons. That's correct figure as far as mine go. (Rather long pause)

Mediator: 31? (Gambon: 31) Something — that's what they said. It's —

Gambon: 24 janitors and 7 matrons. Now, if they say they can't set a rate on them, how 'bout the rest of these?

Mediator: Now, they're — they're — they're against the whole — the principle as a whole x. Now, the — you — that was one of the reasons they gave. (Gambon: Uh-huh) And what I came in to tell you was this. Now, you can take this 2 ways: (1), you can believe me that they're against this thing and start a new tack of negotiations, or we can bring 'em in and let you negotiate this thing out and have all these cross arguments, positions, and see if you can change their mind. I mean, it boils (Gambon: Well —) right down to that.

Gambon: All right. So they're opposed to the fixed bonus. What do they propose to do?

Mediator: There hasn't been any propose-to-do until they know whether the union is standing pat on that. Now, if the union is standing pat on that, that's one thing; if they aren't, then I want to get into the principle of this year contract and <u>get</u> a proposal from them. (Rather long pause)

Gambon: Well, s'pose I generalize, too. The proposition of the 20% fixed bonus is a — is one which the union is adm — is interested in for the purpose of eliminating inequities, Number 1, namely in skilled trades and production workers, Number 2, other day workers and production workers. When we say "other day workers," we have, in our opinion, a great many very good cases for consideration of applying the fixed bonus as it now stands (pause) to many of these[1] jobs, with a possible exception of — put them up in the back there, will you, so those guys can see them, so they get it through their Goddam heads? (rather long pause) — with a possible exception of janitors and matrons. (Rather long pause) Assuming that I recognize for the moment that there are not 31 but possibly 34, counting 3 laborers in the other plant who are all in the same department as these janitors and mat — matrons (pause), are they only opposed to the principle of 20% bonus because they say these people couldn't possibly be rated?

Mediator: No, they're — I — I told you they're opposed to the thing as a whole.

Gambon: Well, but you added "because" —

[Mediator and Gambon talk at once.]

Mediator: That was (Gambon: Yeah) one illustration. (Gambon: Yeah) Now — then I said if you wanta go over these points with (Gambon: H'm) them and negotiate that and find out the why's and where, that's one approach. / The other is —

Gambon: (Over Mediator above) Well, I'll say to you at this point that I am not opposed to lo — leaving the principle of 20% fixed bonus for <u>everybody</u>, at the moment, provided they make an offer that will substantially eliminate the differential that we have — I mean, the inequity we have between day workers and production workers. In other words, well, I'll talk to 'em on the basis of flat cents per hour as they're talking to us now, and at least in a limited basis for 5¢ for skilled trades. (Pause)

Mediator: Say, a word about those signs. (Gambon: Yeah) I'll tell ya why that I don't think that's good. Now, I've been talking to them / xxx. I said —

Gambon: (Over Mediator above) I didn't want them spread all out like that. He could / just have one pile.

Meyer: (Over Gambon above) You said stand 'em up. (One of boys laughs)

Gambon: Well, I meant the whole pile.

Mediator: I've been talking to them — I've been talking to them about sending letters, see.

Gambon: Well — well, they told us they / were gonna send 'em.

---

[1]At this point, 2 of the boys entered with a pile of large "STRIKE" placards which they distributed along the window ledge behind Gambon, facing the management group seats.

Mediator: (Over Gambon above) I know. I know. But I raised that question (Gambon: Uh-huh), see, and I've been arguin'.

Gambon: Do they know they're buckin' a midnight deadline yet?

Mediator: Yeah. (Gambon and someone else say something at once) So that might upset some / of my arguments.

[Over Mediator above, Saunders and another boy talk about how to place the signs.]

Gambon: (Over others above) That I don't go along with ya. Lay it flat on the table.

Saunders: They can see it.

Baker: Upside down, or —

Gambon: No (Saunders: Just over there), leave it there. We're not flauntin' em; they're layin' on the table. / Is that all right with you?

Mediator: (Over Gambon above) It — that's all right. Yeah. Now, go ahead.

Gambon: I'll talk to 'em on the basis of —

Mediator: I couldn't keep my mind on what you were sayin'. All I could see was "STRIKE."

[Several laugh very heartily, and Meyer, also laughing, says something in an aside to Gambon.]

Mediator: I wonder if they were puttin' the pressure on me, Observer? (Meyer and one of boys laugh heartily)

Gambon: I wouldn't think of it, George. / Uh —

Mediator: (Over Gambon above) No, they didn't.

Gambon: I will negotiate on any terms that includes a substantial offer from the company to eliminate the existing inequities between day workers and production workers — or incentive / workers.

Mediator: (Over Gambon above) Well, how else could you do it? How — how could you do anything like that other than a percentage basis?

Gambon: They're offering 5¢. They gave us 5 once before for all day workers. They're now offering 5¢. Incidentally, I mean, to give you an idea of what I'm talking about, I've been doin' a little figurin' here, too, on that very same proposition, and at present they have $3\frac{1}{2}$-cent general wage increase and this 5¢ add for skilled trades, which we estimate at .00284, or a total of .03784 on the table. If the same $3\frac{1}{2}$ would remain where it was and they were to increase the 5 to a 10-cent add, they would only have $.04068 laying on the table. Now, I did that purposely because, as I understood them to say, the difference between their original estimate of $\frac{1}{2}$¢ and the new estimate they now have, because of the dispute we raised, would be given to skilled trades. Since we were talking about and thinking we had a 4-cent offer from the company, I say at this moment their offer, to be realistic on that 4-cent figure, should be $3\frac{1}{2}$-cent general wage increase plus 10¢ to skilled trades only, which will produce a total cost figure of .04068. (Pause) Follow?

Mediator: Uh-huh.

Gambon: Now, that is not sufficient. (Pause) Now, that would be where I — that would be what I would say to them, that I have a right to assume we have here now, taking the total 4-cent figure that they talked about right up to the last minute here. They're getting, on that basis, back to the difference between a 4-cent offer against the union's not 7 but $6\frac{1}{4}$¢. (Pause) Now, I just tried to do a little calculating here,

George, as to what it would cost them on this proposition of the balance of the day workers, some 112 in number. That's outside of the journeymen themselves. (Pause) Got a final figure, and I have to find out what it means. (Rather long pause) In apply — to apply the full 20% to 112 people outside of skilled trades would cost them $1\frac{1}{2}$¢ and 500ths, or 1¢ and 55/100ths, if you wanta call it that. Round figures, let's say a cent and a half. 10%, of course — then we get into a 3/4ths-of-a-cent proposition. If we relate that, or try to relate it, into terms of flat cents per hour, I think we have some guidance on their o — on the .00284 figure here. And using the .00284 cost figure for the 5¢ for skilled trades — or, to get away from that for a moment and back to something more realistic, using an .00568 cost figure as representing a 10-cent add for skilled trades, I think I could then safely say that they could give an additional 10¢ to the other 112 day workers at a cost of not <u>much</u> more than .00 (pause) 4 or 3 — or, for a round package instead of .04068 they could probably offer us at this moment an additional $\frac{1}{2}$¢, or a total package of $4\frac{1}{2}$¢, which should produce $3\frac{1}{2}$-cent general wage increase and 10¢ an hour additional for <u>all</u> day workers. Now, I'm thinking — I'm — I'm — I'm — I don't have those figures in front of me. I'm assuming some things here quickly. (Pause)

Mediator: For a 6- / month —

Gambon: (Over Mediator above) So that i — what they're arguing about at the moment, as I — as I have this package here now, considering that they have said all along a 4-cent package, I can make that produce $3\frac{1}{2}$-cent general increase, which they've had on the board all along, and 10¢ an hour for skilled trades. For an additional $\frac{1}{2}$¢ I can extend that additional 10¢ to the balance of the 112 day workers, and that would take 'em to a total of $4\frac{1}{2}$¢ at the very outside. Maybe it's off 1/10th one way or the other. Now, goin' beyond <u>that</u> point, I think we can begin to develop something here. If they wanta come up to the 7-cent figure without gettin' involved with a 20% bonus, I'll try to — I'll try to work it out with 'em.

Mediator: Now, the 20 — don't mix it up — the 20% is with a (Meyer: A year) — or maybe I — is with a <u>year</u>. Your (?: Yeah) 7¢ was 6 —

Gambon: Oh, yeah. Yeah. I'm talkin' about the 7¢ for the moment — 6 months. And that's what they've been talkin' about. They've given no indication that they're even interested in a year yet, as far (laughing slightly) as I'm concerned (Mediator: Yeah), see. You're workin' on that angle. But for a flat 5-cent-an-hour increase — general increase (pause), 10¢ payroll add for skilled trades, and 10¢ payroll add for the balance of the people, I think it could be wrapped up on a 6-cent offer from them, which is <u>still</u> short (Meyer says something) of our $6\frac{1}{4}$. (Meyer: Yeah) But it — they're becoming very realistic if they come out with something like that.

Mediator: Will you buy that?

Gambon: Can you sell it? (Pause) I'll give it serious consideration (pause) on the 6-month basis, with a reopener.

Mediator: Well, that's what I meant. (Rather long pause) Oh, that — oh, $\underline{6\frac{1}{4}}$?

Gambon: $6\frac{1}{4}$ is our figure. They say — we said 7¢ minimum.

Mediator: Well, what do you say that costs?

Meyer: 6¢.

Gambon: Now (Meyer: About), wait a minute. (Mediator: Oh) Wait'll I make this clear. (Mediator: No) This figure that we're kicking around — this 7-cent minimum that we took, see, was based on half of the 10-cent general increase we wanted and half of their estimated 4¢, which is changed, so that the actual figure — minimum figure is not 7 but $6\frac{1}{4}$. (Mediator: Oh, I see how you're figuring) Now, I — I've said that a 5-cent general wage increase offer from the company, with 10¢ additional for all day workers, would represent a cost of approximately 6¢. Perhaps slightly higher, perhaps slightly lower, but in the neighborhood of 6¢.

Mediator: No, I don't think I could sell that. (Rather long pause) Now, what about the year?

Gambon: Huh?

Mediator: Now, what about the year? What ideas d'you have on a year? (Pause)

Gambon: I think we have to find out whether or not we have any common meeting ground on this question of eliminating inequities. I mean, elimination of inequities does not mean they meet 5¢ even if they extend it to all day workers, particularly in the skilled trades. You can readily see yourself that even with a 16 — 16-cent wage increase produced by a 10% fixed bonus that we would wind up with a $2.38 rate which would still leave us in the position of being in the lower end of the — the area rates for the same kind of shops as ours, let alone th — the jobbing shops, w — in the face of those same shops entering negotiations now. They wouldn't be doing themselves a favor. (One of boys laughs slightly) And I think you ought to investigate this proposition that Les has been talkin' about, because the guys who were talkin' to him about this kind of things and to our skilled trades committee are responsible people. And I've heard this said to me by Henry Duttweiller, who's one of the guys that's been talkin' to him. Told me the same thing back when we were negotiating this contract in '52, that as far as he was personally concerned he'd like to see them get more money instead of having to work 'em overtime to hold the men. (Pause) Now, they're — they're — they're not gonna be able to maintain even a $2.38 rate for any length of time and still try to employ people in this area.

Baker: On quick figures, John, I get 5.6 if you get a 10¢ for all day workers plus $3\frac{1}{2}$¢.

Gambon: Ya get what?

Baker: 10.

[Baker and Saunders talk briefly at once, citing figures.]

Gambon: 5.6? You got me. I got .05568.

Healy: You said $3\frac{1}{2}$¢. He said 5, / didn't you?

Baker: (Over Healy above) That $3\frac{1}{2}$'s in there, / too.

Gambon: (Over Baker above) I said — oh, not — not $3\frac{1}{2}$.

Healy: 5¢.

Baker: 5.6.

[Healy and Meyer talk at once, along with Gambon.]

Gambon: (Over Healy and Meyer above) 5-cent general increase and 10-cent add.

Baker: Oh, oh, oh, / oh.

Gambon: (Over Baker above) See? (Pause) Now, I say roughly about 6¢ that would run to, plus or minus maybe 1/10th somewhere.

Mediator: A what?

Gambon: Plus or minus maybe 1/10th. I mean, it's in the area of a 6-cent proposition, with a 5-cent general increase with a (rather long pause) — h'm, talk about quite a bit of things here. I mean, you can talk in terms of a 4 (pause) — no, let's see (pause) — you can talk in terms of a $4\frac{1}{2}$-cent general increase (pause) if you take the (pause) — no, n — now, wait a minute. (Long pause) No. We won't take a $4\frac{1}{2}$¢. It went down again. To hell with that. (Pause) Are these guys givin' you any reason to believe that they're willin' to try to eliminate these inequities?

Mediator: No, I haven't talked about it. How would they, if they didn't accept the 20%, or a percentage? How would they / do it?

Gambon: (Over Mediator above) But they're indicating some willingness in the sense that they have offered a 5-cent additional wage increase for skilled trades / alone.

Mediator: (Over Gambon above) Oh, I see what you mean.

Gambon: They previously (Mediator: Let's assume that they —) recognized the principle involved in the inequity proposition by giving 'em 5¢ back in March of '52. (Mediator: All right. Let's ass —) They gave it to all the day workers / then.

Mediator: (Over Gambon above) Let's assume they are interested in it.

Gambon: H'm.

Mediator: Go ahead.

Gambon: Well, I'm saying in effect that they oughta start off and talk in terms of at <u>least</u> a 10-cent figure.

Mediator: For what?

Gambon: For (Mediator: 6 months? Year?) all — oh, yeah. Y — yes. 6 months.

Mediator: See, I have to keep — I don't know what you're talkin' about sometimes. I have to fl — / have to come back to the 6 months or the year.

Gambon: (Over Mediator above) Well, let me — look. I'll talk to you on this basis — s. When it comes down to a year, George, I'll talk in terms of splitting the effectiveness of the total increase, part of which shall be effective on April 1st, 1953, and part of it on October 1st, 1953, which — for instance, when you talk about what we — we had as a 12-cent figure, which — what was it? — $12\frac{1}{2}$¢. If you were to take and split that $12\frac{1}{2}$¢, as we were proposing it, see, into a 5-cent general wage increase effective on April 1st, 1953, and another 5-cent general wage increase effective for October 1st, 1953, and in addition to that you had a 10% fixed bonus effective for April 1st, 1953, and the balance of the 10% — or rather, the balance of 20% — effective for October 1st, 1953, while in round figures it's a $12\frac{1}{2}$-cent proposition, the actual cost over a period of one year would be approximately 9-point-some-cents-an-hour cost to the company. Now, in effect that's what I'm saying to you. I'm willin' to bargain on that basis for a year's proposition. In the face of the company's refusal to consider a year's proposition, I'm not setting up any minimums at this point, / since they're confining this to the area of 6 months.

Mediator: (Over Gambon above) Well, my point is this. Assuming we could get a contract for a year without that 20% feature in there, what would you consider?

Meyer: (In <u>very</u> low voice) Uh!

Gambon: Well, you're askin' me what my minimum position is, and I'm
not goin' to (Mediator: No, I didn't mean to — no) offer that now in
the face of the company's / position.
Mediator: (Over Gambon above) No. I meant more — I meant — no.
No, you misunderstood me. I meant (Gambon: H'm) more, how
would it be applied? Not so much the — see, not so much how much.
Gambon: Yeah.
Mediator: Not that. What application could — how — how could you get
around the 20%? You started to talk about it.
Gambon: Well, by putting a flat X cents-per-hour additional in for day
workers, / the same as we've done before and the same as they're
offering now.
Mediator: (Over Gambon above) In other words — in other words — in
other words, as far as application is concerned, your mind would be
open to X amount from April 1 (Gambon: H'm), 1953 (Gambon:
H'm), to October, 1953. (Gambon: Yeah) Uh-h-h (rather long pause
— you do it by X's. Let me listen. X amount, 1953, then to Oc — to
October, 1953, and then X on top of X in — in '5 — in October of '53.
Look. Let's see / if these —
Gambon: (Over Mediator above) Let me take an outside position and
say that since the union is interested in 20% and since I talked to you
in terms of full 20% if it's a year proposition, suppose I put it to ya
this way. The full 20% would result in 32¢ an hour for the top rate.
As an example of what I'm talking about, in terms of straight cents
per hour, forget the percentage propositions, suppose I said that I
would take 16¢ effective on April 1st, 1953, and 16¢ on October 1st,
1953, which would give me the same result without a percentage
proposition involved in any way a'tall. 'Course, my thinking would
follow the same principle for all these day-work jobs in terms of applying a straight cents-per-hour differential in lieu of applying a
fixed bonus. Now, that's a bargainable position as far as I'm con-
cerned as to what X cents shall mean.
Mediator: I see. I get ya. I've got it. That's all right, then. (Long
pause) See you later.
Meyer: Only got 2 hours and (One of girls: 50 minutes) few minutes.
Mediator: What?
One of girls: Tonight?
Gambon: Right!
Meyer: Midnight.
Mediator: What happens at midnight?
Gambon: (One of boys speaks at same time) Their cork gets pulled.
One of girls: That's our deadline.
Mediator: That's a corker (laughing), too.
[All laugh, and several talk at once.]
Mediator: In my — in my years of mediating with labor disputes in this
Service, think of all the corks I've seen pulled out. (Someone laughs
slightly)
Gambon: Well, Atlas hasn't one seen — hasn't seen one pulled since
1936, and the pop's liable to knock 'em off their chair.
Mediator: Well, I'll say this. (Rather long pause) Think I told you once
before you people were good negotiators. (Someone laughs slightly)
That wasn't flattery.

[Meyer bursts into <u>very</u> hearty laughter and continues while Saunders starts to speak and while Gambon, over Saunders and someone else, says, "Thanks, George! I know that, too. The contract proves it."]

Mediator: (Over Gambon above) In other words — in other words, I'm just sayin' that because it's so (laughing slightly).

Gambon: <u>I</u> know that. I (Mediator: Uh —) believe it because it's true, too! (Several laugh heartily)

Mediator: What — what amazes me is that you <u>didn't</u> have a strike, based on the hard kind of bargaining you people do.

Gambon: That becomes a proposition of pointing up that the union is not only fortunate in having good negotiators but a very reasonable group of people who, when the company was in bad straits, recognized that (Mediator: Well, that can be said), and when the union was in a position to put this company out of business, didn't do so! And forewent — for — and in doing so de — refrained from pressing the company for 350,000 bucks that they owe us, see, on a retroactive pay issue. (Meyer says something) That's why I say to you, tell those guys to give us just the 350,000 bucks that we waived at one point back in around '49 that kept 'em in business and got them started to this position where they try spittin' in our eye, see.

Mediator: You know, I's just thinkin'. I was foolish for <u>even starting</u> to compliment (Several laugh heartily, and Meyer says something) you. Look (Gambon: O.K.!) at what I got into! And I've got enough troubles (Gambon: O.K. [laughing]) without havin' — (laughs, as do several others).

Gambon: You see, compliments'll get you nowhere. (Laughs, as do one or 2 others)

Management Caucus - H (9:15 P.M.)

Mediator: Uh (pause) — I think I'm doin' all right on this — I'm punchin' hell outa this 20% thing. (Long pause) We kicked so many figures around — Observer, I want you to — (speaking directly into microphone, and laughing) I want ya — I want ya to pay attention to me and straight ne — me out. We kicked around so many figures in there that I may — if — if I haven't got them in order, you remind me of it. See if — you check me. We got talkin' about a 6-month proposition (pause) and they said (pause) that you could give a 5-cent-an-hour increase — was — was that 4 or 5 on that 6-month, Observer? Do you remember? (Pause)

Observer: 5.

Mediator: 5. That's right. 5¢. You could give a 5-cent-an-hour — or they'd accept — whichever way you wanta put it — 5-cent-an-hour increase (pause), with 10¢ an hour to the skilled — for the skilled workers. (Rather long pause) An additional 5 for the day workers for a 6-month contract, according to their figures, would come to about 6¢ an hour.

Loring: Well, let's see. I think that — that's a xx. (Sighs deeply) Well, yeah. .0612.

Mediator: .0612?

Loring: H'm.

Mediator: Well, then I have that right. That would — so they're <u>down</u>, now, from 7 to — they dropped about 7/10ths of a cent (Loring: Uh-huh) on your 6-month deal. I believe I was successful in neutralizing their position on the 20%. Now, when I say — I should put it this way. Not successful — <u>totally</u> successful, but I think I made an impression to the <u>point</u> where I've got a <u>counter</u>-suggestion. (Loring: Uh-huh) The counter-suggestion would be — and I hit this percentage business pretty hard — but in <u>lieu</u> of that they said they could then do something else other than that, but — to correct inequities, such as give the day workers an additional — and it's (snaps fingers) just what <u>you</u> had proposed — not the figure, but the principle (Loring: Uh-huh) — ya know what I mean, give the — the day workers — y — one of them in your proposals there — there was an additional nickel, wasn't it ?

Loring: Right. Uh-huh.

Mediator: Now (pause), when I heard that I — I — that just fit in nicely. I mean, th — th — as a counter-suggestion, the <u>principle</u> was the same; the <u>how much</u> I don't know yet. See, I won't know that yet for awhile. Uh — (rather long pause).

Loring: Well, wait a minute, George. (Mediator: All right) I — I'm — you've lost me at — at this point. Did you say that they said that they would accept a nickel plus 10 plus 5¢ ?

Mediator: Yeah.

Loring: But then —

Mediator: For 6 months.

Loring: Yeah. Oh, now you're talking about a year. Is that right ?

Mediator: And then I switched to a year. (Loring: Oh. Oh, I see) Now I'm onto a year. Now, on the year proposition, I — I made an impression on them. I neutralized their insistence on 20%. Now, I said <u>not</u> totally I haven't done it. (Loring: Uh-huh) I won't know that until ya — now, I said, "If that is a road-block — 20% — what kind of a proposition could we <u>talk</u> about <u>other</u> than that ?" "Well," he said, "did they at any times — at any time indicate that they were interested in correcting inequities of the day workers ?" I said, "No." He said, "Well, in a way they have! The very fact that they offered something for the skilled workers." "Well," I said, "O.K., if you wanta accept that that's — as a — an indication. O.K." In other words, he answered his own question. (Pause) And <u>then</u> he said, "They could correct the day workters' — day workers' inequity by givin' 'em a flat rate in addition to (voice dies out)." But he / didn't say how much!

Pranis: (Over Mediator above) You say percentage ? You said in addition to a percentage ?

Mediator: No. (Loring: No) (Pranis: Just —) Eliminating the percentage, see (Loring: Uh-huh), which is along the lines that — of your thought to me. Now, that's where we are (pause), see. Now, they said to me, "You know, we've got until 12:00 o'clock." I said, "What's gonna happen at 12:00 o'clock ?" They said, "Why, we're gonna have a strike" — or, no — "We're gonna pull the cork out." I said, "What's a few corks among friends ? I've saw many a cork pulled out, so what's a cork ?" And we just treated it — <u>I</u> treated it lightly. 'Course, you can't (laughing slightly) afford to treat it as (Loring: No. No) lightly as I can. (Laughs)

Loring: That's true, George.

Pranis: I'm gonna be a mediator sometime.

Mediator: Uh — huh?

Pranis: I'm gonna be a mediator some day.

Mediator: Well, we need 'em! (Pranis and Loring laugh) Come on in.
Uh (rather long pause) — so — why?

Pranis: Huh?

Mediator: I forgot to ask ya why.

Pranis: Well, ya got no responsibility. You just kick it back —
[Mediator and Pranis talk briefly at once.]

Mediator: Sure! Sometimes we even spend their money! (Everybody
laughs heartily) (Pause) Uh — tell ya what. I think it's time for a
counter-proposal. (Pause) You got something to spend for a year —
a year contract — 7.1. What can ya cook up at about 6¢? (Pause.
Loring sighs twice) And then what could you do on a 6-month deal?
What would you wanta do?

Loring: Well —

Mediator: Let's look <u>both</u> over.

Loring: Yeah. Now, I — I told you this morning, and — and I've made a
point — I mean, it's usually the way I work — of telling you exactly
our position, George. I haven't held back or given you below my position at any time because I felt you had to know if you're gonna help
me, and it's — Lord knows I (Mediator: Yeah) need the help. This
morning I told you we were authorized to move a c — another cent to
go to 5 on the 6-months' reopener, or we could take a year contract
at 7, from now on. That is, whatever would add up to 7 from now on.
Well, this is about it. If we could get the 6-months' re — reopener —
this — if we could get <u>this</u> reopener settled, and — and I have not
been authorized to do this, but I'd take it on my own responsibility and
go to 5½¢.

Mediator: On the 6-month?

Loring: On the 6-months'. That would mean, say 4½¢ an hour plus 10¢
for the skilled trades plus 5¢ for the day workers. I — I'd go that on
my own responsibility. Uh (rather long pause) — and th — that
would be as much as I could possibly go.

Pranis: For 6 months.

Loring: For 6 months. Now —

Mediator: 4½, t — how much for the skilled?

Loring: 10¢ an hour.

Mediator: 10.

Loring: And 5 for the day workers (Espig starts to speak) — <u>other</u> day
workers.

Espig: If we get up that mu — that high we — should we consider / the
xx?

Loring: (Over Espig above) No, I haven't consulted you fellow — you in
agreement with me or not on this — on a 6-months' reo — on 6-months'
— the <u>present</u> 6-months' opening.

Pranis: What, 5?

Loring: 5½.

Pranis: I'd buy it for that. I — I don't know about the nic — ½¢.

Mediator: Oh, I thought you said 4½.

Loring: Well — well, the total package is 5½, George.

Mediator: Oh! I see.
Loring: It'd be 4½¢ an hour across-the-board.
Mediator: 4½ across-the-board.
Loring: Yeah. Plus / 10¢ an hour for skilled trade.
Pranis: (Over Loring above) And 10¢ an hour for skilled and 5¢ for the rest of 'em. It comes to 5 and a little — 5 —
Loring: .056 (?: Yes) I get.
Mediator: All right. Now, how could we shorten that (slight pause) (Loring: Well —) and make it different what you did offer from their first proposal?
Loring: I mean, that — I — I wouldn't (Mediator: I wanta get in between) go on with that unless it was sure to be accepted.
Mediator: I / wanta —
Pranis: (Over Mediator above) x was ever offered George was 4¢.
Mediator: That's what I mean. 4¢ was your — (slight pause).
Pranis: No. Top.
Mediator: Right. Now, this way you're putting it (Pranis: Well, x —) 4½, 10, and 5.
Pranis: Rather make it 4, 10, and — well (Mediator: Well, let's say ya made it —) — 3½, 10, and f —
Mediator: Let's say ya made it 4, 10, and 5.
Loring: Well, your 4¢ is equal to — it costs 4¢.
Mediator: Well, that would be 5¢.
Espig: That's 5¢.
Pranis: (At same time as Espig above) It'd be 5.1. / 0 —
Loring: (Over Pranis above) .0512.
Pranis: Little better'n / 5.
Mediator: (Over Pranis above) Uh (pause) — what if you made it 4, 5, and 5?
Loring: That would be (pause) .0472.
Pranis: This is no good, George, because we wouldn't be recognizing the inequities.
Mediator: Why not?
Pranis: Remember, we admit the inequities are still there.
Espig: (At same time as Mediator, then Pranis, above) Well, don't forget — don't forget we still got this 4/10ths of a cent on the insurance program.
Pranis: I scratched it, / mentally.
Espig: (Over Pranis above) I don't care whether you scratch it or not, it's there. (Loring: Well —) W — if we're gonna get that high, th — th — why not consider the possibility of the year?
Pranis: The 4¢ we offered had nothing to do with the 60¢ a month. Remember, we scratched it? (Slight pause)
Espig: No. But now, when you're getting past that stage, you're gonna — you're gonna be close to 6¢.
[Tape changed]
Mediator: ... concrete form. Now, I wanted to get from you and not — and I probably won't use it now, but 2 replies, or counters (Loring: Uh-huh), to (1), their 6-month proposition; now — and then the next one the year. Now, on the 6-month proposition you gave me your top picture — pic —
Loring: Except / I said —

Mediator: (Over Loring above) I think you said 5½.

Loring: 5½. / That's right.

Mediator: (Over Loring above) And I don't wanta use that (Loring: Uh-huh) as a counter. I don't wanta use that much. (Loring: Uh-huh) Now, what I'm tryin' to get / from you —

Loring: (Over Mediator above) Let's use this that I gave you before — I mean, which comes to .05.

Mediator: Now, what was that?

Loring: 4¢ an hour, plus 10 and plus 5.

Mediator: Well, that's a jump of a cent.

Loring: It's ha — half — yes, a cent in package. / Yes.

Pranis: (Over Loring above) You're goin' from 4 to 5¢.

Mediator: You're goin' from 4 / to 5.

Loring: (Over Mediator above) Yeah. / That's right.

Pranis: (Over Loring above) Next move's ½¢ on 6 / months.

Loring: (Over Pranis above) It's — / it's speeding it up fast, isn't it?

Espig: (Over Loring above) Why don't you move — why don't you move — if I may suggest, why don't you move to 4¢ — 4½¢ across-the-board, which is a cent — full cent that way, plus 5¢ to the skilled trades, period? To hell this — the — there's no other — there is no other inequities as far as I'm concerned.

Mediator: Well, that makes — that's ½-cent jump / over y — your last offer.

Loring: (Over Mediator above) Well, suppose you did this, George.

Pranis: No, that's a penny jump.

Loring: George, this / will be —

Mediator: (Over Loring above) No, you offered (Espig: A penny?) 4. / Oh, the 5!

Pranis: (Over Mediator above) What's — what's — what's the 5¢ for the skilled trades? Then what's it worth?

Espig: 3/10ths of a cent.

Loring: (At same time as Espig above) .0 — .035.

Pranis: All right. You're gonna pay 8/10ths of a cent, George, actually.

Mediator: Yeah.

Loring: How would this — these are not — just thinking out loud, George. Fo — 4¢ an hour and 10¢ extra to the skilled trades, period; nothing to the other day workers. / This would apply —

Pranis: (Over Loring above) You're — you're a penny high, then.

Loring: That's .047. That's 7/10ths of a cent.

Mediator: Now, in your proposal the 4¢ — you offered 3½ (Loring: Uh-huh) and a nickel, didn't ya?

Loring: And a nickel.

Mediator: Now, what you're sayin' now is 4?

Pranis: But we were proven wrong for the nickel's cost.

Mediator: Yeah.

Loring: 4 across-the-board and 10¢ to the skilled trades, in addition. (Pause)

Espig: That's 4.6.

Loring: 4.7 (Espig: 4.7), including the apprentice (Espig: Huh?) in there.

Mediator: All right.

Loring: Now, is that too far to move? It doesn't leave us too much left.

Mediator: That leaves you —

Loring: Another 8/10ths of a cent.

Mediator: — another 8/10ths of a cent. That's — you — you — you actually moved what, 7 po — tenths?

Loring: 7/10ths.

Mediator: Well, that's splitting it in half. Th — that's all right (Loring: Uh-huh), because, see, you've got — y — you've got about fif — you got 15 points here. You used 7. (Loring: Uh-huh) You've got 8 over (slight pause) you could play with (Loring: Uh-huh), in case you need it. I think that would be as — to have ready, not — not to use but (Loring: Uh-huh) just to have ready. (Loring: Uh-huh) See, we're dealing with a kind of people — this — thi — this kind of bargaining is slow. But you're dealing with this kind of people that you — you — you just can't lay it on the table. (Loring: H'm) You just can't. I don't care what you (pounding table) go in there with now, they'll wanta change. They'll wanta — they'll wanta work something out — they'll wanta get a little more. (Loring: Uh-huh) No — so when you're dealing with those people, you — that kind of negotiating, you just can't give it all! You've got so much to play with; you have to apply it or distribute it so you don't get — destroy its effectiveness (Loring: Yeah. Yeah) or its complete final effective — (slight pause). All right. So much for the 6-month.

Loring: Now, for the year — 12-month — you want somepin' around 6¢?

Mediator: Uh (rather long pause) — yeah. Let's take a look at it.

Loring: (Laughs slightly and then says something but cannot be understood) (Pause)

Espig: 4 and 4 across-the-board?

Loring: Let's see what 4¢ an hour — now would be worth 4; 5¢ to skilled trades (slowly, while calculating) and 5¢ to the others now would be worth .0112; and it'd be .05. We'll do — that's the same; can't be right.

Pranis: What are ya gonna do, give a penny / in October?

Loring: (Over Pranis above) I do — / no. No, wait a minute xx.

Espig: (Over Loring above) You gotta use the same — you've gotta use the same deal for the present time.

Loring: Not — not if you're gonna spread it out.

Espig: Well, you can't get more.

Loring: Well, George's not gonna give 'em these simultaneously, / anyway.

Mediator: (Over Loring above) No, I want this for my own thinking.

Espig: Oh!

Loring: Let's see —

Mediator: I might not use it at all, but I wanta have it ready in case I have to.

Loring: (In low voice, and slowly, while calculating) 5¢ (Pranis: 4 and 4 across-the-board) be 407. Be (Espig: And 5 and 5) .0 (Pranis: 4 and 4 across-the board) 035, .0 / 112.

Espig: (Over Loring above) And 5 and 5 to skilled trades.

Pranis: That's more than 6¢.

Espig: It doesn't matter. It's not enough to worry about.

Loring: (Still in low, slow voice) .0 / 77.

Pranis: (Over Loring above) George said under 6¢. That's over 6¢.

Loring: Hope I'm not makin' a mistake here. (Pause) (Sighs) And then in October another 4¢, which would be equal to 2 now. Musta — gets me right up above it already. (Laughs slightly)

Pranis: You're gettin' 3 and a 3, 10 and f (Espig: H'm) — 3 and 3 and 5 / and 5. Let's cut it at x.

Loring: (Over Pranis above) Prob'ly about x at $3\frac{1}{2}$. (Rather long pause)

Pranis: Well, / 3 and $2\frac{1}{2}$ and 5 — 10 and 5 xxx.

Loring: (Over Pranis above) Plus 2. Have to get down (laughing slightly) to 6, George, just make it look reasonable, unless (Mediator: H'm) we stay at $3\frac{1}{2}$ across-the-board now, which isn't much to induce / them.

Mediator: (Over Loring above) Let's say you did.

Loring: .035, and say 5¢ an hour for all day workers (pause) now would cost us .0427 at this time; then .035, or $3\frac{1}{2}$¢ again in October, would be (slowly) .0175. That'd be just .0602.

Mediator: So $3\frac{1}{2}$ now, 5¢ to all day workers (Loring: Uh-huh), $3\frac{1}{2}$¢ in October.

Loring: 'Cept we're giving up our principle doin' that in that we figure that the skilled trades should (Mediator: Yeah) get preference.

Mediator: And —

Espig: (At same time as Mediator above) Make it 4¢ in October.

Loring: Now, that wouldn't — that wouldn't be too bad. / Suppose — suppose we say —

Pranis: (Over Loring above) Make it 5¢ to all skilled trades and 4¢ in October, Len, and you're keeping your principle clean, which I think is (Loring: Huh?) the idea. $3\frac{1}{2}$¢ now, 5¢ to all skilled trades, and 4¢ in October. You keep your principle the way you want it. (Pause) Remember, we're being pushed into inequities for other than skilled trades. We don't agree / there are such things.

Loring: (Over Pranis above) Well, let me — let me think just a second here. (In low voice) I — (long pause).

Espig: Either resist the day workers completely below the skilled trades, or let's give 'em the damn 20% and get it over with. That's my feeling.

Mediator: Ah-h!

[Several speak at once.]

Pranis: Now, look. (Espig: I mean that!) If you give 'em $3\frac{1}{2}$¢ now (Loring: Uh-huh), 10¢ for skilled trades, $3\frac{1}{2}$¢ in October, what have you got? Ya got $3\frac{1}{2}$ and .0175 is 5 (pause); and what is 10¢ for the skilled trades?

Loring: Well, that — that might (?: 8/10ths) be somepin', Bob. Then we could yield nickel to the other day workers, maybe. That would come out — (long pause).

Pranis: (In low voice) .057 — .0579.

Loring: (In low voice) What have I — what have I got there? .059 — well, that's just under 6 xx.

Pranis: (In low voice) Well, it's close. (Pause)

Loring: Well, the other one — let's try this once more, George.

Mediator: (In low voice) Sure. Go ahead.

Loring: 10¢ for the skilled trades and a nickel for the day workers. That would be .007 (slowly), .0042. (In low voice) That would be 3 (rather long pause); and then — (pause).

Pranis: (In low voice) .0535. (Pause)

Loring: How about that? $3\frac{1}{2}$¢ an hour across-the-board, a dime for skilled workers, a dime for other day workers, and $3\frac{1}{2}$¢ in October across-the-board? (Very long pause)

Mediator: Now, the $3\frac{1}{2}$ across-the-board — you're sayin' $3\frac{1}{2}$ across-the-board, 10¢ for the skilled workers. Now, for the skilled workers that would mean $13\frac{1}{2}$¢.

Loring: Yeah. Uh-huh.

Mediator: 10¢ for the day workers — that would mean $13\frac{1}{2}$ —

Pranis: Fi — 5¢.

Loring: 5. 5.

Mediator: Oh, 5¢! (Loring: Yeah) I see. Fi — that would make $8\frac{1}{2}$¢.

Pranis: Right.

Loring: Right.

Mediator: Then in October, $3\frac{1}{2}$¢ automatically (Pranis: For everybody) on top of that (Loring: Right), which would make 10, 13, 16 for the s — s — the —

Pranis: Skilled trades.

Mediator: — skilled trades, and it would make 5, $8\frac{1}{2}$, $11\frac{1}{2}$, October. I like that. Now, what's that cost?

Loring: That's .0637. (Pause)

Pranis: Gettin' awful close.

Mediator: Yeah, that's whippin' it close. All right. Anything less than that, though, would be the borderline the other way.

Pranis: Yeah. Well, you bleed hard pretty much this (Mediator: Yeah) time to the next move.

Mediator: Yeah. Now (long pause) — now. What I want to get back here — I better put it down on one of these other pages so I don't forget. Now, give me your — the one you gave me before that I's tryin' to remember. 5¢ — (pause).

Loring: Uh — no. $4\frac{1}{2}$¢, George, across-the-board.

Mediator: This is the s — the top package.

Espig: The 6-month / package.

Loring: (Over Espig above) This'd be the top 6-months' package.

Mediator: No.

Espig: (At same time as Mediator above) 6 months of the year.

Loring: Huh? / Oh, in — in a year?

Espig: (Over Loring above but cannot be understood)

Loring: Oh. .04 —

Mediator: Now.

Loring: — now is — now across-the-board, 10¢ for skilled trades now (rather long pause) (Mediator: Uh-huh), and 5¢ for other day workers now (pause), and another 4¢ across-the-board in October. (Pause)

Mediator: Yeah. This is screamingly close! The closeness is the $\frac{1}{2}$¢.

Loring: Right. (Rather long pause)

Mediator: Now, one question, and a big one. (Pause) If they — if they are willing to drop this — if my impression — the impressions I made on them are — were — are — are lasting on — on neutralizin' 'em on this 20%, and if they are willing to drop that and approach — make approaches on the basis of (pause) c — c — y — a fixed (Loring: Uh-huh. Uh-huh) increase for the day workers to correct inequities, as they put it — (pause).

Espig: Wa — wait a minute. Wait a minute. (Pause) A fixed increase
  in some other method / than this.
Mediator: (Over Espig above) No, no. No. This method.
Espig: If they used this method (Mediator: Yeah), O.K. (Mediator:
  That's what I meant to say) But no — but you're not saying that they
  have some other plan of changing (Mediator: No. No) — of meeting
  inequities.
Mediator: No, here's what I mean. They — they used that term.
Espig: Well, I mean, they're not s — they're not asking to set up a fund.
Mediator: No. No, what they're saying is you give 4¢ across-the-board
  or X amount of cents, whatever it is (Espig: Uh-huh), but I'm us —
  reading from your proposal — say 4¢ across-the-board. And then 5¢
  for the day workers would be / getting around the 20% — that kind of
  an application.
Espig: (Over Mediator above) Yeah. H'm. Yeah! Uh-huh. All right.
  Uh-huh. I understand. I wondered.
Mediator: Uh (pause) — assuming that they went for that, would you
  rather have — if they got away from the 20% business and you could
  work out a settlement on this basis — no, this application — would
  you prefer that, with the y — over a year, against the 6-month business at your $5\frac{1}{2}$?
Loring: I prefer the year if it could be bought anywhere near our —
  our figure, George. And m — and why I say near our figure, I mean
  at our figure, ' cause I — I'm — I seriously question whether they'll
  get as good deal in October. I mean, I don't think conditions are
  gonna be that good to get that much better deal than they get now.
  (Pause) (Mediator: Uh-huh) Let me put it this way. In any event, I
  wanta wrap it up, one way or the other. We — we wanta get it wrapped
  up, if we can. We are not against the year contract, but we don't feel
  like payin' through the nose for it, definitely.
Mediator: Which would mean the (slight pause) — oh, you mean in — in
  total / cost.
Loring: (Over Mediator above) In total cost. (Slight pause)
Mediator: Well —
Pranis: (At same time as Mediator above) It has some attraction,
  George, but not a lot.
Loring: It would save us goin' through this sort of thing, and that's about
  all (pause) — I mean, to us, as we see it.
Mediator: Tell you what we'll do. Here's the best approach. Will you
  make notes on this?
Loring: Uh-huh. (Long pause)
Mediator: We'll get this thing started that way. Here's the best way.
  We're dealing in 2 — 2 — we've been dealing in 2 approaches all night.
  (Loring: Uh-huh) Now we'll give answers on 2 approaches. (Loring:
  Yeah) Whichever one they don't want, we'll let them do the dropping.
  (Loring: Uh-huh) Then we'll know which way they really wanta go.
  This will be the test. Now, suppose you do this. I propose that you
  s — you make 2 proposals now. (Loring: Uh-huh) F — the first will
  be — and I think you — you — you can preface, or your opening statement can be that (pause) — that you have been going over all of this
  with me and that I have — an — and — and from that — from this
  c — these caucuses and in the interests of averting a sit — a strike

and getting a contract, in view of the fact that you have been — both
parties have been talking about a 6-month and a 1-year, you're making
this counter-proposal: (1) — taking the 6-month proposition first (long
pause) — that would be (pause) (Pranis says something) $3\frac{1}{2}$?

Pranis: $3\frac{1}{2}$, I think.

Mediator: $3\frac{1}{2}$, 10¢ to the skilled trade, 5¢ to the day workers, and 3¢
automat — oh, no, wait a minute. That's the year's.

Loring: I think we said 4, didn't we, George?

Mediator: 4 and 10 was 4 — 4.7.

Loring: Right.

Mediator: 4 and 10¢ for the skilled people, wasn't it?

Loring: Right.

Mediator: Nothing to the day workers.

Loring: Nothing to the day workers.

Mediator: So that one gives ya 4.7.

Loring: Right.

Mediator: Now, that's — f — that 4 and 10¢ to the skilled workers could
be the first proposal (Loring: Uh-huh), on a 6-month basis. Then
you can submit this on the year basis — the $3\frac{1}{2}$, 10¢ to the skilled
trade, 5¢ to the day workers, $3\frac{1}{2}$ automatic in October. / 6.3.

Espig: (Over Mediator above) H'm! How can — how can you expect 'em to
accept even the — the year's proposal if the money across-the-board
is less than the money across-the-board in the 6-month proposal?

Mediator: Because you're — you're giving 'em an automatic $3\frac{1}{2}$ again,
Erv.

Espig: I don't think so. / I — I —

Mediator: (Over Espig above) It — it says here you are.

Espig: I — I mean I disagree that they — that they can come — that — if
I were in that union, would I go for $3\frac{1}{2}$ / rather than 4¢?

Mediator: (Over Espig above) Yeah, but they're getting 5¢ for day workers in the 2d proposal that they're not getting in the first / proposal.

Espig: (Over Mediator above) That doesn't matter. I'm not i — there's
only — there's only —

Mediator: How many day workers?

Espig: Uh (Loring: 6 —) — 75.

Mediator: Oh!

Pranis: See, they don't — they don't have too many. There are more
skilled tradesmen, / so-called, than are of —

Mediator: (Over Pranis above) Yeah. I see. Right. I kept thinking of
the big group. Forgot about that. (Slight pause)

Espig: I'm sorry to be obnoxious, but / that —

Mediator: (Over Espig above) No, you're not. No, bringing those points
to light are important. (Slight pause)

Espig: I'm interested in a settlement. I'm interested in a settlement
that's gonna buy me what I wanta see (Mediator: Yeah) and not
somepin' worse than what I wanta see.

Loring: (In rather low voice) Well, now, let's see.

Espig: If you're gonna make a proposal of 4 plus 10 in your 6-month,
you gotta make the same kind of (Mediator: 'Fraid ya do) a proposal
in your year.

Mediator: That — and — and in view of the fact that so many are involved
w — in the 4-cent —

Espig: My God, if I — I'm certainly not gonna vote (Mediator: Yeah.
   That —) against myself when — when I go up there. Now, if you
   want the 6-month contract, this is the best way to get it! (Mediator:
   H'm) This is the way to get your 6-months' settlement!
Mediator: Yeah, we were higher on the / front end.
Espig: (Over Mediator above) True! Now, that — I have no objections
   if that's — if that's the — the consensus of opinion.
Mediator: What would it look like if ya put 4¢ on the front on a year
   package and 10¢ to skilled workers (slight pause) (Loring: Well,
   and —), an au — automatic 4 in — well, that would take ya way above.
   No, it wouldn't!
Loring: Not too far. It would be — (slight pause).
Pranis: It's almost your max, though, George.
Mediator: Yeah.
Pranis: 'Member, you said 4, 4, 10, and 5. All you're doing is deleting
   the 5.
Loring: How about (Mediator: Yeah) 4¢ now, 10¢ to skilled trades, and
   $3\frac{1}{2}$¢ in October? (Pause) That would give ya .0645. (Pause)
Mediator: They all knock at the door close, and —
Pranis: Well, they all come close. You're talkin' about your own, George.
   (Mediator: Yeah) Don't let us heckle (laughing) too much here.
Mediator: 4, 10, and what? $3\frac{1}{2}$?
Loring: Uh-huh.
Pranis: Did you say 10, or 10 and 5? (Slight pause)
Loring: Just 10. Skilled / workers.
Pranis: (Over Loring above) 10 and $3\frac{1}{2}$.
Mediator: 4, 10, / $3\frac{1}{2}$.
Loring: (Over Mediator above) Well, you don't have far to move, but —
Espig: Well, you could — y — if you could get the 5 plus 5 on the table
   (pause), that's another story. (Pause)
Mediator: What ya mean?
Espig: Well, at this point they got 10 — they're asking for 10¢ across-
   the-board, effective April 1st. (Slight pause)
Pranis: And 20%. See, that's the last offer you got, George (Mediator:
   Yeah), for a year's contract. (Mediator: Yeah) We don't have 5 and
   5 officially.
Mediator: And you said if you can get a 5 and 5, what?
Espig: Then — then — then we're in a position to get some place to our
   — our max that we gave you, and not too far away. Either party can
   hardly take a strike. They can't take a strike for — what, a cent and
   a half in October? If they can get another $\frac{1}{2}$¢ out of us, they got a
   cent; and we've said we'll go to 4, didn't we? 4 plus 4. (Pause)
Pranis: Well, we said 4 (Mediator: No, you didn't) plus — we said 4
   plus 4, 10, and 5.
Mediator: Yes, you did. Yes, you did.
Pranis: Max. If (Mediator: Yeah, you said —) they got 5 and 5 —
Espig: I mean, this gonna be an arm-twisting game at the end here
   (Pranis: That's right), but, what the hell, uh — uh —
Mediator: All right. Now, if you — if you tossed your 4 and 4 out — 4
   and 10¢ for skilled trades, 4 in October, that's your — that's your / 7.
Espig: (Over Mediator above) Yeah, the max.
Pranis: Except for the 5¢ for the un — / for the rest xxx.

Mediator: (Over Pranis above) Now, is your thinkin' — is it your thinking that if you tossed that out they'd be in a position, well, where they'd
have to decide between where they are now and a strike?

Espig: Well, you've indicated that they would then — that they had some
— John has something else in mind (slight pause) — the 5 plus 5 program. Did we have such a — a —

Pranis: 5 plus 5 plus 10%, which came to / some 9¢.

Loring: (Over Pranis above) Well, you'd get — but what's wrong, Erv,
is you — you hit our ceiling. What can we do / from now on?

Espig: (Over Loring above) Oh, I'm not — I'm not saying go out and
throw it on the table — the 4 plus 4! I'm not saying that!

Loring: Oh, excuse me. I thought that —

Espig: I'm — I'm — I'm trying to get John's counter-proposal back on
the table.

Mediator: Well, in order to get his counter-proposal on the table, we've
got to throw something out that will draw him out. Now, what've we
got to throw out?

Espig: I thought that's what we were developing.

Mediator: Yeah, we are!

Espig: Yeah.

Mediator: Oh, and then I thought / when you was —

Espig: (Over Mediator above) I — I'm guessing at what he'll do.

Mediator: Oh. Oh, I see. (Espig: I'm guessing what he'll do) I thought
you were suggesting that ya throw this out (Espig: Oh, no! Oh, no!)
and then take your chances that he won't strike.

Espig: Oh, no! No. No, I'm not suggesting that a bit. Huh-un. Because
he'd be a cent and (pause) — / what was he?

Loring: (Over Espig above) I'm wondering whether — whether — whether
our throwing out an offer of this kind will bring him down into the area
of 5 plus 5 that —

Mediator: Oh, the answer's Yes. I think it will dr — definitely draw him,
but —

Espig: Well, I'm — I'm afraid it won't draw him as fast as he oughta be
drawn. (Laughs) I'm concerned now with him! (Pause) And yet I
don't know what else to do about it, excepting to take that 10¢ for the
skilled trades out of the picture entirely.

Loring: Well, I mean, / this could —

Espig: (Over Loring above) Use that for a — another counter.

Loring: H — here's another thing, George, we might throw on the table for
the 12 months. Still, this is — doesn't leave us much room. I's gonna
say 4¢ now and a nickel for the skilled workers, and the same thing in
October. (?: H'm) But that's 6½¢ right there.

Espig: O.K! That's (Pranis: No matter what you do, you'll get it back —)
— that — you don't x how you dress it up, you can always shift around.
/ You —

Mediator: (Over Espig above) Yeah. But (Espig: You can shift xx)
Bob has got his finger on it. It — it's so darn close to the max that
the 2d offer might not have too much a — a — attraction, or there
might not be enough left in it to push it over the hump. Better to stay
at a lower figure and have a lot to throw on at the last pitch!

Pranis: Let's assume that (Espig says something) we make this proposal and John says, "I want 5, 5, and (slight pause) 10 and 5" or

somethin' like that (Espig: Uh-huh), which is about 9.6. (Espig: Uh-huh) We're at 7 and somethin'! We're close. (Espig: H'm) We're almost 7. (Espig: Well —) Best we can offer is what? $\frac{1}{2}$¢. Ah! (Pause) I mean, ya got nothin'.

Loring: Well, we're all right on the 6-months' offer, Bob, / xxx.

Mediator: (Over Loring above) Yeah, we're O.K. there. Now, you see what I wanta do in getting a proposal from you on the year, too, is to show them that our minds are open both ways. Then he (tapping table) will cut off one of these — the one he doesn't want — and he'll make his counter-proposal attractive to you. I know he will. It'll definitely work that way. See, what I want you to bring out is the principle more than the figure. Now, the principle would be this. (Pause) At no time have you submitted any proposals on a year contract. Correct?

Loring: Right.

Mediator: You haven't said a thing. So for the first time you'd be saying, "We are willing to go (pause) 4¢ (long pause), 10¢ to the skilled workers, $3\frac{1}{2}$ in October." (Loring: Uh-huh) Comes to what?

Loring: What was that again, George?

Mediator: 4 no — 4¢; 10, skilled workers; $3\frac{1}{2}$, October.

Loring: That's — (pause).

Pranis: (In low voice) 6.7.

Loring: (In low voice) Let's see. $3\frac{1}{2}$ —

Espig: Oh, that's the wrong end. It's worth 4/10ths of a cent, isn't it?

Pranis: H'm.

Mediator: 6.3, did you say? Oh, I thought you —

Pranis: (In low voice) Better'n any 6.3.

Loring: .0645. 4¢ an hour plus 10¢ skilled workers is .047; $3\frac{1}{2}$ in October is equal to .0175 now (Espig: Uh-huh), so that's .0645. Had another thought. (In low voice) Let me see if I — (pause).

Pranis: What are you gonna do with this 60¢ a month? Ya gonna hold that just in case, for the last — sweetening up of the pot? (Pause)

Loring: (In low voice) Uh-huh. (Sighs) This is a toughie, George.

Pranis: What's wrong, George, with giving that number, which is almost the top, to get him out to 5 and 5, or whatever he's gonna put on the table, and / let him eat it?

Mediator: (Over Pranis above) Well, I'm thinking of the same thing, Bob.

Pranis: I mean, we got nowhere else to go.

Mediator: See — and anything lower would be —

Pranis: Silly.

Mediator: — silly. So, let's do that. But I think you oughta give it to him, the both proposals, to let him know that you've been thinking about both of them. Now, we have been talking about — see, they — they s — see, you've got a s — 4 and 7 on the table. (Loring: Uh-huh) Then you've got a new proposal for a year's contract, with a 20% feature for day workers. Now, that's — that feature you don't like. Now, I think we've been — we've made a little headway in knocking it out, or neutralizing it. If that is the case, when you submit this proposal here you will be dignifying both proposals! (Loring: Uh-huh) Now, then he has to make a move. And he's goin' to do this. He's going to say, "Well, look." See, you've showed him in making this move — the 4,

10, and $3\frac{1}{2}$, see — you — you showed him your mind's open on this
thing. For the first time you're willing to consider a year's contract, something that he's been wanting! Now, I'll wager a — a —
a — if I don't miss my guess, he's goin' to say, after he gets both
those proposals, "Let's lay this 6-month thing aside. Let's see
what we can develop <u>here</u>." Then he's goin' to do some talking!
And I think he's gonna try it again to get your 20%, / or he'll touch
on it.

Loring: (Over Mediator above) We're not gonna be euchred into a position where we miss the 6-months' proposal and then get hung up
on the big difference and / x —

Mediator: (Over Loring above) No, <u>both</u> will be on the table.

Loring: Oh.

Mediator: Both will <u>always</u> be on the (Loring: I see. Uh-huh) table.
You're submitting 2, providing — you're submitting the year, providing it can be under these terms. You're not relinquishing 6 — 6 -
month.

Loring: Uh-huh. All right. Now, the 6-months' — what'd you say? 4¢
now and 10¢ to day workers — skilled workers?

Mediator: No. The 6-mo — wait a minute. Now I'm mixed up. The 6-
month — isn't it 4¢ (Loring: That — that's right) and 10 to skilled
/ workers, period?

Loring: (Over Mediator above) Right. (?: Sure) You're right.
Period.

Mediator: Comes to 4.7.

Loring: Right.

?: Uh-huh.

Mediator: The (slight pause) — the other is 4¢, 10¢ to the skilled
workers (Loring: Yeah), $3\frac{1}{2}$ in October.

Loring: O.K.

Mediator: Now, that leaves you later with 4 across-the-board, 10¢ to
the skilled workers, 5¢ to de day —

Pranis: You got 5¢ to the day workers and $\frac{1}{2}$¢ in October to add. Then
you're up to your ears.

Mediator: <u>4</u>¢ in October.

Pranis: Well, it ha — totaled $\frac{1}{2}$¢ more (Mediator: Yeah) here. / Then
you're — then you're finished.

Mediator: (Over Pranis above) Then you're — then you're at the limit.

Pranis: That's right.

Loring: (At same time as Pranis above) Uh-huh.

Pranis: (In low voice) That's — that / xxxx.

Espig: (Over Pranis above) Now, look. I — I think that — I think that it
can be pointed out that the die makers' contract called for 10¢ an hour
average for a year, didn't it?

Mediator: Yeah.

Espig: The die shops.

Mediator: 10¢ an hour.

Espig: So here you're having our skilled people getting 15¢, when actually
the job shops got 10¢.

Mediator: Yeah, but do you know how much (Loring: Eh?) else they
got?

Pranis: Where are they getting 15¢ to —

Mediator: They got — they got a s — s — $16\frac{1}{2}$-cent package.

Espig: Yeah. But they got fringes. (Mediator: Yeah) They didn't get it in the pay envelope necessarily. (Mediator: No) Right?

Mediator: That's right. Total cost, 16½.

Espig: They got about 10¢ in money.

Mediator: 10¢ in cash.

Espig: Well, I think (Mediator: Per hour) — I think that's what we can point out to them, because who knows whether our fringes are as good or bad o — or worse than theirs?

Mediator: 'Course, they may — they may turn around and say, well — well, their rates are different.

Espig: Yes. But we're — we're proportionately covering — if their — if 10¢ — if we were in proportion, as we must be, to the — to the job shops at this point, we are taking up 5¢ difference — giving our people 5¢ more to get them up. If — if the (Mediator: Uh —) die people got 10¢ — if the die shops got 10¢, our people were earning a — let's say our people were earning a dollar and a half and they were earning $1.60, our people would now — would now earn $1.65 and they'll earn $1.70. Right?

Mediator: Uh-huh.

Loring: Now, that's the o — the 2d proposal, George, brings us to .0645 — the 12-month. We'll get about ½¢ to go.

Mediator: Uh-huh. (Rather long pause)

Joint Meeting - F (10:00 P.M.)

Mediator: Uh (pause) — cut all the corners, needless to say both committees know that we've been working with each committee separately, and in the interest of expediency, Len, you take it from here.

Loring: That's O.K. We've been spending a lot of time talking, and Mediator has also spent a lot of time talking with us. Pointed out that there's been 2 proposals on the table from the union; we have considered only one up to this point. He asked us if —

[Tape changed]

... with the 10¢ an hour to skilled workers.

Gambon: In addition.

Loring: In addition. Yes. (Pause)

Gambon: Uh-huh.

Loring: On your 2d proposal to us, we will offer 4¢ an hour across-the-board now, 10¢ an hour to skilled workers now, and 3½¢ an hour across-the-board in October. (Very long pause)

Wollman: That 10¢ is skilled trade, period. Right?

Loring: That's right.

Mediator: Uh (pause) — no. You said 10¢ (Wollman: Yeah, 10 cen —) on top of / the x?

Wollman: (Over Mediator above) No, I mean the 10¢ — when he (Meyer: Yeah) said 10¢ skilled trade, that's / not day workers.

Meyer: (Over Wollman above) That's was between day workers / and the skilled trades.

[Over Meyer above, several, including Mediator, talk at once.]

Mediator: Yeah. (Long pause)

Gambon: Well, the position hasn't been improved too much, Len, from the standpoint of total cost to the company. As against a 4-cent offer that was on the table before, your offer now, on this present reopener, would run about .0456.

Loring: We make it .047, John.

Gambon: No, I — I don't know where we — I'm using the figures that I had here, and you're usin' the ones you (Loring: Right) have. On your general proposal of 4¢ now and 3½¢ later on a general increase basis, with 10¢ now and continue after October, we get a total package prorated over the year of about 6¢.

Loring: .0645 I have, John.

Gambon: Well, I have .06038. (Pause) Well, needless to say, the company's offer on the basis of closing out the negotiations for the entire year are too low. I still consider the fact that (pause) you haven't gone far enough, Len, on the reopener proposition here to wrap this thing up on this reopener itself. What was the figure you had? I have .0456. You said .04 — / what?

Loring: (Over Gambon above) .047, John. (Pause)

Gambon: (In very low voice) I see.

Loring: Skilled workers — we included the apprentices there — apprentices in that group.

Gambon: Oh, I see. Well (Loring: Yeah. That's prob'ly the difference), that's the difference. See, I'm not — I haven't used that a'tall. (Long pause) Well, what is your preference, Len — I mean, i — in order to — for us to know what you wanta bargain about here?

Loring: Well, it's —

Gambon: Do you prefer to still maintain the reopener or do you prefer, now that you've gotten into the discussion about a year's settlement, to do it on that basis?

Loring: John, we're completely open on it. Our primary — our first concern is to — to straighten out the situation now, regardless of which method we can do it by. We can see some — some advantages in — in not going through this again in October, but, frankly, we would just as soon close it up now and — and discuss it in October. (Rather long pause)

Gambon: I would give you a figure, Len (pause), that we would settle for on the basis of closing this out for a year — round figure in terms of total cost to the company (rather long pause), if I can have you agree that I'm not doing it for the purpose of tryin' to bargain with you and I'm not doing it for the purpose of saying, well, this is one figure I'll throw at you and then I'll bargain down with you. If I were to throw this figure to you, it'd be my honest opinion of what I think the company can afford to do for a period of a year from April 1st until the contract expiration and a figure which I think is a — a proper figure when you talk about the union's fair share of the results of the company's business (pause), a figure which I think is contributing to labor peace, particularly for a period of a year, figure which will include (pause) an elimination, to a great extent, of the inequities which now exist without becoming involved in the proposition of fixed bonuses or anything of the like.

Loring: Could you tell me just what you mean by that, John?

Gambon: Well, I mean I — th — the proposals I have to make would be proposals that would do away with inequities between day workers, which, of course, includes skill help, and without using the formula of

a fixed bonus proposition to do it. I mean, it'd be (Loring: Uh-huh)
followin' the same lines that you're talkin' about (Loring: Yeah)
now in addition to (Loring: Uh-huh) in flat cents per hour. (Pause)
Since the hour is getting rather late and we are running into a deadline proposition, taking your offer here, which you rate at .047 in a
6-month period, if you were exactly to double that you'd come up with
a 9.4. Now, my — my figure runs around that kind of a proposition,
Len, and it's not a bargainable proposition. I'm not tryin' to bargain
you up from your 6-cent proposition. I'm trying to say to you, after
having done an awful lot of figuring while you people're out there, as
to just what I can throw to you as being my honest opinion of what
Atlas can afford to pay and what can be accepted by this committee
in order to forestall any strike situation in the plant. And to be exact on my figures, I run around, h'm, .0969. Now, that's less than a
10-cent proposition package, which I'll go into you with to — as soon
as we can get some idea of whether or not you're willing to settle
this whole damn issue on that proposition. My proposition will involve a procedure of putting the increases into effect with 2 separate
breaks (Loring: Uh-huh), one effective for April 1st and another
effective for October fir — 1st, '53. But the total cost to the company over the year would be in that / area there.

Loring: (Over Gambon above) Th — that would be a total cost from
(Gambon: Prorated against the entire year) — from April — from
April 1st on? / Is that —

Gambon: (Over Loring above) Right. Right. (Pause)

Mediator: I — I didn't hear you, John.

Gambon: I say the figure I gave Len here, this .0969 business, is a total
cost to the company over a — prorated for the entire year of April 1st
to April 1st, '54.

Mediator: And did you —

Gambon: I'm withholding, of course, the exact form that I want this in,
because I'm trying to give you an honest figure and I don't wanta get
into a position where you start bargainin' again. I think it's gettin'
too late for this tryin' to jump back and forth, and that's the reason
I'm laying it right cold on the table. I would prefer this kind of a
settlement because I think it will contribute to better labor relations
for a period of a year, at least. It will contribute to better labor relations because you're gonna remove a sore spot in that plant in question of this inequity proposition. Oh, I think it — lot of things'll contribute to a lot of different things in the plant, too, for that matter.
But I also very firmly and honestly believe, Number 1, that the company has the ability to meet that figure, and Number 2, I think it is
the figure which would be properly defined as a fair proposition for
the people in this union to receive from the company as their share
of the company's operations. Now, that's (pause) — that's all I can
say about it at this moment. I — I suggest, Len, that you give it all
the serious consideration that you've given these other propositions.
I think that it can be done. I very honestly believe that. I don't think
there's any question / about the company's ability to meet that figure.

Loring: (Over Gambon above) Well, I want, of course, to give it all the
consideration (Gambon: H'm) we can, John. For that reason I'd like
to discuss it in (Gambon: All right) — in the other room with our

people. As I say, up till now we have been thinking in terms of the 6 — this — this reopener. We came in and gave our thinking on the 12-months' deal because the mediator asked us to. (Gambon: Uh-huh) For that reason I'd like to discuss this (Gambon: All right) with them. And we — we will certainly give it all the consideration we can, John.

Management Caucus - I (10:10 P.M.)

Mediator: We're not gonna stay with ya long. I think we're gonna get a cup of coffee.

Loring: O.K.

Mediator: Give ya time to —

Loring: Uh-huh.

Mediator: Uh (pause) — throwin' it out 2 ways did almost what I said it would do. It would show you what he wants. He wants the year. (Loring: H'm) That's for sure. He's let you know what his cost. (Pause) So, it's getting a little clearer, even though the figures may not be satisfactory. (Loring: H'm) Now I feel a lot better. You (laughing) may not feel (Loring laughs slightly) too good about it, but (slight pause) he's been — all night he hasn't been definite. He's now definite. See, you hit him — when you hit him with the 2 — n — now you can remember this. You can get that 6-month thing for a cost of about $6\frac{1}{4}$. (Pause) See, you're at $5\frac{1}{2}$.

Loring: We're at .047 now but would go to $5\frac{1}{2}$.

Mediator: Yeah. $5\frac{1}{2}$. You can go to (Loring: Yeah) $5\frac{1}{2}$. He may — I don't know. He may even go for $5\frac{1}{2}$, see, rather than strike, but I think his — what he's lookin' for is around 6 or $6\frac{1}{4}$ on a 6-month deal. Now, you can — you can wind it up there and then, of course, reopen in October. And, of course, here you've (pause) — you've got his over-all cost but ya haven't got his application (Loring: Yeah) — how he wants it applied. I think you're goin' to find that his application is pretty much along the same as you — day workers and skilled workers — something for them. How much, or how he intends apply it, I don't — so, from here on, it's your thinking as to what direction you wanta go. (Loring: Uh-huh) He's told you where he wants to (Loring: Yeah) go.

Loring: Well, I mean, that 9¢ is completely out as far as we're concerned. How firm d'you think that is with him? I mean, that would make a difference in what we push for now.

Espig: $9\frac{1}{2}$¢ — gees!

Loring: 9. / 69.

Pranis: (Over Loring above) Plus 9.69. His numbers are low, so it's close to a dime.

Loring: (Espig says something at same time) If you — it — that would be a dime, because his figures are low on the —

Mediator: Yeah. I think he's hittin' — he's knockin' a 10-cent door there.

Pranis: Well, he probably has his 20¢ for skilled me — skilled tradesmen, 10¢ for the other people, and — (pause).

Mediator: What was your offer? / What was your year —

Espig: (Over Mediator above) .071. Requires so that we're payin' 'em inequities for the next time.

Loring: .0 / 712.

Mediator: (Over Loring above) 6 — no, no.

Loring: Oh. Our offer was .0 —

[Tape changed]

Mediator: If figures mean anything (very long pause) — you're $6\frac{1}{2}$. (Pause) Their package comes around 10. Ya got a $3\frac{1}{2}$-cent difference. Half of $3\frac{1}{2}$ —

Loring: 1 3/4.

Mediator: 1 3/4. Your last position was $6\frac{1}{2}$ and add 1 3/4 and ya get 7 — ya get a little over 8. If it worked out that way, ya'd — there's — they might — they might wrap it up for something around 8 or $8\frac{1}{2}$, if his bargaining figures are — if that's really his last — (rather long pause). Well, we'll bring you some coffee.

Loring: Fine.

Mediator: Uh —

[At 10:15 P.M. Mediator withdraws from the management group. Before leaving the building he stops by the union caucus room to tell that group what he is doing. He returns to the management caucus room at 11:05.]

Loring: ... settle tonight?

Mediator: Uh-huh. (Pause) Yeah. (Pause) I think so. (Pause)

Pranis: But at their price.

Mediator: Well, no. xx settle. (Pause)

Loring: We — we were hashing it over a little while you were away. Their .09 or 9¢ — .0989 — whatever it was — is really better than 10, I mean, on our figuring, and that's completely out of the question now. I'm wondering if we shouldn't tell 'em that that's just too much for us to buy and go after the 6-months' closing. On the other hand, maybe you could feel 'em out, see if — how firm he is on it.

Mediator: Uh (very long pause) — yeah, I think you better let me feel 'em out. I think that would be the best / way.

Loring: (Over Mediator above) Now, I'd be willin' to go to — I — I figured out there $4\frac{1}{2}$¢ an hour across-the-board, 10¢ for skilled workers, a nickel for other day workers — that comes to .056.

Mediator: You mean this is on a 6-month.

Loring: On the 6-months'. But now if we go for that, then the other's completely out because we wouldn't — couldn't offer enough to make it sound like anything. (Mediator: Uh-huh) So, if we could get some idea first on the other one. I don't know. I mean, that's the way it hits me.

Mediator: Uh-huh. (Pause)

Espig: The .056 is the limit.

Loring: H'm. (Pause)

Pranis: For 6-months'.

Espig: We ever tell 'em — if we ever ge — put that on the table, we'll tell 'em this is the final.

Mediator: Well, we're gonna get to a point — that point soon, and when we do, that's what we have to do. (Espig: Oh, yeah!) This is it!

Espig: This is just —

Mediator: Whenever we reach that, see. And then, fish or cut bait. It's yours! And then let 'em — then they're stuck with it. They can — if they pull a strike, they pull it / on that.

Espig: (Over Mediator above) They pull it for 7/10ths of a cent. That's what it amounts to (Mediator: Yeah), if we get that far.

Mediator: They won't — they won't do it. Now, on the other — on the year business, you say they're up above 10.

Loring: Well, we've — it must be, because these — these s — skilled-work and day-work things — they're low every time they quote us a figure, and they — their figure is — in itself right now in their figuring was (Espig says something) / .09 —

Pranis: (Over Loring above) .0969.

Espig: .0969.

Loring: .0969, so I'd say it must be at least 10. (Long pause) That's out of our reach. Even with any xxxx.

Mediator: What was your last offer on a year contract amount to?

Loring: .0645.

Mediator: (In low voice) .0645. (Very, very long pause of 50") Let me find out. Uh (rather long pause) — I'll feel around for a while and I'll let 'em know that that's entirely too high and if they're interested in a year contract, they gotta come down and come down fast. And if they're interested, we'll see.

Union Caucus - E (11:12 P.M.)

Mediator: Your year contract proposal is, according to their figures, fraction better than 10¢.

Gambon: What — what year's (Mediator: Your .09 —) proposal? I didn't tell 'em that, huh?

Mediator: What was that?

Gambon: I didn't tell 'em what the hell form it took. I said / I'll put xxx.

Mediator: (Over Gambon above) Regardless, you said — you said it cost this. They said your figures are wrong, that it cost 10 and a fraction.

Gambon: What would?

One of girls: Well, how did they count it?

One of boys: How could they — how could they / know when they don't know what form it is?

Meyer: (Over boy above) You didn't say what he wanted it.

Gambon: I didn't say what I wanted or what form it was in. I said, "The package that I have to offer would cost you approximately 9 and 6 — 9 and si" — / wonder where it is? H'm. (Mumbles to self)

One of boys: (Over Gambon above) 9.69, or somepin' like that, you said.

Gambon: .0969, see. And I didn't say what form / it's in.

Mediator: (Over Gambon above) How the hell could he get that?

Gambon: Huh?

One of girls: That's it. How — what did they count? They didn't — [Several, including Gambon, talk at once. Gambon says, "I don't know what they're — how the hell are they figurin'? What are they figurin'?"]

Mediator: We weren't even in with 'em. We were out. (Pause) [Mediator and Gambon talk at once. Pause.]

Gambon: What — what items is he usin'?

Mediator: (Gambon says something short and laughs slightly, at same time) Wait there. (Pause) Unless — unless he was computing it on a 6-month basis — using that. Wait'll I find out. [Mediator leaves the room briefly, then returns with Loring.]

Gambon: 14 — that's only 7¢.

Loring: George (Gambon: Huh?) asked me — I had indicated to George that I figured your proposal, John, which was .0969, would — would be at least 10¢ in our figuring only on this basis. You mentioned that there would be an adjustment of the day workers and skilled workers (Gambon: Yeah), and our figure that we had computed this afternoon is higher than yours even since then when we've been talking, so I figured 3/10ths of a cent would make it 10, and that's — that's why I said it (Gambon: H'm) must be high.

Mediator: That's the reason.

Gambon: (At same time as Mediator above) My proposal (Loring: Yeah) — the form my proposal would take would be closer to 9¢ than it would be to 10 — I mean, forgetting any figures we kicked around up to this point. / 'Cause I think it would be —

Loring: (Over Gambon above) Uh-huh. Well, I only — I only had what you gave me (Gambon: Yeah), and then this other thought in mind, I figured it must be / 10.

Gambon: (Over Loring above) Uh-huh.

Mediator: It's 9 cent.

Loring: 10.

Gambon: No, it's not that far. (Pause)

[Loring departs at this point.]

Mediator: Now, this much I've — have got straight. The (rather long pause) — the year figure he says is too high. He said they can't buy that. (Pause) He said if the union can't — if that's not negotiable and you can't submit 'em better offer on that, then they'll have to start thinking in the direction of a 6-month contract.

Gambon: What's he mean by a better offer? Why don't he make a better offer? (Pause)

Mediator: It's a good question.

Meyer: Ask him what's the top he'll pay.

Gambon: What's the top on a year's basis that they'll pay (Meyer: Uh-huh), the same as I said I think this is it? I'm not drawin' it out for the purpose of bargaining. What does he think is the — the figure that'd be between what I've given him there and the —

Mediator: I'm goin' to propose to management that management — I'm gonna urge — I don't know whether they'll do it — to come in here and put their last proposal on the table.

Gambon: Yeah. Come o — tell 'em to come in and / stick it around.

Mediator: (Over Gambon above) And I'm going to tell 'em to make it the last one — their rock bottom. I don't care what it is. (Gambon: Their best one, George, tell 'em that) And I'm goin' to tell 'em to submit one that isn't negotiable and to drain the bottom of the barrel, because at this stage (Gambon: Yeah, I still gotta drive for 3 hours) there's no time for x around. Let 'em (?: Uh-huh) throw it on the table and face your xx. (Pause) Well —

[As Mediator is leaving the room, Gambon calls out to him to get the company to name the cents in their package.]

Management Caucus - J (11:15 P.M.)

Mediator: ... It's gonna be in about (Loring: H'm) 20 minutes, one
way or / another.
?: (Over Mediator above but cannot be understood)
Espig: Oh! (Laughs, joined by Pranis and Mediator)
Pranis: Well, it's actually 40 minutes, George (laughing), one way or
another. (Espig laughs again shortly, and Mediator slightly)
Mediator: Why (pause), I told 'em that they're too high. "You can't —
your 9 — your 9-cent figure — whatever you compute that last offer
to be is too high. Company can't buy it." He says (bangs table),
"What will they pay?" Now, I feel the time is here; this is it! Now,
here's what I'd recommend you do. Whatever you want to pay (pause)
— and I told them that I was coming in here to urge you to go in there
and put your last offer n — an offer that cannot be negotiated — on
both proposals. "Now, I mean this. I mean it. Last, and not negotiable." He said, "Fine." He said, "I" — he said, "I think that's
the approach at this point." Now. He said, "When — when he does
so, will you ask him to put it in cost of the package and not so much
the application?" He said, "Maybe we would want to revise that part
of it or modify it by agreement, one way or another." I said, "I'll
c — convey that to him." So (pause), on your 6-month, you know where
you stand on that; you've told me. The other, you make your decision
on that and with the understanding that it's final, because this is your
time. From this point on, there's no need protecting you or your position any longer (Loring: Uh-huh), or theirs. (Loring: Uh-huh)
You're ready. This is it. I think (pause) — and it'll be understood
that — that there's no — no more negotiating. If there is any negotiating, it will be on application. But cost — and that's it! Now, you
think it over. Whatever you want to do on that year thing — whatever
you put down — and I don't care what it is — is all right with me.
Loring: Uh-huh. If you — can you, without violating any confidence, give
us any area that would be acceptable on the year thing, George?
Mediator: Well, you said — I can only — I c — I — I must always follow
that one formula that I said has always worked out. (Loring: Uh-huh)
Very seldom ever misses. An — and for a guidepost — see, I haven't
talked to him about what he would settle for. For a guidepost, you
say your last offer was .0 —
Loring: 645.
Mediator: — 45. And you say — what would you make his? He s — wh —
he said his was —
Loring: He s —
Pranis: (At same time as Loring above) .0969.
Loring: Well, I — 'course, I don't know. I'm only guessing. (Pranis:
Well, you just x —) But I think it's 10, / George.
Mediator: (Over Loring above) We'll — we'll use his number.
Pranis: .0969. 3¢ and a little off. (Long pause)
Loring: We're about 3¢ apart, then.
Mediator: 3.2, around, I think. We'll say 3¢. (Rather long pause) 8¢
(pause) — roughly 7.9.
Espig: Which means that we gotta be careful about the 6-months'.
Pranis: Why? 5.6 for the 6-month / xx.

Espig: (Over Pranis above) Can we ignore the 6-month at this point and go back in on a — just a yearly offer?

Mediator: Yes. Yeah, you could do that.

Loring: Would that be wise?

Mediator: It would show — th — they might think that you're — I — I think since — I think they'd wanta get a look at it. They'd <u>wonder</u> what you were holdin' back. See, they may say — see, you — you submitted your last proposals on 2 (pause) — a 2-point approach. Uh (Espig: Well —) — what was your point in (Espig: The 6) suggesting?

Espig: The 6¢.

Loring: .056?

Mediator: .056?

Espig: .005 — well (Loring: That's what I say), of course, I was figuring insurance.

Pranis: .056, 8¢.

Espig: All right. (Loring: Well —) That's all right!

Loring: Well, you're figurin' the 4/10ths of insurance. (Espig: Yeah) We hadn't agreed that we'd carry / that.

Pranis: (Over Loring above) I'd / say scratch it out. Don't mention it.

Espig: (Over Pranis above) No. No. We scratch that out. Scratch it out under the — under the 6-months' and carry it under the 8¢. / Include it —

Pranis: (Over Espig above) In case ya have to.

Espig: Yeah.

Mediator: Whatever it is (pause), I think at this stage John won't try to negotiate any more.

Pranis: You mean he'll say Yes or, "Here we go."

Mediator: He'll say Yes or he'll say No.

Pranis: That's nice.

Mediator: He will not say No if you come up to anywheres near that, because how can he? Take a strike on that?

Pranis: (In low voice) I don't know.

Mediator: It's impossible! (Pause) I wouldn't wanta be a labor leader (Pranis: I wouldn't, either) that would go out (Pranis: Oh) and take a strike on that. John is no fool. He's not gonna do it. I'll wager you a month's pay he's not. (Loring laughs slightly)

Pranis: No, / I —

Espig: (Over Pranis above) He can — now we got — now we got something worthwhile.

Mediator: Yeah! Now we can —
[Mediator leaves the management caucus group at 11:25 P.M. He is called back by them at 11:28.]

Loring: George, this is our thinking. My committee isn't entirely in agreement with me, but maybe I'm gettin' point where I'm tired. As I told you before, we were authorized to go to 7 on a yearly settlement. I have whatever latitude I — I wanta take upon myself to go beyond that. I'm not authorized to, but if you feel that 8¢ would close it for the year, I'll buy it.

Mediator: Well, let me put it this way. I haven't consulted with them on that. Now, y — common sense and experience tells me that you are at 0. — s —

Pranis: 64 —

Loring: (At same time as Pranis above) 645.

Mediator: — 645. (Pause) He's at 9. You get him o — you got him on
the ropes when you throw out an 8-cent offer. You put him on the
ropes. It's — it's directly — it's down the middle! It splits it right
in half. You couldn't, by negotiation, get it at 8¢. I don't think you
could. But by the — what — what is almo — what almost amounts to
an ultimatum you can get it, because you put him in a — in that position. There it is. That is less. But when you say it, you have to
back it up. You have to be prepared that that is it! Now, I have him
conditioned for whatever it is, it is the last! He knows that. And
(pause) you can toss 'em both out, and (pause) he will — he will go
into a caucus then. I know it! He'll go into a caucus, be — but now
(pause) I think, too, in your opening remarks you ought to tell these
people that I have conveyed to you and recommended that you put out
your last offer, and, "Gentlemen, this is not bargainable! And this
is the last. (Pause) We'll do this, we'll do that. There it is." And —

Loring: Now, shall I just put it in terms of cents / per —

Mediator: (Over Loring above) Of cents per hour. A — and you can —
you can say that — that I conveyed to you a request by the union to
submit it that way, and you considered that request and you're doing
it that way. See, it was a — it was John's last — his request as I was
leaving. You can mention that. (?: Uh-huh) And for that reason you
did, and here it is, bang! (Pause) And make it just as clear as that.
Now, he'll know! And y — y — be prepared that — that that is it. He
can't take no strike on that. (Pause) Can't do it. He can do it, understand (Loring: H'm), but just like I can jump out that window (slight
pause) but I won't! (Pause)

Loring: O.K.!

Mediator: This is it!

Espig: This is it! (Slight pause) What's th — the hooker? (Pause, then
laughs slightly)

Loring: What hooker?

Mediator: What hooker?

Espig: I don't know, but I have a feeling that in any — in that 8¢ flat sum
there is one. I was wondering whether he could think of in terms of
maintaining an 8-cent cost even though people might be laid off at
some time. Is there any such hooker as that, that might come in?

Mediator: (In low voice) Even if people can be laid off?

Espig: Yeah. If some people could be laid off, could there be a possibility of him coming back and saying, "Look. This has reduced your
bill. Therefore we want it" —

Loring: No. It's 8¢ per hour worked.

Mediator: 8¢ per hour.

Espig: All right.

Mediator: You might — you might add, Len — he remi — he — he opened
another door of thought. You might say, too, that, "Submitting it this
way, in an 8-cent — in a cost package, we want to make very clear
that this is contingent upon agreement being reached on the application."

Loring: Uh-huh. Now, the other thing, George. The limit I was wanting
to go on the 6-months' was .056. Shall I give it that way — .0 (Mediator: Yep!) — $5\frac{1}{2}$ — 5¢?

Mediator: $5\frac{1}{2}$.

Loring: $5\frac{1}{2}$. (Pause) You think it's gonna do it, George? (Slight pause)

Espig: Yep.

Loring: Lord, I hope so.

Pranis: Would ya care for a little / 5-and-10 while we wait? (Shuffles cards)

Mediator: (Over Pranis above but cannot be understood) (Laughs)

Espig: I think we'll be out in 10 minutes on the street. I can see the sign.

Pranis: You mean with a sign (laughing heartily)?

Espig: I'm going on strike.

Mediator: What, those signs?

Espig: I want that sign.

Mediator: Oh!

Espig: I want it put right up in my office.

Pranis: What, the one that says "STRIKE" on it? I think (Loring: What do you bet, Observer?) you — you better ask if you can take that if they strike.

Loring: How are you betting?

Observer: H'm! You're gonna have a settlement. Isn't that right? (Loring laughs)

Mediator: That's right!

Pranis: I had sorta hoped we'd give Observer a strike so she could go out of here and say this is a — one of the unsuccessful.

Observer: No. If you had a strike, I'd have to stay till you got it settled.

Loring: Well, this has been a tough one, George.

Mediator: This has been a tough one for a reopener — very tough. But — (slight pause).

Loring: Well, I (Mediator: I —) think we're paying too much. They j — they got us over a barrel on — on the — 'course, we have so many strikes against us.

Mediator: I'll tell you where I think you're payin' too much. I think you're payin' too much on the 6-month. I don't think you're payin' too much on the year. (Pause)

Pranis: Well, he wants a year, George, doesn't he?

Mediator: Yeah. I think $5\frac{1}{2}$, based on averages — figure $5\frac{1}{2}$ for 6 months, 8 for a — a year — for 12 month. I mean, there's your answer right there. (Loring: Uh-huh) Now, if they'd get $5\frac{1}{2}$ now, come 6 months from now, see, regardless of the cost-of-living, whether it's static or whether it goes up or whether it goes down a little, you're gonna be faced with the same problem. Your economic condition, or the number of your orders, your inventory, and so forth is going to de — have a lot to do with your thinking. You may be caught; there's a gamble. You may be then in a position where a strike could do more damage (Loring: That's true) then than now. (Loring: Uh-huh) There are a lot of intent — or unknowns, see, that can — and, of course, you can also say, well, maybe the situation will be such that the union should take a lower figure. But unions don't do that that easily. And I say to any employer, if — if they can buy off a reopener — and actually you are buying this reopener off. $5\frac{1}{2}$ less 8 is $2\frac{1}{2}$¢.

Loring: But that's worth a nickel at that time. I mean, that's worth a nickel in October. I mean, $2\frac{1}{2}$ now (?: Equal —) is equal to a nickel in October.

Mediator: Yes. Oh, yes. Now, you are (pause) — you are closing off
negotiations. If you offer 5½¢ now for a 6-month contract and you're
open again in — in October, well, what you're doing by getting it for
8¢, you're removing all strike threats (Loring: Right) for 2½¢!
(Loring: Uh-huh) You've got an automatic increase. There's no negotiations. And the thing goes on. The only thing, in my opinion,
where you could be in trouble would be where the cost-of-living soars
out of proportion (Loring: Uh-huh) — well, you know it don't —
doesn't do that in 6 months (Loring: No) — to the point where —
well, right with the — the time where employers were calling unions
in. Chrysler started it and gave 'em — m 10¢. You remember? The
index was going up. There was — th — they — their — they were tied
up in contracts, and in order to keep their labor markets the way they
wanted to, they were inviting the unions in and payin' 'em. Well, the
chance of that happening is practically nil today with the changes that
(Loring: Uh-huh) have been made. I think you got — if you can settle
this for a year at 8¢, you got a good deal. You — you're not paying
too much, as negotiations go. Here. We had — Observer was with
me on this one. We had Irving Mining in here. They had a 2-year
contract, so these men had no increases whatever in 2 years. So they
made a 20-cent settlement — 20¢ an hour, of course. Now, you average that out, that's 10¢ a year. (Door opens)
Denk: We want both committees in there, / George.
Mediator: (Over Denk above) O.K. Fine. I'll be right with you. That's
10¢ a year. We just had the ABC in, a 1-year contract, 16¢. I could
go on and on. They're all above a dime. If this thing goes over for
8¢, you are getting a 1-year contract for 8¢. That's — / that's —
Espig: (Over Mediator above) And these others — these others were 1-
year contracts — / ABC —
Mediator: (Over Espig above) All 1-year. (Espig: Uh-huh) Every one
of them were 1-year contracts. And even round this with 8, you
haven't done bad. You've done good. And I'm not tryin' to give you
(Espig: 8¢ plus xx) a consolation prize.

Joint Meeting - G   (11:35 P.M.)

Mediator: Uh (rather long pause) — in meeting with the union before I
went in there this time to meet with the company, I plainly told the
union what the company had relayed to me, that the union's last proposal on the — that the 9-cent figure, isn't it? — for the 1-year contract was not acceptable — 9-point whatever it was — to the company.
After a short discussion with the union, I advised the union that I was
going in to the company and request the company to submit to the
union their last position on these negotiations. The union said to me,
as I was leaving, "If you do, we would like it done in cash, or cents
per hour — submitted on a cents-per-hour package basis." I have
met with the company. Len, you take it from there.
Loring: Well, as the mediator said, he put it on the line to us. He
wanted our complete final offer without reservations. We're actually
prepared to do that. We're getting close to your deadline. I'm willing to throw an offer out on the table which is absolutely the — the

final offer of the company; it's not bargainable. This is it. We will throw it on the table as you have requested the mediator to ask us, that is, in cents per hour worked, contingent upon a mutual agreement as to how it would be applied. (Gambon nods) I think that's only fair. For a 12-month contract, that is, till next April, we're willing to assume a cost of 8¢ per hour. (Pause) For this reopener alone we wil — are willing to assume a cost of $5\frac{1}{2}$¢ per hour. Now, that is final; it's not thrown out to bargain with.

Gambon: Will you give me some further explanation, Len, as to what you mean by contingent on the form it takes? I mean, do I interpret that to mean that you object, for instance, to the fixed bonus principle? Uh —

Loring: We don't like it, John. We'd like to dis — have some discussion with you on it (Gambon: Uh-huh) why — why we don't like / to have it —

Gambon: (Over Loring above) Well, is there anything partic'larly — partic'lar that you would object to in any suggested form we might make?

Loring: We would like anything that you wanta do in the way of adjustment of inequalities to make it on cents per hour for each group.

Gambon: Uh-huh. But that would be the only thing. I mean, it — other than that, if we suggested general increase, additional for skilled trades, additional for day workers, you have no objection to that, so long as it totals to the / figure which I have?

Loring: (Over Gambon above) As long as — I mean, we would like to be in on the discussion of (Gambon: Yeah. Yeah) what those amounts would be.

Gambon: Uh-huh. (Rather long pause) That's 8 on a 12-month and $5\frac{1}{2}$ on the one reopener. Right?

Loring: That's right, John.

Gambon: All right. Will you give us a chance to look this over now?
[Mediator returns with the management group to their caucus room to await a call from the union group. Pranis and Espig put in the time by playing cards. When the union sends Denk to the door of the management caucus room, Mediator leads the management group back into joint meeting.]

Joint Meeting - H (11:45 P.M.)

Gambon: Len, I have a proposition to wrap this thing up. (Rather long pause) This is slightly more than your 8¢. Slightly more. The proposal that I wanted to make would be this kind of a set-up. 5¢ general increase and again 5 on October 1st.

Loring: Let me just get that down, / now, John.

Gambon: (Over Loring above) This is general, now.

Mediator: Do you have a piece of paper there?
[Short interruption follows while one of the girls looks for paper for Mediator. Gambon finally announces, "Here you are, George." Mediator closes the matter with, "O.K. Thanks."]

Gambon: All right. That's 5, April 1st, '53, and 5¢ general increase on October 1st, '53; $7\frac{1}{2}$¢ for skilled trades, in addition, on Oc — April

1st, '53, and again $7\frac{1}{2}$ on October 1st, '53; $2\frac{1}{2}$ for other day workers
on April 1st and again $2\frac{1}{2}$ on October 1st. My estimate on that, Len,
is .084. (Pause) I know you said your 8¢ wasn't bargainable, but so
did I say the .0969 wasn't bargainable. I'm tryin' to find something
(Loring: Uh-huh) that we can — (pause).

Loring: I would like to do this, John. I mean, I'd like — I mean, I'm
(laughing slightly) not sayin' your figures (Gambon: Yeah) aren't
all right, but we've had this little difference as to what the figures
are. I would like to caucus with my group on this.

Gambon: All right. I — I used your figure, by the way, in my estimates
— your — that .047. I think you said that involved the skilled trades.
(Pause)

Loring: Yeah. .007. (Pause)

Gambon: .0 (Loring: 0) 07. That's right. I've been usin' that, now, in
all my figuring here, and I've been using a figure (pause) of .00225,
which would represent that $2\frac{1}{2}$¢.

Loring: Well, as I say, I'd like to (Gambon: Uh-huh) talk with my
(Gambon: All right) committee. I was goin' (Mediator: Before —)
beyond our authorization, and I wanta discuss this.

Gambon: Uh-huh.

Mediator: John, I — ya said 5¢ in April, and then I lost y — then you
said 5¢ general, and (Gambon: This is general increases) I didn't
hear what ya —

Gambon: As far as general increases go, 5¢, April 1st, '53, and another
5¢ on October 1st, 1953.

Mediator: I got it. I see.

Gambon: You got the 2 $7\frac{1}{2}$'s and 2 $2\frac{1}{2}$'s?

Mediator: Uh-huh.

Management Caucus - K (11:50 P.M.)

Mediator: Uh — we'll leave ya for awhile.

Loring: All right, George.

Mediator: We'll be out here somewhere.

Loring: He bargained.

Mediator: I don't like that! But (pause) ya don't have to accept it. It's
up to you. You think it over.

Loring: (In low voice) Uh-huh.
   [Mediator is out of the room until the management caucus group calls
   him back at 11:59 P.M.]

Loring: His bargaining on this bothers me. We figure this is .08595 —
or say .086, 6/10ths of a cent more than we said was our top limit.
And that was our top, believe me. I — I — I went a cent higher than
I was authorized to, to do it.

Mediator: Don't do it! (Rather long pause) Don't do it. (Rather long
pause) Tell 'em you re — you looked it over and you've checked it
and all, and you just can't go! They've gotta fit it in at 8¢.

Loring: What's (Pranis talks at same time) apt to happen at that?

Mediator: Huh?

Loring: What's apt to happen at that?

Mediator: Let's find out!

Espig: We'll suggest to them that they can take $\frac{1}{2}$¢ off either one of those / 5 general —

Pranis: (Over Espig above) You're interested in — you're interested in / 8¢.

Loring: (Over Pranis above) We'll keep it goin', / will —

Mediator: (Over Loring above) Oh, definite.

Loring: Yeah. I — I — I really / can't go in that —

Mediator: (Over Loring above) You got xx — well, ya have to try it! Ya have to find out! / This —

Loring: (Over Mediator above) H'm. I'd rather buy the 6-months' one rather than / this one.

Mediator: (Over Loring above) Uh — and I'll tell ya how you oughta do it, though. This time, instead of me going in there, we all go in, see, 'cause now we're — we're at the important stage. This is that important that you must say it. (Loring: Uh-huh) See, we don't want it to lose any of its (Loring: Yeah) effect. And tell 'em — say, "We — we just cannot — we — we've looked at your proposal; we've checked some other things" — and ya might even help the situation by saying that you checked some of these figures with your people — "and we have — 8¢ is as far as we can go, and we certainly hope that you can find way to f — fit your needs into that 8¢. We just can't do it." And let it go! Hang right there! (Pause)

Loring: O.K.

Mediator: Then we'll — I'll watch it close from there.

Loring: O.K.

Joint Meeting - I (12:01 A.M.)

Gambon: (Addressing 2 of boys, who are joking with each other) All right, wait a minute. All right, wait a minute. Look, time's runnin' out. Let's get goin'.

Loring: O.K., John. We've looked this over. We figured it with figures that we gave you before. Our figuring is that this comes to .0595 — roughly, .086. Now, I wasn't just bargaining when I said 8¢. I went beyond what I'd been authorized to go, but I's willing to take that on myself. This extra 6/10ths of a cent — it — it's just something we won't buy. We're willing to go the 8¢, and I think you could fit in a nice package within the 8¢. But 8¢ is the limit. (Long pause)

Gambon: What's your cost on a holiday, Len?

Loring: Pardon?

Gambon: What's the cost on a holiday?

Loring: On a holiday?

Gambon: Yeah.

Loring: You've got me.

Gambon: Huh?

Loring: You've got me. I don't know. (Pause)

Gambon: Less (Loring: Well —) than a half-cent, isn't it? (Slight pause)

Espig: No. It's about 7/10ths of a cent.

Gambon: Huh?

Espig: About 7/10ths, I think.

Gambon: On the holiday? (Pause)

Meyer: It was that / x —

Gambon: (Over Meyer above) Don't throw in all the f — do-dads and everything else (Espig: No! I — no) that you can think of, now.

Espig: I can get figures from the last, but I think we figured it about 7/10ths of a cent (Loring: Uh —) — 6 or 7/10ths. I'm not sure.

Loring: Let's see. We had figured — oh, wait a minute. Maybe I have it, John. I have .014 for 2 additional holidays. So half of that / would be —

Gambon: (Over Loring above) .014.

Meyer: That would be .00 / 7.

Gambon: (Over Meyer above) .0 / 5 —

Loring: (Over Gambon above) .057, I guess. (Slight pause) Uh — .0057.

Gambon: .0057. Yeah. (Pause)

[There is a period of brief comments from several people, with Pranis pointing out that .014 divided by 2 would produce .007.]

Pranis: 7/10ths, John.

Meyer: Yeah.

[Gambon and Meyer talk at once as Meyer supports Pranis's calculation.]

Pranis: (Over Meyer above) 7/10ths. Yeah. Well, it's .014 for 2, / so —

Loring: (Over Pranis above) Oh, I see.

[Meyer laughs, and Loring and Pranis talk at once.]

Gambon: H'm.

Loring: I never could — should do figuring, anyway. (Laughs slightly)

[Very long pause of 1' follows. Gambon whistles for a little bit, then ceases for some time. Later he hums a little, ceasing again for some time.]

Gambon: What, Len, would your estimates be on a 5-and-5, 7-and-7, $2\frac{1}{2}$-$2\frac{1}{2}$ be? Would that bring it down sufficient to — (pause)?

Meyer: That would be a —

Loring: No, it wouldn't, John.

Gambon: Huh? (Long pause, with Gambon looking at sheets of figures before him) .007 is (slight pause) — figurin' — no, is — no, that wouldn't be right. (Very long pause) I don't know how to figure this to reach that thing exactly.

[Very long pause of over 1' during which Pranis converses in an aside with Loring. He refers at the end to "too much money."]

Loring: John, if you made the general increase in October 1st 4¢, that would bring us down to .081, which we'd buy.

Gambon: 5-4, $7\frac{1}{2}$-$7\frac{1}{2}$. You have .081. I was just lookin' at that one here. I have 0-sa — .0786 on that.

Loring: That — well, we figured it / on those figures that you —

Gambon: (Over Loring above) You said .08 — .081 you / have.

Loring: (Over Gambon above) .081. Yeah. (Long pause)

Gambon: O.K. (Bangs table) It's sold. Let me ask ya a question at this point that's botherin' me. Where are we on this question of these insurance benefits? Does the company propose to reduce it to the $6.00 level? (Pause) Or do you continue them that since you have been paying it since last October without any objections up to this point? I think it was used as a bargaining proposition, to begin (laughing slightly) with.

Loring: It — it really wasn't, John. Uh — / I —

Gambon: (Over Loring above) Maybe not on your part, but Bill Michelsen sure worked it to death.

Loring: I was after Bill e — ever since last Oc — lat — yeah — October to do somethin' about it (Gambon: H'm), and he didn't. (Pause)

Gambon: Well, since you've gone this far with it, Len, I don't see where that could be an objectionable item on the part of the company to carry that until the expiration of the contract and if from experience at that time we find that we can't get the same benefits for the same premium, let's try to work it out. (Pause)

Loring: I'll buy that, John.

Gambon: O.K. All right. Then we'll — look. Get on the — get a-hold of that 3rd shift —
[As tape is changed, Gambon sends Wollman out to stop the 2 shifts from striking; to Loring, he says, "We'll write it this way: 'Present insurance benefits will be continued.' Right?" Rather long pause.]
Continue for duration of contract? (Rather long pause)

Loring: Right. (Pause)

Gambon: (Slowly, while writing) 5¢-per-hour general increase effective April 1st, 1953 (Loring: Right); another 5-cent-per-hour / gen —

Loring: (Over Gambon above) 4¢.

Gambon: Or 4¢. I'm sorry. / xx. I'm persistent, anyhow. (Someone laughs)

Loring: (Over Gambon above) Now, John, October 1st is on a Tuesday. Can we make it on th — the next Monday? I mean, that's just a week out of the way — little less than a week out of the way — if / we — we gave you insurance —

Gambon: (Over Loring above) That's October the 7th. All right. (Pranis starts to speak) (Loring: x) I buy it. 5¢ an hour general increase effective October 7.

Loring: 4¢, you said.

Gambon: 4¢. / Yeah.

Loring: (Over Gambon above) Right. Right.
[Several laugh, at which Gambon asks, "Did I say 5 again?", bringing on a period of general laughing and talking at once. Gambon's final comment is "Always pluggin.' "]

Gambon: Yeah, let's take the 5¢ and change it to October the (One of girls: September 30th) 7th, huh? All right. (Someone laughs) 5¢ general increase effective April 1st, 1953; 4¢ general increase effective October 7, '53. (Loring: Right) In addition, there will be a $7\frac{1}{2}$¢-per-hour increase for skilled trades, which includes the apprentices (Loring: Right) (pause), effective also on April 1st; another $7\frac{1}{2}$¢-per-hour for skilled trades and apprentices effective October 7. (Loring: Right) A $2\frac{1}{2}$-cent additional increase for all other day workers (pause) effective April 1st (pause), 1953, and again another $2\frac{1}{2}$¢-per-hour increase for all other day workers effective October 7 (Loring: Right), 1953. (Rather long pause)

Loring: And this includes a waiver of the / reopener?

Gambon: (Over Loring above) This includes — this (pause) is contingent on the fact that there shall be no reopener on October 1st (Loring: Right) of 1953.

Loring: No reopeners for the duration. / In fact, that —

Gambon: (Over Loring above) All right. No reopeners. (Long pause)
No reopeners for duration of present contract. (Rather long pause)
That it?

Mediator: O.K., ladies and gentlemen. The agreement is reached.
Thanks to both committees for your cooperation. / Wish you luck
with it.

Baker: (Over Mediator above) Can we start on this pie now?

Gambon: Huh? (Several, including Loring, laugh heartily) Might as well
xx. (Laughing continues) Did you wanta cut your pie? He wants to
cut the company in on his pie now. (Laughing continues)

Saunders: Aw, bring it home to the kids. (Several laugh heartily) Bring
it home to the kids, / Les.

Baker: (Over Saunders above) It's already cut.

Loring: Well, ya sure gave / me a workout —

Gambon: (Over Loring above) Huh? I don't want any. I got — / huh?

Loring: (Over Gambon above) You sure gave me a workout for (Gambon: Well —) my first try. (Laughs) Thanks — thanks for (Gambon:
It's a pleasure to deal with ya) treatin' me so — so pleasurably, John.

Gambon: Right.

[Rather long pause, with group preparing to break up. Espig exchanges
comments with someone briefly.]

(Over others above) The only thing I'm mad about is that I still have
to drive to Plattsville, durn it. (Pause) What'd you say, Erwin?

Espig: D'you want a little memo of agreement?

Gambon: Yeah, I think we might draw one up and initial it, if you want
(Espig: I —) to. Is that what you mean?

Espig: Yeah. I mean (Gambon: Well, look. You have —), if — if you
have — look at this, for a moment. (Slight pause) It's r — very rough.
(Pause)

Loring: Boy, I'm beat up. (Laughs, as do one or 2 of boys) (Long pause)

Espig: Tomorrow morning we can type it. You can keep it till tomorrow
morning and send it up to me tomorrow morning. Can't you read it?

Gambon: Yeah. You just got one thing here (Espig: What's that?) that's
botherin' me a little bit. I think — it's not my understanding that that's
the way this works. You got this thing down here on this .025. What's
this business? / I don't —

Espig: (Over Gambon above) Including apprentices.

Meyer: That's way we're —/ they count.

Espig: (Over Meyer above) That — that goes back to the 2 — o — to the
.075. (Meyer: See?) See, this reads — this should read this way:
".075 payroll add for all employ — for all skilled trade employees
on April (Meyer: Including apprentices) 1, 1953 (Gambon: Including
apprentices. I see), including apprentices" (Meyer: Yeah), then
".075 for payroll add for all skilled trades employees effective
October 7th, 1953, including apprentices."

Gambon: Well, that — this is what was throwin' me off. (Espig: Yeah.
You fel —) I thought you were throwin' this thing here / to x.

Espig: (Over Gambon above) No. (Meyer: No) You fellows threw that
in after I had it (Gambon: Oh, I see) dittoed. (Laughs)

Meyer: Subject to ratification by / the —

Gambon: (Over Meyer above) Yeah. This is, of course, subject to ratification / by your membership.

Loring: (Over Gambon above) When will that be, John?

Gambon: Well, we're trying to — we're gonna try to get a meeting together for Monday. (Meyer: Oughta appreciate that) We can't get —
we can't get it before that. Now, one thing that I would ask the company to cooperate with us on and that is that the company does not
give out information as to the possible settlement involved here. I
don't want to have any confusion in the plant. When I say not give it
out, I don't want them to be givin' it out to foremen and supervisors.
Where's Bob Pranis?

One of girls: He's out.

Gambon: I'll (Loring and someone else talk at once) partic'ly want Bob
Pranis to control that end of it out in the factory because we have
lotta leaks (Loring: All right) that way. I mean, you tell your people
and the first thing ya know they're tellin' some special person, and /
before ya know, it's over the shop.

Espig: (Over Gambon above) Well, you wanta hold this until Monday
night. It's gonna / be difficult.

Meyer: (Over Espig above) Yeah, x Monday m —

Gambon: There'll be no trouble about it. There'll be a — there'll be noti-
fications in there, they'll know all about the fact that there's a meeting
on Monday afternoon and one on Monday night — / the 2 meetings.

Loring: (Over Gambon above) Bob, John asked that we not let any information out, even to the supervisors, on this settlement until he has
an opportunity to meet at the general / meeting.

Pranis: (Over Loring above) You mean the details?

Loring: This — details of the settlement.

Gambon: That's right. Because as far as we're concerned, this is an
agreement reached between the 2 committees. It's (Loring: Yeah)
subject to ratification in the membership. (Loring says something)
And I prefer not to have any confusion or have (Loring: Yeah) these
people / getting things and twisting them all over the —

Espig: (Over Gambon above) Well, let's — let's clear one thing. Certainly when you have your first meeting in the afternoon —

Meyer: It'll be out.

Saunders: It'll / be out.

Espig: (Over Saunders above) — it'll be out.

Gambon: Oh, yeah!

Meyer: But they'll be meeting right after work. / One'll — shift'll be
comin' in —

One of boys: (Over Meyer above) They'll — they'll follow, one right
after the other.

[Meyer, Espig, and one of girls talk at once.]

Espig: (Over Meyer above) Things will — things will move fast, and
our foremen are entitled to know about the same time. So what time
will you pract — will you have your meeting? And then (Meyer:
See?) we'll tell our foremen about that same / time.

Meyer: (Over Espig above) 3:00 o'clock in the afternoon.

One of boys: We have one at 3:00 and another one would be around 5:00.
See, it'll be —

Espig: Well, then, if you start your meeting at 3:00, we'll have — we'll —
we'll tell our foremen at 3:00 o'clock. We'll have a meeting of our
foremen at 3:00 o'clock. I think that would be fair to our foremen.

Loring: All right, John?

Gambon: Yep.

[Some time is spent in odds and ends before group disperses. Somewhere during all of this, at 12:15 P.M., Gambon and Loring shake hands over the agreement. Pranis raises the question of checking over the summary Espig drew up, which brings on much laughing and talking and a short repartee between Espig and Gambon. Gambon suggests that the rest of the union committee put their "John Henry's" on the sheet, and Loring assents. Meyer announces, "The people on this committee may be late getting in in the morning, so when you come in at 8:00 o'clock, will you have them sign in for me?" Loring asks for one of the "STRIKE" signs with, "Let me have one of those to take home, John (Gambon: You want a souvenir?), to remind me of this. Not that I need much. Autographed." Gambon writes a long message on one, then signs it, handing it to Loring with, "There you are, boy," whereupon one of the boys inquires, "Do you wanta date that so we don't use it next year?", bringing on laughter from everyone. As Gambon prepares to add the date, he is reminded that it is the "19th now, John," and "12:25 A.M." Someone suggests that "George" may want a sign, too, but Mediator declines with, "No, I'd better let that one stand."]

INDEX